Elizabeth J Beck

Readings in Primary Prevention

of Psychopathology

Primary Prevention of Psychopathology
George W. Albee and Justin M. Joffe, *General Editors*

Readings in Primary Prevention of Psychopathology

Basic Concepts

Justin M. Joffe, George W. Albee, and Linda D. Kelly, editors

Published for the University of Vermont
and the Vermont Conference on
the Primary Prevention of Psychopathology
by University Press of New England
Hanover and London, 1984

University Press of New England

Brandeis University

Brown University

Clark University

Dartmouth College

University of New Hampshire

University of Rhode Island

Tufts University

University of Vermont

RA
790
.A2
R4
1984

LIBRARY OF CONGRESS CATALOGING IN PUBLICATION DATA

Main entry under title:

Readings in primary prevention of psychopathology.
   Selected articles from Primary prevention of psycho-
pathology.
   Includes bibliographical references.
   1. Mental illness—Prevention—Congresses.   2. Social
psychiatry—Congresses.   I. Joffe, Justin M.   II. Albee,
George W.   III. Kelly, Linda D.   IV. University of
Vermont.   V. Vermont Conference on the Primary Prevention
of Psychopathology.   Primary prevention of psychopathology.
RA790.A2R4   1984   616.89'05   83-40557
ISBN 0-87451-295-6
ISBN 0-87451-303-0 (pbk.)

Printed in the United States of America

Contents

vi   Contents

Preface

In the early 1970s, when concern with prevention was beginning to permeate the mental health professions, the attacks of those whose vested interests are threatened by a prevention ideology were spearheaded by an argument on the following lines: "Prevention has no research base, no established methods, no demonstration programs in place, no scholarly underpinning." This was, of course, untrue, but the documentation needed for rebuttal was scattered, unorganized, diffuse, and often not clearly identified as "prevention," so proponents of prevention were vulnerable to these charges.

As enthusiasm for prevention grew, various efforts were made to remedy the situation. Ours consisted of organizing an annual conference—the Vermont Conference on the Primary Prevention of Psychopathology—to bring together people from a diversity of fields to present authoritative overviews of theory, research, and practice in prevention and to discuss new directions. Papers based on the conference presentations have reached an even wider audience through their publication by the University Press of New England. The seven such volumes published to date constitute one of the several major rebuttals of the critics' argument.

We are, of course, delighted at the way the Vermont Conference on the Primary Prevention of Psychopathology has flourished and with the continued widespread enthusiasm for both the conference and the resulting series of books. No longer do we have to scrabble through a dozen fields and a multitude of journals to respond to the question, "Where's the literature on primary prevention?" However, we are, in a sense, now beginning to experience some of the problems of affluence. Certainly clearly identifiable material is now abundantly available to introduce someone to the field of primary prevention, but the seven volumes in our series include 122 papers totaling nearly 3,000 pages—not too handy for people new to the field and needing a route map to find their way around.

This embarrassment of riches is the reason for a book of readings. This book provides a representative sample of the published papers, selected to provide a relatively brief overview of the many facets of primary prevention. The papers we chose are not necessarily better in any way than the ones we did not include, it is simply that as a group they provide an integrated and comprehensive picture of the field as a whole. We not only selected papers, we cut sections of almost all the ones selected in order to be able to include more papers and to improve the book's capacity to act as a guide to the field. The cuts, all of which are indicated by ❖ so that any abruptness or lack of continuity can be blamed on us and not on the authors, were designed to help the reader not lose the wood for the trees. We have omitted those parts of papers containing lengthy presentations of experimental findings, technical details, and—dare we admit it?—repetitive or redundant material.

We have tried to preserve the logic of each paper and to leave its general argument and major concepts intact. We have left reference lists uncut: this results in the minor oddity of there now being bibliographic information on publications that are not mentioned in the text, but we felt this was a small drawback when compared to the advantage of leaving the interested reader with all the references to draw on in case she or he wished to explore any of the topics in greater depth.

To these edited selections from the series of books on primary prevention we have added a prologue—"A Model for Classifying Prevention Programs" (Albee)—to provide a general introduction to the entire field and to orient the reader to the conceptual organization of this book, as well as headnotes for each subsequent section. There is also an epilogue that alerts the reader to the fact that a major dimension of prevention efforts is not addressed in detail in this volume: aspects of the social context and political action needed to ensure the success of prevention efforts are not covered systematically in this book. These issues require more extensive and detailed consideration than space herein allows, and a second book of readings, focused specifically on these issues, is forthcoming.

The result is, we hope, an integrated set of materials suitable for introducing a student or mental health professional to the field of primary prevention or for use as a handy reference book for those involved in writing, research, or practice in the field. We hope, too, that the convenience of having a single comprehensive volume will contribute to the growth of undergraduate and graduate courses in prevention (in psychology and social work departments, in education and psychiatry, and elsewhere) and that instructors will find the readings suitable as an auxiliary text to cover the prevention section of courses in community psychology, social psychiatry, community mental health, abnormal psychology, and others.

To the extent that this book of readings contributes to the development of awareness of the importance of prevention to the entire field of mental health and human development and of the urgency which attends the need to escape the straitjacket of conventional approaches to mental health problems, we will have achieved our objective.

Burlington, Vermont   Justin M. Joffe
March 1984   George W. Albee
                                                                Linda D. Kelly

Prologue: A Model for Classifying Prevention Programs

George W. Albee

The explanation most often used at present to account for mental and emotional disorders emphasizes individual defect. It says that persons exhibit abnormal behavior, or experience unusual thoughts and feelings, because there is something specific wrong inside. This defect, or illness, explanation leads to an approach to intervention that stresses individual therapy and that opposes efforts at social change. As a general rule, one-to-one therapists oriented toward individual treatment, organic or psycho-therapeutic, resist prevention efforts that stress improved social or educational experience.

One frequent criticism opponents level at advocates of primary prevention holds that their efforts are too general, too unfocused, too vague, too nonspecific. Critics of primary prevention also commonly raise one or more of the following specific objections.

It is not possible to prevent mental illness in general. There are many different specific forms of mental illness and we do not yet have clear evidence of the cause of each. Further, these critics argue, it is not possible to mount separate effective prevention programs without a knowledge of the specific cause of each specific form of mental illness.

The answers to this objection are fairly clear. Most forms of "mental illness" are not illnesses in the usual sense. Unlike genuine physical illnesses where a specific microorganism, organic defect, physical malfunction, or other objective toxic or noxious agent can be identified, most mental disorders are identified only by peculiar behavior, unusual ideation, personal report of subjective discomfort, and so forth. Most forms of "mental illness" cannot be identified by laboratory tests or other objective physical measures. Rather, the presence of a mental disorder is inferred from behavioral observation or from the report of the subject about his or her emotional discomfort. Rather than a specific condition being attributable to specific causes, it is well established that any particular stressful life experience may produce any of several different patterns of disturbance. Thus severe marital disruption, for example, may be followed in some people by depression, in others by excessive drinking, in some by alcohol-

X GEORGE W. ALBEE

ism leading to cirrhosis of the liver, in others by social withdrawal and isolation, in others by accident proneness including fatal accidents and/or suicide. Similarly, looking for a single precipitating cause leading to depression, for example, is fruitless, and leads instead to the discovery that this condition results from any of a wide variety of stress-inducing situations. In short, it is most unlikely that a specific cause will ever be identified for each of the 230 different patterns of emotional disturbance described in the American Psychiatric Association's *Diagnostic and Statistical Manual III* (DSM III). Prevention results from stress reduction, particularly those stresses arising out of difficult interpersonal relations, and from improved social coping skills and solid support systems.

In contrast to the objection that we know too little about the causation of mental illnesses to be able to prevent them, another objection argues that most forms of mental illness are a result of genetic defects and/or biochemical imbalances and, as a consequence, are not preventable through social manipulation and environmental change. This argument limits prevention efforts to genetic counseling and suggests that research money might better be spent looking for ways of correcting disturbed brain chemistry and other biological defects. Persons expressing this objection usually attempt to make a distinction between "genuine" mental illnesses, which they hold to be genetic in origin, and problems in living, which they rule out as forms of mental illness. One trouble with this position is that it is often impossible to find a clear organic cause for so-called genuine mental illnesses, like depression or schizophrenia. Further, all of the mental conditions listed in the official psychiatric nomenclature (DSM III) are officially and legally recognized as forms of mental illnesses for purposes of psychiatric treatment and for reimbursement by third-party payments. The same psychiatrists who argue that genuine mental illnesses are organic (which problems of living are not) at the same time accept reimbursement for their treatment of all DSM III conditions, including problems in living, thereby certifying them to be genuine illnesses. It follows then that efforts successful in preventing conditions like adolescent rebellion, school learning problems, tobacco addiction syndrome, and emotional disturbances resulting from marital disruption are indeed preventing conditions officially recognized as psychiatric illnesses.

Another objection cited by opponents of prevention efforts holds that research to demonstrate the effectiveness of prevention programs has not yet produced much in the way of significant positive findings, and therefore it is foolish to expend funds that are in short supply for vague and untested prevention efforts.

One answer to this objection is contained, in significant measure, in this volume, in which selected excerpts have been chosen from the first seven volumes published by the Vermont Conference on Primary Prevention of Psychopathology (VCPPP). This continuing series of books contains papers delivered at the annual Vermont Conference. Each year we have chosen a specific topical area related to primary prevention of psychopathology and have invited distinguished contributors to theory and research to present papers. The resulting annual volume is a record of what is known about prevention in that particular area. It is interesting that critics of prevention apply a distinctly higher standard of evaluation to research in this field than is applied to research in psychiatric treatment. The history of psychiatric treatment is replete with examples of poor research efforts that have been hailed as important breakthroughs and which, after a few years, turn out to be relatively ineffective or even damaging.

Critics of prevention efforts are often disdainful of programs attempting to effect positive social change, to build a more humane and secure society, efforts to make parents more loving and nurturant, schools more supportive and rewarding, work more challenging and interesting, employment more certain, etc. They regard all of these efforts in social change engineering as unrelated to mental health and mental illness. While it may be admirable, they argue, to do our best to improve the lot of humankind, this is really not the major business of workers in the field of mental health who have no special talent or knowledge about political and economic issues.

The answers to this objection, of course, are contained, in part, in this volume. Social stress will be shown to increase emotional disturbance and distress, and the reduction in stress will be followed by a reduced disturbance. Instilling rational attitudes toward sexuality, and providing accurate sexual knowledge, will be shown to be associated with mature sexual behavior, while sexual ignorance and misunderstanding will be shown to be associated with anxiety and pathological sexual disturbances. These and other findings reported in this volume underscore the importance of social change aimed at the reduction of unnecessary stress, at more rational sex education, and toward the fostering of mutual support groups and positive self-esteem. It is the responsibility of the mental health worker continuously to interpret to society, and especially to legislators and persons responsible for social policy and educational programs, the relationship between these societal variables and resulting distress or lack of distress.

Another related objection from those who oppose an environmental model argues that efforts at strengthening mental health, at improving the adaptive skills and potentials of persons by enhancing their coping skills, are really not relevant to the prevention of mental illness. This argument fails to take into account the traditional public health model for disease prevention that has an important lesson for those interested in the prevention of psychopathology. Traditionally public health efforts at the prevention of diseases have involved three strategies: (1) removing or neutralizing the noxious agent, (2) strengthening the resistance of the host, and (3) preventing transmission of the noxious agent to the host. This model has been remarkably successful in reducing or eliminating many of the great plagues that have afflicted humankind in the past. Efforts at removing or neutralizing noxious agents in the water supply have reduced or eliminated diseases such as typhoid fever and cholera. Strengthening the resistance of the host, through vaccination for example, has eliminated smallpox. And preventing transmission, by eliminating mosquitoes that transmit yellow fever or malaria, is a third example of effective prevention. In the field of psychopathology, the noxious agent often is uncontrolled stress. Strengthening the host includes the teaching of coping skills, the enhancement of self-esteem, and the provision of support groups. Preventing transmission may be accomplished by eliminating messages that lead to sexist, racist, ageist, and other pathological attitudes. Illustrations of all of these approaches are contained in the pages that follow.

One of the most common objections to prevention efforts holds that because there is such a limited amount of tax money available for the field of mental health and mental illness it is important to use these scarce funds for the treatment of persons who are currently suffering, rather than diverting money into uncertain and unproven prevention efforts that could have effects only many years later. This objection raises the question of whether the mental health professions now are seeing the persons most in need of help. Let us consider this issue in some detail.

According to most informed estimates (Albee, 1982; Klerman, 1980; the President's Commission on Mental Health, 1978; Ryan, 1969) some 15 percent of the population of the United States exhibit mental conditions described by Klerman as "hard core mental illnesses," and as "serious emotional disturbances" by those who disavow the illness model. Whatever model is used, it is generally agreed that some 32 to 36 million persons in the United States experience conditions such as depression, incapacitating anxiety, addiction to alcohol and drugs, organic mental disorders including chronic brain syndromes in the elderly, as well as the functional psychoses such as schizophrenia. This "hard core group" does *not* include 6 to 7 million other persons classified as mentally deficient or retarded, or millions of persons with psychosomatic physical conditions like hypertension resulting from stress, or the very large number of other persons experiencing acute emotional upset as a consequence of life crises. In recent years in the United States there have been, annually, approximately one million divorces, shown by Bloom (1978) to be a significant source of stress leading to any of several different damaging emotional reactions; in addition the stress of the loss of loved ones through death frequently results in severe emotional distress and/or reactive depression. Large numbers of other persons experience emotional crises. Involuntary unemployment, for example, has been shown (Brenner, 1973, 1977) to produce any of several severe consequences including a rise in admissions to mental health clinics and mental health hospitals, an increased incidence of cirrhosis of the liver, alcoholism, fatal accidents, suicide, and an excess of deaths from all causes.

In 1978 the President's Commission on Mental Health reported on the frightening number of underserved and unserved persons in the field of mental health. Part of the problem results from the maldistribution of professionals who tend to be concentrated in the affluent suburbs of populous states.

Who are these underserved and unserved? They are described in several different places in the commission's report. They include children, adolescents and the elderly—all of whom are identified repeatedly as underserved by mental health professionals. These three groups together represent "more than half" of the nation's population. Then there are the minority groups that include 22 million black Americans, 12 million Hispanic Americans, 3 million Asian and Pacific Island Americans, and one million American Indians and Alaska natives. All of these groups are underserved or, in many instances, inappropriately served by persons insensitive to cultural differences or incompetent in appropriate languages. While these identified groups of 38 million persons clearly overlap somewhat with other groups identified as underserved, we are not yet at the end of the statistical complexities. Five million seasonal and migrant farm workers are largely excluded from mental health care. Moreover, we discover that often women do not receive appropriate care in the mental health system. Neither do persons who live in rural America, or in small towns, or in the poor sections of American cities. Neither do 10 million persons with alcohol-related problems, nor an unspecified but growing number of persons who misuse psychoactive drugs, nor the very large number of children and parents involved in child abuse, nor 5 million children with learning disabilities, nor millions of physically handicapped Americans, nor 6 million persons who are mentally retarded.

The Future Is Worse!

Kramer (1981) has raised some important and alarming questions about what he refers to as "the rising pandemic of mental disorders" throughout the world. He points out that the United States faces, in the decades immediately ahead, a steadily increasing prevalence rate of serious mental disorders, as well as medical diseases involving hypertension and cerebro-vascular accidents. The growth in frequency of these conditions will result from the large increase in the number of persons in those age groups who are at higher risk for their development, as well as the steadily increasing *duration* of such chronic conditions directly resulting from the develop-ment of effective techniques for prolonging the lives of affected individ-uals. In brief, more people, throughout the world, are living into middle age and old age and the chronic mental and physical conditions that are more likely to occur with advancing years are not only occurring but are being treated in ways that prolong their duration.

In a paper entitled *Failures of Success,* Gruenberg (1977) talks about the increase in prevalence rates of conditions that are age specific:

It is obvious that, with increasing duration, we would expect the proportion of the population at any given age group suffering from these conditions to rise. And, in fact, as a result of advances in medical care, we are seeing a rising prevalence of certain chronic conditions which previously led to early terminal infections, but whose victims now suffer from them for a longer period. The goal of medical research work is to "diminish disease and enrich life" (Gregg, 1941), but it produced tools which prolong diseased, diminished lives, and so increased the proportion of people who have a disabling or chronic disease.

That is a major but unintended effect of many technological improvements stemming from health research. These increasingly chronic conditions represent the failures of success. Their growing prevalence and longer duration are a product of progress in health technology.

Among the other "failures of success" we should take note of effective medical techniques for prolonging the lives of the severely retarded, for intervening successfully with severely premature and underweight infants, infants with severe perinatal handicaps and complications, all resulting in a subsequent increase in the prevalence of mentally and physically handi-capped persons. Before the development of antibiotics, the life expec-tancy of severely retarded "crib cases" and other institutionalized retard-ates was fairly short because of the prevalence of infectious diseases in institutions. Now with antibiotics, and de-institutionalization, many severely handicapped individuals have a much expanded life expectancy. The de-institutionalization of persons labeled schizophrenic has increased the number of pregnancies in schizophrenic women, for example, and therefore the number of children born with the risk of being reared with an alleged genetic handicap and/or with a schizophrenic mother. Infants born with phenylketonuria (PKU) are being identified through routine lab tests and are being treated with a special diet, allowing them to live into adult childbearing years with the resulting increase in genetic carriers.

Kramer is not suggesting that we turn back the clock on all of these medical advances, but that we be aware of the serious problems these changes promise to cause in our future. The mechanisms he discusses are occurring world wide, including the less developed regions. Indeed, as Kramer points out, there will be further aggravation of the problem of chronic conditions as developing countries industrialize, as their populations move from rural agrarian to urban industrial areas, and as the pattern of living in extended families shifts to a more nuclear family structure. Kramer sees one of the few hopes to be effective research emphasizing *the prevention of chronic disease.* He points to the current increases in the prevalence rate of schizophrenia, the growing rate of admission to mental health facilities and prisons, to homes for the aged and to nursing homes and suggests that prevention is the only logical solution.

If the prevalence rate of mental and emotional disorders in the United States is about 15 percent then with a population increase of more than 20 percent expected over the next 25 years we will have more than 40 million persons with "hard core" mental disorders by the year 2005. Inasmuch as the prevalence of disorders is a function of both incidence and duration, advances in treatment methods for mental disorders can only have the effect of increasing their prevalence. The proportion of the population over 65 will continue to increase rapidly for both white and nonwhite groups. The increase in the rate of the latter will be more dramatic because of remarkable progress in improving life expectancy for nonwhites in recent decades. The proportion of older persons is not only increasing but the number of them who live alone is also increasing, particularly among females. And, as we know from other studies, the rate of mental and emotional disorders among single (including separated, divorced, and widowed) elderly persons is high and increasing.

It is also worth noting that because of differential birth rates, we can expect a 40 percent increase in new cases of schizophrenia among nonwhites because of the increase in the number of 15 to 34 year olds, the group at highest risk.

Kramer (1981) concludes his frightening analysis with the following:

Although there are many shortcomings and gaps in currently available morbidity and mortality statistics, those that are available are sufficient to illustrate the extraordinary increases that can be expected in the number of persons who will be affected by major problems of disease and disability that are of concern to mental health. This includes persons in every age group, from the youngest to the oldest. Prevalence rates of mental disorders, Down's Syndrome, hypertensive disease, cerebrovascular disease, cirrhosis of the liver, diabetes, visual and hearing impairments, and other chronic conditions are increasing throughout the world. This worldwide increase in the prevalence of mental disorders and chronic disease may be best characterized as a rising chronic disease pandemic. . . .

The number of cases of mental disorder will continue to increase *until effective methods are discovered for preventing their occurrence and equally effective and practical methods are found for their application. It is, therefore, particularly important that our policy makers give the highest priority to the support of research and research training directed toward discovering the preventable causes of those conditions that are increasing in prevalence.* (pp. 27, 28, 31, emphasis added)

We have identified a number of factors associated with increased incidence of mental disorders, and we have also found ways to intervene proactively with groups, especially those at high risk for later psychopathology, to reduce the subsequent incidence. Some of these preventive strategies involve the reduction of noxious agents, and some involve strengthening the resistance of the host. These strategies can be related to incidence according to the following model.

$$\text{Incidence} = \frac{\text{Organic Factors} + \text{Stress} + \text{Exploitation}}{\text{Coping Skills} + \text{Self-esteem} + \text{Support Groups}}$$

To succeed in preventive efforts is to reduce the incidence (the number of new cases) of the various emotional disturbances. There are several strategies for accomplishing such a reduction.

Organic factors. The first strategy is to minimize, or to reduce, the number of the various organic factors that sometimes play a role in causation. The more the negative organic factors can be reduced or eliminated, the lower will be the resulting incidence. Several sections in this volume consider genetic, prenatal, postpartum, and later childhood experiences. We also have included material on the preventive value of working with cardiac patients to prevent or reduce sexual dysfunction, and on the benefits of promoting positive health behaviors.

Stress. A second strategy that is obvious from the formula involves the reduction of unnecessary or avoidable stress. As we move into this area, we discover that relationships become more complex. No longer are there such simple cause and effect relationships as we observed in organic factors. Stress takes many forms. Reducing stress may require changes in the physical and social environment. Environmental stress situations involve a whole complex of interacting variables. Some forms of social stress are a product of deeply engrained cultural values and ways of life that are not easily susceptible to change. Readings are included that deal with stress in general, and with particular, and common, sources of stress.

Exploitation. This factor differs from the others in the formula in an important way. Variations in the degree or type of exploitation affect all the other variables in the model—stress, coping skills, self-esteem, the nature and type of support groups available, and even the incidence of organic factors. For example, in a society in which a power elite exploits the environment for personal profit without regard to the social costs and consequences of their greed, the incidence of birth defects may be increased by environmental contamination or malnutrition, physical health of workers may be damaged, and so on. Since exploitation encompasses all the other variables, as well as being something that itself, with its many faces, contributes to psychopathology, it needs to be considered in both its larger and its smaller sense.

Persons who are victims of exploitation in any of its myriad forms suffer serious emotional damage. The exploitation often involves the use of excessive power by the exploiter to force the victims to conform or to behave in ways that are degrading, demeaning, dehumanizing and/or dangerous. While the experience may well be both stressful and damaging to self-esteem, there is a qualitative difference that justifies separate analysis of this factor. In many societies and throughout the history of many cultures, women and children have been exploited by powerful male patriarchal elites. Rape and the sexual abuse of children are obvious examples of exploitation. But there are many other more subtle ways that people can be subject to daily humiliations.

It is important that we try to learn about a society, or any other group sharing a common culture, those things (like sex roles and class position) taken for granted. What are the unquestioned assumptions, the accepted ways of understanding reality, that never rise above the threshold of conscious awareness because no one feels they can question or examine them?

Damage done through *exploitation*—economic, sexual, through the media, causes increased incidence of emotional pathology. The exploited groups are not responsive to exhortations or to other quick-fix solutions. Certain kinds of exploitation result in low self-esteem and become a kind of self-fulfilling prophecy. Members of ethnic minorities and women, who learn from earliest childhood that their race or sex is regarded as inferior by the white patriarchal culture grow up with lower self-esteem that may be exceedingly difficult to change. Feelings of powerlessness are a major form of stress. Preventive efforts may have to take the form of laws to ensure equal opportunity, public education, changes in the way the mass media portrays these groups, and in pervasive value system changes. Clearly, such efforts often encounter the angry resistance of the power forces that get real benefit from the values being criticized.

A reduction in incidence also may be accomplished by developing feelings of competence—better social coping skills, improved self-esteem, and solid support networks. Each section deals with one of these factors. Wherever possible this material is organized in a developmental sequence within sections.

Overall, the readings that follow should give flesh to the bare bones of the formula outlined. In addition, we hope they will provide a starting point enabling those who see that prevention is our only hope to approach the task with the confidence that comes from being aware of these numerous examples of both the promise and the efficacy of programs to prevent psychopathology and promote human competence. This body of knowledge, of which the present volume is only a sampling, should also help to give the lie to those who would cling to outmoded, ineffective, and, in the long run, inhumane attempts to comfort the victims instead of preventing the casualties.

Scattered throughout this volume are readings that are concerned with aspects of exploitation, primarily in its narrower, more direct sense. The importance of exploitation in its broader sense, as a modifier or determinant of the nature of each of the other variables in the model, is great enough for us to have devoted an entire conference to the issues surrounding the question of prevention through political action and social change. We have decided that it is not possible to do justice to this broader meaning of exploitation in a section of the present volume and consequently a subsequent book of readings will concentrate on this issue.

References

Albee, G. Preventing psychopathology and promoting human potential. *American Psychologist*, 1982, 37, 9, 1043–1050.

American Psychiatric Association. *Diagnostic and Statistical Manual of Mental Disorders* (Third Edition). Washington, D.C.: APA, 1980.

Bloom, B. Marital disruption as a stressor. Chapter 6. In Forgays, D.G. (ed.) *Environmental influences and strategies in primary prevention.* Hanover, N.H.: University Press of New England, 1978.

Brenner, M.H. *Mental illness and the economy.* Cambridge, Mass.: Harvard University Press, 1973.

Gruenberg, E. M. Failures of success. Health and society. *The Milbank Memorial Fund Quarterly,* Winter, 1977.

Klerman, G. Speech at the University of Vermont, March 13, 1980. *Faculty symposium on the social and biological origins of mental illness.*

Kramer, M. The increasing prevalence of mental disorders: Implications for the future. Paper presented at the National Conference on the Elderly Deinstitutionalized Patient in the Community. May 28, 1981.

President's Commission on Mental Health. *Report to the President.* Washington, D.C.: U.S. Government Printing Office, 1978.

Ryan, W. *Distress in the city.* Cleveland, Ohio: The Press of Western Reserve University, 1969.

I. Introduction to Primary Prevention

A book of readings on the basic concepts in primary prevention must begin with some clear definitions. We have chosen three sources of definition of primary prevention that should contribute to a clear understanding of the dimensions of this field.

The first of these is a selection from the Report of the Task Panel on Prevention to the President's Commission on Mental Health. In the spring of 1977 President Carter, fulfilling a campaign pledge, appointed a presidential commission to reexamine the nation's approach to problems of mental health. Rosalynn Carter, who for many years has played an active role in the mental health field, served as Honorary Chairperson.

The commission was composed of twenty people, a majority of them not members of the traditional mental health professions but representing a wide range of backgrounds and perspectives. Each task panel reporting to the commission dealt with a specific aspect of mental health and was composed of persons with specific competency in the subject area. The Task Panel on Prevention included persons from social work, psychology, psychiatry, genetics, law, and education—all actively involved in the field of prevention. The final report of the commission led to the passage of a law establishing a Center on Prevention at the National Institute of Mental Health. The definition adopted by the task panel includes both attempts at reducing stress and efforts at improving the competence of people for handling life's stresses. Selections from the report include, in addition to definitions, an examination of barriers to prevention efforts, a consideration of priorities, and a selection of examples of existing research on competency training, the impact of social systems, and stress reduction.

Stephen Goldston and Emory Cowen were active participants in the deliberations of the Task Panel on Prevention of the President's Commission on Mental Health and both have devoted years of effort to moving prevention efforts to a more central focus in the mental health field. Each has important things to say about the definition of prevention and about the impact of political and social influences on efforts in this field. Excerpts from their papers round out our understanding of the definition of prevention.

Report of the Task Panel on Prevention

❖

SUMMARY

Western society's approach to persons with mental disorders has progressed in a series of steps. Each step has been characterized by increasingly humanitarian concern. For thousands of years the insane were reviled, feared, and rejected. Two hundred years ago, in the first mental health "revolution," they were led by Pinel out of the fetid dungeons, up into the light and into more humane treatment. A second revolution, led by Freud, greatly increased our understanding of the continuity between the insane and the sane. Half a century later, a third revolution was dedicated to providing care in a single comprehensive center accessible to all those at high risk. Now, less than a quarter century later, we are on the threshold of a fourth and most exciting mental health revolution. Its goal is to prevent emotional disorders.

Although each revolution has drawn strength from, and built on, earlier ones, we have come more and more to recognize that widespread human distress can never be eliminated by attempts—however successful—to treat afflicted individuals. We shall continue to do everything we can for persons in pain. But we are also determined to take action to reduce the identifiable causes of later distress, and thereby decrease the incidence of emotional disturbance and disorder.

Primary prevention means lowering the incidence of emotional disorder (1) by reducing stress and (2) by promoting conditions that increase competence and coping skills. Primary prevention is concerned with populations not yet affected by individual breakdown, especially with groups at high risk. It is proactive: it often seeks to build adaptive strengths through education and reduce stress through social engineering.

❖ An important "paradigm shift" must be considered in focusing

---

❖This symbol throughout the text indicates the cutting of original material for the purposes of this volume.

attention on research in primary prevention. There are good reasons to believe that just as an emotional disorder may result from any of several background factors and life crises, so can any specific intense stressful event precipitate any of a variety of mental and emotional disorders. Different life histories and different patterns of strengths and weaknesses among different individuals can and do lead to different reactions to stress. This new paradigm requires that we recognize the futility of searching for a unique cause for every emotional disorder. It accepts the likelihood that many disorders can come about as a consequence of many of the varieties of causes. This paradigm leads to the acceptance of the argument that successful efforts at the prevention of a wide variety of disorders can occur without a theory of disorder-specific positive causal mechanisms.

Our recommendations include a focus on a coordinated national effort toward the prevention of emotional disorder with a Center for Primary Prevention within the National Institute of Mental Health, with primary prevention specialists deployed in each of the ten USPHS Regional Offices, with the establishment of State-level efforts, and with the creation of field stations and model demonstration centers. Because many other relevant government agencies can, and should, be concerned with prevention, we are recommending the coordination of efforts through the proposed NIMH center that is to have convening authority. We are recommending that first priority in primary prevention be directed toward work with infants and young children (and their social environments). We give a number of illustrations of the kinds of programs we have in mind. We take special note of the urgent need to reduce societal stresses produced by racism, poverty, sexism, ageism, and the decay of our cities. We make certain suggestions about funding and about a broadly competent citizen's committee to have a continuing advisory role.

PREAMBLE

The *first* revolutionary change in society's approach to the mentally ill and the emotionally disturbed was the humanitarian concern exemplified by Philippe Pinel who, in 1792, removed the chains binding the insane in the fetid dungeons of Paris. He brought those victims up into the sunlight and showed the world that kindness and concern were defensible and appropriate.

The *second* revolutionary change in our attitudes and values had its origin in Freud's work that stressed the continuities between the sane and the insane, the mind of the child and the mind of the adult, the world of dreams and the world of reality.

The *third* revolution was the development of intervention and treatment centers serving all persons needing help—comprehensive community mental health centers—where, through a single door, everyone could seek and find skilled help for the whole range of human mental and emotional problems.

Unlike political revolutions, each of these mental health revolutions drew strength and inspiration from the earlier ones.

We believe we now stand on the threshold of a *fourth* revolution. Like its predecessors, this revolution will not attempt to displace or replace progress already achieved. The new revolution will involve major societal efforts at *preventing* mental illness and emotional disturbance. It will apply the best available knowledge, derived from research and clinical experience, to prevent needless distress and psychological dysfunction. It will, in the best public health tradition, also seek to build strengths and increase competence and coping skills in populations and thereby reduce the incidence of later disturbance. This fourth revolution, if it happens, will identify our society as a *caring society*—one that both holds out its hand to its unfortunate members and does all it can to prevent misfortune for those at risk.

❖

INTRODUCTION AND RATIONALE

The development and application of primary prevention programs in the field of the emotional disorders is the great unmet mental health challenge of our time. From both a moral and ethical point of view, preventive intervention has the potential for reducing human suffering associated with emotional disorder and the impact of that suffering on family and friends. From an economic point of view, effective primary prevention programs promise to be less expensive in the long run than the direct (fiscal) and indirect (human) costs to society of not providing such services.

The term "primary prevention" refers to a group of approaches that share the common objectives of (1) lowering the incidence of emotional disorders (i.e. the rate at which new cases occur) and (2) promoting conditions that reinforce positive mental health. Primary prevention, in concentrating its efforts on promotion and maintenance of competence, is distinguished from traditional mental health services designed to identify, treat, or rehabilitate persons already disturbed (Kessler and Albee, 1975; Albee and Joffe, 1977; Cowen, 1977; Bloom, 1977; Klein and Goldston, 1977).

One way in which primary prevention works in the mental health field is to eliminate the causes of disorders of known or discoverable etiologies (e.g. cerebral syphilis). Equally or perhaps more important, primary prevention involves building the strengths, resources, and competencies in individuals, families, and communities that can reduce the flow of a variety of unfortunate outcomes—each characterized by enormous human and societal cost. Because primary prevention approaches can be applied flexibly in a variety of situations, they are an especially attractive means for reaching vulnerable, high-risk groups.

Primary prevention activities have two main justifications: (1) the body of evidence supporting the efficacy of these approaches in their own right; and (2) the growing sense of dissatisfaction, as the gap widens between demonstrated need for help and the costly, often unavailable, human resources to meet that need, with mental health's past exclusive reliance on corrective measures.

From a logistical point of view, there can never be a sufficient number of skilled health care providers to meet unchecked intervention needs. And, in any case, no major disorder in a population has ever been eliminated by providing one-to-one treatment, however comprehensive.

Historically, the mental health field has always been unswerving in its definition of mandate, i.e. to understand the complexities of psychological aberration and to contain or minimize dysfunction when called on to engage it. However constructive that mandate is, the service systems developed to meet it cannot be expected to resolve society's mental health problems. Thus, today (1) there are too few resources to deal with mental health problems as defined, (2) distribution of those limited resources is inequitable, following the ironic rule of where help is most needed it is least available, and (3) mental health energies are disproportionately allocated to the exacting and costly task of trying to overcome already rooted, crystallized, "end state" conditions—precisely those that most resist change.

The history of public health in the past century provides ample evidence that programs designed to prevent disease and disorder can be effective and reasonably economical. Infectious diseases that can now be prevented include smallpox, malaria, typhus, cholera, yellow fever, polio, and measles. An equally impressive group of nutritional disorders, including scurvy, pellagra, beriberi, and kwashiorkor, is now also understood and preventable. Imagine what our health bill would be if those diseases were not preventable and society therefore needed to bear the costs of supporting state malaria hospitals, state pellagra hospitals, and state hospitals for polio victims.

Preventive measures have proved to be a vital extension of health care practices in physical health. The mental health field, however, has yet to use available relevant knowledge to develop comparable efforts systematically. Public health approaches offer a sound conceptual and operating framework for undertaking primary prevention in the mental health field.

Primary prevention approaches, on logical, humanitarian, and empirical grounds, thus offer an attractive, sorely needed extension of existing mental health practices that hold promise for reducing the eventual flow of emotional disorder.

In the history of medicine, the response to disease illustrates the relationship between the state of knowledge and what physicians actually do. At a time when few normal physiological processes, let alone the pathological ones, were understood, physicians had to be content with describing what they saw and paltry efforts at palliation. Only with the advance of medical knowledge was it possible to refine descriptions into diagnoses and, with an understanding of etiology, to prescribe disease-specific treatment. As we have become more sophisticated about the nature of illness, efforts to prevent illness have also increased. For diseases with specific etiologies, i.e. in which the pathogenic relationships between causative agent and disease came to be fully understood, prevention efforts were often dramatic. But as most diseases have multiple causes, they required more complex strategies for prevention as well.

Most mental conditions lack the single etiology or definitive understanding of pathogenesis needed for dramatic prevention efforts. That very fact has led many people to despair of *ever* preventing mental disturbance and to continue to advocate an exclusive emphasis on diagnosis and treatment as the only scientifically justifiable approach to mental illness. This broad kind of denial of the possibiltities of prevention has led to widespread indifference toward it both by the medical profession and within society at large. We have thus lived through an era of greater and greater expenditures for treatment and rehabilitation without a much-needed corresponding attention to existing possibilities for prevention.

Prevention in the field of mental health can properly be seen as an integrating perspective that can fuse our best understandings of the etiology of mental disorder, personal and family relationships, and individual psychodynamics on the one hand with a recognition, on the other, of the salient social forces and pressures that combine to produce the individual and collective disorganization we call emotional illness.

❖

DEFINITIONS: WHAT PRIMARY PREVENTION IS AND IS NOT

Primary prevention in mental health is a network of strategies that differ *qualitatively* from the field's past dominant approaches. Those strategies are distinguished by several essential characteristics. This brief section highlights primary prevention's essences using the direct contrast style of saying *what it is* and *what it is not*.

(1) Most fundamentally, primary prevention is *proactive* in that it seeks to build adaptive strengths, coping resources, and health in people; not to reduce or contain already manifest deficit.

(2) Primary prevention is concerned about total populations, especially including groups at high risk; it is less oriented to individuals and to the provision of services on a case-by-case basis.

(3) Primary prevention's main tools and models are those of education and social engineering, not therapy or rehabilitation, although some insights for its models and programs grow out of the wisdom derived from clinical experience.

(4) Primary prevention assumes that equipping people with personal and environmental resources for coping is the best of all ways to ward off maladaptive problems, not trying to deal (how-

ever skillfully) with problems that have already germinated and flowered.

WHAT DO WE SEEK TO PREVENT?

We believe there is sufficient evidence to encourage further development of strategies for the prevention of a wide variety of conditions, such as: the psychoses, especially organic psychoses, neuroses and other social disorders, learning disabilities, child abuse, and other behavioral, emotional, and developmental deviations that fall within the broad range of mental health problems.

One key difference between the human organism and lower animals is the much longer period of time during which the human infant and child must depend on others for survival and support. During that long growth process, successful development can be interfered with by an unusually large number of factors at any point. Thus, under certain unfortunate circumstances, all infants are at risk for subsequent emotional and developmental deviations. Scientific advances have markedly reduced the mortality and morbidity of childbirth. Never before in our history have infants had as good an opportunity as they now do to be born healthy and to thrive. Unfortunately, however, the delivery of a biologically healthy full-term infant does not guarantee smooth psychosocial development forever after. Precisely because interference with optimal development is known to occur with high frequency, and to exact a heavy toll, it is imperative that programs for primary prevention be developed. It is essential to establish priorities, to select infants and children at particularly high risk, and to develop programs to assure optimal continuing development for such target groups. We firmly believe that efforts directed toward infants and young children will provide maximum return in successful prevention.

The Task Panel advocates the establishment of programs designed to prevent persistent, destructive, maladaptive behaviors, i.e. those unfortunate "end states" that result from identifiable stresses for which the individual lacks the necessary coping skills and the adaptive competencies to handle constructively. That critical goal suggests the need to identify (1) agreed-upon behavioral conditions that pose a serious threat to others because of the damage they cause; (2) patterns of behavior that are so distasteful for the affected person that he cries out for relief; or (3) emotional states that lead to withdrawal from meaningful social partipation. Clearly, many such traits or conditions require social value judgments about what is desirable or undesirable behavior, acceptable and unacceptable styles of living. Some of these decisions, in short, may present dangers to liberty and to the freedom of people to follow their own drummers, to be unconventional, and even to be damned fools. There are many historical examples of the tyranny of the majority enforcing patterns of approved behavior and lifestyles, and too many deviants who have been punished, excommunicated, or even killed, for nonconformity. Clearly, preventive efforts must be directed toward those end states that cause either genuine harm to others or genuine unwanted suffering in affected individuals.

Attempts to classify mental conditions have turned out to be far more complex than was originally thought. The exciting successes of medicine and biology during the nineteenth century in classifying physical illnesses were viewed as models that might lead ultimately to successful classification of mental diseases. Indeed, the discovery of specific physical causes for certain mental conditions—the role of the spirochete, and the relationship of untreated syphilis to the subsequent appearance of a serious mental illness called general paresis; relationships between vitamin deficiency and pellagral psychosis; the serious social and behavioral consequences of oversecretion and undersecretion of certain endocrine glands such as the thyroid and the adrenals—each served to strengthen the belief that, eventually, all disturbed behavioral states would be found to have an underlying pathologic organic cause. That view persists even today. Some experts accept Nobel Laureate Linus Pauling's view that there can be no insanity in a healthy brain (1968). Another world famous chemist, Ralph Gerard, said much the same thing: "There can be no twisted behavior without a twisted molecule." Unfortunately, life is not so simple; indeed many everyday observations contradict that view. For example, soldiers under extreme combat stress often show serious emotional disturbances; children of disturbed parents often exhibit serious emotional problems; many persons undergoing naturally occurring life stresses, such as sudden widowhood or marital disruption, experience extreme personal anguish and depression. Yet each of these conditions is reversible. The critical point to be understood is that while all behavior has an underlying physiological *basis*, disturbed behavior need not imply an underlying pathological organic *process*. In short, people react emotionally to stress; they learn to withdraw, to attack, or to distort their relationships with others through normal physical mechanisms.

The Task Panel on Prevention thus advocates a broad-gauged effort in primary prevention directed ultimately to reducing the incidence of the major aberrant conditions and end states that have for years occupied the attention of, claimed the efforts of, and been sources of exasperation to the mental health field: the major childhood behavioral and developmental disabilities, the functional and organic psychoses, symptom and character neuroses, and profound psychosocial disorders such as delinquency and addiction. The Task Panel advocates a vigorous national effort to build health and competencies in individuals from birth, so that each person may maximize his chances for a productive, effective life.

We note especially that any serious national effort at prevention of mental disorders and promotion of mental health must also be addressed to those social-environmental stressors that significantly contribute to the pathology of prejudice. Racism is a particularly noxious influence. Likewise, bias against ethnic minorities, sexism, and ageism must be recognized as placing significant portions of the population at high risk of mental disorder merely by membership in these groups and from the environmental stress that such membership attracts. While outside the direct purview, or immediate special competence, of mental health specialists, elimination of institutionalized and other forms of racism and other biases must continue to be a priority for primary prevention as well as for other aspects of our national interest.

BARRIERS TO PRIMARY PREVENTION EFFORTS

However sensible or rational primary prevention is, however critical it is as a key future strategy for the mental health fields, it is an approach that must surmount powerful barriers, including the following:

(1) Our society is crisis-oriented; we react to here-and-now

pain, blood, and visible suffering. Because primary prevention is future-oriented, many see it as postponable—or if not that, then certainly as having low priority. Because it is oriented so heavily to strengthening people's resources and coping skills rather than addressing current casualty, it lacks a constituency and political clout.

(2) The history, traditions, and past values of the mental health professions have been built on the strategies of repairing existing dysfunction. People are attracted to mental health with that image in mind; moreover, they are trained and they practice in the same mold. That image of self and way of behaving professionally is reinforced because it serves such human needs as the need for status and economic gain and the (understandable) gratifications involved in the process of being personally helpful to distressed others. The question is whether it serves society equally well.

(3) Primary prevention in mental health is threatening to some because its very nature may raise sensitive issues of social and environmental change and/or issues about people's right to be left alone.

(4) Existing mechanisms to support certain mental health activities (e.g. funds for third-party reimbursement, treatment staff, hospital beds) are not geared to primary prevention activities. Accordingly, primary prevention proposals are viewed by some not only as threatening to rooted ways and vested interests but also as competing for resource dollars.

(5) The past lack of recognition of primary prevention as an accepted way in mental health that differs qualitatively from past approaches leaves a series of *Catch-22* residues:

  (a) Fiscal allocations for primary prevention dollars rarely exist, or are at best pitifully small.

  (b) We lack appropriate administrative structures charged with the responsibility of promoting the development of primary prevention.

  (c) Personnel trained in the ways of primary prevention are in extremely short supply. Moreover, they tend to be the last hired and the first fired.

(d) Few professionals are assigned to primary mental health activities on a sustained, full-time basis.

(e) Activities that are labeled primary prevention often, in fact, are not that at all.

(f) There has been virtually no support for research in primary prevention; yet, ironically, critics argue that the field lacks sufficient evidence to warrant programmatic action. One indication of the difference in attitudes toward treatment and prevention is that treatment efforts are mandated even without adequate effectiveness data, whereas prevention efforts are discouraged because of "lack of evidence." With respect to treatment of already identified cases, the social mandate is to "try to be helpful." No such mandate has existed for prevention efforts.

Problems such as the above cannot be engaged, much less resolved, until primary prevention is accorded a place of visibility and importance, backed by leadership with the mechanisms and resources needed to achieve true viability, rather than tokenism.

PRIORITIES

Our Task Panel was asked to order our priorities among a range of prevention interventions and among the variety of target groups for whom primary prevention efforts are possible. It is not easy to set such priorities; indeed, decisions about them could well vary as a function of the weights given to social value judgments versus scientific criteria.

We can try to illustrate the kinds of choices we considered in setting priorities among the large variety of primary prevention programs the Task Panel reviewed. We found ourselves considering:

(1) Programs with high potential for success that affect relatively few people, e.g.

(a) Genetic counseling of persons with a family history of Huntington's Disease, PKU, or Down's Syndrome;

(b) Intensive intervention with blind infants (based on the fact that such children are known to be at high risk for psychosis).

(2) Programs with significant research effectiveness demonstrated on small samples but with good prospects for reaching large numbers, e.g.

(a) Competency training in pre-school settings and early school grades;

(b) Widow-to-widow self-help counseling groups.

(3) Programs with strong *theoretical* promise for success affecting potentially large numbers of people, e.g.

(a) Helping groups for people who experience sudden or extreme stresses such as infant death, job loss, or marital disruption.

(4) Programs aimed at improving broad social situations with potentially great impact on millions of people. Because such conditions are not usually considered part of mental health's purview, considering them might give the Commission the set that the Task Panel has too wide a range of things, i.e. *everything* is primary prevention! Candidly, too, such considerations may involve sufficiently controversial social values that it would be politically wiser to avoid them. Examples include the potentially damaging mental health consequences of:

(a) Unemployment, discrimination, and lack of job security;

(b) Boring and/or dangerous work;

(c) The national epidemic of teen-age pregnancies, unwanted births, premature parenthood;

(d) Smoking and the use of drugs, including alcohol; their effects on unborn children;

(e) Ethnocentrism—racism, sexism, ageism; the damage wrought, the self-fulfilling prophecy, the damaged self-esteem of the persecutor and the persecuted.

Priority-setting may be premature. One rational, possible approach would be to base priorities on three sources of judgment:

(1)   Epidemiological information on prevalence of distress;

(2)   Value judgments solicited from affected groups, e.g. minorities, the aged, the impoverished—all at high risk; and

(3)   Research and demonstrations of effectiveness.

STRATEGIES RESTING ON A RESEARCH BASE

Members of the Task Panel, pulled between the choice of an overinclusive need to cite every relevant study done on primary prevention and the clear realization that brevity and readability were essential, opted for the latter. Somewhat self-consciously, we regarded ourselves as being among the nation's experts on primary prevention. We thus hoped that we might have enough credibility with the members of the Commission to be able to say firmly that the existing evidence indeed supports a major shift in emphasis toward primary prevention. For Commission members who already have the vision that mental health's major new thrusts must be toward the prevention of distress and the building of competence in the citizenry, we need cite only enough data to be reassuring that a broad capability for such an effort truly exists.

At the risk of sounding apocalyptic, the Task Panel believes that a firm, enthusiastic recommendation by the President's Commission for a genuinely accelerated national effort in primary prevention would be a major step forward for humankind. Symbolically, this would mark acceptance of our role as our brothers' and sisters' keepers. It would say that relevant mental health activities must go beyond the here-and-now and would thus move to center-stage a long-term view of benefiting all humankind.

Primary prevention's defining characteristics and mandates necessarily structure its main strategies. With proaction, health and competence-building, and a population orientation among its core qualities, it follows virtually automatically that primary prevention programs must be heavily oriented to the very young. Although the Panel's discussions of programs and strategies have ranged across all developmental stages, we agreed that major primary prevention efforts must be focused on the prenatal, perinatal, infancy, and childhood periods.

The National Association for Mental Health has developed a detailed program of primary prevention that guides efforts from conception through the first months of life. In our recommendations we list a number of other efforts that can be applied at prenatal, perinatal, and subsequent childhood levels. Again, we reemphasize our agreement about the importance of an approach that follows the developmental sequence. In this section, however, we will illustrate the research base with just a few brief programmatic examples.

Let us give a detailed example that involves efforts with children beginning with the pre-school years. Such an approach, consistent with the spirit of primary prevention, has yet to be harnessed systematically by the mental health fields. At the same time, a rapidly growing body of evidence demands that it be taken into serious account.

It has been known for some years that performance on an interrelated group of skills known collectively as interpersonal cognitive problem solving skills (ICPS) consistently discriminates between maladapted clinical or patient groups of children (and adults) and healthy normals (e.g. Spivack and Levine, 1963; Platt, Altmann, and Altmann, 1973; Spivack, Platt, and Shure, 1976; Spivack and Shure, 1977). Such ICPS skills as the ability to "sense" problems, to identify feelings, to use alternative-solution thinking, means-end thinking, and consequential thinking apparently provide a useful cognitive and emotional technology for engaging interpersonal problems effectively. Those who have and use those skills effectively appear to others in interpersonal relations as well adjusted behaviorally. Those who lack or are deficient in such skills are seen as maladjusted—sometimes even with clinically-significant conditions such as neuroses, psychoses, problems of delinquency, antisocial behavior, or addiction. ICPS skills can thus be thought of as mediating effective behavioral adjustment. If that is so, the challenge it presents for primary prevention is to find ways to equip children, as early and effectively as possible, with those skills. The model of ICPS skill-training well illustrates primary prevention's defining attributes: it is health-building, proactive, mass-oriented, and educational. The main theoretical constraint on the ICPS approach is the human organism's limit to profit developmentally from such training. Once that developmental point is reached, only the formats and mechanisms of ICPS training, not its goals, need change for different groups who can be exposed to the approach.

Several research teams have implemented ICPS training programs directed to different target groups that are quite diverse in terms of age, prior history, and sociocultural and ethnic background. Their findings have been instructive—indeed, exciting.

Spivack and Shure (1974) developed one such program consisting of 46 "lessons," given over a ten-week period, for four-year-old Head-Start children. Not only did children in the program acquire the key ICPS skills, but as that happened their behavioral adjustment was also found to improve. Particularly interesting was the fact that the initially most maladapted youngsters both (1) advanced the most in ICPS skill-acquisition and (2) improved the most behaviorally. Spivack and Shure also demonstrated direct linkages between the amount of gain in ICPS skills—particularly in the ability to generate alternative solutions—and improvement in subsequent adjustment. Follow-up of program youngsters a year later, when they had gone on to new class-settings, showed that program improvements were maintained over time (Shure and Spivack, 1975a). In a closely related project (Shure and Spivack, 1975b), it was shown that inner-city mothers given special training in the ICPS method were successful in training their own children in those skills—again with positive radiation to the adjustment sphere. Thus, a potentially powerful primary prevention tool was shown to have coequal applicability in the two settings that most significantly shape a child's early development: home and school.

Several other groups, working within the same general framework, have provided further demonstrations of the applicability and fruitfulness of the ICPS training model as a strategy for primary prevention (Stone, Hinds, and Schmidt, 1975; Allen et al., 1976; Gesten et al., 1977; Elardo and Caldwell, 1976; Elardo and Cooper, 1977). It is beyond the scope of this brief summary to review that body of work in detail. Indeed the main reason for providing the citations is to establish that the efficacy of the approach is not confined to the inputs and wisdom of a single team, working with a particular target group, in a special setting; rather, because the approach has been shown to have generality across diverse settings and age, sex, and ethnic and socioeconomic levels, it stands as an example of a promising generalized strategy for primary prevention.

Findings based on the ICPS approach are in the same research tradition as an earlier set of demonstrations growing out of Ralph Ojemann's pioneering programs (1961, 1969) to train children to think causally. Other workers (Bruce, 1968; Muuss, 1960; Griggs and Bonney, 1970) have shown that successful mastery of causal thinking skills is accompanied by significant gain on measures of (decreased) anxiety, (increased) security and self-concept, and improved overall adjustment status in children.

This broad competence training strategy is limited primarily by its newness and by the minimal investment that has gone into it so far. Thus, the broad range of its potential has scarcely been explored. By broad range is meant the fact that many other competencies besides those that make up the ICPS group may be clearly shown to contribute significantly to behavior adjustment. Examples might include such qualities as healthy curiosity behavior, altruism, role-taking, and the ability to set realistic goals. A promising recent study by Stamps (1975) provides evidence in support of the basic argument. Working with fourth-grade inner-city children, Stamps developed a curriculum, based on self-reinforcement techniques, designed to teach realistic goal-setting skills. Program children learned those skills readily. As their goal setting skills developed, they showed parallel improvements in achievement, in behavioral adjustment, and on personality measures. At the end of training, teachers judged them to have fewer behavior problems than demographically comparable nonprogram controls. Moreover, they showed improvement on measures of openness, awareness, and self-acceptance.

The importance of early competence acquisition can be illustrated at a somewhat different level, i.e. in relationship to a rapidly developing body of knowledge about the efficacy of enrichment stimulation programs for young disadvantaged children (Gottfried, 1973; Horowitz and Paden, 1973; Jason, 1975). Among the most impressive program efforts in the area is that of Heber (1976) and his associates, in Milwaukee—a ten-year longitudinal program with dramatic and exciting findings. Heber's program, directed to the high risk children of mothers with IQs of 75 or less, started immediately after the child was born. An intensive, saturated program emphasizing continual skill training was conducted at a day care center where the children spent all day every day for the first five years of life. Each family was also assigned a home teacher who taught mothers child-rearing and other life skills. Careful comparisons of the program children to matched nonprogram controls, over a ten-year period, have uncovered some remarkable findings. For example, this initially high-risk program sample has not only far outpaced controls, cognitively and linguistically (e.g. at age 7 they had a mean IQ of 121, versus 87 for controls), but they have also run well ahead of expectancies for a normal population of age-peers at large. The key message from this impressive demonstration is that systematic early competence acquisition seems to pave the way for effective later adaptations in key life spheres.

The main sense of the program development and research efforts we are describing here is as follows: We now know that several pivotal competencies, on the surface quite far removed from mental health's classic terrain, can be taught effectively to young children and that their acquisition radiates positively to adaptations and behaviors that are, indeed, of prime concern to mental health. Symptoms and problem behaviors are reduced after acquisition of these skills. Health has been proactively engineered, so to speak, through skill acquisition. This is a message we cannot afford to repress; it is both a paradigmatic example and further mandate for intensified primary prevention efforts.

However promising the competence training approach to date has been, it should be seen as just one model—not as a bible. We urgently need a fuller and clearer understanding of the nature of core competencies in children—how they relate to each other and, even more important, how they may radiate to interpersonal adjustment. We need to understand what changes take place with development in the nature of essential competencies. As competencies that radiate to adjustment are identified, curricula and methods for helping young children acquire them must be developed. The effectiveness of those curricula, as well as their actual behavioral and adjustive consequences, must be carefully evaluated. That is a complex and time-consuming challenge, one that must be met by a concerted effort and not by small, isolated programs or small research grants. The costs will be substantial, but so is the potential reward: a healthier, happier, more effective, better adjusted next generation, on the positive side, and a decrease in the flow of those types of emotional dysfunctions and behavioral aberrations that are at once socially draining, degrading, costly, and destructive of human beings.

Competence training, though unquestionably a powerful tool for primary prevention, is not the only one. A second strategy, also with high potential, is the analysis and modification of social systems. It can be applied at multiple levels, from broad to narrow. It rests on the view that people's (especially children's) development, adaptation, and effectiveness are significantly shaped by the qualities of a relatively few high-impact environments in which they live (e.g. families and schools and communities). Environments can be many things. One thing they cannot be is neutral. Whether planned or by default, they are factors that either facilitate or impede the growth and adaptation of their inhabitants. The following section illustrates research-based efforts to change environments, including social environments, constructively. The first and most impactful social system is the infant-caregiver relationship.

Broussard (1976) has demonstrated, under careful research conditions, negative later outcomes in first-born children whose mothers perceived them negatively shortly after birth and a month later. In those cases in which the mother reported negative attitudes toward the infant at birth and also a month later, follow-up studies through age 11 have shown a high risk of emotional disturbance in these children. Broussard is now engaged in an intervention study with a sample of these high risk infants and mothers using family interviews, home visits, and mother-infant groups up to two years following birth. Preliminary results show significantly better developmental scores for the Intervention children than for Intervention-refused and comparison groups. This set of studies again is illustrative. Viewed together with the Klaus and Kennell studies (1976) showing the critical importance of early bonding experiences between mother (and/or other caregiver) and infant, certain implications for preventive intervention emerge. Conditions designed to maximize optimal positive social perception of the infant are important to the development of a sense of self-esteem and self-worth.

The demonstration of relationships between characteristics of environments and the emotional well-being of people is not at all limited to the infancy period. Indeed, there are examples of such work involving children of all ages during the school years. Illustratively, Stallings (1975) developed a comprehensive framework for assessing class environments for young school children in Project Follow Through. She reported clear relationships between environmental properties and positive outcomes, academic as well as interpersonal (e.g. cooperativeness, curiosity, persistence). Moos and his colleagues at Stanford (Moos, 1973, 1974a, 1974b; Moos and Trickett, 1974; Insel and Moos, 1974) have pioneered the development of measures of a variety of social environments (e.g. hospital wards, schools, military companies, and work units) and have shown consistent relationships between environmental properties and how people feel and behave in those environments. Environments that score high in such relational qualities as involvement and mutual support, compared to their opposites, appear to have occupants who are less irritable and depressed, more satisfied and comfortable, and have higher self-esteem. Specifically, for high schools, Trickett and Moos (1974) demonstrated that students from classes with high perceived student involvement and close student-teacher relationships reported greater satisfaction and more positive mood states than their opposites.

Although qualities of social environments clearly affect what happens to their occupants, it oversimplifies things to assume that those effects are constant for all people. Several observers have stressed the importance of "ecological-matches," i.e. environments that are facilitative for one person can strangle another (Hunt, 1971)—a point that has been documented empirically in several studies (e.g. Grimes and Allinsmith, 1961; Reiss and Dyhdalo, 1975). Especially relevant is the extensive work reported by Kelly and his colleagues (Kelly, 1968, 1969; Kelly et al., 1971, 1977). who have examined, longitudinally, the nature of adaptive behavior in fluid (high annual pupil-turnover) and stable (low annual pupil-turnover) high school environments. Their main finding was that what is adaptive in one environment was not in the other. For example, new students integrated much more readily in fluid environments, where personal development was highly valued. By contrast, status and achievement were more important in stable environments. Insel and Moos (1974) bring the ecological-match question an important step closer to mental health's prime terrain with the following observation: "A source of distress and ill health is in the situation in which a person attempts to function within an environment with which he is basically incompatible."

The purpose of the preceding brief summary is simply to establish that there is already a body of data showing that social climate variation relates to person outcomes on variables of central interest to mental health; moreover, such outcomes may differ for different people. Although we still lack a full understanding of those complex relationships, enough is in place to pinpoint future challenges for primary prevention: What *are* the high-impact dimensions of the important social environments that shape children? How are they best *assessed*? What are the *relationships* between environmental properties and person outcomes, i.e. which qualities facilitate or impede development, and for whom? Ultimately, the goal for primary prevention is to help engineer social environments that optimize development for all people.

Research and demonstration strategies based on impactful social systems must rest on prior or concurrent efforts to provide a sound foundation of good health care and nutrition. Good health care before and at the time of birth has preventive impact. At the time of childbirth, many preventable traumata occur, both physiological and psychological, that can affect the later mental health of the child. Prolonged and difficult births often involve anoxia (lack of oxygen) for the infant. Because low birth weight is known to increase the risk of later difficulties, hospital nurseries must be available for premature infants to prevent damage. Psychologically, support from family members and others is important for the woman at the time of childbirth.

Promoting the health of the expectant mother and child during and after pregnancy, together with sound health care to avoid the complications of pregnancy, including prematurity, can materially reduce the incidence of future mental problems.

Clinical observation of many disturbed people documents the important role played by identifiable environmental social system stresses in precipitating emotional breakdown. Situations involving unusual and intense distress often serve as a kind of "natural experiment" establishing this relationship. Thus, children of parents involved in disrupted marriages, and children moved from foster home to foster home, show a high frequency of emotional disturbance. Adults who lose a job, or who experience the loss of a spouse or child, often show psychological, physiological, and psychosomatic disturbances. (See Holmes and Rahe, 1967; Dohrenwend and Dohrenwend, 1974.)

Although individuals differ in their resistance to environmental pressure, the reduction of environmental stress clearly reduces emotional disturbance. A considerable amount of recent research has related life stresses to subsequent emotional disturbances. The death of a spouse, the loss of a job, going on vacation, marriage, the birth of a child—all are environmental events that may lead to both physical and psychological disturbance.

The individual's social support system is a key factor in determining his or her response to a stressful environmental event. (Caplan and Killilea, 1976; Collins and Pancoast, 1976; Gottlieb, 1976.) We can point to members of identifiable groups and predict a higher than random chance of their later serious emotional disturbance. Children of adults labeled schizophrenic or alcoholic are more likely to be identified later as emotionally disturbed. Primary grade children who are seen by teachers or peers as having adjustment difficulties have been shown to have higher rates of later emotional problems (Cowen et al., 1974, 1975; Robins, 1966; Werner and Smith, 1977).

Research on *stress reduction* is voluminous. Interventions can range from effective sex education for school-age children to anticipatory guidance or emotional inoculation to modeling and/or abreactive approaches before predictable stresses such as elective surgery, all the way through the life cycle to widow-to-widow self-help groups during and following bereavement (Silverman, 1976, 1977). Relationships between stress and emotional disturbance are often much less visible or direct than those between environmental toxins and physical illness. But there are exceptions to this rule, one of which is documented more fully in the paragraphs to follow.

Of all social variables that have been studied in relation to the distribution of psychopathology in the population, none has been more consistently and powerfully associated with this distribution than marital status (Bloom, 1977). Persons who are divorced or separated have repeatedly been found to be overrepresented among the emotionally disturbed, while persons who are married and living with their spouses have been found to be underrepresented. In a recent review of 11 studies of marital status and the incidence of mental disorder reported during the past 35 years, Crago (1972) found that, without a single exception, admission rates into psychiatric facilities were lowest among the married, intermediate among the widowed and never-married adults, and highest among the divorced and separated. This differential appears to be stable across different age groups (Adler, 1953), reasonably stable for each sex separately considered (Thomas and Locke, 1963; Malzberg, 1964), and as true for blacks as for whites (Malzberg, 1956). Supportive evidence of these differentials was provided by Bachrach (1975), who noted that "utilization studies [of mental health services] have generally shown that married people have substantially lower utilization rates than nonmarried people and that the highest utilization rates occur among persons whose marriages have been disrupted by separation or divorce."

Not only are highest admission rates to mental hospitals reported for persons with disrupted marriages, but the differential between those rates and similarly calculated rates among the married is substantial. The ratio of admission rates for divorced and separated persons to those for married persons is on the order of 18:1 for males and about 7:1 for females for public inpatient facilities. In the case of admissions into public outpatient clinics, admission rates are again substantially higher for separated or divorced persons than for married persons. Ratios of these admission rates are nearly 7:1 for males and 5:1 for females (Bloom, 1977).

Although data documenting the adverse mental health correlates of marital disruption are especially extensive and compelling, that is by no means the only area in which linkages between life-stress and emotional upheaval have been shown. Other prominent examples include bereavement, natural disaster, loss of a child, e.g. as in the Sudden Infant Death Syndrome (Goldston, 1977), and job loss. It has been said, with good reason, that life stresses and crises involve both danger and opportunity. Such crises are frequent. They menace—often disrupt—the victim's well-being. They have potentially long-term debilitating effects. The challenge for primary prevention is to develop new program models for at-risk victims of life stresses—programs that minimize the dangers of stress situations and maximize the opportunities they offer for learning effective new ways of coping.

The Task Panel reviewed a very large number of studies of social systems and life events that produce high degrees of stress in large numbers of people. It is important, as noted above, to point out that social stress (from child abuse and marital disruption to racism, discrimination, and unemployment) increases the probability of physical and mental breakdown or disturbance. At the same time, because there are no clear-cut cause-specific connections between single identifiable stresses and a subsequent disturbance, the primary prevention strategist cannot always "produce the convincing evidence" of direct linkages of cause and effect so often demanded by research funding agencies.

It should perhaps be stated explicitly that the Panel's proposals for program development and research in primary prevention involve what philosophers of science call a major new "paradigm shift" (Kuhn, 1970; Rappaport, 1977). The area of social stress illustrates the point. The history of efforts to prevent organic disease shows that one particular research paradigm has been remarkably successful in giving us a sound research base for developing preventive methods. That traditional paradigm may be outlined as follows: (1) define a disease or condition that is judged to be in need of prevention and then develop procedures for reliably identifying persons with the condition; (2) study its distribution in terms of time, place, or person characteristics in the population in order to identify factors that appear to be causally related to it; (3) mount and evaluate experimental prevention programs to test the validity of the hypotheses generated by the previous observations.

That paradigm has been enormously successful; it was used, for example, to develop highly effective preventive programs for smallpox and cholera in the nineteenth century and for rubella and polio in the twentieth century. In the case of the emotional disorders, general paresis is now preventable, as is psychosis following pellagra—both as a result of this approach.

But there are good reasons to believe that new paradigms are now needed. One such reason is that many emotional disorders do not seem to have specific biological causal basis; indeed, most result from a multiplicity of interacting factors. Hence, a paradigm that represents a major departure from the earlier model outlined above is now having a much greater impact on our knowledge base. Its steps may be summarized as follows: (1) identify stressful life events or experiences that have undesirable consequences in a significant proportion of the population and develop procedures for reliably identifying persons who have undergone or who are undergoing such events or experiences; (2) study the consequences of those events in a population by contrasting subsequent illness experiences or emotional problems with those of a suitably selected comparison population; (3) mount and evaluate experimental prevention programs aimed at reducing the incidence of such stressful life events and/or at increasing coping skills in managing those events.

This new paradigm assumes that just as a single disorder may come about as a consequence of a variety of stressful life events, any specific stress event may precipitate a variety of disorders, as a result of differing life histories and patterns of strengths and weaknesses in individuals. For example, an unanticipated death or divorce, or a job loss, may increase the risk of alcoholism in one person, coronary artery disease in another, depression and suicide in a third, and a fatal automobile accident in a fourth. That is, this new paradigm begins by recognizing the futility of searching for a unique cause for every disorder. It accepts the likelihood that many disorders can come about as a consequence of any of a variety of causes. With this acceptance comes the realization that successful efforts at the prevention of a vast array of disorders (particularly emotional disorders) can take place without a theory of disorder-specific causative mechanisms.

This section has presented a brief distillation of some of the current knowledge base in three main areas of primary prevention in mental health: (a) competency training emphasizing developmental approaches, (b) the impact of social systems on individual development, and (c) the reduction and management of naturally occuring life development stresses. All three areas already have substantial, promising knowledge bases that not only justify accelerated primary prevention efforts for the future, but point specifically to areas in which such efforts may be most useful at once.

REFERENCES

Adler, L. M. The relationship of marital status to incidence of and recovery from mental illness. *Social Forces*, 1954, *32*, 185–194.
Albee, George W., and Joffe, Justin M. (Eds.). *Primary prevention of psychopathology. Vol. 1: The Issues.* Hanover, N.H.: The University Press of New England, 1977.
Allen, G. J., Chinksy, J. M., Larcen, S. W., Lochman, J. E., and Selinger, H. V. *Community psychology and the schools: A behaviorally oriented multilevel preventive approach.* Hillsdale, N.J.: Lawrence Erlbaum Associates, 1976.
Bachrach, L. L. *Marital status and mental disorder: An analytical review.*

Washington, D.C.: U.S. Government Printing Office, DHEW Pub. No. (ADM) 75-217, 1975.

Bloom, B. L. *Community mental health: A general introduction.* Monterey: Brooks-Cole, 1977.

Broussard, Elsie. Neonatal prediction and outcome at 10/11 years. *Child Psychiatry and Human Development*, 1976, 7. Winter

Brown, Bertram S. Remarks to the World Federation for Mental Health, Vancouver, British Columbia, August 24, 1977.

Bruce, P. Relationship of self-acceptance to other variables with sixth-grade children oriented in self-understanding. *Journal of Educational Psychology*, 1958, *49*, 229-238.

Caplan, G., and Killilea, M. (Eds.). *Support systems and mutual help: Multidisciplinary explorations.* New York: Grune and Stratton, 1976.

Carter, Jimmy. Hospital cost containment. *National Journal*, 1977, *9*, 964-965.

Carter, Rosalynn. Remarks to the World Federation for Mental Health, Vancouver, British Columbia, August 25, 1977, p. 1.

Collins, A. H. and Pancoast, D. L. *Natural helping networks: A strategy for prevention.* Washington, D.C.: National Association of Social Workers, 1976.

Cowen, E. L., Pedersen, A., Babigian, H., Izzo, L. D., and Trost, M. A. Long-term follow-up of early detected vulnerable children. *Journal of Consulting and Clinical Psychology*, 1973, *41*, 438-446.

Cowen, E. Baby-steps toward primary prevention. *American Journal of Community Psychology*, 1977, *5*, 1-22.

Cowen, E. L., Trost, M. A., Lorion, R. P., Dorr, D., Izzo, L. D., and Isaacson, R. V. *New ways in school mental health: Early detection and prevention of school maladaptation.* New York: Human Sciences Press, Inc., 1975.

Crago, M. A. Psychopathology in married couples. *Psychological Bulletin*, 1972, *77*, 114-128.

Dohrenwend, B. S. and Dohrenwend, B. P. (Eds.). *Stressful life events.* New York: John Wiley and Sons, 1974.

Elardo, P. T., and Caldwell, B. M. The effects of an experimental social development program on children in the middle childhood period. Unpublished.

Elardo, P. T. and Cooper, M. *AWARE: Activities for social development.* Reading, Mass.: Addison-Wesley, 1977.

Gesten, E. L., Flores de Apodaca, R., Rains, M. H., Weissberg, R. P., and Cowen, E. L. Promoting peer related social competence in young children. In M. W. Kent and J. E. Rolf (Eds.), *Primary prevention of psychopathology. Vol. 3: Promoting social competence and coping in children.* Hanover, N.H.: University Press of New England, 1978.

Goldston, S. E. An overview of primary prevention programming. In D. C. Klein and S. E. Goldston (Eds.), *Primary prevention: An idea whose time has come.* Washington, D.C.: U.S. Government Printing Office, DHEW Pub. No. (ADM) 77-447, 1977, pp. 23-40.

Gottfried, N. W. Effects of early intervention programs. In K. S. Miller and

R. M. Dreger (Eds.), *Comparative studies of Blacks and Whites in the United States: Quantitative studies in social relations.* New York: Seminar Press, 1973.

Gottlieb, B. H. Lay influences on the utilization and provision of health services: A review. *Canadian Psychological Review,* 1976, *17,* 126–136.

Griggs, J. W., and Bonney, M. E. Relationship between "causal" orientation and acceptance of others, "self-ideal self" congruence, and mental health changes for fourth- and fifth-grade children. *Journal of Educational Research,* 1970, *63,* 471–477.

Grimes, J. W. and Allinsmith, W. Compulsivity, anxiety, and school achievement. *Merrill-Palmer Quarterly,* 1961, *7,* 247–261.

Heber, R. Research in prevention of socio-cultural mental retardation. Address presented at the 2nd Vermont Conference on the Primary Prevention of Psychopathology. Burlington, Vt., 1976.

Holmes, T. H., and Rahe, R. H. The social readjustment rating scale. *Journal of Psychosomatic Research,* 1967, *11,* 213–218.

Horowitz, F. D., and Paden, L. Y. The effectiveness of environmental intervention programs. In B. M. Caldwell and H. Ricciuti (Eds.), *Review of child development research.* Vol. 3. New York: Russell Sage Foundation, 1973.

Insel, P. M., and Moos, R. H. The social environment. In P. M. Insel and R. H. Moos (Eds.), *Health and social environment.* Lexington, Mass.: Lexington Books, 1974.

Jason, L. Early secondary prevention with disadvantaged preschool children. *American Journal of Community Psychology,* 1975, *3,* 33–46.

Joint Commission on Mental Illness and Health. *Action for Mental Health.* New York: Basic Books, 1961.

Kelly, J. G. Towards an ecological conception of preventive interventions. In J. W. Carter (Ed.), *Research contributions from psychology to community mental health.* New York: Behavioral Publications, 1968.

Kelly, J. G. Naturalistic observations in contrasting social environments. In E. P. Willems and H. L. Raush (Eds.), *Naturalistic viewpoints in psychological research.* New York: Holt, Rinehart, and Winston, 1969.

Kelly, J. G., et al. The coping process in varied high school environments. In M. J. Feldman (Ed.), *Studies in psychotherapy and behavior change. No. 2: Theory and research in community mental health.* Buffalo: State University of New York, 1971.

Kelly, J. G., et al. *The high school: Students and social contexts in two midwestern communities.* Community Psychology Series, No. 4. New York: Behavioral Publications, Inc., 1977.

Kessler, M., and Albee, G. W. Primary prevention. *Annual Review of Psychology,* 1975, *26,* 557–591.

Klaus, M. H., and Kennell, J. H. Maternal-infant bonding. St. Louis: C. V. Mosby Co., 1976.

Klein, D. C., and Goldston, S. E. *Primary prevention: An idea whose time has come.* Washington, D.C.: U.S. Government Printing Office, DHEW Pub. No. (ADM) 77-447, 1977.

Kuhn, T. S. *The structure of scientific revolutions.* 2nd ed. Chicago: University of Chicago Press, 1970.

Malzberg, B. Marital status and mental disease among Negroes in New York State. *Journal of Nervous and Mental Disease,* 1956, *123,* 457–465.

Malzberg, B. Marital status and incidence of mental disease. *International Journal of Social Psychiatry,* 1964, *10,* 19–26.

Mead, Margaret. Conversation with Mrs. Rosalynn Carter, The White House, June 28, 1977, as reported by Mrs. Carter, remarks to the World Federation for Mental Health, Vancouver, British Columbia (August 25, 1977), p. 1.

Moore, Barrington, Jr. *Reflection on the causes of human misery and upon certain proposals to eliminate them.* Boston: Beacon Press, 1970.

Moos, R. H. Conceptualizations of human environments. *American Psychologist,* 1973, *28,* 652–665.

Moos, R. H. *The social climate scales: An overview.* Palo Alto: Consulting Psychologists Press, Inc., 1974. (a)

Moos, R. H. *Evaluating treatment environments: A social ecological approach.* New York: John Wiley and Sons, 1974. (b)

Moos, R. H., and Trickett, E. J. *Manual: Classroom Environment Scale.* Palo Alto: Consulting Psychologists Press, Inc., 1974.

Muuss, R. E. The effects of a one and two year causal learning program. *Journal of Personality,* 1960, *28,* 479–491.

National Association for Mental Health. Primary prevention of mental disorders with emphasis on prenatal and perinatal periods. Action Guidelines. Mimeographed, undated.

Ojemann, R. H. Investigations on the effects of teacher understanding and appreciation of behavior dynamics. In G. Caplan (Ed.), *Prevention of mental disorders in children.* New York: Basic Books, 1961.

Ojemann, R. H. Incorporating psychological concepts in the school curriculum. In H. P. Clarizio (Ed.), *Mental health and the educative process.* Chicago: Rand-McNally, 1969.

Pauling, Linus. Orthomolecular psychiatry. *Science,* 1968, *160,* 265–271.

Platt, J. J., Altman, N., and Altman, D. Dimensions of real-life problem-solving thinking in adolescent psychiatric patients. Paper presented at Eastern Psychological Association Meetings, Washington, D.C., 1973.

Rappaport, J. *Community psychology: Values, research and action.* New York: Holt, Rinehart, and Winston, 1977.

Reiss, S., and Dyhdalo, N. Persistence, achievement and open-space environments. *Journal of Educational Psychology,* 1975, *67,* 506–513.

Richmond, Julius. Remarks made at his swearing-in ceremony as Assistant Secretary of Health, Department of Health, Education, and Welfare, Washington, D.C., July 13, 1977.

Robins, L. *Deviant children grown up.* Baltimore: Williams and Wilkins Co., 1966.

Shattuck. L., et al. Report of the sanitary commission of Massachusetts. Quoted by Jonathan E. Fielding, in Health promotion: Some notions in search of a constituency. *American Journal of Public Health,* 1977, *67,* 1082.

Shure, M. B., and Spivack, G. *A preventive mental health program for young "inner city" children: The second (kindergarten) year.* Paper presented at the American Psychological Association, Chicago, 1975. (a)

Shure, M. B., and Spivack, G. *Training mothers to help their children solve real-life problems.* Paper presented at the Society for Research in Child Development, Denver, 1975. (b)

Silverman, P. R. The widow as a caregiver in a program of preventive intervention with other widows. In G. Caplan and M. Killilea (Eds.), *Support systems and mutual help: Multidisciplinary explorations.* New York: Grune and Stratton, 1976, pp. 233-244.

Silverman, P. R. Mutual help groups for the widowed. In D. C. Klein and S. E. Goldston (Eds.), *Primary prevention: An idea whose time has come.* Washington, D.C.: U.S. Government Printing Office, DHEW Pub. No. (ADM) 77-447, 1977, pp. 76-79.

Spivack, G., and Levine, M. Self-regulation in acting-out and normal adolescents. Report M-4531, National Institutes of Health, 1963.

Spivack, G., Platt, J. J., and Shure, M. B. *The problem-solving approach to adjustment.* San Francisco: Jossey-Bass, 1976.

Spivack, G., and Shure, M. B. *Social adjustment of young children.* San Francisco: Jossey-Bass, 1974.

Spivack, G., and Shure, M. B. Preventively oriented cognitive education of preschoolers. In D. C. Klein and S. E. Goldston (Eds.), *Primary prevention: An idea whose time has come.* Washington, D.C.: U.S. Government Printing Office, DHEW Pub. No. (ADM) 77-447, 1977.

Stallings, J. Implementation and child effects of teaching practices on follow-through classrooms. *Monographs of the Society for Research on Child Development,* 1975, *40* (Serial No. 163).

Stamps, L. W. *Enhancing success in school for deprived children by teaching realistic goal setting.* Paper presented at Society for Research in Child Development, Denver, 1975.

Stone, G. L., Hinds, W. C., and Schmidt, G. W. Teaching mental health behaviors to elementary school children. *Professional Psychology,* 1975, *6,* 34-40.

Thomas, D. S., and Locke, B. Z. Marital status, education and occupational differentials in mental disease. *Milbank Memorial Fund Quarterly,* 1963, *41,* 145-160.

Trickett, E. J., and Moos, R. H. Personal correlates of contrasting environments: Student satisfaction in high school classrooms. *American Journal of Community Psychology,* 1974, *2,* 1-12.

Werner, E. E., and Smith, R. S. *Kauai's children come of age.* Honolulu: University of Hawaii Press, 1977.

Defining Primary Prevention

Stephen E. Goldston

❖

THE MYTHS ABOUT PRIMARY PREVENTION

Until recently there were few dissenters from the prevailing sentiment in the mental health field that primary prevention is unrealistic, virtually impossible to achieve short of total social revolution, illusive, beyond conceptualization, and too difficult to verify. I refer to this view as the myth *about* primary prevention. The literature is replete with broadsides on one hand and homilies on the other directed toward primary prevention. For example, primary prevention has been described as "benevolent gambling" (Panzetta, 1971), "more cost than benefit" (Cumming, 1972), "our Holy Grail" (Brown, 1970), "corraling a cloud" (Isbister, 1975), and a "magical notion," a "woolly notion," and "an illusion" (Henderson, 1975). These phrases are cited to illustrate the rhetoric that has been utilized in place of funds for primary prevention research and practice. Rhetoric aside, primary prevention is neither smoke nor a cloud, nor a rosy vision of a happier tomorrow, but *specific* actions directed to *specific* populations. Before presenting specific primary prevention program activities pursued at the federal level, however, some definitions and a framework for understanding program development and operation are necessary.

DEFINITIONS AND CONCEPTUAL FRAMEWORK

In public health terminology, *prevention* is an all-embracing concept having three distinct levels: primary prevention, referring to actions taken prior to the onset of disease to intercept its causation or to modify its course before man is involved; secondary prevention, meaning early diagnosis and treatment; and tertiary prevention, indicating rehabilitative efforts to reduce the residual effects of illness (Leavell and Clark, 1965). In this conceptualization primary prevention has two aspects: *Health Promotion*, referring to measures concerned with improving the quality of life and raising the general level of health in a population, and *Specific Protection*, denoting explicit procedures for disease prevention—for example, immunizations, prevention of cretinism by adequate iodine intake, and prevention of the sequelae of German measles by vaccination of females prior to pregnancy. Unfortunately, critics of primary prevention are quick to seize on the virtual absence of Specific Protection activities, since the etiologies of most mental illnesses are unknown; these same critics are even more apt to ignore, or be unaware of, Health Promotion as an integral aspect of primary prevention.

This multilevel definition of prevention provides both a broad and a convenient framework for accommodating almost all the activities of health workers as well as a justification for collectively including diagnostic, treatment, and rehabilitative functions under the rubric of prevention. The terminology is confusing and misleading, however, and contributes to the continued neglect and misunderstanding of primary prevention. Some standard meaning of the term *prevention* is needed to avoid semantic difficulties. Accordingly, this writer advocates that *prevention* be used solely to refer to actions which aim either to (1) anticipate a disorder or (2) foster optimal health. In short, only activities that deal with health promotion or health maintenance, or what in the mental health field has been called positive mental health, should bear the label of prevention; the term prevention, then, would be synonymous with primary prevention.

As a function of professional practice and a recognized need for conceptual clarity I have evolved the following definition of primary prevention:

Primary prevention encompasses activities directed toward specifically identified vulnerable high risk groups within the community who have not been labeled psychiatrically ill and for whom measures can be undertaken to avoid the onset of emotional disturbance and/or to enhance their level of positive mental health. Programs for the promotion of mental health are primarily educational rather than clinical in conception and operation, their ultimate goal being to increase people's capaci-

ties for dealing with crises and for taking steps to improve their own lives.

Conceptually, this definition is grounded in crisis theory, which provides a construct for presumptions maintaining that interventions keyed to critical life points can allay the onset of emotional disturbances. These presumptions argue in favor of such primary preventive activities as mental health education, anticipatory guidance, a variety of forms of mental health consultation, and the training of vital caregivers. Within this framework the issue is no longer one of whether what you are doing will prevent mental illness, but a recognition that mental health workers need to view primary prevention efforts and to evaluate them in much broader terms (Bower, 1972):

> *Prevention and promotion in mental health have in the past been so tightly tied to mental illnesses that any foolhardy or misguided adventurer who stumbled into this arena was continually plagued by the question—does what you do prevent mental illness? Unfortunately, mental illnesses are only one of many end points in human failure . . . The modes and roads to human failure are many and varied. Preventive and promotion programs need to be tied into the human condition in all its manifestations.*

Within this public health/crisis theory approach, the stated objective of primary prevention efforts is not the prevention of mental illness. Rather, the goals of primary prevention are twofold: first, to prevent needless psychopathology and symptoms, maladjustment, maladaption, and misery regardless of whether an end point might be mental illness; and second, to promote mental health by increasing levels of "wellness" among various defined populations. The concept of health promotion connotes a socio-psycho-cultural-educational model distinct from a medical model, and the overriding question becomes one involving social competence, coping ability, and ego-strengthening measures rather than criteria of psychiatric symptomatology. The key question becomes, "How well is the individual or community?" rather than "How sick?"

In this connection, the Conference Planning Committee acted astutely when they designated the focus of this meeting in theme and content on the primary prevention of *psycho-pathology* rather than on mental illness. Clarity of labels, foci, and objectives are necessary in order to facilite primary prevention activities and to advance this critical sphere of mental health work.

PRIMARY PREVENTION: AN IDEA WHOSE TIME HAS COME

The past two years have witnessed an unparalleled interest in primary prevention among professional mental health workers and human services groups. This interest has been translated into program activities, conferences, publications, sessions at professional meetings, and the identification of relevant training and research issues—all directly focused on primary prevention. To a large degree, Victor Hugo's famous words of over a century ago could be applied to primary prevention: "Greater than the tread of mighty armies is an idea whose time has come!"

A varied field of forces would appear to be related to the "emergence" of primary prevention as a respectable area for consideration by mental health workers. From a federal perspective, some of the causes and effects that have served to provide primary prevention its present unprecedented prominence include:

(a) The public consumer movement, which has been characterized by a greater sharing of information previously restricted to professional workers and the raising of questions and issues heretofore either ignored or overlooked.

(b) Growing awareness that primary preventive activities can be a major vehicle for eventual reduction of health care costs—for example, hospitalization, etc.—an "ounce of prevention" philosophy with economic considerations.

(c) Genuine interest and growing commitment in the field about translating into action community mental health principles dealing with primary prevention, particularly the notion that community mental health practice implies responsibility for the mental health of an entire population and not merely for the casualties that appear at the doors of the mental health facility.

(d) The identification of prevention as one of five program emphases in the DHEW Forward Plan for Health over the next five-year period. Such official high priority for prevention has been reflected in considerable support for prevention being expressed by key policy-planners and decision-makers within the federal health and mental health establishment.

A more favorable climate for primary prevention is still evolving. Only the sanction has been forthcoming—not the mandate for action. The future directions of primary prevention, from the federal perspective, will be influenced by past events and present activities.

REFERENCES

Bower, E. M. K.I.S.S. and kids: A mandate for prevention. *American Journal of Orthopsychiatry*, 1972, *42*, 556-565.

Brown, B. S. *Mental health and social change*. Austin, Texas: Hogg Foundation for Mental Health, 1970.

Cumming, E. Primary prevention—more cost than benefit. In H. Gottesfeld (Ed.), *The critical issues of community mental health*. New York: Behavioral Publications, 1972.

Henderson, J. Object relations and a new social psychiatry: The illusion of primary prevention. *Bulletin of the Menninger Clinic*, 1975, *39*, 233-245.

Isbister, J. Speech before the Southern Branch, American Public Health Association, Houston, Texas, May 1, 1975.

Kessler, M., and Albee, G. W. Primary prevention. *Annual Review of Psychology*, 1975, *26*, 557-591.

Leavell, H. R., and Clark, E. G. *Preventive medicine for the doctor in his community* (3rd ed.). New York: McGraw-Hill, 1965.

National Institute of Mental Health, Biometry Branch. *Consultation and education services: Federally funded community mental health centers 1973*. (Publication No. (ADM) 75-158). Rockville, Maryland: U.S. Department of Health, Education and Welfare, 1974.

National Institute of Mental Health, Biometry Branch. *Consultation and education services: Federally funded community mental health centers 1974*. In preparation, 1975.

Panzetta, A. F. *Community mental health: Myth and reality*. Philadelphia: Lea and Febiger, 1971.

Demystifying Primary Prevention

Emory L. Cowen

❖

These days, writers treat the concept of primary prevention with reverence. Kelly (1975) says: "In my opinion the topic of primary prevention is a most exciting and overdue challenge for psychology." I feel that way, too.

❖ Although there is some difference of opinion about exactly how to define the concept (Kessler & Albee, 1975) there is enough agreement about its main abstract thrust. Caplan (1964) offers a representative definition:

> *Primary prevention . . . involves lowering the rate of new cases of mental disorder in a population, over a certain period by counteracting harmful circumstances before they have had a chance to produce illness. It does not seek to prevent a specific person from becoming sick. Instead, it seeks to reduce the risk for a whole population so that, although some may become ill, their number will be reduced. (p. 26)*

Sanford (1972) is briefer and more direct. He speaks of it simply as preventing the *development* of disorder. Another definition (Zax & Cowen, 1976) emphasizes three elements: (1) reducing new instances of disorder, (2) reducing irritants to dysfunction before they exact their toll, and (3) building psychological health.

❖

What Mental Health People Can and Cannot Do

My second concern is a by-product of the fact that primary prevention's abstract definition is, indeed, so broad and vague. Caplan (1964) likens it to a motorist's large-scale road map that provides only the grossest directions. The term's connotative meaning ("good") is far clearer than its specific denotative meanings, seen in its actual operations. Things are murkier at the latter level: primary prevention touches many aspects of life; it seeks to improve the quality of life; it requires new combinations of expertise from many fields to be brought off successfully (Zax and Cowen, 1976).

Fortunately or otherwise, people's psychological well-being is not a reified entity, divorced from the rest of their existence. To the contrary, "virtually anything done to improve man's life can also be viewed as primary mental health prevention" (Zax and Cowen, 1976, p. 479). Kessler and Albee (1975) in a recent *Annual Review* chapter on primary prevention provide a tongue-in-cheek rendition of the same point:

> *During the past year we found ourselves constantly writing references and ideas on scraps of paper and emptying our pockets each day of notes on the primary prevention relevance of children's group homes, titanium paint, parent effectiveness-training, consciousness raising, Zoom, Sesame Street, the guaranteed annual wage, legalized abortion, school integration, limits on international cartels, unpolished rice, free prenatal clinics, antipollution laws, a yoghurt and vegetable diet, free VD clinics, and a host of other topics. Nearly everything, it appears, has implications for primary prevention, for reducing emotional disturbance, for strengthening and fostering mental health. (p. 560)*

The statement, incredibly, is absolutely correct. But mental health professionals are limited enough in their own mandated sphere; they are hardly equipped to tackle the "nearly everything" that seems to feed into primary prevention (Bloom, 1965). Sarason, Levine, Goldenberg, Cherlin, and Bennett (1966) inveigh against professional "preciousness"—i.e., the belief of certain groups (take mental health professionals as a random example) that they, and they alone, stand as God's chosen people for stamping out the woes of civilization. We are *not* architects, engineers, nutrition specialists, recreation experts, politicians, or urban planners, nor can we assume a near infinity of such roles. If we are to gain ground in primary prevention, some of the fuzz and mystery must be removed from the concept to provide sharper, more operational answers to the question of what we as mental health specialists are best equipped to contribute to, in the quest for this Holy Grail. Such contributions, we can hope, will go beyond heartfelt vocal support for the platitude of improving the "quality of life."

In sidling up to this challenge, it helped me to dredge up several elemental concepts (dependent and independent variables) from my earlier formation and training. Mental health comes together as a field because of a shared emphasis on certain dependent variables. Although people might quibble a bit about their exact nature, we are talking essentially about such variables as adjustment, adaptation, security, happiness, and self-image—a person's "well-being," if you will. Various people in the extended mental health family engage these dependent variables differently. Historically, the clinical role has been to undo deficit in these states— a casualty-repair orientation. Community mental health (CMH) accepts some of that emphasis, but seeks to streamline the repair process by identifying problems sooner and in more natural settings, and by engaging them more flexibly and realistically. This set moves CMH people away from classic repair institutions (hospitals, clinics, private consulting suites, and so on) into new, community settings (schools, storefronts, and the like).

Although community psychology is oriented to the same dependent measures as traditional clinical practice and community mental health, it seeks to prevent rather than to repair—to build strengths rather than to counterpunch against deficit. That sounds like primary prevention and, indeed, philosophically, it is. But to date it has been a concept in search of operational practices. Troubles start at the level of independent variables. We have already suggested that the answer to the question "Which independent variables materially shape outcomes on mental health's prime dependent measures?" is "Virtually any!" Indeed Kessler and Albee's facetious list of prospective independent variables is far less facetious than it is incomplete. And most of those variables are so far removed from mental health's knowledge and experience bases that we are incapable of engaging them.

There are two ways in which groping, floundering, and probably failure—the failure of trying to shovel water—may be reduced. One, more obvious and hence more often proposed (Kelly, 1973), is that mental health people should strengthen their contacts and collaborative working relationships with specialists who are charged with responsibility for areas (independent variables) that are likely to affect mental health outcomes significantly. These are the same architects, policy-makers, urban planners, and so on who we said above we could not ourselves *be*. Doubtless, much can be done with such people to clarify obscure linkages between decisions and actions in seemingly "remote" areas and mental health outcomes. Indeed, the argument has been carried a step further (Vallance, 1976) with the suggestion that training should be broadened to produce people capable of using psychological knowledge to deal with live social problems as they occur, rather than people who are discipline-bound.

A second, less apparent tack has thus far attracted less attention. From among the multitude of independent variables that have an impact on adjustment, several rather important clusters are *relatively* closer to existing knowledge and competence bases of mental health people. We need to ask which these are, and how their manipulation might promote more positive mental health outcomes. That can be done now; doing so would help both to demystify and to further primary prevention in mental health.

Two broad areas strike me as prime candidates for such a thrust: the analysis and modification of social environments, and competence building. Both exemplify primary prevention in that they are targeted to people-in-general rather than to individuals at known risk.

Social environments

People's (especially children's) development and adaptation are significantly shaped by a limited number of high-impact social environments: communities, churches, schools, and families. In the past we have tended to take properties of these systems for granted and, except for so intimate a system as the family, to overlook their shaping impact. There are, to be sure, exceptions. Barker and Gump (1964) studied the predispositional properties of one significant dimension of physical environment: a school's size. They found that youngsters from small schools. compared to those from large schools, participated in more, and more diverse, activities; were less aware of individual differences; had clearer self-identities; and were more visible. Although Barker and Gump's dependent measures were not all centrally relevant to mental health, the basic question of whether aspects of physical and, more importantly, social environments shape adaptive-adjustive outcomes in people is legitimate and important. Thus, Moos (1974a) says:

*"the social climate within which an individual functions may
have an important impact on his attitudes and moods, his
behavior, his health and overall sense of well-being and his
social, personal and intellectual development." (p.3)*

Several developments are needed to reap full benefit from a
social-environment approach to primary prevention. First, we
must better understand how to assess social environments; we
must also understand their key impact dimensions and how they
vary with respect to them. We then need to establish more clearly
how environmental attributes relate to people's personal development and behavior, both generally and in terms of specific person-
environment matches. This orientation assumes that social systems
are not neutral in their effects on people: they either contribute
to development or impair it. If the whys and wherefores of these
relations can be charted, such information could be harnessed to
engineer health promoting environments (Coelho and Rubenstein,
1972). That seems much preferable to allowing rutted practice to
reign by default.

Rudolf Moos and his co-workers in the Social Ecology Laboratory at the Stanford University Medical School have pioneered
this area. They (Moos, 1973, 1974b) have identified six broad
methodologies (for example, ecological analysis, analysis of
behavior settings, study of psychosocial characteristics) for conceptualizing environmental variables and relating them to behavior. With much perseverance they (Moos, 1974a) have developed
a series of parallel social climate scales, each with 7 to 10 dimensions and 84 to 100 items, to assess nine different types of social
environments ranging from hospital-based treatment programs on
the one hand to correctional and educational settings, work
milieus, family environments, and military companies on the
other. These scales have been used to assess multiple examples of
each of the nine types of settings.

Several fascinating findings emerged from that work. First,
three social climate clusters—relational, personal development, and
system maintenance qualities—have faithfully recurred in describing seemingly diverse environments. Relational factors describe
the nature of interpersonal relations, such as how people affiliate
and the support they provide each other. Personal development
dimensions indicate how people's personal growth and enhance-

ment takes place in terms of such variables as autonomy, amount of competition, and task-orientation. And system maintenance dimensions assess the extent to which environments are orderly, controlling, change-oriented, etc. Moos et al.'s findings suggest that: (a) social climate factors can be reliably measured; (b) a small number of common dimensional clusters well describe superficially different social environments; (c) the scales discriminate well among multiple instances of various environments; and (d) the scales reflect enduring environmental qualities.

Although such information has considerable instrumental value, it is not yet primary prevention. A bridge to the latter is built by considering environmental consequences. That is a challenging area and, as Moos (1974a) points out, one about which we still know very little. But some encouraging, if only suggestive, findings are available. For example, Moos et al.'s data indicate that such social environments as therapy groups and hospital and educational settings, which score high in relational qualities like involvement and support, have occupants who are not irritable and depressed, are satisfied and comfortable, and have high self-esteem (Moos, 1974a, 1974b). Similar early returns suggest that environments high on personal development dimensions, such as autonomy and problem orientation, have positive effects. Trickett and Moos (1974) found that students were happy in classes with high student involvement and a close student-teacher relation. By contrast, some system maintenance dimensions—for example, high control—seem to have negative effects. But the matter may be more complex. Trickett and Moos (1974) found that students from school environments high in competition—a personal development dimension with a negative aura—learned more than students from school environments lower in competition.

Although Moos et al. have been conceptual and methodological leaders in the study of environment effects, others have joined the fray, sometimes defining environmental variables in more macro-molar, less operational ways. For example, a group at the Bank St. College of Education (Minuchin, Biber, Shapiro, and Zimiles, 1969; Zimiles, 1967) has examined some personal correlates of modern versus traditional educational environments. Modern environments were defined as those that encouraged the development of thought and learning process; traditional environments were oriented more to the acquisition of facts. Children educated in modern environments were found to (a) be more identified as children; (b) have greater acceptance of negative impulses; (c) have more differentiated self-concepts; and (d) pursue learning more seriously and analytically. Reiss and Martell (1974) found that children from open-space educational environments surpassed demographically comparable peers from self-contained classes in oral fluency, persistence, and imaginativeness. In a broader, literary way Kozol (1967) describes the disastrously negative consequences of the school environment on slum children in Boston.

Each of the above examples can be thought of as a main-effect consequence of environmental properties. It is insufficient, however, to speak of environmental effects independent of people. A facilitating environment for one person can restrict another. Several examples amplify the point. A study by Allinsmith and Grimes (1961) showed that whereas anxious-compulsive children fared poorly in loosely structured school environments, peers without such characteristics did very well in them. Reiss and Dyhdalo (1975) as part of the research program cited above found that, overall, children from open-space classes compared to those from self-contained environments persisted more on difficult tasks and showed a stronger relation between persistence and academic achievement. On the other hand, nonpersistent (distractible) children from self-contained classes had significantly higher educational achievement scores than those from open environments.

Kelly and his colleagues (Kelly, 1968, 1969; Kelly et al., 1971, 1976) have long stressed the need for this type of ecological orientation, i.e. an emphasis on the person-environment fit. They have focused on the types of adaptations that are encouraged by fluid and stable high school environments (defined by annual pupil turnover rates). They found, for example, that new students were more readily accepted in a fluid, as compared to a stable, environment. Whereas personal development was highly valued in the former, status and achievement were respected in the latter. The same exploratory behaviors that could be adaptive in one environment could be maladaptive in another. Insel and Moos (1974) take the ecological-match question a step closer to mental health: "A source of distress and ill health is the situation in which a person attempts to function within an environment with which he is basically incompatible" (p. 7).

Thus, the evidence suggests not only that social environments can be reliably described and that they vary, but also that these variations relate to person-outcomes on variables important to the mental health domain and, potentially, in different ways for different people. Though we have a long way to go in dotting all the i's and crossing all the t's for these complex relationships, at least this is a brand of knowledge from which bona fide primary prevention efforts can be fashioned. The independent variables involved—system properties—have a high probability for impacting states with which mental health must be concerned. Some mental health professionals already have skills, competencies, and tools to pursue such work. As the knowledge base in the area expands, the pot of gold at the end of the rainbow is the possibility of engineering systems—be they new communities (Barker and Schoggen, 1973; Price and Blashfield, 1975), well-baby clinics, or schools that can build health and resources in people—a true primary prevention.

Several reality constraints, however, bear mention. One is that primary prevention calls for an expanded time perspective. As Kelly (1975) says, "If we wish to understand behavior in relation to primary prevention we will do more work with people over time" (p. 3). There are several reasons why this is so. The manipulations and processes of primary prevention are intrinsically complex, their means-end contingencies are less than immediate, and the target behaviors in question are often ones that change only slowly, over time. Several major studies have been reported recently (Kelly et al., 1976; Hartley, 1972) in which anticipated preventive effects failed to appear initially but became clearer and clearer as time passed.

A second limiting factor is that knowing how to build health facilitating systems and actually being able to build them are two different matters. The latter entails severe practical problems. Once established, systems resist change. Power structures form, vested interests are protected, and system occupants are threatened by the prospect of change. Thus, rooted systems may not be expected to yield passively or graciously to change and, even if we clearly understood the theory and practice of system-change, such change would not be easy. Important economic, psychological, and political determinants quite beyond cold scientific facts influence the social change processes (Sarason, 1972; Fairweather,

Sanders, and Tornatzky, 1974; Rothman, 1974; Rothman, Erlich, and Teresa, 1976).

Competence and Adjustment

A second pathway, different but very attractive, can also be followed in the service of primary prevention. It can be argued that the best possible defense against problems is to build resources and adaptive strengths in people from the start (Murphy and Chandler, 1972). This broad orienting set has been applied at several levels, with instructive findings.

The view assumes that people often become maladjusted because they lack specific skills needed to resolve personal problems. If such skills could truly be taught from the outset there would be less need ever to engage maladjustment. The thrust of this approach is educational rather than restorative, and mass-oriented rather than individual-casualty-oriented. Its key questions are: (1) What core skills undergird positive adjustment? (2) Can curriculum be developed to teach young children these skills? (3) Does acquiring a given competence lead to improved interpersonal adjustment? (4) Do adjustive gains, so acquired, endure? Positive answers to these questions would markedly advance de facto primary prevention.

Ojemann's long-term effort (1961, 1969) to develop causal teaching curricula was an early move in this direction. Although children exposed to this approach, compared to the traditionally educated, were better able to generalize knowledge, weigh alternatives, and understand factors underlying behavior, the program's main thrust has been more toward educational processes and outcomes than toward personal ones (Zax and Specter, 1974).

Recently, through Spivack and Shure's (1974) work, the approach has been brought closer to mental health. These investigators, based on extensive prior research with patients and clinical groups, concluded that social problem-solving skills (for example, sensitivity to human problems, the ability to perceive alternatives and means-end relations, and awareness of the effects of one's behavior on others) critically mediated sound personal adjustment. They reasoned that if they could teach such skills to young children, it would lead to improved behavioral adjustment.

They developed a social problem-solving curriculum for 4-year-old Head-Start children. The curriculum included prior instrumental training in listening and attending skills and in the acquisition of basic building concepts such as negation and similarity, as well as the actual social problem-solving skills. This was done in the form of brief, interesting games and dialogues, covering 10 weeks of daily 5-to-20-minute lessons. After teachers were trained in the approach, they taught the skills directly to the children. Comparisons were made between the experimental group and demographically similar nonprogram control children.

Program children learned these social problem-solving skills readily and were much superior to controls at the end of the program. Their use of irrelevant and forceful problem solutions also decreased significantly. These changes were maintained at followup during the next (kindergarten) school year (Shure and Spivack, 1975a). And a parallel program (Shure and Spivack, 1975b) showed that inner-city mothers could successfully teach social problem-solving skills to their own children.

Among other criterion measures, classroom teachers submitted behavioral and adjustment ratings for all children before the training program started. Some of the study's most significant findings, from the standpoint of primary prevention, came from these data. For example, initially maladjusted program children gained the most in social problem-solving skills. Moreover, there was a direct relation between gain in social problem-solving skills and reduction in maladjustment. Program children also improved significantly on such dimensions as concern for others, ability to take the initiative, and autonomy, with the initially most maladjusted showing the greatest gains. None of these things happened with control children. Implanting social problem-solving skills apparently established a competence beachhead that radiated positively to a cluster of variables that we think of as good mental health.

Spivack and Shure's findings are not isolated. Allen, Chinsky, Larcen, Lochman, and Selinger (1976), as part of a comprehensive three-tiered preventive school mental health program, also did social problem-solving training with fourth-grade children, as their primary prevention component. They too found that the training succeeded and that there were positive spill-over effects: children became more internally oriented and developed more positive expectancies about the school experience.

Although social problem-solving seems to be an important

mediating skill for good adjustment, it is not the only one. How important is it to adjustment to know how to be able to plan ahead, make decisions, take roles, and assert oneself when appropriate? Illustratively, Stamps (1975) used self-reinforcement methods to teach goal-setting skills to deprived inner-city fourth-graders. As a result of this training the children did, indeed, learn to set more accurate goals. Simultaneously, their overall achievement scores improved significantly. These cognitive gains were paralleled by behavioral and personality improvements. Thus, teachers rated program children as having significantly fewer problem behaviors than controls. On test measures, they showed increases in openness, awareness, and self-acceptance and a greater willingness to assume responsibility for negative outcomes on a locus of control measure. Again, rooting a gut competency radiated positively to adjustment.

A child's ability to ask questions, i.e. curiosity behavior, is widely accepted as a positive value (Susskind, 1969). Yet studies of the spontaneous occurrence of curiosity behavior, often measured in terms of children's question-asking behaviors in class, show that it is far less common than what people consider ideal, or estimate to be occurring. Thus, Susskind (1969), using 30-minute classroom observation units, found that teachers on the average asked 20 to 25 times as many questions as an entire class combined. This type of observation lies behind several studies designed both to help teachers augment children's question-asking behavior (Susskind, 1969) and to evaluate approaches (for example, social reinforcement, auto-instruction) designed to increase children's question-asking (Blank and Covington, 1965; Evans, 1971). In one such study (Blank and Covington, 1965) using auto-instruction, not only did children learn to ask more questions, but they also had higher achievement test scores and participated more in class discussions, in comparison to controls who were not so trained.

The primary preventive strategy of enhancing competencies (Riessman, 1967) has been applied at levels that are socially more macromolar. Thus Rappaport, Davidson, Wilson, and Mitchell (1975) developed a setting called the Community Psychology Action Center (CPAC) with the black inner-city poor. CPAC seeks to identify existing competence bases in the community and to support their further development. This program in no way tries to reshape people to conform to regnant systems or to modify people's styles or values. Rather, it takes strength where and as it is, and builds on it, thus enhancing the community's competence base and broadening it to new areas. It is not an anti-problem program. Its goals are to foster independence and positive behaviors, based on the belief that developing resources and competencies is the best way to engage problems and to meet adversity.

The work cited in this section suggests that several pivotal competencies, on the surface removed from the dependent variables of prime concern to mental health, can be taught to people, or strengthened where they already exist. Acquiring these competencies is accompanied by positive radiating effects to adaptations and behaviors squarely related to mental health. That message should not be repressed. Symptoms, or problem behaviors, have been reduced without ever engaging them, through direct training of the critical competencies. Health has been engineered, so to speak, indirectly through skill acquisition. Oriented to people in general, not just troubled people, such efforts model a promising type of primary prevention.

At least one point needs clarification. Up to now, I must confess, I have cheated a bit in suggesting that mental health people already have the wherewithal to bring off these new developments. A few do, perhaps, but the implication that all do is more than charitable. Sociologists and social and organizational psychologists know much more than we about social system analysis and modification, just as developmentalists and educational psychologists may be better versed in competence training. Yet these groups are less knowledgeable about the prime dependent variables of concern. Hence some new marriages are called for, if the chase is to proceed judiciously and efficiently. And, for the future, new training combinations will be needed to produce people genuinely qualified to enrich these areas.

SUMMARY

Nothing in this paper is to suggest that primary prevention is either simple or straightforward. Indeed, what was said earlier about its devilish complexity still holds. The core dilemma is that virtually any manipulation imaginable can affect people's well-being and the so-called quality of life. If we let the matter go at that, the temptation for mental health people will be either to throw up their arms in despair or to traffic in gushy, impalpable platitudes. If as mental health specialists we want a piece of the action, now, we must separate the near-infinity of manipulations and independent variables that could potentially affect well-being into those for which we do, and do not, have a knowledge-and-competence base. If we lack the knowledge base (that is the case for most areas), we shall be limited either to learning more or to working in closer collaboration with people who know more. Where we possess or can readily acquire the necessary competence and technology, we should be getting on with the show.

A major thesis of this paper is that there are at least two broad, very important areas that meet the latter criterion: (a) the analysis and modification of impactful social systems; and (b) competence training. Examples of recent work in these areas have been cited, and linkages have been reported between system qualities and competence as independent variables and criteria of adjustment and well-being. Work in both areas is targeted impersonally to large numbers of people, not to individuals at risk—a desideratum of primary prevention.

Notions of system analysis and modification and competence training are far from new. One difference today is that people are beginning to do things with them concretely rather than just worshiping them from afar. A second difference is that linkages have been found between qualities of social environments and/or the skills people have, and adjustment. These important developments suggest exciting possibilities for restructuring mental health's classic, tunnel-visioned, definition of mandate—to combat pathology. As concrete, operational steps toward primary prevention, which tap skills that are reasonably close to the special backgrounds and training of mental health people, they can help immeasurably to demystify what has always been a deliciously attractive, but very slippery, concept.

REFERENCES

Allen, G. J., Chinsky, J. M., Larcen, S. W., Lochman, J. E., and Selinger, H. V. *Community psychology and the schools: A behaviorally oriented multilevel preventive approach.* Hillsdale, N.J.: Lawrence Erlbaum Associates, 1976.

Allinsmith, W., and Grimes, J. W. Compulsivity, anxiety, and school achievement. *Merrill-Palmer Quarterly,* 1961. *7,* 247-261.

Barker, R. G., and Gump, P. *Big school, small school.* Stanford, Ca.: Stanford University Press, 1964.

Barker, R. G., and Schoggen, P. *Qualities of community life.* San Francisco: Jossey-Bass, 1973.

Blank, S. S., and Covington, M. Inducing children to ask questions in solving problems. *Journal of Educational Research,* 1965, *59,* 21-27.

Bloom, B. L. The "medical model," miasma theory and community mental health. *Community Mental Health Journal,* 1965, *1,* 333-338.

Caplan, G. *Principles of preventive psychiatry.* New York: Basic Books, 1964.

Coelho, G. V., and Rubenstein, E. A. (Eds.). *Social change and human behavior: Mental health challenges of the seventies.* Washington, D.C., U.S. Government Printing Office, DHEW Publication No. (HSM) 72-9122, 1972.

Cowen, E. L., Lorion, R. P., Kraus, R. M., and Dorr, D. Geometric expansion of helping resources. *Journal of School Psychology,* 1974, *12,* 288-295.

Cowen, E. L., Trost, M. A., Lorion, R. P., Dorr, D., Izzo, L. D., and Isaacson, R. V. *New ways in school mental health: Early detection and prevention of school maladaptation.* New York: Human Sciences, Inc., 1975.

Evans, D. R. Social reinforcement of question asking behavior. *Western Psychologist,* 1971, *2,* 80-83.

Fairweather, G. W., Sanders, D. H., and Tornatzky, L. G. *Creating change in mental health organizations.* New York: Pergamon Press, 1974.

Hartley, W. S. *An epidemiologic follow up of a cohort of school children: The Kansas City Youth Development Project experiment in preventive psychiatry.* Kansas City, Kansas: University of Kansas Medical Center, Department of Human Ecology and Community Health, 1972.

Insel, P. M., and Moos, R. H. The social environment. In P. M. Insel and R. H. Moos (Eds.), *Health and social environment.* Lexington, Mass.: Lexington Books, 1974. Pp. 1-12.

Kelly, J. G. Towards an ecological conception of preventive interventions. In J. W. Carter (Ed.), *Research contributions from psychology to community mental health.* New York: Behavioral Publications, 1968. Pp. 75-97.

Kelly, J. G. Naturalistic observations in contrasting social environments. In E. P. Willems and H. L. Raush (Eds.), *Naturalistic viewpoints in psychological research.* New York: Holt, Rinehart and Winston, 1969. Pp. 183-199.

Kelly, J. G. Qualities for the community psychologist. *American Psychologist,* 1973, *26,* 897-903.

Kelly, J. G. The search for ideas and deeds that work. Burlington, Vt., Keynote Address at Vermont Conference on the Primary Prevention of Psychopathology, 1975.

Kelly, J. G., Edwards, D. W., Fatke, R., Gordon, T. A., McGee, D. P., McClintock, S. K., Newman, B. M., Rice, R. R., Roistacher, R. C., and Todd, D. M. The coping process in varied high school environments. In M. J. Feldman (Ed.), *Studies in psychotherapy and behavior change, No. 2: Theory and research in community mental health.* Buffalo, N. Y.: State University of New York, 1971. Pp. 95-166.

Kelly, J. G., et al. *The high school: An exploration of students and social contexts in two midwestern communities.* Community Psychology Series, No. 4. New York: Behavioral Publications, Inc., 1976.

Kessler, M., and Albee, G. W. Primary Prevention. In M. R. Rosenzweig and L. C. Porter (Eds.), *Annual Review of Psychology,* 1975, *26,* 557-591.

Kozol, J. *Death at an early age.* Boston, Mass.: Houghton Mifflin, 1967.

Minuchin, P., Biber, B., Shapiro, E., and Zimiles, H. *The psychological impact of school experience.* New York: Basic Books, 1969.

Moos, R. H. Conceptualizations of human environments. *American Psychologist,* 1973, *28,* 652-665.

Moos, R. H. *The social climate scales: An overview.* Palo Alto, Ca.: Consulting Psychologists Press, Inc., 1974 (a)

Moos, R. H. *Evaluating treatment environments: A social ecological approach.* New York: John Wiley & Sons, 1974. (b)

Murphy, L. B., and Chandler, C. A. Building foundations for strength in the preschool years: Preventing developmental disturbances. In S. E. Golann and C. Eisdorfer (Eds.), *Handbook of community mental health.* New York: Appleton-Century-Crofts, 1972. Pp. 303-330.

Ojemann, R. H. Investigations on the effects of teacher understanding and appreciation of behavior dynamics. In G. Caplan (Ed.), *Prevention of mental disorders in children.* New York: Basic Books, 1961. Pp. 378-397.

Ojemann, R. H. Incorporating psychological concepts in the school curriculum. In H. P. Clarizio (Ed.), *Mental health and the educative process.* Chicago: Rand-McNally, 1969. Pp. 360-368.

Price, R. H., and Blashfield, R. K. Explorations in the taxonomy of behavior settings: Analysis of dimensions and classification of settings. *American Journal of Community Psychology,* 1975, *3,* 335-357.

Rappaport, J., Davidson, W. S., Wilson, M. N., and Mitchell, A. Alternatives to blaming the victim or the environment: Our places to stand have not moved the earth. *American Psychologist,* 1975, *30,* 525-528.

Reiss, S., and Dyhdalo, N. Persistence, achievement, and open-space environments. *Journal of Educational Psychology,* 1975, *67,* in press.

Reiss, S., and Martell, R. Educational and psychological effects of open space and education in Oak Park, Ill.: Final Report to Board of Education, District 97, Oak Park, Illinois, 1974.

Riessman, F. A neighborhood-based mental health approach. In E. L. Cowen, E. A. Gardner, and M. Zax (Eds.), *Emergent approaches to mental health problems.* New York: Appleton-Century-Crofts, 1967. Pp. 167-184.

Rothman, J. *Planning and organizing for social change: Action principles from social science research.* New York: Columbia University Press, 1974.

Rothman, J., Erlich, J. L., and Teresa, J. G. *Promoting innovation and change in organizations and communities: A planning manual.* New York: John Wiley and Sons, 1976.

Sanford, N. Is the concept of prevention necessary or useful? In S. E. Golann and C. Eisdorfer (Eds.), *Handbook of community mental health.* New York: Appleton-Century-Crofts, 1972. Pp. 461–471.

Sarason, S. B. *The creation of settings and the future societies.* San Francisco: Jossey-Bass, 1972.

Sarason, S. B., Levine, M., Goldenberg, I. I., Cherlin, D. L., and Bennett, E. M. *Psychology in community settings.* New York: Wiley, 1966.

Shure, M. B., and Spivack, G. A preventive mental health program for young "inner city" children: The second (kindergarten) year. Paper presented at the American Psychological Association, Chicago, 1975. (a)

Shure, M. B., and Spivack, G. Training mothers to help their children solve real-life problems. Paper presented at the Society for Research in Child Development, Denver, Colo., 1975. (b)

Spivack, G., and Shure, M. B. *Social adjustment of young children.* San Francisco: Jossey-Bass, 1974.

Stamps, L. W. Enhancing success in school for deprived children by teaching realistic goal setting. Paper presented at Society for Research in Child Development, Denver, Colo., 1975.

Susskind, E. C. Questioning and curiosity in the elementary school classroom. Unpublished Ph.D. dissertation, Yale University, 1969.

Trickett, E. J., and Moos, R. H. Personal correlates of contrasting environments: Student satisfaction in high school classrooms. *American Journal of Community Psychology,* 1974, *2,* 1–12.

Vallance, T. R. The professional nonpsychology graduate program for psychologists. *American Psychologist,* 1976, *31,* 193–199.

Zax, M., and Cowen, E. L. *Abnormal Psychology: Changing conceptions.* 2nd Edition. New York: Holt, Rinehart, and Winston, 1976.

Zax, M., and Specter, G. A. *An introduction to community psychology.* New York: Wiley, 1974.

Zimiles, H. Preventive aspects of school experience. In E. L. Cowen, E. A. Gardner, and M. Zax (Eds.), *Emergent approaches to mental health problems.* New York: Appleton-Century-Crofts, 1967. Pp. 239–251.

II. Organic and Physical Factors Affecting Incidence

Several different forms of psychopathology clearly result from organic conditions. This section includes readings dealing with organic and physical factors across the life span that have an important bearing on the development of emotional distress and psychopathology.

In an extensive review, Justin M. Joffe examines genetic, chromosomal, prenatal, and perinatal factors that are associated with reproductive risk and with deviant development. He examines whether or not prenatal and perinatal events produce deleterious effects in the absence of adverse postnatal circumstances and finds that the very theoretical premises on which this question is based provide support for the significant contribution of prenatal events. He leads the reader to a reexamination of the utility of current modes of thinking about risk and proceeds with an analysis of the various kinds of intervention that can reduce deviant development of mental outcomes and points to the need to consider the larger network of societal variables when considering risk factors.

Thomas F. McNeil and Lennart Kaij report on Swedish efforts at attempting to reduce the risk of damage occurring during pregnancy and throughout the neonatal period that might affect later behavior. They describe the Swedish system of providing complete prenatal care, excellent delivery facilities, and state-supported well-baby clinics. Despite the resulting low infant mortality, they identify a number of potential problem areas that are a consequence of the system itself.

Tiffany M. Field presents data from a series of studies on the effects of early compensatory experiences on groups of infants considered at risk for one or more reasons. The group of studies taken together constitutes powerful evidence for the preventive effects of interventions early in the lives of infants considered at risk. Even relatively simple and inexpensive techniques can be remarkably beneficial, particularly those that are focused on the parent rather than aimed directly at the infant. She demonstrates that the rate of return on an intervention investment is much greater if the intervention increases the parents' transactional skills, presumably because the effects of changing a parent have pervasive effects on the child and persist well beyond the end of the formal intervention.

In the final paper in this section, Nathan Maccoby reports on research at the Stanford Heart Disease Prevention Program. He reviews the evidence of a link between life-style and cardiovascular disease and notes that the prevention of this major health problem depends upon self-management of behavior. He examines the question of controlling behavioral risk factors associated with cardiovascular disease at reasonable cost and discusses the effectiveness of some of the unconventional health campaign tactics developed by the program he codirects. Behavioral skills, not just health facts, are taken out of the clinic and the message is brought to the community with the help of the mass media. His findings are an encouraging demonstration for other preventive education programs.

Approaches to Prevention of Adverse Developmental Consequences of Genetic and Prenatal Factors

Justin M. Joffe

Both hereditary factors and prenatal events influence the survival and the development of organisms. The purpose of this chapter is to consider what steps can be taken to minimize the chances of genetic, chromosomal, maternal constitutional, and prenatal and perinatal environmental factors having deleterious effects on intrauterine and postnatal development. In order to explore the issues relating to preventing disorders of prenatal origin, it is necessary first to indicate the nature and assess the importance of genetic, chromosomal, prenatal, and perinatal factors that are associated with deviant development of various kinds and with reproductive risk. To provide such an overview two categories of influences are distinguished, namely genetic and chromosomal factors on the one hand and environmental events on the other.

Prenatal Influences

Genetic and Chromosomal Factors.

Almost 2,000 autosomal dominant and recessive and X-linked disorders had been catalogued by 1970 (McKusick, 1971), and the number had risen to 2,336 by 1975 (Elinson and Wilson, 1978). Individual disorders due to single gene defects are rare, but together they are estimated to affect about 1 percent of children born (Elinson and Wilson, 1978; Motulsky, Benirschke, Carpenter, Fraser, Epstein, Nyhan, and Jackson, 1976). Many of these conditions—which include galactosemia, maple syrup urine disease, Hurler's syndrome, genetic thyroid defects, and phenyl

I am very grateful to George Albee, Daryll Joffe, and Philip Kitcher for their helpful comments on an earlier draft of this paper. They are not responsible, of course, for misunderstandings that I still entertain. And also to Josephine F. Beach for her Herculean labors in retyping successive drafts of this paper.

ketonuria—are associated with mental retardation (Kopp and Parmelee, 1979; Nitowsky, 1975). Multifactorial or polygenic disorders may account for the largest number of genetically determined deviant outcomes. Brent and Harris (1976), on the assumption that these play a role in producing not only congenital malformations but also schizophrenia and manic-depressive disorders and susceptibility to various common adult disorders such as high blood pressure, diabetes, and arteriosclerosis, estimate that they may affect as many as 10 percent of *all births*.

As are genetic disorders, individual chromosomal disorders are infrequent. Their effects range from intrauterine death through severe malformations with or without mental retardation to sterility and mild intellectual impairment; some have no known clinical effects (Harris, 1975). The most common "chromosomal disease" is Down's syndrome with a frequency of about 1 in 600 births (Motulsky et al., 1976) but other less prevalent chromosomal abnormalities such as Turner's syndrome (1 in 5,000 births) can have dramatic effects on development. The overall incidence of chromosomal anomalies is estimated at about 6.7 per 1,000 births (Elinson and Wilson, 1978). Considerably more detailed treatment of genetic and chromosomal factors can be found in the volumes edited by Brent and Harris (1976) and by Milunsky (1975a).

How large a problem overall do genetic and chromosomal factors present for those concerned with development? It is difficult to provide exact estimates of the overall involvement of hereditary factors in developmental defects and susceptibility to dysfunction. Even if one limits one's attention to relatively clearcut outcomes such as birth defects, only rough approximations are available. It is estimated that about 25 percent of birth defects are the result of genetic transmission and chromosomal aberrations (Brent, 1976; Wilson, 1977a), an estimate that does not include anomalies due to genetic-environmental interactions. Generally accepted estimates of the incidence of congenital malformations run from 3 to 5 percent at birth, a rate which rises to about 10 percent when malformations ascertained from birth to 2 years of age are included. Given an annual total of a little over 3,000,000 births in the United States in recent years (National Center for Health Statistics [NCHS], 1978), these estimates imply that each year about 300,000 children are born with congenital malformations, amongst whom about 75,000 are malformed as the result of genetic or chromosomal factors. Genetic and chromosomal conditions constitute the second most frequent cause of death prior to one year of age (NCHS, 1978). Alarming as these figures may be, however, they seriously underestimate the scope of the problem with regard to prevention. In the first place, these figures should more accurately be termed prevalence rather than incidence figures since no estimate is possible of the extent of chromosomal damage in the approximately 50 percent of conceptuses that die within 17 days of fertilization before pregnancy is recognized (Hertig, Rock, and Adams, 1956), and it is probable that many defective conceptuses do not reach an age where their disorder is recognized. A majority of embryos and fetuses with chromosomal abnormalities are spontaneously aborted, and it is estimated that a minimum of 7 percent of all *recognized* pregnancies involve a conceptus with a chromosomal abnormality (Motulsky et al., 1976).

More important, as Slone, Shapiro, and Mitchell (1980) state in discussing the effects of prenatal chemical events, congenital malformations probably represent only the tip of the iceberg of hereditary or environmentally induced developmental anomalies because, in addition to malformations, genetic and chromosomal factors and environmental agents can produce prenatal and perinatal mortality, postnatal functional aberrations (biochemical, physiological, neurological, intellectual, and behavioral) and congenital neoplasms in addition to various reproductive disorders that are themselves associated with suboptimal neonatal outcomes.

In addition, the relevance of genetic and chromosomal factors to morphological and functional characteristics in the "normal" range is seldom explicitly considered, although chromosomally determined characteristics such as an individual's gender and genetically influenced characteristics such as temperament (Thomas, Chess, and Birch, 1968) and cognitive ability play a major role in modifying important features of the postnatal psychosocial environment. These aspects of prenatal influences will be discussed in more detail later.

Environmental Factors

In discussing environmental agents two overlapping categories need to be included, maternal characteristics and agents in the external environment. Maternal characteristics such as the development of the reproductive system or metabolic disorders are factors influencing the intrauterine environment of the conceptus. This can, in addition, be affected by agents in the maternal environment such as stressors and drugs. Furthermore, not only is the mammalian organism susceptible to the effects of an astonishing range of physical, chemical, and biological agents during the period from conception to birth, but for a complete understanding of outcome, events occurring prior to pregnancy and during the birth process itself have to be taken into account.

For many reasons, it is impossible to provide an exhaustive list of environmental agents that affect human development. In the first place, in the case of most of more than 1,000 agents that have been reported to be mutagenic, teratogenic, or carcinogenic in animals, evidence is simply unavailable on humans. Second, failure to recognize until recently that an agent may affect development even when encountered prior to conception either by the mother or the father has resulted in a paucity of evidence on the effects of agents prior to conception and on paternal drug effects. Third, if the effects of an agent are mild (for example, subclinical intrauterine growth retardation), the outcome may not even be recognized as anomalous (Redmond, 1979). Fourth, even in the case of clear structural malformations it is often difficult to establish a causal relationship between an agent and an outcome: identical outcomes can result from either genetic or environmental factors, and particular agents can produce a variety of outcomes (Barnes, 1968), probably as a result of variations in time and duration of exposure and of dosage or as a result of individual differences in susceptibility. The absence of a distinctive defect or pattern of defects, particularly in the absence of a large number of cases, means that a teratogenic agent is unlikely to be recognized (Wilson, 1977a). Even if an agent results in a distinctive defect, if the effect is found only in susceptible individuals, unless the defect is otherwise very rare, the relationship may not readily be detected (Redmond, 1979).

These difficulties in establishing that an agent affects development are exacerbated in the case of functional alterations and delayed effects (that is, those not manifested or ascertained at birth). Not only does delay in the manifestation of the condition mean that a prenatal event is less likely to be suspected, but, in the case of functional alterations, postnatal events can produce effects identical to both genetic factors and prenatal events. Animal experiments can be of only limited help in clarifying causal relationships because there are enormous species and strain differences in susceptibility.

Nevertheless, a listing of the types of agents that affect development helps to illustrate the scope of the problem (see Table 1). More details, including summaries of probable effects and references to supporting data can be found in Brent (1976, 1977), Catz and Yaffe (1976), Goldman (1980), Grabowski (1977), Wilson (1977a, 1977b), and Winick (1976).

In view of the difficulties involved in establishing that an agent affects development, the agents listed in Table 1, particularly drugs and chemicals, probably constitute a minimum estimate of relevant environmental variables, and it is probably appropriate to regard any drug or chemical as potentially embryo-toxic until it is demonstrated not to be: "The burden of proof must be on those who wish to believe that a drug is safe during pregnancy" (Redmond, 1979, p. 7). In Table 1 no attempt is made to identify sequelae associated with the agents listed. As discussed, effects depend on a number of other factors, perhaps the most important of which is the time the event is encountered. An overview of the periods during which the environmental agents can produce effects adds another

Table 1 Environmental Causes of Developmental Defects

Radiation
Drugs and Hormones[a] (including obstetric medication)
Chemicals
Infections[b]
Maternal metabolic disorders
Pregnancy, labor, and delivery complications
Nutrition
Maternal stress and emotions
Intrauterine physical factors (e.g. uterine structure)
Miscellaneous (e.g. maternal hypoxia, mechanical trauma)

NOTE. The table includes both agents in the maternal environment (e.g. radiation, drugs, and chemicals) and maternal factors (e.g. metabolic disorders) that alter the intrauterine environment of the conceptus.

[a]Specific teratogens are discussed by Catz and Yaffe (1976), Goldman (1980), Wilson (1977a); agents causing intrauterine growth retardation by Redmond (1980); and effects of obstetric medication by Brackbill (1979).

[b]Specific agents are discussed by Wilson (1977b)

---

dimension to one's appreciation of the scope of the problem presented by environmentally produced developmental defects.

Prior to conception.

Agents such as radiation and possibly some hormones and drugs can cause chromosome damage in sperm or ova and thus act as determinants of embryonic death or developmental defects well before conception. In the case of damaged ova such events could exert their effect decades in advance of fertilization since the development of human ova begins while the mother herself is a fetus. In the case of the sperm, the susceptible period is up to about 64 days prior to fertilization, the time required for maturation of a sperm cell (Goldman, 1980). Consequently, some proportion of chromosomal disorders are attributable to environmental events, including events long before the conception of the affected embryo.

In addition, agents acting prior to conception can affect development without apparently producing chromosomal damage. Drugs and chemicals administered to *males* have been associated with deleterious effects on their progeny in both experiments on animals (Table 2) and clinical investigations of humans (Table 3). There appears to be sufficient evidence to conclude that risks associated with maternal exposure to drugs and chemicals extend also to those ingested or encountered by the father. Three effects emerge with considerable consistency in the animal research: decreased litter sizes, decreased birth weights, and increased neonatal mortality. Similar effects have been reported in humans.

Table 2 Summary of Adverse Effects of Drugs and Chemicals Administered to Male Mammals, Prior to Mating, on their Progeny: Experimental Studies

Species	Effects	Reference and year
Lead		
Rabbit	Decreased litter size, birth weight, and survival	Cole & Bachhuber, 1914
Guinea pig	Decreased birth weight, survival, and weight gain	Weller, 1915
Rat	Decreased litter size, birth weight, and survival	Stowe & Goyer, 1971
Rat	Decreased learning ability—T-maze	Brady et al., 1975
Morphine		
Mouse	Decreased weight—F_1 + F_2 generations	Friedler, 1974
Rat	Decreased survival	Smith & Joffe, 1975
Methadone		
Rat	Decreased litter size, birth weight, and survival	Smith & Joffe, 1975 Joffe et al., 1976 Soyka et al., 1978a, b, 1980a
Ethanol		
Guinea pig	Intrauterine deaths, decreased post-natal survival (F_1 − F_3 generations)	Stockard, 1913
Mouse	No significant effects on sex ratio or prenatal mortality	MacDowell et al., 1926 a,b MacDowell & Lord, 1927 Durham & Woods, 1932
Guinea pig	No significant effects on birth weight, sex ratio, or prenatal or postnatal mortality	Durham & Woods, 1932
Mouse	Intrauterine deaths	Badr & Badr, 1975
Rat	Decreased litter size and fetal size	Klassen & Persuad, 1976
Caffeine		
Hamster	Skewing of sex ratio toward females	Weathersbee et al., 1975
Rat	Decreased birth weight of males, decreased survival	Soyka et al. (un-published)
Propoxyphene		
Rat	Decreased survival	Soyka et al. (un-published)
Thalidomide		
Rabbit	Decreased birth weight, decreased litter size survival, increased malformations	Lutwak-Mann, 1964 Lutwak-Mann et al., 1967

SOURCE: Joffe, 1979.

Table 3 Summary of Adverse Effects of Drug Exposure on the Reproductive Performance of Men

Agent	Effects	Reference and year
Lead	Increased spontaneous abortions, neonatal mortality	Paul, 1860
	Reduced family size	Chyzzer, 1908
	Increased spontaneous abortions	Rudeaux, 1910
	Increased spontaneous abortions, still-births, neonatal mortality	Reid, 1911
Anesthetic gases	Increased spontaneous abortions, congenital anomalies	Ad Hoc Committee, 1974
	Increased spontaneous abortions	Cohen et al., 1975
Cigarettes	Increased incidence of low-birthweight (LBW) infants, increased neonatal mortality, and congenital anomalies in LBW infants	Yerushalmy, 1971
Caffeine	Increased reproductive loss (spontaneous abortions, stillbirths, premature births)	Weathersbee et al., 1977

SOURCE: Soyka and Joffe, 1980b

Factors operating prior to conception can also operate through the mother to affect development. The quality of reproductive performance (as indicated by perinatal mortality, delivery complications, and prematurity) is associated with maternal height (Baird, 1949; Baird and Illsley, 1953; Thomson, 1959; Yerushalmy, 1967) with taller women having better outcomes—a relationship that holds across social classes (Baird, 1964). The relationship between height and reproductive performance may be mediated by the association of height with health and general physique (Thomson and Billewicz, 1963) and with pelvic development (Bernard, 1952) and possibly with other changes in the reproductive and endocrine systems. Although there may be some genetic contribution to height differences, secular changes in populations and differences between immigrants and native stock indicate that nutrition plays a major role (see Birch and Gussow, 1970, Ch. 5). In addition, in epidemiological studies of anencephaly and spina bifida, in which an inverse relationship between maternal stature and rates of anencephaly has been demonstrated, rates are unrelated to the social class of the father but significantly related to the social class of the maternal grandfather (Carter and Evans, 1973) and peaks of occurrence were found to be due largely to births to women who were themselves born during periods of severe economic depression (Baird, 1974). Emanuel (1976) suggests that epidemiological data are consistent with growth disturbance during childhood being perhaps the major environmental influence on the occurrence of anencephaly and spina bifida. In short, nutritional deficiencies during the development of the mother may affect the development of her offspring by affecting her reproductive competence.

Animal research suggests that it may not be possible to compensate for such effects in a single generation. Cowley and Griesel (1966) maintained rats on low-protein diets from weaning until their offspring were weaned; the offspring were placed on rehabilitation diets at weaning (with some attenuation of the effects on growth, development, and behavior) and then mated to produce a third generation. The offspring of mothers that had been adequately fed while growing to maturity and producing young were lighter at birth, showed developmental lags (incisor eruption, unfolding of pinnae, eye opening, righting response), and made more errors than controls on a maze-learning task at maturity.

In addition to rendering the mother less biologically competent to provide her unborn child with an optimal prenatal environment, factors operating prior to pregnancy could obviously affect her competence to do so psychosocially, making her less informed about, or able to cope with, potential hazards or the need for adequate care.

Zygotic and early embryonic period (fertilization to gastrulation).

During the first 3 weeks of human gestation the embryo is relatively resistant to teratogenesis. The most likely effect, if any, of environmental agents during this period is death of the embryo with subsequent abortion, but if it survives it is not generally deformed although some evidence indicates that some chemicals and drugs and possibly radiation can produce nonfatal teratogenic effects during this period (see Goldman, 1980; Joffe, 1969, p. 64).

Embryonic period.

From 4 to 9 weeks of gestation the embryo is highly susceptible to teratogens and to lethal effects of toxic agents. Anomalies produced by an agent are likely to differ according to the exact time of administration, since different organs are susceptible at different times. Different agents can produce similar morphological effects either by interfering in the same way with organ formation or by acting on different developmental processes of which the normal progress of each is necessary for a normal outcome. With increasing age both individual organs and the embryo as a whole become increasingly resistant to teratogenic influences, and larger doses of drugs, chemicals, hormones, or radiation are needed to produce effects. These generalizations are derived principally from research on the effects of radiation, drugs, chemicals, and hormones on morphological development, including the development of the nervous system. It is probable, but not established, that they apply also to other agents and to other adverse developmental outcomes that may or may not be accompanied by morphological anomalies.

Fetal period.

The period from 9 weeks of gestation to birth is largely one of growth and development and because organogenesis is completed prior to the fetal period teratogenesis in the strict sense cannot occur (Wilson, 1965). However, growth retardation of the fetus as a whole or of particular organs, damage to organs, prematurity or abortion, and alterations of function can result from environmental agents encountered during the fetal period. Sequelae such as growth retardation and functional changes are precisely the ones that are least likely to be noticed or to be regarded as anomalous unless the effects are extreme. Consequently these effects of environmental agents are likely to be underestimated unless they are specifically sought in carefully controlled studies (Redmond, 1979).

Many of the agents listed in Table 1 can produce effects if encountered during the fetal period, with the retarding effects of drugs and hormones on intrauterine growth being among the best documented in humans (Redmond, 1979). Intrauterine growth retardation is associated with increased perinatal morbidity and mortality, and surviving small-for-date infants are at greater risk of impaired postnatal development.

Intrapartum period.

The period from the onset of labor to the emergence of the neonate in the extrauterine world is not unique in terms of vulnerability to environmental agents but is worth delineating as a separate period since it is one of altered probability of exposure to environmental agents such as obstetric medication and hypoxia-producing events. In the course of a comprehensive and careful review of available evidence on effects of obstetric medication on infant behavior, Brackbill (1979) summarized the evidence as follows: "Drugs given to mothers during labor and delivery have subsequent effects on infant behavior . . . . The direction of the effect is consistent across studies in showing behavioral degradation or disruption. No study has demonstrated functional enhancement following obstetrical medication" (p. 109). She found that behavioral effects were not transient, being found in some cases in infants of 1 year of age, and that the most pronounced defects was seen in areas of cognitive function and gross motor abilities.

As in the case of genetic and chromosomal factors, it is difficulty to assess the extent of the involvement of prenatal environmental factors in deviant development. About 10 percent of developmental defects (principally malformations) are estimated to be caused by environmental agents (Brent, 1976; Wilson, 1977a). However, the causes of about two-thirds of all defects are at present unknown, and it seems likely that many of these will turn out to be attributable to multiple causes with environmental components. Teratogenic effects of a drug, for example, may be dependent on other environmental agents (such as temperature, diet, or stress), maternal factors (such as age and parity), other pharmacological agents, or maternal or fetal genetic factors (Fraser, 1977). In addition, estimates do not include any allowance for prepregnancy environmental influences on reproductive function. Unless a large proportion of defects is attributable to spontaneous errors in development, environmental factors will probably turn out to have a causal role in over 60 percent of malformations.

In any event, as was pointed out in relation to genetic factors, congenital malformations are only one of the more obvious adverse consequences of prenatal events, which can also result in perinatal mortality and morbidity and a wide range of adverse delayed and functional effects.

Even if it were clearly the case that prenatal and perinatal factors had only limited effects in the absence of adverse postnatal events there are two reasons why this would not diminish their importance in development. First, there is considerable evidence to indicate that the incidence of hazardous prenatal and perinatal events is higher among the poor and among oppressed ethnic minorities. Some of this evidence is inferential. For example, blacks in the United States are more likely to have babies at ages when complications of labor are more prevalent and to have poor obstetric care during pregnancy; the latter implies that prenatal and perinatal problems are less likely to be diagnosed and treated and is, in any case, associated with higher rates of prematurity (Birch and Gussow, 1970, Chs. 4 and 7). Furthermore, insofar as outcomes such as birth weight and perinatal mortality are indicative of adverse prenatal events, a mass of evidence indicates that such events occur more frequently among the disadvantaged: stillbirths, neonatal deaths, birth weight, and prematurity are clearly related to family income, father's occupation, and other measures of socioeconomic status (Birch and Gussow, 1970, Chs. 2 and 3). In addition there is more direct evidence: Pasamanick, Knobloch, and Lilienfeld (1956) reported that while the rate of complications of pregnancy was only 5 percent in the white "upper economic fifth" it was 14.6 percent in the "lower economic fifth" and 50.6 percent in the nonwhite group. Furthermore, nutrition during pregnancy is likely to be less adequate among the poor (Birch and Gussow, 1970, Ch. 6). In other words, it is precisely those groups—the poor, the disadvantaged—who are least likely to be able to provide ameliorating postnatal environments who suffer higher incidences of hazardous prenatal events.

There is a second reason for arguing that prenatal and perinatal events would be of considerable significance even if their effects waned in the absence of adverse postnatal environmental circumstances. Briefly, the reason is that the prenatal events themselves may indirectly help to provide just such postnatal circumstances. Aside from the reasonable possibility that a stressful pregnancy might affect the mother's (and father's) care and treatment of the infant, the effects of the prenatal events on the infant's functioning and behavior are likely themselves to alter the way it is treated—the child's characteristics are themselves important determinants of his or her psychosocial environment. Indeed, this is precisely the point made by Sameroff and Chandler (1975) in their argument that development should be conceptualized as a process of *transactions* between the child and the environment and one which was made about animal development even before such a model was proposed for human development (Joffe, 1969, pp. 22–23). Perhaps surprisingly, the possibility that offspring characteristics might affect parental behavior was considered—and demonstrated—in research on animals (Ressler, 1962; Young, 1965) well before it was generally discussed in relation to human development. An interesting "taxonomy" of genotype-environment correlations suggested by Plomin, Defries, and Loehlin (1977) might be adapted to provide a systematic approach to phenotype-environment interactions of the sort involved in parent–infant relationships.

A good example of how, in the context of the transactional model, even transient effects of prenatal events might impair development is provided by Ferreira (1978), who analyzed the way in which malnutrition might interact with socioeconomic conditions to impair mental development:

The family in a deprived social environment is usually burdened with socioeconomic and health problems. In these circumstances, the child will rarely find in its immediate environment a person available and prepared to "syntonize", i.e., to tune in to him, and to be stimulating and responsive to his behavior. At the same time, children born in this environment, because of malnutrition and other ailments, will often be biologically less able to be stimulating and responsive to the caregivers. These children show apathy, irritability, and loss of interest in the social environment. Their behavior is often more disorganized and less predictable than that of the controls, requiring a special effort from those who interact with them to achieve syntony and synchrony with them. The combination of these conditions, acting throughout the child's early years, creates a cycle of interactional deprivation, which inhibits its intellectual development. (p. 207)

In contrast to the situation of the biologically vulnerable child in the deprived environment, Ferreira suggests that the child of normal prenatal development born into the same environment will be better able to elicit a 'healthy transaction", and the impaired child in a favorable environment has a better chance of having parents who can make the necessary effort to respond to the child in a way that compensates for the initial effects of the adverse prenatal and perinatal events.

In brief, Sameroff and Chandler's (1975) transactional model of development itself suggests that adverse conditions and hazardous prenatal and perinatal events might have considerable significance for development even if the direct effects of such conditions and events were transient.

Before turning to a discussion of issues relating to prevention of adverse outcomes it should be noted that the perspective in which prenatal and perinatal factors have been viewed thus far is one of prevention of defects rather than promotion of optimal development. Much concern has focused on avoiding adverse effects, very little on whether prenatal development takes place in an environment that fosters even more favorable outcomes than usual. Should we reach a point where our "control" group is not one defined by the absence of adverse conditions during prenatal life but rather by the presence of favorable conditions—those optimizing neonatal status and functioning—it may emerge that the children who experience hazards have lost more than we thought and that the rebound that sometimes occurs in favorable postnatal environments does not bring the children to the level of functioning that we might assume them to have been capable of reaching. If such is the case we will have to give greater weight to the primary prevention of prenatal hazard than we currently do. As long as we think we can compensate postnatally for the consequences of prenatal disadvantage, there is a danger that we will not give sufficient attention to prenatal development.

Prevention

In this section some of the approaches to intervening to reduce the incidence of deviant outcomes of prenatal origin—death, malformations, stunting of growth, functional aberrations—will be considered. Issues of *what* can be done are often inseparable from questions about *how* they should be done and questions of desirability are linked with both of these, but the focus in this section is primarily on characterizing types of interventions that could reduce deviant outcomes and discussing the extent to which they can be regarded as preventive measures. Three general approaches to the task, distinguishable initially largely by the time at which they are implemented, are diagrammed in Figure 1. The first is postnatal intervention which, in principle, could be applied generally or could be restricted to groups considered to be at high risk for deviant development on the basis of measures of neonatal status or on the basis of factors (for example, socioeconomic status) that are associated with an increased probability of the child encountering circumstances that lead to less than optimal development. Depending on the nature of the risk factors the interventions might be intended to do one or both of the following:

- To interrupt the causal chain linking already encountered events to undesirable outcomes or to compensate for their effects; this might be classified as prevention of sequelae or early treatment.

- To obviate the child's encountering events that might not be conducive to optimal development, or to improve the child's ability to cope with such events in a manner that does not deflect such development.

Postnatal approaches are essential for continued optimal development in even the healthiest of neonates, and until such time as we have intervened with complete success prior to birth, postnatal measures to minimize the anticipated deleterious effects of adverse prenatal events—to treat them, to prevent their sequelae—will be essential. Since we may always have a residue of unpreventable neonatal outcomes for which we will need to implement ameliorative postnatal programs, concern for definitional purity (see Kessler and Albee, 1975; Bloom, 1980) may have to take a back seat to practical concerns. Postnatal interventions are the subject of detailed consideration elsewhere in this volume and will not be further discussed here.

In any case, intervention prior to birth is obviously more attuned to the notion that the purpose of primary prevention is to obviate negative events and promote positive ones (Bloom, 1980), not "to reduce or contain already manifest deficits" (Task Panel on Prevention, 1978, p. 1833).

Even limiting our concern to interventions prior to birth we are left with at least two general approaches: We can consider ways of minimizing the likelihood of adverse neonatal outcomes in the presence of threatening prenatal events—roughly characterizable as "high-risk approaches"—as well as ways of preventing the occurrence of such events (see Figure 1). In any case, we will see, once again, that distinctions between prevention and treatment are not straightforward. In considering each approach, three questions underlie the discussion. What kinds of techniques are available—that is, what can we do? How effective are these techniques—in particular, to what extent are they *preventive?* And how do we know when, or to whom, to apply them?

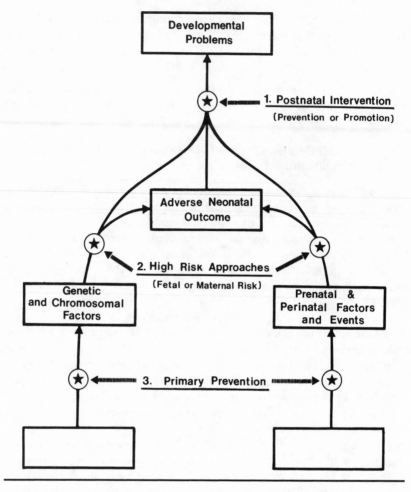

Figure 1. Approaches to prevention of adverse outcomes of prenatal and genetic factors.

High-Risk Approaches

Similar general principles apply to prenatal intervention whether the disorders are of genetic or nongenetic origin and for this reason, and because many prenatal problems are of unknown or multifactorial origin, genetic and environmentally determined disorders will not be considered separately. Despite the risk of oversimplification, a rough distinction between the techniques and the treatments used when the concern is with identifying sick embryos or fetuses as opposed to identifying sick mothers is of some help in organizing a discussion of these approaches. In fact, of course, the two categories overlap and many of the matters discussed in the section on fetal disorders are relevant to prenatal disorders in general.

Fetal disorders.

Ingalls (1953), in discussing what he termed "preventive prenatal pediatrics", wrote:

The nearly insurmountable obstacle to clinical study of prenatal sickness arises in the fact that the patient voices no complaint, remembers nothing about his illness, hides himself from view, and puts off his visit to the doctor until the last possible moment. (p. 34)

This statement illustrates what are still unique difficulties in dealing with problems in perinatal development, although technical progress since the 1950s has made the unborn organism far less inaccessible than it was when Ingalls wrote. The development of procedures of visualizing the fetus using indirect techniques such as sonography and improved radiographic methods or direct ones such as fetoscopy, and the concurrent development of procedures of obtaining samples of fetal tissue and blood or of amniotic fluid (Golbus, 1978; Kushnick, 1979), have made it more difficult for fetuses to hide themselves from view. Advances in our ability to read the messages in amniotic and fetal fluids and cells and in maternal blood and urine have helped provide the fetus with a voice. We have, in fact, entered an era where a variety of fetal disorders, including neural tube defects and biochemical disorders of metabolism, have been, or are capable of being, diagnosed prenatally (Golbus, 1978; Kushnick, 1979; Milunsky and Atkins, 1975).

Aside from the need for technical and scientific advances to make the techniques safer, more accurate, cheaper, and capable of detecting even more disorders, we need to consider two problems of some importance. The first is the question of what is to be done when congenital disorders are detected—and is it prevention?—and the second relates to efficient and effective use of our technology. How do we know when to resort to prenatal diagnosis?

When prenatal diagnosis detects genetic or other prenatal disease, few options are available. The first, intrauterine therapy, is at present available in only a limited number of disorders. Therapy can take the form of preventing toxic changes in maternal physiology (as, for example, in dietary control in maternal phenylketonuria), of intrauterine fetal transfusion (as treatment in cases of rhesus incompatibility), and of prevention of toxic changes in the fetus (as, for example, in the use of intrauterine corticosteroids to treat congenital adrenal hyperplasia) (Hsia, 1975). Compared with postnatal treatment these approaches have the advantage of being applicable early enough to prevent changes that may be irreversible if left until after birth (Hsia, 1975). However, they are clearly no different in principle from postnatal interventions and even though they comprise earlier and potentially more effective treatment, they do not constitute prevention of the conditions themselves.

The second option in the event of prenatal diagnosis of fetal disorder is abortion. Although this is clearly primary prevention of the chronic stress that may be experienced by parents and family of an affected child, when the focus is on the condition itself, whether abortion is regarded as primary prevention or not is a matter of definition. It can reduce the prevalance of a disorder but does not affect incidence, unless one adopts birth as the point at which incidence is determined. Although it obviously prevents the birth of an infant with a given condition, it does not prevent the occurrence of the condition. Furthermore it is possible that detection and abortion of affected fetuses could result in an increase in the number of abnormal genes in the population as a whole since parents may tend to replace affected fetuses with normal infants, about two-thirds of whom will be unaffected carriers of the condition (Harris, 1975). In the case of many congenital disorders abortion is, at present, the only method available to avoid the birth of an affected child. An intriguing alternative approach is contained in the suggestion that we find ways of improving the natural mechanisms that already result in the discarding of a large proportion of damaged embryos (Fraser, 1978; Smithells, 1978), an approach that Warkany (1978) has termed "terathanasia". When prenatal diagnosis *excludes* the possibility that the fetus is defective, its findings could be said to constitute primary prevention since they eliminate a source of parental apprehension and anxiety that might affect development.

A problem that presents other kinds of difficulties for practical application of prenatal diagnosis and from the point of view of obviation or prevention of the conditions rather than their treatment is related to decisions about the circumstances in which prenatal diagnosis should be used. One possibility is to attempt to implement prenatal diagnosis universally. Such an approach would encounter formidable technical, economic, service delivery, psychological, legal, and ethical obstacles (many of which are discussed in the volume on preventing genetic disease and mental retardation edited by Milunsky, 1975a). The more practicable approach is to use prenatal diagnostic techniques only when there are a priori reasons to suspect genetic or congenital abnormalities. At present, indications for undertaking prenatal diagnosis include the following (Kushnick, 1979):

•For chromosomal abnormalities: advanced parental age, chromosomal abnormalities in a parent; previous chromosomally abnormal child or abortus

•For metabolic diseases: known maternal metabolic disorders; both parents known carriers; mother known or suspected carrier of X-linked disorder; previous affected child.

• For neural tube defects: raised maternal alpha-fetoprotein; previous affected child.

• For erythroblastosis: Rh negative mother.

The presence of indicators of these kinds defines a pregnancy in which the risk of a child with significant impairment is substantially greater than it is in the population at large. As indicated, if the aim is primary prevention, prenatal diagnosis, for whatever reason it is carried out, has limitations. Even its effective use as a method of secondary prevention is compromised as long as issues relating to the availability of adequate medical attention and the resources and knowledge to seek it remain unresolved. In addition, there are somewhat different implications for prevention depending on the kind of risk indicator which determines that diagnostic methods are invoked.

Indicators like parental age and manifest metabolic disorder offer the best possibility for prevention since they provide a way of identifying couples at risk before the birth of an affected child. Age of parents and, for some disorders, ethnicity (sickle cell anemia, Tay-Sachs disease, and so forth) can provide indications of risk before the disorders have appeared in the family. Recognized metabolic disorders in a family, although no strictly "pre-proband" indicators, at least are potentially capable of indicating risk before an affected child is born to the couple. By contrast, when risk indicators that depend on the prior birth—or miscarriage—of an affected child are relied upon, "only limited reduction in the overall postnatal incidence of the disease could be expected" (Kaback, 1975, p. 95), since the majority of cases of genetic disease tend to occur in families without a previous history of the disorder.

The final category of risk indicators includes such things as knowledge that the parents are carriers of a genetic disorder or knowledge of correlates of fetal defects, such as raised maternal serum alpha-fetoprotein. Discussion of these indicators can be recursive: unless we rely on postproband identification of at-risk couples, with its attendant drawbacks, or screen entire populations (and this may be feasible for some disorders: see Scriver and Laberge, 1978), we need to determine on the basis of what indicators (of possible possession of deleterious genes) we will look for indicators (of prenatal disorder).

These questions as to whom to apply techniques are important not only in the context of prenatal diagnosis but also for using pre-proband identification techniques to obviate the *conception* of children with genetic disorders, a topic that will be discussed in the section on primary prevention.

Maternal risk factors.

The rationale of an approach to prevention based on maternal risk factors is that through adequate prenatal care to reduce the occurrance of disorders of pregnancy or labor or through identification and subsequent treatment or management of such disorders, adverse neonatal outcomes can be avoided or the severity of the disorders reduced. There is no shortage of risk factors that can be used to identify high-risk pregnancies: For example, McNeil and Kaij (1977) list 20 criteria used to identify obstetric risk groups in need of specialist care in the Swedish health system; Meier (1975) identifies 26 risk factors spanning maternal variables and complications during pregnancy and delivery; and Chez, Haire, Quilligan, and Wingate (1976), in the course of their comprehensive review of the relationships between prenatal and perinatal factors and adverse neonatal outcome, provide a table that contains a total of 69 pregnancy risk factors (not counting 19 fetal-maternal and neonatal factors).

A list of the categories of variables other than fetal-maternal and neonatal ones that Chez et al. (1976) present illustrates the variety of factors that can be involved in this approach:

●socioeconomic factors (for example, father's occupation, housing conditions, minority status, early prepregnancy malnutrition)

●demographic factors (for example, maternal age, weight, familial genetic disorder, poor obstetric history)

●maternal medical factors (for example, lack of prenatal care, toxemia, hypertensive disorders, mental retardation, emotional disturbance)

●placental and membrane factors (for example, vaginal bleeding, placental insufficiency, abruptio placentae)

●labor and delivery factors (for example, premature labor, prolonged labor, high mid-forceps delivery).

It seems clear that the efficacy of interventions based on the presence of risk factors of these kinds is dependent upon their being obviated entirely or treated as early as possible. This in turn depends upon the availability of prenatal care that people can afford and a recognition by consumers of the need to seek such care as early as possible. In practice it is just those groups that are at highest risk on socioeconomic criteria—the poor, the unmarried, the oppressed minorities—who are least likely to seek early care, as well as those least likely to receive adequate care when they do (Birch and Gussow, 1970). Experience in Sweden indicates that such problems may arise even when services are readily available; according to McNeil and Kaij (1977), "the women who do not take advantage of the [parent education] classes are to a large extent the very ones who need the most help—the young, the poorly informed, and foreigners" (p. 99).

In the event that risk factors are recognized, a variety of medical and "psycho-obstetric" (McNeil and Kaij, 1977) interventions are available to reduce the probability of miscarriage of embryonic or fetal damage. Depending on the nature of the condition, intervention may take the form of evaluating the condition of the embryo or fetus (perhaps followed, if indicated, by treatment or abortion) or implementing one or other form of medical management of the condition. Given the diversity of the risk factors involved, it is difficult to provide an overall characterization of the preventive status of the approach. Much depends on the nature of the risk factors.

When maternal medical or placental or membrane factors are involved, the approach can be said to constitute primary prevention insofar as the conditions can be corrected and the potential threat to the unborn child expeditiously removed; the only qualification would pertain to the question of whether the condition itself could have been prevented through earlier intervention. When the measures are palliative, as with medical or obstetric disorders that can only be ameliorated or their consequences monitored to enable treatment to be instituted expeditiously—perhaps maternal diabetes and placenta praevia constitute examples of such disorders—the approach might be termed partial prevention. When the maternal risk factors result in prenatal examination of the fetus and subsequent fetal therapy or abortion, the approach, as discussed earlier, constitutes early treatment. Similarly, when labor and delivery factors are involved, interventions will often have to be directed at neonatal amelioration of the effects on the infant.

Socioeconomic and demographic risk factors are different from the other factors considered, both in the sense of being antecedents of other risks and in being unamenable to alteration by the types of techniques used to deal with complications of pregnancy and delivery. Demographic variables may predict a greater probability that complications will occur but variables like family income, maternal age or stature, and poor obstetric history are not treatable in the same way as medical disorders. Aspects of this dilemma will be discussed later.

Primary Prevention

In discussing high-risk approaches we mostly considered methods of ameliorating or eliminating the early consequences of genetic and chromosomal factors on the one hand and prenatal and perinatal factors and events on the other. These approaches cannot be considered to be primary prevention insofar as they deal with disorders after their occurrence: in many cases the very presence of high-risk groups constitutes evidence that primary prevention measures have either not been implemented or have failed.

If we are actually to prevent risk—that is, to eliminate the occurrence of conceptuses with chromosomal and genetic disorders, women who are reproductively incompetent, the occurrence of prenatal and perinatal events that harm the unborn child—we need to identify and eradicate the factors that result in their occurrence or to alter those exposed to them in a way that makes them immune to the effects. In brief, we have to identify and control the *causes of the causes*, the events and conditions that fill the empty boxes in Figure 1. Causal chains are long and complex, and it is in the nature of scientific inquiry to be selective about which links to investigate in detail. In addition, causal chains tend to acquire more and more interlinking strands as one moves away from the effect one wishes to understand, making it less likely, and certainly more difficult to demonstrate, that earlier links constitute necessary and sufficient conditions for the occurrence of the "effect". Consequently, once important links are identified, there is a tendency to concentrate study on subsequent links rather than antecedent ones, so that the "causes of the causes" are relatively neglected.

The subsequent discussion attempts to demonstrate the greater effectiveness of directing more effort at dealing with earlier links, first briefly in considering genetic and chromosomal disorders and then at more length in considering environmentally related prenatal and perinatal factors and events.

Genetic and chromosomal disorders.

We know a considerable amount about the antecedents of chromosomal and genetic disorders. Some chromosomal abnormalities (and genetic mutations) are the result of environmental agents, which are considered in the next section. In other cases we can identify causally relevant variables, those that may not constitute immediate antecedents of chromosomal abnormalities, but that are predictive of an increased likelihood of such abnormalities. An obvious example is the relationship between maternal and paternal age and Down's syndrome (Abroms and Bennett, 1979), with considerably increased risk of chromosomal nondisjunction in older parents. Intervening to ensure that people confine child bearing to their lower risk years would presumably constitute a preventive measure although recent decreases in mean age of child-bearing women in England, Canada, the United States, and other industrialized nations (Holmes, 1978) have not, however, been accompanied by a decreased incidence of Down's syndrome, possibly indicating an improvement in ascertainment or a biological change (see Bennett and Abroms, 1979). It is interesting to note that such an approach, despite its apparent simplicity, has many ramifications. At the very least, to be maximally effective, it requires widespread educational measures and the availability (and acceptability) of contraceptive measures; it is little use telling women over

35 not to have babies unless steps have been taken to ensure that they have had the number of children they want before then (and unless they have the means of preventing further conceptions and the willingness to use them). Ensuring that a desired family size is attained during the optimal years for childbearing in turn depends in part on socioeconomic conditions and on social support services since family planning is affected by a couple's ability to afford the loss of income resulting from interruption of work and by the question of whether or not there are affordable and adequate alternatives to one member rearing the child rather than being employed outside the home.

We know enough to prevent a great many genetic disorders too. We can, as yet, do little, even if we wish to, about the ultimate causes of genetic defects, mutation, and natural selection, but we could, in many cases, take steps to deal with the proximate cause of genetically affected embryos, the mating of genetic carriers. People affected with dominant genetic disorders or X-linked ones pose a threat to their offspring regardless of the genotype of their mate, while individuals heterozygous for some autosomal recessive disorder (unaffected carriers) pose a threat only if their mate is also a carrier (Reilly, 1975). Provided such individuals can be identified, intervention to reduce the incidence of genetic disorders is possible, with the potential efficacy of intervention substantially greater in cases in which identification can be made prior to the birth of an affected child (as was discussed earlier). At present, only one preventive method is available in such cases, the prevention of reproduction—either the abortion of the conceptus or the prevention of conception. In principle, such an approach could be extremely effective: "Mass screening for genetic disease, when coupled with appropriate mating prohibitions, could permit the reduction of all identifiable disorders to mutation level in a single generation" (Reilly, 1975, pp. 430–431). Aside from technical and economic considerations (Harris, 1975), mass screening (and effective use of the information obtained) poses a variety of legal questions (Reilly, 1975). In addition, the design and implementation of programs to reduce the frequency of "deleterious" genes—negative eugenics—through voluntary or compulsory restrictions on procreation raise troubling ethical issues, the difficulties of which are exacerbated by geographic, ethnic, and class-related concentrations of certain genes and by lack of knowledge of what constitutes eugenic improvement (Lappé, 1975). Similar issues arise, though less pointedly, in attempts to apply the same preventive method on a smaller scale, through the use of genetic counseling (Milunsky, 1975b). At present, expanded availability of genetic counseling in conjunction with increased public awareness of its role probably represent the least controversial approach to the primary prevention of genetic disorders. In combination with improved techniques of identification and mass screening it has the potential to reduce markedly the incidence of such disorders.

Environmental factors and events.

In abstract terms, the process of prevention can be stated very simply: once the damaging agent is identified, any one of three actions can be taken to prevent its effects—removal of the agent, strengthening the host to increase resistance to the agent, or preventing contact between agent and host (Roberts, 1970). In the case of deleterious prenatal and perinatal environmental factors and events, we have a great deal of knowledge about the agents involved. This knowledge takes two apparently disparate forms: information about factors that cause adverse outcomes (see Table 1) and information about variables correlated with such outcomes. In neither case does the information alone seem to enable us to determine ways of removing agents, strengthening the host, or preventing contact between agent and host. In each case we seem to have to do something further with the information to design prevention programs. The remainder of this paper will briefly examine the form that these attempts take and argue that the "causes" are less relevant to prevention than the correlated variables and that the reluctance to deal directly with these variables is based on misconceptions.

First, then, we examine the prenatal "causes" of adverse development. Table 1 lists categories of causes and we can provide detailed lists of agents in each category, yet these do not, in themselves suggest what can be done. The problem seems to result from the fact that exposure to any of the agents in Table 1 could arise in many different ways, each involving multiple determinants. In practice, what we seem to do to design prevention programs is to look for these determinants—in effect, to identify the causes of the causes. We might, for example, inquire about why a pregnant woman took a prescription drug during pregnancy, and identify among the causes failures in medical education; ignorance of the patient (of the risk or of the fact that she was pregnant); too-ready reliance on chemical solutions to problems of living (in the case of a tranquilizer, say) in both doctor and patient; the overconcern of the pharmaceutical industry with profit; the unavailability, inaccessibility, or unaffordability of alternative means of dealing with problems for which the tranquilizer was resorted to; and so on. The number and scope of "prevention programs" suggested by even a casual analysis of this kind is dizzying and could involve anything from revising the medical school curriculum and increasing the number of public service messages in the media to nationalizing the pharmaceutical industry.

This kind of approach is nothing if not fruitful and does offer potential benefits, but they may be slow in coming and each program may in itself be able to show only negligible results. As Fraser (1978) suggested about the prevention of teratogenic effects, "no one preventive measure will bring about a dramatic drop in frequency. . . . We must keep on chipping away . . . ; each small decrease in the burden will be vitally important to some families, and the cumulative effect will be eventually visible" (p. 398). The practical difficulties of obtaining funding for programs that only chip away are substantial; many otherwise admirable programs will founder on the fiscal rocks given their low expectations of benefits in relation to costs. In attempting to prioritize programs we will be in danger of spending the little that is available for prevention (Albee, 1979) on pilot projects.

Parenthetically, this approach represents something of a methodological paradox. Normally, compounded variables correlated with a particular outcome are subjected to further dissection, by experimental study whenever possible, to identify "causal variables" entangled in the correlations. Yet it seems that to develop effective prevention programs we may have to go from the kinds of physical, chemical, and biological variables we have already identified to the larger network of variables that encompass them.

The second approach, which starts with the larger, correlated variables usually suggests programs that are indistinguishable from those arrived at by the first, but the process differs. In this approach, we start with the demographic variables that correlate with the outcome we wish to prevent, those variables encompassed by answers to questions about who does and does not suffer from a given condition and when and where the condition is or is not found. When we do this, we find that our best predictors are global and complex variables like ethnic group and socioeconomic status. With regard to prenatal factors, for example, the variables in the Collaborative Perinatal Project (Broman et al., 1975) with the highest correlations with IQ at age 4 were socioeconomic index and mother's education (there was also a 13 point IQ difference between black and white children) and in the Kauai study (Werner and Smith, 1977) low level of maternal education and low standard of living were among the key predictors of poor developmental outcomes at 2 years and of learning and behavior problems at 10 and 18.

What do we do with such information? The short answer is, anything but deal with the factors identified. We claim that the only proper use of such data is to look for variables within the demographic correlates that account for the effects and that it is misguided to consider that prevention might best be served by dealing with them directly. They can be unravelled in plausible ways. For example: "The poor woman having a baby may be at risk because of her age, her nutritional status, her probable poor growth, her excessive exposure to infection in the community

which she inhabits, her poor housing, and her inadequate medical supervision, as well as because of complex interactions between these and
other potentially adverse influences" (Birch and Gussow, 1970, p. 175).
Such unravelling is useful in suggesting prevention programs: we can design programs to improve prenatal care in urban ghettos; to provide vitamin supplements for poor women; to reduce drug abuse; and so on.
These are very much the kinds of programs suggested by the first approach, in which the reasons people are exposed to the proximate causes
of poor developmental outcomes are analyzed.

An interesting question arises, however. Since the broad demographic
variables seem to encompass something closer to ultimate causes, and
since we seem to be better able to design prevention programs when we
deal with causes of causes, why do we choose the middle ground? Why
do we ask: What is it about poverty that produces increases in birth defects, prematurity, perinatal death, instead of designing programs to prevent poverty?[1] Why do we ask, what is it about powerlessness that produces breakdown, misery, and violence, instead of trying to redistribute
power?

We seem to be given three reasons why we should leave the broader
variables alone: They are not the real causes of the problems, we are not
competent to deal with them, and it would not solve the problem if we
did. The first reason has to do with a particular concept of what constitutes a causal relationship and implies that attempting to deal with global
factors is scientifically misguided. For example:

Efforts at prevention will not succeed . . . unless we establish specific interventions that work on the causes of specific kinds of psychopathology. . . . Without
an understanding of causes, we are in the position of relying on serendipity—
surely a poor substitute for the solid knowledge that research can provide—or
relying on vague hopes that broad, often unsubstantiated social action programs
will automatically decrease the rate of mental illness by correcting social woes
and increasing the general psychological well-being. Arnhoff (1975) noted,
"Somewhere along the line, a problem as old as man, that of mental illness, was
absorbed into the pursuit of global mental health" (p. 1281). It is this confusion of
objectives that has led some workers to formulate the issue of primary prevention
in terms of eliminating poverty, slums, and economic insecurity—among other
commendable but nebulous proposals. (Erlenmeyer-Kimling, 1977, p. 86)

It seems that we think we have two kinds of variables: the "real
causes"—things like drug abuse, marital problems, lack of parenting
skills—that we can deal with as professionals, and the global and nebu-

---

[1] For example: "The important question . . . is: in what way do adverse socio-economic
conditions produce the disorders of pregnancy and delivery?" (Joffe, 1969, p. 269). I was
writing at the time about methodological issues but cannot now defend the narrowness of
focus that makes analysis of the variables entwined in socioeconomic status *the* important
question.

lous factors, like poverty, ignorance, and powerlessness that we know correlate with the causes but do not themselves constitute causes. The dichotomy is misleading in implying that the variables we can deal with have a unique scientific status—it cloaks our bias and ignorance in a scientific rationalization.

In fact, the "real causes" do not appear to be quite as different from "mere correlations" as we seem to find it convenient to believe, and if this is the case, we cannot be excused on scientific grounds from dealing with the correlated variables. This is not the place to undertake a philosophical disquisition of the nature of causation. However, it is pertinent to point out that the distinction between "genuine causes" and "merely correlated" variables is more complex than seems to be appreciated by many of those who wish to make this kind of distinction with a view to de-emphasizing the kinds of variables the importance of which I want to stress. If one takes the simplest approach, that variables have to be individually necessary and sufficient in order to be regarded as causal, one will find that very few causes have been identified in the biological and social sciences—or even in physics for that matter. In many cases we cannot claim that what we regard as a causal variable is either necessary *or* sufficient. In fact, we appear to recognize a causal relationship when we see that in the presence of a particular factor the probability of a certain outcome is increased and we have no reason to believe that both are dependent on a third variable. Given these considerations, brief as they may be, unless one has evidence that both are due to a third (genetic?) variable, there is no reason not to say that poverty and powerlessness (see Albee, 1980) cause disease—and birth defects.

Variables like age, ethnic group, socioeconomic status, education, housing conditions, and so on are not second-class scientific variables and attending to them may, in fact, enable us to design more effective prevention programs than we can when we give all our attention to *mere causes*.

The second reason we are given why we have no business with social reform is that we have no particular competence in this area and that involving ourselves in the arena of social reform detracts from our credibility and effectiveness as professionals. For example:

Instead of focusing narrowly on the environmental stressors that are likely to be amenable to the intervention of mental health specialists with community decision makers, they become preoccupied by such major and global problems as poverty and racial prejudice, and they embark themselves on quixotic remedial campaigns as revolutionaries and social agitators. Unfortunately, they are no more skilled in social action than in community mental health practice; on the one hand they make inflated rhetorical promises about putting the bad world right which eventually bring inevitable discredit, or they lead inept marches on

City Hall on behalf of the downtrodden, and get repudiated both by their disappointed clients and by the municipal authorities who pay their salaries. In any event, primary prevention for which they have ostensibly been fighting, gets a bad name. (Caplan, 1978 p. 10).

Indeed we may have no special competence as professionals to solve social problems—even if we do seem to be able to identify them—but the modesty we assume when talking about poverty and injustice seems to be put aside when we attempt to influence public policy to achieve what we claim as professional goals. Do we not claim special competence in identifying needs and implementing solutions when it comes to influencing legislation or acquiring funding for prevention programs of other kinds? Is it that we define as within our professional sphere those actions and aims that we approve of, while those we disapprove of are "political"? Furthermore, with whom do we lose credibility when we attempt remedial campaigns? It seems that our inaction, rather than action, in the social arena is more likely to compromise the credibility of our efforts as professionals. Or do we believe that our efforts as professionals excuse us from working for social change? If primary prevention is to have any hope of success, it needs a more committed stance than that represented by an "I gave at the office" philosophy.

The third reason we are given why we should not attack social evils is that even if we succeeded we would not have eradicated deviance, unhappiness, or the birth of infants with impaired potential. This, too, may be true, but there are reasons to believe that this approach will achieve more than piecemeal one-small-problem-at-a-time approaches. If we are realistic, we acknowledge that each proximate cause is the outcome of complex interactions of variables and that, as Vance (1977) pointed out, "the greater the number of relevant interactions, the smaller the groupings for which a single treatment will be appropriate" (p. 208). If this is so, then either we resign ourselves to designing myriads of low-payoff prevention programs or we lay siege to the broader variables that encompass the complex interacting variables. Dealing with variables like socioeconomic status and ethnicity deals simultaneously with factors giving rise to hazardous prenatal and perinatal events, those enhancing susceptibility to such events, and those that ensure postnatal conditions that at best fail to alleviate the consequences of prenatal hazards and at worst exacerbate their efforts. In addition, the broader variables are also more promising in terms of the timing of intervention. They exert their effects earlier than the proximate causes of adverse neonatal outcomes so their eradication has a greater change of obviating problems before they occur. A further advantage to putting emphasis on prevention that can be achieved through attention to demographic variables is that the approach encompasses both prevention and promotion: Removal of the global causes of dysfunction at the very least should result in a population with the means and the desire to pursue improved function. Removing external barriers strengthens people and provides conditions in which they can direct their strength toward the removal of further barriers.

None of this is to argue that social change will solve all the problems but rather that without such change much of whatever else we do may be futile. We will have to do it over and over again. Social change may not be sufficient, but it is necessary. Even if social change brought equitable programs to prevent genetic disease, reduce reproductive incompetence, and minimize environmental hazards, we would still be left with an apparently irreducible minimum of developmental defects. The perspective of primary prevention might be defined as never concluding that the minimum has been reached.

References

Abroms, K. I., and Bennett, J. W. Parental age and Trisomy-21. *Down's Syndrome,* 1979, *2,* 6–7.

Ad Hoc Committee on the Effect of Trace Anesthetics on the Health of Operating Room Personnel. Occupational disease among operating room personnel: A national study. *Anesthesiology,* 1974, *41,* 321–340.

Albee, G. W. The prevention of prevention. *Physician East,* April 1979, 28–30.

Albee, G. W. Politics, power, prevention, and social change. In J. M. Joffe and G. W. Albee (Eds.), *Prevention through political action and social change,* Vol. 5: *Primary prevention of psychopathology.* Hanover, N.H.: University Press of England, 1980.

Arnhoff, F. N. Social consequences of policy toward mental illness. *Science,* 1975, *188,* 1277–1281.

Badr, F. M., and Badr, R. S. Induction of dominant lethal mutation in male mice by ethyl alcohol. *Nature,* 1975, *253,* 134–136.

Baird, D. Social class and foetal mortality. *Lancet,* 1949, *1,* 1079–1083.

Baird, D. The epidemiology of prematurity. *Journal of Pediatrics,* 1964, *65,* 909–924.

Baird, D. Epidemiology of congenital malformations of the central nervous system in (a) Aberdeen and (b) Scotland. *Journal of Biosocial Science,* 1974, *6,* 113–137.

Baird, D., and Illsley, R. Environment and childbearing. *Proceedings of the Royal Society of Medicine,* 1953, *46,* 53–59.

Barnes, A. C. The fetal environment: Drugs and chemicals. In A. C. Barnes (Ed.), *Intrauterine development.* Philadelphia: Lea and Febiger, 1968.

Bennett, J. W., and Abroms, K. I. Changing perspectives on Down's syndrome. *Journal of the Louisiana Medical Society,* 1979, *131,* 305–307.

Bernard, R. M. The shape and size of the female pelvis. (Transactions of the Edinburgh Obstetrical Society) *Edinburgh Medical Journal,* 1952, *59,* 1–16.

Birch, H. G., and Gussow, J. D. *Disadvantaged children: Health, nutrition and school failure.* New York: Harcourt, Brace, and World, 1970.

Bloom, M. A working definition of primary prevention related to social concerns. *The Journal of Prevention,* 1980, *1,* 15–23.

Brackbill, Y. Obstetrical medication and infant behavior. In J. D. Osofsky (Ed.), *Handbook of infant behavior*. New York: Wiley, 1979.

Brady, H., Herrera, Y., and Zenick, H. Influence of parental lead exposure on subsequent learning ability of offspring. *Pharmacology, Biochemistry and Behavior*, 1975, *3*, 561–565.

Brent, R. L. Environmental factors: Miscellaneous. In R. L. Brent and M. I. Harris (Eds.), *Prevention of embryonic, fetal, and perinatal disease*. DHEW Pub. No. (NIH) 76-853. Washington, D.C., 1976.

Brent, R. L. Radiations and other physical agents. In J. G. Wilson and F. C. Fraser (Eds.), *Handbook of teratology*. Vol. 1: *General principles and etiology*. New York: Plenum, 1977.

Brent, R. L., and Harris, M. I. Summaries. In R. L. Brent and M. I. Harris (Eds.), *Prevention of embryonic, fetal, and perinatal disease*. DHEW Pub. No. (NIH) 76-853. Washington, D.C., 1976.

Broman, S. H., Nichols, P. L., and Kennedy, W. A. *Preschool IQ: Prenatal and early developmental correlates*. Hillsdale, N.J.: L. Erlbaum Associates, 1975.

Caplan, G. *The primary prevention of mental disorders in children: Developments during the period 1962–1977*. Lecture, University of Leuven, Belgium, May 26, 1978.

Carter, C. O., and Evans, K. Spina bifida and anencephalus in Greater London. *Journal of Medical Genetics*, 1973, *10*, 209–234.

Catz, C. S., and Yaffe, S. J. Environmental factors: Pharmacology. In R. L. Brent and M. I. Harris (Eds.), *Prevention of embryonic, fetal, and perinatal disease*. DHEW Pub. No. (NIH) 76-853. Washington, D.C., 1976.

Chez, R., Haire, D., Quilligan, E. J., and Wingate, M. B. High risk pregnancies: Obstetrical and perinatal factors. In R. L. Brent and M. I. Harris (Eds.), *Prevention of embryonic, fetal, and perinatal disease*. DHEW Pub. No. (NIH) 76-853 Washington, D.C., 1976.

Chyzzer, A. Des intoxications per le plumb se presentant dans le ceramique en Hongrie Budapest XLIV, Chir. Presse, 1908, 906. (Quoted by Weller, 1915).

Cohen, E. N., Brown, Jr., B. W., Bruce, D. L., Cascorbi, H. F., Corbett, T. H., Jones, T. W., and Whitcher, C. E. A survey of anesthetic health hazards among dentists. *Journal of the American Dental Association*, 1975, *90*, 1291–1296.

Cole, L. J., and Bachhuber, L. J. The effect of lead on the germ cells of the male rabbit and fowl. *Proceedings of the Society for Experimental Biology and Medicine*, 1914, *12*, 24–29.

Corah, N. L., Anthony, E. J., Painter, P., Stern, J. A., and Thurston, D. L. Effects of perinatal anoxia after seven years. *Psychological Monographs*, 1965, *79*, 3 (Whole No. 596).

Cowley, J. J., and Griesel, R. D. The effect on growth and behavior of rehabilitating first and second generation low protein rats. *Animal Behaviour*, 1966, *14*, 506–517.

Durham, F. M., and Woods, H. M. Alcohol and inheritance: An experimental study. *Medical Research Council Special Report Series*. London: H.M.S.O., No. 168, 1932.

Elinson, J., and Wilson, R. W. Prevention. In *Health, United States, 1978*. U.S. Department of Health, Education and Welfare. DHEW Pub. No. (PHS) 78-1232. Hyattsville, M.D., 1978.

Emanuel, I. Problems of outcome of pregnancy: Some clues from the epidemiologic similarities and differences. In S. Kelly, E. B. Hook, D. T. Janerich, and I. H. Porter (Eds.), *Birth defects: Risks and consequences*. New York: Academic Press, 1976.

Erlenmeyer-Kimling, L. Issues pertaining to prevention and intervention of genetic disorders affecting human behavior. In G. W. Albee and J. M. Joffe (Eds.), *Primary prevention of psychopathology*, Vol. 1: *The issues*. Hanover, N.H.: University Press of New England, 1977.

Ferreira, M.C.R. Malnutrition and mother-infant asynchrony: Slow mental development. *International Journal of Behavioral Development*, 1978, *1*, 207–219.

Fraser, F. C. Interactions and multiple causes. In J. G. Wilson and F. C. Fraser (Eds.), *Handbook of teratology*, Vol. 1: *General principles and etiology*. New York: Plenum, 1977.

Fraser, F. C. Future prospects—clinical. In J. W. Littlefield, J. DeGrouchy, and F.J.G. Ebling (Eds.), *Birth defects. Proceedings of the fifth international conference, Montreal, Canada, 21–27 August 1977*. Amsterdam: Excerpta Medica, 1978.

Friedler, G. Morphine administration to male mice. Effects on subsequent progeny. *Federation Proceedings*, 1974, *33*, 515.

Golbus, M. S. Prenatal diagnosis of genetic defects—where it is and where it is going. In J. W. Littlefield, J. DeGrouchy, and F.J.G. Ebling (Eds.) *Birth defects. Proceedings of the fifth international conference, Montreal, Canada, 21–27 August 1977*. Amsterdam: Excerpta Medica, 1978.

Goldman, A. S. Critical periods of prenatal toxic insults. In R. H. Schwarz and S. J. Yaffe (Eds.), *Drug and chemical risks to the fetus and newborn*. New York: A. R. Liss, 1980.

Graham, F. K., Ernhart, C. B., Thurston, D. L., and Craft, M. Development three years after perinatal anoxia and other potentially damaging newborn experiences. *Psychological Monographs*, 1962, *76*, 3 (Whole No. 522).

Graham, F. K., Matarazzo, R. G., and Caldwell, B. M. Behavioral differences between normal and traumatized newborns: II. Standardization, reliability, and validity. *Psychological Monographs*, 1956, *70*, 21 (Whole No. 428).

Graham, F. K., Pennoyer, M. M., Caldwell, B. M., Greenman, M., and Hartman, A. F. Relationship between clinical status and behavior test performance in a newborn group with histories suggesting anoxia. *Journal of Pediatrics*, 1957, *50*, 177–189.

Grabowski, C. T. Atmospheric gases: Variations in concentration and some common pollutants. In J. G. Wilson and F. C. Fraser (Eds.), *Handbook of teratology*, Vol. 1: *General principles and etiology*. New York: Plenum, 1977.

Harris, H. *Prenatal diagnosis and selective abortion*. Cambridge, Mass.: Harvard University Press, 1975.

Hertig, A. T., Rock, J., and Adams, E. C. A description of 34 human ova within the first 17 days of development. *American Journal of Anatomy*, 1956, *98*, 435–459.

Holmes, L. B. Genetic counseling for the older pregnant woman: New data and questions. *New England Journal of Medicine*, 1978, *298*, 1419–1421.

Hsia, Y. E. Treatment in genetic diseases. In A. Milunsky (Ed.), *The prevention of genetic disease and mental retardation*. Philadelphia: W. B. Saunders, 1975.

Ingalls, T. H. Preventive prenatal pediatrics. *Advances in Pediatrics*, 1953, *6*, 33–62.

Joffe, J. M. *Prenatal determinants of behavior*. Oxford: Pergamon, 1969.

Joffe, J. M. Influence of drug exposure of the father on perinatal outcome. In L. F. Soyka (Ed.), *Clinics in perinatology*, Vol. 6, No. 1: *Symposium on pharmacology*. Philadelphia: W. B. Saunders, 1979.

Joffe, J. M., Peterson, J. M., Smith, D. J., and Soyka, L. F. Sublethal effects on offspring of male rats treated with methadone. *Research Communications in Chemical Pathology and Pharmacology*, 1976, *13*, 611–621.

Kaback, M. M., Heterozygote screening for the control of recessive genetic disease. In A. Milunsky (Ed.), *The prevention of genetic disease and mental retardation.* Philadelphia: W. B. Saunders, 1975.

Kessler, M., and Albee, G. W. Primary prevention. *Annual Review of Psychology,* 1975, *26,* 557–591.

Klassen, R. W., and Persaud, T.V.N. Experimental studies on the influence of male alcoholism on pregnancy and progeny. *Experimental Pathology,* 1976, *12,* 38–45.

Kopp, C. B., and Parmelee, A. H. Prenatal and perinatal influences on infant behavior. In J. D. Osofsky (Ed.) *Handbook of infant development.* New York: Wiley, 1979.

Kushnick, T. Antenatal diagnosis. In H. A. Kaminetzky, L. Iffy, and J. J. Apuzzio (Eds.), *New techniques and concepts in maternal and fetal medicine.* New York: VanNostrand Reinhold, 1979.

Lappé, M. Can eugenic policy be just? In A. Milunsky (Ed.), *The prevention of genetic disease and mental retardation.* Philadelphia: W. B. Saunders, 1975.

Lutwak-Mann, C. Observations on progeny of thalidomide-treated male rabbits. *British Medical Journal,* 1964, *1,* 1090–1091.

Lutwak-Mann, C., Schmid, K., and Keberle, H. Thalidomide in rabbit semen. *Nature,* 1967, *214,* 1018–1020.

MacDowell, E. C., and Lord, E. M. Reproduction in alcoholic mice: Treated males. Study of prenatal mortality and sex ratios. *Archiv fur Entwicklungsmechanik der Organismen,* 1927, *110,* 427–449.

MacDowell, E. C., Lord, E. M., and MacDowell, C. G. Heavy alcoholization and prenatal mortality in mice. *Proceedings of the Society for Experimental Biology and Medicine,* 1926, *23,* 652–654. (a)

MacDowell, E. C., Lord, E. M., and MacDowell, C. G. Sex ratio of mice from alcoholized fathers. *Proceedings of the Society for Experimental Biology and Medicine,* 1926, *23,* 517–519. (b)

McKusick, V. A. *Mendelian inheritance in man. Catalogs of autosomal dominant, autosomal recessive, and X-linked phenotypes* (3rd ed.). Baltimore: The Johns Hopkins Press, 1971.

McNeil, T. F., and Kaij, L. Prenatal, perinatal, and post-partum factors in primary prevention of psychopathology in offspring. In G. W. Albee and J. M. Joffe (Eds.), *Primary prevention of psychopathology,* Vol. 1: *The Issues.* Hanover N.H.: University Press of New England, 1977.

Meier, J. H. Early intervention in the prevention of mental retardation. In A. Milunsky (Ed.), *The prevention of genetic disease and mental retardation.* Philadelphia: W. B. Saunders, 1975.

Milunsky, A. (Ed.). *The prevention of genetic disease and mental retardation.* Philadelphia: W. B. Saunders, 1975. (a)

Milunsky, A. Genetic counseling: Principles and practice. In A. Milunsky (Ed.), *The prevention of genetic disease and mental retardation.* Philadelphia: W. B. Saunders, 1975. (b)

Milunsky, A., and Atkins, L. Prenatal diagnosis of genetic disorders. In A. Milunsky (Ed.), *The prevention of genetic disease and mental retardation.* Philadelphia: W. B. Saunders, 1975.

Motulsky, A., Benirschke, K., Carpenter, G., Fraser, C., Epstein, C., Nyhan, W., and Jackson, L. Genetic diseases. In R. L. Brent and M. I. Harris (Eds.), *Prevention of embryonic, fetal, and perinatal disease.* DHEW Pub. No. (NIH) 76-853. Washington, D.C., 1976.

National Center for Health Statistics. *Facts of life and death*. U.S. Dept. of Health, Education and Welfare. DHEW Pub. No. (PHS) 79-1222. Hyattsville, MD., 1978.

Nitowsky, H. M. Heterozygote detection in autosomal recessive biochemical disorders associated with mental retardation. In A. Milunsky (Ed.), *The prevention of genetic disease and mental retardation*. Philadelphia: W. B. Saunders, 1975.

Nuckolls, K. B., Cassel, J., and Kaplan, B. H. Psychosocial assets, life crisis, and the prognosis of pregnancy. *American Journal of Epidemiology*, 1972, *35*, 431–441.

Pasamanick, B., Knobloch, H., and Lilienfeld, A. M. Socioeconomic status and some precursors of neuropsychiatric disorders. *American Journal of Orthopsychiatry*, 1956, *26*, 594–601.

Paul, C. Archives generales de Medecine, 1860, *1*, 513. (Quoted by Weller, 1915).

Plomin, R., DeFries, J. C., and Loehlin, J. C. Genotype-environment interaction and correlation in the analysis of human behavior. *Psychological Bulletin*, 1977, *84*, 309–322.

Redmond, G. P. Effect of drugs on intrauterine growth. In L. F. Soyka (Ed.), *Clinics in Perinatology*, Vol. 6, No. 1: *Symposium on pharmacology*. Philadelphia: W. B. Saunders, 1979.

Reid, G. Report of the Departmental Commission on the dangers attendant on the use of lead. Quoted by T. Oliver, Lecture on lead poisoning and the race. *British Medical Journal*, 1911, *1*, 1096–1098.

Reilly, P. The role of law in the prevention of genetic disease. In A. Milunsky (Ed.), *The prevention of genetic disease and mental retardation*. Philadelphia: W. B. Saunders, 1975.

Ressler, R. H. Parental handling in two strains of mice reared by foster parents. *Science*, 1962, *137*, 129–130.

Roberts, C. A. Psychiatric and mental health consultation. *Canadian Journal of Public Health*, 1970, *51*, 17–24.

Rosen, G. *Preventive medicine in the United States 1900–1975: Trends and interpretations*. New York: Science History Publications, 1975.

Rudeaux, P. La Clinique, 1910. Quoted by Thompson in *The occupational diseases*. New York: Appleton, 1914.

Sameroff, A. J. Early influences on development: Fact or fancy? *Merrill-Palmer Quarterly of Behavior and Development*, 1975, *21*, 267–294.

Sameroff, A. J. Concepts of humanity in primary prevention. In G. W. Albee and J. M. Joffe (Eds.), *Primary prevention of psychopathology*, Vol. 1: *The issues*. Hanover, N.H.: University Press of New England, 1977.

Sameroff, A. J., and Chandler, M. J. Reproductive risk and the continuum of caretaking casualty. In F. D. Horowitz, M. Hetherington, S. Scarr-Salapatek, and G. Siegel (Eds.), *Review of child development research*, Vol. 4. Chicago: University of Chicago, 1975.

Scriver, C. R., and Laberge, C. Genetic screening. An outlook en route. In J. W. Littlefield, J. DeGrouchy, and F.J.G. Ebling (Eds.), *Birth defects. Proceedings of the fifth international conference, Montreal, Canada, 21–27 August 1977*. Amsterdam: Excerpta Medica, 1978.

Slone, D., Shapiro, S., and Mitchell, A. Strategies for studying the effects of the antenatal environment on the fetus. In R. H. Schwarz and S. J. Yaffe (Eds.), *Drug and chemical risks to the fetus and newborn*. New York: A. R. Liss, 1980.

Smith, D. J., and Joffe, J. M. Increased neonatal mortality in offspring of male rats treated with methadone or morphine before mating. *Nature,* 1975, *253,* 202–203.

Smithells, R. W. Future prospects: Environmental factors. In J. W. Littlefield, J. DeGrouchy, and F.J.G. Ebling (Eds.), *Birth defects. Proceedings of the fifth international conference, Montreal, Canada, 21–27 August 1977.* Amsterdam; Excerpta Medica, 1978.

Soyka, L. F., and Joffe, J. M. Influence of concurrent testosterone on the effects of methadone on male rats and their progeny. *Developmental Pharmacology and Therapeutics,* 1980, *1,* 182–188. (a)

Soyka, L. F., and Joffe, J. M. Male mediated drug effects on offspring. In R. H. Schwarz and S. J. Yaffe (Eds.), *Drug and chemical risks to the fetus and newborn.* New York: A. R. Liss, 1980. (b)

Soyka, L. J., Joffe, J. M., Peterson, J. M., and Smith, S. M. Chronic methadone administration to male rats: Tolerance to adverse effects on sires and their progeny. *Pharmacology, Biochemistry and Behavior,* 1978, *9,* 405–409. (a)

Soyka, L. F., Peterson, J. M., and Joffe, J. M. Lethal and sublethal effects on the progeny of male rats treated with methadone. *Toxicology and Applied Pharmacology,* 1978, *45,* 797–807. (b)

Stockard, C. R. Effect on the offspring of intoxicating the male parent and transmission of the defects of subsequent generations. *American Naturalist,* 1913, *47,* 641–682.

Stowe, H. D., and Goyer, R. A. The reproductive ability and progeny of F_1 lead-toxic rats. *Fertility and Sterility,* 1971, *22,* 755–760.

Task Panel on Prevention. *President's Commission on Mental Health* (Vol. 4). Washington, D.C.: U.S. Government Printing Office, No. 040-000-00393-2, 1978.

Thomas, A., Chess, S. and Birch, H. *Temperament and behavior disorders in children.* New York: New York University, 1968.

Thomson, A. M. Maternal stature and reproductive efficiency. *Eugenics Review,* 1959, *51,* 157–162.

Thomson, A. M., and Billewicz, W. Z. Nutritional status, physique and reproductive efficiency. *Proceedings of the Nutrition Society,* 1963, *22,* 55–60.

Tizard, J.P.M. Pre-natal and perinatal factors. In J. W. Littlefield, J. DeGrouchy, and F.J.G. Ebling (Eds.), *Birth defects. Proceedings of the fifth international conference, Montreal, Canada, 21–27 August 1977.* Amsterdam: Excerpta Medica, 1978.

Vance, E. T. A typology of risks and the disabilities of low status. In G. W. Albee and J. M. Joffe (Eds.), *Primary prevention of psychopathology,* Vol. 1: *The issues.* Hanover, N.H.: University Press of New England, 1977.

Warkany, J. Terathanasia. *Teratology,* 1978, *17,* 187–192.

Weathersbee, P. S., Ax, R. L., and Lodge, J. R. Caffeine-mediated changes of sex ratio in Chinese hamsters, *Cricetulus griseus. Journal of Reproduction and Fertility,* 1975, *43,* 141–143.

Weathersbee, P. S., Olsen, L. K., and Lodge, J. R. Caffeine and pregnancy: A retrospective study. *Postgraduate Medicine,* 1977, *62,* 64–69.

Weller, C. V. The blastophthoric effect of chronic lead poisoning. *Journal of Medical Research,* 1915, *33,* 271–293.

Werner, E. E., Bierman, J., and French, F. *The children of Kauai: A longitudinal study from the prenatal period to age ten.* Honolulu: University Press of Hawaii, 1971.

Werner, E. E., Bierman, J. M., French, F., Simonian, K., Connor, A., Smith, R., and Campbell, M. Reproductive and environmental casualties: A report on the 10 year follow-up of the children of the Kauai pregnancy study. *Pediatrics*, 1968, *42*, 112–127.

Werner, E. E., Simonian, K., Bierman, J. M., and French, F. Cumulative effect of perinatal complications and deprived environment on physical, intellectual and social development of preschool children. *Pediatrics*, 1967, *39*, 490–505.

Werner, E. E., and Smith, R. S. *Kauai's children come of age*. Honolulu: University Press of Hawaii, 1977.

Wilson, J. G. Embryological considerations in teratology. *Annals of the New York Academy of Sciences*, 1965, *123*, 219–227.

Wilson, J. G. Embryotoxicity of drugs in man. In J. G. Wilson and F. C. Fraser (Eds.), *Handbook of teratology*, Vol. 1: *General principles and etiology*. New York: Plenum, 1977. (a)

Wilson, J. G. Environmental chemicals. In J. G. Wilson and F. C. Fraser (Eds.), *Handbook of teratology*, Vol. 1: *General principles and etiology*. New York: Plenum, 1977. (b)

Winick, M. Maternal nutrition. In R. L. Brent and M. I. Harris (Eds.), *Prevention of embryonic, fetal, and perinatal disease*. DHEW Pub. No. (NIH) 76-853. Washington, D.C., 1976.

Yerushalmy, J. Biostatistical methods in investigations of child health. *American Journal of Diseases of Children*, 1967, *114*, 470–476.

Yerushalmy, J. Relationship of parents' cigarette smoking to outcome of pregnancy—implications as to the problem of inferring causation from observed observations. *American Journal of Epidemiology*, 1971, *93*, 443–456.

Young, R. D. Influence of neonatal treatment on maternal behavior: A confounding variable. *Psychonomic Science*, 1965, *3*, 295–296.

Prenatal, Perinatal, and Post-Partum Factors in Primary Prevention of Psychopathology in Offspring

Thomas F. McNeil and Lennart Kaij

The topic we are addressing here is primary prevention of psychopathology in offspring based on factors in the mother during pregnancy, delivery, and the postpartum period. We touch upon a variety of areas: general preventive medical systems and lessons from the Swedish system, individuals' needs within the formal system, the particular needs and characteristics of mothers with histories of mental disturbances, and further needs for research on primary prevention. We have based our presentation on published literature, on experiences (our own and others') within the Swedish obstetric-psychiatric-pediatric system, on our series of retrospective studies on psycho-obstetrics and obstetro-psychiatrics,† and our ongoing prospective study of the offspring of psychotic women and never-psychotic control women.

If the question were asked, "What factor during the pregnancy-postpartum period has most often been shown to be associated with subsequent psychopathology in the offspring?" the best answer would probably be, "obstetric complications" (OCs). The series of studies by Pasamanick and Knobloch (1961) led to

Our research has received support from NIMH Grant No. 18857, Grant No. 3793 from the Swedish Medical Research Council, and the Grant Foundation Inc. We wish to thank the following people for their help in providing information for this presentation: Lennart Jacobson, Ylva Laurell-Borulf, Bengt Bjerre, Signe Jansson, Iris Hugoson, Bertha Katz, and Lars Svanberg.

†By the term *obstetro-psychiatrics* we mean the study of the effects of obstetric factors on the mental (psychiatric) condition of the offspring and mother.

their positing a continuum of reproductive casualty extending from death through varying degrees of neuropsychiatric disability. OCs were found to be related to subsequent cerebral palsy, epilepsy, tics, mental deficiency, behavior disorders, and reading disabilities. Other researchers have provided evidence for the association between OCs and epilepsy (Churchill, 1959, 1966), cerebral palsy and spastic paraplegia (Plum, 1956, 1962), and broader ranges of mental or behavioral disorders (McNeil et al., 1970; Pollack, 1967). A number of studies have found positive OC histories for schizophrenics (Bender and Faretra, 1961; Gittelman and Birch, 1967), especially as compared with their normal siblings (Vorster, 1960; Whittam et al., 1966), with their nonschizophrenic monozygotic twins (Pollin et al., 1966), with matched controls and siblings (Taft and Goldfarb, 1964), and with neurotic children (Osterkamp and Sands, 1962). Other studies show high OC rates in the histories of autistic children (Kanner, 1957; Keeler, 1957; Knobloch and Pasamanick, 1962). Not all empirical studies have found positive OC histories for mentally disturbed samples (Terris et al., 1964; Pasamanick et al., 1956; Eisenberg and Kanner, 1956; Lotter, 1967; Rimland, 1964; Schain and Yannet, 1960), but the general conclusion may be drawn that an important factor in primary prevention of psychopathology is the prevention of OCs. The presentation and evaluation of an existing system for primary prevention of OCs is thus relevant.

Furthermore, existing systems for primary prevention in obstetrics, have considerable value as models for early attempts at primary prevention of psychopathogy. Obstetrics has made considerable progress even in prevention of conditions (e.g. toxemia) whose etiology is not necessarily fully understood (Page, 1972; Brody, 1970); and primary prevention of psychopathology will often have to contend with a similar uncertainty about etiological factors. In addition, existing systems provide lessons regarding the behavior of both patients and staff within a preventive system. Reproduction is a topic of great emotional loading—as is psychopathology—and human response to medical systems regarding primary prevention within obstetrics may give some clues to anticipated human response regarding primary prevention of psychopathology.

SWEDISH PRENATAL AND CHILD HEALTH CARE SYSTEM
(Socialstyrelsen, 1970)

The Swedish system for health care of women during pregnancy and postpartum and of children from birth to school age has been established by law since 1937. The system has broadened over time: approximately 80 percent of all pregnant women were covered in the beginning of the 1960's, compared with 95 to 98 percent since 1970. The purpose is "to prevent, through both physical and mental health care, the development of diseases and disturbances in mothers and children" (p. 5). All examination and care related to the system during this period are free of charge, as is delivery and postpartum care at the obstetric departments. Participation is voluntary; but, though both outpatient prenatal and pediatric examinations are available from a number of private physicians (in many regions), the vast majority of pregnancies and children are cared for through the standardized system.

Prenatal and OB System

All deliveries are performed at the centralized hospitals. Prenatal care is given through the Prenatal Clinics (PNCs), which are associated either with the hospitals (in large cities) or with district physicians (in smaller cities and the countryside). The pregnant woman's entry into the system is very simple: she calls the clinic on the telephone and makes an appointment. Her primary contact with the PNC is through highly trained midwives (RNs) or, in some cases, district RNs with special training in prenatal care. The scheduled prenatal care for normal cases includes three examinations by a physician: usually once in the third month, once after quickening (fifth month), and once in the eighth month. From quickening through the eighth month, examinations by midwives are conducted every other week at the PNC, and, from the eighth month until delivery, once a week. Thus, for the normal pregnancy the mother is examined approximately 15 times at the PNC.

Women fitting into the established risk categories, as described below, or showing other complications are referred to specialists in OB/GYN. Hospitalization is suggested currently for a broad spectrum of risk cases: multiple pregnancies, toxemias, premature labors, bleeding, and so on. The extent of hospitalization varies in different areas, but in Malmö (population 250,000, with about 3,000 deliveries per year) approximately half of all beds in OB are occupied by nonterm pregnant women (B. Bjerre, personal communication, 1975). This means that more than 10 percent of all pregnant women are prophylactically hospitalized at some time during pregnancy (L. Jacobson, personal communication, 1975).

The policy concerning legal abortion has been liberal in Sweden since the early 1960's. But since January 1975 a pregnant woman has been given the sole right, through the eighteenth week of pregnancy, to decide whether she will have an abortion. Prior to the thirteenth week, only a physician's examination is required, and from the thirteenth through the eighteenth week consultation with a social worker is an additional requirement. (Legal abortions after the eighteenth week are approved only by the governing medical board and only on grounds of serious physical or mental illness.) All legal abortions are free of charge.

By law, parent education classes are made available, taught by midwives, covering information about pregnancies, deliveries, and fetal development and including preparatory physical exercises. In recent years, methods of psychoprophylaxis (Lamaze, 1956) have been taught in many areas.

All deliveries take place at centralized hospitals. Normal deliveries are performed by midwives. Complicated cases are handled jointly by the midwives and the physician on duty at the delivery department. Strong emphasis is placed on natural delivery; in 1974, for example, 84.4 percent of the deliveries at Malmö General Hospital were vaginal noninstrumental deliveries. The remainder consisted of 6.6 percent by Caesarean section, 8 percent by vacuum extraction, and 1 percent by forceps.

The pediatrician or physician on duty is called to attend any delivery where problems are anticipated in the neonate (as with premature births, Caesarean sections, or ablatio placentae); and the physician is, of course, available when such additional problems as respiratory difficulties are encountered. The newer hospitals have placed infant intensive care units contiguous to the delivery departments. About 7 percent of newborns are transferred to the pediatric department for care or observation, 5.5 percent of these being premature.

The mother and baby typically remain at the delivery department until two hours postpartum, and are then transferred to the puerperal ward, where the usual stay is four to six days before discharge home. A number of rooming-in, self-care puerperal units are available at many hospitals and are very popular among mothers, especially I-parae. Pediatric examinations of the baby are typically conducted on the first day after birth and on the day of discharge, with additional examinations if problems arise during the stay at the puerperal unit.

Given the extensive schedule of examinations for all pregnant women, not every woman can be examined by obstetric "specialists."* The following 20 criteria have been established to provide guidelines for choosing obstetric risk groups to receive specialist care: (1) 35-year-old or older O-para; (2) woman with more than 8 years since last delivery; (3) woman with 4 or more deliveries; (4) woman with previous child with birthweight more than 4,500 grams; (5) woman with history of involuntary infertility or repeated miscarriages; (6) woman with history of complicated pregnancy or delivery (premature infant, stillbirth, toxicosis, Caesarean section, etc.); (7) multiple pregnancy; (8) breech presentation after thirty-fourth week of pregnancy; (9) woman undelivered by 14 days after expected term; (10) contracted pelvis; (11) Rh-immunization; (12) chronic medical disease (diabetes, circulatory illness, kidney disease, etc.); (13) uterine or vaginal malformation; (14) toxicosis (at least one among proteinuria, noteworthy oedema or quick weight gain, and blood pressure more than 140/90); (15) bleeding during pregnancy; (16) previous bleeding or coagulation disturbance; (17) hydramniosis; (18) abnormal fetal position; (19) anemia of $\leqslant 10$ g percent (65 percent) which is unresponsive to iron supplement; (20) other conditions: allergies, suspected drug effects on the fetus, large discrepancy between fetal development and length of pregnancy, notably poor psychosocial conditions, unusual attitude toward delivery, and so on.

Our contact with obstetricians and midwives has led to the following observations regarding these obstetric risk criteria and their use.

(a) In practice, these 20 criteria are supplemented by other risk-group criteria, for example premature labor; and criteria

*All pregnant women are examined by physicians who may be general practitioners in the smaller towns and countryside or not yet specialized physicians working in the departments of obstetrics in the centralized hospitals.

indicating fetal risk, such as growth retardation and signs of placental insufficiency, are increasingly used.

(b) The 20 criteria are effective in identifying women with higher somatic risk; few other categories could be suggested, and some might well be modified or further restricted.

(c) The criteria should be used as a preliminary screening device to identify women needing further evaluation on an individual level. "Once at risk" defined by a general criterion is not necessarily "always at risk," and a comparable formal system may be needed for removing individuals from risk groups.

(d) The designation "at somatic risk" in terms of the 20 categories places a relatively large proportion of mothers at risk; estimates of this proportion range from about 20 to 40 percent, and the more extensive the screening, the higher the proportion of mothers found to be at risk.

(e) The designation "at risk" according to the 20 categories calls for varying degrees of intervention. For example, category 9, "post-term pregnancy," usually results in initiation of labor. Other categories, for example 1 through 5, generally call for increased observation of the woman during pregnancy and at delivery. Being "at risk" does not necessarily call for intervention but rather for further observation and evaluation.

(f) The twentieth category, which provides the possibility of defining risk in terms of psychosocial or psychic conditions, is very seldom used as compared with the other nineteen. In our opinion, women deserving special consideration during the pregnancy-postpartum period are very young mothers, those without a stable relationship with the biological father, those with an abnormally strong fear of the delivery, those with a history of serious mental disturbance (as discussed below), those with an openly negative or ambivalent attitude toward the pregnancy, and especially those who desired an abortion but were unable or unwilling to obtain it. Some data suggest that these groups have an increased risk for OCs (Brody, 1970) and for widespread disturbance in the offspring (see Forssman and Thuwe, 1966, regarding the offspring of women refused an abortion), but further systematic study is needed regarding the risk-increasing properties of psychological and social situations surrounding this period. The steps taken to help women defined as risk cases on these bases need, of course, to be appropriate to the existing problems, which may be of a completely different nature from those embodied in the somatic risk criteria.

(g) The specialists who care for women designated as "at somatic risk" do not feel that labeling the mother as at risk has caused any problems for the women; most women either are unaware that they are in a special risk group or seem to appreciate the extra care and attention they receive.

Well-Baby Clinics

Upon birth of the child, the Well-Baby Clinic covering the residential area of the child is automatically informed of the birth and engaged in the care of the child. A personal relationship is established between the parents (mother) and the pediatric nurse in the district where the parents live. The nurse visits the home on a number of occasions to become familiar with the baby's home environment and give advice and support to the parents. Health check-ups for the baby are performed by a pediatrician a recommended four to seven times during the first year of life, twice during the second year, and once per year thereafter up to seven years of age, when school health services take over responsibility for health care of the child. The parents have 24-hour reference service through the emergency services of the pediatric departments. The Well-Baby Clinics have regular telephone hours for advice and consultation regarding the child and its care. The health system described here concerns normal cases; sick babies are not brought to the Well-Baby Clinics. The identification of health problems requiring treatment leads to referral of the mother or infant to the relevant facility—the department for obstetrics, pediatrics, ENT, child psychiatry, or whatever is appropriate. The system described can thus be considered to represent routine attempts to identify incipient problems or situations and take steps against the problems before they become worse; and it thus has the essential characteristic of a structure for primary prevention of illness and disturbance.

LESSONS OF THE SYSTEM

The Swedish prenatal system described above provides a good opportunity to make the following observations about standardized systems and people's responses to them.

(a) The system is extensively used. Between 95 and 99 percent of all pregnant women receive prenatal care. All women come to the delivery departments for births. On a nationwide basis, at least 95 percent of all children are taken to the Well-Baby Clinics during the first year of life and 85 percent continue with the scheduled health check-ups during the second year of life (A. Baude, personal communication, 1975).

(b) The system is both expensive and inexpensive. The prenatal clinic in Malmö cost $325,000 (1.3 million kronor) in 1974, which gives an approximate per-pregnancy cost of $110—quite inexpensive considering the large number of examinations. The cost of the Well-Baby Clinic in Malmö in 1974 was $1,150,000 (4.6 million kronor); again, this is reasonably inexpensive considering the service for approximately 18,000 children up to seven years of age (about $65 per child per year). On the other hand, prophylactic hospitalization of nonterm pregnant women was used extensively in Malmö and cost about $1.5 million (6 million kronor) for 1974, or more than the cost of the prenatal and Well-Baby Clinics combined.

(c) In terms of perinatal mortality,* the system is among the best in the world (Brody, 1970). The mortality figures in Malmö for 1974 were 1.06 percent. Perinatal mortality statistics are obviously not the only relevant measure of the effectiveness of the system, and primary preventive systems that take such mortality as the ultimate criterion may unintentionally cause a great number of psychological and social problems (see below regarding twins).

(d) Since participation is voluntary, the very relevant question may be raised whether those who most need help are those who use the services of the system. Whereas at least 95 percent of all pregnant women receive somatic prenatal care, acceptance of other services offered appears to be more selective. By law, mothers who should be given the most attention in parent education classes are the young and the unmarried. Roughly 50 percent

*Perinatal mortality is here defined as fetal-neonatal death from the twenty-ninth week of gestation through the first seven days after birth.

of all women registered at the PNC in Malmö in 1974 chose to attend parent education classes (I. Hugoson, personal communication, 1975). The women who do not take advantage of the classes are to a large extent the very ones who need the most help—the young, the poorly informed, and foreigners (S. Jansson, personal communication, 1975).

(e) The production-line approach to prenatal care has functioned reasonably well in providing a large amount of somatic screening for all pregnant women. At the same time, the experience has led both patients and medical staff to desire smaller, decentralized units with the opportunity for more personal contact between patient and staff, such as is possible in the small countryside units. In the large city clinics, the psychological needs of the patients (and staff) have often not been met by the production-line approach, and as a result a number of helpful changes have been made in the necessary compromise between cost, amount of contact, and quality of personal contact. In Malmö, mothers have been assigned to a given midwife so that there is continuity of contact, however brief, on each occasion. A social worker assigned as a permanent staff member at the prenatal clinic is a helpful reference person for mothers with social and psychological problems and need for additional personal contact. Thus, providing adequate somatic examination and care for the vast majority of pregnant women may be the first goal in the primary prevention of OCs, but this needs to be supplemented at some level by opportunities for meaningful personal contact.

(f) The effects of preventive measures need to be viewed in their totality. In Malmö, for example, prophylactic hospitalization for all women with multiple pregnancies is standard practice from the thirtieth through the thirty-sixth week of pregnancy, the gestational period bearing the highest risk for premature births with nonsurviving fetuses. With a twin frequency of one per 80 births, this means that in about 37 cases a year the policy results in a guaranteed six-week separation of the woman from her family, often including small children.* Estimates of the number of twin infants saved in Malmö range from 1 to 5 per year; as yet, no

---

*It should be noted that the mother is not completely isolated from her family during this period; she has opportunities for living at home on the weekends and receiving frequent family visits (including small children) at the OB department.

systematic evaluation has been done of the psychological and intrafamilial consequences of this separation. And multiple pregnancy is only one of the indications for such extensive hospitalization. Cases have been seen where marginal marital adjustments have been ruined by the separation; where the woman and her family cannot cope economically or practically with the separation; and where the woman's psychological balance has been seriously (if temporarily) endangered by guilt feelings about her family and by the experience of being in a monotonous hospital environment concentrated solely on her preganancy. Perinatal mortality figures are definitely thought to be served by extensive prophylactic hospitalization, but the total costs and benefits to the families have not yet been weighed.

(g) The broad use of nondoctor medical personnel has allowed a preventive system that would be entirely impossible if doctors alone were to conduct prenatal examinations and check-ups and deliver babies. About four midwives can be hired for the cost of one obstetrician; this provides considerable economic savings, since 80 to 90 percent of all deliveries are conducted by midwives, as are 80 percent of the scheduled prenatal examinations.

(h) Use of the psychoprophylactic method (PPM) can make an important contribution to prevention of OCs and postpartum problems. Systematic studies of the effects of PPM (Enkin et al., 1972; Huttel et al., 1972) suggest that PPM is associated with reduced use of medications during labor and delivery, less operative intervention, more favorable parental experience of labor and delivery, and less maternal depression postpartum. The studies also stress the very helpful effect of the father during the labor and delivery. The preliminary results of a Swedish study (Jansson et al., 1975) support the earlier findings. PPM can be effective both on a somatic basis and on a psychological level as a supportive part of the labor-delivery program. Given that PPM is effective in reducing OCs, important topics for primary prevention of OCs are the questions of why certain parents cannot effectively use PPM in spite of considerable advance practice, how these parents can be identified during pregnancy, and what kind of extra help or intervention may allow them to profit from PPM during labor-delivery.

(i) Effective primary prevention of psychopathology on a large scale is likely to require some type of primary screening of individuals regarding risk characteristics (psychologic, somatic, social) associated with higher risk for psychopathology. This primary screening would probably have to be done by teachers, nurses, and social workers rather than by psychiatrists or psychologists. The extent of systematization and thoroughness of such screening is undoubtedly going to vary from area to area; but both primary screening and effective management of incipient problems require theoretical and practical knowledge of psychopathology, of the criteria to be used for identifying risk cases, and of the potential benefits of primary prevention.

Lack of education and understanding can easily frustrate all attempts at primary prevention (a) by a resulting increase rather than decrease in the dangers to the individual through such screening and (b) by the inability and/or unwillingness to identify the relevant conditions or problems. Taking examples from the prenatal-postpartum period, a history of mental disturbance for the mother can lead delivery personnel, because of their own fear of mental illness, to overmedicate the mother during labor and/or to terminate the delivery as quickly as possible through medical or operative intervention. In some cases such practices may be justified, but the decision should be made after careful consideration of the mother's and fetus' current condition and should not be based solely upon her mental history (sometimes rather ancient history). To cite another example, psychologically enlightened delivery personnel feel emphatically that they could profit from knowing which mothers have an unusually strong fear of the delivery, so that they could be aware of the mothers' need for extra support and consideration; the information should be contained in the medical record that is sent in advance from the prenatal clinic to the delivery department. But the midwives at the prenatal clinics are generally unwilling to "mark" a mother by writing anything in the record about her fears or psychological condition. Our experience is that if a mother communicates fears and apprehension to the personnel at the PNC, she is seeking help and is not opposed to the delivery midwife's knowing about her fears and giving extra help. Thus, the potentially effective use of a preventive system may be frustrated as a consequence of unwillingness to record important psychological conditions.

Similar examples may be taken from the puerperal wards. We have received reports that some women cry all day long for several days and that the personnel ignore it or dismiss attempts to call it to their attention, saying, "Everyone feels a little blue the first days after delivery." We have observed other mothers with clear perceptions of changed sex ("I feel like a man") and with the highly unusual behavior of walking all night with the baby in her arms; when we asked whether the mother might need special help, the response was that "the mother is just a little tired." Such inability or unwillingness to recognize problems not only hinders effective care of mothers and infants during this period, but will hinder effective primary prevention when such prevention is theoretically possible. Education of professional workers and society in general must be given very high priority by those interested in promoting primary prevention.

(j) We may learn something about difficulties of primary prevention by considering the rate of success in preventing unwanted pregnancies—an easily diagnosed somatic condition with known etiology and highly developed methods for primary prevention. Sweden, by contrast with other countries, has had a very liberal attitude toward disseminating sexual information and education; contraceptives are available everywhere and are even free in certain areas. As a result, one might expect to find an effective birth control rate. The real figures, however, suggest that primary prevention of unwanted pregnancies is not very successful. In Malmö in 1974, for the roughly 3,000 births and 300 spontaneous abortions, 1,200 legal abortions took place; thus, 1,200 (26.6 percent) among 4,500 identified pregnancies were terminated deliberately. A recent prospective study by Nilsson (1970) in Lund showed that of 151 women who did not terminate their pregnancy, 39.4 percent reported during pregnancy that the pregnancy was not desired and 57.3 percent said it was not actively planned. These figures accord with an earlier study by Nilsson et al. (1967) showing 30 percent with undesired pregnancies, as reported postpartum. Thus a general estimation of the rate of unwanted and intentionally terminated pregnancies is 65 percent. This should lead us to consider the difficulties of preventing psychopathology, where the causes are less well known and most probably multifactorial and the particular measures are less specific or available.* It is well to

*One is tempted to imagine a future where one can buy a "contra-psychotic" from a vending machine for 25 cents or get an IHD (Intra-Head

remember in this context that real progress has been made in primary prevention (for example, the control of cholera and typhoid fever) through societal and political implementation of preventive procedures and not by the mere development of appropriate techniques and procedures.

SPECIAL CONSIDERATIONS REGARDING WOMEN WITH HISTORIES OF SERIOUS MENTAL DISTURBANCES

We wish to share a number of ideas and observations regarding reproduction among women who have had psychoses or other serious mental disturbances. The topics discussed are: (1) criteria for designating such women as obstetric risk cases, to receive extra care during reproduction; and (2) problems associated with postpartum mental disturbances.

Criteria for Designating Women as Obstetric Risk Cases

Should women with a history of serious mental disturbance be considered obstetric risk cases and receive extra somatic care or attention during pregnancy and birth? We can find four different bases upon which such women might be categorized as at obstetric risk.

Criterion I: If They Have Increased Rates of OCs. Since premorbid identification of future mental patients is, as yet, impossible within the context of OB systems, the relevent question concerns whether women already identified as having (had) serious mental disturbance have increased rates of OCs during subsequent reproductions. A great many data exist regarding OCs in all reproductions for mental patients, but few exist comparing reproductions of already identified patients as against reproductions of controls. We therefore review the three types of empirical studies which bear relevance to this criterion.

i. Comparison of controls vs. all reproductions of patients.

Device) fitted by the family physician. The question would still remain whether people who apparently wished to avoid mental disturbance would actually use the preventive measures as inefficiently as they currently use contraceptives.

Studies including reproductions both before and after onset of illness show complex results, with some studies of schizophrenics and other psychotics showing significantly increased rates of OCs (Sameroff and Zax, 1973; Paffenbarger et al., 1961; Wiedorn, 1954; Mura, Mednick, Schulsinger, and Mednick, 1973; Mednick and Schulsinger, 1968), while others show none (Mizrahi Mirdal, Mednick, Schulsinger, and Fuchs, 1974; Mednick et al., 1971; Soichet, 1959; McNeil and Kaij, 1973a, 1974). Sameroff and Zax (1973) found increased rates of OCs in reproductions of neurotically depressed women. Our own study (McNeil and Kaij, 1974) of all hospitalized female patients showed no significant increase in OCs for all patients or any diagnostic group. The results of these studies thus provide no uniform answer. Even different studies by the same authors on the same diagnostic groups (for example, Mednick and Schulsinger, 1968, compared with Mednick et al., 1971) or on subgroups of the same sample (for example, Mizrahi Mirdal, Mednick, Schulsinger, and Fuchs, 1974, compared with Mednick and Schulsinger, 1968) show different results. Within the context of the clinical question raised here, it must be remembered that findings based on all reproductions may be unrepresentative for reproductions after onset of illness (of interest here), especially since some diagnostic groups—process schizophrenics, for example—appear to have proportionally few reproductions after onset.

 ii. Within-group comparisons of patients before vs. after illness onset. One position recently taken (Mednick and Lanoil, 1975; Mednick, 1975) is that schizophrenics have more OCs in reproductions before, as contrasted with after, onset of illness. A close look at the studies that have presented within-group comparisons shows that currently available results are very complex and contradictory. Wiedorn (1954), studying samples with almost unparalleled rates of toxemia (from 22.2 percent for controls up to 83.3 percent for O-parae schizophrenics), found significantly higher rates of toxemia for schizophrenics before, as contrasted with after, the first psychotic episode. (There appears to be no basis in this study for comparison to the other studies cited in terms of obstetric background and psychiatric diagnostic practices.) Mednick, Mura, Schulsinger, and Mednick (1971, p. S110) found that although "character disorder" mothers showed more pregnancy and delivery complications after than before onset of illness, schizophrenic mothers showed more pregnancy complications before than after onset of illness (data unpublished, statistical significance unstated). In contrast, the original Mednick-Schulsinger schizophrenic sample, as studied by Mizrahi Mirdal, Mednick, Schulsinger, and Fuchs (1974), showed no significant difference in mean OC score, mean severity of OCs, or mean number of OCs before as against after onset of illness.

Our own research showed similar complexity of results among different OC variables. We found significantly more prenatal developmental deviations in reproductions *before* than after first psychiatric hospitalization for endogenous psychotics (McNeil and Kaij, 1974) and for process schizophrenics (McNeil and Kaij, 1973a) but significantly more neonatal disturbances *after* first hospitalization for both endogenous psychotics and all psychiatric patients (McNeil and Kaij, 1974). Schizophrenic-like psychotics, as a specific diagnostic group, showed significantly more birth complications and neonatal disturbances plus a trend toward more pregnancy complications *after* first hospitalization (McNeil and Kaij, 1973a). Age- and parity-matched controls did not show the same significant results in our study, thus hindering simplified explanations of the above results.

Within the clinical perspective of the current question, it must be noted that within-group comparisons of type "before vs. after onset" do not necessarily indicate the absolute magnitude of OCs after onset nor their relevance for disturbance in the offspring. Existing differences of a before-after-onset nature, whether statistically significant or not, may be of little clinical importance. To take one example, Mizrahi Mirdal et al. (1974) stated that there was a tendency toward more complicated births in the birth-before-breakdown group, but there may be little clinical relevance in an average of 0.23 points more severe OCs in births before illness onset. OCs exist in abundance for reproductions during all life periods in the studies cited, and clinical efforts should be aimed at reducing these.

iii. Direct comparison of controls vs. patients in reproductions after illness onset. Sameroff and Zax (1973) found that small samples of both schizophrenic and neurotically depressed mothers had significantly more OCs than did controls. Schachter (according to Garmezy, 1974) found significantly more birth complications for 23 schizophrenic women as contrasted with controls; no significant differences were found between the groups in pregnancy complications or offspring birthweights. A number of current prospective studies, including our own, should in the future provide more data regarding this specific comparison, which is most relevant to the question raised here. Data existing now appear contradictory, but the safest conclusion (from a clinical point of view) is perhaps that enough studies have shown significantly increased OC rates to justify considering such women as "at somewhat increased risk for OCs."

Criterion II: If OCs Associated with Such Reproductions Are Especially Damaging to the Fetus. The theoretical position underlying this criterion is that an OC of a given type and degree may have varying effects on different fetuses, and that fetuses of psychotic mothers may have selective sensitivity to OCs. For example, in the Mednick-Schulsinger study (Mednick and Schulsinger, 1974, p. 110) of the offspring of schizophrenic and normal mothers, OCs were found to be significantly associated with short latency of the galvanic skin response (GSR) in the schizophrenics' offspring but not in control offspring. These data suggest an interaction between genetic risk and OCs, while other data from the same study suggest an additive effect (for example, on GSR amplitude) of genetic risk and OCs. These findings are very interesting, but far more data are needed, and independent replication of the results should be awaited before drawing extensive theoretical conclusions.

Criterion III: If the Mother and the Family Are Not in a Good Position to Accept and Support a Perinatally Damaged or Preterm Infant. A perinatally damaged or premature baby can be a considerable stress for even the most adequate, trouble-free family. The integration of the baby into the family is hindered by premature birth, which results in at least some separation of the baby from the family. In families already having to contend with current or threatened recurrent mental disturbance in the mother, all steps should be taken to reduce problems in the offspring. Furthermore, although most parents tend to blame themselves for reproductive problems and failures, the mother who needs psychopharmacological drugs during pregnancy and at delivery and is aware of their potentially harmful effect on the fetus (as are almost all Swedish mothers) is put in a special conflict between her own needs and those of the baby; this conflict increases her guilt feelings when something goes wrong with the reproduction.

Reversing the argument, one can say that the perinatally damaged or preterm infant may not be in a good position to enter a disturbed family. A study by Drillien (1964) showed that prematurity appeared to render children more vulnerable to the effects of family stress and difficulty, thus resulting in increased behavioral disturbance in the children. Even in the absence of genetic risk for disturbance, children entering families with a psychotic parent should be provided as good a start as possible.

Criterion IV: If the Mother Is Psychologically (or Somatically) Less Able to Withstand the Effects of OCs With our focus upon the effects of OCs on the fetus-infant, we must bear in mind that OCs often mean the mother is sick or at least very concerned about the course of the pregnancy or delivery. Many OCs and the resulting treatment procedures are stressing, irritating, frightening, tiring, or depressing, not to mention endangering to the mother's general somatic health. Preventing OCs is advisable for the mother's own well-being, which is presumably relevant to the prevention of psychopathology in the offspring.

In combination, these four criteria suggest that women with histories of serious mental disturbances should receive fully adequate (extra, that is, if what is usual would fall short) somatic examination and consideration during pregnancy and delivery. Although the scientific evidence that would define these women as "at obstetric risk" is still ambiguous, such extra care may be indicated on the basis of the general "at risk" situation surrounding the women and the offspring.

Certain practical considerations should be mentioned in association with extra care for such women.

(i) Judging from the difficulty of finding large samples for research, treating these women as obstetric risk cases is not going to place an enormous burden on prenatal care resources.

(ii) How is one to identify the women needing this extra service? In one of our retrospective studies (McNeil and Kaij, 1973b), about 50 percent of women who had been psychiatrically hospitalized withheld this information from the medical history given to the prenatal clinic. If further research provides more sophisticated criteria for judging which disturbance histories (diagnostic type and severity, for example) indicate real obstetric risk and which do not, the question of obtaining relevant anamnestic information becomes even more pressing.

(iii) We must consider the effects of labeling a pregnant woman in this way. We have seen many cases of entirely normal maternal behavior which were interpreted as abnormal because the medical personnel were aware of the mother's previous mental disturbance. Also important is the effect on the patient's self-perception. A number of women with whom we have had contact have been hesitant to accept extra benefits—however attractive—that they feel identify them as deviant or unusual. Furthermore, many are reluctant to have any contact with medical personnel, and their attendance at the regular prenatal examinations is irregular. If such women are to accept extra care, they must be convinced of its importance; and this, in turn, raises the possibility that telling a woman she or her offspring is at risk will actually increase the risk.

(iv) Many of the patient's problems uncovered in the process of considering a history of mental illness as an OB risk criterion are not somatic but psychological, intrafamilial, economic, or the like. Facilities are needed for dealing with these problems, but our experience from Sweden suggests they are not typically available within routine prenatal and obstetric systems. Identifying problems without having the capacity to deal with them may be frustrating for both patients and personnel.

Problems Associated with Postpartum Mental Disturbances

As mothers are well aware, the postpartum period carries an increased risk for maternal mental disturbance of varying degree. Women with psychosis histories have often had mental disturbances associated with previous reproductions, and fear of recurrent psychosis is well founded: whereas the general population risk for postpartum psychosis is about 1 per 1,000 reproductions, the risk is about 1 in 7 reproductions for women with a previous postpartum psychosis and 1 in 4 for those with previous psychosis both postpartum and in other life periods (Arentsen, 1966; Kaij and Nilsson, 1972).

Many mothers with previous psychotic episodes are afraid not only of recurrent disturbance but also of being separated from the baby and thus missing a period which is of great importance to them. Separation of mother and baby for any reason during the early period is problematic for the relationship; but where the cause is mental illness, the mother is at a special disadvantage on two counts. The disturbance itself interferes with the emotional relationship; and she feels guilty because she cannot take care of the baby. Many of our subjects with postpartum psychoses have expressed the feeling of irreparable loss. They feel inadequate as mothers and say they "never got off on the right foot" with the child. Where relatives are able to care for the baby, the mother is spared having it placed in an institution, but she still must live with her own maternal inadequacy. She feels the baby is not really hers. Well-intentioned relatives who rush in to take over the care of the baby—leaving the cleaning and household chores to the mother—reinforce these feelings. Our own bias is toward separating mothers and babies as little as possible: hospitalizing the baby with the mother, supporting the mother substantially in the home, and intruding as little as possible on the mother-baby relationship.

Fear of recurrent mental disturbance in the mother is also a serious concern for the father. If the mother must be absent, he is responsible for her, for himself, and for the baby. And if he cannot cope with the baby and must place it temporarily in an institution, both he and the mother can develop feelings of guilt and failure. We have seen a number of postpartum disturbances in fathers which may be related to this problem of paternal adequacy, and the threat of mental disturbance in the mother exacerbates the problem.

The important question arises whether to initiate discussion of the topic with expectant parents who have histories of mental illness and what to tell them about postpartum risk. Should the same principles apply at all periods—before pregnancy, during the early weeks when legal abortion is possible, and after the legal abortion period is past? Some practical examples may help to illustrate difficulties.

One of our subjects with a previous postpartum psychosis consulted her psychiatrist before she became pregnant about her chances of becoming ill again. According to her, the psychiatrist assured her she would not get sick again, and so the pregnancy was initiated. But after delivery, she did become seriously depressed and was hospitalized for four months, while her baby was cared for in an institution. At our most recent contact, she and the baby were at home but she was unable to cope with anything beyond feeding the child.

Another of our subjects had lost custody of a child during divorce proceedings on grounds of her mental illness; and in a new marriage she became pregnant in order to replace her lost baby. The psychiatrist told her early in pregnancy that whether or not she would be allowed to keep the new baby depended upon whether or not she remained mentally healthy postpartum. By the time of our contact with her during pregnancy, she was extremely paranoid toward the researcher and broke down with our project midwife because of the tremendous pressure to stay healthy.

In contrast, another subject had developed a "catastrophe plan" with her family, relatives, and neighbors in the event she became ill again; she had also received assurance from the psychiatric clinic that she was welcome if she needed help. As a result, she was unusually calm about the possibility of becoming ill again. This example strongly suggests that a realistic approach to coping with the practical difficulties of recurrent disturbance may contribute to the mother's mental health during pregnancy and postpartum.

IDEAS REGARDING RESEARCH RELATED TO PRIMARY PREVENTION

Careful, methodologically sound research on the effects of preventive or interventive efforts must be given high priority. Much of the work we have seen is done unsystematically and with some apparent resistance toward evaluating the effects of the prevention. Unless the work is evaluated, important side effects will be missed, resistance toward all prevention will increase, and costs will be extended beyond what is necessary for the most effective elements within generalized preventive efforts. Control groups are of great importance, both for obtaining evidence of possibly positive effects and for guarding against the spurious apparent increases in deviation that result from increased evaluation for mental deviation. Effective primary prevention makes good financial sense, but we need sound evidence that it *is* effective if we are to compete against current, manifest problems to obtain funds for prevention of events or conditions which after all are not certain—only highly probable.

In the service of effective primary prevention, research needs to develop adequate scoring and interpretation systems for risk-identifying characteristics and events. Even the type of risk characteristics obtained from such fascinating studies as Pollin and Stabenau's (1968) compilation of characteristics of monozygotic twins discordant for schizophrenia begin to pale in the face of contact with subjects in prospective studies. In our current prospective study of high- and low-genetic risk children, few subjects—including controls—go through the pregnancy-birth-neonatal sequence without showing some event or characteristic that would have been highly interesting if seen retrospectively in a schizophrenic patient. The more complete the data, the more critical the problem of adequate scoring, weighting, and inter-pretation. Multivariate studies are crucial both because they tend to reflect better the complexity of reality and because they provide the possibility of finding combinations of characteristics and factors which enable us to identify groups needing primary prevention.

REFERENCES

Arentsen, K. *Om psykoser opstået efter fødsler med saerligt henblick på prognosen* (On psychoses beginning after childbirth with special consideration of prognosis). Odense: Andelsbogtrykkereit, 1966.

Bender, L., and Faretra, G. Pregnancy and birth histories of children with psychiatric problems. *Proceedings of the Third World Congress of Psychiatry*, 1961, *2*, 1329-1333.

Brody, S. *Obstetrik och gynekologi*. Stockholm: Almqvist and Wiksell, 1970.

Churchill, J. A. The relationship of epilepsy to breech delivery. *Electroencephalography and Clinical Neurophysiology*, 1959, *11*, 1-12.

Churchill, J. A. On the origin of focal motor epilepsy. *Neurology*, 1966, *16*, 49-58.

Drillien, C. M. *The growth and development of the prematurely born infant*. Edinburgh: Livingstone, 1964.

Eisenberg, L., and Kanner, L. Early infantile autism, 1943-55. *American Journal of Orthopsychiatry*, 1956, *26*, 555-565.

Enkin, M. W., Smith, S. L., Dermer, S. W., and Emmett, J. O. An adequately controlled study of the effectiveness of PPM training. In *Psychosomatic medicine in obstetrics and gynaecology*. Basel: Karger, 1972.

Forssman, H., and Thuwe, I. One hundred and twenty children born after application for therapeutic abortion refused. *Acta Psychiatrica Scandinavica*, 1966, *42*, 71-88.

Garmezy, N. Children at risk: The search for antecedents of schizophrenia. Part II. Ongoing research programs, issues, and intervention. *Schizophrenia Bulletin*, 1974, No. 9, pp. 55-125.

Gittelman, M., and Birch, H. G. Childhood schizophrenia: Intellectual, neurological status, perinatal risk, prognosis, family pathology. *Archives of General Psychiatry*, 1967, *17*, 16-25.

Huttel, F. A., Mitchell, I., Fischer, W. M., and Meyer, A. E. A quantitative evaluation of psychoprophylaxis in childbirth. *Journal of Psychosomatic Research*, 1972, *16*, 81-92.

Jansson, S., Kask-Esperi, I., and Kaij, L. Effekten av den psykoprofylaktiska metoden (PPM) vid förlossningen (Effect of the psychoprophylactic method of delivery). Preliminary manuscript, 1975.

Kaij, L., and Nilsson, Å. Emotional and psychotic illness following childbirth. In J. G. Howells (Ed.), *Modern perspectives in psycho-obstetrics*. Edinburgh: Oliver and Boyd, 1972.

Kanner, L. *Child psychiatry*. Springfield, Ill.: Thomas, 1957.

Keeler, W. R. Discussion of paper presented by L. Kanner. *Psychiatric Research Reports of American Psychiatric Association*, 1957, *7*, 66-88.

Knobloch, H., and Pasamanick, B. Etiologic factors in "early infantile autism" and "childhood schizophrenia." Paper presented at the Tenth International Congress of Pediatrics, Lisbon, Portugal, 1962.

Lamaze, F. Introduction au dernier stage. *Encyclopedie medico-chirurgicale*. Paris, 1956.

Lotter, V. Epidemiology of the autistic condition in young children: II. Some characteristics of the parents and children. *Social Psychiatry*, 1967, *1*, 163-173.

McNeil, T. F., and Kaij, L. Obstetric complications and physical size of offspring of schizophrenic, schizophrenic-like, and control mothers. *British Journal of Psychiatry*, 1973, *123*, 341-348. (a)

McNeil, T. F., and Kaij, L. Obstetric notations of mental or behavioral disturbance. *Journal of Psychosomatic Research*, 1973, *17*, 175-188. (b)

McNeil, T. F., and Kaij, L. Reproduction among female mental patients: Obstetric complications and physical size of offspring. *Acta Psychiatrica Scandinavica*, 1974, *50*, 3-15.

McNeil, T. F., Wiegerink, R., and Dozier, J. E. Pregnancy and birth complications in the births of seriously, moderately, and mildly behaviorally disturbed children. *Journal of Nervous and Mental Disease*, 1970, *151*, 24-34.

Mednick, S. Discussion. WHO Conference on Primary Prevention of Schizophrenia in High-Risk Groups, Copenhagen, 1975.

Mednick, S. A., and Lanoil, G. W. Efforts at prevention in high-risk children. First Vermont Conference on Primary Prevention of Psychopathology, Vermont, 1975.

Mednick, S. A., Mura, E., Schulsinger, F., and Mednick, B. Perinatal conditions and infant development in children with schizophrenic parents. *Social Biology*, 1971, *18*, Supplement, 103-113.

Mednick, S. A., and Schulsinger, F. Some premorbid characteristics related to breakdown in children with schizophrenic mothers. In D. Rosenthal and S. S. Kety (Eds.), *The transmission of schizophrenia*. London: Pergamon Press, 1968.

Mednick, S. A., and Schulsinger, F. Studies of children at high risk for schizophrenia. In S. Mednick et al. (Eds.), *Genetics, environment and psychopathology*. Amsterdam: North-Holland, 1974.

Mizrahi Mirdal, G. K., Mednick, S. A., Schulsinger, F., and Fuchs, F. Perinatal complications in children of schizophrenic mothers. *Acta Psychiatrica Scandinavica*, 1974, *50*, 553-568.

Mura, E., Mednick, S. A., Schulsinger, F., and Mednick, B. Erratum and further analysis. Perinatal conditions and infant development in children with schizophrenic parents. Manuscript, 1973.

Nilsson, Å. Paranatal emotional adjustment. A prospective investigation of 165 women. Part I. *Acta Psychiatrica Scandinavica*, 1970, Supplement 220.

Nilsson, Å., Kaij, H. L., and Jacobson, L. Postpartum mental disorder in an unselected sample. IV. The importance of the unplanned pregnancy. *Journal of Psychosomatic Research*, 1967, *10*, 341-347.

Osterkamp, A., and Sands, D. J. Early feeding and birth difficulties in childhood schizophrenia: A brief study. *Journal of Genetic Psychology*, 1962, *101*, 363-366.

Paffenbarger, R. S., Steinmetz, C. H., Pooler, B. G., and Hyde, R. T. The picture puzzle of the postpartum psychoses. *Journal of Chronic Diseases*, 1961, *13*, 161-173.

Page, E. W. On the pathogenesis of pre-eclampsia and eclampsia. *Journal of Obstetrics and Gynaecology of British Commonwealth*, 1972, *79*, 883-894.

Pasamanick, B., Constantinou, F. K., and Lilienfeld, A. M. Pregnancy experience and the development of childhood speech disorders: An epidemiologic study of the association with maternal and fetal factors. *American Journal of Diseases of Children*, 1956, *91*, 113-118.

Pasamanick, B., and Knobloch, H. Epidemiologic studies on the complications of pregnancy and the birth process. In G. Caplan (Ed.), *Prevention of mental disorders in children*. New York: Basic Books, 1961.

Plum, P. Cerebral palsy: A clinical survey of 543 cases. *Danish Medical Bulletin*, 1956, *3*, 99-108.

Plum, P. Early diagnosis of spastic paraplegia. *Spastic Quarterly*, 1962, *11*, 4-11.

Pollack, M. Early "minimal brain damage" and the development of severe psychopathology in adolescence. *American Journal of Orthopsychiatry*, 1967, *37*, 213-214.

Pollin, W., and Stabenau, J. R. Biological, psychological and historical differences in a series of monozygotic twins discordant for schizophrenia. In D. Rosenthal and S. S. Kety (Eds.), *The transmission of schizophrenia*. London: Pergamon Press, 1968.

Pollin, W., Stabenau, J. R., Mosher, L., and Tupin, J. Life history differences in identical twins discordant for schizophrenia. *American Journal of Orthopsychiatry*, 1966, *36*, 492-509.

Rimland, B. *Infantile autism*. New York: Appleton-Century-Crofts, 1964.

Sameroff, A. J., and Zax, M. Perinatal characteristics of the offspring of schizophrenic women. *Journal of Nervous and Mental Disease*, 1973, *157*, 191-199.

Schain, R. G., and Yannet, H. Infantile autism. *Journal of Pediatrics*, 1960, *57*, 560-567.

Socialstyrelsen. *Normalreglemente för mödra- och barnhälsovården* (Regulations for prenatal and child health care). Stockholm: Kungl. Boktryckeriet, 1970.

Soichet, S. Emotional factors in toxemia of pregnancy. *American Journal of Obstetrics and Gynecology*, 1959, *77*, 1065-1073.

Taft, L., and Goldfarb, W. Prenatal and perinatal factors in childhood schizophrenia. *Developmental Medicine and Child Neurology*, 1964, *6*, 32-34.

Terris, M., LaPouse, R., and Monk, M. The relation of prematurity and previous fetal loss to childhood schizophrenia. *American Journal of Psychiatry*, 1964, *121*, 475-481.

Vorster, D. An investigation of the part played by organic factors in childhood schizophrenia. *Journal of Mental Science*, 1960, *106*, 494-522.

Wittam, H., Simon, G. B., and Mittler, P. J. The early development of psychotic children and their sibs. *Developmental Medicine and Child Neurology*, 1966, *8*, 552-560.

Wiedorn, W. S. Toxemia of pregnancy and schizophrenia. *Journal of Nervous and Mental Disease*, 1954, *120*, 1-9.

Infants Born At Risk:
Early Compensatory Experiences

Tiffany M. Field

Infants born at risk are generally considered at risk for developmental problems due to reproductive casualties, caretaking casualties, or both. Examples of infants on the reproductive casualty continuum, first defined by Pasamanick and Knobloch (1966), include those born with congenital disorders such as the mentally retarded and cerebral palsied and those who are born too soon or too small. On the not necessarily separate caretaking casualty continuum—described by Sameroff and Chandler (1975)—are infants who may experience developmental problems secondary to being parented by adults stressed by emotional or socioeconomic problems. These might include infants born to lower socioeconomic-status (SES) mothers or teenage mothers. Infants at risk because of both reproductive and caretaking casualties are, for example, preterm infants of teenage mothers, twins, and infants born to schizophrenic mothers.

Although retrospective studies of developmentally handicapped children ranging from those who are profoundly retarded to those who are abused reveal a number of reproductive and caretaking casualties in the histories of their subjects (e.g., a heightened incidence of prematurity among handicapped and abused children) the prospective studies of the last couple of decades on these same casualties reveal a surprisingly less negative picture.

❖   This chapter describes a number of examples of data which demonstrate these compensating influences. Among these studies are (1) a comparison between early survivors and later survivors of RDS, illustrating the varying effects of different intensive care technologies; (2) effects of supplemental stimulation on preterm RDS infants; (3) a comparison between low birthweight twins and their normal weight co-twins among discordant pairs and the apparent compensating treatment provided for the weaker twin; (4) a comparison of preterm infants born to middle versus lower SES parents to illustrate stressful and nonstressful parenting effects; (5) the effects of a very minimal parent-training intervention; and (6) more extensive parent-training interventions for infants at risk because of both reproductive and caretaking casualties, that is, preterm infants born to lower SES teenage mothers. These separate studies are presented to illustrate the potential compensatory influences of postnatal environments on infants born at risk because of reproductive and caretaking casualties.

❖ Summary

There appear to be a number of compensating factors that may attenuate anticipated developmental problems, although we might expect morbidity problems associated with reproductive casualties such as preterm delivery, low birthweight, or complications such as RDS or might predict caretaking casualties associated with teenage, lower SES parenting.

The comparison between earlier and more recent survivors of RDS suggests that medical technology and new neonatal care practices may facilitate more optimal development in addition to reducing mortality. Newer forms of ventilation, parent education, prettier nurseries, and increased parent visiting may all mediate more optimal development.

A simple intervention such as providing a pacifier during tube feedings appears to contribute to fewer feedings, smoother bottle feedings, and probably happier parents for both lower hospital costs and easier to feed babies at discharge.

The smaller, sicker, preemie twin does not appear to be rejected by his or her parents, rather he or she appears to be specially treated. Although we do not know whether parents do, in fact, treat this twin differently, the data suggest some compensation has occurred for the twin to excel in some areas during infancy despite the disadvantage at birth.

The power of parenting is further suggested by the dramatic developmental effects of simply showing mothers the skills of the newborn on a Brazelton. The teenage mother, through education and support posthospitalization, not only appears to change her attitudes and developmental expectations but also her interactive behaviors with her infant. Many of the reported effects are suggestive of a transactional phenomenon whereby teaching parents other ways or altering their perceptions, attitudes, and behaviors appears to mediate developmental strides in their infants, which, in turn, reinforce and elicit more of the parenting skills necessary for fostering development.

Thus some infants born at risk appear to escape the gross insults of reproductive and caretaking casualties, perhaps because there are these compensatory experiences. There are, however, a number who do not experience these, as well as others who fail despite compensatory treatment. In addition, there are the unknown effects of being treated specially. While the low birthweight twin out performs his/her normal birthweight co-twin, parents anecdotally report the weaker twin as more difficult to manage behaviorally. Our RDS sample at 4 years achieved normal IQ scores but were extremely difficult to test because of limited attention span, restlessness, and hyperactivity. Some suggest that learning disabilities are mediated by early behavioral problems such as restlessness and hyperactivity. Thus a very large question is whether our treatments—the compensatory experiences we provide such as supplemental stimulation, enriched environments, parent training and, in general, very special treatment of the high-risk infant which are reducing mortality and serious morbidity—also mediate undesirable later childhood behaviors such as being a "brat" or writing backwards. The neonatologist's and psychologist's concerns too often cease with healthy weight gains and normal IQ scores, while the more subtle uninvestigated problems may remain with parents, teachers, and the child.

References

Allen, M., Greenspan, S., and Pollin, W. The effect of parental perceptions on early development in twins. *Psychiatry*, 1976, *39*, 65–71.

Allen, M. G., Pollin, W., and Hoffer, A. Parental birth and infancy factors in infant twin development. *American Journal of Psychiatry*, 1971, *127*, 1597–1604.

Als, H., Tronick, E., Adamson, L., and Brazelton, T. B. The behavior of the full-term yet underweight newborn infant. *Developmental Medicine and Child Neurology*, 1976, *18*, 590–594.

Badger, E. Effects of parent education program on teenage mothers and their offspring. In K. Scott, T. Field, and E. Robertson (Eds.), *Teenage parents and their offspring*. New York: Grune and Stratton, 1980.

Bauer, C. Effects of neonatal intensive care: A follow-up study of multiple births. *Pediatric Research*, 1977, *11*, 374.

Bayley, N. *Manual for the Bayley Scales of Infant Development*. New York: Psychological Corporation, 1969.

Bee, H. L., VanEgeren, L. F., Streissguth, A. P., Nyman, B. A., and Lockie, M. S. Social class differences in maternal teaching styles and speech patterns. *Developmental Psychology*, 1969, *1*, 726–734.

Brazelton, T. B. *Neonatal Behavioral Assessment Scale*. London: Spastic International Medical Publications, 1973.

Burroughs, A. K., Asonye, I. O., Anderson-Shanklin, G. C., and Vidyasagar, D. The effect of nonnutritive sucking on transcutaneous oxygen tension in non-crying preterm neonates. *Research in Nursing and Health*, 1978, *1*, 69–75.

Cornell, E. M., and Gottfried, A. W. Intervention with premature human infants. *Child Development*, 1976, *47*, 32–39.

DeLissovoy, V. Child care by adolescent parents. *Children Today*, 1973, *2*, 22–25.

Doll, E. A. *Vineland Social Maturity Scale*. Minnesota: American Guidance Service, 1965.

Field, T. *Effects of providing preterm infants a pacifier during Brazelton examinations*. Unpublished manuscript, University of Miami, 1978. (a)

Field, T. The three Rs of infant-adult interactions: Rhythms, repertoires, and re-sponsivity. *Journal of Pediatric Psychology*, 1978, *3*, 131–136. (b)

Field, T. Games parents play with normal and high-risk infants. *Child Psychiatry and Human Development*, 1979, *10*, 41–48. (a)

Field, T. Interaction patterns of high-risk and normal infants. In T. Field, A. Sostek, S. Goldberg, and H. H. Shuman (Eds.), *Infants born at risk*. New York: Spectrum, 1979. (b)

Field, T. Interactions of preterm and term infants with their lower and middle class teenage and adult mothers. In T. Field, S. Goldberg, D. Stern, and A. Sostek (Eds.), *High-risk infants and children: Adult and peer interactions*. New York: Academic Press, 1980.

Field, T., Dempsey, J., and Shuman, H. Developmental assessments of infants surviving the respiratory distress syndrome. In T. Field, A. Sostek, S. Goldberg, and H. Shuman (Eds.), *Infants born at risk*. New York: Spectrum, 1979.

Field, T., Dempsey, J., Hallock, N., and Shuman, H. H. Mothers' assessments of the behavior of their infants. *Infant behavior and development*, 1978, *1*, 156–167.

Field, T., and Pawlby, S. Early face-to-face interactions of British and American working- and middle-class mother-infant dyads. *Child Development*, 1980, *51*, 250–253.

Field, T., and Widmayer, S. *Infant twin-mother interactions: Bigger is not always better.* Paper presented at the International Conference on Infant Studies, New Haven, Connecticut, April 1980.

Field, T., Widmayer, S., Stringer, S., and Ignatoff, E. Teenage, lower class black mothers and their preterm infants: An intervention and developmental follow-up. *Child Development*, 1980, *51*, 426–436.

Fitzhardinge, P. M., Pape, K., Arstikaitis, M., Boyle, M., Ashby, S., Rowley, A., Nettley, C., and Swyer, P. R. Mechanical ventilation of infants of less then 1,501 gm birthweight: Health, growth, and neurologic sequelae. *Journal of Pediatrics*, 1976, *88*, 531–541.

Gifford, S., Murawski, B. J., Brazelton, T. B., and Young, G. C. Difference in individual development within a pair of identical twins. *International Journal of Psychoanalyses*, 1966, *47*, 261–268.

Goldberg, S. The pragmatics and problems of longitudinal research with high-risk infants. In T. Field, A. Sostek, S. Goldberg, and H. H. Shuman (Eds.), *Infants born at risk*. New York: Spectrum, 1979.

Grant, A. R., Vidyasagar, D., and Anderson, G. C. The effect of self-regulatory sucking upon behavioral state in restless newborn infants. Unpublished manuscript, University of Florida, Gainesville, 1978.

Gross, M. B., and Wilson, W. C. *Minimal brain dysfunction*. New York: Brunner/Mazel, 1974.

Ignatoff, E., and Field, T. *Effects of nonnutritive sucking during tube feedings on the clinical course and behavior of ICU preterm neonates.* Paper presented at the International Conference on Infant Studies, New Haven, Connecticut, April 1980.

Johnson, J. D., Malachowski, N. C., Grabstein, R., Welsch, D., Daily, W. J. R., and Sunshine, P. Prognosis of children surviving with the aid of mechanical ventilation in the newborn period. *Journal of Pediatrics*, 1974, *88*, 272–276.

Kilbride, H. W., Johnson, D. L., and Streissguth, A. P. Social class, birth order and newborn experience. *Child Development*, 1977, *48*, 1686–1688.

Lambesis, C. C., Vidyasagar, D., and Anderson, G. C. The effects of surrogate mothering upon physiologic stablization of the transitional newborn. In G. C. Anderson and B. Raff (Eds.), *Newborn behavioral organization: Nursing research* and implications. National Foundation/March of Dimes. *Birth Defects: Original article series* (Vol. 15). New York: Liss, 1979.

Lewis, M., and Wilson, C. D. Infant development in lower-class American families. *Human Development,* 1972, *15,* 112–127.

Littman, B., and Parmelee, A. H. Medical correlates of infant development. *Pediatrics,* 1978, *61,* 470–474.

Masi, W. Supplemental stimulation of the premature infant. In T. Field, A. Sostek, S. Goldberg, and H. H. Shuman (Eds.), *Infants born at risk.* New York: Spectrum, 1979.

Measel, C. P., and Anderson, G. C. Nonnutritive sucking during tube feedings: Effect upon clinical course in premature infants. *Journal of Obstetric, Gynecologic and Neonatal Nursing,* 1979, *8,* 265–272.

Miller, S. A., and Dymsza, H. A. Artificial feeding of neonatal rats. *Science,* 1963, *141,* 517–518.

Neligan, G. A., Kolvin, I., Scott, D. Mcl., and Garside, R. F. *Born too soon or born too small.* Philadelphia: J. B. Lippincott, 1976.

Nichols, R. C., and Bilbro, W. C. The diagnosis of twin zygosity. *Acta Genetica,* 1966, *16,* 265–275.

Pasamanick, B., and Knobloch, H. Retrospective studies on the epidemiology of reproductive casality: Old and new. *Merrill-Palmer Quarterly,* 1966, *12,* 7–26.

Quay, H., and Peterson, D. R. *Manual for the behavior problem checklist.* Miami: University of Miami Press, 1975.

Rowe, D. C., and Plomin, R. Temperament in early childhood. *Journal of Personality Assessment,* 1977, *41,* 150–156.

Sameroff, A. J., and Chandler, M. J. Reproductive risk and the continuum of caretaking casualty. In F. D. Horowitz, M. Hetherington, S. Scarr-Salapatek, and G. Siegel (Eds.), *Review of child development research* (Vol. 4). Chicago: University of Chicago Press, 1975.

Sroufe, L. A., and Wunsch, J. P. The development of laughter in the first year of life. *Child Development,* 1972, *43,* 1326–1344.

Stringer, S., and Field, T. *Effects of nonnutritive sucking stimulation on preterm infants' feeding performance.* Paper presented at the International Conference on Infant Studies, New Haven, Connecticut, April 1980.

Terman, L. M., and Merrill, M. A. *Stanford-Binet Intelligence Scale.* Boston: Houghton-Mifflin, 1972.

Tjossem, T. D. Early intervention: Issues and approaches. In T. D. Tjossem (Ed), *Intervention strategies for high-risk infants and young children.* Baltimore: University Park Press, 1976.

Tulkin, S., and Kagan, J. Mother-child interaction in the first few years of life. *Child Development,* 1972, *43,* 31–41.

Widmayer, S., and Field, T. Effects of Brazelton demonstrations on early interactions of preterm infants and their mothers. *Infant Behavior and Development,* 1980, *3,* 79–89.

Wilson, R. S., Brown, A. M., and Matheny, A. P. Emergence and persistence of behavioral differences in twins. *Child Development,* 1971, *32,* 1381–1398.

Promoting Positive Health Behaviors in Adults

Nathan Maccoby

One of the principal causes of mental illness is physical illness. Multiple sclerosis, which makes people into wheelchair patients, is likely to make people stop trying to function and spend their time bemoaning their cruel fate. Survivors of a heart attack or stroke are similarly inclined to resign from life when it might well be possible for them to continue to make important contributions to self-fulfillment, family, and society: we have had at least two presidents in this century who continued in office long after undergoing severe myocardial infarctions. Other crippling diseases often require a severe mental adjustment.

Although it is frequently possible to succeed in rehabilitating such patients through both physical and mental therapy, how much better it would be if the physical disease could be prevented from happening. Many disabling diseases are to a considerable extent preventable. Interestingly enough, however, changes in life style, a psychological adjustment, are required for such prevention. In other words, reducing the incidence of cardiovascular disease, our single largest cause of premature death, can be accomplished by changes in behavior. The reduction of early deaths would certainly reduce mental illness among closely affiliated survivors. Since about half of the victims of heart attacks survive their first attack, the reduction of such attacks would also help prevent the occurrence among victims of post-heart-attack psychological adjustment problems.

It turns out that the self-management of behavior is the key to prevention of both cardiovascular disease and of psychological maladjustment (Mahoney and Thorensen, 1974). Just as successful adjustment requires self-management of behavior rather than the constant direction of a therapist, so the changes in behavior that can result in reduced risk of cardiovascular disease can be accomplished by self-directed and self-managed behavior changes.

The leading cause of death in this country and, for that matter, in almost all of the other highly developed countries is cardiovascular disease (American Heart Association, 1977). Most of the gains in longevity attained in this century due to advances in public health practices and improvements in medicine have been largely offset by enormous increases in particular diseases (Feinlieb, 1975). Most noticeable among these diseases are the cardiovascular ones, for some time now the leading killer. There has also been a phenomenal risk in the incidence of certain cancers—mainly in lung cancer, an "almost always" fatal disease (Surgeon General's Report, *Smoking and Health*, 1979).

During the last ten years there have been substantial reductions in the number of deaths induced by cardiovascular disease. The reasons for this consistent improvement are not fully known, but the reduction of smoking and reduction of serum cholesterol among middle-aged men may be important factors. Although the causes of atherosclerosis (diseases of the arterial inner walls) the leading form of cardiovascular disease, are not yet fully understood, risk factors and the probable ways in which these risk factors increase the likelihood of occurrence of cardiovascular events are, in at least some instances, clearly identifiable. High blood pressure, smoking, high blood lipids (fats), and particularly low-density lipoproteins (serum LDL cholesterol) are clearly associated with a high incidence of heart attacks and strokes, the leading events in cardiovascular disease. It is important for psychologists to remember that the medical term "hypertension" refers not to stress but to the stretching of the walls of arterial blood vessels due to the filling of the inside openings (lumens) of the arteries with fatty deposits. Stress may in some as yet unknown manner contribute to hypertension, but the term hypertension simply means high blood pressure. Essential hypertension means high blood pressure whose cause is not known.

Epidemiological studies show that combinations of risk factors have a multiplicative relationship to cardiovascular events (Truett, Cornfield, and Kannel, 1967). Thus even a moderately high systolic blood pressure—well below what might be labeled hypertension—when combined with cigarette smoking or moderately high blood cholesterol (LDL) results in considerable risk—much greater than the sum of each risk that these values would suggest. Thus all measures of risk should be regarded as continuous distributions, with some risk beginning at relatively low values and increasing with larger values. The distribution of serum cholesterol indicates that the mean cholesterol value in the United States would be near the top of the distribution in Japan. Almost all of those in the United States have high enough serum cholesterol to have some risk of a cardiovascular event. Secondary risk factors include being overweight, lack of exercise and improper diet—for example, too much salt or sugar—and probably persistent psychological stress.

There is additional epidemiological evidence to support the hypothesis that cardiovascular disease is at least strongly influenced by factors of life style (Intersociety Commission for Heart Disease Resources, 1970). Cross-cultural studies of morbidity and mortality rates assignable to cardiovascular diseases reveals considerable variation from country to country. Finland and the United States lead the list, and Japan, among the developed countries, has very low rates. When the Japanese in California are compared with those in Japan, their rates are much higher, with Japanese in Hawaii showing intermediate values. Dietary factors appear to be strongly implicated in these differences in morbidity and mortality, and cultural hereditary factors seem relatively less important (Kagan, Harris, Johnson, Hiroo, Syme, Rhoads, Gay, Nichamen, Hamilton, Tillotson, and Winkelstein, 1974).

Thus, while the precise mechanisms by which these risk factors contribute to cardiovascular disease is not fully specifiable, the prudent person is clearly wise to take steps to keep blood pressure low, maintain a reasonably lean body, not smoke cigarettes, and observe certain dietary precautions (Keys, Anderson and Grande, 1965). The problem we at the Stanford Heart Disease Prevention Program have undertaken now is to help people adopt and maintain a prudent life style, and how to do this in a reasonably cost-effective and effort-effective manner.

In 1971 the Stanford University Heart Disease Prevention Program undertook a three-community study in order to discover a method for risk reduction which would be generally applicable. Why did we pick a community as the unit of education for reducing risk of cardiovascular disease? (1) If an individual therapist-instructor is used with either one person at a time or even with a small group of persons, the problem of general risk reduction is just too large to manage. Such an undertaking would be very expensive, and the number of therapist-instructors needed would be astronomically high. (2) Risk reduction involves behavior changes that have a very long-term—even a lifetime—duration. Cessation of smoking or not beginning to smoke cigarettes is behavior that has to last if it is going to make a contribution to the reduction of risk of disease. Similarly, changes in diet involving reductions in dietary cholesterol, saturated fats, salt, and calories generally call for changes in eating habits that are permanent for the remainder of the life cycle. (3) These changes need to take place not in the clinic but in the context of the environments in which people live. Furthermore, the community nexus can contribute greatly to the maintenance of changes in life style. The home, the school, the work place (Meyer and Henderson, 1974) and other community settings are the environments in which such behavior occurs, and therefore it must be practiced there. Furthermore, these institutions are potential sources of support for new behavior, or they can constitute obstacles to such change (Farquhar, 1978).

Diffusion of changed behavior and social support are potentially important sources of strength for the formation and maintenance of new habits. Peers can play a very important role in the process. For example, school children can be influenced not to begin cigarette smoking if peer models occupy visible roles as nonsmokers (McAlister, Perry, and Maccoby, 1978).

We were interested in discovering a method for helping people to change their life styles so as to reduce their risk of suffering a cardiovascular event such as a myocardial infarction—a heart attack—or a stroke. We were searching for a method that would accomplish this objective, would not require overwhelming numbers of therapists, and would be relatively inexpensive per person assisted.

In 1972 our group (Farquhar, Maccoby, Wood, Alexander, Breitrose, Brown, Haskell, McAlister, Meyer, Nash and Stern, 1977)—investigators at the School of Medicine and the Institute for Communication Research at Stanford University—began a field experiment in three northern California communities in order to study the modification of risk factors in cardiovascular disease through community education. The major tactical choices for such a campaign are mass media, face-to-face instruction, or combinations of the two. Study of previous mass-media campaigns directed at large open populations has established the potential effectiveness of the media in transmitting information. altering some attitudes, and producing small shifts in behavior, by means of choices among consumer products, but has failed to demonstrate that the media alone substantially influence more complex behavior (Bauer, 1964; Cartwright, 1949; Robertson, Kelley, O'Neil, Wixom, Eisworth and Haddon, 1974; Star and Hughes, 1950). Yet the habits influencing cardiovascular risk factors are very complex and long standing, are often reinforced by culture, custom, and continual commercial advertising, and are unlikely to be very strongly influenced by mass media alone. Face-to-face instruction and exhortation also have a long history of failure, particularly with respect to recidivism, as noted above, in efforts to influence diet (Stunkard, 1975) and smoking (Bernstein and McAlister, 1976).

After considering the powerful culture forces which reinforce and maintain the health habits that we wished to change, and in view of past failure of health education campaigns, we designed a heretofore untested combination of extensive mass media with a considerable amount of face-to-face instruction. We chose this method not so much because it was potentially widely applicable, but because it was a method that we judged most likely to succeed (Mendelsohn, 1973). We could then compare a more generally applicable treatment, though one not quite so promising of results, with the more sure one. Therefore, another community was selected in which we administered treatments via mass media alone. We also chose to include three elements typically ignored in health campaigns: (1) the mass media materials were devised to teach specific behavioral skills, as well as to perform the more usual tasks of offering information and affecting attitude and motivation; (2) both the mass media and, in particular, the face-to-face instruction were designed to embody many previously validated methods of achieving changes in behavior and self-control training principles; and (3) the campaign was designed on the basis of careful analysis of the specific needs and the media consumption patterns of the intended audience. Our overall goal was to create and evaluate methods for effecting changes in smoking, exercise, and diet which would be both cost-effective and applicable to large population groups.

RESEARCH DESIGN

Since our media campaigns were directed at entire communities, random assignment of individuals to the treatment or control condition was not feasible. An equally rigorous experimental method, treating a large number of entire geographically defined populations as single units and randomly assigning some of these communities to treatment and some to control conditions, was prohibitively expensive. Thus we concluded that the most realistic compromise between feasibility and rigor was a quasi-experimental research approach with a small number of experimental units. Three roughly comparable communities in northern California were selected. Tracy was chosen as a control because it was relatively distant and isolated from media in the other communities. Gilroy and Watsonville, the other two communities, share some media channels (television and radio), but each town has its own newspaper. Watsonville and Gilroy received different strategies of health education over a period of two years. Gilroy received health education through the mass media alone; Watsonville also received health education through the mass media, except that there we also carried out a randomized experiment with a sample of persons at higher levels of risk for cardiovascular disease, employing intensive face-to-face instruction for two thirds of this group and using the remaining people in this group, exposed only to health education through the media, as a control against intensive instruction under a mass media umbrella.

MASS MEDIA AND INTENSIVE FACE-TO-FACE INSTRUCTION CAMPAIGN

The experimental design involved development and application of a mass media and face-to-face instruction campaign. These communication efforts were designed to overcome deficiencies in previous unsuccessful campaigns to change behavior. Each campaign was intended to produce awareness of the probable causes of coronary disease and of the specific behaviors that may reduce risk. The campaigns also aimed at providing the knowledge and skills necessary to accomplish recommended behavior changes. Lastly, the campaigns were designed to help the individual become self-sufficient in maintaining new health habits and skills. Dietary habits recommended for all participants were those which, if followed, would lead to a reduced intake of saturated fat, cholesterol, salt, sugar, and alcohol. We also urged reduction in body weight through caloric reduction and increased physical activity. Cigarette smokers were educated on the need and methods for ceasing or at least reducing their daily rate of cigarette consumption.

For the mass media campaign a coordinated set of messages was prepared for the lay audiences in Gilroy and Watsonville. Over time these basic messages were transformed into a variety of media (e.g., TV spots, bus cards, etc.) and released to the target audience through a variety of the most generally available media channels. A broad range of materials was produced. For example, about 50 television spots, three hours of television programming, over 100 radio spots, several hours of radio programming, weekly newspaper columns, newspaper advertisements and stories, billboards, printed material sent via direct mail to participants, posters, and other assorted materials. Because of the sizable Spanish-speaking population in the communities, the campaign was presented in both Spanish and English. The media campaign began two months after the initial survey and continued for nine months in 1973, stopped during the second survey, and then continued for nine more months in 1974 and on a very reduced basis in 1975 (Maccoby, Farquhar, Wood, and Alexander, 1977).

The dominant characteristic of the mass media campaign structure was its organization as a total integrated information system such that its primary functions (the creative transformation of the medical risk-reduction messages into media events, the formative evaluation of those events, their distribution in coordinated packages over time, and their cumulative effectiveness in promoting change) could all interact to improve and refine decisions on how best to allocate the remaining available resources. The management of this system was put into operation by a process of continuous monitoring of the target audience's existing knowledge, beliefs, attitudes, risk-related behavior, and media use. At the onset of the campaign, decisions were based primarily on data gathered at the initial survey, from the pretesting on local audiences of various media productions, and on the practical considerations arising from the likely availability of privately owned mass media for our purposes. While the campaign was under way, further guidance was obtained from the second annual survey and from a series of systematic but informal small-scale information-gathering efforts designed to provide media planners with immediate feedback on the public's awareness and acceptance of specified sets of media events, as well as to gauge the progress to date. Thus the total campaign could be seen as a set of phased media events where the information obtained from monitoring was used to refocus priorities, reset directions, and modulate the course of the campaign in the desired direction.

The intensive face-to-face instruction program was directed at a randomly selected two thirds of the Watsonville participants whom we identified as being in the top quartile of risk of coronary heart disease according to the multiple logistic formula. These individuals and their physicians were informed by letter of their relatively high risk status, and this was considered as part of the treatment for the group. Their spouses were also invited to participate. The educational effort was launched six months after the first baseline survey and was conducted intensively over a ten-week period. A less intense effort was conducted during the second year. A total of 107 of 113 participants originally assigned to receive intensive instruction were successfully recruited for treatment, and 77 high risk individuals (and 34 spouses) completed all three interviews and examinations.

The intensive instruction program was composed of education and persuasion in the context of social learning and self-control training procedures designed to achieve the same changes in cholesterol and fat consumption, body weight, cigarette smoking (Meyer, Maccoby, and Farquhar, 1977), and physical exercise that were advocated in the media campaign. It was conducted by a team of graduate students in communication, physicians, and specialist health educators trained in behavior modification techniques. The protocols were pretested in a controlled setting before being applied in the field. The basic sequential strategy was to present information about the behavior that influences risk of coronary heart disease, stimulate personal ayalysis of existing behavior, demonstrate desired skills (e.g., food selection and preparation), guide the individual through tentative practice of those skills, and gradually withdraw instructor participation. The expectation was that the behavior would be maintained in the group setting without the instructor. During the initial stage, intensive instruction was conducted in group classes and home counseling sessions. During the second year the frequency and amount of contact was successively reduced. A less intensive educational campaign was conducted in the summer months of the second year, which consisted primarily of individual counseling in difficult problem areas—for example, smoking (Frederickson, 1968) and weight loss—and such social activities as parties, picnics, and hikes, which were intended primarily to encourage participants to maintain changes that had been produced during the first stage of instruction. Very little follow-up occurred in 1975.

In previous studies of weight loss, blood pressure detection and control, smoking cessation, and dietary composition changes, selected persons have served as subjects. In this study entire communities were the subjects of education for change. The data reported above were from probability samples of those communities. However, loss of sample subjects in successive waves of measurements may well limit the unbiased nature of the findings. In addition, there were notable lacks of success. Sustained weight loss did not occur, and cessation of smoking occurred primarily among intensive instructees.

In spite of these shortcomings, the changes that did take place are impressive. In general, the changes in knowledge, behavior, and—most important—physiological end points achieved in the first year were maintained and actually improved in the second year of education. Even during the third year, when educational efforts all but ceased, most changes were maintained, especially in the community containing intensive instructees.

This study demonstrates that mass media when appropriately used can increase knowledge and help people to adopt improved health habits. The results led us to believe, however, that the power of this method could be considerably enhanced if we could devise ways of employing the media to stimulate and coordinate face-to-face instructional programs in natural settings in such communities as schools, places of work, and community groups. This study led, therefore, to a further investigation designed to test these ideas.

We believe that media can be powerful, but that their effects can be augmented by community organization. Interpersonal influence can have a multiplicative effect in helping people to change their behavior. Community organizations can expand and improve the educational effort in ways that can improve community-wide risk reduction. They can publicize and support this effort. Most important, community organizations can help the process of community adoption of risk-reduction programs as their own programs and thus increase both the immediate and the long-term educational effectiveness of health education programs in their cities. Our media efforts will include both an improved program of mass media aimed directly at the public and little media packages such as video and audio tapes, booklets, slides, etc. for the use of community educators.

The early part of the human life cycle is clearly the place to begin the development of health habits. To that end our current study includes an emphasis on helping young people to adopt appropriate food consumption, weight control, exercise, and smoking habits. Our strategy is to experiment on a small scale with selected subjects or schools before applying these methods to the communities at large.

The method of temptation-resistance training appears to be a promising approach, especially when the training is conducted by older peers. Studies in schools employing these methods have yielded preliminary findings which suggest that the onset of smoking can at least be delayed and at best, we hope, be prevented from occurring altogether. Training methods for other health habits are being explored similarly in "pre-field" settings.

Although this discussion has been focused on the prevention of cardiovascular disease, it is evident that the methods employed could be adapted to the reduction of other important diseases. The second largest killer in our society is cancer. The etiology of cancer even more than cardiovascular disease, is obscure. As in the case of CVD, however, there are sufficiently identifiable precursors that can be dealt with. Cigarette smoking is not the sole cause of lung cancer, and many people who smoke do not get it, while many who do not smoke do become victims of lung cancer. Clearly, however, from the recent Surgeon General's Report (*Smoking and Health*, 1979), it can be seen that not smoking considerably reduces the risk of contracting lung cancer. It is generally held also that the likelihood of falling victim to other cancers may be decreased by changes in food habits. The linkage of obesity to breast cancer and relation of fiber in the diet to cancer of the colon are two additional examples. The more that we learn about helping people to adopt healthful habits, the more this knowledge can be applied to the reduction of disease generally.

REFERENCES

American Heart Association. *Heart facts.* New York: American Heart Association, 1977.

Bauer, R. A. The obstinate audience: The influence process from the point of view of social communications. *American Psychologist*, 1964, *19*, 319-328.

Bernstein, D. A., and McAlister, A. L. Modification of smoking behavior: . Progress and problems. *Addictive Behavior*, 1976, *1*, 89-102.

Butts, W. C., Kuehneman, M., and Widdowson, G. M. Automated method for determining serum thiocyanate to distinguish smokers from nonsmokers. *Clinical Chemistry*, 1974, *20*, 1344-1348.

Cartwright, D. Some principles of mass persuasion. *Human Relations*, 1949, *2*, 253-267.

Farquhar, J. W. The community based model of life style intervention trials. *American Journal of Epidemiology*, 1978, *108*, 103-111.

Farquhar, J. W., Maccoby, N., Wood, P., Alexander, J. K., Breitrose, H., Brown, B., Haskell, W., McAlister, A., Meyer, A., Nash, J., and Stern, M. Community education for cardiovascular health. *Lancet*, 1977, *1*, 1192-1195.

Feinleib, M. Changes in life expectancy since 1900. *Circulation*, 1975, *52* (111), 16-17.

Frederickson, D. T. How to help your patient stop smoking. *Diseases of the Chest*, 1968, *54*, 196-202.

Griffiths, W., and Knutson, A. The role of mass media in public health. *American Journal of Public Health*, 1960, *50*, 515-523.

Intersociety Commission for Heart Disease Resources. Primary prevention of the atherosclerotic diseases. *Circulation*, 1970, *45*, A55-A95.

Kagan, A., Harris, E. R., Johnson, K., Hiroo, K., Syme, S. L., Rhoads, G., Gay, M., Nichamen, M., Hamilton, H., Tillotson, J., and Winkelstein, W.

128   NATHAN MACCOBY

Epidemiological studies of coronary heart disease and stroke in Japan, Hawaii, and California: Demographic, physical, dietary, and biochemical characteristics. *Journal of Chronic Diseases*, 1974, *27*, 345–364.

Keys, A., Anderson, J. T., and Grande, F. Serum cholesterol response to changes in the diet. *Metabolism*, 1965, *14*, 747–787.

Maccoby, N., Farquhar, J. W., Wood, P., and Alexander, J. K. Reducing the risk of cardiovascular disease. *Journal of Community Health*, 1977, *3*, 100–114.

Mahoney, M. J., and Thorensen, C. E. *Self control: Power to the person.* Monterey: Brooks-Cole, 1974.

Mendelsohn, H. Some reasons why information campaigns can succeed. *Public Opinion Quarterly*, 1973, *37*, 50–61.

Meyer, A. J., and Henderson, J. B. Multiple risk factor reduction in the prevention of cardiovascular disease. *Preventive Medicine*, 1974, *3*, 255–236.

Meyer, A. J., Maccoby, N., and Farquhar, J. W. The role of opinion leadership in a cardiovascular health education campaign. In B. D. Ruben (Ed.), *Communication yearbook* (Vol. I). New Brunswick: Transaction Books, 1977.

Miller, N. E. The evidence for the antiatherogenicity of high density lipoprotein in man. *Lipids*, 1978, *13*, 914–919.

McAlister, A., Perry, C., and Maccoby, N. *Systematic peer leadership to discourage onset of tobacco dependency.* Paper presented at American Psychological Convention, Toronto, August 1978.

Robertson, L. S., Kelley, A. B., O'Neill, B., Wixom, C., Eisworth, R., and Haddon, W. A controlled study of the effect of television messages on safety belt use. *American Journal of Public Health*, 1974, *64*, 1071–1080.

Smoking and health: A report of the Surgeon General. Washington, D.C.: Department of Health Education and Welfare, 1979.

Star, S., and Hughes, H. M. Report of an educational campaign: The Cincinnati plan for the United Nations. *American Journal of Sociology*, 1950, *55*, 389–400.

Stern, M. P., Farquhar, J. W., Maccoby, N., and Russell, S. Results of a two-year health education campaign on dietary behavior: The Stanford three-community study. *Circulation*, 1976, *54*, 826–833.

Stunkard, A. J. Presidential address—1974: From explanation to action in psychosomatic medicine: The case of obesity. *Psychosomatic Medicine*, 1975, *37*, 195–236.

Truett, J., Cornfield, J., and Kannel, W. A multivariate analysis of the risk of coronary heart disease in Framingham. *Journal of Chronic Diseases*, 1967, *20*, 511–524.

iii. Stress and Stress Reduction

Stressful life events, social interactions, and social institutions together constitute a major set of variables that contribute to the incidence of psychopathology. Control of the nature and severity of stressors can, we believe, have the effect of reducing the incidence of aberrant behavior and the likelihood of people living unfulfilling and unhappy lives. It is not obvious that positive results are achievable by providing an environment free of stress, even were this possible, since "stress" is a complex concept encompassing events and occurrences which, under certain circumstances and in appropriate "doses," appear to have beneficial rather than disruptive effects on human development and functioning. This section provides insights into the conceptual complexity of the concept of stress as well as information on the effects of various kinds of stress on the lives and functioning of those exposed to it.

Richard S. Lazarus provides an analysis of stress and coping that emphasizes the complexity of the ideas. Drawing on his productive and imaginative research, he points out that the static unidimensional model of stress needs to be replaced by an interactional model, and that stress may have benign or even positive effects as well as deleterious ones. He reminds us that there is little clear knowledge of what patterns of coping are likely to work for particular individuals in specific circumstances. Before we attempt to change people's coping responses, a better understanding is needed of which deleterious responses are ameliorated and which exacerbated by such changes.

Michael Rutter discusses the interactive effects of stressors on children's development and the factors that offer protection against disruption. Both chronic and acute stressors can be withstood by children, but a combination of stressors produces disturbances more frequently than can be predicted from the separate effects of each. This indicates the value of eliminating whatever stressors we can, even if we cannot eliminate all. Rutter goes on to discuss differences in vulnerability to stress and identifies factors that have protective effects. Although much remains to be discovered, it seems that we can say with some confidence that variables that fit the categories in the denominator of our prevention equation — "competence and coping skills," "self-esteem," and "support groups" — are of major importance in protecting the individual from adverse consequences when she or he is exposed to stress.

In the next paper in this section, Gisela Konopka vividly delineates the stresses and strains particular to the adolescent experience. She asserts that adolescence is not a passage between life stages but rather a stage in itself. Drawing from years of experience with adolescents, about whom she has written extensively, Konopka illustrates their strong desire for responsibility and for the facts needed to make decisions. In her view, stress results from adolescents being forced to make decisions without experience and from being prevented from acting on their own behalf. Regardless of whether adolescents are assimilated into their world or protest against it desperately, Konopka feels that their underlying motive is confirmation of self-value.

Bernard L. Bloom's review of the effects of marital disruption as a stressor moves us to a later but equally problematic stage of life. He documents the size of the problem — the large and increasing numbers of people encountering marital breakdown and divorce — and the severity of its effects: marital disruption is associated with an increased risk of an astonishing range of disorders. Breakdown of marriage, possibly to a greater extent than most life events, represents a double threat to adaptive functioning; it involves considerable stress and at the same time disrupts an intimate and powerful support system. Bloom explores the complexities of the process and makes a strong case for the value of studies of marital discord that aim at using the occasion for effective preventive intervention.

Continuing the analysis of stressors in adult life, Harry Levinson, who has written extensively on various aspects of work, stress, and mental health, addresses the contradictions that emerge from large sample surveys of satisfaction with work. From a largely psychodynamic perspective, he examines circumstances causing stress, emphasizing the joint contributions of the environment and the individual. He goes on to focus on typically unrecognized factors within individuals that precipitate dissatisfaction and to recommend specific techniques that may promote the ability to cope with such problems.

The Stress and Coping Paradigm

Richard S. Lazarus

❖

STRESS AND COPING, CIRCA 1950

When I first came on the scene, psychologists viewed stress mostly as a disrupter of skilled performance. In clinical psychology and psychiatry, anxiety was conceived of as the major drive source of pathological modes of adaptation. Stress (or anxiety) was thought to generate inherently pathological defensive operations, such as repression, denial, isolation, undoing, intellectualized detachment, projection, and so on, leading to a distortion of reality. Such defenses reduced drive tension (anxiety), and the reductions made them refractory to unlearning or deconditioning. In short, psychopathology was considered, in large measure, to result from intense and/or prolonged stress which, in especially vulnerable persons, was comprised of dysfunctional ways of living and adjusting. Moreover, the origins of such pathogenic stress were commonly considered to be mainly intrapsychic and conflict-laden (endogenous) rather than lying in the environment (exogenous) (see also Roskies and Lazarus, 1979).

The central research questions my associates and I (e.g., Lazarus, Deese, and Osler, 1952) then asked were: "Under what conditions of stress does deterioration of functioning occur?" and "Who are the people most vulnerable to such deterioration?" During the Korean War and World War II, in which under battle conditions men developed diverse emotional disorders and even failed to fire their weapons, such a question was of great practical importance. But even in ordinary life such effects were observed to be common. For example, severe anxiety and blocking of thought and speech commonly occur in school examinations and other kinds of evaluative circumstances. It was obviously important to discover the general rules about how stress impaired human functioning.

Soon, however, we discovered that three kinds of results occurred under stress: (1) no measurable effect, (2) impairment of performance, and (3) facilitation of performance. Try as we might, the key factors making for these differences in result remained highly elusive, despite the generation of theories having limited utility in a narrow range of settings (e.g., Child and Waterhouse, 1953; Easterbrook, 1959; Spence and Spence, 1966; Yerkes and Dodson, 1908). The traditional linear S-R perspective could not be made to work well enough to produce usable rules that would link stress and performance, especially in natural settings. The terms of our original questions therefore had to be changed, and I came to believe that we would never understand the way stress affected performance until we began to treat individual differences as mediators of the reaction to stressful conditions. Our choice of mediators at that time included motivational and emotional traits and their interaction with task demands (Lazarus et al., 1952).

My own approach to stress and coping is explicitly cognitive-phenomenological. The questions I now ask have changed, as have to some extent the variables and how they are defined and interrelated. For example, whereas in 1950 coping was almost universally viewed as a product of emotion and emotion viewed as a drive, my colleagues and I press the argument that emotions (and stress) are products of cognition, that is, of the way a person appraises or construes his or her relationship with the environment. This does not mean, however, that the relationship goes only one way—that is, from cognition to emotion; rather, once aroused, emotions can also affect cognition. Moreover, motives and modes of thought influence the cognitive appraisal of all adaptational encounters.

MAJOR TENETS OF STRESS AND COPING THEORY TODAY

There are four such tenets, dealing respectively with (1) the naturalistic emphasis, (2) transaction and process, (3) multiple levels of analysis, and (4) ipsative-normative ways of studying people. Although these tenets actually evolved from a substantive-cognitive theory emphasis, it is best to defer review of that theory for last.

The Naturalistic Emphasis

❖

There are at least five serious limitations in laboratory research on stress and coping that should be noted:

(a) The laboratory cannot provide descriptive data on sources of stress in people in general or in subgroups of persons based on age, sex, type of community, socioeconomic status, subculture, and personality type. After all this time in which stress has been of multidisciplinary interest, we still do not know the stressors ordinary people or special subgroups face, their daily hassles, sources of positive feeling, or their patterns of daily emotional response. In the absence of such basic ecological information, how can we expect to know much about how these stressful encounters and their emotional outcomes are generated (their socio- and psychodynamics), or about their adaptational outcomes as in somatic health, morale, and social functioning? And how can we respond knowledgeably to the implications of a poetic statement by Charles Bukowski (1972) in "Shoelace" that:

> It's not the large things that send a man to the madhouse . . .
> No, It's the continuing series of small tragedies
> that send a man to the madhouse . . .
> not the death of his love
> but a shoelace that snaps
> with no time left . . . (p. 114)

Although I believe it is true that people can be distressed over what seem at the moment to be trivialities, they are not really trivial at all in meaning, for they symbolize things that are very important to a person. The shoelace might break, but a major part of the psychological stress created thereby is the implication that one cannot control one's life, that one is helpless in the face of the most stupid of trivialities, or, even worse, that one's own inadequacies have made the obstacle occur in the first place. This is what brings the powerful, stressful, and pathogenic message that breaks one's morale. In any case, how is one to evaluate such a momentous issue in the traditional style of laboratory stress research? No way.

(b) By the same token, laboratory research cannot create the full range of coping processes, the conglomeration of thoughts and actions that people ordinarily employ in dealing with both the small stresses of living and the major ones, like bereavement. The laboratory permits us to explore single or at best a few such coping processes, and only the few suitable to laboratory analogues at that, leaving obscure the overall patterning of coping processes routinely used in nature.

(c) Adaptational outcomes, such as somatic health/illness, morale, and social functioning, emerge over an extended time period from stressful encounters with which we continually struggle to cope, not in the short periods in which we have the laboratory subject at our disposal. With experimental stressors, we may produce momentary elevations in blood pressure, say, but such research is not capable of creating the health-related effect in which we are most interested, namely, the shift from a momentary rise in blood pressure to the chronic disease of hypertension (Herd, 1977; Lazarus, 1978; Stahl, Grim, Donald, and Neikirk, 1975). To study the mechanisms linking stress to disease or dysfunction requires time and can only be accomplished in the field study or field experiment in which we observe concurrently the ups and downs of an adaptational outcome along with the ongoing, causal psychological and social processes (Lazarus, Cohen, Folkman, Kanner, and Schaefer, 1980; Luborsky, Docherty, and Penick, 1973). Usually we cannot follow the human subject around to observe the daily adaptational encounters as can sometimes be done with animal species (e.g., Schaller, 1964; van Lawick-Goodall, 1971; Washburn and DeVore, 1961). However, we can develop other naturalistically oriented methods. One that my colleagues and I are using is to work regularly with human subjects and over an extended period of time, to reconstruct from memory important recent adaptational encounters. The message has been spreading that more naturalistic research on stress and coping, on adaptational outcomes, and in human psychological research in general, is badly needed (cf. Willems and Raush, 1969).

(d) Perhaps the most obvious limitation of the laboratory is the impossibility, for ethical and practical reasons, of subjecting humans to the kinds and degrees of stress that are encountered in everyday life. The stresses produced in the laboratory are pale shadows of the real thing, and as such, rules derived from them may not be stable or valid in the natural setting.

(e) Last, and most exasperating of all, much of what we take to be precise control over measurement and confounding variables is illusion, particularly when one's concerns are psychodynamic or sociodynamic. Yet this supposed control is presumably the primary virtue of the laboratory. Our *saying* that a given experimental stimulus is the basis of a subject's response does not make it so. Confounded with this stimulus are a host of irrelevant but potent factors, including what the subject thinks is happening, the complex, intrapsychic, adaptational processes, and the changing relationship with the experimenter. Much of what is psychologically important occurs in these other, unintended relationships, and these most commonly are unacknowledged and unmeasured. We must be wary of treating this type of research with veneration, as having some special precision and dependability beyond well designed and thoroughly analyzed naturalistic field studies in which the "ecological validity" is far greater.

Transaction and Process

No one seriously doubts that the way a person thinks, feels, or acts is a product of the interaction of external situation characteristics and person characteristics. Person characteristics are forged over a lifetime and nestled in a genetically shaped physical constitution; a situation contains three important elements to which persons can attend and react: demands, constraints, and resources (Klausner, 1971). In stress and adaptation a person with a given set of beliefs, values, commitments and skills encounters such a situation. To survive and flourish, countless such encounters must be experienced by a person over a lifetime. When a person construes an encounter as damaging, threatening or challenging, we speak of psychological stress; when it is evaluated as positive, a positively toned emotional state usually accompanies or follows it. Psychological stress (as well as positive experiences) resides neither in the situation nor in the person, though it depends on both. It arises from the adaptational relationship as it is appraised by the person. Such a relationship is best termed a "transaction."

In psychological stress theory as I elaborate it, various kinds of appraisal define the relationship through the subjects' eyes, as it were. It is one of harm/loss, threat, or challenge. The term "threat" expresses a new unit of psychological analysis. It refers to neither the person nor the environment alone, but to both, fused into a special kind of relationship described by the word "threat." Thus "transaction," in addition to implying mutuality of influence—which, incidentally, the term "interaction" could do adequately—implies the fusion of person and environment into a unit, a relationship, a system. Although "system" would be perfectly appropriate as an overarching term, I prefer transaction because system is very general while transaction is clearly concerned with a specific kind of system, namely, a person-environment relationship in an adaptational encounter.

A transactional view of stress and coping has one other important characteristic that should be identified. Rather than focusing exclusively on what is stable in the person-environment relationship, the emphasis is on process or dynamics—that is, on what is actually happening in any given stressful encounter and how what is happening changes. Thus, as I use the word, "process" refers to what happens over time or across encounters. It contains two elements: first, an actual interchange between the person and the environment (or among forces within the person); and second, the flow and transformation of the interchange over time, either as the encounter gets under way, proceeds and ends, or during its transformation across diverse encounters.

The first element—namely, an actual interchange—can be illustrated by a research study on the way surgical patients coped with the threat of surgery and how this affected postsurgical recovery (Cohen and Lazarus, 1973). We were able to dimensionalize patients into those with the trait of avoidance and denial at one extreme, and vigilance at the other, by using a traditional trait measure, the Epstein and Fenz (1967) version of Byrne's scales of repression-sensitization (Byrne, 1961, 1964). In addition, we obtained a process measure based on an interview with the patient the evening before the surgery. In the interview patients were asked to tell what they knew about their illness, the strategy of treatment, and their postsurgical expectations. Some knew a great deal and sought more; others knew little or nothing and seemed to avoid such information. This is a process measure in the first sense noted above because, rather than trying to assess patients' usual coping style (trait), measurement was centered on how they were *actually* coping with the *specific threat* at the moment it was happening. It turned out that the trait measure bore no relationship to either the process measure or the post-surgical outcome. Moreover, the process measure modestly predicted such outcome, with persons coping by avoidance-denial having a shorter hospital stay, fewer minor complications, and less distress than those who coped by vigilance.

The second element in understanding what is meant by "process," a key one in my estimation, is an emphasis on *flux and change*, over time or in diverse encounters. In stressful transactions psychological events are constantly moving and changing. Depending on what happens in the environment and within the person, anger gives way to anxiety or guilt, or it melts or grows stronger with each successive interchange. A stressful episode is not just a momentary, static stimulus in the environment to which the person gives a single response, say, a thought, act, or somatic reaction, as in the analogy of a single still photo; rather, it is a continuous flow of events over time, sometimes a short time as in an argument that quickly ends when one party leaves the room, at other times a long, tortuous, complex, sometimes repetitive process of achieving a new equilibrium in a relationship.

❖   *SUBSTANTIVE COGNITIVE AND COPING CONCEPTS*

As I noted at the start, the cognitive orientation in psychology has had a marked resurgence in recent years. Psychology has always been concerned with the relations between cognition, emotion, and motivation, but the nature of these relationships has been differently conceived at different times. It is only recently, however, that emotions and motivation have been seen as clearly shaped by the way a person construes ongoing relationships with the environment—in effect, by cognitive processes (cf. Lazarus, 1966; Lazarus, Averill, and Opton, 1970; Lazarus and Launier, 1978). There is a growing group of theorists (Arnold, 1960, 1970; Mandler, 1975), including the cognitive behavior therapists (e.g., Beck, 1971; Ellis, 1962; Goldfried, 1979; Mahoney, 1977; Meichenbaum, 1977), which accepts the premise that emotions are products of cognitive activity. In such a view, emotions are outcomes of, or reactions to, cognitively mediated transactions with the environment, actual, imagined, or anticipated. The term I have consistently employed since 1966 to express this idea is "cognitive appraisal," of which there are two main kinds, primary and secondary.

Primary Appraisal and Reappraisal

The process of evaluating the significance of a transaction for one's wellbeing is referred to as *primary appraisal*. Such appraisals come in three forms—judgments that the transaction is either (1) irrelevant, (2) benign-positive, or (3) stressful. There are three subtypes of stressful appraisals: (a) harm/loss, (b) threat, or (c) challenge. Harm/loss refers to injury or damage already done, as in bereavement, loss of physical function, social esteem, self-esteem, existential meaning, etc. Threat can refer to the same kinds of injuries, but the term signifies also that they have not yet occurred but are anticipated. Challenge means an opportunity for growth, mastery, or gain. The distinction between harm/loss, threat, and challenge may be very important not only in affecting the coping process itself and the effectiveness with which coping skills are utilized in social transactions, but also in their divergent consequences for morale and somatic health (Lazarus et al., 1980a).

We know too little about the kinds of people who typically appraise stressful encounters as challenging rather than threatening and vice versa, the types of stress situations that encourage challenge as opposed to threat appraisals and vice versa, and the adaptational consequences of each of these types of appraisal. A working hypothesis about the causal antecedents of threat and challenge is that the former is more likely when a person assumes that the specific environment is hostile and dangerous and that he or she lacks the resources for mastering it, while challenge arises when the environmental demands are seen as difficult but not impossible to manage, and that drawing upon existing or acquirable skills offers a genuine prospect for mastery. In addition to assumptions about specific environments, people may have very general belief systems about themselves and the environment (cf. Bandura, 1977; Ellis, 1962; Lazarus, 1966), systems that also influence appraisal of specific encounters.

Psychological stress, over all, refers to demands (or conflicts among them) which tax or exceed available resources (internal and external) as appraised by the person involved. Cognitive appraisal by an individual is what makes this definition of stress a psychological one. The key element is that a person senses in some way, consciously or unconsciously, that he or she is in jeopardy. In parallel fashion at the social level, stress involves demands from without or within which tax or exceed the resources of a social system. And at the somatic level, stress consists of proximate physical demands (even when they originate distally at the social or psychological level) which tax or exceed the resources of a tissue system—that is, stress is not an environmental stimulus, a characteristic of a system (e.g., a person), or a response; it is a *relational concept*, a balance between demands and the power to deal with them without unreasonable or destructive costs (as pointed out earlier).

At the bottom line of psychological stress analysis, then, primary appraisal determines the intensity and quality of the emotional response to any transaction. A benign-positive appraisal results in a positively toned emotional reaction, such as joy, exhilaration, love, contentment, relief. A stressful appraisal produces negatively toned emotions, such as anxiety, fear, anger, guilt, envy, jealousy, disgust. Each emotional quality and intensity has its own appraisal pattern (see also Beck, 1971). Anxiety, for example, involves an anticipated harm (threat) that is ambiguous, either as to what is to happen or what can be done about it, and is, compared with fear, largely symbolic (Lazarus & Averill, 1972).

Primary appraisal also involves the possibility of feedback from changes in the person-environment relationship and from reflection as the transaction proceeds, thus potentially allowing for changes in the quality and intensity of the emotion. I have called this cognitive activity *reappraisal*. A research example can be found in a study by Folkins (1970) in which experimental groups of subjects await an electric shock, each for a different period of time varying from 30 seconds to 20 minutes. Their intrapsychic processes were later reconstructed through interviews. Psychophysiological stress reactions were found to differ in magnitude depending on the duration of the waiting period, being highest at about one minute, lowest at three and five minutes, then rising again when the time period for waiting was 20 minutes. The interview evidence suggested strongly that this variation depended on what subjects thought about during the waiting period. For example, one minute was long enough for the subject to assimilate the threatening idea that he was going to feel pain when the shock came, but not long enough to develop doubts about the threat. However, if the subject had five minutes to think about it, he began to reflect on or reappraise the situation, saying to himself, for example, "A college professor surely would not expose me to severe pain," or "I have had shock before from a laboratory inductorium and it was hardly anything to worry about." At 20 minutes, the dimensions of the problem seemed to change. Subjects commonly began to feel anxious, perhaps thinking that so long a wait must portend something of major import. Throughout life we are constantly appraising and reappraising encounters with respect to their relevance and meaning. This is one reason why emotions are always in flux from moment to moment, changing both in intensity and quality depending on how the changing portents of the situation are being "read" by the person.

At this writing I have come across a tragic instance of the appraisal and reappraisal processes that illustrates well how they can work. A 45-year-old woman was supposed, after shopping, to meet her husband and daughter at home to go to a local ball game. On the way home she passed a scene of an auto accident to which she paid little attention, and on arrival home, discovered that her husband was not there. For some reason she felt impelled, with some apprehension, to go back to the scene of the accident with her daughter. On first passing the accident she had apparently noticed marginally that the color of the car was the same as that of her husband's. As soon as she and her daughter arrived at the scene of the accident it was clear that it was, indeed, her husband's car. An ambulance had already taken him away. Even though the policemen at first did not mention it, and although the car did not seem badly damaged, somehow she understood that he was already dead. He had had a heart attack. In retrospect she observes that what gave her the clue was that the policemen seemed in no hurry to do anything, or even to get the wife and daughter to the hospital. In effect, it was all over, and without anything having been said she knew this from the manner in which people were acting.

Here we see an interesting series of appraisal and reappraisal processes based on situational cues. Without knowing more about the person, we cannot identify the personal dispositions and knowledge that might also have shaped the cognitive activity. We do not know, for example, whether she had any intimation of his cardiovascular vulnerability. There was the initial marginally registered recognition that the car in the accident was the color of her husband's. When she had arrived home and her husband, usually a prompt man, was not yet there, the earlier, casual recognition now took on new salience—the accident could have happened to her husband. On arrival, and confirming that it was, indeed, her husband's car, she did not have to be told that he was already dead because of the behavior of the people at the scene of the accident. Further talk could only confirm what she already knew. The whole incident involves, in addition to any emotion felt, a series of appraisals and reappraisals as the events unfolded. A new set of appraisals, particularly related to coping with bereavement, eventually would be set in motion by the discovery of her husband's untimely death.

Secondary Appraisal

Primary appraisal concerns the significance of a transaction for well-being, a question of "Is there anything at stake here?" If the answer is that "I am in jeopardy," that is, facing harm/loss, threat, or challenge, a key adaptational process is called into being, namely, *coping*. Whether consciously and deliberately, or unconsciously and automatically, a decision is made about what to do. Since most important stressful transactions are comprised of numerous specific encounters stretching out over time, as in grieving, in bolstering damaged or threatened self (or social) esteem, or in managing chronic interpersonal difficulties, the person needs information about personal and social resources which can be drawn upon, the adequacy of fit between one or many types of coping and the stressful demands, and the possibility that new problems will be created by coping activities. Obviously, all this requires a set of complex cognitive appraisal processes devoted to coping decisions. I have called these cognitive appraisal processes *secondary appraisal* to distinguish their function of evaluating coping options and resources from primary appraisal functions. A fuller account of this may be found in Lazarus and Launier (1978), in which various types of secondary appraisal are illustrated and their consequences for action indicated.

In a dynamic, time-oriented cognitive system such as I am describing, secondary appraisal and primary appraisal processes are interdependent, and even seem to fuse. Their only difference consists of the contents to which they are addressed. For example, to the extent that one identifies a coping course of action that has a high likelihood of success in overcoming a harm, mastering a threat, or being equal to a challenge, primary appraisal of threat is itself changed. One is no longer greatly threatened when it is realized that a potential harm is readily preventable. On the contrary, if a search for information on which to predicate adaptive action turns up little or nothing, or leads to the conviction that there is nothing to be done, threat is apt to be greatly enhanced, and the options for coping are evaluated accordingly.

One can see such a dynamic interplay in the gradual discovery that an illness is not merely a minor breast cyst but a malignant tumor. Surgical removal may once again alter the intensity of the threat, but later evidence of new growthlike symptoms elsewhere alters the threat appraisal a third time, and if this growth turns out to be metastatic, options for mastery of the illness are now severely curtailed, leading to a greatly enhanced sense of injury and threat, and greater reliance may have to be placed on intrapsychic coping processes of denial, efforts to preserve hope, and efforts at acceptance than on actions to change the situation through action.

The concept of cognitive appraisal troubles some because it appears circular—that is, known only after the fact, by inference or by self-report. That is untrue. When I first discussed this concept (Lazarus, 1966), I pointed out that, as with any psychological process, the determinants of appraisal lie in the interaction of the environmental situation and person variables. A number of possible environmental factors probably contribute to appraisal, including the imminence of harm, its ambiguity (cf. Folkman et al., 1979), the power of the environmental demands to do harm, and the duration of the demands. With respect to duration, for example, chronic stress seems more likely to result in gastric ulcers than acute stress (Mahl, 1952, 1953), and there is much evidence that the hormonal and psychological responses to stress also depend on the chronic-acute distinction (Gal and Lazarus,

1975). Among person-centered determinants, two are particularly important: general and specific beliefs about oneself and the environment, and the pattern and strength of values and commitments.

This is not the place to give additional details on the determinants of appraisal, nor is our knowledge of them great. It is important to point out, however, that the mediating concept of cognitive appraisal is fully capable of cause-and-effect research on its determinants, and to emphasize what is often forgotten in actual research, that it is the interaction of both sets of determinants, person and environment, which determines whether a transaction will be appraised as irrelevant, benign-positive, or stressful, and if the last, then whether harm/loss, threat, or challenge.

Coping

In my view, stress itself as a concept pales in significance for adaptation compared with *coping*. As noted elsewhere (Roskies and Lazarus, 1979), stress is ubiquitous, an inevitable feature of normal living, though some persons do indeed experience more frequent, severe, or sustained stressful encounters than others. What makes the major difference in adaptational outcome is coping, and so we should give special attention to it in our research on human functioning. I will first deal with the main functions of coping, then, in order, offer a rough classification of coping modes.

Functions of coping.   One major difference I have with the cognitive behavior therapists, such as Albert Ellis (1962), with writers on coping, such as Haan (1977), and with the traditional psychiatric approach, is that I do not assume that the best coping is necessarily realistic, although I am convinced that coping must be flexible. If, as Ellis does, one assumes that the pathology of emotional life rests on false or irrational assumptions or beliefs about life, then therapy must try to make such beliefs realistic, and coping must ultimately be predicated on accurate testing of reality. I agree, of course, that actions to change a troubled relationship with the environment are often of crucial importance to the outcome, especially so in anticipatory coping under conditions in which there is some possibility of evading or preventing the harmful confrontation. However, there are many encounters in which little or nothing can be done even when one has obtained all the available information about a problem. Under such conditions, living optimally or even adequately requires that we tolerate a high degree of ambiguity, or even that we engage in some self-deception (cf. Hamburg and Adams, 1967). Therefore, to the problem-solving or the instrumental function of coping, we must add another important function, in a sense the antithesis of instrumentality—namely, the self-regulation of emotional distress.

Two major functions of coping must therefore be considered: first, to change the situation for the better if we can, either by changing one's own offending action (focus on self) or by changing the damaging or threatening environment; and second, to manage the somatic and subjective components of stress-related emotions themselves, so that they do not get out of hand and do not damage or destroy morale and social functioning. These functions are not always contradictory, but when they are, there is danger of maladaptation. For example, we make ourselves feel better in the face of harm or threat by such palliative modes of coping as denying, intellectualizing (achieving detachment), avoiding negative thoughts, or taking drugs (e.g., alcohol, pain killers, and tranquilizers). Although these make us feel better, they do not change the actual person-environment relationship. Under certain conditions, when it does not countermand needed adaptive actions, this may help greatly.

For example, in the study cited above by Cohen and Lazarus (1973) on coping with surgical threat, avoidance-denial modes of coping were associated with better postsurgical outcomes than vigilance. Given the circumstances of being hospitalized, there is no evident value in vigilance because there is no action available to master the problem of recovering. On the other hand, research by Katz, Weiner, Gallagher, and Hellman (1970) reveals the other side of this issue: palliative coping obstructed or delayed actions required to protect people against serious illness. They observed that one of the most common ways women coped with the threat of having discovered a breast lump was a pattern of avoidance-denial which resulted in delay in seeking medical evaluation. If the growth was malignant, excessive delay could result in metastasis and a much poorer medical outlook. Similarly, Hackett and Cassem (1975) observed men who, during symptoms of a heart attack, did vigorous pushups or ran up and down some flights of stairs, on the reasoning that they could not be having a heart attack because the exercise did not kill them. These men were trying to feel better psychologically (palliation) at the expense of taking the adaptive action of getting medical attention. As it turned out, they were, indeed, having a heart attack and they did survive, but the coping process clearly endangered their lives.

The two functions of coping—problem-solving and regulation of emotional distress (palliation)—have been commented on by many writers (e.g., Kaplan, Cassel, and Gore, 1973; Mechanic, 1962; Parsons and Bales, 1955; Pinneau, 1976). Although they are sometimes in opposition, especially when the palliative function preempts adaptationally necessary actions, often one supports the other. For example, if one is not too distressed in an examination or a performance before an audience (because of use of a tranquilizer or engaging in some intrapsychic process that lowers the anxiety), performance can be much improved or at least less impaired. Furthermore, actions that resolve the person-environment problem—say, by preventing the harmful confrontation or compensating for an injury—also reduce or eliminate emotional distress. It is a worthwhile working assumption that, despite our society's value preference for reality testing and direct action, effective copers typically engage in forms of coping that achieve both of these functions, and that effective copers use both direct actions and palliative coping modes.

Coping modes. In a recent treatment of coping (Lazarus and and Launier, 1978), four main coping modes were identified, each serving both problem-solving and emotion-regulatory functions, each capable of being oriented to the self or the environment, and each concerned with either past or present (harm/loss) or future (threat or challenge). The four modes are: information-seeking, direct action, inhibition of action, and intrapsychic processes.

Information-seeking involves scanning the characteristics of a stressful encounter for knowledge needed to make a sound coping decision or to reappraise the damage or threat. In addition to providing a basis of action (problem-solving function), information-seeking can also have the function of making the person feel better by rationalizing or bolstering a past decision (Janis, 1968; Janis and Mann, 1977). Ironically, this palliative function is contrary to the assumptions usually made about decision-making by information-processing researchers (cf. Folkman et al., 1979). Palliation often calls for ignoring the negative implications of what one knows or of information one receives or seeks. Moreover, the regulation of emotional distress often requires accepting ambiguity (the obverse of information) as a natural feature of living. At times such ambiguity or uncertainty is even a balm rather than a source of anxiety.

Anything one does (except cognitively) to handle stressful transactions falls within the rubric of *direct action*. Such actions are as diverse as the environmental demands and personal goals people have to manage, including expressing anger, seeking revenge, fleeing, suicide, building storm shelters, taking medication, jogging to preserve one's health, etc. The list is virtually unlimited. Direct coping actions can also be aimed at the self or the environment, since either is potentially capable of being changed, thereby altering the stressful person-environment relationship for the better. The action can be aimed at overcoming a past injury—as when a grieving person becomes buried in work or seeks a new love relationship—or at a future danger. In the light of their great importance in human adaptation, too little attention has been devoted to anticipatory coping actions.

It may seem strange to cite *inhibition of action* as a coping mode, since it implies inaction, but effective coping often calls more for holding back action impulses that will do harm than taking action that poorly fits the requirements of a transaction. In a complicated social and intrapsychic world, every type of action is capable of coming into conflict with moral, social, or physical constraints and dangers, and choice is possible only if strong natural impulses to act (as in anger and fear) can be held back in the interest of other values.

All the cognitive processes designed to regulate emotion—in

effect, the things a person says to himself or herself, as it were—
are included in *intrapsychic modes*, making this, too, a highly
varied category. Not only does it encompass self-deceptive mechanisms or defenses, such as denial, reaction formation, and projection, but it also includes avoidance and efforts to obtain detachment or insulation (as in isolation, undoing, and intellec-
tualization) from a threat to achieve a feeling of control over it.
These modes are mostly palliative in that they make the person
feel better by reducing or minimizing emotional distress. As in
the case of the other coping modes, they can be oriented to the
past, as in the reinterpretation of a traumatic event, or to the
future, as in the denial that one is in danger. They can also be
focused on the self ("I am not inadequate or evil"), or on the
environment ("This situation is not dangerous").

❖
SUMMARY OF IMPLICATIONS FOR THE STUDY OF HUMAN FUNCTIONING

It only remains now to point out the implications of this stress
and coping paradigm for research on human functioning. These
implications, and others, are already embedded in this paper, but
it will help the reader keep them in mind to touch briefly on
each of the major implications once more, this time separated
from the paradigmatic system from which they arise.
❖
    As I see it, there are at least seven important implications of
what I have said for the study of human functioning. They follow
briefly:
    1. Stress per se cannot be regarded simplistically as causal in
human maladaptation, because it generates a variety of coping
processes and, in turn, is as much a product of inept coping as of
environmental demands or stressors (cf. Lazarus and Cohen,
1977). Therefore, it is not fruitful to blame pathology strictly
on stress, except perhaps in extreme situations of environmental
deprivation and human cruelty in which little or no opportunity
is allowed for the development or utilization of effective coping.
One example would be the concentration camp (Dimsdale, 1980),
wherein coping could have little or nothing to do with survival;
that depended heavily on luck and other factors outside the per-

son's control. From the perspective of this paper, to relate stress to maladaptation requires emphasis not so much on stressors as on the cognitive and coping processes mediating the reaction.

2. The view presented here is that the greatest need is for naturalistic research on stress and coping. Such research, however, should not be limited to the clinical context of psychopathology and treatment, but should seek knowledge about the day-to-day stresses as well as positive experiences of ordinary people and those who function optimally, and about how such people cope. There are serious conceptual and empirical dangers connected with an exclusive reliance on the context of pathology or dysfunction, the most serious of which is the tendency to equate effective functioning with accurate reality testing, and to underestimate the value of palliative modes of coping, and positive emotions. Even if one doubts the validity of this assertion, it cannot be evaluated without intensive studies of coping patterns in normal and optimally functioning persons and groups.

3. In such research much more attention should be given to pure theoretical description of the transactions of a person with the environment. In the recent past, description has taken a back seat to cause-and-effect research on determinants (interaction), with the result that we do not know how to describe and measure the fundamental processes whose determinants we also need to identify. We have virtually no process measures of coping and other transactional concepts, such as threat and challenge.

4. With respect to causal determinants of human dysfunction, the transactional perspective shifts our attention from strictly endogenous or intrapsychic variables and processes to exogenous ones. The important Freudian discoveries of unconscious, intra-psychic processes and their impact on thought, feeling, and action also got clinicians frozen into the study of internal processes exclusively, but we now cycle back toward a recognition of the important role played by environmental influences in adaptation and maladaptation. Indeed, it would hardly be suitable to cycle back and forth between either extreme from one period to another. The separation of personality from social psychology is an unfortunate consequence of this either/or pattern in thought and research. Transaction implies the somewhat banal conclusion that we must look at both, though the banality is somewhat

mitigated by the fact that mainly lip service has been given to so obvious a conclusion in actual research and theory.

5. Explanation of and research on human functioning more often should include three levels of analysis: the social, psychological and physiological simultaneously, without reductionism and without the perennial and mistaken tendency to use measurement at one level to stand for events at another level. Only when these levels are simultaneously examined can the principles of their relationships be explored. Studied correctly, the mechanisms of psychosomatic disease, and the links between social system and psychological processes, can be identified. Maladaptation always reflects some form of poor fit between the person (psychologically and physiologically) and the social system, and all levels contribute to a full account of human functioning.

6. Two research styles can be profitably combined in the study of human functioning. One of these (normative) selects large representative cohorts of persons chosen through survey methods and categorized on the basis of social or personality variables of interest to us. In stress research such variables include patterns of life change, daily hassles, cognitive appraisals of these, beliefs, commitments, etc. The second style involves study of a single individual or a few individuals over time or across various life circumstances requiring coping and adaptation. We need an in-depth look at the individual as he or she struggles with the tasks of living, and as the processes unfold that will ultimately determine the adaptive outcome in respect to somatic health, morale, and social functioning.

Survey or assessment approaches are designed to identify very general properties of persons, giving us little or no real chance to observe how a resourceful, flexible individual reacts in a variety of adaptive transactions in a changing environment. They are designed for representativeness and economy—we measure what we want to know in one or two limited testing or survey sessions. If such approaches worked ideally or even well in providing us with a reasonably complete portrait of the person, or with an accurate prediction of how he or she reacts emotionally or copes with the conditions of life that must be faced, there would be no inherent problem with structurally oriented strategies. The economy would, in fact, then be very welcome. However, when we want to construct a working portrait of the stresses to which an individual or class of persons is exposed, modes of coping, and the stability and variation of these processes, there are severe limitations to a nomothetic and survey-oriented approach.

The alternative of studying a single individual or several persons is also unacceptable by itself, since it does not allow us to generalize to others with any assurance. Intensive or in-depth study of many individuals over time and across diverse life situations is very costly. A compromise, however, could permit us to study sufficient numbers of subjects and at the same time give us the in-depth information we should need to describe and analyze the processes of stress and coping. In such a compromise the strategy of large cohorts and survey methods for statistical analysis could be retained, while at the same time selecting limited subsamples for more intensive study. Research designs should be ipsative as well as normative—that is, the individuals studied intensively would be observed time and time again, over many life contexts and encounters. By such ipsative or repeated study of the same individuals, the ongoing processes involved in reacting to and coping with stressful transactions—those leading to health/illness, effective/impaired social functioning, and high/low morale—could be examined as they were taking place. In addition, intensive study could capitalize more fully on the advantages of the human relationship between subject-participant and researcher, encouraging more candor and self-examination, as well as the use of clinical skills to infer defenses, ambivalences, and hidden neurotic agendas.

7. Finally, although I have said little about it, the proper study of human functioning requires the evaluation of such functioning. We must be able to indicate how well a coping pattern used by the person facilitates survival and helps him or her to flourish, or is in some sense counterproductive. To intervene in prevention, treatment, or education in the interests of aiding the development of coping effectiveness and social competence means that we have some notions and evidence about the strategies that are effective and the ones that are ineffective. The answer may vary with the kind of person, the context, or the situation, and depend on our values about health and pathology. Optimal functioning might mean that all three categories of adaptational outcome—namely, social functioning, morale, and somatic health—be in harmony in the ideal case. The trouble is that some coping strategies may work

well for one value—say, morale—but poorly in generating effective instrumental actions. Or an individual's coping actions might provide maximum mileage in getting along or succeeding socially and occupationally, but cost greatly in somatic health. Until we are in a better position to evaluate such matters in varying types of persons and situations, we will be operating almost blindly in our intervention efforts, whether these be directed at prevention, treatment, or education. Although there are plenty of ideas about such matters, they are not well bolstered by empirical observations because little research is being mounted today along these lines. Correcting this state of affairs is more easily said than done.

At the present time no author of a paradigm for theory and research on human functioning has reason to crow loudly. We need to seek innovative approaches and travel pathways not well trodden in the past. There is no single stress and coping paradigm, and certainly not one on which there is substantial agreement. I would like to believe that I have described here a meaningful conceptual analysis and a workable set of methodological principles that could and should be tried out and ultimately judged heuristically.

REFERENCES

Allport, G. W. The general and the unique in psychological science. *Journal of Personality*, 1962, *30*, 405–422.

Altman, I. Environmental psychology and social psychology. *Personality and Social Psychology Bulletin*, 1976, *2*, 96–113.

Arnold, M. *Emotion and personality* (2 vols.). New York: Columbia University Press, 1960.

Arnold, M. (Ed.). *Feelings and emotion*. New York: Academic Press, 1970.

Bandura, A. Self-efficacy: Toward a unifying theory of behavioral change. *Psychological Review*, 1977, *84*, 191–215.

Beck, A. T. Cognition, affect and psychopathology. *Archives of General Psychiatry*, 1971, *24*, 495–500.

Berne, E. *Games people play*. New York: Grove, 1964.

Bolles, R. C. Cognition and motivation: Some historical trends. In B. Weiner (Ed.), *Cognitive views of human motivation*. New York: Academic Press, 1974.

Bower, E. M. Mythologies, realities, and possibilities in primary prevention. In G. W. Albee and J. M. Joffe (Eds.), *Primary prevention of psychopathology, Vol. 1: The issues*. Hanover: University Press of New England, New England, 1977.

Broverman, D. M. Normative and ipsative measurement in psychology. *Psychological Review*, 1962, *69*, 295–305.

Bukowski, C. *Mockingbird wish me luck*. Los Angeles: Black Sparrow Press, 1972.

Byrne, D. The repression-sensitization scale: Rationale, reliability and validity. *Journal of Personality*, 1961, *29*, 334–349.

Byrne, D. Repression-sensitization as a dimension of personality. In B. A. Maher (Ed.), *Progress in experimental personality research* (Vol. 1). New York: Academic Press, 1964.

Carlson, R. Where is the person in personality research? *Psychological Bulletin*, 1971, *75*, 203–219.

Carlson, R. Personality. In M. R. Rosenzweig and L. W. Porter (Eds.), *Annual Review of Psychology*, 1975, *26*, 393–414.

Cassel, J. Psychosocial processes and "stress": Theoretical formulations. *International Journal of Health Services*, 1974, *4*, 471–482.

Child, I. L., and Waterhouse, I. K. Frustration and the quality of performance: II. A theoretical statement. *Psychological Review*, 1953, *60*, 127–139.

Clark, M. M. The anthropology of aging, a new area for studies of culture and personality. *The Gerontologist*, 1967, *7*, 55–64.

Cohen, F., and Lazarus, R. S. Active coping processes, coping dispositions, and recovery from surgery. *Psychosomatic Medicine*, 1973, *35*, 375–389.

Cronbach, L. J. The two disciplines of scientific psychology. *American Psychologist*, 1957, *12*, 671–684.

Cronbach, L. J. Beyond the two disciplines of scientific psychology. *American Psychologist*, 1975, *30*, 116–127.

Dember, W. N. Motivation and the cognitive revolution. *American Psychologist*, 1974, *29*, 161–168.

Dimsdale, J. E. (Ed.). *Survivors, victims and perpetrators: Essays on the Nazi holocaust*. Washington, D.C.; Hemisphere, 1980.

Dollard, J., and Miller, N. E. *Personality and psychotherapy*. New York: McGraw-Hill, 1950.

Easterbrook, J. A. The effect of emotion on cue utilization and the organization of behavior. *Psychological Review*, 1959, *66*, 183–201.

Eibl-Eibesfeldt, I. *Ethology: The biology of behavior* (trans. E. Klinghammer). New York: Holt, Rinehart, and Winston, 1970.

Ellis, A. *Reason and emotion in psychotherapy*. New York: Lyle Stuart, 1962.

Epstein, S., and Fenz, W. D. The detection of areas of emotional stress through variations in perceptual threshold and physiological arousal. *Journal of Experimental Research in Personality*, 1967, *2*, 191–199.

Erikson, E. H. The problem of ego identity. *Journal of the American Psychoanalytic Association*, 1956, *4*, 58–121.

Folkins, C. H. Temporal factors and the cognitive mediators of stress reaction. *Journal of Personality and Social Psychology*, 1970, *14*, 173–184.

Folkman, S., Schaefer, C., and Lazarus, R. S. Cognitive processes as mediators of stress and coping. In V. Hamilton and D. M. Warburton (Eds.), *Human stress and cognition: An information processing approach*. London: Wiley, 1979.

Frankl, V. *The doctor and the soul*. New York: Knopf, 1955.

Frankl, V. *Man's search for meaning*. New York: Washington Square Press, 1963.

Gal, R., and Lazarus, R. S. The role of activity in anticipating and confronting stressful situations. *Journal of Human Stress*, 1975, *1*, 4–20.

Gergen, K. J. Stability, change, and chance in understanding human development. In N. Datan and H. W. Reese (Eds.), *Life-span developmental psychology: Dialetical perspectives on experimental research*. New York: Academic Press, 1977.

Goldfried, M. R. Anxiety reduction through cognitive-behavioral intervention. In P. C. Kendall and S. D. Hollon (Eds.), *Cognitive-behavioral interventions: Theory, research, and procedures*. New York: Academic Press, 1979.

Haan, N. *Coping and defending*. New York: Academic Press, 1977.

Hackett, T. P., and Cassem, H. Psychological management of the myocardial infarction patient. *Journal of Human Stress*, 1975, *1*, 25–38.

Hackett, T. P., and Weisman, A. D. Reactions to the imminence of death. In G. H. Grosser, H. Wechsler, and M. Greenblatt (Eds.), *The threat of impending disaster*. Cambridge: The MIT Press, 1964.

Hamburg, D. A., and Adams, J. E. A perspective on coping: Seeking and utilizing information in major transitions. *Archives of General Psychiatry*, 1967, *17*, 277–284.

Herd, J. A. *Cardiovascular correlates of psychological stress*. Paper presented at Conference on the Crisis in Stress Research, Boston, October 20–22, 1977.

Hinkle, L. E. The concept of "stress" in the biological and social sciences. *Sciences, Medicine, and Man*, 1973, *1*, 31–48.

Holt, R. R. Individuality and generality in the psychology of personality. *Journal of Personality*, 1962, *30*, 377–404.

Janis, I. Stages in the decision-making process. In R. Abelson, E. Aronson, W. McGuire, T. Newcomb, M. J. Rosenberg, and P. Tannenbaum (Eds.), *Theories of cognitive consistency: A sourcebook*. Chicago: Rand McNally, 1968.

Janis, I., and Mann, L. *Decision making*. New York: The Free Press, 1977.

Kaplan, B. H., Cassel, J. C., and Gore, S. *Social support and health*. Paper presented at American Public Health Association Meetings, San Francisco, November 9, 1973.

Katz, J. L., Weiner, H., Gallagher, T. G., and Hellman, L. Stress, distress, and ego defenses. *Archives of General Psychiatry*, 1970, *32*, 131–142.

Klausner, S. Z. *On man in his environment*. San Francisco: Jossey-Bass, 1971.

Klein, G. S. (Ed.). *Assessment of human motives*. New York: Holt, Rinehart, and Winston, 1958.

Klein, G. S., and Schlesinger, H. Where is the perceiver in perceptual theory? *Journal of Personality*, 1949, *18*, 32–47.

Klinger, E. Consequences of commitment to and disengagement from incentives. *Psychological Review*, 1975, *82*, 1–25.

Kuhn, T. S. *The structure of scientific revolutions*. Chicago: University of Chicago Press, 1970.

Lazarus, R. S. *Psychological stress and the coping process*. New York: McGraw-Hill, 1966.

Lazarus, R. S. The concepts of stress and disease. In L. Levi (Ed.), *Society, stress and disease* (Vol. 1). London: Oxford University Press, 1971.

Lazarus, R. S. Psychological stress and coping in adaptation and illness. *International Journal of Psychiatry in Medicine*, 1974, *5*, 321–333.

Lazarus, R. S. A strategy for research on psychological and social factors in hypertension. *Journal of Human Stress*, 1978, *4*, 35–40.

Lazarus, R. S., and Averill, J. R. Emotion and cognition: With special reference to anxiety. In C. D. Spielberger (Ed.), *Anxiety: Current trends in theory and research* (Vol. 2). New York: Academic Press, 1972.

Lazarus, R. S., Averill, J. R., and Opton, E. M., Jr. Toward a cognitive theory of emotion. In M. B. Arnold (Ed.), *Feelings and emotions*. New York: Academic Press, 1970.

Lazarus, R. S., and Cohen, J. B. *The study of stress and coping in aging*. Paper presented at the 5th WHO Conference on Society, Stress and Disease: Aging and Old Age, Stockholm, June 14–19, 1976.

Lazarus, R. S., and Cohen, J. B. Environmental stress. In I. Altman and J. F. Wohlwill (Eds.), *Human behavior and the environment: Current theory and research* (Vol. 1). New York: Plenum, 1977.

Lazarus, R. S., Cohen, J. B., Folkman, S., Kanner, A., and Schaefer, C. Psychological stress and adaptation: Some unresolved issues. In H. Selye (Ed.), *Guide to stress research*. New York: Van Nostrand Reinhold, 1980. (*a*)

Lazarus, R. S., Deese, J., and Osler, S. F. The effects of psychological stress upon performance. *Psychological Bulletin*, 1952, *49*, 293–317.

Lazarus, R. S., Kanner, A. D., and Folkman, S. Emotions: A Cognitive-phenomenological analysis. In R. Plutchik and H. Kellerman (Eds.), *Theories of emotion*. New York: Academic Press, 1980. (*b*)

Lazarus, R. S., and Launier, R. Stress-related transactions between person and environment. In L. Pervin and M. Lewis (Eds.), *Perspectives in interactional psychology*. New York: Plenum, 1978.

Lorenz, K. *King Solomon's ring*. New York: Crowell, 1953.

Luborsky, L., Docherty, J. P., and Penick, S. Onset conditions for psychosomatic symptoms: A comparative review of immediate observation with retrospective research. *Psychosomatic Medicine*, 1973, *35*, 187–204.

Mahl, G. F. Relationship between acute and chronic fear and the gastric acidity and blood sugar levels in macada mulatta monkeys. *Psychosomatic Medicine*, 1952, *14*, 182–210.

Mahl, G. F. Physiological changes during chronic fear. *Annals of the New York Academy of Science*, 1953, *56*, 240–249.

Mahoney, M. Cognitive therapy and research: A question of questions. *Cognitive Therapy and Research*, 1977, *1*, 5–17.

Mandler, G. *Mind and emotion*. New York: Wiley, 1975.

Marceil, J. C. Implicit dimensions of idiography and nomothesis: A reformulation. *American Psychologist*, 1977, *32*, 1046–1055.

Mason, J. W. Specificity in the organization of neuroendrocrine response profiles. In P. Seeman and G. M. Brown (Eds.), *Frontiers in neurology and neuroscience research: First International Symposium of the Neuroscience Institute*. Toronto: University of Toronto Press, 1974.

Mason, J. W., Maher, J. T., Hartley, L. H., Mougey, E. H., Perlow, M. J., and Jones, L. G. Selectivity of corticosteroid and catecholamine responses to various natural stimuli. In G. Serban (Ed.), *Psychopathology of human adaptation*. New York: Plenum, 1976.

Mechanic, D. *Students under stress*. New York: The Free Press of Glencoe, 1962.

Meichenbaum, D. *Cognitive-behavior modification: An integrative approach*. New York: Plenum, 1977.

Moos, R. H. Psychological techniques in the assessment of adaptive behavior. In G. V. Coelho, D. A. Hamburg, and J. E. Adams (Eds.), *Coping and adaptation*. New York: Basic Books, 1974.

Parsons, T., and Bales, R. F. *The family: Socialization and interaction process*. Glencoe, Ill.: The Free Press, 1955.

Pearlin, L. I. Status inequality and stress in marriage. *American Sociological Review*, 1975, *40*, 344–357.

Pervin, L. A. Performance and satisfaction as a function of individual-environment fit. *Psychological Bulletin*, 1968, *69*, 56–68.

Pinneau, S. F., Jr. *Effects of social support on occupational stresses and strains*. Paper presented at American Psychological Association Convention, Washington, D. C., September 1976.

Riegel, K. F. Time and change in the development of the individual and society. In H. W. Reese (Ed.), *Advances in child development and behavior* (Vol. 7). New York: Academic Press, 1972.

Riegel, K. F. (Ed.). *The development of dialectical operations*. Basel: Karger, 1975.

Roskies, E., and Lazarus, R. S. Coping theory and the teaching of coping skills. In P. Davidson (Ed.), *Behavioral medicine: Changing health life styles*. New York: Brunner/Mazel, 1979.

Schaller, G. B. *Year of the gorilla*. Chicago: University of Chicago Press, 1964.

Skinner, B. F. *The behavior of organisms*. New York: Appleton-Century-Crofts, 1938.

Smelser, N. J. *Theory of collective behavior*. New York: The Free Press of Glencoe, 1963.

Spence, J. A., and Spence, K. W. The motivational components of manifest anxiety: Drive and drive stimuli. In C. D. Spielberger (Ed.), *Anxiety and behavior*. New York: Academic Press, 1966.

Stahl, S. M., Grim, C. E., Donald, S., and Neikirk, H. J. A model for the social sciences and medicine: The case for hypertension. *Social Science and Medicine*, 1975, *9*, 31–38.

Tinbergen, N. *The study of instincts.* New York: Oxford University Press, 1951.

Van Lawick-Goodall, J. *In the shadow of man.* New York: Dell, 1971.

Vogel, W., Raymond S., and Lazarus, R. S. Intrinsic motivation and psychological stress. *Journal of Abnormal and Social Psychology,* 1959, *58,* 225–233.

Washburn, S. L., and DeVore, I. The social life of baboons. *Scientific American,* 1961, *204,* 62–71.

Weisman, A. D. *On dying and denying.* New York: Behavioral Publications, 1972.

White, R. W. Motivation reconsidered: The concept of competence. *Psychological Review,* 1959, *66,* 297–333.

Willems, E. P., and Raush, H. L. *Naturalistic viewpoints in psychological research.* New York: Holt, Rinehart, and Winston, 1969.

Yerkes, R. M., and Dodson, J. D. The relation of strength of stimulus to rapidity of habit formation. *Journal of Comparative and Neurological Psychology,* 1908, *18,* 459–482.

Protective Factors in Children's Responses to Stress and Disadvantage

Michael Rutter

There is a regrettable tendency to focus gloomily on the ills of mankind and on all that can and does go wrong. It is quite exceptional for anyone to study the development of those important individuals who overcome adversity, who survive stress, and who rise above disadvantage. It is equally unusual to consider the factors or circumstances that provide support, protection, or amelioration for the children reared in deprivation. This neglect of positive influences on development means that we lack guides on how to help deprived or disadvantaged children. It is all very well to wish for the children to have a stable, loving family which provides emotional support, social stability, and cognitive stimulation. But we are almost never in a position to provide that. All we can do is alleviate a little here, modify a little there, and talk to the child about coming to terms with his problems. On the whole, the benefits that follow our therapeutic endeavors are pretty modest in the case of severely deprived children. Would our results be better if we could determine the sources of social competence and identify the nature of protective influences? I do not know, but I think they would. The potential for prevention surely lies in increasing our knowledge and understanding of the reasons why some children are *not* damaged by deprivation. My purpose in this paper is to consider some of the very limited evidence so far available on the topic.

Among children in Britain today about one in six live in conditions of extreme social disadvantage characterized by poverty *and* poor housing *and* family adversity (Wedge and Prosser, 1973). Nearly half of these children are well adjusted, one in seven has some kind of outstanding ability, and one in eleven shows above average attainment in mathematics. Thus, in spite of profound social deprivation, some of these children not only develop adequately but are well above average in their educational attainments.

Even in a deprived neighborhood, it is unusual for a child to suffer the constellation of disadvantages of parental criminality, bad child-rearing, poverty, low intelligence, and large family size (West and Farrington, 1973, 1977). Yet, of the children who do experience all these sources of risk, over a quarter show no evidence of any kind of delinquent or antisocial behavior as assessed in multiple ways on several occasions during a longitudinal study.

It is difficult to imagine the dreadful stresses experienced by youngsters who are brought up by mentally disturbed parents with a lifelong personality disorder whose marriages show extreme discord, hostility, and disruption. Everything appears against them, but a proportion of such children developed normally without any evidence of disorder at any time during the course of an intensive four-year longitudinal study (Rutter, Quinton, and Yule, 1977).

The three studies I have quoted all placed great emphasis on the severe risks for later psychosocial development which attend being brought up in grossly deprived or disadvantaged family circumstances. Their research findings provide ample evidence of the extent of the risks. Children who suffer in this way are much more likely than other children to develop psychiatric disorder, become delinquent, or remain educationally retarded. Nevertheless, as the figures I have quoted illustrate, some children do come through unscathed. This is a phenomenon shown by all investigations, but it has been systematically studied only rarely. In particular, although various writers have drawn attention to the importance of coping skills in children at risk and their resistance to stress (e.g. Hersov, 1974; Murphy, 1962; Garmezy, 1974; Anthony, 1974; Rutter, 1974, 1977a), there have been very few attempts to determine why and how some children appear relatively invulnerable.

❖

INTERACTIVE EFFECTS BETWEEN STRESSES

The first point to make is the very great importance of interactive effects. We tend to overlook their importance because several stresses so often come together, and most research data are not analyzed in such a way as to reveal the cumulative and inter-active effects of single stresses. The usual approach is to take account of intercorrelations between variables by some form of statistical regression or standardization procedure. The resulting comparison shows whether or not a particular stress still has an effect after taking into account its associations with other forms of stress or disadvantage. However, it is necessary to appreciate that while the result shows whether the stressor has an effect over and above that of other factors, it does not show whether the stressor has an effect when it occurs entirely on its own.

We looked at this point in relation to the data collected in the Isle of Wight and inner London epidemiological studies (Rutter et al., 1975a, 1975b) of 10-year-old children. First, we identified six family variables all of which were strongly and significantly associated with child psychiatric disorder: (1) severe marital dis-cord; (2) low social status; (3) overcrowding or large family size; (4) paternal criminality; (5) maternal psychiatric disorder; and (6) admission into the care of the local authority (Rutter and Quinton, 1977). Next we separated out families which had none of these risk factors, those with only one risk factor, those with two, and so on. We then compared these groups in terms of the rates of psychiatric disorder in the children.

The results, summarized in Figure 1, were interesting and sur-prising. The children with just one risk factor—that is, those with a truly isolated stress—were no more likely to have psychiatric dis-order than children with no risk factors at all. It appeared that even with chronic family stresses the children were not particularly at psychiatric risk so long as it was really a single stress on its own. On the other hand, when any two of the stresses occurred together, the risk went up no less than fourfold. With yet more concurrent stresses, the risk climbed several times further still. In other words, the stresses *potentiated* each other so that the combination of chronic stresses provided very much more than a summation of the effects of the separate stresses considered singly.

These findings refer to interactions between chronic stresses. It appears that much the same thing may also apply to acute stresses. In the same set of studies we examined the long-term effects of hospital admission. We found, as had Douglas (1975) previously, that there were no detectable long-term sequelae of *single* admissions to hospital regardless of the age at which they

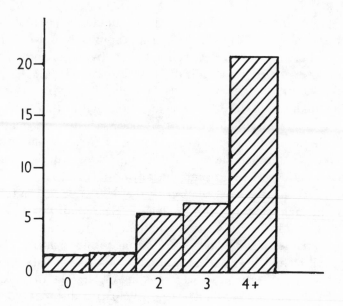

Figure 1. Multiplicity of Risk Factors and Child Psychiatric Disorder

occurred (Quinton and Rutter, 1976). On the other hand, we found, as had Douglas, that *multiple* hospital admissions were associated with a substantially (and significantly) increased risk of psychiatric disorder in later childhood.

This finding is of interest from several points of view. First, it demonstrates the greatly increased effects of a cumulation of stresses. One hospital admission did no long-term harm, but two admissions were damaging. An interaction effect again. Secondly, there were two quite different types of associations between chronic stresses and hospital admission. On the one hand, children from deprived and disadvantaged families were more likely to *have* multiple admissions to hospital. In other words, the presence of chronic family stress meant that the children were more likely to experience a series of multiple acute stresses during development. Sameroff (1975) has called this a transactional effect.

On the other hand, there was also a potentiating or interaction effect. Not only were children from disadvantaged homes more likely to have multiple admissions, they were also more likely to suffer from the long-term adverse effects. In other words, children from more favored homes were less likely to develop psychiatric disorder following multiple admissions. It seemed that a favorable home environment exerted a protective effect in relation to the stresses of recurrent hospitalization.

GENETIC EFFECTS

Another kind of interaction is seen in connection with hereditary or genetic influences. There is good evidence that genetic factors play a significant role in determining individual differences in personality characteristics and intelligence (Shields, 1973 and 1977). Sometimes this effect is interpreted as meaning that we can do little to influence development by manipulation of the environment. Of course this is wrong, because environmental variables in fact also account for a good deal of the variance. However, it is also wrong for a more interesting reason. It appears that one of the ways in which genetic factors operate is through an influence on responsiveness to environmental stresses. This effect was suggested in our own studies by the finding that the children most likely to be damaged by the effects of severe family discord were those whose parents had a lifelong personality disorder (Rutter, 1971). However, our data did not allow a clear distinction between genetic and environmental influences. The interaction between the two was shown more clearly in the recent studies of adopted and fostered children by Hutchings and Mednick (1974) and by Crowe (1974).

Hutchings and Mednick (1974) use a naturally occurring cross-fostering design to study criminality. They found that when the adoptive father was criminal but the biological father was not, the rate of criminality in the offspring was no higher than when neither the biological nor the adoptive father had a crime record. In contrast, when the biological father had a criminal record but the adoptive father did not there was a twofold increase in criminality among the children. This difference clearly points to a biological genetic effect (presumably on personality traits rather than on crime as such). On the other hand, the highest rate of criminality in the children was found when *both* the adoptive father and the biological father had a crime record. In this case the rate of criminality showed a three-and-a-half-fold increase. The implication is that the environmental stress of having a criminal adoptive father had no significant effect in individuals who were not genetically predisposed. But in those persons who were genetically susceptible, by virtue of having a criminal biological father, the environmental stress had a very considerable impact. It seems then that environmental factors have their greatest effect on people who are genetically vulnerable.

Much the same was shown in Crowe's (1974) study of 46 children of female offenders who had given up their babies for adoption. The group was compared with an appropriately matched control group. Again, a genetic effect was shown. Also, however, within the group of those who were presumably genetically vulnerable as a result of having a criminal mother (who had not reared them), the development of antisocial problems was related to various adverse experiences in early life. This environmental effect was not found in the control group, again suggesting that genetic endowment had acted in part by rendering the children more vulnerable to environmental traumata.

It is difficult to obtain a really clean differentiation of genetic and environmental influences, and both studies have limitations. The numbers were too small to examine interaction effects reliably and the findings fell short of statistical significance. It is therefore particularly necessary that the findings be replicated. Even so, the results certainly imply that the extent to which individuals are likely to be damaged by stressful experiences is determined in part by genetic factors which influence how they adapt and respond to their environment.

INDIVIDUAL DIFFERENCES: TEMPERAMENT AND SEX

It should be added that constitutional factors also help determine how the environment responds to the individual. That seems a curious and paradoxical thing to say, but it is true nevertheless. What I mean is that the way all of us respond to another person is determined to a considerable extent by what the other person is like. This has been shown in several quite different studies of adult-child interaction (see Rutter, 1977b). For example, adults' behavior is much influenced by the child's level of spoken language (Moerk, 1974), by his level of nutrition (Chavez et al., 1974), and by his dependency (Osofsky and O'Connell, 1972). Our own studies looked at temperamental characteristics (Graham et al., 1973) which we found to be strongly associated with the later development of psychiatric disorder. One of the ways they exerted their effect was by modifying the child's experiences. Even in quarrelsome and discordant homes, the temperamentally easy child tended to avoid much of the negative interchange. When parents are depressed and irritable they do not take it out on all their children to the same extent: often, one is more or less scape-goated. The target child tends to be the temperamentally difficult one. We found that children with adverse temperamental charac-teristics were twice as likely as other children to be the target of parental criticism (Rutter, Quinton, and Yule, 1977). Altogether, then, it seems that the kinds of social environments experienced by children is determined in part by their personal characteristics. In this way genetic variables to some extent shape environments. These findings are in accord with Sameroff's (1975) transactional model.

One other personal variable that requires mention is sex. It has usually been found that boys are more likely than girls to be damaged by family discord and disruption (Rutter, 1970; Wolkind and Rutter, 1973). It is well established that males are more vul-nerable to physical stresses; and they appear in some respects to be also more susceptible to psychosocial traumata. One protective factor in stress circumstances, it seems, is to be a girl! But the relative invulnerability of girls does not apply to all stresses. For example, girls are equally likely to suffer from the ill effects of an institutional upbringing (Wolkind, 1974). Moreover, the sex dif-ference is abolished when there is gross damage to the brain (Rutter, Graham, and Yule, 1970; Shaffer et al., 1975). Little is known about why boys and girls seem to respond differently to deprivation and disadvantage (Rutter, 1970); the topic requires much further study.

Let me summarize the findings so far. The first point is the importance of interaction effects in the cumulation of stresses; this implies that it may be of considerable value to eliminate some stresses, even if others remain. Second, with at least some aspects of development, environmental traumata are most damaging to genetically vulnerable individuals. That is, the presence of a genetic predisposition makes it more important—not less so—to do everything possible to improve environmental circumstances. Third, there are marked individual differences (with respect to both sex and temperament) in how children respond to deprivation or disadvantage. While we have only a very limited understanding of how these individual differences exert their influences, one effect seems to be that they shape other people's responses to the children. Accordingly, their impact on other persons is potentially modifiable and relevant to programs dealing with the primary prevention of psychopathology.

INFLUENCES OUTSIDE THE HOME

So far I have largely focused on patterns of adverse factors. It is time now to turn attention to the modifying effect of positive influences or protective factors. The first observation to make is that children's development is shaped by experiences outside the home as well as by those inside the family. The school environment has been shown to be particularly important. Obviously, education is influential with respect to scholastic attainment, but here I am concerned rather with schools as social institutions which have an impact on children's behavior and emotional development.

Many studies in Britain have shown wide variations between schools on all sorts of measures of behavior: absenteeism, delinquency, teacher ratings of behavior, psychiatric referrals, and even patterns of employment after leaving school (Power et al., 1967, 1972; Reynolds and Murgatroyd, 1974; Reynolds et al., 1976; Gath et al., 1977; Rutter et al., 1975b). For example, Gath et al. (1977) found that mean annual delinquency rates in nonselective secondary schools varied from 4 to 152! In an entirely different area, Reynolds et al. (1976) showed a variation from 3.8 to 10.5. It is clear that the differences between schools are large and important. The question arises, however, whether the differences reflect the differing influence of schools or whether they are merely an artefact of variations in the proportion of difficult or disturbed children admitted to the schools.

In our own studies we tackled that problem by assessing the behavior and attainments of an entire age cohort of 10-year-old children in the year before they transferred to secondary school

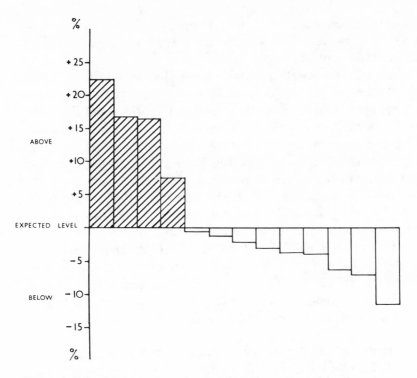

Figure 4. School delinquency rates in relation to expected level

and then following them over the next 7 years during their time at secondary school. A variety of behavioral measures were obtained using observations in the school, teacher ratings, police records, school attendance registers, and interviews with the children themselves. Because we had systematic assessments of the children's behavior before they entered secondary school, we could determine statistically what each school's level of disturbance might be expected to be on the basis of their intake. We could then observe whether schools were doing better or worse than expected on any of the outcome measures. Substantial school variations remained even after controlling for differences in intake, as shown in Figure 4 with respect to delinquency. The *expected* delinquency rate per school varied between 11 percent and 18 percent, whereas the *observed* rates ranged between 0 percent and 35 percent—from 11 percent below expectation to 22 percent above expectation. Some schools that had rather high proportions of children who had shown behavioral deviance in primary school, nevertheless had rather low delinquency rates. Good schools can and do exert an important protective effect.

Obviously the next questions are, What makes for a good school? and, What can schools do to ensure that they facilitate the normal development of children from deprived and disadvantaged homes? It is clear that the answers do not lie in such factors as size, staff-pupil ratio, or quality of buildings. Rather, the crucial differences are to be found in the atmosphere of the schools and their qualities as a social institution. So far we lack the data to be more precise about what that means in actuality, but it may soon be possible to take the matter a little further. We are now nearing the end of an intensive comparative study of 12 schools known to differ in their effects on children. During the last two and a half years, we have made detailed assessments of all aspects of school life, interviewing staff and pupils, observing in the classroom and the playground, and making use of records of all kinds. Analysis of this large amount of data is currently under way.

In adult life, work may be the equivalent of school. Brown et al. (1975) found that women in full- or part-time employment were less likely than those without jobs to become depressed following severe acute stresses or major chronic difficulties. It appeared that employment had a protective function. Why it did so is more difficult to determine. It could be through improved economic circumstances, the alleviation of boredom, an increase in social contacts, an enhanced sense of personal worth, or a variety of other mechanisms. According to Brown et al. (1975), the women's comments suggested that a sense of achievement might be crucial. If this is so, presumably different jobs vary in how far they lead to satisfaction and self-esteem. This is another topic worth further study.

SELF-ESTEEM

My own interest in the possible importance of self-esteem in childhood was much increased by the findings of the Isle of Wight survey (Rutter, Tizard, and Whitmore, 1970). Two results stood out in this connection. First, there was the observation, based on behavioral information from both parents and teachers, that highly intelligent children were less likely to show behavioral deviance than children of average intelligence. Second, it was found that children of average intelligence with specific reading retardation had a much increased rate of conduct disorders. We suggested that children who do not learn to read lost confidence in themselves, failed to maintain normal self-esteem, and reacted with antagonism and sometimes delinquency. Our findings and those of other investigations (Varlaam, 1974) pointed to the psychiatric vulnerability of children with low scholastic attainments. In the present context, however, the question is how far superior attainments serve to protect children from psychiatric disorder in the presence of family stress or adversity.

We were able to examine this question in the epidemiological study of 10-year-old children in inner London (Rutter et al. 1975a and 1975b; Berger et al., 1975), where we had measures of scholastic attainment, children's behavior and psychiatric state, and family functioning. In both cases the rates of disorder are considerably less among children of above average attainment. Good scholastic attainment appears to have a protective effect even after the children's family circumstances have been taken account of. These findings refer to children's behavior in the classroom, but the pattern is much the same with assessments of the child's behavior at home. The only difference is that, for obvious reasons, the effects of family adversity are relatively greater and the effects of reading skills relatively less.

These results, however, do not necessarily mean that the protective effect is mediated through high self-esteem and a sense of achievement. Maybe it is just that the more intellectually able children are constitutionally more resilient.

STRUCTURE AND CONTROL

One of the striking features of most studies of multiproblem families is the chaotic state of their patterns of supervision and discipline. Moreover, poor supervision has been one of the common antecedents of delinquency in most investigations (West and Farrington, 1973; Glueck and Glueck, 1959). Less attention has been paid to the converse: that is, the extent to which good supervision and well balanced discipline can serve to protect children from a high risk background. Wilson's (1974) findings from a study of severely disadvantaged families suggest that it warrants further exploration. She found that, in conditions of chronic stress and poverty, strict parental supervision of the children's activities was more effective in preventing delinquency than was a happy family atmosphere. As Wilson points out, some of the supervision was merely part of good parenting with a sensible setting of limits and a reasonable set of expectations; some, on the other hand, appeared intrusive and restrictive, but even so, it seemed to have benefits in terms of preventing delinquency. Strict supervision was what seemed of value—not extreme punitiveness.

Of course, there are many unanswered questions. In the first place, the findings should be replicated before they form the basis of policies. In the second place, outcome was assessed only in terms of delinquency, so that the costs in other aspects of development remain unknown. Nevertheless, children probably need a degree of structure and control, and it may be (as Wilson suggests) that this is more important in conditions of severe deprivation, chaos, and uncertainty. At any rate, the possibility deserves study. The same issue arises with respect to schooling, and that is one of the aspects of school life we are investigating in our study of 12 schools.

BONDS AND RELATIONSHIPS

Much of the research on maternal deprivation (Rutter, 1972) has concentrated on the ill effects of impaired, broken, or deviant family relationships. Accordingly, it seems appropriate to look at the other side of the coin and examine the possibility that one good relationship might serve as a protective function at times of deprivation, stress, or disadvantage. There are several studies of children in institutions suggesting that a stable relationship with an adult (not necessarily the parent) is associated with better social adjustment (Conway, 1957; Pringle and Bossio, 1960; Pringle and Clifford, 1962; Wolkind, 1974).

In our own studies we investigated the matter in connection with children brought up by their own families. The sample consisted of children with at least one parent who had been under psychiatric care, and the rate of discord and disharmony in these families was high. In order to study the possibly protective effect of one good relationship, we focused on children who were living in severely quarrelsome, discordant, unhappy homes. From these we isolated children who had a good relationship with one parent — defined in terms of both the presence of high warmth and the absence of severe criticism. These children were then compared to those who did not have a good relationship with either parent (see Figure 6). We found that a good relationship did indeed provide quite a substantial protective effect. Of the children with a good relationship only a quarter showed a conduct disorder, compared with three-quarters of those lacking such a relationship. Whether close and harmonious relationships with someone outside the immediate family could have a similar protective effect is not known; this should be studied in the future.

We do know from other work (Rutter, 1972 and 1977c) that children develop bonds and attachments to a variety of people other than their two natural parents. The findings suggest that these bonds have the same psychological effect in spite of persistent differences in their strength. The matter requires further investigation, but from the evidence to date it seems likely that the protective effect will prove to depend more on the quality, strength, and security of the relationship than on the particular person with whom the relationship happens to be formed.

The next question is how far good relationships and family harmony continue to serve the same protective effect at all stages in the child's development. This may be examined from several points of view. In our longitudinal study of the family of mentally ill parents (Rutter, 1971) we studied the effects of new-found family harmony in later childhood by focusing on children who had been separated from their parents in early childhood as a result of family discord or severe family problems. Within this group, all of whom had experienced marked family stress and disharmony, we compared two subgroups: those still living in homes characterized by discord and disharmony, and those who were now in harmonious, happy homes. As shown in Figure 7, conduct disorders were much less frequent among the children now experiencing good family relationships. A change for the better in family circumstances was associated with a marked reduction in psychiatric risk for the child.

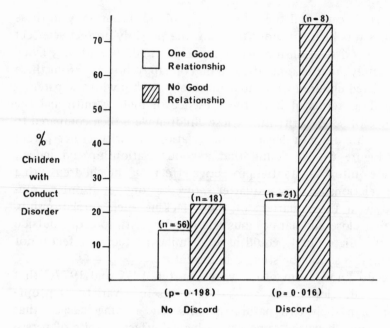

Figure 6. 'Protective' effect of at least one good relationship

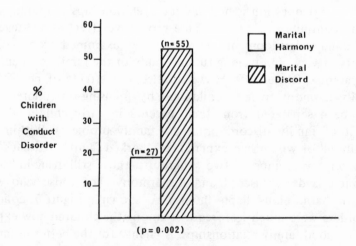

Figure 7. 'Protective' effect of improved family circumstances in children with stressful separations when young.

A different approach was followed by Brown and his colleagues (1975) in their studies of depression among women. They found that severe-stress events played an important role in the genesis of depression but also that stresses were significantly less likely to lead to depression when the woman had a close, intimate, and confiding relationship with someone (usually her husband). An intimate relationship served as a powerful protective factor. Interestingly, both frequency of contact with other people and practical support were not protective. It was a close confiding relationship which seemed to be important.

Another issue, too, concerns the importance of a child's early bonding. Children who are reared in institutions from infancy tend to experience a very large number of caretakers, none of whom lasts long enough to allow the formation of an enduring bond with the child. As shown by the studies of both Tizard (Tizard and Rees, 1975; Tizard and Hodges, 1977) and my colleague, Dixon (1977), such children are less likely to show deep ties and more likely to show disturbed social behavior at school, compared with children reared in ordinary families. An important question examined by Tizard (Tizard and Hodges, 1977) is how far adoption *after* these early years can make up for what was previously missing in close interpersonal relationships. What she found was very interesting. Compared with the children who remained in institutions or those who returned to a deprived home environment, the adopted children had generally done well in terms of their behavior at home. The great majority of them had formed close ties with their adoptive parents and they showed no more problem behavior than controls. To that extent even late adoption had made up for earlier lacks and had facilitated normal development. On the other hand, teachers reported high rates of socially disruptive behavior among the adopted as well as among the institutional children. Both tended to be attention-seeking, disobedient, restless, and unpopular. Dixon's (1977) observations of institutional children in the classroom confirmed the teachers' reports. Although the children are still only 8 years old and it is far too early to judge their final social development, the results so far suggest that whereas late adoption helps, it does not make up for the lack of early bonding. In spite of a currently good home environment, the adopted children still showed social problems which were linked with their early years in institutional care.

It seems, then, that warm close personal relationships have a powerful protective effect at all ages through childhood and into adult life. At the same time, it may well be that although later relationships can build on earlier bonds, initial bonding must still take place in early childhood if there are not to be later social deficits.

COPING SKILLS

The last variable I wish to mention is coping skills. Some years ago Lois Murphy (1962) emphasized the importance of children learning to cope with the variety of new situations they encounter as they grow up. She noted the link between mastery over the environment on the one hand and self-pride, esteem, and pleasure in life on the other. White (1967), similarly, has pointed to the role of competence and mastery in normal social development. It is relevant, too, that adaptability and malleability are among the chief temperamental characteristics which protect against psychiatric disorder in childhood (Rutter et al., 1964; Graham et al., 1973).

In spite of this, there has been very little direct attempt to study the importance of children's coping skills in dealing with acute or chronic stresses. Their possible relevance is suggested by the Stacey et al. (1970) study of children's responses to hospital admission. They found that children who had had brief normal separation experiences (such as staying overnight with friends or relatives, having baby sitters, attending nursery school, or being left all day with a familiar person) were less likely than other children to show behavioral disturbance in hospital. The finding needs to be replicated, but it appears that brief, graded separations in happy circumstances can help protect children from the stresses of later unhappy separations. The mechanisms remain uncertain. In part it is likely to be a reflection of the situation being a less strange one because these children are already used to a variety of environments other than their family homes. In part, too, it may be that they are less distressed by the separation because they have already learned from previous separations that their parents always return. In this way, their uncertainty and feeling of loss are likely to be less than those of children separated for the first time. In a sense, all of this can be thought of as learning to cope with separations. Presumably there must be coping skills of both similar and different kinds which can be acquired and which apply to other forms of stress. Such skills have yet to be identified but coping mechanisms certainly deserve further study.

CONCLUSIONS

The exploration of protective factors in children's responses to stress and disadvantage has only just begun. We are nowhere near the stage when any kind of overall conclusions can be drawn. What is clear, though, is that there is an important issue to investigate. Many children do *not* succumb to deprivation, and it is important that we determine why this is so and what it is that protects them from the hazards they face. The scanty evidence so far available suggests that when the findings are all in, the explanation will probably include the patterning of stresses, individual differences caused by both constitutional and experiential factors, compensating experiences outside the home, the development of self-esteem, the scope and range of available opportunities, an appropriate degree of environmental structure and control, the availability of personal bonds and intimate relationships, and the acquisition of coping skills.

REFERENCES

Anthony, E. J. The syndrome of the psychologically invulnerable child. In E. Anthony and C. Koupernick (Eds.), *The child in his family*. Vol. 3, *Children at psychiatric risk* (New York: Wiley, 1974), pp. 529–544.

Aronson, E., and Mettee, D. R. Dishonest behavior as a function of differential levels of induced self-esteem. *Journal of Personality and Social Psychology*, 1968, *9*, 121–127.

Berger, M., Yule, W., and Rutter, M. Attainment and adjustment in two geographical areas. II. The prevalence of specific reading retardation. *British Journal of Psychiatry*, 1975, *126*, 510–519.

Brown, G. W., Bhrolchain, M. N., and Harris, T. Social class and psychiatric disturbance among women in an urban population. *Sociology*, 1975, *9*, 225–254.

Chavez, A., Martinez, C., and Yaschine, T. The importance of nutrition and stimuli on child mental and social development. In J. Cravioto, L. Hambracus, and B. Vahlquist (Eds.), *Early malnutrition and mental development*. Symposia of the Swedish Nutrition Foundation. Stockholm: Almquist and Wilksell, 1974.

Conway, E. S. *The institutional care of children: A case history*. Unpublished Ph.D. thesis, University of London, 1957.

Coopersmith, S. *The antecedents of self-esteem*. San Francisco: W. H. Freeman and Co., 1967.

Crowe, R. R. An adoption study of antisocial personality. *Archives of General Psychiatry*, 1974, *31*, 785–791.

Dixon, P. Unpublished data. 1977.

Douglas, J. W. B. Early hospital admissions and later disturbances of behaviour and learning. *Developmental Medicine and Child Neurology*, 1975, *17*, 456–480.

Garmezy, N. The study of competence in children at risk for severe psychopathology. In E. Anthony and C. Koupernick (Eds.), *The child in his family*. Vol. 3, *Children at psychiatric risk* (New York: Wiley, 1974), pp. 77–98.

Gath, D., Cooper, B., Gattoni, F., and Rockett, D. *Child guidance and delinquency in a London Borough*. Institute of Psychiatry. Maudsley Monograph No. 24. London: Oxford University Press, 1977.

Glueck, S., and Glueck, E. *Predicting Delinquency and Crime*. Cambridge: Harvard University Press, 1959.

Graham, P., Rutter, M., and George, S. Temperamental characteristics as predictors of behavior disorders in children. *American Journal of Orthopsychiatry*, 1973, *43*, 328–339.

Hersov, L. Introduction: Risk and mastery in children from the point of view of genetic and constitutional factors and early life experience. In E. J. Anthony and C. Koupernick (Eds.), *The child in his family*. Vol. 3, *Children at psychiatric risk* (New York: Wiley, 1974), pp. 67–76.

Hutchings, B., and Mednick, S. A. Registered criminality in the adoptive and biological parents of registered male adoptees. In S. A. Mednick et al. (Eds.), *Genetics, environment, and psychopathology*. Amsterdam: North-Holland, 1974.

Jahoda, M. *Current concepts of positive mental health*. New York: Basic Books, 1959.

Moerk, E. Changes in verbal child-mother interactions with increasing language skills of the child. *Journal of Psycholinguistic Research*, 1974, *3*, 101–116.

Murphy, L. B., and associates. *The widening world of childhood: Paths toward mastery*. New York: Basic Books, 1962.

Offer, D., and Sabshin, M. *Normality: Theoretical and clinical concepts of mental health*. New York: Basic Books, 1966.

Osofsky, J. D., and O'Connell, E. J. Parent-child interaction: Daughters' effects upon mothers' and fathers' behaviors. *Developmental Psychology*, 1972, *7*, 157–168.

Power, M. J., Alderson, M. R., Phillipson, C. M., Schoenberg, E., and Morris, J. N. Delinquent schools? *New Society*, 1967, *10*, 542–543.

Power, M. J., Benn, R. T., and Morris, J. N. Neighbourhood, school and juveniles before the courts. *British Journal of Criminology*, 1972, *12*, 111–132.

Pringle, M. L. K., and Bossio, V. Early prolonged separations and emotional adjustment. *Journal of Child Psychology and Psychiatry*, 1960, *1*, 37–48.

Pringle, M. L. K., and Clifford, L. Conditions associated with emotional maladjustment among children in care. *Educational Review*, 1962, *14*, 112–123.

Quinton, D., and Rutter, M. Early hospital admissions and later disturbances of behavior: An attempted replication of Douglas' findings. *Developmental Medicine and Child Neurology*, 1976, *18*, 447–459.

Reynolds, D., Jones, D., and St. Leger, S. Schools do make a difference. *New Society*, 1976, *37*, 223–225.

Reynolds, D., and Murgatroyd, S. Being absent from school. *British Journal of Law and Society*, 1974, *1*, 78–81.

Rutter, M. Sex differences in children's responses to family stress. In E. J. Anthony and C. Koupernick (Eds.), *The child in his family*. Vol. 1, (New York: Wiley, 1970), pp. 165–196.

Rutter, M. Parent-child separation: Psychological effects on the children. *Journal of Child Psychology and Psychiatry*, 1971, *12*, 233–260.

Rutter, M. *Maternal deprivation reassessed*. Harmondsworth, England: Penguin, 1972.

Rutter, M. Epidemiological strategies and psychiatric concepts in research on the vulnerable child. In E. J. Anthony and C. Koupernick (Eds.), *The child in his family*. Vol. 3, *Children at psychiatric risk* (New York: Wiley, 1974), pp. 167–180.

Rutter, M. Early sources of security and competence. In J. S. Bruner and A. Garton (Eds.), *Human growth and development*. London: Oxford University Press, 1977. (a)

Rutter, M. Individual differences. In M. Rutter and L. Hersov (Eds.), *Child psychiatry: Modern approaches* (Oxford: Blackwell Scientific, 1977), pp. 3–21 (b)

Rutter, M. Maternal deprivation 1972–1977: New findings, new concepts, new approaches. Paper read at the Biennial meeting, Society for Research in Child Development, New Orleans, 16–20 March 1977. (c)

Rutter, M., Birch, H. G., Thomas, A., and Chess, S. Temperamental characteristics in infancy and the later development of behavioural disorders. *British Journal of Psychiatry*, 1964, *110*, 651–661.

Rutter, M., Cox, A., Tupling, C., Berger, M., and Yule, W. Attainment and adjustment in two geographical areas. I. The prevalence of psychiatric disorder. *British Journal of Psychiatry*, 1975, *126*, 493–509. (a)

Rutter, M., Graham, P., and Yule, W. *A neuropsychiatric study in childhood*. Clinics in Developmental Medicine 35/36. London: Heinemann/SIMP, 1970.

Rutter, M., and Madge, N. *Cycles of disadvantage*. London: Heinemann Educational, 1976.

Rutter, M., and Quinton, D. Psychiatric disorder: Ecological factors and concepts of causation. In H. McGurk (Ed.), *Ecological factors in human development*. Amsterdam: North-Holland, 1977.

Rutter, M., Quinton, D., and Yule, B. *Family pathology and disorder in children*. London: Wiley, 1977.

Rutter, M., Tizard, J., and Whitmore, K. (Eds.). *Education, health and behaviour*. London: Longmans, 1970.

Rutter, M., Yule, B., Quinton, D., Rowlands, O., Yule, W., and Berger, M. Attainment and adjustment in two geographical areas. III. Some factors accounting for area differences. *British Journal of Psychiatry*, 1975, *126*, 520–533. (b)

Sameroff, A. J. Early influences on development: Fact or fantasy? *Merrill-Palmer Quarterly of Behavior and Development*, 1975, *21*, 267–294.

Sameroff, A. J. Concepts of humanity in primary prevention. In G. W. Albee and J. M. Joffe (Eds.), *Primary prevention of psychopathology*. Vol. I, *The issues* (Hanover, N.H.: University Press of New England, 1977), pp. 42–63.

Shaffer, D., Chadwick, O., and Rutter, M. Psychiatric outcome of localized head injury in children. In R. Porter and D. FitzSimons (Eds.), *Outcome of severe damage to the central nervous system*. Ciba Foundation Symposium 34 (new series). Amsterdam: Elsevier-Excerpta Medica-North Holland, 1975.

Shields, J. Heredity and psychological abnormality. In H. J. Eysenck (Ed.), *Handbook of abnormal psychology*, 2nd ed. London: Pitman Medical, 1973.

Shields, J. Polygenic influences. In M. Rutter and L. Hersov (Eds.), *Child psychiatry: Modern approaches*. Oxford: Blackwell Scientific, 1977, pp. 22–46.

Stacey, M., Dearden, R., Pill, R., and Robinson, D. *Hospitals, children, and their families: The report of a pilot study*. London: Routledge and Kegan Paul, 1970.

Tizard, B., and Hodges, J. The effect of early institutional rearing on the behaviour problems and affectional relationships of eight year old children. *Journal of Child Psychology and Psychiatry*, 1978, *19(2)*, 99–118.

Tizard, B., and Rees, J. The effect of early institutional rearing on the behaviour problems and affectional relationships of four year old children. *Journal of Child Psychology and Psychiatry*, 1975, *16*, 61–74.

Varlaam, A. Educational attainment and behaviour at school. *Greater London Intelligence Quarterly*, 1974, No. 29, December, pp. 29–37.

Wedge, P., and Prosser, H. *Born to fail?* London: Arrow Books, 1973.

West, D. J., and Farrington, D. P. *Who becomes delinquent?* London: Heinemann Educational, 1973.

West, D. J., and Farrington, D. P. *The delinquent way of life*. London: Heinemann Educational, 1977.

White, R. W. Competence and the growth of personality. *Science and Psychoanalysis*, 1967, *11*, 42–49.

Wilson, H. Parenting in poverty. *British Journal of Social Work*, 1974, *4*, 241–254.

Wolkind, S. N. Sex differences in the aetiology of antisocial disorders in children in long-term residential care. *British Journal of Psychiatry*, 1974, *125*, 125–130.

Wolkind, S. N., Kruk, S., and Chaves, L. P. Childhood separation experiences and psychosocial status in primiparous women: Preliminary findings. *British Journal of Psychiatry*, 1976, *128*, 391–396.

Wolkind, S. N., and Rutter, M. Children who have been "in care": An epidemiological study. *Journal of Child Psychology and Psychiatry*, 1973, *14*, 97–105.

Stresses and Strains in Adolescents and Young Adults

Gisela Konopka

❖ It is my thesis that the period of adolescence is as significant a period in life for the development of the total personality as are the first years in childhood.

It is a time of rebirth. It is sometimes questioned whether adolescence is purely an artificial concept born out of recent, urban western society. I find this questioning futile. Any division of the life cycle and the conceptualization of various age periods are artificial in the sense that we cannot separate them out, nor are they exactly the same in all cultures. Adulthood, old age, all such periods are different in different cultures. We must look at the life cycle, and the different environments and systems in which human beings grow up, and then try to understand what is specific about these periods.

To me—and here I differ from many textbook descriptions—adolescence does not represent merely a preparation for adulthood, nor should it be a no-man's land between childhood and adulthood. Adolescents are not just pre-adults, pre-parents, or pre-workers but human beings participating in their particular way in the activities of the world around them.

Adolescence is not a passage to somewhere but an important stage in itself, though all stages of human development connect with each other. There is an "adolescenthood."

The key experiences of adolescence (which always include stresses and strains) are certain *firsts* which need to be worked through. They may occur in different individuals at various times with varying intensity, and perhaps not *all* of them apply to every person, but they do exist.

It must be understood that no generalization about human beings ever applies exactly to any one person and that in working with people, we have to take a fresh look at the human being with whom we interact.

Some of the "firsts" of adolescence are:

Experiencing physical sexual maturity. A phenomenon particular to adolescence that never occurs again in the life of the individual is the process of *developing* sexual maturation, different from the state of *accomplished* sexual maturation. Biologically this is a totally new experience. Its significance is due both to its pervasiveness and to the societal expectations surrounding it. It creates in adolescents a great wonderment about themselves and a feeling of having something in common with all human beings. It influences all their relationships with one another, male or female. Entering this part of maturity also stimulates them to a new assessment of the world.

Experiencing withdrawal of and from adult benevolent protection. Along with the biological maturity attained in adolescence come varying degrees of withdrawal of, and from, the protection generally given to dependent children by parents or substitutes. We know that some young people were never protected, even as children; but whatever the degree of previous protection, the adolescent is moving out from the family toward interdependence (not independence, *inter*dependence) in three areas: (a) with peers his or her own generation; (b) with elders, but on an interacting or questioning level instead of a dependent level; and (c) with younger children, not on a play level but on a beginning-to-care-for-and-nurture level. This process of moving away from dependency creates tensions and emotional conflicts.

Consciousness of self in interaction. The development of self and the searching for self starts in childhood, but the intellectual and the emotional consciousness of self in interaction with others is a particular characteristic of adolescence. It is a time when personal meaning is given to new social experiences. Young people define for themselves what they are experiencing in their relationships with others. This is no longer done *for* them by adults, or, if it is done, it is questioned by most adolescents. The categories they used as children to figure out the world begin to break down. What may have been clear and explicable may suddenly become inexplicable. This makes for inner excitement, frightening yet enjoyable.

Reevaluation of values. Though the formation of values is a life-long developmental process, it peaks in adolescence. It is related to both thinking and feeling, and is influenced by human interaction. In our culture, where young people are likely to be exposed to a variety of contradictory values, questioning begins even in childhood. Adolescents engage in reevaluation of values that have been either accepted at an earlier age or simply rejected because of individual resistance. They move beyond simple perception (for example, "if I burn my hand, it hurts") to seeing things in a morally good or bad framework. They become moral philosophers concerned with "shoulds" and "oughts" and they may be subtle or outspoken about it. Value confrontations are inevitable in this age period. The young, because of their intensity, tend to be uncompromising. They may opt clearly for a thoroughly egalitarian value system, or they may give up and become cynics. They often are true believers and therefore feel deeply hurt when others do not accept their value system.

Becoming an active participant in society. Adolescents encounter their world with a new intellectual and emotional consciousness. They meet it less as observers who are satisfied with this role than as participants who actually have a place to fill. I see this wish to *participate* as a most significant "first" in adolescence. In the old, mostly European textbooks it appears as the adolescent quality of rebellion, and for years we have considered rebellion an inevitable attribute of adolescence. I think that this is true in authoritarian societies—and we are still, partially, an authoritarian society—but basically it is not rebellion that characterizes adolescence but an extraordinary new awakening to the fact that one must develop one's values, and not only by imitation. This is a terribly hard task and brings with it enormous stress.

Life Force. Adolescence is an age of extraordinary physical capacity, enormous life force. This is sometimes at variance with the emotional development, and that again makes for great strain. It is an age where the mood swings with utmost intensity from omnipotence to despair. Adolescents can go without sleep for a long time; they run, jump, dance. In one of our Youth Polls done by the Center for Youth Development and Research in which the subject of health was at issue, it became clear that adolescents define health as "activity and energy." One said, "I think I am healthy when I am able to walk and run and run around all day and not be tired." Another, "When you are energetic, lively, active, and not run down." And another, "When you are feeling strong and able to run and laugh."

Being *not* healthy is a total experience because of this extraordinary life force: One defined it, "I feel unhealthy when I don't feel like doing anything." And another, "It's when you feel like you don't cope with anything, or feel like you don't have anything to live for" (Hedin, Wolfe, Garrison, and Fruetel, 1977).

CONTENT AREAS OF LIFE SIGNIFICANT TO ADOLESCENCE

The major institutions in which adolescents move have begun to be the same all over the world. Cultures change rapidly. For example, the teenage Bedouin, until recently, had to develop predominantly within the extended family and handle stresses within this system. The boy's work environment was static in terms of its tasks, namely herding goats, but it was changing geographically because of the tribe's nomad existence. The girl had no decisions to make, only to obey. Yet today most of the Bedouin teenagers have to deal with a smaller family unit, with school, with a variety of work tasks, and with less nomadic movement. These changes impinge on both sexes.

The most significant institutions in adolescent life today are: (a) the family; (b) the school; (c) the place of work; and (d) the peer group.

The Family

It is a myth that North American young people do not care for the family. In every survey that the Center for Youth Development and Research has made, the yearning for close family ties emerges clearly.

❖

The major frustration for an adolescent within the family is to suffer the role of an inferior at an age when the wish to be taken seriously, and as an equal, is very intense. Frustrating experiences range from being treated "like a kid" to serious abuse. And additional frustration can result from the youth's keen awareness of problems between the parents. Younger children suffer deeply from strife between parents, but adolescents often feel they have to *do* something about it, that they have to take on the responsibility in the situation. I found again and again a deep resentment of divorce, and at the same time a feeling that the adolescent should have done something to prevent it. Also, adolescents, unlike younger children, begin to look to the future. Many expressed a wish to start a family, but also feared it.

The School

Some of the dynamics in the family apply as well to the relationship of the adolescent to school. Again, the strong sense of self comes in conflict with possible violation of the vulnerable self-integrity. The youth wants to be seen as an individual as expressed by the wishes: "There should be a one to ten ratio of teachers to students." "If the teachers understood the students better, they could help the students with their problems." They should treat young people "like adults, not like two-year-olds, unless students just don't cooperate. Discuss all material that will be tested. Make every effort to answer all questions. Do best to help each student by keeping classes smaller. Not like we are their slaves or workers, and they are the boss." "To understand that we are people too and not just dumb kids to whom they can attach a number" (Hedin, 1978).

There are other stresses in school. It is the place where students expect to learn. Adolescents in their own way begin to question whether they need what they learn. One expressed it this way: "Teach us things that will help us to live in the real world—life and health facts. These are the students' main interests. They should be able to decide what they need to learn along with what the teachers think they have to know" (Hedin, 1978).

School experience also includes the questioning of one's intellectual capacity. As students put it: "The students who get the most attention are the ones with special problems, the 'normal' ones get left alone."

The Place of Work

Many adolescents do work while in school, though others see it as part of the future. We found in our observations a generally strong work ethic. Two students expressed themselves: "looking forward to starting a job because it gives one a sense of responsibility." "Want to work . . . because we've trained for it for so long and we're anxious to start" (Hedin, Wolfe, Bush, and Fruetel, 1977). Contrary to popular assumption, adolescents felt a responsibility for the work they were doing. They frequently regretted not having an opportunity to work on something that would prepare them for a future career. Young people can rarely find work related to special interests. A 16-year-old volunteered to work in the Rape Center of the Attorney General's Office, and saw this as an opportunity not only for feeling significant at that particular time in her life, but also to find out what her specific interests would be. But a study done last summer on CETA jobs showed that usually adolescents felt frustrated because their jobs had no connection with their interests and were not realistic experiences.

The Peer Group

For adolescents the peer group is most important. In our culture this world exists within organized institutions and in informal encounters. School is seen by practically all adolescents as the major formal institution where they can find friends. But for others, school may mean the unpleasant strain or, for a variety of reasons, painful rejection by one's peers. Youth organizations may also provide friends along with very positive experiences.

The world of peers is the life blood of adolescence. Friendships with both sexes, intensified by growing sexual maturity, are exceedingly important—and complex; they demand decision-making about oneself, about others, about the present and the future. Decision-making is written large all through adolescence, and no decisions are more important than those of peer relationships.

How Do Human Beings in General Cope with Stresses and Strains?

All human beings have to deal with the stresses and strains of life. The answers to life's pain spontaneously range from withdrawal to violent attack on one's self or others. "Coping" means "dealing with." It is more than a reflex; it includes thinking and doing. When we talk about a person being able to cope with life's events, we are not using the term in a neutral sense. We are giving it a value-connected meaning. We do mean the capacity to withstand, to resist, to live through adversity without damage to one's own personality or to the personalities of others. It is important that we are clearly talking about a value judgment. We can cope with stress by denying it and then finally breaking under it, or by blaming others for it and making them miserable, or by demanding incessant support, or by fleeing into drugs or alcohol. We see those ways of "coping" as negative. We wish people to have the capacity to accept stress and strain as an inevitable part of life, to be able to acknowledge it, and then to work their way through it. We do not expect this of the infant. The infant responds to pain and frustration simply by expressing the hurt, by screaming. Increasingly, children learn to handle pain in various new ways, usually with the protective help of adults. This development of new ways, and the acknowledgment of what one can *do* about the stresses and strains, and accepting them as inevitable are the real business of life, and the development of philosophy. These adjustments never end. Only in old age is another ingredient, perhaps reassurance, added to the coping process, namely the knowledge that "it will not be so long anymore."

Coping in Adolescence

The coping process is most significant in adolescence. (A friend of mine said of youth, "They don't yet have anything in the bank," meaning that they have not yet experienced how to live through severe stress.) Because of stresses that are new and because of their intense life energy, adolescents often react to personal or institutional strain with extreme behavior. Some throw off the frustration of an unhappy love experience by totally denying it, by pretending that it never happened. Teachers know the "shrug of the shoulder kid," who seems to be untouched by anything. Some respond to frustration with physical violence. Zvi Eisikovits (1977) studied a number of violent teenage offenders in the State of Minnesota. He found that frequently the victim of violence was not the person who had frustrated the youth, but somebody related to that person whom the adolescent felt more capable of destroying. Adolescents' frustration and anger, and frequently the sense of being totally demeaned, become so overwhelming that sometimes they cannot cope with their emotional and physical revulsion in any way other than to destroy someone.

Despair about life's frustrating events leads to running away, drugs, and suicide. The second leading cause of death in adolescence in Minnesota was suicide (Minnesota Center for Health Statistics, 1975). Drugs and alcohol are frequently taken because of a sense of rejection at home or by a close friend. A 17-year-old said: "I sniffed paint, glue, mainly paint . . . I figure a lot of that happened when I was fighting with my parents" (Konopka, 1976, p. 104). Another said, "I take drugs when I get depressed or when I get upset or when I feel I can't handle a problem, or when I really got a bad problem on my mind" (Konopka, 1976, p. 106).

When there has been no experience dealing with serious life events, the doors seem closed and one cannot cope: "My boy friend, he didn't give me as much attention as I needed so I cut my wrists . . ." (Konopka, 1976, p. 97). And, "I am being pushed around from institution to foster home several times. What have you got to live for? No place to go—no place to stay where you are at? Nothing to want to get up in the morning for. I always feel lonely" (Konopka, 1976, p. 98).

Loneliness is the curse of humans at any time in life. In adolescence the need to have peers who can confirm your own value, and at least one adult whom you can trust, is very great. Loneliness presents a desperate strain then. During our survey of needs of adolescent girls, we often heard them quote a verse: "Loneliness is a silent jail, Without cellmates, parole, or bail" (Konopka, 1976, p. 98).

What are some of the positive ways of coping in adolescence? It rarely is a well thought-out philosophy, but we can speak of four means: (a) communication with contemporaries; (b) communication with adults who understand, often of "the grandparent generation"; (c) religion; and (d) creative expression of emotions, as in songs, poetry, and painting.

Communication with contemporaries. This means talking about one's problems, but also holding each other, crying together, dancing, and sexual relationships. All of these represent some form of coping with problems.

Communication with adults. The wish to find a willing ear of an adult and also to hear what the adult has to say (if he or she is not judgmental) is very great. Again and again, adolescents express a need to be listened to. Among the girls we interviewed, mothers were still the ones that they thought of most often as confidants and from whom they wanted help; if they could not get it from this source, the strain increased. Grandparents, or people of that age group, were often sought out because they seemed to be more patient and less judgmental. Adolescents seemed to understand well that one needs to talk about problems in order to deal with them. In fact, not communicating feelings to others was regarded by them as behavior harmful to one's health.

In general, young people do not consider going to professionals for help, partly because of their own overconfidence and partly because they distrust professionals. As one youth put it: "It's hard to tell your problems to a perfectly strange person. It's hard to let everything out" (Hedin et al., 1977). Adolescents often worry that doctors or nurses might not keep their problems confidential, might tell their parents.

The young person has a very specific difficulty in coping with serious problems, and for two reasons:

(a) They feel that there are many expectations laid upon them and that they will let people down if they do not live up to them.

(b) In spite of these expectations, they are treated as dependent children, and frequently cannot get services by themselves. The wish, for instance, to get medical care without having to go with their parents was expressed very frequently. For instance, the girl who has to cope with a pregnancy out of wedlock deals with an extraordinarily severe life problem. Yet even today she faces not only the problem of how to deal with her own body and the future of her child, but also with the hostility of the human environment. (I know there are exceptions, but this is still the rule.)

Religion. As either a traditional way of dealing with stresses and strains or as a new emotional experience, religion is on the increase among adolescents. The revival of fundamentalist religion and the popularity of various new sects among American youths express a need to deal with a life that is not always happy or satisfying. This renewal also represents an acceptance of authority, but from sources other than the ones with which they grew up.

A society that does not prepare children and young people early for thinking through a problem and making decisions, but considers obedience a higher value, is vulnerable to the embrace by its young of a dangerous authoritarianism.

Creative response. This seems to involve far more youth than we have ever assumed. Young people often keep it hidden. That may be due partly to the fact that art is considered erudite, and they cannot believe that they themselves can produce anything worthwhile, and partly because of impossibly high expectations laid upon them. For example, I found excellent poetry written by girls in delinquency institutions, but they hesitated to share it because the grammar and spelling were not perfect. Yet whether they shared this writing with others or not, for the young people themselves it was a very positive means of coping with frustration and loneliness.

Coping with institutions. When adolescents deal with institutional frustrations (as, for instance, school or correctional institutions) another form of coping is to cheat—a method well known among adults. It is a way of circumventing the source of strain to prevent any further hurt and this is done by "playing the games" that adults expect of them.

For instance, in institutions where constant group involvement or confrontation was the expected form of treatment, adolescents played the game of "involvement," "confrontation," or whatever was demanded and did so superbly. If individual "baring of the soul" was expected, they also knew how to do this. Adolescents are good actors, and they can cope with hurt by pretending to live up to almost any expectations. They know what they are doing. In one institution, a young man asked me cynically: "Well, what do you want me to be or to do, so that you can have success?" Part of their response is based on the philosophy of retaliation which makes it possible to live through frustration: "If teachers would treat us nicely and like adults, we would treat teachers the same way. With respect, etc. A famous saying, An eye for an eye and a tooth for a tooth. That's our philosophy for these questions, about teachers treating us and students treating teachers" (Hedin, 1978).

Help with Coping in Adolescents

It behooves the professional not only to understand, but to use this understanding to prevent illness or to enhance health. To prevent serious damage to the individual adolescent and achieve the human interaction necessary for positive quality of life in our society, we must draw conclusions on how to help young people deal with stress and strain.

We have to accept each specific stage of adolescence with its strength and its problems. The vigorous life force, the wide mood swings, the sense of omnipotence as well as despair—all have to be taken as reality to which one must say "yes." We do not want people to become immune to stress. We want people to be sensitive to whatever life brings, but to be able to cope with it. We therefore do not want to give them drugs to dull their senses. We do not want to develop people who expect life to be a rose garden and are therefore unable to accept imperfection. We should create for adolescents an environment that allows them to be *participating* members of society, so that they actively learn the reality of life. There are many tasks they can fulfill which will give them a sense of worth and accomplishment and strengthen them to work through stress. We must accept their mistakes and let them know it:

> You are now on your way, so of course all the mistakes are ahead—all the wonderful mistakes that you must and will make. No matter what the mistakes are that you must make, do not be afraid of having made them or making more of them. (Saroyan, 1943, p. 144)

We adults should also admit mistakes in daily life as well as in clinical encounters with youth. The notion of maturity as a kind of perfection does not help adolescents to learn to cope with life. They must know that coping is a never-ending struggle and that all of us at any time may fail to do it well.

We must let young people know reality not only with its joys but also with its problems. The fiction of a "life of happiness" raises expectations that sap the strength of people.

We have to consciously talk philosophy with young people from their earliest ages. It was a five-year-old with whom I had to discuss death as part of life when my own husband died. It would not have helped this child to develop the capacity to work through other problems in his life if I had put him off with generalities. We had to talk about what it meant to be dead, and also what it meant to keep people alive in memory, and how one gains strength by thinking of other people. Someone else might have discussed this in somewhat different terms. The major point I am making is that I had to work with this child on his level to talk through his own pain and mine as well as to learn about strength in human beings. In adolescence one truly needs to develop a philosophy of life. It should become the basis of thinking, action, and feelings. The sentimental search for a comforting religion that makes no demands arises partially out of experience with an adult world that does not share its problems. Some of us were still very young and comparatively close to adolescence when the unspeakable terror of the Nazi concentration camps and Holocaust came upon us. We could live through those experiences because we had arrived at a meaning in life. This was the basic help that made coping possible. An additional one for some came through their sense of inner creativity. I remember vividly the poetry I quoted in solitary confinement, poetry I had read and poetry I myself created, though there was no way of writing it down. Art and imagination are superb gifts provided for human beings, and we should develop them increasingly in our young people.

Finally, adults themselves will have to accept pain as an important part of life without glorifying it or purposely inflicting it. Yet we cannot let young people grow up thinking that one must avoid it. John Steinbeck wrote beautifully in one of his letters:

> we have learned no technique nor ingredient to take the place of anguish. If in some future mutation we are able to remove pain from our species we will also have removed genius and set ourselves closer to the mushroom than to God.
> (Steinbeck, 1975, p. 604)

I underline that I do no preach death, pain, and stress as ideals, but I see them as necessary ingredients in life; ingredients that cannot be seen merely as catastrophe but also as an opportunity to grow. We will help young people to cope if we form a truly supportive but not sentimental society. A 17-year-old writes it better than I can say it:

I am growing, world.
I am reaching and touching and stretching
and testing
And finding new things, new wonderful
Things.
New frightening things.
I'm just growing, world, just now.
I'm not tall, I'm not strong. I'm not
Right.
I'm just trying to be.
I'm a person, I'm me!
Let me test, let me try, let me reach,
Let me fly!
Push me out of my nest (but not too fast).

There is much I don't know.
There are things that I want—don't
hide me from the sight of the world.
Give me room give me time. There
are things I'm not frightened
To try.
Let me tumble and spring, let me go
Let me be. Wait and see. . . .
I am growing, world
Water me with wisdom of
Your tears.

(Konopka, 1976, p. 14)

REFERENCES

Brokering, B. *Requirements for healthy development of adolescent youth: With examples from a summer youth employment program* (Center for Youth Development and Research). Unpublished manuscript, University of Minnesota, 1978.

Eisikovits, Zvi C. *Youths committed to the State Department of Corrections of Minnesota for offenses against persons.* Unpublished doctoral dissertation, University of Minnesota, 1977.

Hedin, D., Wolfe, H., Garrison, K., and Fruetel, J. *Youth's views on health* (Minnesota Youth Poll, No. 3, Center for Youth Development and Research). Unpublished manuscript, University of Minnesota, 1977.

Hedin, D. *A poll of Eisenhower High School students on their views of the school's philosophy* (Minnesota Youth Poll, Center for Youth Development and Research). Unpublished manuscript, University of Minnesota, 1978.

Hedin, D., Wolfe, H., Bush, S., and Fruetel, J. *Youth's views on work* (Minnesota Youth Poll, No. 2, Center for Youth Development and Research). Unpublished manuscript, University of Minnesota, 1977.

Konopka, G. *The adolescent girl in conflict.* Englewood Cliffs, N.J.: Prentice-Hall, 1966.

Konopka, G. *Young girls: A portrait of adolescence.* Englewood Cliffs, N.J.: Prentice-Hall, 1976.

Minnesota Center for Health Statistics. *Minnesota health statistics.* Minneapolis, Minnesota,: Author, 1975.

Saroyan, W. *The human comedy.* New York: Pocket Books, 1943.

Steinbeck, J. *Steinbeck: A life in letters.* In E. Steinbeck and R. Wallsten (Eds.), New York: Viking Press, 1975.

Yevtushenko, Y. *Selected Poems* (R. Milner-Gulland and P. Levi, Eds. and trans.) New York: Dutton, 1962.

Marital Disruption as a Stressor

Bernard L. Bloom

❖ A very large proportion of psychopathology, particularly the milder forms, seems to be brought about as a consequence of psychological rather than biological factors, and a variety of psychological strategies for preventing emotional disorders are currently being developed and tested. The efforts fall into two major categories. First, and most common, are efforts to decrease people's vulnerability to specific stresses; second, considerably less common, are efforts to reduce these stresses at their source.

❖ In 1975 more than three million persons were directly involved in a legally defined marital disruption in the United States. There were over one million divorces during this time period, and in each divorce an average of 1.22 children. Thus, two million adults and over one million children were affected by divorce in a single year, representing 1½ percent of the total United States population (Glick, 1975; U.S. Bureau of the Census, 1974; and U.S. Department of Health, Education, and Welfare, 1976).

These figures might have little interest to any group other than demographers were it not for the growing body of evidence that marital disruption often constitutes a severe stress, the consequences of which can be seen in a surprisingly wide variety of physical and emotional disorders. Persons undergoing marital disruption have been shown to be at excess risk for psychiatric disorders, suicide, homocide, motor vehicle accidents, and a variety of forms of disease morbidity and disease mortality (see Bachrach, 1975; Bloom, Asher, and White, Note 1).

❖ In considering the research studies linking marital disruption to physical and emotional disorders, it would be useful to keep in

This paper draws on material copyrighted by the American Psychological Association and published in the *Psychological Bulletin*. Permission to make use of this material is gratefully acknowledged.

mind four general hypotheses that have been invoked to account for the obtained relationships. First, if physically or emotionally handicapped persons marry, their preexisting handicaps may reduce the likelihood that they will remain married. Second, physical or emotional disorders arising after marriage in either spouse may significantly reduce the likelihood that the marriage will continue. Third, the status of being married and living with one's spouse may reduce vulnerability to a wide variety of diseases or emotional disorders. Fourth, marital disruption may be a life stressor which can precipitate physical or emotional disorders in married people presumably already vulnerable to them but not yet affected. Since these hypotheses are not mutually exclusive, and in fact may all be true to some extent, it has been understandably difficult to develop research designs whose conclusions could support them differentially.

Of all the social variables whose relationships with the distribution of psychopathology in the population have been studied, none has been more consistently and powerfully associated with this distribution than marital status. Persons who are divorced or separated have been repeatedly found to be overrepresented among psychiatric patients, while married persons living with their spouses are underrepresented. In a recent review of eleven studies of marital status and the incidence of mental disorder reported during the past 35 years, Crago (1972) did not find a single exception to the following summary statement: admission rates into psychiatric facilities are lowest among the married, intermediate among widowed and never-married adults, and highest among the divorced and separated. The differential appears to be stable across different age groups (Adler, 1953), reasonably stable for each sex separately considered (Thomas and Locke, 1963; Malzberg, 1964), and as true for blacks as for whites (Malzberg, 1956).

Not only are highest admission rates reported for persons with disrupted marriages, but the differential between these rates and similarly calculated rates among the married is very substantial. In the most recent data available on a national level (for the year 1970), Redick and Johnson (1974) have shown that the ratio of admission rates for divorced and separated persons to those for married persons is around 18 to 1 for males and about 7 to 1 for females. In the case of admissions into public section outpatient clinics, admission rates are also substantially higher for persons with disrupted marraiges than for married persons—nearly 7 to 1 for males and 5 to 1 for females.

Another view of the magnitude of these differences can be seen from data we collected between 1969 and 1971 in the city of Pueblo, Colorado (Bloom, 1975). Data from public and private inpatient facilities were combined but analyzed separately by sex and by whether the patient was admitted for the first time or had a prior history of inpatient psychiatrric care. In all cases, admission rates are substantially higher for patients with disrupted marriages (divorced and separated patients combined) than for patients married and living with their spouses. Specifically, with first admissions, rates for males with disrupted marriages are nine times higher than for males with nondisrupted marriages; among the females, the difference is around three to one. Among patients with histories of prior psychiatric care the differentials by marital status are greater for both sexes: 16 to 1 for males and 6 to 1 for females.

Another way of viewing the Pueblo data is to note that while divorced and separated males constitute only 6.5 percent of ever-married males age 14 and above, they constitute 46 percent of evermarried patients of both sexes in the same age span. Similarly, divorced and separated females constitute 8 percent of ever-married females age 14 and above but 32 percent of all ever-married patients in this age span. More than 7 percent of males with disrupted marriages are hospitalized annually because of a psychiatric condition—indeed, a quiet epidemic.

Two important sources of data serve to link marital disruption and suicidal behavior. First, Schneidman and Farberow (1961) have compared some personal characteristics of attempted and committed suicides from the year 1957 in Los Angeles County.* Thirteen percent of committed suicides were divorced and 8 percent were separated. Both of these figures are more than double what would have been expected from the proportion of divorced and separated persons in the general population of Los Angeles County. Furthermore, while about the same proportion of attempted and committed suicides are married and while about twice as

---

*Data regarding committed suicides were obtained from the Los Angeles coroner's office, and for attempted suicides from Los Angeles physicians, records of the Los Angeles County General Hospital, and records from the sixteen Los Angeles municipal emergency hospitals.

large a proportion of single persons attempt as commit suicide, the divorced, separated, and widowed are significantly over-represented among those who commit suicide and significantly underrepresented among those who attempt it. Schneidman and Farberow suggest that "it seems probable that the losses and disturbances in dyadic relationships occurring among the older groups, where more divorced, separated, and widowed appear, are also more likely to result in more lethal suicidal behavior" (p. 30). In a related study, Litman and Farberow (1961), proposing a strategy for undertaking emergency evaluations of self-destructive potentiality, note that "many suicide attempts, especially in young persons, occur after the separation from a spouse or loved one. . . . When there has been a definite loss of a loved person, such as a spouse, parent, child, lover, or mistress, within the previous year (by death, divorce, or separation), the potentiality for self-destruction is increased" (p. 51).

The second source of data linking suicide with marital status comes from the continuing reports of the National Center for Health Statistics. The most recent report (National Center for Health Statistics, 1970) covers the period 1959–61 and is based on an analysis of total U.S. mortality data. With particular reference to deaths from suicide, among white females the rate is higher among the divorced than any other marital status category and is more than three times the rate found in the married, while for white men it is also highest among the divorced and is more than four times as high as for married persons. For nonwhite females, the suicide rate is highest in the widowed and second highest in the divorced, where it is twice that of the married; and finally, among nonwhite males, it is highest in the divorced and is nearly two and one-half times as great as among the married.

The figures for deaths from homicide are even more striking. In both sexes and among both whites and nonwhites, risk of death by homicide is far higher for the divorced than for any other marital status group. With white women the risk is more than four times higher among the divorced than the married and with white men, more than seven times higher. Among nonwhites, the risk is twice as high among women and three times as high among men.

Two studies demonstrate excess vulnerability to motor vehicle accidents among the divorced. The analysis of total U.S. mortality data published by the National Center for Health Statistics (1970) shows that in both sexes and for whites and nonwhites alike, automobile fatality rates are higher among the divorced than among any other marital status group, averaging about three times as high as among the married. Second, a study by McMurray (1970) demonstrated that the accident rate of persons undergoing divorce doubled during the period between the six months before and the six months after the divorce date.

A variety of studies have attempted to link stress experiences to disease morbidity. Indeed, such linkages form the empirical basis of psychophysiological disease hypotheses. Holmes and Rahe (1967; also Rahe, McKean, and Arthur, 1967; Rahe, 1968; and Theorell and Rahe, 1970) have developed a measure of stressful life events based on the amount of readjustment required by each such event and have shown that this measure (in which marital disruption figures heavily) distinguishes persons likely to become ill from those not likely to become ill (see also Cline and Chesy, 1972).

Two recent studies suggest that alcoholism (both acute and chronic) is more prevalent among the divorced than among the married, a finding that corroborates much earlier literature. Wechsler, Thum, Demone, and Dwinnel (1972), studying the blood alcohol level of over 6,000 eligible consecutive admissions to the emergency service of Massachusetts General Hospital, found that "in both sexes, the divorced or separated had the highest proportion with positive Breathalyzer readings. . . . Divorced or separated men included 42 percent with positive alcohol readings" (p. 138). Widowers had the lowest proportion with positive readings (10 percent), and single (24 percent) and married (19 percent) men were intermediate. Rosenblatt, Gross, Malenowski, Broman, and Lewis (1971) contrasted first admissions with readmissions for alcoholism and concluded that their results "reveal a significant relationship between disrupted marriage and multiple hospitalizations for the acute alcoholic psychoses at ages below 45" (p. 1094); also see Woodruff, Guze, and Clayton, 1972).

Both the widowed and the divorced have higher age-adjusted death rates for all causes combined than do married persons of equivalent age, sex, and race. With respect to specific diseases, death rates from tuberculosis and cirrhosis of the liver are consistently higher among the divorced. Among white men and nonwhites of both sexes, death rate is higher among the divorced than among the married from malignant neoplasm of the respiratory system, and among nonwhite males it is higher among the divorced for diabetes mellitus and arteriosclerotic heart disease.

Finally, an extensive literature testifies to the generally negative consequences of marital disruption for the children in the disrupted family. While empirical studies are not numerous, there is some equivocal support for this general assertion, although few studies report data from control children in nondisrupted families, and many are based on a very limited number of cases.

❖   A review of the American literature suggests six specific stresses associated with marital separation. First, the psychological and emotional problems associated with a marriage breakup appear to be intense. The termination of a marriage is the death of a relationship, requiring constructive mourning and a coming to grips with the resulting sense of failure, shame, and low self-worth. Second, particularly among women, there often are stresses associated with the need to think about employment, career planning, or additional education preparatory to establishing an independent economic existence. Third, legal and financial problems often occur, creating additional stress. Separated women often find it impossible to get loans or establish charge accounts. Parental rights are often poorly understood. Fourth, with the change from a two-parent to a one-parent family setting, child-rearing problems frequently emerge. Fifth, particularly among men, problems regarding housing and homemaking appear. And sixth, for both men and women—particularly if they are beyond the early adult years—there are often serious difficulties in finding adequate social groups and experiences.

In spite of the fact that there is a large body of research and opinion regarding the stressful character of marital disruption, a careful search of the published literature of the past fifteen years has failed to uncover a single controlled study designed to reduce those stresses.

It is important to acknowledge at the outset that the concept of a "good divorce," that is, the idea of divorce counseling in contrast to marriage counseling, remains controversial in the literature. In fact, the existence of the controversy may help explain the lack of evaluated intervention programs for persons undergoing marital disruption. Basic to the anti-divorce counseling position is the fact that reconciliation is often seen as a far more desirable outcome to marital conflict than divorce. Rutledge (1963), for example, argues that "seldom does a divorce solve the fundamental personality problems resident in a marital situation" (p. 320), and Bodenheimer (1970) suggests that with the liberalization of divorce laws many couples turn to divorce rather than trying to rebuild their marriages. She urges that "care should be taken to avoid a complete swing of the pendulum from yesterday's marriage breakdown without recourse to divorce, to today's divorce without breakdown" (p. 219).

It would now be appropriate to examine more closely the four hypotheses that have been advanced to account for the associations found between marital disruption on the one hand and various physical and emotional disorders on the other. First, it has been asserted that persons with physical or emotional disorders who marry will be less likely to maintain a successful marriage than persons without preexisting disabilities. Our review of the literature indicates that data have not been collected in such a way that the validity of this hypothesis can be distinguished from that of the second hypothesis, which proposes that marital disruption may be significantly increased as a consequence of disabilities arising after marriage. These hypotheses suggest that psychopathology is the cause and marital disruption the consequence.

Turner describes the hypothesized relationship linking emotional disorder with subsequent marital disruption in terms of the incipient character of psychopathology that "makes marriage less likely and, given marriage, is likely to speed divorce or separation" (1972, p. 365). Srole and his colleagues make a similar point when they indicate that "elements of mental health may be crucially involved in determining whether or not individuals choose to marry; if they do so choose, whether or not they are successful in finding a spouse; and, if they are successful in this respect, whether or not the marriage is subsequently broken by divorce" (1962, p. 175). Briscoe and his colleagues, interpreting findings in their research, suggest that "one of the implications of finding such a significant amount of psychiatric illness in a divorced population is that psychiatric illness is probably a significant cause of martial breakdown" (Briscoe et al., 1973, p. 125).

Crago, in her review of research studies linking marital disruption and psychopathology, raises the same possibility, stating: "Studies of hospitalization rates and marital status are sometimes criticized because the differences in rates may be due to effects of mental disorders on the marital status of individuals before they are admitted to a mental hospital. For example, if mental disorders tend to lead to divorce, this would boost the rate of mental disorders among the divorced and at the same time decrease the rate for married persons" (1972, p. 115).

These two hypotheses can be tested through a single prospective research design that would assess physical and psychological functioning in individuals as well as couples at the time of marriage. The first hypothesis could be evaluated by following such a cohort over a number of years, by means of an annual physical and psychological evaluation determining the relationship between pre-existing disability and marital adjustment and success. In addition, by identifying couples with postmarital onset of emotional or physical disability in a group judged healthy at the time of marriage, the second hypothesis could be evaluated. In this case one would need to examine the temporal relationships between disability onset after marriage and marital dissatisfaction or disruption. Undoubtedly, the cost and personal commitment required to complete a longitudinal study lasting perhaps a decade or longer have been a major reason why such studies have not been undertaken. Yet without them, it is possible neither to evaluate the hypotheses individually nor to differentiate between them.

The third hypothesis is that the status of being married reduces vulnerability to a wide variety of illnesses. Turner, for example, suggests that different marital statuses may place an individual in different social systems which may vary in their supportive character, and thus that the "marriage state . . . is seen as protective against hospitalization" (1972, p. 365). In an interesting report by Dupont, Ryder, and Grunebaum (1971) regarding their study of 44 married couples in which one spouse had been diagnosed as psychotic and hospitalized, a surprisingly large number of couples reported that the problems associated with coping with the psychosis strengthened their marriages.

Syme has recently reviewed the statistics linking disease mortality and marital status and has concluded:

It may be instructive to recall the very wide range of conditions for which married people have lower mortality rates. The list of such conditions includes lower death rates for respiratory tuberculosis, stroke, influenza, pneumonia, and cancer of almost all sites including cancer of the buccal cavity and pharynx, the digestive organs, the respiratory system, the breast, and the urinary system. While the possibility cannot be ruled out, it is difficult to see how people who die of a stroke when they are 70 or 80 years old were less likely to have gotten married 50 years earlier. Further, if the marital state provides an environment which reduces the risk of death from this long list of conditions, it must be that a very profound and important influence is at work which is certainly worthy of prompt and careful study. By such detailed study of marital status and its varied disease consequences, we may be able to develop a whole set of insights about social processes and health status. (1974, p. 1045)

The notion of the special protective power of being married suggests that never-married persons and divorced and separated persons matched for age and sex might have similar disease morbidity and mortality experiences. But the data clearly indicate that never-married persons are at lower risk for most disorders than persons undergoing marital disruption. Another hypothesis suggested by this explanatory concept is that in people equated for age, length of marriage might be inversely related to a variety of morbidity or mortality risks. To our knowledge, this hypothesis has not been definitely examined.

Research intended to examine the hypothesis that marriage is a special protective environment could be accomplished retrospectively and has in fact been done with respect to certain disorders. The Pueblo study (Bloom, 1975), for example, linked psychiatric admissions rates to marital history. What is significant about this research is that marital history data and not merely marital status data were collected at the time of admission, thus allowing analysis not only of the relationship of current marital status to a specific disorder (the approach taken in most of the available literature) but also of the effect of patterns of marital history on the evolution of a specific disorder. We found that six patterns were sufficient to identify the marital histories of 93 percent of ever-married psychiatric inpatients (1975, p. 223) and that first inpatient admissions and patients with prior histories of psychiatric inpatient care differed significantly in the distribution of these martial history patterns. Through an analysis of marital history it is possible to address the questions of whether the benefits of the protective power of being married are outweighed by the relative stress of separation and divorce and whether total length of marriages, or time since separation and divorce, are related to subsequent vulnerability to physical and emotional disorder.

The fourth hypothesis is that the marital disruption constitutes a significant stressor. This hypothesis can be viewed within the rubric of crisis theory (see Caplan, 1964; Parad, 1965) and, of course, it is this hypothesis that has the greatest implication for primary prevention. The national psychiatric admission rate statistics already cited, which show a substantially higher admission rate for separated persons than for divorced persons, support this hypothesis.

Perhaps, more generally, contemporary role theorists would look for stress associated with particular status assignments and would see being separated or divorced as having particularly stressful role attributes. In 1960, for example, national mental health service statistics indicated that married women had mental illness rates twice as high as those of married men. In contrast, there were no appreciable sex differences between the admission rates of divorced or separated men and women. Gove (1972) used these figures to postulate a special vulnerability associated with the role of married women in western society. More recent statistics suggest that his hypothesis may no longer be tenable. In admission rates reported since 1970, sex differences for married patients have disappeared and sex differences for separated and divorced persons have emerged, with the male admission rate far higher than the female. What has remained stable over this time period, however, is the excessive admission rate, in both sexes, of the separated and divorced when contrasted with admission rates among the married.

Research in the area of marital disruption as a life stress has been further complicated by the fact that the data support the notion that marital disruption and physical and emotional disorders are clearly interactive, in the sense that each has the potential to influence the other. These interactions have yet to be explored empirically, not only because of the methodological difficulties but also, in part, because of the complexity of the task (see B. P. Dohrenwend, 1975). One needs to identify and follow a cohort of married persons who differ in marital satisfaction but not in psychological well-being to determine if differential rates of psychopathology are subsequently generated. In a companion research program one needs to identify and follow married psychiatric patients to determine how their psychopathology has a subsequent effect on marital adjustment and disruption. Improved measures of marital adjustment, marital satisfaction, and mental health need to be developed before these programs can be successfully mounted.

Perhaps the most appropriate interpretation of the research that has been reviewed is that an unequivocal association between marital disruption and physical and emotional disorder has been demonstrated and that this association probably includes at least two interdependent components: first, illness (physical or emotional) can precede and can help precipitate marital disruption; and second, marital disruption can serve to precipitate physical and psychiatric difficulties in some persons who might otherwise not have developed such problems. Conversations with newly separated persons leave no doubt that separation is an important stressor.

When the history of twentieth-century efforts to control mental disorders is written, the great contribution of the last third of the century may well turn out to be the movement away from considering predisposing factors in mental illnesses toward concern with precipitating factors. This movement, away from a concern with the past and toward a concern with the present, has come about in part from a sense of frustration with our efforts at remediation. But in addition, a growing accumulation of empirical evidence has turned our attention away from the past. Kohlberg, LaCrosse, and Ricks (1972, p. 1233), for example, reviewing the literature linking childhood behavior and adult mental health, comment:

> To conscious experience, moods change, anxieties disappear, loves and hates fade, the emotion of yesterday is weak, and the emotion of today does not clearly build on the emotion of yesterday. The trauma theory of neurosis is dead; the evidence for irreversible effects of early-childhood trauma is extremely slight. Early-childhood maternal deprivation, parental mistreatment, separation, incest—all seem to have much slighter effects

*upon adult adjustment (unless supported by continuing depri-
vation and trauma throughout childhood) than anyone seemed
to anticipate.*

In our concern with the development of effective preventive
intervention programs, we find ourselves inexorably drawn to the
simple dictum of Barrington Moore (1970, p. 5): "Human society
ought to be organized in such a way as to eliminate useless suffering."

REFERENCES

Adler, L. M. The relationship of marital status to incidence of and recovery from mental illness. *Social Forces*, 1953, *32*, 185-194.

Aponte, J. F., and Miller, F. T. Stress-related social events and psychological impairment. *Journal of Clinical Psychology*, 1972, *28*, 455-458.

Bachrach, L. L. Marital status and mental disorder: An analytical review. DHFW Publication No. (ADM) 75-217. Washington, D.C.: U.S. Government Printing Office, 1975.

Baguador, E. *Separation: Journal of a marriage.* New York: Simon and Schuster, 1972.

Bloom, B. L. The medical model, miasma theory, and community mental health. *Community Mental Health Journal*, 1965, *1*, 333-338.

Bloom, B. L. *Changing patterns of psychiatric care.* New York: Behavioral Publications, 1975.

Bloom, B. L., Asher, S. J., and White, S. W. Marital disruption as a stressor: A review and analysis. *Psychological Bulletin* (in press).

Bloom, B. L., Hodges, W. F., Caldwell, R. A., Systra, L., and Cedrone, A. R. Marital Separation: A Community Survey. *Journal of Divorce*, 1977, *1*, 7-19.

Bodenheimer, B. M. New approaches of psychiatry: Implications for divorce reform. *Utah Law Review*, 1970, 191-220.

Briscoe, C. W., Smith, J. B., Robins, E., Marton, S., and Gaskin, F. Divorce and psychiatric disease. *Archives of General Psychiatry*, 1973, *29*, 119-125.

Brown, G. W., Sklair, F., Harris, T. O., and Birley, J. L. T. Life events and psychiatric disorders: 1. Some methodological issues. *Psychological Medicine*, 1973, *3*, 159-176.

Caplan, G. *Principles of preventive psychiatry.* New York: Basic Books, 1964.

Cline, D. W., and Chesy, J. J. A perspective study of life changes and subsequent health changes. *Archives of General Psychiatry*, 1972, *27*, 51-53.

Cochrane, R., and Robertson, A. The life events inventory: A measure of the relative severity of psycho-social stressors. *Journal of Psychosomatic Research*, 1973, *17*, 135-139.

Crago, M. A. Psychopathology in married couples. *Psychological Bulletin*, 1972, *77*, 114-128.

Dohrenwend, B. P. Sociocultural and social-psychological factors in the genesis of mental disorders. *Journal of Health and Social Behavior*, 1975, *16*, 365-392.

Dohrenwend, B. P., and Dohrenwend, B. S. *Social status and psychological disorder: A causal inquiry*. New York: Wiley-Interscience, 1969.

Dohrenwend, B. P., and Dohrenwend, B. S. Social and cultural influences on psychopathology. *Annual Review of Psychology*, 1974, *25*, 417-452.

Dohrenwend, B. S. Life events as stressors: A methodological inquiry. *Journal of Health and Social Behavior*, 1973, *14*, 167-175. (a)

Dohrenwend, B. S. Social status and stressful life events. *Journal of Personality and Social Psychology*, 1973, *28*, 225-235. (b)

Dohrenwend, B. S., and Dohrenwend, B. P. *Stressful life events: Their nature and effects*. New York: Wiley and Sons, 1974.

Dupont, R. L., Ryder, R. G., and Grunebaum, H. U. An unexpected result of psychosis in marriage. *American Journal of Psychiatry*, 1971, *128*, 735-739.

Gardner, R. A. *The boys and girls book about divorce*. New York: Science House, Inc., 1970.

Glick, P. C. *Some recent changes in American families*. (Current Population Reports, Series P-23, No. 52. Bureau of the Census.) Washington, D.C.: U.S. Government Printing Office, 1975.

Gove, W. R. The relationship between sex roles, marital status, and mental illness. *Social Forces*, 1972, *51*, 34-44.

Holmes, T. H., and Rahe, R. H. The social readjustment rating scale. *Journal of Psychosomatic Research*, 1967, *11*, 213-218.

Hudgens, R. W., Robins, E., and Delong, W. B. The reporting of recent stress in the lives of psychiatric patients. *British Journal of Psychiatry*, 1970, *117*, 635-643.

Hunt, M. M. *The world of the formerly married*. New York: McGraw-Hill, 1966.

Hunt, M. M. Review of *Marital separation*, by R. S. Weiss. *New York Times Book Review*, Nov. 30, 1975, p. 4.

Kellam, S. G., Branch, J. D., Agrawal, K. C., and Ensminger, M. E. *Mental health and going to school: The Woodlawn program of assessment, early intervention, and evaluation*. Chicago: University of Chicago Press, 1975.

Klassen, D., Roth, A., and Hornstra, K. Perception of life events as gains or losses in a community survey. *Journal of Community Psychology*, 1974, *2*, 330-336.

Kohlberg, L., LaCrosse, J., and Ricks, D. The predictability of adult mental health from childhood behavior. In B. Wolman (Ed.), *Manual of child psychopathology*. New York: McGraw-Hill, 1972.

Krantzler, M. *Creative divorce: A new opportunity for personal growth*. New York: M. Evans and Co., 1973.

Lantz, H. R., and Snyder, E. C. *Marriage: An examination of the man-woman relationship* (2nd ed.). New York: Wiley and Sons, 1969.

Litman, R. E., and Farberow, N. L. Emergency evaluation of self destructive potentiality. In N. L. Farberow and E. S. Schneidman (Eds.), *The cry for help*. New York: McGraw-Hill, 1961.

Malzberg, B. Marital status and mental disease among Negroes in New York State. *Journal of Nervous and Mental Disease*, 1956, *123*, 457-465.

Malzberg, B. Marital status and the incidence of mental disease. *International Journal of Social Psychiatry*, 1964, *10*, 19-26.

McMurray, L. Emotional stress and driving performance: The effect of divorce. *Behavioral Research in Highway Safety*, 1970, *1*, 100-114.

Mindey, C. *The divorced mother: A guide to readjustment*. New York: McGraw-Hill, 1969.

Moore, B., Jr. *Reflections on the causes of human misery and upon certain proposals to eliminate them*. Boston: Beacon Press, 1970.

Morrison, J. R., Hudgens, R. W., and Brachha, R. G. Life events and psychiatric illness. *British Journal of Psychiatry*, 1968, *114*, 423-432.

National Center for Health Statistics. *Mortality from selected causes by marital status*. (Series 20, No. 8A and B. U.S. Department of Health, Education, and Welfare.) Washington, D.C.: U.S. Government Printing Office, 1970.

National Center for Health Statistics. *100 years of marriage and divorce statistics: United States, 1867-1967*. (Vital and Health Statistics, Series 21, No. 24. Washington, D.C.: U.S. Government Printing Office, 1973. (a)

National Center for Health Statistics. *Remarriages: United States*. (Vital and Health Statistics, Series 21, No. 25.) Washington, D.C.: U.S. Government Printing Office, 1973. (b)

Parad, H. J. (Ed.). *Crisis intervention: Selected readings*. New York: Family Service Association of America, 1965.

Prokopec, J., Dytrych, Z., and Schuller, V. Rozvodova chovani a manzelsky nesoulad (Divorce and marital discord). *Vyzkumny Ustav Psychiatricky Zpravy*, No. 31, 1973.

Rahe, R. H. Life-change measurement as a predictor of illness. *Proceedings of the Royal Society of Medicine*, 1968, *61*, 44-46.

Rahe, R. H., McKean, J. E., Jr., and Arthur, R. J. A longitudinal study of life-change and illness patterns. *Journal of Psychosomatic Research*, 1967, *10*, 355-366.

Redick, R. W., and Johnson, C. *Marital status, living arrangements and family characteristics of admissions to state and county mental hospitals and outpatients psychiatric clinics, United States 1970*. (Statistical Note 100, National Institute of Mental Health.) Washington, D.C.: U.S. Government Printing Office, 1974.

Reid, D. D. Precipitating proximal factors in the occurrence of mental disorders: Epidemiological evidence. In E. M. Gruenberg and M. Huxley (Eds.), *Causes of mental disorders: A review of epidemiological knowledge, 1959*. New York: Milbank Memorial Fund, 1961.

Rohner, L. *The divorcee's handbook*. Garden City: Doubleday, 1969.

Rosenblatt, S. M., Gross, M. M., Malenowski, B., Broman, M., and Lewis, E. Marital status and multiple psychiatric admissions for alcoholism: A cross-validation. *Quarterly Journal of Studies on Alcohol*, 1971, *32*, 1092–1096.

Rubin, Z., and Mitchell, C. Couples research as couples counseling: Some unintended effects of studying close relationships. *American Psychologist*, 1976, *31*, 17–25.

Rutledge, A. L. Should the marriage counselor ever recommend divorce? *Marriage and Family Living*, 1963, *25*, 319–325.

Schneidman, E. S., and Farberow, N. L. Statistical comparisons between attempted and committed suicides. In N. L. Farberow and E. S. Schneidman (Eds.), *The cry for help*. New York: McGraw-Hill, 1961.

Spanier, G. B. Further evidence on methodological weaknesses in the Locke-Wallace Marital Adjustment Scale and other measures of adjustment. *Journal of Marriage and the Family*, 1972, *34*, 403–404.

Srole, L., Langnor, T. S., Michael, S. T., Opler, M. K., and Rennie, T. A. C. Mental health in the metropolis: The midtown Manhattan study. New York: McGraw-Hill, 1962.

Stewart, C. W. Counseling the divorcee. *Pastoral Psychology*, 1963, *14*, 10–16.

Syme, S. L. Behavioral factors associated with the etiology of physical disease: A social epidemiological approach. *American Journal of Public Health*, 1974, *64*, 1043–1045.

Theorell, T., and Rahe, R. H. Life changes in relation to the onset of myocardial infarction. In T. Theorell (Ed.), *Psychosocial factors in relation to the onset of myocardial infarction and to some metabolic variables—a pilot study*. Stockholm, Sweden: Department of Medicine, Seraphimer Hospital, Karolinska Institutet, 1970.

Thomas, D. S., and Locke, B. Z. Marital status, education and occupational differentials in mental disease. *Milbank Memorial Fund Quarterly*, 1963, *41*, 145–160.

Turner, R. J. The epidemiological study of schizophrenia: A current appraisal. *Journal of Health and Social Behavior*, 1972, *13*, 360–369.

U.S. Bureau of the Census. *Current population reports*, Series P-20, No. 271. *Marital status and living arrangements: March, 1974*. Washington, D.C.: U.S. Government Printing Office, 1974.

U.S. Bureau of the Census. *Current population reports*. Series P-20, No. 287. *Marital status and living arrangements: March, 1975*. Washington, D.C.: U.S. Government Printing Office, 1975.

U.S. Department of Health, Education, and Welfare. Births, marriages, divorces, and deaths for 1975. *Monthly Vital Statistics Report*, 1976, *24*, (12), 1–8.

Vinokur, A., and Selzer, M. L. Life events, stress, and mental disorders. *Proceedings, 81st Annual Convention, American Psychological Association*, 1973, 329–330.

Wechsler, H., Thum, D., Demone, H. W., Jr., and Dwinnel, J. Social characteristics and blood alcohol level. *Quarterly Journal for the Study of Alcoholism*, 1972, *33*, 132–147.

Weiss, R. S. *Marital separation*. New York: Basic Books, 1975.

Weissman, M. M. The assessment of social adjustment. *Archives of General Psychiatry*, 1975, *32*, 357–365.

Woodruff, R. A., Jr., Guze, S. B., and Clayton, P. J. Divorce among psychiatric out-patients. *British Journal of Psychiatry*, 1972, *121*, 289–292.

An Overview of
Stress and Satisfaction:
The Contract with Self

Harry Levinson

Much attention has been given to work satisfaction and its relationship to productivity, accidents, absenteeism, psychological symptoms and the quality of working life. Morale and attitude surveys and climate studies are an organizational commonplace. However, large sample surveys of satisfaction with work seem to be self-contradictory. For the past twenty years 80 percent of the people surveyed by the Institute of Social Research of the University of Michigan say that they are satisfied with their work (Quinn, Mangione, and Baldi de Mandelovito, 1973). Yet up to 60 percent report that they would change to another occupation if they could (Campbell, Converse, and Rodgers, 1976). Job satisfaction as a concept, as expressed in public opinion surveys, has questionable meaning (Campbell, 1977; Kanter, 1978). Why is this so? How then can we speak of satisfaction, and what relationship does it have to stress? There are a number of possible reasons for the contradictions:

(1) A simple one is that people can respond in a perfunctory way. Ask a person walking down the street, "How are you?," and he or she is likely to respond, "Fine" even though he may be suffering from acute intestinal pain or dying of cancer. Most surveys seem to assume that how people *say* they feel is what they really feel.

(2) Asked what they *might* do, for example if they would change jobs, people may well respond in terms of fantasy, even though their responses to their present situations may reflect simultaneously a realistic assessment of the present. As an analogy, to entertain the fantasy of moving to a distant resort area does not

necessarily reflect serious discontent with one's present living circumstances.

(3) As Sarason (1977) has pointed out, many people in high status roles are indeed satisfied with their jobs. Even if they are not, they must say so because they are doing so well. However, simultaneously they can be dissatisfied because in an open and mobile society they have developed many competences, and the concurrent expectation that they will do the many things they promised themselves they would do. To have achieved competence in only one occupational role leaves them dissatisfied with that *one*.

(4) When they respond to a question about their present jobs, inevitably people are taking into consideration a configuration of forces: what they expect this job will bring; what lies ahead of them; whether it is a necessary step in a career; their feelings about their work relationships; comparative experiences in their previous jobs; their relative success or failure; their position vis-à-vis peers; and so on.

(5) The questioners have their own, often unconscious, political biases. That somebody asks about a given topic and somebody else responds says nothing about the degree of importance of the topic to the latter person (see, for example, Flanagan, in this volume). Nor does the questioner's interpretation of the responses as reflecting the wish for a given set of conditions necessarily genuinely reflect that wish. For example, highly dependent people might well answer a questionnaire in such a way as to indicate that they want and should have greater autonomy and to actualize themselves. As a matter of fact, probably they would be much more effective, if not much more contented, in a highly structured environment in which they were told what to do. Perhaps both issues could be important to the researcher but less relevant to the respondent.

No doubt there are many other reasons for contradictory findings and why it is difficult to measure satisfaction, to speak about it in any reasonably clear, conceptual way, and to relate it to stress (Zaleznik, Ondrack, and Silver, 1970). The same is true with respect to happiness or well-being (Campbell, 1977). Yet we know from many contemporary circumstances, including strikes and physical symptoms, that there are indeed many dissatisfactions in work situations.

❖

Studies of stress indicate that symptoms are inversely correlated with community or organizational status levels (Hollingshead and Redlich, 1958; Kornhauser, 1965; Srole, Langner, Michael, Opler, and Rennie, 1962). Stress seems to be higher, and therefore we must infer that satisfaction is lower, when people feel responsible for others and when there is greater role ambiguity (Kahn, Wolfe, Quinn, Snoek, and Rosenthal, 1964).

In sum we cannot infer much about satisfaction from mass surveys. We often do not know what is being measured in surveys. However, there is much evidence of stress from which we can infer considerable dissatisfaction.

What do we make of all this?

THE EGO IDEAL AND SELF-IMAGE RELATIONSHIP

When we ask people whether they are satisfied, we are asking implicitly about how they see themselves in the present with respect to some ideal anticipated view of themselves in the future. In psychoanalytic terms, we are talking about the difference between the ego ideal (how one perceives oneself at one's ideal best) and the self-image (how one sees oneself in the present). Both have powerful roots in, and evolve out of, unconscious fantasy as well as from developmental circumstances. Certainly both are affected by contemporary events. The greater the gap between the ego ideal and the self-image, the lower the self-esteem and the greater the self-directed aggression or anger with self. This might be expressed in a formula like this:

$$\text{Self Esteem} = \frac{1}{\text{Ego Ideal} - \text{Self-Image}}$$

Thus stress and satisfaction are very closely and inversely related to each other. To be dissatisfied or aggrieved with one's work or job situation is to be angry in varying degrees (disappointment, frustration, disillusionment, defeat) both with the environment (job, organization, career) and with oneself for being in such a position.

THREE CIRCUMSTANCES PRECIPITATING STRESS

There are three circumstances when psychological stress is increased and satisfaction diminished:

(1) When feelings of helplessness or inadequacy increase. This may happen as a product of being moved arbitrarily, of lowered status, of significant deprivations, and of other organizational actions. The fact that people experience being demeaned is reflected in a wide range of studies, expecially those having to do with status. There is also widespread evidence of the significance of loss of support, of life change events, of unemployment, and similar factors which leave the individual feeling more psychologically helpless and alone.

Organizational pyramidal structures, with their heavy emphasis on winners and losers, on one track to success, demean people. People in many specialities must shift from those specialities into managerial ranks in order to attain structural success, although they may be less competent as managers than as specialists. This is as much a problem for teachers who must become principals and superintendents, or nurses who must become nursing administrators, or college professors who must become deans and presidents. This problem is compounded by inadequate appraisal systems which do not speak to people's work performance and behavior on the job but to abstractions like promotability (Levinson, 1976). When, on the basis of inadequate appraisal, people are graded on curves that do not meet the required underlying statistical assumptions, they are arbitrarily defined as successful or unsuccessful when objectively their behavior on the job or their occupational performance is quite acceptable.

Another force that contributes to the lowered self-image in organizations is simply the behavioral consequence of the aging process. Most organizations have no effective or systematic way of describing and defining tasks in such a way as to place people at different ages or life stages in roles which most fit where they are physically and psychologically.

A major problem in many work organizations, if not all, is that phenomena widely recognized in the family tend to get played out in those organizations. Components of organizations, like members of a family, are scapegoated. Frequently, the trained observer sees the splitting phenomenon: people or groups are arbitrarily separated into the black hats and white hats. There is sadistic and overcontrolling behavior, as well as often bitter intra-organizational strife, sometimes chronic, sometimes resulting in the extrusion of some organization members.

Unrelenting pressure for production, managerial inability, or unwillingness to solve frustrating problems, or simple inefficiency, produce feelings of hostility toward the organization and toward the self for putting up with such conditions. The inability of organizations to recognize the devastating effects of change and to build in systematic methods of supporting people through the process of change further compounds the sense of loss, magnifies the feelings of helplessness, and undermines the self-image.

Change takes many forms. A combination of aging and obsolescence may make people less desirable in an occupational marketplace. People who are no longer technically up-to-date feel themselves to be less adequate and more readily threatened. Merger, retirement, transfer, promotion all disrupt previous relationships and produce losses. People do not easily reestablish ties or adapt to new experiences as they age. Therefore they tend to become increasingly isolated as a function of the aging process, making it likely that they will focus more intensely on work. Thus they necessarily develop a greater dependency on work as a source of gratification, and are more vulnerable to the effects of whatever decisions are made about them.

(2) When people's values and personal rules of behavior are violated. Violations of values precipitate feelings of guilt. People are then angry with themselves or the organizations in which they work. Violation of personal standards occurs repeatedly, and people frequently complain about such violations. Advertising people will write books criticizing their own profession, teachers will complain about schools, and former CIA agents about the activities of their agency. Some people have exposed the dishonesty of their company's actions; others have reported on how they have fudged figures. All respond to internal standards, and the guilt and anger for violation of those standards.

People feel guilty and angry also when they are required to assume responsibilities which they cannot discharge adequately. A significant source of managerial guilt is the appraisal process itself. When managers and supervisors are asked to evaluate or appraise others, they usually feel they are being destructive. This is reflected in the fact that organizations are continuously changing performance-appraisal systems not only because they are unsatisfactory but also because, despite much training and pressure, it is difficult to get managers and supervisors to make evaluations. A fundamental reason is that evaluating others touches off ancient primary process feelings: to think something or to feel it is the same as to do it. Thus to critically evaluate is to be aggressive; unconsciously to be aggressive is to destroy. This problem is exacerbated when younger people are placed in supervisory or managerial roles over older people, as increasingly is the case with higher levels of education and ever more youthful management. Carrying out judgmental criticism under these circumstances becomes much like attacking one's own parents, thus reviving ancient oedipal anxieties, unconscious guilt, and the fear of retaliation. Fear is already exacerbated in organizations by the intense rivalry for places in the organization hierarchy. It is compounded even further by placing people in supervisory positions over others who were previously rivals or supervisors, thus recapitulating the worst fantasies of early childhood.

Changes in organizations which must adapt in turn require people to adopt new styles of behavior. Authoritarian managers are no longer permitted either by their subordinates or by their superiors to be as authoritarian as they once were. Many of us may applaud that phenomenon, but the change is hard on the people involved. There are other less dramatic demands for change in personal style. People who are accustomed to administering by not taking charge, as often is the case in management of mental health clinics or art museums or hospitals, are now being compelled to take charge and to become more efficient, to control people rather than merely consult with them. Employees who formerly were encouraged to be dependent now are frequently being required to become more aggressive as more organizations shift from technical or manufacturing orientations to marketing orientations. Thus the long-term pursuit of the ego ideal for such people is undermined and the fact that they must go off in other occupational directions frequently presents them with a self-image that is anathema to them.

(3) When people feel they are not moving toward their ego ideals. People will be angry with themselves (and therefore depressed) and with their work organizations when they do not have a sense of forward movement. The expected movement toward the ego ideal is implicit in studies that reflect the wish for greater autonomy, opportunity, growth, and challenge.

In addition to negative organizational events, movement toward the ego ideal may be inhibited by social and cultural forces. All cultural units, whether flocks or families, tribes or nations, have pecking orders. The males who are more dominant in the pecking order, presumably for Darwinian reasons, have greater access to food and females. Thus there is a certain inevitability about the way social structures evolve and power is distributed, regardless of economic systems. There is also a certain inevitability about people's willingness to attribute status or "better than" to one kind of work as contrasted with another. The leather workers of India and Japan are drawn only from the lowest castes. In our own country, as well as others in the western world, fewer people are willing to perform personal services, and those who do are now more often immigrants from less developed countries. Repeated surveys of the status of occupations indicate that professions are highest ranked. Within given professions there are also well defined hierarchies. Therefore, even in autonomous professional practices, a sense of hierarchy prevails and people scale themsleves, thereby significantly affecting their own self-images.

Although it is true that one's position in an organization hierarch usually governs one's social position in one's community, nevertheless, even if there were no organizations, there would be competition for social position. As noted earlier, social class studies indicate that the lower a person is in the community social structure, the more likely he or she is to have symptoms of mental and physical illness.

In addition there are, of course, the inevitable socioeconomic forces which go beyond what organizations do of their own accord. When school enrollments decline, some teachers lose their jobs. When brokerage houses merge, there is a surplus of security analysts. When one or another kind of work becomes obsolete, its practitioners are compelled to adapt and to give up their ego ideal pursuits in that particular profession. Then there are problems of racial, ethnic, and educational discrimination which not only do permanent damage to the self-image but also inhibit the move toward the ego ideal.

All this is compounded when there is inadequate information from the organization and repetitive change in organization structures. These result in inadequate support from superiors to deal with both the organization and external reality. Coping both with losses and new demands requires simultaneously taxing adaptation (Holmes and Rahe, 1967). This effort is complicated by role ambiguity. In the absence of information and role definition and without an adequately delegated charge and necessary support, people are more likely to be hyper-self-critical, more defensive, more distressed, more overcontrolled, and increasingly at risk of external criticism from superiors.

People attribute to superiors in their work organizations many of the same qualities they experienced in their relationships with their parents. Superior-subordinate relationships thereby take on powerful psychological overtones, especially these days when young people come to organizations expecting to be helped toward careers. But organizations do not adequately recognize the symbolic representation of superiors as parental surrogates. Nor do work organizations recognize that people can develop mutually supporting work groups around their leadership.

A conspicuous feature in the literature having to do with the precipitants of stress and dissatisfaction to which I have just referred is the assumption in all of these studies that the environment is the problem. Therefore, it follows that if you change the environment, you will change the balance of forces in the equation and people will therefore be better satisfied and have less stress. There is much to this thesis. In fact, if I did not accept the thesis as having a certain validity, I would not do much of what I presently do in organizational consultation. It is clear from all kinds of therapy as well as studies in organizations that people do indeed feel better about themselves when they have a greater effect on the forces that in turn affect them and when they have greater control over their environments. This conviction has led to the contemporary movement loosely labeled "Improving the Quality of Work Life."

But those of us who are clinicians or whose work is rooted in clinical theory and practice, know that people make their own psychological beds, so to speak. All of us are always engaged in maintaining our psychological equilibria, and therefore in making much of our own psychological environments. One way of doing that is by choosing our occupations and the kinds of organizations we work in, however unconsciously. We create psychological contracts with our organizations (Levinson, Price, Munden, Mandl, and Solley, 1962). We are not merely passive agents to be shaped by the organization or the organizational role alone. Furthermore, specific environmental circumstances and events have idiosyncratic meaning for individuals, as reflected in their varying reactions to the same events. Therefore, the sophisticated behavioral scientist must always see a person in context, always engaged in psychological negotiation with his or her environment and key figures in it. However, to assert that the individual has an effect on his or her environment—for example, that the assembly line worker indeed enters into a psychological contract with General Motors—is to risk being accused of blaming the victim, or of taking the extreme position that *everything* that happens to a person is willed by that person. I do not propose to be in either one of those camps.

So while organizations do indeed precipitate dissatisfaction and stress, one cannot take the position that dissatisfaction/stress is altogether the fault of the organization. Not only does the culture have an impact but also individuals bring their own ego ideals and self-images, their own values and expectations to the organization, and thereby their own vulnerabilities. It follows that one cannot readily say that organizations would attain significantly higher levels of satisfaction *if only* they were to change the environment (the organization structure, the political system, the work place, etc.) in a more positive direction.

UNRECOGNIZED FACTORS

Efforts to improve the quality of work life may indeed give rise to greater satisfaction and thereby presumably to less stress. However, there are important factors within individuals which precipitate dissatisfaction and stress which seem to be largely unrecognized. Chief among them is a fundamental phenomenon, primary narcissism (Freud, 1914/1957).

Given the ego ideal/self-image phenomenon, none of us is as

good in his own eyes as he or she would like to be. A subtle, unconscious, but nevertheless important aspect of the ego ideal is the wish to attain omnipotence or perfection. None of us comes close. Some think they have a chance and pursue that illusory goal unremittingly in compensatory behavior. To varying degrees, therefore, we will be happy with ourselves for thinking we are coming close. Those who feel they must drive themselves to that end do so in vain. Continuously failing, they are perennially angry with themselves. One of the more commonplace ways of dealing with the obverse of happiness, namely, unhappiness or anger with self, is to displace it onto others. Scapegoating, racial prejudice, and denigration of stereotyped individuals or groups are wisely recognized to be such displacements.

If work in our society is significantly the basis of self-esteem, then dissatisfaction with self is likely to be readily displaced onto work. If by one's own standards one is not as good as one would like to be and one works in an organization, then that organization is likely to be a displacement object. After all, the organization is bigger than the person, has more resources, more information, and more capacity for coping with the environment; and therefore, by definition, it should be more effective than the individual. When the individual sees the organization's ineffectiveness, just as when the child sees the imperfections of the parent, the dissatisfaction with self will be displaced onto the organization. The individual will be easily able to identify those aspects of the organization which "make" him or her feel dissatisfied and therefore be put under stress, when as a matter of fact these elements or forces or events may not be nearly as powerful or stressful as the individual indicates. Indeed, they may be magnified in his or her eyes purely as a product of the individual's psychic conflicts. As an analogy, if a person with an obsessive character structure married another with an hysterical character structure and then they criticize each other for characterological shortcomings, are the shortcomings objective failures or do they lie in the eyes of the respective beholders? How much of the beholders' stress then is self-created? How much do they need each other to live out certain fantasies?

Sarason's (1977) observation, noted earlier, that the higher a person's attainment, even when highly satisfied, the greater the likelihood that he or she will be simultaneously unsatisfied because he or she has not done as much as he or she promised himself he or she would do, supports this point. Again, not having come close to the ego ideal and therefore angry with oneself, one can easily displace such hostility onto the job.

Studies of life stages are now in vogue (Erikson, 1963; Gould, 1978; Levinson, 1977). As adults move through the various stages of adult life, however defined, there are shifts in value emphases and therefore in activities which are more gratifying and more appropriate at different stages of life. There are new and different responsibilities. There are changed expectations of self. For example, now that retirement limits have been lifted for many people, they expect to be able to continue to produce at the same high level as when they were younger. In many instances they will not be able to do so. It will be easier to blame the work organization than to confront that narcissistic injury which is the lowered self-image which accompanies the incapacities of aging.

Finally, we are confronted with another curious dichotomy. Human beings are greatly preoccupied with death. All religions have at their root an effort to understand and cope with death. Great philosophical movements, such as existentialism, have been preoccupied with that issue (Toynbee, 1968). Great authors, too. Isaac Bashevis Singer (1978) says, "in literature, as in our dreams, death does not exist." Alfred Kazin (1978) says of Sylvia Plath, "As a poet, she would not become alive and frightening until she faced her fascination with her own death." The current vogue for counseling the dying (Kübler-Ross, 1969) testifies to another form of the same preoccupation. Historically, the cosmetic business has prospered from the wish to mask one's aging and therefore increasing proximity to death.

Although we are powerfully preoccupied with mortality, we seem not to take this preoccupation into account when we speak of satisfaction in our lives and with our work, which is such a crucial component of both our lives and our satisfaction. Nowhere in the satisfaction/stress literature is this pervasive issue recognized, although it is clear that reported happiness declines with age (Campbell, 1977).

It is a clinical commonplace that primary narcissism is a fundamental protection against the helplessness of the infant and the basis for establishing relationships with others. The infantile wish to be omnipotent, to be able to live forever, never leaves us. We see its effects perennially in the denial of the impact of smoking and similar self-destructive activities. It is this belief in our own omnipotence which is deflated by the aging process, by the vicissitudes of life, and always by the underlying threat of death (nobody knows whether he or she is going to be alive tomorrow). Rubin (1977) remarks on how often working-class men and women, still in their twenties, use the phrase "When I was young." Not only do they feel loaded down early with family responsibilities, but also they feel early on they have "had it" in life. They have to either explode or withdraw, she says. She notes that the men and women she met recall parents, especially fathers, who were taciturn and unresponsive, withdrawing into silence (in my view, dying).

Our anger at the narcissistic injury (the recognition that we are not omnipotent and are not going to live forever) is likely to be displaced onto the most important and easily available activities and social structures in which those activities occur. We see much of this in the middle-age crisis and in the symptoms and the breakup of marriages which follow it.

I contend that much of the dissatisfaction with work is also a displacement from the same phenomenon. Our work, which is the source of so much of our coping effort, ultimately, it turns out, is not going to enable us to master the external environment fully or be fully in control of our fate. In only a few cases is it going to enable us to live forever in the form of great artistic or scientific achievement or great organizational entities. Even then we will endure only symbolically.

In other words, each of us has a contract with himself. Many primitive, infantile elements of that contract having to do with the wish to attain perfection and to live forever are inevitably doomed to nonfulfillment. The underlying disappointment in the failure to understand, let alone fulfill, the contract with the self is a significant component of dissatisfaction and therefore of stress. That fundamental disappointment is exacerbated, in turn, by environmental forces which causes work organizations to violate other elements of that contract (e.g., violations of conscience). It is further magnified by those which become a counterforce or barrier to attaining the more conscious expectations of the self. I say exacerbated because I think the fundamental issues, those of primary narcissim and the wish to endure forever, will not be gratified no matter what happens in the external environment, and therefore there will always be significant elements of dissatisfaction and of stress.

I do not mean to imply that narcissistic injury is all there is to stress or that it is not worth mitigating the precipitating events or configurations of forces that give rise to diminished self-images, problems of conscience, or inhibition of career aspiration. I do mean to say that I think the results people expect from such efforts alone are likely to be both elusive and disappointing. We will continue to find contradictory evidence in morale studies and attitude surveys, and a shift of the focus of discontent from one issue to another as long as the facts of narcissistic injury and displacement are not recognized. The organizational changes that are built on such data will probably continue to yield limited and temporary results.

THE COPING PROCESS

Coping with stress involves coping with one's own character defenses in the face of tasks that are age-specific, stage-specific, and congenial to one's equilibrium-maintaining efforts. Coping involves managing one's drives, the distance between self-image and ego ideal, and focal conflicts, in the face of institutional requirements. Those requirements may magnify or intensify intrapsychic struggles or conversely make certain kinds of defenses incongruous in certain situations. How then do we help people cope with such a phenomenon?

First, by significant public education efforts. We need to help people understand both the sources of and the elements of irrational expectations of self, as well as the consequences of these expectations, e.g., depressive orientations to life, compensatory drives to power, drivenness, unrewarding life experiences despite intense effort to achieve gratification, etc. We need to help them understand the crises of normal development as people pass from one life stage to another, giving up youth and the gratifications of earlier years, and having increasingly to face the realization of mortality as they do so. We need to help them understand the relationship between the consequent disappointment and the appearance of physical, even life-threatening illnesses like cancer. We need to help them understand why there are different value emphases at different points in the life stage curve.

Second, we need to establish better mechanisms through which people can give more thoughtful attention to their careers as they mature. We need to encourage people not merely to seek jobs but to take initiative to develop their own independent occupational activities which they, themselves, may be able to control and, with continuing education, to change as they wish. While this will not cope with the underlying phenomena I have described, it will tend to reduce some of the sense of helplessness and dependency that people feel too often in organizations in which they work. They will be less vulnerable to the feeling of being defeated and destroyed as they age. But they will have to learn to cope with the feeling of being alone in their work, without the comfort of organizational support.

These two together—(1) Greater understanding of the underlying concern with mortality and the displacement phenomenon, and of the transition through life stage events and the experiences of loss, and (2) Greater control over one's work and career—can be fostered through the further development of a contemporary self-help mechanism, namely, mutual-support groups. If we can help people understand and recognize depression, which is anger with self and therefore the core of the emotional stress I have been examining, then we can also help them understand the need for forming more mutual-support groups to deal with specific problems. We already have Weight Watchers, Parents Without Partners, Alcoholics Anonymous, and so on. In only a few instances have there been mutual-support groups of people who have lost their jobs or people who have different kinds of illnesses. These could well proliferate in every community. Indeed, perhaps it should be a major function of community mental health centers to form them.

Finally, we can help bring such understanding into work organizations where it can become part of employee and managerial education. The contemporary vogue of concern with executive stress, relaxation mechanisms and devices, and cathartic relief could well become something more conceptually and professionally solid. For example, there might be systematic education in the formation of various support groups within the organizational structures as well as in the community at large to anticipate, to alleviate, and to ameliorate stress.

Executives, managers, and supervisors could be helped to understand what it means psychologically to be in positions of power over others, and what is required of them as symbolic parental surrogates. Work organizations particularly need to help managers and supervisors understand the guilt involved in performance appraisal and other supervisory actions, and to work out some of those feelings in management training programs.

Executives might be helped to understand the need to evolve multiple paths to achievement, using devices other than the ordinary hierarchical model, and to evolve more structured ways of funneling rivalry into task accomplishment, rather than pitting people against each other. Organizations must increasingly evolve more specific behavioral job descriptions, clearly defining what behavior is to be required of people and how they will know when those requirements are met. I refer specifically to actual behavior rather than to simple objectives.

More organizations might undertake and maintain continuous career counseling—including, particularly, counseling in the middle-age transition and through the preretirement period, specifically taking account of important psychological issues such as those that I have outlined here. They also should have devices for helping people prepare for multiple careers so they can make choices more readily and move into new occupational tracks when they become satiated with the previous work or reach dead ends in their present work or need to seek renewed stimulation.

Organizational leaders need to learn more about managing change in such a way as to alleviate potential stress and enable people to be effectively in charge of what is happening to them.

Finally, work organizations might well provide continuing education programs to support these efforts.

REFERENCES

Campbell, A. Subjective measures of well-being. In G. W. Albee and J. M. Joffe (Eds.), *Primary prevention of psychopathology. Vol. 1: The issues.* Hanover, N. H.: University Press of New England, 1977.
Campbell, A., Converse, P. E., and Rodgers, W. L. *The quality of American*

life: Perceptions, evaluations and satisfactions. New York: Russell Sage Foundation, 1976.

Erikson, E. H. *Childhood and society*, 2nd ed. New York: Norton, 1963.

Freud, S. On narcissism: An introduction. In J. Strachey and A. Tyson (Eds.), *The standard edition of the complete psychological works of Sigmund Freud* (Vol. 14). London: Hogarth Press (1957). (Originally published in 1914).

Gould, R. *Transformations.* New York: Simon and Schuster, 1978.

Hollingshead, A. B., and Redlich, F. C. *Social class and mental illness.* New York: Wiley, 1958.

Holmes, T. H., and Rahe, R. H. Social adjustment and rating scale. *Journal of Psychosomatic Research*, 1967, *11*, 213–223.

Kahn, R., Wolfe, D., Quinn, R., Snoek, J., and Rosenthal, R. *Organizational stress: Studies of role conflict and ambiguity.* New York: Wiley, 1964.

Kanter, R. M. Work in a New America. *Daedalus*, 1978, *107*, 47–78.

Kazin, A. *New York Jew.* New York: Knopf, 1978.

Kornhauser, A. W. *Mental health of the industrial worker: A Detroit study.* New York: Wiley, 1965.

Kübler-Ross, E. *On death and dying.* New York: Macmillan, 1969.

Levinson, D. J. *The seasons of a man's life.* New York: Pantheon, 1977.

Levinson, H., Price, C. R., Munden, K. J., Mandl, H. J., and Solley, C. M. *Men, management and mental health.* Cambridge: Harvard University Press, 1962.

Levinson, H. Appraisal of *what* performance? *Harvard Business Review*, 1976, *54*, 30–46.

Quinn, R. S., Mangione, T. W., and Baldi de Mandelovito, M. S. Evaluating working conditions in America. *Monthly Labor Review*, 1973, *96*, 32–41.

Rubin, L. *Worlds of pain.* New York: Basic Books, 1977.

Sarason, S. *Work, aging and social action.* New York: Free Press, 1977.

Singer, I. B. *A young man in search of love.* New York: Doubleday, 1978.

Srole, L., Langner, T. S., Michael, S. T., Opler, M. K., and Rennie, T. A. C. *Mental health in the metropolis: The Midtown Study* (Vol. 1). New York: McGraw-Hill, 1962.

Toynbee, A. (Ed.). *Man's concern with death.* New York: McGraw-Hill, 1968.

Zaleznik, A., Ondrack, J., and Silver, A. Social class, occupational mental illness. In A. McLean (Ed.), *Mental health and work organizations.* Chicago: Rand McNally, 1970.

iv. Increasing Competence and Coping Skills: Models and Approaches

In this section we move from the numerator of the prevention equation to the denominator, from the amelioration or elimination of variables that increase psychopathology to the fostering of individual characteristics and social systems that counteract it. In a sense, we are moving from the prevention of disorder to the promotion of healthy functioning. Competence promotion is a concept that represents not only a strategically more promising approach to preventing psychopathology than the idea of obviating or removing psychopathogenic influences, but one that entirely redefines the debate between treatment and prevention and between "medical models" and psychobiosocial models of disturbed functioning. The development of the concept of promotion is part of a process of shifting emphasis from individual aberrations as a cause of disturbance to a consideration of institutional determinants such as socioeconomic conditions.

George W. Albee's paper, which introduces this section, provides a bridge from the past to the future, from prevention to promotion. He is critical of psychology and related professions for perpetuating an illness or defect model of mental disturbance. Why has a flawed and inadequate model persisted for so long? Albee argues that the reasons are to be found in professional jealousy, profit, professional status, and ethnocentrism, rather than in scientific fact. A competence model, as he envisages it, depends on an egalitarian political and moral philosophy, the prime prerequisite for fostering competence. Mental health professionals can help to enhance competence by redirecting their attention to environmental causes of psychopathology and by adopting models of human development and functioning that avoid "blaming the victim."

Robert W. White, to whom we owe the modern concept of competence, discusses its meaning as an aspect of personal growth. He reminds us of two important facts. First, competence is primarily a biological concept. Humans, White argues, have an urge to act effectively on the environment, and a primary factor in developing competence is how rewarding one's behavioral initiatives are to the individual. Becoming socially competent, that is, requires the experience of success in social initiatives. Thus if competent behavior is inherently self-initiated and self-rewarded, it may be that no outside agents can teach it to another person. White sounds another cautionary note for those who would combine the concept of *social* competence with primary prevention. Competence implies skills, but social competence implies value judgments regarding standards of acceptability and morality. According to White, the histories of modern societies provide abundant evidence of periodic radical redefinitions of socially competent behavior. Thus White is wary of interventions whose outcomes can be judged only by future generations.

Luis M. Laosa expands on the theme of cultural relativity inherent in the concept of competence, emphasizing the need for a model that "includes important sociocultural dimensions and reflects the diversity present within complex and changing societies." Identifying the universal components of competence cross-culturally requires a complex and subtle model of development. Laosa integrates several developmental theories to provide a definition of social competence and attempts to identify means by which any society can maximize its children's acquisition of culturally valued psychosocial competencies at each developmental stage.

Lynne A. Bond's paper helps sharpen the distinction between "prevention" and "promotion" and clarifies the importance of one's model of development to the approach one takes to promoting competence. She points out the limitations of the historically accepted goal of preventing the development of negative outcomes and urges a focus on the more general aim of promoting positive development. Programmatic constraints have typically led us to focus on predominantly preventive measures and hence to implement isolated, short-lived, expensive programs when disaster is impending. Bond argues that the shift toward promotion is best accelerated by incorporating promotive features into the typical normal activities of our society. Bond outlines the nature and bases of her approach to development, which she views as a product of the organism's own interaction with the environment. Consequently, efforts at promotion need to foster the individual's propensity to engage in such interactions. Her review thus elaborates on Robert W. White's notion of an intrinsic motive to achieve effective interaction and suggests the need to address the self-sustaining motivational processes that underlie a sense of efficacy.

Steven J. Danish and Anthony R. D'Augelli continue the discussion of the issues raised by the distinction between "prevention" and "promotion." They explain the reasons for their pessimism about the potential effectiveness of primary prevention in today's helping systems and suggest that the prevention movement has overemphasized the absence of pathology as its goal and in the process has given insufficient consideration to the dimension of *health*. Their own human developmental model of competence holds that "stressful" life events can be important opportunities to enhance development. They point out that people are learning ways of enhancing their lives—promoting competence—not from professionals but in other ways. The self-help movement is spurred by natural caregivers in communities and by the dispensing of life skilis through the mass media, and Danish and D'Augelli advocate a pyramid model of human service delivery that capitalizes on people helping each other in their own communities.

A Competency Model Must Replace the Defect Model

George W. Albee

Frequently a revolution in scientific thinking occurs when some widely accepted premise, some "historical truth," is seen finally as inaccurate or incorrect. Our minds explore the crowded spaces created by the walls of fixed ideas until eventually we question why the walls are there at all. With the expanse of space that comes into view as the old conceptual walls are torn down, completely new kinds of explorations are possible. The simple step of abandoning an old habitual pattern of thinking often leads to a whole new way of dealing with a problem.

The *sickness* or *defect* or *illness* explanation of disturbed behavior has been ascendant for a century. It has been questioned repeatedly over the years, but only recently has the intellectual climate become favorable to the growth of disbelief. Now the harvest of doubt is ready.

One of the most important factors forcing our reevaluation of the *illness* model is a growing concern with the primary prevention of emotional disturbance. To prevent something we must first identify or describe what it is that we wish to prevent; then we must identify the causative forces that lead to the undesirable state or process, and try to remove them—or, as another strategy, we must do other things that "strengthen the host" to resist successfully the causative agent.

The illness model has come to be seen increasingly as inappropriate to meaningful efforts at primary prevention. Mental illnesses are not objective facts. They are not identifiable diseases to be confirmed in the laboratory through diagnostic tests. There is, with rare exceptions, no organic pathology to be discovered. These conditions are not easily identified and are not reliably diagnosed. They do not follow the usual public health paradigm of prevention where an identifiable disease is traced back to a predictable cause that can be removed or defended against. Rather we are concerned with problems in living, problems often created by blows of fate, by the damaging forces of a racist, sexist, ageist society where preparation for competent adaptation is minimal.

❖ Henderson (1975), writing in the *Bulletin of the Menninger Clinic*, sees a "fading" of community psychiatry, decries "the magical notion of 'primary prevention' " (p. 235), and points to "the striking advances of biological medicine" (p. 235) in both treatment and prevention. Persons are naive when they talk about prevention (says Henderson) because there are "only a few conditions in psychiatry (brain syphilis and PKU perhaps) that are well . . . (enough) understood to be preventable" (p. 235). He concludes: "it makes little sense to divert millions of dollars from treatment to a 'woolly' notion of primary prevention" (p. 236).

❖ In spite of one hundred years of increasingly massive attempts at educating the general public about mental illness, the person in the street, in contrast to the highly educated, does not interpret most disturbed behavior as "illness." In the late 1950's the Joint Commission on Mental Illness (sic) and Health (see *Action for Mental Health*, 1961) reported an extensive study, done by Shirley Star, of a nationwide sample survey to determine what is recognized by most people as "mental illness." On the basis of 3500 interviews she concluded that there is a large "tendency to resist labeling anyone as mentally ill" (by the general public) except as a last resort (pp. 74–75).

❖ If the general public has not been sold on the sickness explanation, and if our research data fail to support this explanation, why do we continue to emphasize the illness model in our professional intervention centers and professional training programs? If emotional problems are learned in a social context, why do we continue to pretend that people with these problems are sick? If emotional problems have been and continue to be shown to result from the interaction of environmental stress and learned ability to cope with stress (competence), why is our clinical model still medical? Who benefits?

Bertrand Russell suggested that anything worth *stating* is worth *overstating*. I will be following that principle. First let me state my own position. I believe the *competence model* demands an egalitarian political and moral philosophy. If we believe that every person, female and male, of whatever race, nationality, age, or ethnic origin, deserves every possible opportunity to maximize his or her competence and coping skills, we must free ourselves of the prejudices that are so much a part of Western thought. We must accept the position that everyone has the potential for growth and the right to personal maximization of competence to deal with stress.

This moral position is and will be highly threatening to the authoritarians and to those who accept a defect model. I want to argue that a competency model is incompatible with the position that certain persons are emotionally defective, that certain groups are defective because of genetic or organic factors, that women are inferior to men, blacks inferior to whites, southern Europeans inferior to Nordics, and that there is something *inherently* different about Jews, Orientals, French Canadians, Bantus, or whatever groups. I am not arguing against the concepts of individual differences and statistical variability. I am arguing against prejudice, ethnocentrism, and elitism. A competency model will be opposed, subtly or overtly, by those who favor meritocracy, divine right, or separate and unequal kinds of interventions for separate groups. A competency model is anti-categorical and anti-elitist.

I warn you that acceptance of a competency model will be dangerous to your comfort. There are many powerful forces that are threatened by such a model; and as these forces have the power to punish those espousing it, it will be dangerous if we go too far down this road. There is a safe, dillettantist position we can play: the artificial competency training of persons who are imbedded in an authoritarian system that is loaded with injustice. This is comparable to polishing brass on the *Titanic*. But if you accept the position that most emotional distress develops as a result of the unequal battle between individual resistance to stress and competency to deal with stress, on the one side, and on the other, the overwhelming injustice and dehumanization that is part of our consumer-oriented industrial society, then clearly the strategy is to strive to change the society and its values if we are to make a competency model more promising for success in prevention.

My thesis is that excessive industrialization requires the dehumanization of work and the submergence or elimination of individuality, of individual creativity, of a sense of identity and of personal competence. We are merely dealing with a small part of the problem when we try to build competencies into children who are destined to take their places as workers in endlessly boring and routine jobs in manufacturing, sales, service, and agribusiness. The modern industrial state has defined human existence into rigid poles, emphasizing efficient production and mindless consumption. In the process competent individuality has been all but lost (Albee, 1977).

❖ Let me make clear my position on prevention. In developing a model for primary prevention we should focus our attention on the following formula:

$$\text{Incidence} = \frac{\text{Organic causes and stress}}{\text{Competence, coping skills, self esteem, and social support systems}}$$

I must point out that this model can accommodate efforts in the organic and psychotherapeutic modes as well—it depends on whether the focus is on an individual or a population. The point I want to make is that building competence through increasing coping skills will reduce incidence—so long as we do not assume the presence of an unmodifiable organic defect, as long as we have some control over excessive social and economic stress, and as long as we do not have a society that destroys self esteem and/or social support systems. But focusing on competence, important as it is for prevention, must be part of a larger effort at social and political change.

❖ The illness model of mental disturbance is *evil*. It restricts the field of therapy to a small elite band by setting artifically high, nonfunctional, educational criteria for helpers. If one works directly with *sick patients*, then one must have prestigious training and high status. It demands that every person receiving help be given a medical diagnosis—a damaging label that can be a self-fulfilling prophecy and that may be a life-long Scarlet Letter. It ensures that the large sums of money that a trusting society thinks it is appropriating for the relief of human suffering wind up in the pockets of a small and powerful elite group whose underlying purpose is to support the status quo. It denigrates and ridicules efforts at prevention that suggest the importance of social change and competence building.

The medical model has other faults. It focuses our attention on one-to-one patchwork symptom reduction as the best way to help. Finding ways to prevent cancer would destroy one of the major American growth industries! Accepted epidemiological doctrine says that no mass disorders afflicting humankind have even been eliminated with one-to-one intervention with afflicted persons. In the case of genuine diseases the principle always operates. Smallpox, typhoid fever, polio, and measles were not dealt with successfully by training enough physicians to treat sufferers individually. These scourges afflicting humankind were brought under control by discovering their causes and by effective efforts at primary prevention. An analogy can be drawn with emotional problems. They are so common, so damaging to effective living, and so endemic that we cannot expect to have enough professional people to intervene with each disturbed person on a one-to-one basis; rather we ought to devote our efforts to documenting the social origins of psychopathology and to making the social changes necessary to reduce the incidence of these problems, and to increase the competency of people to deal with problems in living. The defect model diverts our attention from the social origins of disturbance and it camouflages the need for radical social change.

I have another complaint about psychiatry and the medical model; it, too, relates to prevention. One of the several major myths that has been promulgated with great intensity in recent years has it that the deinstitutionalization of persons who have been locked for years in the state hospitals is a result of dramatic discoveries in psychiatry and improvements in the field of psychotropic medication. This is unmitigated nonsense, but it affects our attitudes about prevention.

If the decarceration of hundreds of thousands of inmates of mental hospitals has *not* been the result of the effectiveness of the new psychotropic drugs, then what *has* led to it? Scull (1977) gives the answer with devastating clarity: it is *cheaper for the states*. With the gradual shift in the cost of public welfare to the Federal Government, the states, particularly the conservative administrations of certain states, discovered that it is far less expensive to get people out of mental hospitals that are supported by state monies and into communities where they can be supported on medicare, daycare, and the welfare roles. No matter that these poor unfortunates are herded into the poverty ghettos of the city slums, where they are preyed on by others. No matter that they must lead lives of terror, subject to the rapaciousness of profiteering group-home and nursing-home operators. In short, the "revolution in the care of the mentally ill" touted by the mass media as a triumph of modern psychiatric and pharmacological research is little more than a way for the states to cut their losses and shift the burden onto the Federal Government. Scull (1977) points out: "The pervasiveness, intensity, and mutually reinforcing character of the pressures to adopt a policy of decarceration are shown to be intimately connected to the rise of welfare capitalism" (p. 12).

Mechanic (1969) has also shown that the accelerating tendency in England to release mental cases from institutions was observed *before* the introduction of the psychotropic drugs. Scull summarizes a number of studies that make it clear "that the tremendous change that took place is due largely to alterations in administrative policies" (p. 82). Data on the length of hospitalization make it clear that *before* the marketing of chlorapromazine the average duration of stay in mental hospitals in England had already dropped significantly. At the Vermont State Hospital the number of schizophrenics admitted did not essentially vary between 1948 and 1958, but the number of schizophrenics discharged increased four times during this period—*before* drugs were in use!

❖ Of all the professions that have been developed to provide for the social control of deviants, psychiatry has been most successful. By allying itself with medicine and by labeling deviants as having *diseases* based on underlying (as yet undiscovered) organic conditions and defects, psychiatry has achieved great social power. Persons judged insane can be deprived of their liberty without a trial, on the basis of psychiatric testimony about their *dangerousness*—even though research evidence has established clearly the unreliability of such a prediction. Stone (1975), a professor of psychiatry and law at Harvard, studied this evidence and concluded:

It can be stated flatly on the basis of my own review of the published material on the prediction of dangerous acts that neither objective actuarial tables nor psychiatric intuition, diagnosis, and psychological testing can claim predictive success when dealing with the traditional population of mental hospitals. (p. 33)

So far I have had some highly critical things to say about psychiatry. Let me give equal time to the evils of psychology. May I commend to your reading Leon Kamin's incisive book *The Science and Politics of IQ* (1974). Kamin documents in incredible detail the lengths to which prominent American psychologists were willing to go to prove their tenacious beliefs in the inheritance of a fixed entity called intelligence and in the inferiority of non-Nordics and other groups who were so inferior genetically that they threatened to destroy the existence of the early sturdy stock of the United States. The roster of these psychologists is a Who's Who in American psychology. They were leaders of the APA, and their intellectual offspring are still at work in our most prestigious universities today. Terman (1917), for example, was convinced that Spanish-Indian and Mexican families in the Southwest, and Negroes, had deficient intellects.

Repeatedly we find psychologists arguing that poor people are poor because they are defective and not for environmental reasons. Terman favored eugenic solutions and he observed pointedly that organized charities often allow these feebleminded individuals to survive when otherwise they would not be able to live and reproduce. Henry Goddard (1917) in an invited address at Princeton University spelled out the reasons why workmen with low intelligence did not merit the same living standards as persons on higher mental levels. Robert Yerkes, another president of APA, was active in the eugenics movement. His group educated the Congress and the state legislatures on the importance of passing sterilization laws. Kamin (1974) concludes: "The mental testers pressed upon the Congress scientific IQ data to demonstrate that the 'new immigration' from Southeastern Europe was

genetically inferior" (p. 12). The evidence from the mental testers
was used to change the pattern of immigration, to shut off, insofar
as possible, immigration from Southern and Eastern Europe.
Goddard in 1912 went to Ellis Island with his Binet test and
administered this and other performance tests to a representative
sample of what he referred to as the great mass of average immigrants. He found that 83% of the Jews, 80% of the Hungarians,
79% of the Italians, and 87% or the Russians were 'feeble
minded' " (Kamin, 1974, p. 16).

❖   Kamin points to the interesting parallel between the statements
made about the Italians by Pintner in his 1923 text *Intelligence
Testing* and the statements made today about blacks. Jensen
(1969) argues that "Negroes" average about one standard deviation (15 IQ points) below the average of the white population. Is
it not highly probable that this finding is as valid as the earlier
observations by psychologists that 83 percent of Jewish immigrants were feebleminded or that the average IQ of the Italian was
84?

❖   The Jensen position is a modern version. It is antithetical to
a competency model. Jensen's monograph (1969) argued that
compensatory education may be considered a failure. For him,
some people simply do not have it. He acknowledges that his conclusion, if true, amounts to a death sentence for the ideal of
egalitarianism, a powerful influence in contemporary Western
society. He says:

> There is an increasing realization among students of the psy-
> chology of the disadvantaged that the discrepancy in their average
> performance cannot be completely or directly attributed to
> discrimination or inequalities in education. It seems not un-
> reasonable, in view of the fact that intelligence variation has a
> large genetic component, to hypothesize that genetic factors
> may play a part in this picture. But such an hypothesis is
> anathema to many social scientists. The idea that the lower
> average intelligence and scholastic performance of Negroes could
> involve, not only environmental, but also genetic, factors has
> indeed been strongly denounced e.g., Pettigrew (1964). But it has
> been neither contradicted nor discredited by evidence.
>   The fact that a reasonable hypothesis has not been rigorously
> proved does not mean that it should be summarily dismissed.

It only means that we need more appropriate research for putting it to the test. *I believe such definitive research is entirely possible but has not yet been done.* (Italics added; p. 82)

These paragraphs bear careful study. What Jensen is saying is that there are hints and clues that support the position that there are differences in intelligence between the races that are due to genetic factors. But he makes it clear that definite scientific evidence in support of this hypothesis has not yet been accumulated. He urges more research on the question. Yet having disposed of this scientifically necessary qualification, he goes on to draw conclusions and make recommendations for changes in social policy as if the difference had been scientifically established. In a truly scientific approach one never rejects the null hypothesis until the evidence is in, and then only in terms of stated probability limits. The psychologists referred to seem to be rejecting the null hypothesis (that there are no differences between races that cannot be accounted for by environmental differences) but with no real certainty. This is a cardinal scientific sin.

The organic model of retardation, like the organic model of "mental illness" is contradicted by a great many facts. The first of these is that it is very very hard to find "mildly retarded" children before schooling begins. Frequently someone decides to do early intervention with mildly retarded preschoolers in order to see if such efforts can reduce the child's later learning problems in school. In most efforts of this sort it turns out to be impossible to locate "mildly retarded" preschoolers. If one asks pediatricians in public clinics, or faimly doctors, or public health nurses, all of these professionals can identify the more seriously retarded children in the community. But no one knows (with reliable knowledge) who the mildly retarded are. So researchers must work with groups of "high risk" children—say, all the children of mothers with low IQs—to find *some* children who will receive the label when they get to school.

It has also been observed that the IQs of inner city children often decline while they are in school, and they wind up being called "mildly retarded" when they get to junior high, or high school—having gone through regular classes in elementary school. Lane and Albee (1970) found that inner-city school children tested as part of a routine group testing program in the Cleveland schools showed a decline from second to sixth grade that averaged more than 10 points! These children were in the normal range in second grade and were at the borderline or mildly retarded level four or five years later. Obviously this had to be *pseudo-retardation*.

The model we adopt affects directly the kind of people we help and the kind of institutions we develop for intervention and prevention. These in turn dictate the kind of people we use to deliver care. With a social-developmental model focused on social reform and competence building, our state hospitals and public clinics would be replaced by social intervention centers, largely staffed by people at the bachelor's level—more like special education teachers and social welfare workers, potentially available in vastly greater supply than psychologists and psychiatrists. For prevention, people like ourselves would be needed as teachers, researchers, and especially as radical social activists proselytizing for changes in our society to make it more supportive, less dehumanized.

The massive deterioration of the fabric of industrial society and its institutions results in a complex tangle of pathology which includes especially the destruction of the emotional integrity of the family. Let me emphasize something that you already know very well. Many significant research breakthroughs have already been made. Many of the discoveries are already in. We know, for example, that the emotional climate that surrounds the infant and young child is of critical importance in determining his or her future—including the kind, the severity, and perhaps even the biological concomitants of later disturbance.

Such knowledge is dangerous. We usually shut our eyes to its implications. We go on trying to fix up damaged adults in one-to-one relationships when a more proper professional function would be to spend a considerable portion of our energies trying to fix up our society in ways that will increase the strength and stability of the family, thereby affecting positively the mental health of generations to come.

Most efforts at prevention focus on the forces that have produced disturbance. Another approach for investigators is to try to define and measure "adaptive potential." This approach argues that certain individuals develop highly skilled patterns of competent adaptation to a wide range of situations. Offer and Sabshin

(1963) did a study of adolescents without gross psychopathology—they all showed a high level of mastery of developmental tasks and effective coping skills in their relationships with others. Grinker, Grinker, and Timberlake (1962) studied mentally healthy young males and found that "homoclites" (optimally adjusted men) tended to be self-confident goal-seekers with a strong sense of self-worth, warm family relationships, and an action orientation. This model would suggest that preventive efforts be focused on the development and competence and coping skills in contrast with the more life-history oriented model that focuses on the elimination of pathological experiences. Obviously the two models are not separate and even complement each other.

Poser (1970) has discussed a behavioral model for prevention. This approach focuses attention on the role of learning processes in the development of adaptive and maladaptive behavior. The approach suggests that specific learning experiences can be identified and that behavioral approaches effective in leading to behavioral change can also be identified. Some persons may actively learn to behave in a maladaptive way, while others may passively learn, through modeling ineffective social and interpersonal skills. Both groups are then more vulnerable to later stress situations and so are at higher psychological risk. This approach stresses more careful delineation of specific behavioral problems and draws heavily on the concepts of behavioral psychology.

Other examples in this area include the work of Seligman (1975), whose study of learned helplessness has had such a widespread impact. He suggests that giving individuals early experience with stress situations that they can learn to control may reduce their susceptibility to later feelings of helplessness in uncontrollable aversive situations. Suinn, Jorgensen, Stewart, and McGuirk (1971) gave groups "anxiety management training," and Meichenbaum (1975) used a cognition-training procedure that he called "stress inoculation" as a defense against later anxiety. All of these approaches involve some form of practice in the management of stress so as to increase the person's ability to deal competently with later stress.

Others in this volume are concerned at greater length with the issue of competence. I remind you that competent persons often are turned into incompetent persons as a result of the operation of social and economic forces outside of their control.

Forcing persons into an incompetent role or life style when in fact they are competent in another role or life style has to be a major source of stress contributing to emotional disturbances and other forms of psychopathology. I will cite two examples:

In many parts of the United States, particularly in Southern states, laws are *written* in such a way that competent black farmers can be forced off the land they have long regarded as their own, land that has been in their family for several generations. There is a proper legal mechanism involved. In the past, black farmers have often died without a will, and their land has been inherited, share and share alike, by children and/or other relatives. After two or three such generations the legal title to the land is so clouded that persons and corporations coveting the land (the value of which may be increasing rapidly) can use any of several strategems to force a Sheriff's sale. As a result, many competent black farmers and their families are being forced out of a way of life in which they are self-respecting and self-supporting into cities where they have few salable skills and where they are forced to become part of the welfare roll. Critics of the "growing welfare burden" do all sorts of dehumanizing things to add to the stresses placed on these families, with resulting emotional disturbance, crime, delinquency, and premature pregnancy.

Here is a second example. Impoverished women throughout our society, and especially throughout the third world, are being encouraged to feed their infants with powdered formula in bottles. Propaganda and social pressure for bottle-feeding by women who are perfectly competent to breast feed their infants is fostered and augmented by the formula manufacturing companies, who often have arrangements with local physicians and governmental health educator officials. These give new mothers free samples of powdered infant formula that last long enough for the mother's breast milk to dry up, after which she is then obligated to pay a significant portion of the family income for the formula. In areas where water supplies are contaminated, infants often receive disease-laden formula, or they are given inadequate quantities of the powdered milk as their mothers seek to stretch the formula because of its excessive cost. As a consequence, thousands of infants are failing to thrive, dying, or not developing proper growth of the central nervous system. A major source of stress, of course, is the sickness and death of these infants. Again we see competent people turned into incompetent people as a result of social pressures and economic manipulation.

Many serious, sober, and far-from-radical observers today believe the problem at the heart of our social malaise is the primacy of corporate profits over long-range planning for the public good. Short-run success is all that is important to the mindless corporation. In pursuit of these immediate rewards our environment is devastated, our people are brainwashed into becoming mindless consumers or thrill-seeking robots, and the pleasures of human contact have been subordinated to the pleasures of material consumption.

One of the most fearsome aspects of this situation is the seeming hopelessness of the system ever changing itself. Enormous corporations and conglomerates defy government control. The cost of running for federal office has grown to the point where successful candidates must be supported by these giant corporate powers in order to be elected. The conglomerates and cartels are more powerful than governments, and power structure extends around the earth.

Blame is one of the most useless human activities. I do not propose to blame solely the corporations or the people who run them for the dehumanization that is a prominent part of the conglomerate society. But we must all point to them as a major source of our pollution, environmental and human, and then seek, coldly and rationally, to change the system.

Back in the early days of this century, before the psycho-dynamic-sickness model had assumed its current total primacy, there was little ambiguity among mental health professionals about where evil was to be found. It was clearly recognized that human beings were damaged, dehumanized, and destroyed by the mindless and indifferent forces of free-enterprise-industrialization. And it was clear that social causes of emotional disturbance demanded social action as a remedy.

Jane Addams back in 1910 was merciless in her criticism of professionals who failed to recognize the relationship between industrialization and poverty. She urged those in her own field of social work to come together with "the Radicals" to fight for better social conditions. In her view, social work, to achieve its goals, had to engage in social and political action. It was no accident that the economic reforms and labor legislation proposed in the 1912 platform of Theodore Roosevelt's Bull Moose party read like Jane Addams' program for social action. She was on the platform and seconded his nomination.

When did we switch from an *evil-is-in-the-system* social reform philosophy to the more conservative *evil-is-inside-the-person* individual-treatment philosophy? Probably sometime in the decade of the 1920's. Psychiatry and social work focused on individual need, on psychic determinism, and on the one-to-one intervention method. The early involvement of social workers in social action — storming the citadels of the establishment, organizing the poor, working with the unions, leading and encouraging tenant strikes, gave way to the ascendant psychiatric notion that evil is inside the person, and that if we can get the person across a desk from us, we can somehow patch up the problem. Our training programs all teach this model, which serves as a support for reaction. If evil is inside the person, then we do not need to change anything except the person, and the damaging status quo is left intact.

Let us recognize that these training fictions influence the moral attitudes and ethical values of professional workers, and they in turn significantly influence both the form of intervention and the prevention we choose to use, and the way we are perceived by society. The fundamental professional decision is whether we *represent the client* or whether we *represent the agency*, institution, and society that pays the salary.

The professional worker in the human services fields is faced with severe personal role conflicts which are continuing and inescapable. Each professional worker must decide to whom he or she is responsible, the *Establishment* or the *victim*. Professional workers are overwhelmingly drawn from the middle-class and are notoriously timid about fighting for social change. Middle-class professionals are educated in middle-class colleges and universities and are exposed to an endless indoctrination which rewards conformity and control and punishes extremism and originality. The lock-step system of education from the earliest school years through college and professional training continuously weeds out rebels and deviants so that professionals completing their training are a highly selected group of middle-of-the-roaders. Yet once one begins to work with the emotionally disturbed, the so-called insane, the rebels against the system, the alcoholics, the drug addicts, the juvenile delinquents and criminals, one begins to see that many of these problems are caused by the faults and defects of the economic system. Is this knowledge enough to counteract our years of training in conformity? Is it enough to affect our attitudes toward prevention?

The professional must continuously decide whether he or she is a defender of the established order or must become an advocate for the victims of the established order. Those who opt for the traditional pattern of pinning diagnostic labels on disturbed people and explaining their deviant behavior in terms of a sickness originating in a defective brain or endocrine system or chromosomal defect are clearly defenders of the status quo, particularly in the absence of any compelling evidence for such a defect explanation. This whole approach has been well labeled by William Ryan (1971) as *Blaming the Victim*. The poor are to blame for their poverty, and the insane are to blame for the insanity, and the criminals are to blame for their rebellion.

On the other hand, the professionals who see disturbed people as victims of an exploitative and dehumanizing system are quickly made visible and are themselves labeled as radicals or rebels with emotional problems (probably caused by some internal defect). We need unanimity in these matters, or we will be picked off one by one!

Kenneth B. Clark (1974) has pointed out that "any form of rejection, cruelty and injustice inflicted upon any group of human beings by any group of human beings *dehumanizes* the victims overtly and in more subtle ways dehumanizes the perpetrators" (p. 144). He called on psychology to stop avoiding the moral and survival problems of the human race and try to enhance the human capacity for creativity and progress. He argued that it is imperative for psychology to seek to control the destructive forces within society.

Professionally, we also know that a person with the strongest hunger for power, with power needs that lead to an insatiable drive for authority and control over others, is not ordinarily the most empathic person. If those who avidly seek positions of power are drawn from the more neurotic, then perhaps we should apply what we know about intervention in neurosis (which is to make the unconscious conflicts conscious). This suggests that we continue to interpret to political leaders the causes of their most dehumanizing actions, and that we seek to secure whatever legal checks and balances we can to minimize the damage they do to those who cannot help or protect themselves.

Professionally, we also know something about the development of empathy, that feeling we experience when we put ourselves in the place of others. Those with a mature and well developed conscience are capable of empathy. Empathy is the source of most humanistic actions and concerns. Yet we know, too, that empathy is most likely to appear when specific, real, and concrete objects for empathy are clearly perceivable. Many bomber pilots found it hard to empathize with abstract people who might or might not have been in jungle villages thousands of feet below their planes. Neither can polluters feel empathy for unknown people who might be damaged hundreds of miles distant, or several generations hence. Knowing this, it seems to me that we must find ways to make known the sufferings of people—those who are the victims of human actions and policies.

By all of this I am suggesting that we should consider assuming more active efforts to change society. I make this suggestion with some trepidation because I anticipate protest from those who will point to our lack of enough firm knowledge, at the grandiosity implicit in this proposal, and at the inappropriateness of small and precious groups attempting such a formidable task. But our social problems are all human problems, and we are the experts on those.

We must do more than simply make our knowledge available to the decision-makers of our society. As ethical social scientists, we must advocate, assert, urge, and proselytize. Each of us must decide how he or she can best contribute to the reduction of the dehumanizing forces in our society and the enhancement of the human competence that is possible. But we must first agree that the problem is in the system, not in the victim.

REFERENCES

Albee, G. W. The protestant ethic, sex, and psychotherapy. *American Psychologist*, 1977, *32*, 150–161.

Albee, G. W. A manifesto for a fourth mental health resolution? A review of the Report of the President's Commission on mental health, 1978. *Contemporary Psychology*, 1978, *23*, 549–551.

Brigham, C. C. *A study of American intelligence.* Princeton: Princeton University Press, 1923.

Brill, H. and Patton, R. E. Psychopharmacology and the current revolution in mental health services. In *Proceedings of the Fourth World Congress of Psychiatry*, Amsterdam: Excerpta Medica Foundation, 1966.

Carstairs, G. M. Preventive psychiatry—is there such a thing? *Journal of Mental Science*, 1958, *104*, 63–71.

Chesler, P. *Women and madness.* New York: Avon Books, 1973.

Clark, K. B. *Pathos of power.* New York: Harper and Row, 1974.

Deutsch, A. The first U.S. census of the insane (1840) and its use as pro-slavery propaganda. *Bulletin of the History of Medicine*, 1944, *15*, 469–482.

Eisenberg, L. Primary prevention and early detection in mental illness. *Bulletin of the New York Academy of Medicine*, 1975, *51*, 118–129.

Fromm, E. Boredom and aggression. *The New York Times Magazine*, February 27, 1972, pp. 80, 81, 84, 85.

Goddard, H. H. Mental tests and the immigrant. *Journal of Delinquency*, 1917, *2*, 271.

Grinker, R. R., Sr., Grinker, R. R., Jr., and Timberlake, J. A. Study of "mentally healthy" young males (homoclites). *Archives of General Psychiatry*, 1962, *6*, 405–410.

Henderson, J. Community tranference review: With notes on the clinic-community interface. *Journal of the American Academy of Psychoanalysis*, 1974, *2*, 113–128.

Henderson, J. Object relations and a new social psychiatry: The illusion of primary prevention. *Bulletin of the Menninger Clinic*, 1975, *39*, 233–245.

Jarvis, E. *Idiocy and lunacy in Massachusetts. Report of the commission on lunacy.* Boston: William White, Printer to the State, 1855. (reprinted Cambridge: Harvard University Press, 1971).

Jenson, A. R. How much can we boost I.Q. and scholastic achievement? *Harvard Educational Review Monograph*, 1969, *39*(1), 1–123.

Joint Commission on Mental Illness and Health. *Action for mental health.* New York: Basic Books, 1961.

Kamin, L. *The science and politics of I.Q.* Potomac, Md.: Lawrence Erlbaum Associates, 1974.

Klerman, G. Psychotropic drugs as therapeutic agents. *Hastings Center Studies*, 1974, *2*, 81–93.

Lane, E. A., and Albee, G. W. Intellectual antecedents of schizophrenia. In M. Roff and D. Ricks (Eds.), *Life history research in psychopathology.* Minneapolis: University of Minnesota Press, 1970.

Mechanic, D. *Mental health and social policy.* Englewood Cliffs, N.J.: Prentice-Hall, 1969.

Meichenbaum, D. Self-instructional methods. In F. H. Kanfer and A. P. Goldstein (Eds.), *Helping people change.* New York: Pergamon, 1975.

Mercer, J. *Labeling the mentally retarded.* Berkeley: University of California Press, 1973.

Offer, D., and Sabshin, M. The psychiatrist and the normal adolescent. *American Medical Association Archives of General Psychiatry*, 1963, *60*, 427–432.

Pettigrew, T. *A profile of the Negro American*. Princeton: Van Nostrand, 1964.

Pintner, R. *Intelligence testing: Methods and results*. New York: Holt, 1923.

Poser, E. G. Toward a theory of behavioral prophylaxis. *Journal of Behavioral Therapy and Experimental Psychiatry*, 1970, *1*, 39–43.

Ryan, W. *Blaming the victim*. New York: Pantheon Books, 1971.

Scull, A. *Decarceration*. Englewood Cliffs, N.J.: Prentice-Hall, 1977.

Seligman, M. *Helplessness: On depression, development, and death*. San Francisco: Freeman, 1975.

Stone, A. A. *Mental health and the law: A system in transition*. DHEW Publication No. (ADM) 76-176. Washington, D.C.: U.S. Government Printing Office, 1975.

Suinn, R. M., Jorgensen, G. T., Stewart, S. S., and McGuirk, F. D. Fears as attitudes: Experimental reduction of fear through reinforcement. *Journal of Abnormal Psychology*, 1971, *78*, 272–279.

Terman, L. S. Feeble-minded children in the public schools of California. *School and Society*, 1917, *5*, 161–165.

Competence as an Aspect of Personal Growth

Robert W. White

❖ *COMPETENCE IN GENERAL*

I arrived at the concept of competence some twenty years ago when trying to write a chapter on motivation for a book on personality. At that time the two leading theories, behaviorism and psychoanalytic theory, were in essential agreement that behavior was motivated by drives. The hunger drive was the model most commonly used by behaviorists, and the erotic instinctual drive was the favorite with psychoanalysts. The drive formula seemed to me seriously inadequate to account for the ceaseless activity, play, and exploration that are so obvious in young animals and in young children. Why are young creatures so busy and full of life when they might perfectly well sit back and wait for the next prodding of hunger or discomfort? This activity, it appeared to me, must have served a clear purpose in evolutionary history. Exploration and play enabled young animals to increase their knowledge of the environment and their competence in dealing with it. In contrast to a creature that sat idle until activated by a drive, an animal with restless curiosity would acquire extensive information about hiding places, escape routes, and its own prowess for combat and flight, in advance of the time when danger or acute need made this competence critical for survival.

Of all animals the human, with its capacious brain, seems most specialized for learning. We start life with little useful competence, but we have great resources for acquiring it. As babies we can only squirm and cry when too warm, but as adults we cope with the problem through air-conditioning. We start without language, but only seventeen years later we may produce an abstruse freshman essay on existentialism. To me it seems easier to understand these achievements if we picture our brains as living, restless organs that require occasional sleep but that otherwise need to be doing something. What they need to be doing shows in such behaviors as exploring objects with eyes and hands, which results eventually in eye-hand coordination, or trying different combinations of sound, which leads presently to speech, or practicing the far from simple coordinations required to throw and catch a ball—these and hundreds of other activities leading to the development of useful skills.

❖ Being effective, being able to have effects, seemed to be the heart of the matter. After some search of dictionaries I chose to call this simply *competence* and to speak of playful and exploratory behavior as exhibiting a general *urge toward competence.*

❖ Animal psychologists had begun to speak of an exploratory drive, a manipulative drive, even a drive to activity. Among psychoanalysts, Hartmann (1958) had written about adaptive behavior, Hendrick (1942) had postulated an instinct to master, Mittelmann (1954) had described a motility urge, and Bettelheim (1960) had stressed self-initiated activity to which he gave the name autonomy. In the older American tradition of functional psychology William James had favored such an idea, and John Dewey's notable contributions to education rested on the activity and potential interest which he assumed to be basic in human nature. I was safe from the Columbus complex. I was talking about something that was hardly more than common sense, something that everybody knew about—everybody, that is, except the behaviorists and strict Freudians who at that time dominated psychological theory.

It is now generally accepted that we are curious, probing, learning, coping, adapting creatures who build up competence through action on our surroundings. However we choose to conceive of these tendencies, they are essential to understanding such presently prominent topics as cognitive development and information processing. Less obvious, perhaps, is the effect of competence on the growth of personality as a whole. Yet, there is much reason to suppose that a sense of competence is a highly important ingredient of self and of self-esteem. When we interview young adults about their plans, hopes, and self-conceptions, we discover how often they refer to what they can and cannot do. Certain kinds of action they view with confidence, feeling sure they can have desired effects on their surroundings. In other spheres their experience may have led them to judge that the environment is intractable, which makes them feel inferior, helpless, and possibly anxious. You have a strong bastion of self-esteem if you feel confident you can do the things that matter most, that in these ways you can affect your environment and thus influence the course of your own life. People who feel this way are unlikely to wonder about their identity.

It is of the greatest importance to remember that competent behavior is self-rewarding. As Karl Groos (1901) long ago expressed it, there is "joy in being a cause." There is joy for a child in stamping in a puddle and seeing the widespread effect. The concept of intrinsic reward (Deci, 1975), now a popular topic of research, is nowhere better illustrated than in the discovery of our own competence.

This does not mean that extrinsic rewards in the form of encouragement and praise are without value. They can play a part, but if a real sense of competence is going to develop, the subject himself must experience his own action, his own initiative, in relation to the ensuing effects. No one else can confer this experience. No one can give another person a sense of competence.

People in the helping professions, who typically want to give and feel that they have much to give, are apt to be frustrated by this conclusion. And there are certainly things they can do to promote a growth of competence. But ultimately the sense of competence, being rooted in one's own action, has to come from within.

SOCIAL COMPETENCE

So much for competence in general. Let us now turn to the specific problem of social competence. Human beings are a vital part of the environment. They lead the child to the same questions as inanimate objects do: what are their properties, what can one do with them, what effects is it possible to have on them? The baby exploring the features of the mother's face, the one-year-old testing the properties of the word "No" when addressed to an older sibling, are all finding out by exploratory action what effects one can produce in one's human surroundings. A continuing history marked by extensive success in such endeavors may produce a highly confident adult who expects favorable responses to social initiative and who flourishes in the company of others. A history of the opposite kind may lead to a pervasive sense of helplessness, most dramatically seen in schizophrenics, where other people are seen as intrusive, perhaps dangerous, and no way can be found to fend them off. Up to a point, dealing with the inanimate environment and dealing with the human environment are wholly similar.

The human environment, however, from the start involves extra complications. Trying to exert influence is not usually just a matter of playful exploration but is mingled with other needs: to be fed, comforted, helped, supported, loved and esteemed. We find it difficult to distinguish the element of competence, of being able to have an influence, from these other needs to which it is instrumental. Because of this, we have tended to describe social behavior in terms of love and hate, acceptance and rejection, social enjoyment, and other affective goals without much reference to competence. What meaning, then, should we try to attach to social competence?

Now, when I lecture on this subject, it is here that I customarily perceive audience chill. Being competent sounds like a good thing when it refers to mastering the material world, but phrases like "influencing people" and "having effects on people" are bad: they call to mind manipulative mothers, domineering fathers, authoritarian teachers, tyrannical bosses, and the sorry business of shaping public opinion to make us think less and buy more. Are we trying to prevent psychopathology by increasing what may become a rampant and destructive desire for power?

Of course not. Competence, as I am using the term, is a biological concept, not a moral one. The ability to influence people can be used for bad ends as well as good. The great villains of history have been highly competent; that is how they could do so much harm. Competence can be used for sheer love of power as well as for giving expression to love. When we describe a helping person—a counselor or a child care worker—as competent, we mean effective in work; we do not imply a misuse of skills for personal glory.

What concerns us in connection with the general theme we are addressing is that low degrees of social competence in children seem to be importantly related to psychopathology. Children thus handicapped need to acquire enough sense of competence to make true interaction possible and in this way allow social needs to be satisfied. This is where we can hope to accomplish something for prevention.

THE OLDER CAMPAIGN FOR SOCIAL ADJUSTMENT

How do we go about promoting social competence in children who seem to lack it? So that we can all avoid the Columbus complex on this subject, I think it is important to realize that this is no new undertaking. Mental health teaching for fifty years has been singing the anthem of social adjustment. Reversing an earlier belief that it is well to keep children out of each other's mischievous company, we have urged that they be constantly plunged among their peers. We have come to regard first grade, when this happens anyway, as far too late. There must be kindergarten, there must be nursery school, there must be pre-nursery play groups. And the campaign must not weaken as children advance through school and into adolescence. The suburban mother must accept her role as full-time chauffeur, taking children to this or that opportunity for further mingling, and the school teacher must be a group worker who organizes clubs to fill the time after classes. For a child to be alone was positively dangerous. Solitude was a step down the seductive path to daydreaming and thence to schizophrenia.

The sad truth is that in our earlier attempts at mental health education we overshot the mark and gave parents a terrific scare about social adjustment. Two experiences that I had when lecturing to parents brought home to me the force of their anxiety. At a meeting of nursery school parents I happened to say that the social curriculum was a long one, extending over many years, so they need not be upset if their child did not exhibit instant social virtuosity at nursery school. Signs of joy, sighs of relief, and favorable comments from the audience showed me how strong their anxiety had been over three-year-old social ineptitude. On another occasion, meeting with junior high school parents, I was besieged for advice on what to do when one radical parent allowed her children various privileges for which the other parents felt their children were too young. Apparently these parents did not feel able to influence the radical parent—a commentary on their own sense of social competence—but they dared not risk spoiling their children's social adjustment by insisting on rules that did not apply fairly to everyone.

You may be surprised and not altogether pleased that I have sketched the campaign for social adjustment in such unflattering terms, emphasizing its excesses and the anxiety behind them. But we can learn something important, I believe, by inquiring into the consequences. As already mentioned, our first products seemed to be a generation of other-directed conformists who had trouble becoming aware of who they were. We should not overlook, however, the social virtues of many of the young people of the sixties and seventies who, despite certain troublesome outbreaks, seem able to get along well together and to meet people of all ages with a relaxed, attractive friendliness. Perhaps we dare take some credit for this happy result, and I am always touched by the seriousness with which young people try to make their relations authentic— true expressions of true feelings. But if their social learning had been perfect, it is paradoxical that they have to struggle so for purity of feeling. It is strange that, as a generation, they express such a strong desire for more social training, such a hunger for encounter groups, T-groups, marathon weekends, group psychotherapy, as if they still had to learn how they affect other people and how other people affect them.

The conclusion is hard to escape that there were grave defects in the old campaign for social adjustment. Thinking of the end as vitally important, we failed to make a proper analysis of the means. We tried to teach children to swim by throwing them overboard. All our emphasis fell on getting children together, and we did not sufficiently consider the kinds of situations that would be most conducive to the growth of real social competence. This is what we need—insight into means—in order to achieve our goals.

INHERENT DIFFICULTIES IN SOCIAL INTERACTION

The first point to consider is what may be called the inherent danger contained in human interactions. If there are elements of felt danger in the company of others, children placed among their peers may well learn not social interaction but defenses against social interaction. Before they have time to feel comfortable and to satisfy some of their social inclinations they may develop protective strategies that effectively block these inclinations. Social competence cannot become established if the necessary initiative is inhibited by anxiety.

Children potentially have much to gain and much to enjoy from interaction with the people around them. But first the child must dare to interact. This is the point which I believe we have not perceived with enough sharpness. As products of the Freudian revolution we were convinced that the dreadful family tended to saddle children with anxieties that crippled their whole development. Then, as if to compensate for our disillusionment with families, we spread a rosy romantic glow over peer groups, hopefully entrusting them with the socializing functions that were no longer safe in parental hands. Peer groups were a way out, an avenue of escape from the oppressive family. Thus they entered the mental health message in a saving role, with little thought of what they are really like.

It is easy to puncture the dream by calling to mind the peer education that goes on in a disadvantaged urban ghetto. Rivalry, aggression, and mistrust are well taught, but they leave little room for the enjoyment of social inclinations. More benign environments still exhibit grave faults as agents for social development. Sullivan (1953) described the crudeness in interpersonal relations characteristic of the years from six to ten as a time of "shocking insensitivity to feelings of personal worth in others." Even at nursery school, a planned benign environment with the teacher quick to intervene, children usually experience some of the activities of their peers as damaging to their well-being.

Social initiative, then, typically develops in circumstances that contain elements of danger. But there is a second difficulty that may impede the growth of social competence: the difficulty of recognizing the results of one's actions. Many children, and indeed many adults, are not held back by possible risks. On the contrary, they speak and act impulsively but seem to be little aware of the effects they have on others. A husband of the bull-in-the-china-shop type, tired from work, storms into the house with a bombardment of critical and demeaning comments and then, when his wife bursts into tears, asks in wonderment, "What did I say? " Now that we are alerted to hyperactive children, we can see that understanding the consequences of one's social initiatives may be a matter of real difficulty. Just as physical competence will not improve if a child fails to register the connection between throwing a ball too hard and its going too far, so interpersonal competence will not grow if there is failure to notice the responses. And social responses are often harder to perceive correctly than are physical ones.

With these difficulties in mind, I am going to describe three general patterns of social incompetence which I shall call *social anaesthesia, social isolation* and *social enslavement.*

Social Anaesthesia

The psychological basis of social anaesthesia is that some of our behavior is simply a blind expression of feeling. The tired husband who slams the door, aims a kick at the dog, and shouts at the children as well as insulting his wife, is not really in focus on his environment. He is trying to deal with his own feelings of frustration, and his explosions may actually make him feel better provided the environment does not hit back too hard. Many of a child's expressions, like crying, hitting, and tantrums, are only vaguely directed at the environment. These actions are forced out by strong feelings almost regardless of who is there. Under these circumstances it is an advantage not to register the real effects. A pleasant catharsis of aggression is spoiled if the victim lashes back or shows hurt and makes you feel guilty. Workers with hyperactive and emotionally disturbed children give reports which I believe justify the metaphor of social anaesthesia. The child who tears down the party decorations as fast as the other children put them up is giving vent to a vast anger, and perhaps securing some inner relief, but this is surely not the way to increase social competence. The emotional necessities swamp any rewards that might be gained by effective influence of the other children.

People who are impulsive, whether by nature or by high emotional need, will have greater difficulty in recognizing the social consequences of their acts. They will therefore be slower to develop social competence even though their initiatives come easily. Earlier mental health messages, emphasizing permissiveness, tended to make impulsiveness a virtue, and did not recognize that it might interfere with real social growth.

The procedure by which social anaesthesia can be modified is symbolized in the words of the nursery school teacher who says: "Look, Michael, if you push Karen so hard that she falls down, it hurts her." Clarifying the consequences may be worth trying when a child seems not to be registering them. At the adult level there is group psychotherapy and all its training offshoots, where the participants learn, through interacting, the unsuspected effects other people have on them. Most people who experience these procedures learn a good deal that they did not know before.

Social Isolation

By social isolation I do not refer primarily to an avoidance whereby the child simply stays alone. Physical withdrawal from company has long been described by the artistically and philosophically inclined as a necessity for creative accomplishment. By many people, however, withdrawal is seen as selfish, sinful, and an insult; we are hurt that anyone should prefer solitude to our charming and wonderful company. Mental health workers, scenting schizophrenia, have joined in this harsh attitude toward withdrawal. But it is not often possible, in the well-filled modern world, to withdraw in this literal sense. The experience of most children is that parents, peers, teachers, counselors, and group workers are united in pushing for social participation; it is something of a miracle to get off by oneself. Thus social isolation more commonly takes the form of not being away from other people but of being with people while wanting to be away. If danger is felt in human company, the desire to be away may take precedence over inclinations to interact. You undoubtedly know adults who illustrate this pattern. We often describe them as giving nothing of themselves and as not being really there.

Being in company while wanting to be elsewhere has a highly damaging effect on social competence. There is obviously no wish to prolong the meeting. In adult terms, it is risky to introduce an interesting topic; it will lead to conversation. Mention of any controversial matter will lead to argument. Expressions of interest in what the other person is saying will encourage more extended exposition. The only safe tactic is to agree quickly with whatever is said and make plausible excuses to be elsewhere. Neither of these actions yields any sense of social competence. No desired effects are produced on the other person's behavior, and there is no sense of control over the interaction. The only pride that can develop is in one's increasing adroitness at bringing social contacts to an end.

This pattern of meeting dangers is likely to be soon complicated by aggressive feelings. If other people are felt as intrusive, and you have no sense of competence to deal with them, you soon find them annoying. The approach of another person, far from being welcome, fills you with resentment and may even make you suspect hostile intentions. I believe this is the explanation of what psychoanalytic workers with schizophrenics have reported: a touchy aggression just beneath the seemingly indifferent surface. Even if the analyst is sensitive, benign, and apparently liked, it takes almost nothing to transform him into an intrusive outsider who is hated.

If such a pattern becomes established in a child, it sets a trap for social development. The essential avoidance of real interaction blocks the normal growth of a sense of interpersonal competence. There is no attempt to become interested and involved, no putting forth of effort to have an effect on the other person, even so mild an effect as pleasing or entertaining. Thus there is no finding out what effects it might be possible to have; other people stay in the category of intractable and intrusive objects. In the course of time a kind of compromise may develop in which superficial social amenities are learned and physical mingling is not wholly avoided, but relations with others remain formal, distant, and certainly lacking in warmth. But it may be that a child cannot reach even this compromise, continuing to feel anxious tension and not much else in human company. This blocking of interaction may well lead to a pathological outcome.

One practical conclusion at once follows. This problem is not going to be overcome by immersion in the company of peers. We can suspect that it is even created by too early and too insistent an immersion that left no time for initial anxieties to subside. The company of several other children is not propitious for getting over anxiety. Parents and professional workers, noticing the social awkwardness, may think that mingling will teach the needed skills. So it might do for a child who merely felt lonely and wanted to find friends. But it will not have this effect when anxiety and aggression have fixed a defensive pattern. In such a case the first need is for a basic sense of social competence, an elementary power of initiative, which may eventually lead to acquiring the skills. Initiative toward others must be found possible and rewarding, and this is not best encouraged by a peer group.

The extreme form of social isolation is found in the children we call autistic. Treatment is almost ruled out because the therapist is part of the intractable human world. But if the therapist waits with long patience, the time may come when the child will try to have an effect on him. These attempts will be curiously hedged against the danger of unexpected responses. The therapist will be required to copy each movement made by the child, but not allowed to introduce movements of his own. The therapist will be expected to repeat whatever his patient says, but not permitted to intrude with utterances of his own. Primitive as they are, these are real initiatives on the part of the autistic patient. If such first stabs prove to be successful, the child may advance to more varied and playful forms of interaction.

We can take a hint from these extreme cases as to what is propitious for loosening the social isolation pattern. We can take a hint also from instances of spontaneous loosening, as reported by anxiously shy children in the biographical literature. Typically such a child, perhaps nearing or beyond puberty, discovers a sympathetic companion with whom it suddenly proves easy to talk in a personal way, exchanging experiences and confidences hitherto carefully guarded.

Essential to such discovery is a special attitude in the other person, who is in some way drawn and attracted and whose sympathetic interest offsets the usual mobilization of defense. Telling about yourself is a kind of initiative, an attempt at influencing another person to accept you as you are; when acceptance occurs, an increment is added to one's sense of competence. As in treating autistic children, the favorable condition is a single unusually sympathetic companion with whom initiatives can be risked. Even two companions would be too much of a crowd for such ventures.

To summarize: the social isolation pattern is a defensive maneuver that prevents initiative toward others. The experience of social competence is thus blocked at its source, and change depends on conditions that will overcome the basic fear of initiative.

Social Enslavement

I turn now to another protective pattern: social enslavement. In contrast to the isolation pattern—being perforce in company but wanting to be out of it—in this case the person wants to be in company but is afraid of being thrown out of it. There is desire to be accepted coupled with lively fear of being rejected. This fear dictates doing nothing that could possibly give offense. The range of safe actions includes being pleasant, agreeing, helping, and going along with whatever seems to be expected. These placating tactics leave little room to express wants of one's own. Initiatives are risky; they may lead to ridicule, rejection, even punishment. There is thus limited room for exerting influence on others and little chance of developing a sense of social competence. Safety lies in leaving initiative to others.

Perhaps this sounds less like pathology than it does like the way a lot of us get along in a lot of our social relations. It is simply Riesman's other-directed pattern; and surely it does no harm, when you are in company, to go along with the expectations of the group. Some of our conformities, like our conventional politeness and our role-dictated interactions, seem to be harmless concessions to the convenience of living. Even so, such well-meant conventions may do a little harm to all of us. Our children must notice the gap between what we say to our neighbors when they are present and after they have left, and conclude that neighbors are dangerous and must not be offended. Thus we may enact and pass along a more anxious picture of human relations than we intend.

As I have said, there is a certain inherent danger in social interaction. One semester when I was teaching at Harvard, three days a week at eleven, I descended in the elevator from my fifteenth-floor office to the ground-floor lecture room. At the fourteenth floor I was usually joined by a group of students who had just finished a class conducted as a T-group. They would still be interacting vigorously. One day, however, to my surprise, they were totally silent. My colleague—a veteran of much teaching by this method—explained to me later that this was the inevitable day when they ordered him out of the room because he was interfering with their interaction. Symbolically killing your teacher must give rise to misgivings! Another day, the class had decided to hold a marathon meeting the following weekend, but one girl demurred. Her classmates questioned her insistently: why not? When she hesitantly murmured that it was a long time to be together, one of the others demanded, "Don't you like our company?"

The incident is instructive. Even in this group of young people who were becoming unusually sophisticated about their interactions and unusually dedicated to improving them, there was anxiety when they did not agree: anxiety on the part of the girl who expressed a divergent opinion, anxiety on the part of the others that they were being rejected and not loved. Even our most civilized social interactions have their margins of danger. We may not make the impression we want, we may be caught in a misstatement, we may drop a brick, we may give grounds for silent ridicule or contempt. We are all probably bound to be a little socially enslaved.

When the enslavement pattern is strong, it has two possible connections with psychopathology. In the first place, a person so dependent on acceptance and so fearful of losing it is a vulnerable person. Membership in a group, or even in a small circle of friends, cannot always be harmonious. There will be frictions and momentary rejections, and these may prove traumatic to a person who has specialized in placating and who knows no other competent way to repair the situation. Some schizophrenics appear to have been sociable before breakdown, but perhaps they were only socially enslaved, so that when things go wrong they have as little sense of social competence as if they had been isolates. In other cases, friction or the break-up of a hitherto congenial group may set off feelings of desertion and depression which are not counterbalanced by confidence that something can be done.

In the second place, the pattern of social enslavement is capable of inflicting grave damage on other aspects of personal growth. Too great a dependence on the company of others may seriously interfere with an independent sense of self. When approval is such an urgent matter, it may be hard to become aware of being or wanting anything except what others expect.

Much of what has been written in recent years about the problems of youth points to social enslavement and alienation from self. This is the essence of the other-directed character, and certainly the discovery of a sense of identity will be much hampered if you are a stranger to your own inclinations. Recent research on locus of control enables us to contrast those who believe they have some internal control over their behavior with those who think their behavior is pretty much determined by outside forces. The former, the internalists, do in fact make greater efforts to master the environment, and they show greater self-control. Among the latter, the externalists, there is a greater frequency of psychopathology (Phares, 1976; Lefcourt, 1976). Counselors describe clients who seem to have no experience of reaching decisions, making up their minds, assuming responsibility for what they do. Such clients sound as if their lives thus far had been experienced as happening around them and to them, without any sense of themselves as agents. This basic helplessness fits well with looking for an outside agent, such as a drug, to make you feel better and expand your consciousness. It fits well with a resigned cynicism; the world is all wrong, but nothing can be done about it. It does not fit at all with democracy's basic tenet that concerned citizens can have some influence on their fate.

There are, of course, many influences in our society that tend to make this form of pathology widespread. I need not recite the familiar list, but I think it is important that we professionals, as exponents of mental health, should be sure to get our influence on the right side. Historically we have clamored too loud for social adjustment. We have not been sensitive to the dangers of throwing children together regardless of their anxieties and their own social needs. We have been enchanted with peer groups, as if the highest form of social behavior were getting along with age-equals, the relation where competition is most salient. We take it as bad adjustment, for instance, when someone gets along well only with younger and older people and is uncomfortable with peers. As most of the people in our adult lives are either older or younger, we might better judge this person as showing fine promise, certainly more promise than one who thrives only with peers and treats older and younger people as if they did not exist. Or we join unthinkingly with those who nip intimacy in the bud by trying to break up child and adolescent pairs, as if a close warm relationship were poisonous. This is what I mean by being on the wrong side and failing to declare for what is truly good and valuable in human relations.

I hope that the idea of social competence will help us to be regularly on the right side. But it is not a panacea; competence plays merely an instrumental part in social development. I think we can believe that there are many people who would express more social interest, more sympathy, more appreciation, more helpfulness, and more love if they dared. They do not dare because too much anxiety has entered into their social training. They have not dared to risk the initiatives through which they might discover that others can be responsive and that a truly rewarding interaction is possible. They need to attain the level of social competence that is required to make and keep this discovery. The question of how this learning can best be encouraged is treated in subsequent chapters of this volume.

REFERENCES

Bettelheim, B. *The informed heart.* New York: Free Press, 1960.

Deci, E. L. *Intrinsic motivation.* New York: Plenum Press, 1975.

Erikson, E. H. *Childhood and society.* New York: Norton, 1950.

Groos, K. *The play of man.* New York: D. Appleton, 1901.

Hartmann, H. *Ego psychology and the problem of adaptation.* New York: International Universities Press, 1958.

Hendrick, I. Instinct and the ego during infancy. *Psychoanalytic Quarterly,* 1942, *11,* 35–58.

Lefcourt, H. M. *Locus of control: Current trends in theory and research.* Hillsdale, N.J.: Erlbaum, 1976.

Mittelmann, B. Motility in infants, children and adults. *Psychoanalytic Study of the Child,* 1954, *9,* 142–177.

Phares, E. J. *Locus of control in personality.* Morristown, N.J.: General Learning Press, 1976.

Piaget, J. *The construction of reality in the child.* New York: Basic Books, 1954.

Riesman, D. *The lonely crowd: A study of the changing American character.* New Haven: Yale University Press, 1950.

Sullivan, H. S. *The interpersonal theory of psychiatry.* New York: Norton, 1953.

White, R. W. Adler and the future of ego psychology. *Journal of Individual Psychology,* 1957, *13,* 112–124.

White, R. W. Motivation reconsidered: The concept of competence. *Psychological Review,* 1959, *66,* 297–333.

White, R. W. Ego and reality in psychoanalytic theory. *Psychological Issues,* 1963, *3,* No. 3.

White, R. W. The experience of efficacy in schizophrenia. *Psychiatry,* 1965, *28,* 199–211.

White, R. W. *The enterprise of living: A view of personal growth.* 2nd ed. New York: Holt, Rinehart, and Winston, 1976.

Social Competence in Childhood: Toward a Developmental, Socioculturally Relativistic Paradigm

Luis M. Laosa

This chapter presents an evolving conceptualization of the development of social competence. One does well to consider at the start the implications of such an undertaking. The study of human development is a highly challenging enterprise. In addition to being a scientific discipline, it touches on the most significant and far-reaching aspects of culture and society: the rearing of the young. For all that it is a psychological science, it is also a policy science—that is, one which provides the underlying framework for decisions concerning not only the formulation of problems, the framing of hypotheses, and the kinds of research carried out but also the types of societal programs developed and implemented and the way public institutions are designed to run. In socializing and educating the young, society is continuously required to make decisions about such courses of action (Bruner, 1974). The study of human development, therefore, mirrors two major concerns: how to define a socially competent human being, and how to socialize and educate the young to become socially competent.

❖   The model offered here considers developmental as well as sociocultural differences and contextual variation. I refer to this evolving perspective of human behavior and development as *the developmental, socioculturally relativistic paradigm*. As we will see, this view draws from several recent theoretical positions that have had significant impact on my conceptualization of the environment and of the child's interaction with it. These theories have provided varied views of the environment, they have emphasized different dimensions of early experience, and they have arrived at different notions of the organism. Although each has a distinctive emphasis, there are some basic similarities and complementary aspects. The conception presented here translates selected aspects of these views into a general framework for a paradigm of human development. The point of departure is the need for a model that includes important sociocultural dimensions and reflects the diversity present within complex and changing societies.

THE ACTIVE ORGANISM

One emphasis here that is common to several theoretical approaches is stimulus seeking. The child is seen as an active organism who elicits stimulation and response from others. The nature of the effects sought and the aspects of the environment acted upon vary with developmental level as well as with the nature of the available environment. The child assimilates the environment with his or her currently existing psychological structures and modifies these structures by accommodating to the demands of the environment, thus evolving in cognitive and social functioning. There is, then, a dynamic, ongoing interaction between child and environment.

The child is viewed as having an intrinsic motivation to explore the novel (White, 1959) and to act on the environment. This inherent natural tendency is seen to be *susceptible, however, to modification by environmental contingencies*. Contingency, a key concept in operant learning theory (Skinner, 1953), emphasizes the importance of a responsive environment. The impact on environmental events depends on their temporal relation to behavior. Activities that are typically followed by a rewarding response will tend to be repeated; those that are not, or that are followed by painful stimulation, will tend to occur less. Seligman (1975) recently has called attention to a class of behaviors that he labeled "learned helplessness." Helplessness is the psychological state frequently observed in an organism when none of its actions produces an effect on a given event. When an event is thus uncontrollable (that is, when the event occurs independently of all the organism's responses), the organism ceases to respond and becomes passive. Learned helplessness disrupts the learning process and results in emotional disturbance.

EARLY EXPERIENCE

Early research on children undergoing severe deprivation of human and other sensory stimulation, such as the studies of children living in orphanages (Dennis, 1960; Spitz, 1946), showed dramatically the severely detrimental effects of extreme environmental deprivation on development. Children who were otherwise normal did not attain the fundamental milestones of social competence that nearly all children reared in less extreme circumstances reach spontaneously. There is no longer any doubt that extreme environmental deprivation is severely detrimental to the child.

The evidence shows, moreover, that within the *normal* range of environmental variation, certain experiences are more important than others in influencing children's development along specific dimensions of cognition, perception, language, and personality. The current emphasis, therefore, is to examine the effects of experiences that fall within this range—a shift from a "deficit" or pathology-oriented model to one that recognizes a great range in normal variation. Furthermore, early experiences are now viewed as complex events. We are aware of a continuum of effects that vary with many of the organism's characteristics as well as with the quality, intensity, and patterning of the environmental stimuli (Yarrow, Rubinstein, and Pedersen, 1975). It is becoming increasingly apparent that, to arrive at an adequate theory of child development, one must begin with a model that represents development as a series of complex, interacting events involving characteristics of the organism and the environment.

INTERNAL CONSTRUCTION OF THE WORLD

I give special emphasis to the internal representation of contingent responsiveness—that is, psychological structure. A constructivist view posits that the organism actively constructs an internal representation or map of what events or behavior lead to what outcomes (Kelly, 1955; Sigel, 1977). By direct experiences of contingencies and by observing what happens to others, as well as through didactic teaching, the child acquires a given set of psychological structures—a model of what the world is like, what the payoff is for particular actions. As in social learning theory (Bandura, 1977), experiences that bear on the development of psychological structures are here considered to be sometimes mediated by contingencies experienced vicariously. Of course, internal representations of what the world is like (also referred to as cognitive constructs, psychological structures, internal constructions, belief systems, internal map of the world, personality structure, behavioral dispositions, expectancies, and so on) are not always, and not always totally, available to the immediate awareness of their possessors.

The child is born with a minimal set of species-specific functional structures (anatomical and neurological) which permit transactions with the environment. As these take place, the child incorporates experiences and stimulation—otherwise he or she would not develop. The child actively takes in and "digests" environmental properties. The consequences are physiological change, psychological change, or both. Physiological structures, of course, can only assimilate environmental properties for which they have appropriate physiological organs. In the same manner, the organism can only assimilate experience and information for which it has appropriate psychological structures. Thus the person's existing psychological structures selectively determine the character of transactions and the significance of experience. Conversely, the range of possible experiences is determined by the nature of the environment, that is, the range of possibilities for interaction and the contingencies in the (social and nonhuman) environment. The experiences encountered, in turn, feed back upon the child's functional structures that were involved in the earlier stages of that transaction (Langer, 1970; Werner and Kaplan, 1963). In ways that remain little understood, such feedback leads to qualitative alterations of the child's current psychological development and provokes a next stage of *organism-environment organization*. In this sense the process of development has dialectical properties.

The nature of the transactions that occur between child and environment is here seen to be influenced by the psychological structures of the individuals. This view is partly consistent with Sigel's (1977) radical constructivism and with Sameroff's (1975b) notion that the mother's level of cognitive complexity determines the nature of the transactions between mother and child. Individuals with whom the child interacts will construe or interpret the child's actions and characteristics in a manner consistent with their own psychological structures or belief system. The internal constructions or belief system held by a person in the child's milieu about children in general, or about that child in particular, will determine how that person acts toward the child. Much of the response occurs because of expectations. The belief system of a parent and a teacher will include categorical expectations and standards against which they will evaluate a given child's actions and characteristics. Such expectations and standards will determine much of how the child is perceived and evaluated and of how the person will act toward the child. Thus, the psychological structures of people in the child's milieu are seen to act as mediators of their interactions with the child. Conversely, the child's evolving structures or constructions about given elements in the environment mediate or influence the child's interactions with those aspects of the milieu. A dialectical process appears to be involved in these reciprocal interactions, which affects the evolution of psychological structures of the individuals involved. Psychological structures or belief systems are subject to change over time, partly as the result of interactions with other individuals. The dialectical process is seen to involve relationships not only in the individual-psychological domain (i.e. psychological structures, actions) but in three others. I will refer to these four domains in Riegel's (1975) terms: the individual-psychological, the inner-biological, the cultural-sociological, and the outer-physical. The dialectical process involving them, seen here to underlie human development, is discussed more fully below.

ORGANISM-ENVIRONMENT INTERACTION

Many investigators and practitioners proceed on the assumption that is is possible to identify particular characteristics of either the child or the environment that will account for the course of later development (Sameroff, 1975a). Indeed, it would seem logical to assume that a given characteristic in the child, if associated at all with later development, would have a similar developmental outcome for all children who share it. But such a generalization does not appear to hold. For instance, early characteristics resulting from physical trauma or biological complications during the perinatal period appear to be consistently related to later physical and psychological development *only* when combined with and supported by persistently poor environmental conditions (Werner, Bierman, and French, 1971, cited in Sameroff, 1975a).

Moreover, as Bell (1968, 1971) has noted, the child is more involved in determining the nature of his or her interpersonal relationships than was once supposed. Many parent behaviors are *elicited* by the child's own characteristics and behaviors. Nevertheless, much research and practice are based on the assumption of unidirectionality, examining the influence of, say, parental behavior on the child's development, while ignoring the possible influence the child has on the parents' actions. As an extreme example of how a child's characteristics may elicit others' actions, consider the work of Sameroff and Chandler (1975), who seem to have found support for the hypothesis that certain characteristics of the child may predispose the parents to battering or neglect.

But in order to account adequately for the developmental process, we must do more than invoke the concept of reciprocity. It appears, for instance, that a given child characteristic will not elicit the same reaction from all parents if the parents differ from one another on a critical variable. This view receives support from recent evidence that constitutional variability in children affects the parents' attitudes and care-giving styles. Thomas, Chess, and Birch (1968) studied changes occurring in the child's temperament as a function of the family environment characteristics. They described a temperament constellation labeled "the difficult child." Difficult infants are those characterized by low thresholds for arousal, intense reactions when aroused, poor adaptability, and irregularity in biological functioning. What made the difference in such children's later development appeared to be their parents' characteristics. If the parents were able to adjust to the child's difficult temperament, a good developmental outcome was likely; if not, the difficulties were exacerbated and behavior disturbance often resulted.

Several years ago I proposed an interactional model to explain the process of development as it occurs in the classroom (Laosa, 1974b). The model is based on the assumption that much of what a child learns there is a function of an interaction* between the teacher's actions and the student's characteristics. Thus, teacher X's actions toward student S1 and student S2 may be identical; but if the two students differ in a key characteristic, they will evidence different learning outcomes (even assuming that everything else is held constant). Interindividual variation in cognitive styles and in learning and teaching strategies is one area where one may fruitfully apply this interactional model.

Cognitive styles are conceptualized as stable attitudes, preferences, or habitual strategies determining a person's typical *manner* of processing and organizing information—that is, of perceiving, remembering, thinking, and problem solving (see, for example, Messick, 1976). There is evidence suggesting that, depending on a person's cognitive style, he or she will use particular teaching and learning strategies for given tasks (see, for example, Goodenough, 1976; Cohen and Laosa, 1976; Laosa, 1977a; Witkin, 1976; Witkin, Moore, Goodenough, and Cox, 1977). It appears, moreover, that some learning is a function of an interaction between the teacher's teaching strategy and the learner's learning strategy. Persons who employ a given learning strategy will learn particular tasks faster and better if they have a teacher who employs a teaching strategy that maximizes learning for that learning strategy. This would call for an interactionist model to explain the outcomes of the teaching-learning process. Such a model is presented below. Each of the four quadrants represents students' learning or other developmental outcomes on a given task. Students with

Student Learning Strategy

		A	B
	C	Good	Bad
Teacher Teaching Strategy			
	D	Bad	Good

*The term "interaction" as used in this chapter applies to two somewhat different concepts. In one sense, it refers to a transaction between two persons or between a person and an object in the environment, and to the mutually influencing relationship between two dimensions within the individual,

learning strategy *A* will show better learning on a given task if paired with a teacher who employs teaching strategy *C* than if paired with a teacher who uses teaching strategy *D*. On the other hand, students with learning strategy *B* will show a better outcome with teaching strategy *D* than with *C*. According to this general model, then, a given learning or developmental outcome, or level of functioning, may be reached through a variety of pathways.

The interactionist model substantially increases our efficiency in predicting developmental outcomes and in understanding the developmental process, and is particularly appealing for making relatively short-term developmental predictions. It seems adequate for understanding some types of learning or other developmental outcomes associated with contexts in which the child spends a relatively short time, such as classroom environments. The interactionist model may be insufficient, however, to facilitate our understanding of longer-term and more inclusive developmental processes (Sameroff, 1975a). The major reason a different model is needed for an inclusive account of human development is that neither child characteristics nor environmental characteristics are necessarily constant over time (Lewis and Lee-Painter, 1974; Sameroff, 1975a). At each moment, month, or year, the characteristics of both the child and the environment (social and non-human) change in important ways. The temporal parameters associated with the changes are assumed to vary along dimensions as yet undetermined. The child alters the environment and in turn is altered by the changed world he or she has created. *In order to incorporate these progressive interactions, one must expand the interactionist model to include the changes in the characteristics of both child and environment that result from their continual interplay over time.* One implication of such a dynamic interactionist model is that, if one is to understand development, one's methodology must provide for a continuous assessment of the transactions between child and environment to elucidate the processes that facilitate or hinder adaptive integration as both child and surroundings change and evolve.

---

i.e. between two psychological structures or between a psychological and a biological structure. In a different sense, it has a statistical meaning. The interaction between teacher teaching strategies and student learning strategies (independent variables) to produce student learning outcomes (dependent variables) is an example.

DIALECTICS AND DEVELOPMENT

The conceptualization proposed here considers that human development consists of a dialectical process, characterized by asynchronies in the interactions involving progressions along dimensions in and outside of the individual. As Riegel (1975) exhorted, an inclusive, dialectical approach to human development must embrace both inner and outer dialectics.

For an inclusive account of human development, I consider dimensions in the following domains, within and outside of the individual, to be of importance.

Domains Within Individual	*Domains Outside of Individual*
(a) Psychological structures	(a) Sociocultural structures and events
(b) Biological structures	(b) Actions by the individual
(c) Biochemical events	(c) Actions by other individuals in the environment
	(d) Physical events (e.g. climate and terrain)

Thus the processes that underlie the evolving restructuring and reorganization of the person-environment organization involve more than just people's actions and psychological structures. There is a simultaneous progression of events along dimensions in the various domains within and outside the individual. The changing events along dimensions in domains within the individual interact with and influence one another, as do events along dimensions in domains outside the individual. Moreover, the changing, mutually interacting events within the individual interact with the changing, mutually interacting events outside the individual. Thus, events within and outside the individual constitute a complex system of interdependent, mutually influential progressions. The result is a continually evolving restructuring of the person-environment organization.

My current conceptualization of the child's development during his or her transactions with the environment contrasts sharply with three other views: (a) of the child as a relatively passive recipient of stimulation; (b) of new or modified behaviors as being merely added on in continuous temporal order as the organism grows; and (c) of considering only the child's developmental status and conceptualizing it as more or less independent of the environment or context. The theoretical model proposed here considers the developmental status of the *child-environment organization* as reflected in the nature of the child's transactions with the environment.

The present view necessitates an explanation of why an organism that is well adapted at one stage of organization ever progresses to reorganizing toward a subsequent stage. The Wernerian concept of evolution as a synthetic process that interweaves two antithetical tendencies is useful here (Langer, 1970; Werner and Kaplan, 1963). It follows from this concept that there are two simultaneous tendencies in the organism: (a) to maintain continuity in order to preserve one's integrity or current organizational coherence; and (b) to generate transformations of the current stage toward a relatively mature state. The present conceptualization emphasizes viewing the child's activities as directed toward producing effects on various aspects of the environment. In every person-environment system, then, contradictions or asynchronies are generated. These provide much of the impetus leading the organism to higher levels of organization.

Development of the person-environment organization represents the coordination or synchronization of progressions along dimensions in the internal and external domains discussed above. When the synchrony of these dimensions in a given person-environment organization breaks down because a progression or other change occurred at a different rate in one or several dimensions, the result is conflict, contradiction, or discordance. The organism reestablishes synchrony or coordination among progressions in all domains by restructuring the person-environment organization. Therefore, under the widest and most propitious range of conditions, the child-environment organization undergoes transformations toward greater articulation and integration; that is, it moves toward more advanced developmental status.

SOCIOCULTURAL VARIABILITY

An adequate conceptualization of children's development of social competence must allow for an inclusive and integrated account of the variability existing among cultural groups within a society and throughout the world. The terms "culture," "subculture," and "socioculture" are applied here to an organized body of "rules" about how individuals in a population communicate with one another, think about themselves and their environments, and behave toward one another and toward objects. Although the rules are not universally constant for a given group, or conscious to every individual, they are generally followed by all of its members; and the rules limit the range of variation in patterns of belief, value, and social behavior within the group.

Most views of children's development of social competence have dealt with cultural variability either by ignoring it or by invoking the concept of "deficit" or "social pathology." Typically, "social competence" has been defined as a *unitary* set of standards or norms. Almost without exception, the norms have tended in the United States to represent the characteristics of the modal white middle-class male. A person is judged socially competent if his or her characteristics match this set of norms; persons deviating from them are considered deficient or pathological. Because of this reliance on a unitary set of standards representing the values of a single, dominant group, the prevalent orientation clearly has been aggressively ethnocentric.

The term "ethnocentrism" is most generally understood to refer to an attitude or outlook in which values derived from one's own cultural background are applied to other cultural contexts where different values are operative (LeVine and Campbell, 1972). In the most naive form of ethnocentrism, termed "phenomenal absolutism" (Segall, Campbell, and Herskovits, 1966), people unreflectively take their own culture's values as objective reality and automatically use them as the context within which they judge unfamiliar objects or events. As in the Piagetian stage of egocentric thought, the absolutist cannot conceive of other points of view. At a more complex level, the ethnocentric outlook acknowledges the existence of multiple points of view but dismisses other cultures as incorrect, inferior, or immoral (LeVine and Campbell, 1972).

The conceptual model proposed here postulates that individual differences in psychological structures underlie differences in observed behavior—that is, there is individual variation in the person-environment organization. Some of this variability may be rooted in the cultural group. A number of contemporary complex societies, including the United States, are composed of multiple cultural groups living side by side. Each group has a unique culture, although there are many areas of similarity. Even within groups there are subpopulations with distinctive cultural characteristics. There is, of course, individual variability within each subgroup and overlap among all groups and subgroups. Cross-cutting the differences are religious and regional distinctions as well as those associated with socioeconomic status, sex, and age.

A child, then, is perceived as socially competent or incompetent in the context of specific roles and value judgments. The dominant group, however, has determined the characteristics that define a competent child. Moreover, for minority children, typically someone unfamiliar with the child-environment organization in the child's minority socioculture has defined (a) the context or situation in which performance is assessed and (b) the content and form of the tasks employed to assess competence.

SITUATIONAL EFFECTS ON PERFORMANCE

The sociocultural context or situation in which a psychological structure is developed represents an integral part of that structure. Several writers (Mischel, 1968, 1977; Sigel, 1974) have emphasized the need to examine the effects of the context or situation on performance. Performance on tasks typically employed to assess competence can be subject to the influence of situational or contextual effects. As Sigel (1974) has noted, tasks on a test are usually taken out of their natural contexts and presented in a specified (standardized) set of conditions. It is typically assumed (a) that the task (i.e. the test items) represents a sample of items from a universe of tasks; and (b) that responses to the items represent a sample of the individual's proficiency. But how is one to interpret a response to an item that has been taken out of its natural context? Does it represent the individual's response to a similar task in its natural context?

Compelling evidence of the effects of the context on performance comes from the work of Labov (1970). Cole and Bruner (1971) have described a relevant facet of his work:

One example of Labov's approach is to conduct a rather

standard interview of the type often used for assessment of language competence. The situation is designed to be minimally threatening; the interviewer is a neighborhood figure, and black. Yet, the black eight-year-old interviewee's behavior is monosyllabic. He is a candidate for the diagnosis of linguistically and culturally deprived.

But this diagnosis is very much situation dependent. For, at a later time, this same interviewer goes to the boy's apartment, brings one of the boy's friends with him, lies down on the floor, and produces some potato chips. He then begins talking about clearly taboo subjects in dialect. Under these circumstances the mute interviewee becomes an excited [competent] participant in the general conversation. (p. 86)

Here it is important to distinguish between *proficiency* and *performance*. Performance is what a child actually does in a particular situation. Proficiency is what the child would do under conditions that are optimally conducive to eliciting what he or she is capable of doing.

That some behaviors may be partially associated with specific situations is not a difficult view to accept within the conceptualization offered here. A person's psychological structures should become articulated or refined enough so that the total configuration of stimuli in a situation is associated with a particular set of expectations for certain actions having certain consequences in that situation. A context or situation is not defined solely or even necessarily by the physical setting (e.g. living room, sidewalk) or by person combinations (e.g. child and mother, child and sibling); rather, they are constituted of what people are doing and when and where they are doing it (Erickson and Schultz, 1977).

In order to behave in a manner acceptable to others, children and adults must "know" what context they are in and when contexts change. That is, one must be able to exhibit the form of verbal and nonverbal behavior that is appropriate in a given social context. The capacity to thus "monitor" contexts is an essential feature of social competence (Erickson and Schultz, 1977). To prevent the misunderstandings and ensuing social and mental health problems that can result from not being able to monitor given contexts correctly, individuals must learn the "rules" for assessing them and behaving appropriately in them. Thus, a prerequisite competency for persons who work with children from sociocultural backgrounds different from their own is to "know" the rules that apply in the children's sociocultures and behave accordingly. They must also be able to "teach" children the rules for behaving appropriately in the diverse contexts in which the children will be required to function.

❖

COMPETENCE AND PERFORMANCE

Having discussed the potential effects of the situation or context on performance, let us consider other common pitfalls in interpreting the performance of individuals from sociocultural groups about whose psychological and sociological aspects we know relatively little.

It is often accepted as fact that particular kinds of tests or experimental situations diagnose particular cognitive capacities or processes (Cole and Scribner, 1974). Particularly with ethnic minorities (or other groups whose socioculture is not highly familiar to us), we should not always assume that a test is measuring some generalized, underlying capability such as "intelligence"; we must pay close attention to the possible limitations inherent in the tasks employed to demonstrate competence. A simple yet dramatic illustration of the legitimacy of this caveat is provided by the research of Cole and his colleagues (Cole, Gay, Glick, and Sharp, 1971). They found that American adults performed more poorly than nonliterate Kpelle (Liberian) farmers on the task of sorting leaves into categories according to whether they came from vines or trees. This finding, of course, says nothing about Americans' "capacity for understanding and other forms of adaptive behavior" (*American College Dictionary*, 1959, definition of "intelligence"). It is ironic that we readily make generalizations about the "intelligence" of individuals from groups other than the white American middle-class on the basis of tasks and situations familiar to and relevant for the latter but sometimes not the former.

Another potential pitfall lies in the syntax of the role relation between the person being evaluated and the evaluator. An individual's performance in an evaluative situation may be inextricably embedded in his or her role relationship to the evaluator. There appear to be cultural and possibly other sources of individual differences in these role relationships (Holtzman, 1965, 1968). Evidence comes from a recent study of children in Mexico and the United States (Holtzman, Díaz-Guerrero, and Swartz in collaboration with Lara-Tapia, Laosa, Lagunes, Morales, and Witzke, 1975; Laosa, Lara-Tapia, and Swartz, 1974). These cross-cultural investigators found that, when faced with standardized testing situations, the average Mexican child appeared cautious and seemed to look for ways to please the examiner. The average Anglo American child, on the other hand, seemed to approach the testing situation as a challenge to be mastered, an opportunity to show how much he or she could do. Such differences in role relations and approaches to the task may conceivably affect performance and lead to inaccurate judgments.

❖   By employing methods of inquiry and data collection that do not take cultural differences into account, the field of human development has not provided the understanding of developmental processes that would otherwise be possible. This constricted approach has yielded relatively little in the way of adequate theory and data to help understand cultural differences in children's development of social competence and coping. On the basis of recent empirical and theoretical evidence (see, for example, Cárdenas and Cárdenas, 1973; Cole and Bruner, 1971; Cole and Scribner, 1974; Baratz and Baratz, 1970; Kleinfeld, 1973; Laosa, 1974a, 1974b, 1977d; Laosa, Burstein, and Martin, 1975; Lesser, Fifer, and Clark, 1965; Tulkin and Konner, 1973), there is increasing acceptance of the view that there are differences between minority and nonminority children and among the various cultural and subcultural communities. There is, of course, wide variability *within* any one ethnic or cultural group (see, for example, Laosa, 1975; Laosa, 1978, b; LeCorgne and Laosa, 1976; Laosa, Swartz, and Witzke, 1975), and one may find instances of deficiencies in any group. *The important point, however, is not to mistakenly equate cultural characteristics with deficiencies or mistakenly define as a deficiency a characteristic that may actually represent a cultural difference.*

In the present conceptualization of social competence, psychological processes are *not* seen as properties (such as intelligence) that a person does or does not "have," *independent of the particular context or situation.* It is *not* assumed, in the absence of empirical evidence, that performance on any task always indicates what the person may be capable of doing on a similar item under different circumstances, nor that it indicates capability in a task of a different nature, in a problem meaningful in the person's everyday sociocultural environment, or on the kind of performance demanded by the environment in which the person has evolved his or her psychological structures.

ADAPTATION AND CONTINUITY

A perspective that takes sociocultural relativism into account is particularly necessary when one is dealing with environment, development, and performance of children from ethnic minority families. I consider that for many minority children, the sociocultural context of the home and neighborhood is different from that of the "mainstream" socioculture, and therefore different from many of its institutions, including the school.* The difference is greater for some families than others. A key concept here is adaptation. Functional adaptation to the characteristics of a particular environment is what enables the person to operate effectively in that environment. The minority child is faced with having to develop functional adaptation to two sets of environments—to the home and neighborhood on the one hand and to the larger "mainstream" society, particularly the school, on the other. Each environment may have a different set of functional adaptation demand characteristics, and the child's degree of success in the school environment depends on how much overlap there is between the two sets of cognitive and personality demand characteristics. In general, the greater the overlap, the greater the child's success in school. It follows that one must be cautious of value generalizations about what constitutes "adequate" performance. A child who can cope effectively in the home/neighborhood environment may not yet have developed the specific cognitive and personality characteristics to cope with and benefit from the school environment. Hence, any statement about a person's degree of competence must always be followed by (a) a description of the task or situation on which performance was assessed; (b) a description of the

---

*This is not to say, of course, that nonminority children do not experience discontinuity between the home and institutions outside the home. I suggest that the discontinuity is, on the average, greater and more abrupt for minority than nonminority children (see Laosa, 1977d).

environment in which the person has developed; and (c) the person's level of functioning of adaptation in the context of his or her natural environment.

What happens when a child is taken out of the environment in which he or she has been developing as an integral part of the organism-environment organization, for example the home, and put in a different environment, for example the school? The answer is that a new child-environment organization begins to be created. The child will be able to profit from the new environment in proportion to the degree of *articulated continuity* between the two environments. If the new environment is too abruptly different, or different in critical ways, the child's psychological structures developed over time in (competent) adaptation to the usual environment might not allow for successful assimilation of the new environment. Therefore, the continued differentiation of psychological structures and their ensuing accommodation that would typically occur if there were a greater degree of articulated continuity between the usual and new environments might not occur; instead, development may be stunted. This is why it is so important, for primary prevention, to learn about the development of the child-environment organization in minority families. With valid and accurate knowledge, psychologists, educators, child development experts, policy makers, program designers, and others may make children's extrafamilial environments developmentally continuous—that is, compatible and articulated with, yet progressively different from, the child-environment organization of the home. Thus, extrafamilial institutions, programs, and services may be able to provide services for the child's continued development.

RIGIDITIES AS OBSTACLES TO DEVELOPMENT

The dialectical principle is seen here to underlie development. Discordances or contradictions between components of a system are resolved, in the course of normal development, when a synthesis of the discordances is achieved. Such syntheses represent a restructuring, coordination, or reorganization of the system at a higher level of integration and organization.

Sometimes, however, there are obstacles. These occur when there is *rigidity* in (or impermeability in the boundaries of) one or more of the system's components. The concept of rigidity is considered here very important to the understanding of anomalies in development. A component of a system is rigid when it exhibits extreme resistance to the normal dialectical course. That is, when a component resists the synthesizing process in the face of tension created by discordances, the synthesis—and thus the restructuring and reorganization of the system at a higher level of integration that would occur normally (i.e. in the absence of rigidity)—fails to occur.

Let us consider an example. As discussed above, individuals construct their own internal conception of the world. Thus, each parent has as part of his or her own psychological structures, a particular conception of his or her child. This conception includes a belief system of what the child can do, should do, and so on; this mediates the parent's expectations and actions vis-à-vis the child. As the child's biological and psychological structures (e.g. what the child can do) develop, potential conflicts are created between the child's developmental status and the parent's conception of the child. Further development of the child-environment organization calls for these discordances to be resolved. In the course of normal development, the parent's conception of the child is modified, or evolves, to accommodate changes in the child; with each change, the modified conception mediates new parental actions which, in turn, influence the individual-psychological development of the child. This process involves a continuous evolution of the elements in the system and thus in its organization.

What happens when the parent's psychological structures vis-à-vis the child are rigid and do not accommodate to the changes occurring in the child? A possible developmental solution is that the child adapts to the now inadequate and unchanging expectations and actions of the parent and thus fails to fully realize his or her potential.

Let us now consider another example. Certain characteristics of some ethnic minority individuals may be viewed as adaptations to societal reality. Reduced opportunity has been a hard reality for many minority persons. For them, it may be a realistic solution to have low academic and occupational aspirations and to believe they have relatively little control over their own lives. Such a situation may, understandably, lead to hopelessness and, accordingly, to an alienation from the goals and activities that constitute criteria for success in the dominant group.

Characteristics resulting from such negative forms of adaptation are both functional and dysfunctional. They are functional in that they represent an adaptation in the face of an insurmountable obstacle to optimal development—that is, in the face of rigidity in one component of the person-environment organization (i.e. in the dominant group). Development of such characteristics provides a state of coordination within the person-environment system. But such an adaptation is also dysfunctional. The component of the system that so adapts cannot develop optimally. For instance, in the face of real obstacles to academic development, the minority child may give up trying. Moreover, such a limit to optimal development occurs not only in the component of the system that makes the adaptation (i.e. the minority child); there is a blockage as well to the development of the rigid component and of the system as a whole (i.e. the society), since the dialectical developmental process is not permitted to progress. Rigidity does not allow for synthesis, and thus the whole system fails to progress to the higher levels of integration and organization that would take place without rigidity. When and if the rigidity is dissolved, the dialectical process is allowed to continue.

Rigidities in a developing system frequently occur also in institutional responses to culturally rooted characteristics of ethnic minority individuals. A minority child may possess such characteristics which, in the context of his or her own home/neighborhood socioculture, constitute a successful and healthy adaptation and are criteria of social competence in that environment. When the minority child enters a different environment, where the "rules" for human interaction (Byers and Byers, 1972; Getzels, 1974; Laosa, 1975, 1977a, 1977b, 1977d) are different, the same characteristics are often not valued or considered useful or, worse, they may be evaluated negatively (see Laosa, in press, a). As components of the child-environment system, institutions outside the minority child's home often are rigid and do not allow an accommodative process that would result in a child-environment organization that synthesizes both sociocultures.

As seen in the conceptualization of human development presented here, the task of primary prevention is to identify rigid elements in developing systems and to find ways to dissolve them. Once this is done, the dialectical process can proceed on its normal course, and the system can progress to higher levels of integration and organization.

RIGIDITIES IN THE FIELD OF HUMAN DEVELOPMENT

The dialectical principle not only underlies development at the individual level but also operates in the development of fields of study and of society as a whole.

The field of human development can be viewed as containing rigidities with regard to sociocultural differences. Reluctance to carefully investigate sociocultural variation has limited our ability to understand a great portion of humanity and stunted the growth of knowledge. Why this failure to understand and include sociocultural differences in our theorizing, research, and practice (aside from political and historical factors that place various cultural and ethnic groups in bitter competition)? If significant developmental experiences are limited to those of a single socioculture, the development of psychological structures that would allow the assimilation of pluralistic concepts and evidence is also limited. The concept of and evidence for sociocultural differences are much more easily grasped by those with extensive experience of living in more than one socioculture. It is thus understandable that those who lack a cross-cultural experiential base as part of their development dismiss sociocultural differences and relativity as unimportant or even nonexistent. Yet there is evidence in the anthropological, psychological, and sociological literature that sociocultural differences not only exist but go much beyond such surface manifestations of culture as dress, foods, music, and speech habits. Underneath the surface there appear to exist wide, complex, and subtle differences in cognitive, perceptual, and personality structure and in socialization and person-environment organization.

The development of certain groups has been subordinated to the development of a dominant group much as the development of the woman in the traditional family has been subordinated to that of her husband. Today, however, rapidly increasing numbers of subordinated groups are assertively claiming recognition, equality, and mutual respect vis-à-vis the dominant groups. As once occurred with many liberation movements in the history of the world, minorities and women are now demanding that society integrate into policy and practice values that are dear and important to them. They seek to exercise their right to generate fundamental knowledge that will underlie important societal decisions, to apply their perspectives to interpreting this knowledge, and to participate at all levels in making decisions. Among the concerns are their as-yet-unfulfilled desires to maintain and transmit the richness of diverse cultural values, to exercise a wider range of societal roles, and thus to contribute to the definition of what a socially competent human being is and how a child is to be raised in order to become one. Moving effectively toward the fulfillment of these goals will undoubtedly be a significant step toward the primary prevention of psychosocial pathology.

REFERENCES

Anderson, S., and Messick, S. Social competency in young children. *Developmental Psychology*, 1974, *10*, 282-293.

Bandura, A. *Social learning theory.* Englewood Cliffs, N.J.: Prentice-Hall, 1977.

Baratz, S. S., and Baratz, J. C. Early childhood intervention: The social science base of institutional racism. *Harvard Educational Review*, 1970, *40*, 29-50.

Bell, R. Q. A reinterpretation of the direction of effects in studies of socialization. *Psychological Review*, 1968, *75*, 81-95.

Bell, R. Q. Stimulus control of parent or caretaker behavior by offspring. *Developmental Psychology*, 1971, *4*, 63-72.

Bruner, J. S. *Patterns of growth.* Oxford: Clarendon Press, 1974.

Byers, P., and Byers, H. Nonverbal communication in the education of children. In C. Cazden, V. John, and D. Hymes (Eds.), *Functions of language in the classroom.* New York: Teachers College Press, 1972.

Cárdenas, B., and Cárdenas, J. A. Chicano, bright-eyed, bilingual, brown, and beautiful. *Today's Education*, 1973, *62*, 49-51.

Chomsky, N. *Cartesian linguistics.* New York: Harper and Row, 1966.

Cohen, A., and Laosa, L. M. Second language instruction: Some research considerations. *Journal of Curriculum Studies*, 1976, *8*, 149-165.

Cole, M., and Bruner, J. S. Cultural differences and inferences about psychological processes. *American Psychologist*, 1971, *26*, 867-876.

Cole, M., Gay, J., Glick, J. A., and Sharp, D. W. *The cultural context of learning and thinking.* New York: Basic Books, 1971.

Cole, M., and Scribner, S. *Culture and thought: A psychological introduction.* New York: John Wiley and Sons, Inc., 1974.

Dennis, W. Causes of retardation among institutional children. *Journal of Genetic Psychology*, 1960, *96*, 47-59.

Díaz-Guerrero, R. *Psychology of the Mexican: Culture and personality.* Austin: University of Texas Press, 1975.

Erickson, F., and Schultz, J. When is a context? Some issues and methods in the analysis of social competence. *The Quarterly Newsletter of the Institute for Comparative Human Development,* Vol. 1, No. 2. New York: The Rockefeller University Press, 1977.

Getzels, J. W. Socialization and education: A note on discontinuities. *Teachers College Record,* 1974, *76,* 218–225.

Goodenough, D. R. The role of individual differences in field dependence as a factor in learning and memory. *Psychological Bulletin,* 1976, *83,* 675–694.

Hogan, R., DeSoto, C. B., and Solano, C. Traits, tests, and personality research. *American Psychologist,* 1977, *32,* 255–264.

Holtzman, W. H. Cross-cultural research on personality development. *Human Development,* 1965, *8,* 65–86.

Holtzman, W. H. Cross-cultural studies in psychology. *International Journal of Psychology,* 1968, *3,* 83–91.

Holtzman, W. H., Díaz-Guerrero, R., and Swartz, J. D., in collaboration with Lara-Tapia, L., Laosa, L. M., Morales, M. L., Lagunes, I. R., and Witzke, D. B. *Personality development in two cultures: A cross-cultural longitudinal study of school children in Mexico and the United States.* Austin: University of Texas Press, 1975.

Kagan, S., and Madsen, W. C. Cooperation and competition of Mexican, Mexican-American, and Anglo-American children of two ages under four instructional sets. *Developmental Psychology,* 1971, *5,* 32–39.

Kelly, G. *The psychology of personal constructs.* Vols. 1 and 2. New York: Norton, 1955.

Kleinfeld, J. S. Intellectual strengths in culturally different groups: An Eskimo illustration. *Review of Educational Research,* 1973, *43,* 341–359.

Kuhn, T. S. *The structure of scientific revolutions.* Chicago: University of Chicago Press, 1962.

Labov, W. The logic of nonstandard English. In F. Williams (Ed.), *Language and poverty.* Chicago: Markham Press, 1970.

Langer, J, Werner's theory of development. In P. H. Mussen (Ed.), *Carmichael's manual of child psychology.* Vol. 1. New York: Wiley, 1970.

Laosa, L. M. Cross-cultural and subcultural research in psychology and education. *Interamerican Journal of Psychology,* 1973, *7,* 241–248. (a)

Laosa, L. M. Reform in educational and psychological assessment: Cultural and linguistic issues. *Journal of the Association of Mexican American Educators,* 1973, *1,* 19–24. (b)

Laosa, L. M. Child care and the culturally different child. *Child Care Quarterly,* 1974, *3,* 214–224. (a)

Laosa, L. M. Toward a research model of multicultural competency-based teacher education. In W. A. Hunter (Ed.), *Multicultural education through competency-based teacher education.* Washington, D.C.: American Association of Colleges for Teacher Education, 1974. (b)

Laosa, L. M. Bilingualism in three United States Hispanic groups: Contextual use of language by children and adults in their families. *Journal of Educational Psychology*, 1975, *67*, 617–627.

Laosa, L. M. Cognitive styles and learning strategies research: Some of the areas in which psychology can contribute to personalized instruction in multicultural education. *Journal of Teacher Education*, 1977, *28*, 26–30. (a)

Laosa, L. M. Maternal teaching strategies in Mexican American families: Socioeconomic factors affecting intra-group variability in how mothers teach their children. Paper presented at the annual meeting of the American Educational Research Association, New York City, 1977. (b)

Laosa, L. M. Nonbiased assessment of children's abilities: Historical antecedents and current issues. In T. Oakland (Ed.), *Psychological and educational assessment of minority children*. New York: Brunner/Mazel, 1977. (c)

Laosa, L. M. Socialization, education, and continuity: The importance of the sociocultural context. *Young Children*, 1977, *32*, 21–27. (d)

Laosa, L. M. Inequality in the classroom: Observational research on teacher-student interactions. *Aztlán International Journal of Chicano Studies Research*, in press. (a).

Laosa, L. M. Maternal teaching strategies in Chicano families of varied educational and socioeconomic levels. *Child Development*, 1978, *49*, 1129–1135.

Laosa, L. M., Burstein, A. G., and Martin, H. Mental health consultation in a rural Chicano community: Crystal City. *Aztlán International Journal of Chicano Studies Research*, 1975, *6*, 433–453.

Laosa, L. M., Lara-Tapia, L., and Swartz, J. D. Pathognomic verbalizations, anxiety, and hostility in normal Mexican and United States Anglo-American children's fantasies: A longitudinal study. *Journal of Consulting and Clinical Psychology*, 1974, *42*, 73–78.

Laosa, L. M., Swartz, J. D., and Witzke, D. B. Cognitive and personality student characteristics as predictors of the way students are rated by their teachers: A longitudinal study. *Journal of Educational Psychology*, 1975, *67*, 866–872.

LeCorgne, L. L., and Laosa, L. M. Father absence in low-income Mexican-American families: Children's social adjustment and conceptual differentiation of sex role attributes. *Developmental Psychology*, 1976, *12*, 470–71.

Lesser, G. S., Fifer, G., and Clark, C. Mental abilities of children from different social class and cultural groups. *Monographs of the Society for Research in Child Development*, 1965, *30*, (4).

LeVine, R. A. *Culture, behavior, and personality*. Chicago: Aldine, 1973.

LeVine, R. A., and Campbell, D. T. *Ethnocentrism: Theories of conflict, ethnic attitudes, and group behavior*. New York: Wiley, 1972.

Lewis, M., and Lee-Painter, S. An interactional approach to the mother-infant dyad. In M. Lewis and L. Rosenblum (Eds.), *The effect of the infant on its caregiver: The origins of behavior*. Vol. 1. New York: Wiley, 1974.

Messick, S. Personality consistencies in cognition and creativity. In S. Messick (Ed.), *Individuality in learning*. San Francisco: Jossey-Bass, 1976.

Mischel, W. *Personality and assessment*. New York: Wiley, 1968.

Mischel, W. On the future of personality measurement. *American Psychologist*, 1977, *32*, 246–255.

Pepper, S. C. *World hypotheses*. Berkeley: University of California Press, 1942.

Piaget, J. *The origins of intelligence in the child*, 1936, Rev. ed. New York: International Universities Press, 1953.

Raizen, S., and Bobrow, S. B. *Design for a national evaluation of social competence in Head Start children*. Santa Monica, CA: The Rand Corporation, 1974.

Reese, H. W., and Overton, W. F. Models of development and theories of development. In L. R. Goulet and P. B. Baltes (eds.), *Life-span developmental psychology: Research and theory*. New York: Academic Press, 1970.

Riegel, K. F. The influence of economic and political ideologies upon the development of developmental psychology. *Psychological Bulletin*, 1972, *78*, 129–141.

Riegel, K. F. Toward a dialectical theory of development. *Human Development*, 1975, *18*, 50–64.

Sameroff, A. J. Early influences on development: Fact or fancy? *Merrill-Palmer Quarterly*, 1975, *21*, 267–294. (a)

Sameroff, A. J. Transactional models in early social relations. *Human Development*, 1975, *18*, 65–79. (b)

Sameroff, A. J., and Chandler, M. J. Reproductive risk and the continuum of caretaking casualty. In F. D. Horowitz, E. M. Hetherington, S. Scarr-Salapatek, and G. M. Siegel (Eds.), *Review of child development research*. Vol. 4. Chicago: University of Chicago Press, 1975.

Segall, M. H., Campbell, D. T., and Herskovits, M. J. *The influence of culture on visual perception*. Indianapolis: Bobbs-Merrill, 1966.

Seligman, M. E. P. *Helplessness: On depression, development, and death*. San Francisco, W. H. Freeman, 1975.

Sigel, I. E. When do we know what a child knows? *Human Development*, 1974, *17*, 201–217.

Sigel, I. E. Radical constructivism and teacher education. Paper presented at the annual meeting of the American Educational Research Association, New York City, April 1977.

Skinner, B. F. *Science and human behavior*. New York: Macmillan, 1953.

Spitz, R. A. Hospitalization: An inquiry into the genesis of psychiatric conditions in early childhood. *Psychoanalytic Study of the Child*, 1946, *1*, 53–74.

Thomas, A., Chess, S., and Birch, H. *Temperament and behavior disorders in children*. New York: New York University Press, 1968.

Tulkin, S. R., and Konner, M. J. Alternative conceptions of intellectual functioning. *Human Development*, 1973, *16*, 33–52.

Werner, E. E., Bierman, J. M., and French, F. E. *The children of Kauai*. Honolulu: University of Hawaii Press, 1971.

Werner, H., and Kaplan, B. *Symbol formation*. New York: Wiley, 1963.

White, R. W. Motivation reconsidered: The concept of competence. *Psychological Review*, 1959, *66*, 297–333.

Witkin, H. A. Cognitive style in academic performance and in teacher-student relations. In S. Messick (Ed.), *Individuality in learning*. San Francisco: Jossey-Bass, 1976.

Witkin, H. A., Moore, C. A., Goodenough, D. R., and Cox, P. Field-dependent and field-independent cognitive styles and their educational implications. *Review of Educational Research*, 1977, *47*, 1–64.

Yarrow, L. J., Rubenstein, J. L., and Pedersen, F. A. *Infant and environment*. New York: Wiley, 1975.

From Prevention to Promotion:
Optimizing Infant Development

Lynne A. Bond

❖   This chapter discusses an orientation for reconceptualizing primary prevention in terms of the promotion of development. Emerging from a transactional, constructivist perspective of the nature of development, this paper suggests that promoting optimal development might best be approached by promoting the motivational system underlying infants' own active, adaptive interaction with the environment. Following a review of the research on infants' intrinsic motivation toward effective interaction, this chapter examines empirical literature that supports the notion that this motivational system is modified by contingency-related experiences and, in turn, has impact upon developmental competence. At the same time, it is stressed that a similar framework underlies the larger, multilevel transactional network (involving caregivers, family, community, etc.) of which infant development is only a part. This chapter concludes by discussing the implications of this model for structuring programs designed to optimize infant development.

Let us distinguish between the notion of prevention and the more general notion of enhancement or promotion. While prevention typically focuses upon avoiding negative outcomes, defects, or disease, promotion aims toward facilitating growth and adaptation. In discussing the philosophy of medicine, for example, Hoke (1968) points out that *"curing* disease and *preventing* disease . . . are but two aspects of a single orientation—the disease orientation. The focus is on disease and its causes. The object is, through therapeutics, to cure the disease or, through hygiene, to keep it away" (p.269). He suggests that while "health and disease have been regarded as polar opposites with health being the absence of disease" (p.269), to the contrary, "they are not mutually exclusive, dualistic, entities. . . . Promotive medicine seeks to promote healthy, positive adaptive responses. . . . Health is not a static end-point but a way of pursuing one's goals" (p.270).

❖   The focus on prevention not only assumes a limited perspective of optimal development but also generates serious constraints in the programs it inspires. With its orientation toward avoiding the development of disorders, prevention typically is translated into a framework in which stress is seen as a negative factor and stressful events are to be avoided. This denies the constructive, growth-enhancing potential of crises and stress situations (e.g., Danish, 1977; Danish and D'Augelli, 1980; Danish et al., 1980; Lazarus, 1980; Riegel, 1975). It further presupposes a static model of human nature in which the goal is simply "problem reduction," that is, returning to conditions that existed prior to the problem (Danish and D'Augelli, 1980).

❖   All of this is not to say that we should diminish our concern for high-risk populations or that we should abandon specific efforts directed toward these groups. But I would argue that the needs of these groups and the population at large might be better met if considered within the broader context of promotion, enhancement, and optimization of positive growth. It is only in this manner that we will move beyond the short-term interventions that are implemented intermittently when disaster seems impending to focus on broad-scale, long-term restructuring toward self-sustaining supportive systems as integral parts of our lives.

How shall we proceed? How can society go about the task of promoting optimal growth? The goal of prevention in its narrowest sense, averting the development of negative outcomes, appears ominous in magnitude. Working within the broader context of promoting positive growth may present more overwhelming difficulties given the absence of a consensus on definition. What is it that we want to or need to promote? Notions such as competence, life satisfaction, and positive quality of life come to mind. What do these entail? How do we promote them? As Ansbacher (1978) and others have suggested, it may be precisely this lack of a definition of positive mental health that has led us to focus our energies on dealing with negative environmental influences and negative outcomes. In attempting to specify our goals, Hoke's (1968) description of promotive medicine seems pertinent.

Promotive medicine . . . will require understanding health in *process* terms rather than in static or ontologic terms . . . . [It] views health, not as an entity that is lost or gained, nor a quantity, but as a developmental process involving multi-level responses to a total environment. (p.270)

This focus on process terms rather than static terms also appears in descriptions of "competence." Connolly and Bruner (1974) explain that "when we talk about competence we are talking about intelligence in the broadest sense, operative intelligence *knowing how* rather than simply *knowing that.* For competence involves action, changing the environment as well as adapting to the environment" (p.3). Mason (1970) describes intelligence as the process by which the organism adjusts as a whole; intelligent behavior involves the process of bringing a fit between the needs of the organism and the restrictions of the environment. Murphy and Frank (1979) report: "The outcomes of interactions between vulnerabilities and the environment . . . will not depend solely on how benign the efforts of others in behalf of the beleaguered child or adult may be, but on how the vulnerable person uses the environment along with his or her own resources" (p.198). They see the "process of restoring and maintenance of equilibrium as a basic aspect of coping which goes beyond culturally recognized and demanded cognitive and social skills" (p.203). Thus, although a shift from prevention to promotion might lead us to the problem of "how to structure a child's world so that experience has the maximum positive effect on growth and development" (White, 1967, p.204), it appears that promotive efforts require we proceed from our understanding not only of the pattern of human development but of the very processes underlying this development. We will see that a promotive rather than preventive approach fits well with our current conceptualization of the nature of development, and it is from this conceptualization that we can attempt to redefine our task of promotion.

Constructivist Perspective

There has been a move from empiricist and nativist arguments toward a constructivist notion of development "which holds that human organisms actively build their constructs, knowledge base, and views of reality through engagement with the environment" (Sigel and Cocking, 1977, p.225). Inspired by Piagetian theory and subsequent work by Kelly (1955), this perspective is best articulated by Sigel and Cocking (1977). Individuals are seen neither as passive shapes waiting to be molded nor as preprogrammed machines with a fixed developmental plan. Rather, humans are recognized as active processors of information who construct their own realities. The individual does not learn through the passive absorption of information; one's perception or understanding is not a carbon copy of some external reality. Instead, an individual's reality is constructed through active physical and mental manipulation of the environment. Organisms assimilate new experiences to their existing conceptual frameworks as a function of the interaction which, in turn, leads to restructuring these frameworks and hence new levels of environmental manipulation. Thus development is a product of the interactional process itself, not only in social and cognitive domains but in motor and perceptual activities as well (e.g., Held and Hein, 1963; Kohler, 1962; White, 1969). If we construe the term "understanding" in the broadest sense of perceiving, feeling, acting, and knowing, it appears to be the case that "to understand is to invent" (Piaget, 1976, p.1).

Transactional Perspective

The roots of the transactional approach go at least as far back as the turn of the century (e.g., Baldwin, 1902) with the recognition that "persons become both factors and products in the social organizations of which they are a part" (Cairns, Green, and MacCombie, 1980, p.80). Certainly, much of the work of Piaget and Bowlby also portrays infants as active organisms "born with behavioral propensities and tendencies that shaped their experiences and contributed to their own development" (Lamb, 1979, p. 68). And Cairns et al. point to the transactional perspective, long espoused in research on nonhuman development (e.g., Kuo, 1967; Schneirla, 1966).

There is now widespread acknowledgment of the transactional nature of human development with much recent attention to the work of Sameroff and his colleagues (e.g., Sameroff, 1975a, 1975b, 1977; Sameroff and Chandler, 1975). It is recognized that individuals play an active role in shaping their environment and are simultaneously affected by the environment they are altering. Thus the infant–caregiver interaction is not simply a matter of each individual impacting on the other but rather, this interaction involves "the changing pattern of the mutual perceptions and behaviors of both infant and caretaker vis-à-vis each other as a result of their respective previous mutual perceptions and behaviors vis-à-vis each other" (Rosenthal, 1973, p.302), and, of course, vis-à-vis other animate and inanimate aspects of their environments. Parent and child characteristics change over time. Each changes the environment and is changed by the changes each has created. As Beckwith (1979) has summarized, development may well proceed "through a sequence of regular restructurings within and between the infant and his/her environment" (p.700). Thus the child's individuality and his/her environment are placed in a common reciprocal system. Individual functioning is "the outcome of an interactive process in which the infant's characteristics are only one of the multiplicity of factors in the social context of development" (Beckwith, 1979, p. 700).

Perhaps as a function of the methodological and statistical difficulties involved in reliable observation and assessment of behavioral transactions (e.g., see discussion by Packer and Rosenblatt, 1979), research and interventions have lagged behind theory in adopting a transactional perspective. Nevertheless, research and intervention techniques are slowly reorienting in this direction. Consider, for example, the focus on family systems theory and family-oriented education or intervention programs (Schaefer, 1970). Or consider the focus on reciprocity, synchrony, and dialogue in the context of the infant–caregiver relationship. For example, Kaye (1977) studied the emergence of "turn-taking" by mother and infant during feeding situations where the bursts and pauses of the infant's sucking and the jiggling by the mother show the controlled and controlling characteristics, that is, the mutual regulation of adult dialogue. Green, Gustafson, and West (1980) have demonstrated the increasing emergence of give-and-take games through infancy, with infants initiating more interactions from 6 to 12 months and mothers increasingly presenting games in which the infant is required to be an active participant. Thus, as Cairns et al. (1980) suggest, "developmental changes in young pace changes in their environments, which, in turn, feedback to produce subsequent alterations in their behaviors" (p.92).

To summarize, human infants are highly competent organisms who are capable of interacting with, processing information from, and responding to the environment as well as affecting it. Their development is transactional in nature with the infant and environment constantly in the process of mutual influence and regulation. The infant's development is best conceptualized in the context of a whole, organized, interrelated system of influence.

❖

Thus, we come to recognize human infants and their environments in the context of a larger system of biological and behavioral adaptation. It is from this conceptualization, the adaptive behavioral system, that we can orient toward promoting positive growth within the structure of the lives of the population at large. Although we could identify and support specific skills associated with competency, this approach is not easily adapted to broad-scale implementation and the continually changing nature of individuals' needs. We must abandon our search for "experts" who will enhance the lives of the "masses". We cannot hope to provide each infant with some optimal pattern of stimulation even if such an unlikely formula were to exist. Instead, we must emphasize self-sustaining supportive systems within the population at large. That is, we need to focus on promoting the individual's own adaptive response system to allow for the unique and changing demands of the individual's development. The active, selective behavior of each individual leads to transactions which are the bases of the individual's growth and construction of reality, the process by which development occurs. Thus, to promote the optimal development of each individual, we can encourage the individual's own propensity toward creating those conditions conducive to its own development. These conditions involve the individual's active, adaptive interaction with the environment.

Toward Infant-Environment Interaction

What is it that affects the infant's tendency to interact with the environment? Noting the persistent, selective, directive nature of the infant's behavior, R. W. White (1959) proposed the existence of an intrinsic motivation to attain "competence", that is, "to interact effectively with [the] environment" (p. 297). Citing rich illustrations from the work of Piaget (1952), White suggested that the child seems to select "for continuous treatment those aspects of his environment which he finds it possible to affect in some way" (p. 320). That is, there appears to be an intrinsic motive to explore the consequences of one's behavior upon the environment and the effects which the environment has upon oneself. This was alternatively described as a motive to develop an "effective familiarity" with the environment (White, 1959, p. 321) and labeled more precisely, "effectance motivation."

> Effectance motivation must be conceived to involve satisfaction—a feeling of efficacy—in transactions in which behavior has an exploratory, varying, experimental character and produces changes in the stimulus field. Having this character, the behavior leads the organism to find out how the environment can be changed and what consequences flow from these changes. (White, 1959, p. 329)

Effectance motivation, manifested in characteristics such as curiosity and exploration, was presumed to propel much of the infant's interaction with the environment. Effectance motivation would lead to exploration of one's effects upon the environment (i.e., mastery attempts). The perception of effects that are contingent upon one's behavior would result in feelings of efficacy. Feelings of efficacy appeared to be intrinsically reinforcing and therefore would serve to increase or sustain the effectance motivation. Thus competent (i.e., effective) behavior was seen as self-rewarding and leading to an adaptive, self-sustaining cycle which perpetuated infant–environment transactions.

Thus the infant's interaction with the environment is propelled, in part, by a tendency to explore its effective relationships and is perpetuated by the intrinsically reinforcing properties associated with perception of efficacy. The consequent interaction provides the nutriment for growth and adaptation; it is the process whereby the infant constructs its reality. Therefore as one's tendency to explore and develop effective familiarity with the environment increases or decreases, so may one's developmental progress.

The Effective Infant

Over a decade ago, Lewis and Goldberg (1969) suggested that mothers who respond promptly and contingently to their infants do more than merely reinforce the specific preceding infant behavior. The mother also fosters the development of a generalized expectancy of effectiveness on the part of the child, that is, the infant learns the rule that its behavior has environmental consequences. The generally reinforcing effects of this sense of self-efficacy promote novel responding and exploration in new situations as well. This ensuing interaction leads to the discovery of new environmental consequences, promoting the sense of self-efficacy and motivation toward further interaction.

The results of experimentally manipulated contingency experiences confirm interpretations of naturalistic observations. Early associations with response-contingent stimulation influence the infant's subsequent tendency to explore and discover contingent relationships (e.g., Finkelstein and Ramey, 1977; Papoušek, 1967; Ramey and Finkelstein, 1978; Watson and Ramey, 1972). For example, experience with response-noncontingent mobile turning led to significant difficulty in learning to affect a response-contingent mobile even 6 weeks later while response-contingent mobile turning enhanced infants' subsequent ability to effect such consequences (Watson and Ramey, 1972). Furthermore, the facilitory effects of early contingency experiences not only transfer from one task to another (Finkelstein and Ramey, 1977), but from one behavioral setting to another as well (Ramey and Finkelstein, 1978).

Thus, we have found that experiences with response-contingent and noncontingent stimulation modify the infant's pursuit of an effective familiarity with the environment. Meanwhile, it is this pursuit which propels transactions with the environment, the substance from which development emerges. Therefore, the responsiveness of the infant's early environment should have a significant impact upon the infant's developmental progression.

The responsiveness of the infant's social environment (maternal responsiveness in particular) has been associated with enhanced development of infants' social and cognitive skills (e.g., Clarke-Stewart, VanderStoep, and Killian, 1979; Cohen and Beckwith, 1979). Latency of maternal response to infant crying or vocalization is inversely related to the infant's habituation rate to repeated stimulation, a measure of early concept development and predictive among 1-year-olds of Stanford Binet IQ score and concept formation performance at 3½ years (Lewis and Goldberg, 1969). Maternal responsiveness to infant behaviors, vocalization, and distress is also associated with the following:

- superior psychomotor (Yarrow et al., 1975) and mental development scores on the Bayley (Clarke-Stewart, 1973; Yarrow et al., 1975)
- gross and fine motor skills and cognitive-motivational measures (Yarrow et al., 1975)
- indices of object and person permanence (Bell, 1970)
- initiation, number, variety, and clarity of infant communication signals (Ainsworth and Bell, 1974; Bell and Ainsworth, 1972; Yarrow et al., 1975).

In summarizing her own extensive observational research, Clarke-Stewart (1973) stated:

Maternal responsiveness was, in fact, more highly related to measures of the child's general competence and motivation than it was to the frequency of the specific infant behaviors responded to (looking at mother, vocalizing to her, approaching her, giving or showing her objects). Responsiveness was related to the child's Bayley mental score, to his speed of processing information, and to his schema development, as well as to language, social, and emotional indices of competence. This finding is one step toward confirming the suggestion that contingent responsiveness to an infant's behavior does more than reinforce specific behaviors, that it created in the infant an expectancy of control which generalizes to new situations and unfamiliar people. (p.71)

Although much of the support for the promotive impact of contingency relationships has come from research examining maternal responsiveness to infant distress in particular, Clarke-Stewart (1973) suggested that maternal responsiveness to the infant's social signals (other than distress) may reveal an even stronger relationship to the enhancement of social and intellectual competencies and motivation. In a report on a longitudinal study of premature babies, Beckwith, Cohen, Kopp, Parmelee, and Marcy (1976) state:

Infants who were assessed at 9 months as more skillful in sensorimotor performance had at 1 month more mutual caregiver–infant gazing, at 3 months more interchanges of smiling during mutual gazing and more contingent response to their fuss cries, and at 8 months experienced greater levels of social interaction including more contingent responsiveness to their nondistress vocalizations. The significant dimension appears to be reciprocal social transactions, that is, transactions that occur contingently to the infant's signals, either simultaneously as in mutual gazing or successively as in contingency to distress or contingency to nondistress vocalizations. (pp. 585–86)

They propose that their study revealed "an effective similarity of contingent behaviors, although each contingent behavior acquired salience at different ages" (p. 586).

The infant's exploration of its control of and control by the environment is fundamental to the emergence of reciprocal turn taking within the caregiver–infant dyad. The development of these caregiver–infant "dialogues" or reciprocal exchanges is receiving growing attention as the basis of early communication (e.g., Brazelton, Koslowski, and Main, 1974; Newson, 1977, 1979; Richards, 1974; Trevarthen, 1977) and as the precursor to mature language and general social dialogue (e.g., Bruner, 1977; Cairns et al., 1980; Jones, 1979; Kaye, 1977; Schaffer, 1977a, 1977b). As Lamb (1979) remarked:

It is evident . . . that infants must develop concepts of themselves as effective social beings (i.e., individuals whose behaviors affect those with whom they are interacting) as well as expectations regarding the behavior of others before they can be viewed as intentionally social beings rather than persons whose behavior has unanticipated social significance . . . . [Some] have argued that, by assuring responses to the infant's actions, parental sensitivity permits babies to develop notions of their own effectance as well as expectations regarding the mode and predictability of others' behavior. (p.70)

This preverbal dialogue may serve as the mechanism whereby the infant's actions acquire meaning and intentionality for the infant as well as for others (Jones, 1979; Newson, 1979; Richards, 1974). Caregivers tend to interpret the infant's behavior in the same way that they interpret the behaviors of others engaged in a social dialogue and respond discriminately to those infant behaviors that have meaning in a typical social exchange. Thus a nonresponsive parent not only decreases an infant's tendency to explore its surroundings but also interferes with the cultural mediation of socially significant gestures and the phasing and reciprocity critical to the development of mature social exchange. That is, both the structure and the content of social dialogue may be influenced.

The Effective Dyad

Armed with this knowledge, how do we proceed toward the goal of optimizing infant development? Surely we could design individualized infant stimulation programs that would include extensive contingency experience. But such an approach is inadequate for broad-scale promotion. It returns us to the gross inefficiencies of one-to-one interventions and, in fact, becomes an absurd impossibility when targeting the general population. Furthermore, infant development occurs via transactions that are nested within larger systems. Thus we need to focus on restructuring the system rather than the individual, with the further goal of promoting a self-sustaining system. Expanding simply to the point of the caregiver–infant dyad or family triad lends a new perspective to the task of promotion.

Goldberg (1977) has emphasized that caregivers' experiences affect their feelings of efficacy, as well. Adults embark upon parenthood with both general feelings of self-efficacy relevant to their pursuit of life goals, career, relationships, and so forth and certain specific expectations of their abilities to interact effectively with their baby. As with infants, caregivers' feelings of efficacy affect their tendencies to initiate responses; the expectation of being effective encourages the exploration of responses which may produce desired consequences. Feelings of self-efficacy also promote the caregiver's tendency to attend to and analyze the infant's behavior in terms of its contingent relationship to the caregiver's, allowing subtle changes in the infant's behavior to be used as cues for subsequent contingent responding by the caregiver.

As we speak in terms of the "responsive caregiver" and the "responsive, predictable, readable infant," it becomes clear that we are not referring to independent characteristics of parent or child but rather to mutually dependent and evolving characteristics of an infant–caregiver transactional system (nested within still broader systems). The notion of a competent or effective dyad emerges (Ainsworth and Bell, 1974; Goldberg, 1977). Perceptions of efficacy not only influence the individual's tendency to explore and initiate responses but they simultaneously lead to behaviors that are effective in eliciting responsive behaviors from others. The effective, responsive individual (caregiver or infant) behaves in a manner that is more likely to elicit effective responsive interaction with others, which, in turn, increases both the individual's and the others' perceptions of efficacy and subsequent tendency for future exploration and effective interaction. Meanwhile, the least effective infants and caregivers, those in most need of feedback regarding their own effects, behave in a manner least likely to elicit such experiences from others. Thus, the competent dyad fosters increasing growth and efficacy on the part of both members, while the incompetent dyad experiences spiralling decreases in feelings of effectiveness, which presumably decrease dyadic interaction and transactions in general.

❖   In summary, the caregiver's sensitivity and responsiveness to the child will vary with the caregiver's psychological and physiological state, expectations of the child's performance, and perceptions of, or affective feelings toward, the child. An infant's sensitivity and responsiveness to the caregiver will depend upon the infant's perceptual abilities, autonomic maturity, motor ability, and abilities to sustain an alert responsive state (Packer and Rosenblatt, 1979). But while the characteristics of infant and caregiver affect those of the other, they are simultaneously altered by their consequences in a manner which continually shapes the ability of each to interact effectively.

Promoting Optimal Development

How do we go about the task of promoting optimal development? We are coming to recognize the inherent dangers of attempting to prescribe the enhancement of specific skills or characteristics (e.g., Bruner and Connolly, 1974). For example, in appraising past efforts to promote social competence, White concludes that "mental health workers have rushed in where shrewder observers feared to tread" (1979, p.5). He explains that the term "social competence" has assumed different meanings through history as a function of the changing values of society. What we choose to enhance in one decade may be considered far less significant in another. Thus, it appears wiser to focus on more basic, nonspecific emotional and intellectual characteristics, which, being neither situation- nor task-specific, allow the individual to monitor circumstances relevant to his or her own particular environment (see Laosa, 1979).

Interventionists have begun to consider Hunt's (1961, 1965) concept of the "problem of match" in their intervention designs; they have pointed to the importance of diagnosing the individual's level of functioning before determining the environmental circumstances optimal for promoting the individual's growth. From this perspective, it is claimed that a particular intervention cannot be expected to affect all people uniformly given the variations in "match" (e.g., Ulvund, 1980). Although this argument is certainly valid, it may be interpreted as calling for the development of unique formulas of optimal stimulation for each individual. Such a scheme is simply not feasible on a broad-scale basis. Moreover, the dialectics of development are such that the child's orientation toward producing effects upon the environment continually generates contradictions or asynchronies that move the individual toward greater articulation and integration (Laosa, 1979). Therefore, the optimal match for each individual continues to change, requiring constant reformulation. Thus, while the match between environment and child or parent and child may contribute significantly to development, it appears more fruitful to enhance the underlying tendency of the individual to seek circumstances that continually allow for growth. At the same time, while we can try to educate parents about their children's needs and the manner in which to meet them, it seems more productive to maximize parents' own tendencies to seek out and continually analyze the effectiveness of their varied behavioral transactions with their children.

I think we have reached a consensus that it is *enduring influences* which have enduring effects (e.g., Clarke and Clarke, 1976). Therefore, we need to focus upon promoting the self-sustaining and hence enduring characteristics of the individual and environment which underlie growth and development. Given the multidirectional, transactional nature of development, the variations within and between individuals, and the changing life task demands across the life span and across cultures, we cannot provide each individual with an "optimal" environment. Thus, we need to promote individuals who are more likely to promote optimal conditions for their own development, whatever their environment may be. Enhancing feelings of effectiveness and contingency seeking and analyses on the part of both members of the parent–infant dyad may be one important step toward optimizing development within the general population since these factors appear to underlie the individual's interaction with the environment which is, in turn, the basis of development.

Promoting self-sustaining feelings of efficacy within the dyad is not a simple task in our society. For example, in other cultures and other times, individuals developed confidence as effective, competent caregivers in their youth through observing practices of the extended family and by caring for younger siblings. Today parents are choosing to have fewer children. Furthermore, the population is typically segregated by age in education, social gatherings, and employment; the old and the young are rarely incorporated into the mainstream of economic, political, and social spheres. With the industrialization of our economy and the increased mobility of the population, we find increasing isolation of the nuclear family. Connolly and Bruner (1974) reported that 50 years ago more than half the families in Massachusetts had an older relative living with them, or within one mile of the home whereas fewer than 1 in 20 families were so situated in 1974. There has been a dramatic increase in single parenting, particularly as a result of divorce. Political, cultural, and economic changes have led to increased pressure for women and men alike to be employed in full-time jobs. Our society gives little prestige to those fully occupied with caregiving activities, whether professionally or otherwise. In sum, the situation is not conducive for either parents or children to observe and engage in childrearing activities and to develop expectations of competence in this role. There has been a change in the role of the family as a principal support system both of the young and the adult.

Compounding these problems is the increasing technology of the childrearing business. Childbirth has grown into a massive medical industry which has taken much control and responsibility for the young out of parents' hands. The message is that parents are not capable of providing adequate care for the newborn. Even parents of healthy, full-term babies are often deprived of opportunities for early continuous interaction with their neonates. The opportunity to become acquainted with the infant and develop early parenting skills is often delayed until the parents are home and without the support of professionals. The proliferation of childrearing theories, guides, educational toys and paraphernalia contrasts the "guesswork" of parenting with the "facts" and "knowledge" of the "experts." It is no wonder that adults lack confidence about their abilities as effective caregivers.

Therefore, just as the infant must be considered as a part of a larger caregiver–infant system, the dyad must be recognized within the context of a larger family system that is part of a community which, in turn, is enmeshed within a larger social structure. If we intend to promote optimal development on a broad-scale, long-term basis, it will mean restructuring the many levels of the social system so that people have more control of and impact on their own lives; they must recognize themselves as competent problem seekers and problem solvers.

The task of promotion may be approached simultaneously through many levels of systems, and it is this multilevel approach which seems to be most promising. Beyond certain obvious implications of our discussion for promotion efforts, broad guidelines for the content and structure of these activities emerge as well.

Parent-centered and family-centered problem-solving orientation.

An emphasis upon parents as effective caregivers and problem solvers suggests a move from child-centered programs to parent- or family-centered programs. Since enduring influences have enduring effects, not surprisingly we find that family-centered intervention programs will have the most positive and long-lasting effects (e.g., Bronfenbrenner, 1974; Lazar and Darlington, 1978; Ramey, Sparling, and Wasik, 1979; Schaefer, 1970; Weikart and Lambie, 1970). This conclusion has led to programs in which parents rather than professionals are trained to implement curricula that have been carefully designed by specialists. But this move alone is not a solution since parents continue to be treated as actors reading someone else's script; they are encouraged to depend upon the recipes of experts with little thought toward the process of creating their own. Given the multilinear, multidimensional character of development, it is important not to promote one "optimal" course of behavior. Furthermore, deviation from that path then denotes parental "failure". Parents themselves must develop confidence and skills as "curriculum designers" with the recognition that the curriculum will be continually under reconstruction by both parent and infant. Just as there is no single formula for optimizing the development of all individuals, no single plan remains optimal for an individual across time and circumstances. Caregivers themselves need to be effective detectors, analyzers, and synthesizers of information (see Ramey, Sparling, and Wasik, 1979, and Shure and Spivack, 1978 for two successful applications of this notion).

In sum, positive, enduring impact is most likely to come about through programs and institutional restructuring directed not only toward the parent or family but also toward the processing and problem-solving skills of the caregiver. Of course, this orientation is an integral part of any attempt to enhance caregiver responsiveness and sensitivity to infant responsiveness. Again, the discovery of the self as a competent problem solver leads to behaviors that are more likely to confirm and sustain this self-image.

Development of self-help groups, natural caregivers, and support systems.

An inherent part of self-help groups is the implication that individuals are competent in diagnosing and affecting their own circumstances. Self- and peer-reliance are emphasized rather than dependence upon professionals; individuals are recognized as capable of contributing to both their own and others' development. Thus, the very structure of the self-help group enhances the individual's sense of efficacy and skills as a problem solver (e.g., see Silverman, 1978).

Huntington (1979) points out that parents learn best from each other. Increasing numbers of programs have capitalized upon this notion by employing former program participants as "trainers" for new members. These trainers occupy their roles for only a limited period at which time a new group of recent participants assume their jobs. This procedure prevents the emergence of a cadre of indoctrinated "experts" and emphasizes the expertise of each participant.

At the same time, mental health professionals are beginning to take advantage of the great potential of natural caregivers and support systems by promoting their development. Neighbors and friends remain the most common and accessible resource for help with problems of living. Farsighted programs are already supporting the skills of these native helpers (e.g., Collins and Pancoast, 1976; Danish and D'Augelli, 1980).

Promotion of behaviors relevant for changing the social system.
Hess (1974) noted that studies of social development often dwell upon "person-relevant" behaviors, that is, those which relate persons to one another or to small groups. In contrast "system relevant" behaviors which "relate individuals to institutions and to political and social systems" (1974, p. 283) are rarely considered. We have seen that competence involves both adaptation to, as well as modification of, the environment. Individuals need to be effective both in coping with institutions and in altering those structures to meet their needs. Hess's (1974) analysis of elementary school social studies texts revealed that major sources of national tensions were infrequently mentioned and were portrayed as capable of resolution by the current social system, thus encouraging the status quo and the maintenance of ongoing tensions and stress rather than promoting skills in effecting productive societal changes.

Just as increased feelings of efficacy regarding person-relevant behaviors lead to actions that are likely to confirm effectiveness with others, increased feelings of efficacy regarding system-relevant behaviors may promote skills that support institutional and societal effectiveness. In an analysis of nursery settings, Tizard (1974) found that both staff behavior and child development were significantly related to social organization. Institutional structures that fostered staff feelings of autonomy and control appeared to lead to more effective staff behavior. With regard to families, Kagan (1970) argued that "a sense of control over one's future and a stake in the next day are likely to develop if the parent *believes* that a specific set of changes in daily practices is reasonable and the parent knows that he or she has the option to choose the procedures" (p. 24).

In summary, promoting competent individuals involves supporting individual's feelings of efficacy with regard to both person- and system-relevant behaviors. The self-supporting characteristics of efficacy are most likely to encourage the wide-scale, enduring promotion of development which we seek. Central to our concern is a recognition that we must view this process within the context of a multilevel response system. This takes us beyond the individual infant or infant–caregiver dyads (or triads) to consider the structures of the family, community, and society. If we hope that primary prevention in the broadest sense of promotion will become a way of life, we have to integrate responsive, supportive systems into our social structure; that is, we must work toward a society which itself is growth-promoting, one in which individual and group efficacy is real.

References

Ainsworth, M. D. The development of infant–mother attachment. In B. M. Caldwell and H. N. Ricciuti (Eds.), *Review of child development research* (Vol. 3). Chicago: University of Chicago, 1973.

Ainsworth, M. D., and Bell, S. M. Mother–infant interaction and the development of competence. In K. J. Connolly and J. S. Bruner (Eds.), *The growth of competence*. New York: Academic Press, 1974.

Albee, G. W. The fourth mental health revolution. *Journal of Prevention,* 1980, *1*(2), 67–70.

Ansbacher, H. L. What is positive mental health? In D. G. Forgays (Ed.), *Primary prevention of psychopathology,* Vol. 2: *Environmental influences.* Hanover, N.H.: University Press of New England, 1978.

Appleton, T., Clifton, R., and Goldberg, S. The development of behavioral competence in infancy. In F. D. Horowitz (Ed.), *Review of child development research* (Vol. 4). Chicago: University of Chicago Press, 1975.

Badger, E. A mother's training program—The road to a purposeful existence. *Children,* 1971 *18*(5), 168–173.

Badger, E. A mother's training program—A sequel article. *Children Today,* 1972, *1*(3), 7–12.

Baldwin, J. M. *Social and ethical interpretations in mental development: A study in social psychology* (3rd ed.). New York: Macmillan, 1902.

Baltes, P. B. (Ed.). *Life-span development and behavior* (Vol.1). New York: Academic Press, 1978.

Baltes, P. B., and Brim, O. G., Jr. (Eds.). *Life-span development and behavior* (Vol.2). New York: Academic Press, 1979.

Baltes, P. B., Reese, H. W., and Lipsitt, L. P. Life-span developmental psychology. *Annual Review of Psychology,* 1980, *31,* 65–110.

Beckwith, L. Relationships between infants' social behavior and their mothers' behavior. *Child Development,* 1972, *43,* 397–411.

Beckwith, L. Prediction of emotional and social behavior. In J. D. Osofsky (Ed.), *Handbook of infant development.* New York: John Wiley, 1979.

Beckwith, L., Cohen, S. E., Kopp, C. B., Parmelee, A. H., and Marcy, T. G. Caregiver-infant interaction and early cognitive development in preterm infants. *Child Development,* 1976, *47,* 579–587.

Bell, R. Q. A reinterpretation of the direction of effects in studies of socialization. *Psychological Review*, 1968, *75*, 81–95.

Bell, R. Q. Stimulus control of parent or caretaker behavior by offspring. *Developmental Psychology*, 1971, *4*, 63–72.

Bell, S. M. The development of the concept of object as related to infant-mother attachment. *Child Development*, 1970, *41*, 291–311.

Bell, S. M., and Ainsworth, M. D. Infant crying and maternal responsiveness. *Child Development*, 1972, *43*, 1171–1190.

Beller, K. Discussant. In F. Palmer (Chair), *Persistence of preschool effects: Evidence of impact*. Symposium presented at the meeting of the Society for Research in Child Development, San Francisco, March 1979.

Bond, E. K. Perception of form by the human infant. *Psychological Bulletin*, 1972, *77*, 225–245.

Bower, T. G. *Development in infancy*. San Francisco: W. H. Freeman, 1974.

Brazelton, T. B., Koslowski, B., and Main, M. The origins of reciprocity: The early mother-infant interaction. In M. Lewis and L. A. Rosenblum (Eds.), *The effect of the infant on its caregiver*. New York: Wiley, 1974.

Brazelton, T. B., Tronick, E., Adamson, L., Als, H., and Weise, S. Early mother-infant reciprocity. In Ciba Foundation Symposium 33, *Parent-infant interaction*. Holland: Elsevier, 1975.

Bronfenbrenner, U. Is intervention effective? *Teachers College Record*, 1974, *76*, 279–304.

Broussard, E. Neonatal prediction and outcome at 10/11 years. *Child Psychiatry and Human Development*, 1976, *7*, 85–93.

Broussard, E. R., and Hartner, M. S. Further considerations regarding maternal perception of the newborn. In J. Hellmuth (Ed.), *Exceptional infant*, Vol. 2: *Studies in abnormalities*. New York: Brunner/Mazel, 1971.

Bruner, J. S. Discussion: Infant education as viewed by a psychologist. In V. H. Denenberg (Ed.), *Education of the infant and young child*. New York: Academic Press, 1970.

Bruner, J. S. Early social interaction and language acquisition. In H. R. Schaffer (Ed.), *Studies in mother-infant interaction*. New York: Academic Press, 1977.

Bruner, J. S., and Connolly, K. J. Competence: The growth of the person. In K. J. Connolly and J. S. Bruner (Eds.), *The growth of competence*. New York: Academic Press, 1974.

Cairns, R. B., Green, J. A., and MacCombie, D. J. The dynamics of social development. In E. C. Simmel (Ed.), *Early experiences and early behavior: Implications for social development*. New York: Academic Press, 1980.

Caplan, G. *Principles of preventive psychiatry*. New York: Basic Books, 1964.

Charlesworth, W. R. The role of surprise in cognitive development. In D. Elkind and J. H. Flavell (Eds.), *Studies in cognitive development: Essays in honor of Jean Piaget*. New York: Oxford University Press, 1969.

Chavez, A., Martinez, C., and Yaschine, T. The importance of nutrition and stimuli on child mental and social development. In J. Cravioto, L. Hambraeus, and B. Vahlquist (Eds.), *Early malnutrition and mental development*. Uppsalla, Sweden: Almquist and Wiksell, 1974.

Clarke, A. M., and Clarke, A. D. B. *Early experience: Myth and evidence*. London: Open Books, 1976

Clarke-Stewart, K. A. Interactions between mothers and their young children: Characteristics and consequences. *Monographs of the Society for Research in Child Development*, 1973, *38* (6–7, Serial No. 153).

Clarke-Stewart, K. A., VanderStoep, L. P., and Killian, G. A. Analysis and replication of mother-child relations at two years of age. *Child Development,* 1979, *50,* 777–793.

Cohen, L. B., DeLoache, J. S., and Strauss, M. S. Infant visual perception. In J. D. Osofsky (Ed.), *Handbook of infant development.* New York: John Wiley, 1979.

Cohen, S. E., and Beckwith, L. Preterm infant interaction with the caregiver in the first year of life and competence at age two. *Child Development,* 1979, *50,* 767–776.

Collins, A. H., and Pancoast, D. L. *Natural helping networks: A strategy for prevention.* Washington, D.C.: National Association of Social Workers, 1976.

Connolly, K. J., and Bruner, J. S. (Eds.). *The growth of competence.* New York: Academic Press, 1974.

Danish, S. J. Human development and human services: A marriage proposal. In I. Iscoe, B. L. Bloom, and C. C. Spielberger (Eds.), *Community psychology in transition.* New York: Halstead, 1977.

Danish, S. J., and D'Augelli, A. R. Promoting competence and enhancing development through life development intervention. In L. A. Bond and J. C. Rosen (Eds.), *Competence and coping during adulthood.* Hanover, N.H.: University Press of New England, 1980.

Danish, S. J., Smyer, M. A., and Nowak, C. A. Developmental intervention: Enhancing life-event processes. In P. B. Baltes and O. G. Brim, Jr. (Eds.), *Life-span development and behavior* (Vol.3). New York: Academic Press, 1980.

Eimas, P. D., Siqueland, E. R., Jusczk, P., and Vigorito, J. Speech perception in early infancy. *Science,* 1971, *171,* 303–306.

Eisenberg, R. B. Auditory behavior in the neonate. I. Methodological problems and the logical design of research procedures. *Journal of Auditory Research,* 1965, *5,* 159–177.

Finkelstein, N. W., and Ramey, C. T. Learning to control the environment in infancy. *Child Development,* 1977, *48,* 806–819.

Fraiberg, S. Intervention in infancy: A program for blind infants. *Journal of Child Psychiatry,* 1971, *10,* 381–405.

Goldberg, S. Social competence in infancy: A model of parent–infant interaction. *Merrill-Palmer Quarterly,* 1977, *23,* 163–177.

Goldberg, S. Premature birth: Consequences for the parent-infant relationship. *American Scientist,* 1979, *67,* 214–220.

Goldston, S. E. Defining primary prevention. In G. W. Albee and J. M. Joffe (Eds.), *Primary prevention of psychopathology,* Vol. 1: *The issues.* Hanover, N.H.: University Press of New England, 1977.

Gordon, T. Parent effectiveness training: A preventive program and its delivery system. In G. W. Albee and J. M. Joffe (Eds.), *Primary prevention of psychopathology,* Vol 1: *The issues.* Hanover, N.H.: University Press of New England, 1977.

Green, J. A., Gustafson, G. E., and West, M. J. The effects of infant development on mother–infant interactions. *Child Development,* 1980, *51,* 199–207.

Gunnar, M. R. Control, warning signals, and distress in infancy. *Developmental Psychology,* 1980, *16,* 281–289.

Gunnar-vonGnechten, M. Changing a frightening toy into a pleasant toy by allowing the infant to control its actions. *Developmental Psychology,* 1978, *14,* 157–162.

Gustafson, G. E., Green, J. A., and West, M. J. The infant's changing role in mother-infant games: The growth of social skills. *Infant Behavior and Development,* 1979, *2,* 301–308.

Haaf, R. A., and Bell, R. Q. The facial dimension in visual discrimination by human infants. *Child Development,* 1967, *38,* 893–899.

Harter, S. Effectance motivation reconsidered: Toward a developmental model. *Human Development,* 1978, *21,* 34–64.

Harter, S., and Zigler, E. The assessment of effectance motivation in normal and retarded children. *Developmental Psychology,* 1974, *10,* 169–180.

Held, R., and Hein, A. Movement-produced stimulation in the development of visually guided behavior. *Journal of Comparative and Physiological Psychology,* 1963, *56,* 872–876.

Hess, R. D. Social competence and the educational process. In K. J. Connolly and J. S. Bruner (Eds.), *The growth of competence.* New York: Academic Press, 1974.

Hoke, B. Promotive medicine and the phenomenon of health. *Archives of Environmental Health,* 1968, *16,* 269–278.

Hunt, J. McV. *Intelligence and experience.* New York: Ronald, 1961.

Hunt, J. McV. Intrinsic motivation and its role in psychological development. In D. Levine (Ed.), *Nebraska Symposium on Motivation* (Vol. 13). Lincoln: University of Nebraska Press, 1965.

Huntington, D. S. Supportive programs for infants and parents. In J. D. Osofsky (Ed.), *Handbook of infant development.* New York: John Wiley, 1979.

Jennings, K. D., Harmon, R. J., Morgan, G. A., Gaiter, J. L., and Yarrow, L. J. Exploratory play as an index of mastery motivation: Relationships to persistence, cognitive functioning, and environmental measures. *Developmental Psychology,* 1979, *15,* 386–394.

Jones, O. H. A comparative study of mother-child communication with Down's syndrome and normal infants. In D. Shaffer and J. Dunn (Eds.), *The first year.* New York: John Wiley, 1979.

Kagan, J. On class differences and early development. In V. H. Denenberg (Ed.), *Education of the infant and young child.* New York: Academic Press, 1970.

Kaye, K. Toward the origin of dialogue. In H. R. Schaffer (Ed.), *Studies in mother-infant interaction.* New York: Academic Press, 1977.

Kelly, G. A. *The psychology of personal constructs* (Vol.1). New York: Norton, 1955.

Klein, D. C., and Goldston, S. E. (Eds.). *Primary prevention: An idea whose time has come.* Rockville, MD: ADAMHA, 1977. DHEW Publication No. (ADM)77-447.

Kohler, I. Experiments with goggles. *Scientific American,* 1962, *206,* 62–86.

Korner, A. F. Conceptual issues in infancy research. In J. D. Osofsky (Ed.), *Handbook of infant development.* New York: John Wiley, 1979.

Kuo, Z. Y. *The dynamics of behavior development: An epigenetic view.* New York: Random House, 1967.

Lamb, M. E. Social development in infancy: Reflections on a theme. *Human Development,* 1979, *22,* 68–72.

Laosa, L. M. Social competence in childhood: Toward a developmental, socioculturally relativistic paradigm. In M. W. Kent and J. E. Rolf, *Primary prevention of psychopathology,* Vol. 3: *Social competence in children.* Hanover, N.H.: University Press of New England, 1979.

Lazar, I., and Darlington, R. B. (Eds.). *Lasting effects of preschool.* Final report, HEW Grant 90C-1311 to the Education Commission of the States, 1978.

Lazarus, R. S. The stress and coping paradigm. In L. A. Bond and J. C. Rosen (Eds.), *Competence and coping during adulthood.* Hanover, N.H.: University Press of New England, 1980.

Levitt, M. J. Contingent feedback, familiarization, and infant affect: How a stranger becomes a friend. *Developmental Psychology*, 1980, *16*, 425–432.

Lewis, M., and Goldberg, S. Perceptual-cognitive development in infancy: A generalized expectancy model as a function of the mother-infant interaction. *Merrill-Palmer Quarterly*, 1969, *15*, 81–100.

Lewis, M., and Rosenblum, L. A. *The effect of the infant on its caregiver*. New York: John Wiley, 1974.

Mahrer, A. R., Levinson, J. R., and Fine, S. Infant psychotherapy: Theory, research, and practice. *Psychotherapy: Theory, Research and Practice*, 1976, *13*, 131–140.

Mason, W. A. Early deprivation in biological perspective. In V. H. Denenberg (Ed.), *Education of the infant and young child*. New York: Academic Press, 1970.

McCall, R. Exploratory manipulation and play in the human infant. *Monographs of the Society for Research in Child Development*, 1974, *39* (2, Serial No. 155).

Miller, G. A. Psychology as a means of promoting human welfare. *American Psychologist*, 1969, *12*, 1063–1075.

Murphy, L. B., and Frank, C. Prevention: The clinical psychologist. *Annual Review of Psychology*, 1979, *30*, 173–207.

Newson, J. An intersubjective approach to the systematic description of mother-infant interaction. In H. R. Schaffer (Ed.), *Studies in mother-infant interaction*. New York: Academic Press, 1977.

Newson, J. Intentional behavior in the young infant. In D. Shaffer and J. Dunn (Eds.), *The first year of life*. New York: John Wiley, 1979.

O'Keefe, A. An overview of the El Paso National Head Start Conference—Parents, children and continuity. *Head Start Newsletter*, 1977, 1–16.

Osofsky, J. D. (Ed.), *Handbook of infant development*. New York: John Wiley, 1979.

Packer, M., and Rosenblatt, D. Issues in the study of social behavior in the first week of life. In D. Shaffer and J. Dunn (Eds.), *The first year of life*. New York: John Wiley, 1979.

Papoušek, H. Conditioned head rotation reflexes in infants in the first months of life. *Acta Paediatrica*, 1961, *50*, 565–576.

Papoušek, H. Experimental studies of appetitional behavior in human newborns and infants. In H. W. Stevenson, E. H. Hess, and H. L. Rheingold (Eds.), *Early behavior: Comparative and developmental approaches*. New York: Wiley, 1967.

Papoušek, H. Individual variability in learned responses in human infants. In R. J. Robinson (Ed.), *Brain and early behavior*. London: Academic Press, 1969.

Papoušek, H., and Bernstein, P. The functions of conditioning stimulation in human neonates and infants. In A. Ambrose (Ed.), *Stimulation in early infancy*. London: Academic Press, 1969.

Papoušek, H., and Papoušek, M. Interdisciplinary parallels in studies of early human behavior: From physical to cognitive needs, from attachment to dyadic education. *International Journal of Behavioral Development*, 1978, *1*, 37–49.

Piaget, J. *The origins of intelligence in children*. New York: International Universities Press, 1952.

Piaget, J. *To understand is to invent: The future of education*. New York: Penguin Books, 1976.

Provence, S., and Lipton, R. C. *Infants in institutions*. New York: International Universities Press, 1962.

Ramey, C. T., and Finkelstein, N. W. Contingent stimulation and infant competence. *Journal of Pediatric Psychology*, 1978, *3*, 88–96.

Ramey, C. T., Hieger, L., and Klisz, D. Synchronous reinforcement of vocal responses in failure-to-thrive infants. *Child Development*, 1972, *43*, 1449–1455.

Ramey, C. T., Sparling, J. J., and Wasik, B. H. Creating social environments to facilitate language development. In R. Schiefelbusch and D. Bricker (Eds.), *Early language intervention*. Baltimore: University Park Press, 1979.

Ramey, C. T., Starr, R. H., Pallas, J., Whitten, C. F., and Reed, V. Nutrition, response-contingent stimulation, and the maternal deprivation syndrome: Results of an early intervention program. *Merrill-Palmer Quarterly*, 1975, *21*, 45–53.

Richards, M. P. The development of psychological communication in the first year of life. In K. J. Connolly and J. S. Bruner (Eds.), *The growth of competence*. New York: Academic Press, 1974.

Richards, M. P. Effects on development of medical interventions and the separation of newborns from their parents. In D. Shaffer and J. Dunn (Eds.), *The first year of life*. new York: John Wiley, 1979.

Riegel, K. F. Toward a dialectical theory of development. *Human Development*, 1975, *18*, 50–64.

Riksen-Walraven, J. M. Effects of caregiver behavior on habituation rate and self-efficacy in infants. *International Journal of Behavioral Development*, 1978, *1*, 105–130.

Roberts, C. A. Psychiatric and mental health consultation. *Canadian Journal of Public Health*, 1970, *51*, 17–24.

Rosenthal, M. The study of infant-environment interaction: Some comments on trends and methodologies. *Journal of Child Psychology and Psychiatry*, 1973, *14*, 301–317.

Rossetti Ferreira, C. M. Malnutrition and mother-infant asynchrony: Slow mental development. *International Journal of Behavioral Development*, 1978, *1*, 207–219.

Sameroff, A. J. Early influences on development: Fact or fancy? *Merrill-Palmer Quarterly*, 1975, *21*, 267–294. (a)

Sameroff, A. J. Transactional models in early social relations. *Human Development*, 1975, *18*, 65–79. (b)

Sameroff, A. J. Concepts of humanity in primary prevention. In G. W. Albee and J. M. Joffe (Eds.), *Primary prevention of psychopathology*, Vol. 1: *The issues*. Hanover, N.H.: University Press of New England, 1977.

Sameroff, A. J., and Chandler, M. J. Reproductive risk and the continuum of caretaking casualty. In F. D. Horowitz, M. Hetherington, S. Scarr-Salapatek, and G. Siegel (Eds.), *Review of child development research* (Vol. 4). Chicago: University of Chicago, 1975.

Schaefer, E. S. Need for early and continuing education. In V. Denenberg (Ed.), *Education of the infant and young child*. New York: Academic Press, 1970.

Schaffer, H. R. (Ed.). *Studies in mother-infant interaction*. New York: Academic Press, 1977. (a)

Schaffer, H. R. *Mothering*. Cambridge: Harvard University Press, 1977. (b)

Schaffer, H. R. Acquiring the concept of dialogue. In M. H. Bornstein and W. Kessen (Eds.), *Psychological development from infancy*. New York: Erlbaum, 1979.

Schneirla, T. C. Behavioral development and comparative psychology. *Quarterly Review of Biology*, 1966, *41*, 283–302.

Seligman, M. *Helplessness: On depression, development, and death*. San Francisco: Freeman, 1975.

306   LYNNE A. BOND

Shure, M. D., and Spivack, G. *Problem solving techniques in childrearing.* San Francisco: Jossey-Bass, 1978.
Sigel, I. E., and Cocking, R. R. *Cognitive development from childhood to adolescence: A constructivist perspective.* New York: Holt, Rinehart and Winston, 1977.
Silverman, P. R. *Mutual help groups: A guide for mental health workers.* Rockville, MD: ADAMHA, 1978. DHEW Publication No. (ADM)78-646.
Sroufe, L. A., and Waters, E. The ontogenesis of smiling and laughter: A perspective on the organization of development in infancy. *Psychological Review,* 1976, *83,* 173–190.
Sroufe, L. A., and Wunsch, J. A. The development of laughter in the first year of life. *Child Development,* 1972, *43,* 1326–1344.
Stern, D. N. A micro-analysis of mother–infant interaction behavior regulating social contact between a mother and three-and-a-half-month-old twins. *Journal of the American Academy of Child Psychiatry,* 1971, *10,* 501–517.
Stern, D. N. Mother and infant at play: The dyadic interaction involving facial, vocal, and gaze behaviors. In M. Lewis and L. A. Rosenblum (Eds.), *The effect of the infant on its caregiver.* New York: John Wiley, 1974.
Stern, D. N., Beebe, B., Jaffe, J., and Bennett, S. L. The infant's stimulus world during social interaction: A study of caregiver behaviours with particular reference to repetition and timing. In H. R. Schaffer (Ed.), *Studies in mother-infant interaction.* New York: Academic Press, 1977.
Stone, L. J., Smith, H. T., and Murphy, L. B. (Eds.). *The competent infant: Research and commentary.* New York: Basic Books, 1973.
Task Force on Prevention. G. Albee, coordinator. *Report to the President's Commission on Mental Health* (Vol.4). Washington, D.C.: U.S. Government Printing Office, No.040-000-00393-2, 1978.
Tizard, B. Do social relationships affect language development? In K. J. Connolly and J. S. Bruner, *The growth of competence.* New York: Academic Press, 1974.
Trevarthen, C. Descriptive analyses of infant communicative behavior. In H. R. Schaffer (Ed.), *Studies in mother-infant interaction.* New York: Academic Press, 1977.
Ulvund, S. E. Cognition and motivation in early infancy: An interactionist approach. *Human Development,* 1980, *23,* 17–32.
Wachs, T. D. The relationship of infants' physical environment to their Binet performance at 2½ years. *International Journal of Behavioral Development,* 1978, *1,* 51–65.
Wachs, T. D., Uzgiris, I. C., and Hunt, J.McV. Cognitive development in infants of different age levels and from different environmental backgrounds: an explanatory investigation. *Merrill-Palmer Quarterly,* 1971, *17,* 283–317.
Wagenfeld, M. O. The primary prevention of mental illness. *Journal of Health and Social Behavior,* 1972, *13,* 195–203.
Watson, J. S. The development and generalization of contingency awareness in early infancy: Some hypotheses. *Merrill-Palmer Quarterly,* 1966, *12,* 123–135.
Watson, J. S. Smiling, cooing and "The Game." *Merrill-Palmer Quarterly,* 1972, *18,* 323–340.
Watson, J. S. Perception of contingency as a determinant of social responsiveness. In E. B. Thoman (Ed.), *Origins of the infant's social responsiveness.* New York: Erlbaum, 1979.
Watson, J. S., and Ramey, C. T. Reactions to response-contingent stimulation in early infancy. *Merrill-Palmer Quarterly,* 1972, *18,* 219–229.

Weikart, D. P., and Lambie, D. Z. Early enrichment in infants. In V. H. Denenberg (Ed.), *Education of the infant and young child*. New York: Academic Press, 1970.

White, B. L. An experimental approach to the effects of experience on early human behavior. In J. P. Hill (Ed.), *Minnesota Symposium on Child Psychology* (Vol. 1). Minneapolis: University of Minnesota Press, 1967.

White, B. L. The initial coordination of sensorimotor schemas in human infants—Piaget's ideas and the role of experience. In D. Elkind and J. H. Flavell (Eds.), *Studies in cognitive development*. New York: Oxford University Press, 1969.

White, R. W. Motivation reconsidered: The concept of competence. *Psychological Review*, 1959, *66*, 297–333.

White, R. W. Competence as an aspect of personal growth. In M. W. Kent and J. E. Rolf (Eds.), *Primary prevention of psychopathology*, Vol. 3: *Social competence in children*. Hanover, N.H.: University Press of New England, 1979.

Yarrow, L. J., Pedersen, F. A., and Rubenstein, J. L. Mother-infant interaction and development in infancy. In P. H. Leiderman, S. R. Tulkin, and A. Rosenfeld (Eds.), *Culture and infancy: Variations in human experience*. New York: Academic Press, 1977.

Yarrow, L. J., Rubenstein, J. L., and Pedersen, F. A. *Infant and environment: Early cognitive and motivational development*. New York: Halstead, 1975.

Promoting Competence and Enhancing Development through Life Development Intervention

Steven J. Danish and Anthony R. D'Augelli

❖ In this chapter, we will present a new paradigm that can direct the future development of mental health services. In particular, the approach presented will be offered as an alternative to primary prevention, a concept with much intuitive appeal which has yet to be consistently operationalized. The promotion of competence through life development intervention, in contrast to the remedial or preventive model, is explicitly based on theories of human development (Baltes and Danish, 1980). Such theories, often implicit in mental health activities, suggest different timing for intervention, goals for intervention, and processes for intervention. Therefore, before describing our model of intervention, we will elaborate our conceptual framework and the theory of development that guides the framework.

❖ *PRIMARY PREVENTION AND HUMAN DEVELOPMENT*

Toward Enhancement of Human Development

Most conceptions of primary prevention focus on problem prevention. Although one cannot prevent problems without implicitly identifying goals, most mental health interventions do not have explicit goals other than to alleviate problems or prevent

We owe thanks to Paul Baltes, Carol Nowak, and Michael Symer for identifying a number of issues presented here, and to Margaret Plantz and Rachel Pruchno for their constructive comments.

them from recurring. As such, these interventions assume a homeostatic (Danish, 1977) or equilibrium (Riegel, 1975b) model of human functioning. In other words, the goal of these interventions is a return to the conditions existing prior to the problem. From this perspective, human development is a steady line interrupted by crisis points. These crises can vary in duration, intensity, and severity, and some are likely to result in psychopathology. The return to a steady line indicates successful problem resolution or coping. Primary prevention theoretically protects an individual from experiencing these crisis periods in such a way that debilitating psychological distress results.

An alternative model of human development must have at least two characteristics. The first is a model of behavior which presupposes continuous growth and change. One such model is a life-span human development orientation. This orientation has been characterized by Baltes (1973) and Danish (1977) as one which:

(1) incorporates statements about desirable goals or end-states of behavior;

(2) focuses on sequential change;

(3) emphasizes techniques of optimization;

(4) considers the individual or system as an integrative bio-psychosocial unit (Ford, 1974) and therefore is amenable to a multidisciplinary focus; and

(5) views individuals or systems as developing in a changing biocultural context.

The second characteristic of an alternative model is that crises are not considered by definition pathological or problematic. Part of the problem lies in the language used to describe crisis. Riegel described the dilemma of labeling and conceptualizing a new model:

Searching through my vocabulary, I thought for a while that terms like "developmental leaps," "critical choice points," or "existential challenges" might somewhat better describe the condition under concern. Failing to convince myself of the preference for these substitutions, I began to realize that it would be necessary to devote (time) to an analysis of the concept of crisis and its underlying philosophical model and ideology. The concept of crisis is antithetically connected with those of equilibrium, stability, consonance, and balance. The notion of equilibrium as a desirable goal has thoroughly penetrated the thinking of behavioral and social scientists and defines crisis in a negative manner. (1975a, p. 100)

A more appropriate view is that growth is preceded by a state or imbalance or crisis which serves as the basis for future development. In fact, without crises, development is not possible. Caplan (1964) recognized this quality of crisis in arguing that the way crises are resolved has a major impact on their ultimate role in mental health. In striving to achieve stability during crises, the coping process itself can result in the achievement of a qualitatively different "stability." Thus, contrary to the view that crises are destructive, we contend that they may initiate a restructuring process toward further growth (Danish, 1977). If crises can result in either negative or positive outcomes, the goal of intervention is not to prevent crises, but rather to *enhance* or *enrich* individuals' abilities to deal constructively with these events. Enhancement activities would be designed to enable individuals to use crises as opportunities for growth.

Incorporating the notion of enhancement in mental health program development introduces a new conception of paradigm-like dimensions, the optimization of human development. Not only is the medical model finally discarded, but the noble intentions of those espousing the need for primary prevention can find a direct avenue for widespread implementation. To provide a concrete illustration, it is likely that attendance at "parent effectiveness training" groups would drop quickly if they were labeled as "child abuse prevention groups" or, for that matter, "neurotic parents' discussion groups."

To espouse enhancement as a framework calls for an elucidation of a theory of human development that describes "desirable" behavioral functioning. Given the view that enhancement activities provide an opportunity to optimize human functioning, it is necessary to identify end-states or markers for the life course. A heuristic concept, that of critical life events, is helpful in this regard.

A Critical Life Events Conception of Development

The concept of critical life events has become central to the study of adult development. Interest in life events comes from diverse sources, and research in the area has grown rapidly. Two divergent lines of research are important to review. The first is the investigation of stressful life events and subsequent illness (Rahe, 1974) or psychopathology (Dohrenwend and Dohrenwend, 1974). The second area is the use of life events as markers for adult development (Neugarten and Hagestad, 1976; Nowak, 1978). Both areas clarify the linkage between the occurrences of events and their consequences for individuals. This linkage is important because enhancement activities are targeted to this causal chain. Only a very brief review will appear here; for more detail, the reader is referred to Datan and Ginsberg (1975) and Hultsch and Plemons (1979).

1. Stressful life events. Attempts to identify correlates of stress in the form of physical illness and psychopathology have comprised many of the available studies on stressful life events and their concomitants. From this viewpoint, Selye (1956) postulated that psychological stress and physical stress are similar in sequence. In the same tradition, Holmes and Rahe (1967) have quantified psychological stress in terms of the numbers and types of significant life changes in an individual's experience. Rahe, McKean, and Arthur (1967) suggest that the additive effects of such life changes can be serious enough to predict the need for medical attention in the near future. They developed a checklist of Life Change Units scaled according to alterations in life style needed to readjust to a life event. The readjustment may be to a positive event (such as marriage or birth of a wanted first child) or a negative event (such as death of a spouse or being fired from a job). From this perspective a negative event does not necessarily require more change than a positive one. Their work has indicated that yearly life-change unit totals correlate positively with the risk of major health problems in the following year.

2. Events as markers of life development. Although the critical life concept is most commonly associated with the stressful life events orientation, its use in the field of adult development has become increasingly significant, for it engenders a conceptual shift from a biological to a social clocking of adult development. Effort has been expended in identifying events as societal markers, checking their occurrence for "correct" or normative timing, placing the event in an individual's social and cultural context, and describing the attitudes and moods of individuals during the events (Neugarten, 1976; Neugarten and Hagestad, 1976; Nowak, 1978). As Neugarten (1976) notes:

> There exists a socially prescribed timetable for the ordering of major life events: a time in the life span when men and women are expected to marry, a time to raise children, a time to retire. The normative pattern is adhered to, more or less consistently, by most persons within a given social group—although the actual occurrences of major life events are influenced by various contingencies and although the norms themselves vary somewhat from one socioeconomic, ethnic, or religious group to another. (p. 16)

She later says:

> The fact that regularities of change through the life cycle are demonstrable along biological, social, and psychological dimensions leads to the question of adaptation and the concept of a normal, expectable life cycle. (p. 18)

When events are a priori defined as debilitatingly stressful, the focus of study has been on the parameters of the event itself, and not on the event within the context of the individual's total development. Events are then less useful as markers along the life course. Nowak (1978) has differentiated between the study of life events as stimuli and the study of the structure of the event. She identifies a number of dimensions that may affect an event's impact: timing, intensity, duration, sequencing, and the degree of interference with other developmental events. When the events are considered within the context of the life course rather than discretely, they become targets for enhancement efforts aimed at optimizing adult development. This is not to imply that everyone encounters each event, or that the events always occur in the same sequence. However, informal norms develop about events and when they are likely to be experienced. Contrasting their own experience with such norms, individuals may expect certain events at certain times and experience dissatisfaction if they are "off time" in experiencing an event (Elder, 1975).

Earlier we noted that a human development orientation must contain desirable goals or end-states of behavior. From the perspective of societal norms, life events serve as markers (Lowenthal and Chiriboga, 1973) to chart adult development. An appropriate set of end-states is the ability to confront the life events successfully regardless of whether they are normative or nonnormative. The intuitive appeal of this approach and the documented stress associated with life events suggests that they are highly appropriate targets for intervention.

ENCOUNTERING CRITICAL LIFE EVENTS

Overview

In previous sections we have stressed that critical life events can have either positive or negative outcomes. This section will review the literature on determinants of the outcomes of life events.

Hultsch and Plemons (1979) have identified three factors which affect an individual's reaction to an event: biological, psychological, and contextual. However, these factors take on different significance depending upon the person's position in the life cycle and the specific event. Thus, authors who have considered certain factors as invariably correlated with a certain kind of outcome may not recognize that a factor which may be a resource for one event may be a deficit in another. For example, Lieberman (1975) reported that older adults who adapted well to new living arrangements tended to be aggressive, irritating, and demanding, behaviors generally not associated with successful life adaptation. A second problem with identifying factors influencing the quality of a response to life event is the difficulty in isolating the effects of individual elements and unraveling dependent from independent variables. Identifying what are resources and what are irrelevant factors, then, is not as clear cut as it seems. Despite the difficulties in partialing out the factors (resources) which influence positive responses to events, to do so is essential, since it may provide guidelines for intervention.

In our review of the work on life events, two factors seem prominent: the individual's past history of responding to events and the individual's social support. These two factors seem consistent with Caplan's (1964) conception of psychosocial "supplies."

Past History of Response to Events

When a stressful life event is encountered, one's history and life style influence the impact of the event. Despite qualitative differences in events, the subjective assessment of threat will decrease with greater experience in dealing with generally complex life situations. For example, Birren (1964) suggests that experience in coping with stressful life events leads to enhanced coping ability in the future. Lawton and Nahemow (1973) propose that an individual's response to an external stressor is dependent on the context of the stressor *and the individual's past history with similar phenomena*. They suggest that experience with similar events increases one's competence, thus providing the capacity to cope successfully with a wider range of environmental demands. In fact, they contend that highly competent individuals may find themselves dissatisfied with low levels of demands, finding moderate or higher levels more challenging. This contention is similar to the concept of optimal discrepancy proposed by Hunt (1961). Atchley (1975) and Janis (1971) propose models similar to Lawton and Nahemow (1973).

In sum, when an individual confronting a critical event, such as loss of a job, bereavement, or marriage, encounters the event with a history of success, the likelihood of a positive outcome increases. The past experience has provided both constructive attitudes about the event and behavioral competencies that were reinforced by the success experience. Because of this, the new event is not perceived as overwhelming because psychosocial resources can be drawn upon. Over the course of the life span, a pattern of successful copings would successively decrease the individual's vulnerability to crises.

The ability of an individual with a past history of effective responses to events to respond well to present events can be partly explained by *intra-individual similarity* in reactions to events. Individuals who respond effectively may recognize the similarity between the event they are presently encountering and both past and future events in their lives. Thus they understand that they have experienced similar situations previously. At a cognitive level, they know they *can* deal with the event. At a behavioral level, they employ a behavioral sequence successful in the past. As such the *psychological* uniqueness of the event becomes deemphasized, and properties common to similar experiences are highlighted. This process avoids internal distress and behavioral disability.

Social Support Systems

The impact of critical life events may also be altered by the quality of the support system available to the individual. Gore (1973) reported that stress associated with unexpected unemployment produced fewer negative consequences for men with highly supportive spouses and friends. In a study of life events and complications during pregnancy, by Nuckolls, Cassel, and Kaplan (1972), support measures such as the marriage relationship, quality of interaction with extended family, and adjustment within the community were examined. The results indicated that while neither the past history of events nor support resources alone predicted ease of pregnancy, women with much event experience and high support had one third the complication rate of women with many events and low support. Adams and Lindemann (1974), Hamburg, Coelho, and Adams (1974), and Maddox (1977) also have pointed out the importance of supportive networks and interpersonal resources for an individual dealing with a life event.

LIFE DEVELOPMENT TRAINING: A MODEL FOR INTERVENTION

Overview

An intervention model can be derived from the framework developed in the initial sections of the paper. The model must have the following attributes: (1) an enhancement orientation, (2) a central focus on life events, (3) a concern with the experience of encountering a number of life events as a resource to developing competence, and (4) an emphasis on the development of a support system. In the following sections, the model will be detailed in the context of mental health service delivery.

The Present Delivery of Human Services

The current mental health delivery system, based on a problematic paradigm, can be characterized as an overworked, fairly ineffective remedial system. The problems of the system have been duly chronicled elsewhere, but one example is worth noting. In Boston, Ryan (1969) reports, a city with one of the highest concentrations of mental health professionals, most individuals experiencing emotional problems do not receive professional mental health assistance. Ryan found that 150 of every 1000 individuals are experiencing mental health problems and that of this 150, 10 are seen in mental health settings (five in hospitals, four in clinics, and one privately). Of the remaining 140, two fifths are seen by physicians without mental health training. Srole, Langner, Michael, Opler, and Rennie's (1962) Midtown Manhattan survey contains similar findings. Thus in urban settings where professional help is assumedly readily available, most individuals in need of help do not see mental health professionals.

If not even most individuals with "serious problems" worthy of traditional remediation are being seen by professionals, what is happening to individuals undergoing life crises? As mentioned above, such crises may indeed become serious problems. Furthermore, if this pattern of low utilization of professionals exists in urban settings, what is happening in rural areas where professionals are scarce? In other words, if people are not seeing professional helpers, who are they seeing? Warren (1976) in his analysis of community helping in Detroit found neighbors and friends to be the primary source of help. Young, Giles and Plantz (1978) found similar patterns in rural Pennsylvania, where helping is primarily a community activity performed by neighbors and friends. This is true for serious problems, problems of living, or everyday concerns! In conclusion, despite the noble intentions of mental health professionals, most help occurs outside the mental health system through informal social systems. If most helping is done not by professionals but by "natural care-givers," it is essential that the role of these care-givers be maximized. Professionals must avoid suggesting to their communities that such help is ineffective, insufficient, and possibly dangerous. (Restrictive licensure laws may implicitly do this. See Danish and Smyer, 1978.)

❖

Life Development Intervention and Enhancement

Our perspective focuses on the course of adult development using life events as markers. We do not intend, however, that intervention be designed to deal with each life event as it occurs. Not only would this be a prohibitively expensive venture, it also could encourage excessive dependence on human service providers. An alternative that avoids these problems starts with an assumption of significant similarity across life events. Although the *content* of the events is different, the skills, risks, and attitudes necessary to encounter events overlap considerably. For example, the life events of marriage and retirement require different information but call for related skills—making decisions about present and future behaviors, risk taking, and so on.

It is necessary to help individuals recognize the similarity among past, present, and future events. What an individual did to encounter successfully a past event must be recalled. The past success experience can help in the present *if the individual can make the connection between one event and another.* Lazarus (1979) called this anticipatory coping. If the person's past experience was not entirely satisfying, it is worth asking now what he or she might have done to be more effective and *then helping the person make the connection between past and present events.* This *intra-individual similarity* can be a potent factor in helping people to deal with life events. Our perspective, then, is that there are a limited number of generic skills of value in many life events. If the skills are known to an individual, use of these skills will enhance the person's development.

❖

Clearly knowledge about life events can be disseminated *outside of the professional helping system,* and if skills that accompany the knowledge can be provided, intervention can then proceed more rapidly. The knowledge can be provided via media; generic skills can be taught and used across events. In this way the markers become something one *can prepare for,* and intervention is explicit anticipatory socialization. As one becomes more skillful in encountering each event, encounters with events become opportunities for growth, and the situations (events) become viewed as challenging. *Life Development Intervention* is teaching individuals *planfulness* in dealing with life events. Our end-state, then, is *not* a particular outcome with an event but *the ability to be planful in confronting life events*.

To recapitulate briefly, in our conceptual model individual critical life events can become problems of living if not resolved. If personal goals for any event can be identified, it becomes necessary to determine why goals are not achieved and what the roadblocks to achievement are. We believe only three roadblocks can exist. They are a lack of knowledge, a lack of skill, or an inability to assess the risks involved in changing behavior.

In implementing life development intervention, we subscribe to an educational model of service delivery. Such a model has been described by Danish (1977) and Guerney (Guerney, 1977; Guerney, Guerney, and Stollack 1971/1972; Guerney, Stollack, and Guerney, 1971). The educational model takes the school as its model, and instruction as its method of enhancement (D'Augelli, 1978). The helper acts in a consultative way, working with the individual or group to develop a specific enhancement program or to adapt an existing one. Programs on parenting, marital communication, sexual functioning, and decision-making have been developed using this approach (see Authier, Gustafson, Guerney, and Kasdorf, 1975, for a recent review). What is important here is not the context of the intervention as much as the role of the helper. In other words, not only do we reject a medical-disease orientation for a learning one, but we reject the *clinical treatment model* in favor of a *mass teaching model*.

❖

IMPEDIMENTS TO IMPLEMENTING LIFE DEVELOPMENT INTERVENTION

We began this chapter by discussing the difficulties of initiating change in human services systems. In clarifying our conceptual underpinnings and in providing a model for implementation, we hope to avoid some of the pitfalls human service innovations seldom escape. We anticipate, however, that some of the policies of the mental health establishment will obstruct the implementation of a life development orientation as well. Broskowski and Baker (1974) have identified professional, organizational, and social barriers to the implementation of primary prevention. Some of these same barriers are applicable to life development intervention.

Professional Barriers

Professionals have tended to assign a lower status to attempts to *prevent* rather than to *cure* problems (Danish, 1977; Gurevitz and Heath, 1969; Snoke, 1969). As reimbursement for mental health activities becomes more common, programs aimed at reducing the number of potential consumers may be administratively counterproductive. Furthermore, the demystification of the helping process by employing an educative focus runs counter to the professionals' needs to maintain a heightened aura of mystery around helping activities.

However, professional barriers extend beyond the negative attitudes of some professionals. Most professionals are untrained to deliver such services. For example, despite evidence that the need for preventive services is increasing and the demand for direct services decreasing (Miller, Mazade, Muller, and Andrulis, 1978), the education and training of most professionals still virtually ignores such indirect activities as consultation, training, and education. Few new professionals have either a conceptual perspective or practical experience with these activities. Therefore, to suggest that agencies adopt a life skills enhancement model raises serious attitudinal and pragmatic problems.

Organizational Barriers

Helping people avoid remedial professional services through proactive intervention poses significant difficulties for mental health administrators. As funding to community mental health centers decreases annually—as much as 10 to 20 percent with the reduction of the federal staffing grants—the costs of maintaining a specified level of operations becomes increasingly difficult. State costs appear fixed, counties find it difficult to increase their share of the cost given other demands, and the burden of maintaining operations is placed increasingly on third-party reimbursements. A community mental health center designed to provide services that are clearly reimbursable becomes very much like a traditional outpatient clinic. Both enhancement and prevention activities may be benignly neglected because they keep people out of the reimbursement system and therefore adversely affect operations. The number of client-hours remains a powerful index of a center's effectiveness when funding is sought. It is conceivable that the problem dictates a radical solution, namely that life development services are best not offered in a mental health context at all. The tendency toward subtlely shaping such services into a referral system for direct services may be too powerful, fueled as it is by historical precedent and staff training backgrounds. In any event, an administrative structure that gives primacy to life development services is a requirement.

Social Barriers

Social impediments are the most damaging for the implementation of life development intervention efforts. Groups concerned about combating mental illness have presented the "disease" through the media as a terrible illness, far more dangerous and damaging than cancer or other dreaded physical diseases. Just as the behavioral and social sciences have begun to reject the concept of mental illness (Szasz, 1961), we are more firmly reinforcing its existence to the public. The disease view of mental illness portrayed to the public may arouse sympathy for the "afflicted"; a more pernicious outcome, however, is that the public will be "protected" from the notion that psychosocial problems result from difficulties in life planning. Therefore, the public will not link "mental illness" and problems of living and consequently will not recognize that they must learn to deal more effectively with the critical events in their own lives to prevent problems of living. The public's view of "mental illness" is such that there is no demand or constitutency for developing programs on life planning.

Life planning services can be made appealing to the public, more so than can remediative or preventive services. Individuals are likely to be eager to deal effectively with typical problems of living if they are provided with relevant skills. When the focus of intervention is either prevention or remediation, the danger of defining problems of living as mental illness is perpetuated. A delivery system orienting around illness must create "patients" to "diagnose" and "treat." Although such a system might "prevent" as well, potential patients at risk must be detected. Our argument has been that progress in mental health service delivery will occur only if this trap is avoided. We must remove problems of living from the mental health/mental illness arena and place them in a context of human development.* When a human development perspective becomes accepted, life development enhancement strategies will be used, and the stigma associated with coping with personal problems will be eliminated. A new era of human services for human development will begin.

REFERENCES

Adams, J. E., and Lindemann, E. Coping with long-term disability. In G. V. Coelho, D. A. Hamburg, and J. E. Adams (Eds.), *Coping and adaptation*. New York: Basic Books, 1974.

Atchley, R. C. Adjustment to loss of job at retirement. *International Journal of Aging and Human Development*, 1975, *6*, 17-27.

Authier, J., Gustafson, K., Guerney, B. G., and Kasdorf, J. A. The psychological practitioner as a teacher: A theoretical-historical and practical review. *The Counseling Psychologist*, 1975, *5*, 31-50.

Back, K. W., and Taylor, R. C. Self-help groups: Tool or symbol? *Journal of Applied Behavioral Science*, 1976, *12*, 295-309.

Baltes, P. B. Prototypical paradigms and questions in life-span research on development and aging. *Gerontologist*, 1973, *13*, 458-467.

*It has been suggested by some (Illich, 1976) that perpetuating the notion that problems of living are mental health/mental illness issues is a self-serving social policy supported by the mental health establishment. To prevent the public from becoming aware of the differences between mental illness/mental health and problems of living, conceptions might be labeled *illnessism*. Certainly in the mental health area, the maintenance of illnessism as a "public relations" message is very powerful, since it links mental health with the expertise and prestige of the medical establishment. Although the mental health establishment typically follows medicine's dubious lead in this area, it is clear that mental health professionals are as myopic as physicians in discarding iatrogenic conceptions. We recognize that the perpetuation of illnessism is not purposeful, as many instances of racism, sexism, and ageism are not purposeful social injustices. Nevertheless, the effects of illnessism may be as debilitating as these other social injustices.

Baltes, P. B., and Danish, S. J. Intervention in life span development and aging: Issues and concepts. In R. R. Turner and H. W. Reese (Eds.), *Life-span developmental psychology: Intervention*. New York: Academic Press, 1980.

Birren, J. E. *The psychology of aging*. Englewood Cliffs, N. J.: Prentice-Hall, 1964.

Blumer, H. Social movements. In B. McLaughlin (Ed.), *Studies in social movements: A social psychological perspective*. New York: The Free Press, 1969.

Bower, E. M. K.I.S.S. and kids: A mandate for prevention. *American Journal of Orthopsychiatry*, 1972, *42*, 556-565.

Broskowski, A., and Baker, F. Professional, organizational, and social barriers to primary prevention. *American Journal of Orthopsychiatry*, 1974, *44*, 707-719.

Caplan, G. *Principles of preventive psychiatry*. New York: Basic Books, 1964.

Cowen, E. L. Baby steps toward primary prevention. *American Journal of Community Psychology*, 1977, *5*, 1-22. (*a*)

Cowen, E. L. Psychologists and primary prevention: Blowing the cover story. *American Journal of Community Psychology*, 1977, *5*, 481-490. (*b*)

Cowen, E. L., Trost, M. A., Lorion, R. P., Dorr, D., Izzo, L. D., and Isaacson, R. V. *New ways in school mental health: Early detection and prevention of school maladaption*. New York: Behavioral Publications, 1975.

Danish, S. J. Human development and human services: A marriage proposal. In I. Iscoe, B. L. Bloom, and C. C. Spielberger (Eds.), *Community psychology in transition*. New York: Halsted, 1977.

Danish, S. J., D'Augelli, A. R., and Hauer, A. L. *Helping skills: A life development training program*. New York: Human Sciences Press, 1979.

Danish, S. J., and Hauer, A. L. *Helping skills: A basic training program*. New York: Human Sciences Press, 1973.

Danish, S. J. and Smyer, M. A. *The unintended consequences of requiring a license to help*. Unpublished manuscript, Pennsylvania State University, 1978.

Danish, S. J., Smyer, M. A., and Nowak, C. A. Developmental intervention: Enhancing life-event processes. In P. B. Baltes and O. G. Brim, Jr. (Eds.), *Life-span development and behavior*, Vol. 3. New York: Academic Press, in press.

Datan, N., and Ginsberg, L. H. (Eds.), *Life-span developmental psychology: Normative life crises*. New York: Academic Press, 1975.

D'Augelli, A. R. Paraprofessionals as educator-consultants: A new training model. *Professional Psychology*, 1978, *9*, 18-23.

Dohrenwend, B. S. Social status and stressful life events. *Journal of Personality and Social Psychology*, 1973, *28*, 225-235.

Dohrenwend, B. S., and Dohrenwend, B. P. (Eds.), *Stressful life events: Their nature and effects*. New York: Wiley, 1974.

Elder, G. H., Jr. Age differentiation and the life course. *Annual Review of Sociology*, 1975, *1*, 165-190.

Ford, D. H. Mental health and human development: An analysis of a dilemma. In D. Harshbarger and R. Maley (Eds.), *Behavior analysis and system analysis: An integrative approach to mental health programs.* Kalamazoo, Mich.: Behaviordelia, 1974.

Gartner, A., and Riessman, F. *Self-help in the human services.* San Francisco: Jossey-Bass, 1978.

Goldston, S. E. Defining primary prevention. In G. W. Albee and J. M. Joffe (Eds.), *Primary prevention of psychopathology. Vol. 1: The Issues.* Hanover, N.H.: University Press of New England, 1977.

Gore, S. *The influence of social support and related variables in ameliorating the consequences of job loss.* Unpublished doctoral dissertation, University of Pennsylvania, 1973.

Gurevitz, H., and Heath, D. Prevention and professional response. In H. Lamb, D. Heath, and J. Downing (Eds.), *Handbook of community mental health practice.* San Francisco: Jossey-Bass, 1969.

Guerney, B. G. Should teachers treat illiteracy, hypocalligraphy, and dysmathematica? *The Canadian Counselor,* 1977, *12*, 9–14.

Guerney, B. G., Guerney, L. F., and Stollak, G. E. The potential advantages of changing from a medical to an educational model in practicing psychology. *Interpersonal Development,* 1971/72, *2*, 238–245.

Guerney, B. G., Stollak, G. E., and Guerney, L. F. The practicing psychologist as educator—An alternative to the medical practitioner model. *Professional Psychology,* 1971, *2*, 276–282.

Hamburg, D. A., Coelho, G. V., and Adams, J. E. Coping and adaptation: Steps toward a synthesis of biological and social pe:spectives. In G. V. Coelho, D. A. Hamburg, and J. E. Adams (Eds.), *Coping and adaptation.* New York: Basic Books, 1974.

Holmes, T. H., and Rahe, R. H. The social readjustment rating scale. *Journal of Psychosomatic Research,* 1967, *11*, 213–218.

Hultsch, D. F., and Plemons, J. K. Life events and life-span development. In P. B. Baltes and O. G. Brim, Jr. (Eds.), *Life-span development and behavior* (Vol. 2). New York: Academic Press, 1979.

Hunt, J. McV. *Intelligence and experience.* New York: Ronald Press, 1961.

Illich, I. *Medical nemesis.* New York: Random House, 1976.

Janis, I. L. *Stress and frustration.* New York: Harcourt Brace Jovanovich, 1971.

Kessler, M. and Albee, G. W. Primary prevention. *Annual Review of Psychology,* 1975, *26*, 557–591.

Lawton, M. P., and Nahemow, L. Ecology and the aging process. In C. Eisdorfer and M. P. Lawton (Eds.), *The psychology of adult development and aging.* Washington, D.C.: American Psychological Association, 1973.

Lazarus, R. S. The stress and coping paradigm. In L. A. Bond and J. C. Rosen (Eds.), *Primary prevention of psychopathology. Vol. 4: Competence and coping during adulthood.* Hanover, N.H.: University Press of New England, 1980.

Lieberman, M. A. Adaptive processes in late life. In N. Datan and L. H. Ginsberg (Eds.), *Life-span developmental psychology: Normative life crises.* New York: Academic Press, 1975.

Lieberman, M. A., and Borman, L. D. Self-help groups: A special issue. *Journal of Applied Behavioral Sciences*, 1976, *12*, 261–463.

Lowenthal, M. F., and Chiriboga, D. Social stress and adaptation: Toward a life-course perspective. In C. Eisdorfer and M. P. Lawton (Eds.), *The psychology of adult development and aging*. Washington, D.C.: American Psychological Association, 1973.

Maddox, G. L. Community and home care: United States and United Kingdom: The unrealized potential of an old idea. In A. N. Exton-Smith and J. G. Evans (Eds.), *Care for the elderly*. London: Academic Press, 1977.

Miller, F. T., Mazade, N. A., Muller, S., and Andrulis, D. Trends in community mental health programming. *American Journal of Community Psychology*, 1978, *6*, 191–198.

Neugarten, B. L. Adaptation and life cycle. *The Counseling Psychologist*, 1976, *6*, 16–18.

Neugarten, B. L., and Hadestad, G. O. Age and the life course. In R. H. Binstock and E. Shanas (Eds.), *Handbook of aging and the social sciences*. New York: Van Nostrand Reinhold, 1976.

Nowak, C. *Research in life events: Conceptual considerations*. Paper presented at the 31st Annual Scientific Meeting of the Gerontological Society, Dallas, November 1978.

Nuckolls, K. B., Cassell, J., and Kaplan, B. Psychosocial assets, life crisis, and the prognosis of pregnancy. *American Journal of Epidemiology*, 1972, *95*, 431–441.

Rahe, R. The pathways between subjects' recent life changes and their near-future illness reports: Representative results and methodological issues. In B. S. and B. P. Dohrenwend (Eds.), *Stressful life events: Their nature and effects*. New York: Wiley Press, 1974.

Rahe, R. H., McKean, J. D., and Arthur, R. J. A longitudinal study of life-change and illness patterns. *Journal of Psychosomatic Research*, 1967, *10*, 355–366.

Riegel, K. F. Adult life crises: A dialectic interpretation of development. In N. Datan and L. Ginsberg (Eds.), *Life-span developmental psychology: Normative life crises*. New York: Academic Press, 1975. (*a*)

Riegel, K. F. From traits and equilibrium toward developmental dialectics. *The Nebraska Symposium on Motivation* (Vol. 24). Lincoln: University of Nebraska Press, 1975. (*b*)

Riessman, F. How does self-help work? *Social Policy*, 1976, *7*, 41–45.

Ryan, W. *Distress in the city*. Cleveland: Case Western Reserve University Press, 1969.

Seidman, E., and Rappaport, J. The educational pyramid: A paradigm for training, research, and manpower utilization in community psychology. *American Journal of Community Psychology*, 1974, *2*, 119–130.

Selye, H. *The stress of life*. New York: McGraw-Hill, 1956.

Snoke, A. The unsolved problem of the career professional in the establishment of national health policy. *American Journal of Public Health*, 1969, *59*, 1575–1588.

Srole, L., Langner, T. S., Michael, S. T., Opler, M. K., and Rennie, T. A. C. *Mental health in the metropolis: The midtown Manhattan study.* New York: McGraw-Hill, 1962.

Szasz, T. *The myth of mental illness.* New York: Harper and Row, 1961.

Warren, D. I. *Neighborhood and community contexts in help seeking, problem coping and mental health.* Ann Arbor, Michigan: Program in Community Effectiveness, 1976.

Young, C. E., Giles, D. E., and Plantz, M. *Help seeking patterns in rural communities.* Unpublished manuscript, Pennsylvania State University, 1978.

v. Increasing Competence and Coping Skills: Applications

Having discussed the concepts of competence and coping skills, and having covered some of the models and approaches consistent with these concepts, we turn in this section to an examination of how these concepts have been translated into specific programs. This section includes reports of applied research projects that are relevant to primary prevention. Some involve field tests of methods of promoting social and cognitive development that serve as methodological models for future community-based projects. The projects described do not exhaust the range of efforts in this area, however.

In the first two papers, interventions that effectively prevented mental retardation in infants are described. In the first, F. Rick Heber provides the only publicly available report on the well-known Milwaukee Project, which used environmental manipulation to offset developmental delays among a sample of infants at high risk for mental retardation. In the second paper, Marie Skodak Crissey reports dramatic findings on the effects of stimulating environments on children who, to all appearances, would otherwise have been doomed to a life of serious mental retardation. These two studies constitute powerful evidence for the preventive effects of intervention early in the lives of infants considered at risk.

The programs described in the next two papers have carefully focused on a specific facet of measured competence, namely social problem solving, which is believed to be crucial to a child's overall psychological well-being. Myrna B. Shure and George Spivack review research on social cognition and consider how cognitive problem solving can be taught as a developmental skill.

In the next paper, Willard W. Hartup examines the effects of peer interaction with toddlers and older children, with specific attention to the role of peer play in shaping social competence. Hartup presents a number of provocative implications for primary prevention.

The remaining papers in this section address the issue of promoting competence and coping throughout adulthood. Lillian B. Rubin's paper is concerned with the relationship between coping and competence and the family. Rubin goes beyond the assumptions and stereotypes of the "empty nest syndrome" to analyze the ways in which women in fact deal with the midlife transition surrounding the end of their "active mothering years."

Ruth Glick examines the faltering emergence of retirement planning in America. Her analysis of the current social and psychological conditions of older Americans provides a framework for considering the potential role of retirement planning in the promotion of competence and coping.

Sociocultural Mental Retardation: A Longitudinal Study

F. Rick Heber

❖   Our research, which has come to be known as the Milwaukee Project, was designed to add to our factual knowledge of the etiology of cultural-familial mental retardation and its susceptibility to preventive measures. Those adhering to either the hereditary or the social deprivation hypothesis have cited virtually the same data in support of their respective positions: principally epidemiological data on population and family group incidence frequencies of mental retardation.

It should be obvious, however, that simple awareness of the high frequency of mental retardation in areas where the economically or otherwise disadvantaged are concentrated is sufficient neither to validate the prepotence of genetic determinants nor to conclude that social deprivation in the slum environment causes the retardation encountered there. Such a generalization ignores the fact that most children reared by economically disadvantaged families are by no means mentally retarded. In actual fact, a majority of children reared in city slums grow and develop and learn relatively normally in the intellectual sense.

Before we could begin any prospective research it was necessary to learn more about the distribution of cultural-familial mental retardation. We conducted a series of surveys in a residential

Research supported in part by Grant 16-P-56811/5-11, from the Social and Rehabilitation Services of the Department of Health, Education, and Welfare.

Dr. Heber has produced a thirty-minute color film showing the interaction patterns between his trainees and the children in the experimental group of the Milwaukee Project, described in this paper. Inquiries should be directed to Dr. Heber at the University of Wisconsin, Waisman Center on Mental Retardation and Human Development, Madison, Wisconsin.

section of Milwaukee, a city of 800,000, characterized by census data as having the lowest median family income, the greatest population density per living unit, and the greatest rate of dilapidated housing in the city. For the United States it was a typical urban slum of the 1960's and it yielded by far the highest prevalence of identified mental retardation among school children in the city. In our first survey, all of the families who had a newborn infant and at least one other child of up to the age of six were selected for study.

The major finding relevant to this discussion is that the variable of maternal intelligence proved to be by far the best single predictor of the level and character of intellectual development in the offspring. Mothers with IQ's of less than 80, although comprising less than half the total group of mothers, accounted for almost four-fifths of the children with IQ's below 80 (see Table 1).

It has been generally acknowledged that slum-dwelling children score lower on intelligence tests as they grow older. However, the mean measured intelligence of offspring of mothers with IQ's above 80 is relatively constant. And it is only the children of mothers with IQ's below 80 who show a progressive decline in mean intelligence as age increases.

Further, the survey data showed that the lower the maternal IQ, the greater the probability of offspring scoring low on intelligence tests. For example, as Table 2 shows, the mother with an IQ below 67 had roughly a fourteen-fold increase in the probability of having a child test below 67 as compared with the mother whose IQ fell at or above 100.

These population survey data have been taken by some as support for the prepotence of hereditary determinants of cultural-

Table 1

Distribution of Child IQ's as a Function of Maternal Intelligence

Mother's IQ	Percent of Mothers	Children's IQ		
		%>90	%80-90	%<80
>80	54.6	65.8	47.3	21.9
<80	45.4	34.1	52.7	78.2

> = greater than   < = less than

familial mental retardation. Our simple casual observation, however, suggested that the mentally retarded mother residing in the slum creates a social environment for her offspring which is distinctly different from that created by her next-door neighbor of normal intelligence.

Most importantly, these survey data suggested that it would be feasible to conduct the longitudinal, prospective research essential to achieving a more adequate understanding of what determines the kind of retardation that perpetuates itself from parent to child in the economically deprived family. That is, the survey data suggested that parental intelligence could be utilized as a tool to select a sample which would be small enough for practical experimental manipulation but would still yield a sufficient number of cases who would later become identifiable as mentally retarded.

As a consequence of the survey data, we took maternal IQ as a basis for selecting a group of newborns, confident that a substantial percentage would be identified as mentally retarded as they grew older. By screening all mothers of babies born in our survey area over a period of a little over a year, we identified mothers of newborns with IQ's less than 75. Forty of these mentally retarded mothers were assigned to either an experimental or a control group.

Although our geographic study area was racially mixed, our sample was confined to black families because of the substantially lower mobility of the black population in that section of Milwaukee. Obviously, a longitudinal study is seriously weakened when its test sample is decimated by attrition.

The 20 Experimental families were entered into an intense rehabilitation program with two primary emphases: (1) education, vocational rehabilitation, and home and child care training of the mother; and (2) an intense, personalized intervention program for their newborn infants which began in the first few weeks of life. The objective of the intervention was to displace all of the presumed negative factors in the social environment of the infant being reared in the slum by a mother who is herself retarded. Our goal was to test the social deprivation hypothesis of etiology by attempting to determine whether it is possible to prevent retardation in the offspring of these retarded mothers.

It was our contention that if the experimental children should reach school age and exhibit normal intelligence, we would know that it is indeed possible to prevent mental retardation from occurring at the present high frequency in this group. Should they exhibit a retarded level of functioning, at least we would know that their intensive exposure to learning experiences of the type we provided was not sufficient to displace their genetic or other biologic predispositions for intellectual functioning.

Initially, each experimental family was assigned one special teacher whose responsibility was to establish rapport, gain the family's confidence, and work with both the mother and the newborn child in the home.

Once the mother trusted the teacher, the infant began to attend our infant center every day from 9 until 4, five days a week, on a year-round basis. The mother began her own rehabilitation program when the child began participation in our infant intervention program.

One of the major purposes of the maternal program was to alter the manner in which the economically and intellectually disadvantaged mother interacted with her children and operated within the home and within the community. At the outset, a major obstacle was the attitude of many of the mentally retarded mothers themselves: they were hostile and suspicious toward social agencies and had a sense of economic despair. It was hoped that as the mother's rehabilitation proceeded, her improved employment potential and increased earnings and self-confidence would bring about positive changes in the home.

Over the course of the maternal rehabilitation program, the emphases changed. At the beginning, the focus was on the mother's vocational adjustment. Since a number of the families did not have a stable income-producing father, occupational training and placement was of major importance. After formal vocational training and placement was completed, increased emphasis was given to remedial education and homemaking and child-care skills. As we established rapport with the parents, they called on us increasingly to intervene and assist in internal family crises and, not uncommonly, in conflicts with the community.

The occupational training program used two large private nursing homes in Milwaukee. These were chosen because of the appropriate job skill areas they offered, the availability of professional staff with some understanding of rehabilitation programs, and the employment opportunities available in nursing homes and other chronic care facilities. The basic remedial academic curriculum emphasized reading, writing, and arithmetic—that is, basic literacy training. In addition, the curriculum included child care techniques, home economics, community oriented social studies, interpersonal relations, and home management.

Although our maternal efforts were a success in many dimensions, they by no means put an end to all of the mother's internal family and community conflicts. We attempted to evaluate the effectiveness of the maternal program through a number of measures.

The Experimental mothers showed some significant changes in behavior and attitude in dealing with their children. On experimental task measures of mother-child interaction, they encouraged reciprocal communication with their children; that is, given a behavior by one, there was a greater certainty of the behavior of the other. This relationship did not occur within the Control families. Also, this behavior change was reflected in the Experimental mother's greater tendency to engage in verbally informative behaviors as compared to the non-task-oriented physical behaviors shown by the Control mothers and by the Experimental mothers at the beginning of the program.

On the Wechsler Adult Intelligence Scale (WAIS) eight years after their initial testing, there was no significant change for either Experimental or Control groups.

The Experimental mothers are significantly superior to the Control mothers in basic literacy but remain relatively low—roughly at fourth-grade level.

By every measure, the most effective component of our maternal program was the vocational one. We succeeded in placing all mothers in employment where the family situation made this feasible. And their record of job stability and work performance is distinctly superior to that of the Controls. For mothers in both groups who are presently working, salary favors the Experimental mother by an average of $40 per week.

Our direct infant intervention program was initiated when the children were about three months of age and continued, on an all-day 5-day-a-week year-round basis, until the children entered public school. The general goal was to provide an environment and a set of experiences which would foster the acquisition of cognitive skills and allow each child to develop socially, emotionally and physically. The program focused heavily on developing language and cognitive skills and on maintaining a positive and responsive learning environment for the children.

Throughout the intervention program, the curriculum was concerned with three main areas of growth: perceptual-motor development, cognitive-language development, and social-emotional development. During infancy (0–2), a period characterized by the rapid development of perceptual-motor skills, we provided a wealth of varied experiences designed to enable the child to refine his perceptual acuity, especially the ability to differentiate between visual and auditory stimuli. At the same time, attention was given to developing motor behavior by providing considerable opportunity for the children to practice newly developing skills and explore their environment.

Because infancy is a crucial time for laying the foundations of cognitive and language development, the program made use of the rapidly developing perceptual-motor skills as a vehicle through which cognitive and language experiences (size, color, relations) could be systematically introduced. We attempted to meet the social-emotional needs of the developing infant by providing a consistent one-to-one teacher-child relationship throughout the child's first year in the program. During the preschool years (2–6), the educational program continued to focus upon the same three areas of growth, but increased emphasis was placed on the cognitive-language area—gradually broken down into the three traditional academic areas of reading, language, and math/problem-solving. By this time, groups of 10 to 12 children had come together with three teachers into a more traditional classroom setting. Within the classroom, there were three learning areas and a free-flowing or free-choice area. At specified intervals during the day, small groups of children would meet with teachers to engage in teacher-planned activities at each of the three learning centers. In addition, there was opportunity for science, art, music, and gross motor activities in the free-choice area.

The general intervention program is best characterized as having a cognitive-language orientation implemented through a planned environment utilizing informal prescriptive teaching techniques. By this latter we mean that in planning appropriate activities, each teacher would (1) make direct observation of the child's strengths, weaknesses, preferences; (2) gear tasks and experiences specifically for this child; and (3) evaluate the effect of the task or experience on the child.

Most importantly, the program gave major emphasis to the social and emotional development of the children. Although language and cognitive development were the foundation, it was recognized that motivation—the child's desire to utilize these skills—was essential to making the system work. We attempted to develop achievement motivation by designing tasks and creating an atmosphere which would maximize interest and provide success experiences and supportive and corrective feedback from responsive adults, and which would gradually increase the child's responsibility for task completion.

ASSESSMENT OF DEVELOPMENT

In order to assess the effects of this six-year comprehensive intervention in the natural environment of the infant and his retarded mother, we undertook an ambitious schedule of measurements consisting of medical evaluations, standardized and nonstandardized tests of general intelligence, experimental learning tasks, measures of mother-child interaction, and various measures of language development.

Both the Experimental and Control subjects were on an identical measurement schedule keyed to each child's birth date. Assessments were carried out every two months from age 6 months to 24 months, and then monthly through age 6. The particular measure administered at a given session depended upon the predetermined schedule of measures for that age level. Each test or task was administered to both the Experimental and Control subjects by the same persons. The testers, who were both men and women, white and black, were not involved in any component of the maternal or child intervention program.

Medical evaluations of our research children have shown no significant differences in height, weight, or other specific medical tests (See Fig. 2). Gesell data illustrate some of the earliest differences between Experimental and Control infants. Though reasonably comparable through the fourteenth month of testing, the Control group fell three to four months below the Experimental group, although still performing close to test norms. At

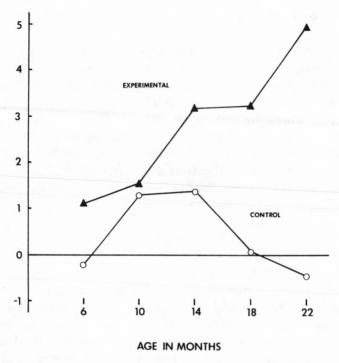

Figure 2. Comparison of experimental and control children on Gesell growth norms.

22 months, the Experimental group was 4½ to 6 months in advance of the Control group on all four Gesell schedules and the Control group had fallen below Gesell norms on the Adaptive and Language schedules.

On Z transformations of scores from a number of measures, administered at varying age levels, there is a sustained differential in performance in favor of the Experimental children.

In the learning-performance tasks, such as color-form, probability matching, and oddity discrimination, the Experimental group was superior to the Control group on all tasks and all testings between 2½ and 6 years of age. The important aspect of the differential in performance, however, was the development of more sophisticated and more consistent response behaviors by the Experimental children. Generally, the Experimental children's responses demonstrated that they tended to use strategies or hypothesis-testing behavior and were sensitive to feedback information from their responses. The Control children, on the other hand, showed a marked tendency to response stereotypy, often perseverating in their responses with no attempt to use a strategy. They also tended to be passive and unenthusiastic in their response behavior. This early learning performance had potential implications for future development: the Experimental child's approach to problem-solving could be facilitative, while the Control child's behavior style could interfere with the ability to learn and perform.

The first significant difference in language performance appeared at 18 months on the language scale of the Gesell. By 22 months the Experimental children were over 4 months ahead of the norm and 6 months ahead of the Control children. This early and dramatic trend of differential language development continued throughout the program across a wide array of measures, including an analysis of free-speech samples, a sentence repetition test, a grammatical comprehension test, tests of morphology, and the Illinois Test of Psycholinguistic Abilities (ITPA). We can summarize by saying that the language development of the Experimental children tended to be substantially in advance of that of the Control group by age (see Tables 7 and 8). The results of our analysis of the children's spontaneous speech give a conservative estimate of the differences in language development between the two groups. There is, for example, a year's difference in mean length of utterance (MLU).

Our free-speech results have been corroborated and extended by a wide variety of language tests which we gave at regular intervals over periods ranging from one to two-and-a-half years (Table 8). On these tests, which covered the three main aspects of language acquisition—comprehension (The Grammatical Comprehension Test), imitation (Sentence Repetition Tests I and II), and production (The Picture Morphology and Berko Morphology tests)—there was as much as two years' difference in age between Experimental and Control group children. Levels achieved by the Experimental children at age 3½ years on the Grammatical Comprehension Test, for instance, were reached by the Control children only at age 5½ years.

We have been careful to ensure that we are not merely measuring differences resulting from different degrees of dialect usage.

Table 7
Free-speech Analysis for the Experimental (E) and Control (C) Children for the First Five Years

AGE	MEAN LENGTH OF UTTERANCE		MEAN CUMULATIVE VOCABULARY	
	E	C	E	C
2	2.1	1.7	78	33
2.5	2.9	2.4	174	89
3	3.4	3.1	281	208
3.5	4.3	3.4	338	249
4	4.4	3.4	396	303
4.5	4.8	4.0	458	363
5	5.2	4.5	510	414

The diagonal lines represent the age differential between groups achieving similar performance levels.

Our tape recordings of their conversational speech show that the children from both groups speak the dialect referred to as "Black English"; where there was any possibility, however, that test scores could be influenced by dialect patterns, we devised alternative scoring systems to reduce the possibility. One such system was used in the Sentence Repetition Tests to arrive at the "Structures Preserved" measure. This measure makes allowances for errors in repetition resulting from such dialect patterns as the omission of past tense and plural markers and of the copulative verb *be*—recognized features of Black English. As Table 8 shows, the two groups differed in the same manner and to the same degree on this measure as on all the other language measures used. Our findings indicate that it is not dialect usage that underlies the difference in performance levels between the two groups, but rather a difference in the grasp of the concepts and relationships that are expressed or implied in syntactic structures.

The ITPA was administered to all children when they were 4½ and again when they were 6½. The results are consistent with our experimental measures of language. At 6½, the difference between the groups found at 4½ had been maintained: the Experimental subjects performed six months above their mean CA, while the Control subjects performed 11 months below their mean CA. The mean Psycholinguistic Quotient (PLQ) for the Experimental group was 108.3, that for the Control group was 86.3—a difference of 22 points. In Figure 3 we have derived the distribution for the performance of the two groups on the ITPA. The difference between groups is quite apparent: there is virtually no overlap between distributions.

As a group, the Experimental children have an aptitude for language substantially greater than that of their counterparts in the Control goup. The readiness with which they grasped and acquired new linguistic structures appeared to be a manifestation of their readiness to learn structures in general, and suggested enhanced awareness of their surroundings and of their ability to express themselves in relation to these surroundings. What is perhaps more important is that they entered school with the language skills and aptitudes needed for further learning.

We attempted (perhaps somewhat feebly) to measure mother-child interactions, using Hess and Shipman (1968) techniques. In the mother-child interaction, most of the sophisticated behavior

Table 8
The Results of Various Language Tests for the Experimental (E) and Control (C) Children for the First 6½ Years

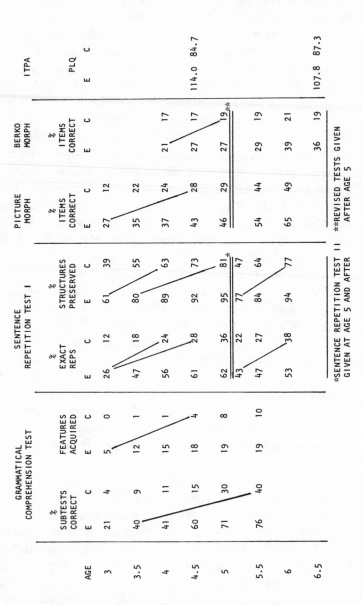

AGE	Grammatical Comprehension Test — % Subtests Correct E	C	Features Acquired E	C	Sentence Repetition Test I — % Exact Reps E	C	% Structures Preserved E	C	Picture Morph — % Items Correct E	C	Berko Morph — % Items Correct E	C	ITPA PLQ E	C
3	21	4	5	0	26	12	61	39	27	12				
3.5	40	9	12	1	47	18	80	55	35	22				
4	41	11	15	1	56	24	89	63	37	24				
4.5	60	15	18	4	61	28	92	73	43	28	21	17	114.0	84.7
5	71	30	19	8	62 / 43	36 / 22	95 / 77	81* / 47	46	29	27	17		
5.5	76	40	19	10	47	27	84	64	54	44	27	19**		
6			19		53	38	94	77	65	49	39	21		
6.5											36	19	107.8	87.3

*SENTENCE REPETITION TEST II GIVEN AT AGE 5 AND AFTER   **REVISED TESTS GIVEN AFTER AGE 5

is done by the mother—initiating problem-solving by verbal clues and verbal prods, organizing tasks with respect to goals in problem-solving situations, and so on. Where the mother has a low IQ, the interaction is often more physical and less organized, and less direction is given to the child. Such was the case in the Control group mother-child dyads. The Experimental dyads transmitted more information than the Control dyads, but this appeared to be a function of the quality of the Experimental child's verbal behavior. The Experimental children supplied more information verbally and initiated more verbal communication than Controls. The children in the Experimental dyads took responsibility for guiding the flow in information, providing most of the verbal information and direction. Experimental and Control mothers showed little difference in their teaching ability during the testing session. However, in the Experimental dyads the children structured the interaction session either by their questioning or by teaching the mother. The Experimental mothers appeared to model some of the behaviors of their children and, consequently, used more verbal positive reinforcement and more verbal responses. This finding suggested that, in fact, our Experimental children, rather than their mothers, may have assumed the role of "educational engineer."

From 24 months to 72 months the Experimental group has maintained better than a 20-point difference over the Control group on the Cattell and Stanford-Binet, and at the mean age of 72 months the Experimental group's mean IQ is 120.7 (SD = 11.2) compared to the Control group mean IQ of 87.2 (SD = 12.8), a difference of over 30 IQ points. These levels have been substantiated by an independent testing service using a "double blind" procedure. (Figure 4).

One should be cautioned not to overinterpret these IQ values. There is without doubt an effect of undetermined magnitude of repeated practice on the Binet under conditions of maximum motivation and where test-taking skills for both groups have been enhanced. What is to be viewed as of significance is the differential in performance between the two groups.

Recall that our intervention program terminated at school entry. Figure 5 presents post-intervention performance on the Wechsler Intelligence Scale for Children (WISC) at roughly one, two, and three years after school entry. One major question is the extent to which the gains of intervention will be maintained

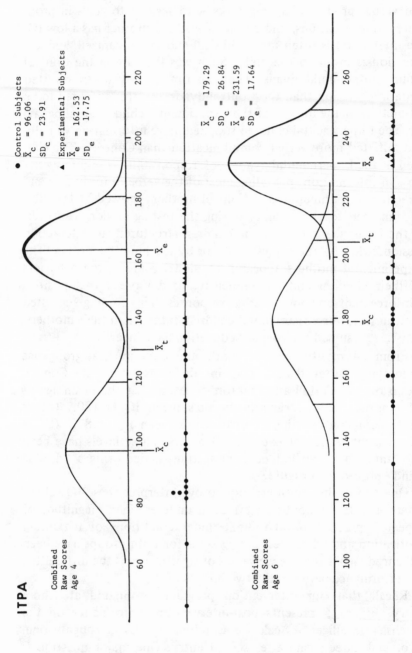

Figure 3. ITPA scores for the Experimental (▲) and Control (●) children at ages 4½ and 6½ years.

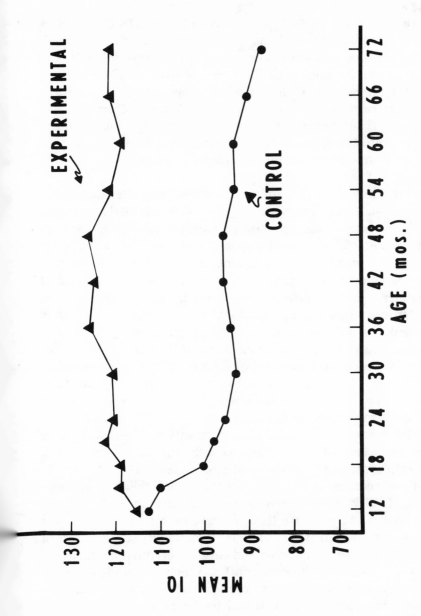

Figure 4. Mean IQ performance for Experimental (▲) and Control (●) children.

as time goes on. It is apparent that up to this point, at least, the WISC differential of around 20 IQ points has been maintained over a three-year follow-up to age nine.

We are asked repeatedly about any diffusion effects on siblings of our Experimental children. There is, in fact, a small but significant difference between Experimental and Control sibling IQ's in favor of the Experimentals. The Control group of siblings shows the typical pattern of declining IQ as age increases (consistent with the pattern of our original survey data.) And among older siblings of our research subjects, approximately twice as many from Control families as from Experimental families have been placed in special classes for the mentally retarded (17 of 59, as against 9 of 68).

How do we view our results some three years after the conclusion of our family intervention? First, it is absolutely clear that our intervention children were extraordinarily well prepared to enter public school as compared with their less fortunate Control peers. On virtually every behavioral measure, Experimental children were distinctly superior to Controls, and in a number of measures there was little or no overlap in performance between the groups. Three years into follow-up, Experimental children continue to perform in the normal range, while Controls as a group perform at the borderline level. At 96 months (where our scores are complete) one-third of the Control group tested below (WISC) IQ 75, a traditional test score criterion for placement in special classes for the mentally retarded. By contrast, the lowest IQ scores for Experimental children at 96 months are two of 88.

With respect to our maternal intervention program, we have been quite successful in the essential task of preparing the mothers for employment which has proven to be reasonably stable. The mothers' verbally stated aspirations for all their children have been distinctly elevated as a result of their participation in the Milwaukee Project. At the same time, we have been far less effective in changing each mother's social patterns, her ability to remain free of conflict with her community, and most importantly, her modes of interacting with her children. Conflicts which we were able to assist in resolving through crisis aid as part of intervention now continue unabated and are perhaps increased. By these I mean social conflicts involving the mother within the family, conflicts involving her

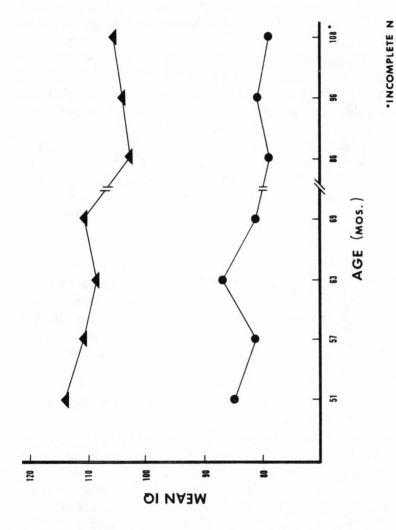

Figure 5. Mean IQ's for the two groups of subjects taken at various times from approximately four to nine years of age. ▲ = Experimental Group; ● = Control Group. Tests used were WPPSI and WISC.

friends outside the family, conflicts between school and parent, and conflicts involving the police and other community agencies.

For example, while children attended the intervention center, they were given breakfast, lunch, and an afternoon snack. Some of the children now report going to school hungry or inappropriately dressed. Where the parent has become aware of minor school adjustment problems, she may respond by physical beatings or by threatening to "send him south to live with his father."

Based on comments teachers have written on report cards, one-third of our Experimental children have some social or behavioral difficulty in the school setting. Often these difficulties can be translated to mean "the child talks too much." The Experimental children display the same behavioral problems as their Control counterparts but in addition are able to confront the teacher and their classmates verbally. Above all else, the Milwaukee Project children were given confidence, skill, and practice in the use of language as an effective tool for interacting with the adults in their lives. Whether this will be seen as an asset or a liability to the children is yet to be determined.

But we have seen geniune problems of adjustment emerge as well. With frequently poor communication between school and parent, simple problems are exaggerated to the detriment of the children. For example, notes are frequently sent home requesting a meeting and our mothers often do not respond; the public school teacher is inclined to believe the mother is not interested, rather than understanding that she may be unable to read or that the note's request is not clearly stated. On the mother's part, unquestioning attitudes of "schools know best" have led to decisions of placement for the children with no parental input.

For example, one little girl of the Experimental group tested at the 96th percentile in reading on a pre-first-grade achievement test. During her first two months of school she decided that she did not want to speak. Possibly she was angry about no longer being with her preschool teachers. Her teacher had decided to place her back in kindergarten because her parents offered no support for the first grade adjustment problem she was having. Luckily, just before the change was to be made, the child walked up to the teacher's desk, opened a book, and fluently read from it. A shocked teacher called in her supervisors to witness the event. From then on she has been a model student.

It is our subjective judgment that parent-school incompatibilities and disrupted family living environments will continue to erode the high hopes engendered by our Experimental childrens' performance at the end of our intervention effort. Nevertheless, the performance of our Experimental children three years into follow-up is such that it is difficult to conceive of their ever dropping to the performance standards of the Control group. Those of us who have participated in this experience have witnessed a capacity for learning on the part of these children dramatically in excess of their epidemiologically based expectations. At the same time, we are rapidly approaching the view that intervention and support for children reared with the intellectually inadequate parent and living in a disrupted family environment must continue throughout the child's school as well as preschool years. Nevertheless, our data to this time do nothing to inhibit the hope that it may indeed prove possible to prevent the high frequency of mental retardation among children reared by parents of limited intellectual competence under circumstances of severe economic deprivation.

Prevention in Retrospect: Adoption Follow-Up

Marie Skodak Crissey

The primary prevention of what is identified in later life as psychopathology will ultimately be governed by the integrated findings from a variety of research efforts. Some of these will emanate from laboratories and some from experimental conditions in defined settings, but perhaps the most significant will come from field observations of people reacting to, and behaving in, real-life circumstances. It is frustrating to experimental scientists that a real-life situation has so many uncontrolled and elusive impacts whose influence cannot be quantified or even identified until after the event, or until their influence has become a part of the individual's behavior repertoire and is in constant modification in response to changing events.

Nevertheless, evidence from real-life situations can lead to general principles, applicable in broader terms to people in similar circumstances. Studies of families in which the individuals experience a generally continuing kind of environment and interpersonal treatment, for example, have shown a continuing thread of similarity in educational and vocational achievement, intelligence, incidence of pathology, and so on. These observations do not, however, give evidence on the modifiability of human development or behavior in response to marked changes in environment or interpersonal relations. One real-life situation in which it is possible to observe the effects of a marked alteration in life circumstances is adoption. Many adoptions, particularly those by step-parents or relatives (which in fact constitute the majority of legal adoptions), do not produce significant changes in life circumstances. One middle-class family functions in general about like another; one that is low in the socioeconomic scale is similar to its neighbor. It is when marked disparity is found between the natural and the adoptive parent and family that evidence regarding human modifiability is uncovered. Intellectually average or superior parents who adopt children from families of distinctly lesser competence can set the stage for a field experiment with implications for primary prevention.

The majority of adoption studies have covered relatively short periods of time, usually one initial and one follow-up observation. They have also been characterized by intensive statistical manipulation of data having dubious validity or reliability. Educational level, occupation, and IQ are themselves dependent on many factors: opportunity, motivation, chance encounters, constitutional differences, or genetic predispositions, to name a few. To leap from data of this kind to controversy about genetic inheritance, or the relative contributions of nature versus nurture, is not only hazardous by virtue of being based on fragile data, but contributes little or nothing that is useful to practices or policies with potentially ameliorative social applications. The state of the art is such that inspecting life histories—studying similarities and differences in outcome, following differences in initial or ongoing conditions—may quite possibly prove more useful than laboratory methods. Pure research methods may not really be applicable to the variability of human beings in real-life situations. This unsophisticated, nontechnical approach is used here to look at data that have been previously reported in other contexts and are now examined with a view to preventing psychopathology, specifically mental retardation.

Most individuals in this country are born into families and remain with them, experiencing a continuity of life style set by their parents and their parents' parents before them. Adoptees, by contrast, have had a different experience. None of the adoptees discussed here remained with their natural families; in fact, few had any contact with them whatever, having gone directly from the hospital ward to an orphanage hospital ward.

I would like to explore with you the life pattern of these children, beginning with information about the natural family and the events that precipitated the changes in family setting, followed by descriptions of the family setting in which the adoptees grew up. Repeated cross-sectional glimpses of the children's development follow them into adulthood. Regrettably, there are gaps in the information, but even so, the data may be useful.

Four groups are discussed. The first group, 13 children, was one in which the natural mothers had IQ's of 70 to 79 and the children were placed in adoptive homes before the age of 6 months. The second group, 11 children, had mothers with IQ's between 53 and 69 and the children were placed in adoptive homes before the age of 6 months. The third group, 13 children, had been identified as retarded in infancy and experienced a planned environment in infancy and preschool ages. The fourth group, 12 children, had been identified as normal in infancy and remained in an orphanage for "normal" children.

The study covers a space of some 40 years. It may be useful to describe the setting in which it began.

Iowa, in the late 1920's and early 1930's, was one of the midwest states suffering from drought and a major economic depression. Though incomes were low and farm foreclosures were frequent, the general life standard of families was not as severely affected as in urban states. Iowans had been used to hard work and home gardens, and chickens and pigs were raised for meat even in cities. Help for neighbors in need had been a long tradition. In many respects the inhabitants of the state suffered less personal hardship and deprivation than people in industrial states to the east or in more drought-stricken states to the south and west. There was little evidence, for example, that more infants were referred for state care than in years preceding or following the Great Depression. It should be recalled that there was no social security at that time, no unemployment supplements or aid to dependent children, no reliable contraceptives or casual acceptance of sex relations. There were few alternatives for out-of-wedlock pregnancies. Some infants were legitimized by marriage; a few were accepted by the maternal family, at great emotional cost to everyone. An unknown proportion, but probably the majority, were placed for adoption. The few private child-placing agencies in the state were selective primarily on the basis of religion, and they tended to reject unwed applicants from the lowest economic and cultural strata and offer care first to girls from "better family backgrounds." Consequently, referrals to the state agency for child care tended to consist mostly of infants no one else wanted. Since no costs to family or local welfare agencies were involved, the majority of these births occurred at the University Hospital, with a direct transfer to the state child caring agency. From there, through a network of essentially untrained placement workers, the children were placed in adoptive homes. The usual stay in the orphanage hospital was two to three months while family selection and the inevitable paper work were completed. In those days before antibiotics, infections and illnesses occasionally delayed placement or removed a child from the placeable list.

Through a liaison between the Board of Control of State Institutions and the Child Welfare Research Station of the State University of Iowa, a series of studies of various aspects of child development were made possible. Among them was a study of the mental development of all children admitted to state care, and specifically all children placed for adoption. Arrangements were made for repeat examinations, and eventually 125 children were followed over a period of nearly 40 years. It was from this latter number that the four groups discussed here were selected.

When the study began, there was no intention of preventing retardation. The infants were simply accepted by the orphanage as dependent children. At that time there were only two alternatives: adoptive placement or retention in the orphanage. Other, more sophisticated child-caring agencies would have looked askance at such histories and would have placed with reluctance if at all, but not so this orphanage.

Adoptive applications, accompanied by medical, ministerial, and financial references and screened locally by untrained field workers, were reviewed by a placement committee and a child was selected on the basis of parental request for sex, coloring, and religion, in that order. The committee—made up of the orphanage superintendent, the head of the state child welfare program, the head nurse of the receiving hospital ward, and later the state psychologist—were influenced primarily by their own impressions of the quality of the baby, as seen in a brief walk through the nursery ward.

The First Group

The first group, of 13 children, had mothers whose IQ's were between 70 and 79, with a median IQ of 76, based on individual 1916 Stanford Binet tests. In addition to the score, comments by the psychologists who gave the tests described the mothers with such comments as "dull, sluggish, with poor memory." All the infants were illegitimate and comments were frequent that the burden of child rearing would be beyond the capabilities of the mothers. Among them were several known to have been promiscuous. The families were not merely "depression welfare" families, but had long records of inadequacy. Although some family members were regarded as slow, the families were not generally labeled as feeble-minded. Other studies, however, have shown that children from such maternal and social backgrounds are at high risk for slow development, poor school progress, and mental ability on the borderline of dull normal levels as adolescents.

Of the 13 infants in this group, all were placed under 6 months of age and most under 3 months. One was placed in a professional (medical services) home, 5 in homes of independent business men or minor professions, 3 in skilled trades or technical homes, and 4 in the homes of farm owners or operators. The contrast in level of families is obvious: the occupational level of all but one of the original families (whether maternal or alleged paternal) was at the unskilled, laborer, or unemployed level. The one exception was a student still in school, and this paternity was not verified.

Examined at age 2, the 13 children had a mean IQ of 121, with none below 102. At age 4, the mean IQ was 108, at 7 years 117, and at 13 years 114. IQ's at age 13, the last formal testing, ranged from 78 and 82 (a pair of twins) to 141. Of the 13, seven had IQ's of 120 to 141 on the 1937 Terman-Merrill test. Interviewed some 20 to 30 years later, it was found that all 13 children, originally qualifying as at high risk, graduated from high school. Four went no further. Of these 4, two are homemakers, one married to a farmer and one to a salesman. One man has made a career in the military service as a cook, with a proud file of commendations for excellence in both quality of meals and sanitation. He has also taken many courses in military law and takes an active role in helping his buddies circumvent unwanted regulations. The fourth high school graduate is a man who had an IQ of 140 at age 13. His family moved to a singularly unstimulating community and he had the misfortune to land in several dead-end military assignments in spite of high aptitude scores. Abandoning a military career short of retirement, he returned to civilian life and within three weeks had advanced to a responsible job in a manufacturing company.

Two others had one year of college and one had two years (one is now a warehouse manager and two are homemakers). One had three years of special training and is now vice president of an advertising firm. One had four years of college and is a specialty salesman, one completed seventeen years' training and is a medical specialist; and one has a two-year master's degree in educational administration.

Of special interest are the two girls who had the lowest IQ's at age 13 and who seemed to be following the pattern that would have been predicted from the natural family background. Throughout their lives they have had spectacular health histories, including near death from ingesting a household chemical, and a fractured skull in a travel accident. They spent a year or two in special remedial classes and in addition had intensive tutoring (two to four hours daily) through elementary school and junior and senior high school. They graduated and attended a two-year college, taking a secretarial course. After working as secretary and receptionist, they subsequently married. The husband of one is now a senior military officer and the other is vice president of a sizable firm. In spite of the stormy beginning—more extensive than this account allows—neither is retarded or maladjusted. Each has three children, all doing well in school.

The singularly successful post-high-school achievement and adjustment would not have been predicted from either the natural family history or the early developmental pattern and educational progress. It does suggest the value of early counseling. When the relative delay of these children was observed, and the educational expectations of the family were clarified, several additional psychological evaluations were arranged and the results and their implications discussed with the parents. Since the children would need additional help to compete with others, this help was arranged at the time it was needed. Instead of being held as a college fund, the investment was made during the earlier years, and with an attitude of help rather than pressure. The supportive nature of the interpersonal relations in the adoptive family was clearly evident in every contact and has implications beyond these two exemplary cases.

There was no evidence of major maladjustment in any of these 13 adults. All were married to people comparable to themselves in education and family socioeconomic level. One (the cook) had a child estimated to be slow or with a learning disability, but all the others were in appropriate grades for their ages, and their report cards (shown with considerable pride) indicated at least average and usually superior progress.

The Second Group

The second group, of 11 children, had mothers whose IQ's were from 53 to 67, with a median of 63. Educational level was commensurate with this degree of retardation. Not only were the mothers described as retarded or mentally defective, but in fact several were, had been, or subsequently became residents of state institutions for the retarded. The general family backgrounds of these mothers were measurably inferior to those of the previous group.

The placement committee was understandably somewhat more cautious in placing these children. Two nevertheless went into the homes of teachers, one into the home of an office worker, 4 into skilled or sales workers' homes, 2 into homes of farmers, and 2 into homes of semi-skilled factory workers. Describing these homes is substantially more difficult, since subsequent to the adoptive placement major problems emerged. The interplay between characteristics of the home and characteristics of the child, and possibly some knowledge of natural family characteristics, becomes too complex to be unraveled on the basis of the information available.

For example, one child had a mother "retarded with psychosis," plus about seven siblings, most of whom have spent at least part of their lives in state institutions. The alleged father was a psychiatric patient. The child was placed in a modest home, where the adoptive mother soon became totally deaf, with accompanying personality changes. The adoptive father immersed himself in his job. As an adolescent, the girl was at loose ends. She married to legitimize a pregnancy, became the mother of four in rapid succession, and broke down, with hospitalization needed for over a year. She has since continued out-patient treatment, with good results; she is an adequate, though slightly demanding, mother and has completed most of a two-year college program. Her husband is a long haul truck driver, her children range from 107 to 135 in IQ, and her home, while disorganized, is full of books, science projects for the children, and a stream of pets which come and go. Erratic and emotionally fragile, she is nevertheless a pillar of the local P.T.A. and a willing helper of the needy in her area.

One child placed in a teacher's home completed a two-year post-high-school technical program. He is married and has two bright children and a fine career as a creative artist. The adoptive father completed a doctorate and the home is comparable to the warmest and most supportive to be found anywhere.

Another child placed in another teacher's home is, to all intents and purposes, psychotic. Unfortunately both adoptive parents are so marginally adjusted that every assessment by the various clinics that have had contact with the family has carried a poor prognosis for the future. "Unworkable" has been the kindest description of them. The adoptee has had about three unsuccessful marriages, has a neurologically involved, maladjusted son, and keeps house for the adoptive parents, who have developed other business and professional activities since giving up teaching. The entire menage is self-sufficient and manages to remain in the community, but hardly qualifies as mentally healthy.

Still another, whose mother had an IQ of 53, is divorced, has been hospitalized, and now lives with her adopted mother in a remote community. Both she and the preceding adoptee had been recognized as seriously disturbed when they were children and had been returned briefly to the agency. Both were reclaimed by the respective adopting parents. Thus the home was reconstituted in spite of the children's poor adjustment and the evident problems of the family; and the adoptees have both gone on to verify the prognosis of poor adulthood made in infancy.

Of the total group of 11 children, two left school at tenth or eleventh grade, but all the others graduated from high school. Six went no further; these are now all housewives. Two had done some office work, two some factory work. One, as mentioned, had two years of specialized training, and two completed college; one of these has since earned a master's degree in education. The other is in a minor profession in which continuing special training is required.

The lot of these 11 children is less neatly successful. On the whole they are not as successful—in middle-class terms—as the children of borderline mothers. At least three have had psychological/psychiatric help and probably three more would benefit from it. None are currently hospitalized; all are doing some useful work. One has not married and two have been divorced. Of the 11, six are known to have good solid marriages.

When success is evaluated, one must ask "Compared to what?" These were indeed high risk children, who went into homes many of which had less than optimum strengths. That 6 of the 11 can be described as at least reasonably well adjusted may still be regarded as speaking for adoption as a preventive measure.

The Third Group

The third group consists of 13 children who had been admitted to the orphanage before the age of three years but were subsequently recognized to be retarded. They were not considered for adoptive placement but were held for observation to determine whether there was some physiological basis for the slow development and whether they might respond to the care available in the orphanage. Medical reasons were not established, and they did not improve in the orphanage.*

In the normal course of events, retarded children were transferred from the orphanage to institutions for the mentally handicapped when space became available for them. Two of these children were regarded as urgently in need of special care, and since no other room was available, each was placed on a ward of older girls and women. Each little girl was the only young child on the ward. To the astonishment of everyone, the two children showed remarkable improvement, not only in appearance, health, and behavior, but in IQ as well. When this improvement endured over a period of two years, a planned program of intervention was initiated with the hope that similar gains could be duplicated with other children. Eventually a total of 13 children were involved in a program which removed mentally retarded preschool children from an orphanage for normals to an institution for the mentally retarded with the specific goal of improving their intelligence.

Instead of being placed on wards according to chronological

*The following two groups have been reported in more detail in Harold M. Skeels, Adult status of children with contrasting early life experiences, *Monographs of the Society for Research in Child Development, 31*, No. 3 (1966).

age, which was the usual practice, the project stipulated that the children be placed as individuals on wards where there would be maximum stimulation. On the wards with older girls (ages 15 to 50) these singleton infants received a great deal of attention from both inmates and staff, were played with almost constantly, were talked to incessantly, had a wealth of toys, were given all kinds of extra experiences, and were regarded as highly desirable and eminently successful individuals. In addition to the general attention from all, an individual attachment developed between each child and some particular adult who became a mother substitute.

The children remained in the institution for the retarded for periods of five and a half to fifty-two months. From an initial average IQ of 64 at the age of 18 months all had gained in IQ by the end of their stay from 7 to 45 points, with a mean gain of 28 points. At the end of the "experiment" the range of IQ's was from 70 to 113 with a mean IQ of 92.

The experiment was ended for each child when it appeared that he had attained maximum benefit from the experience in the institution for the mentally retarded. One child who was at the institution when the project closed was returned to the orphanage before she was believed to be ready, and as an adolescent she was again returned to the institution. One remained in the institution for the retarded until adulthood, and later, as an adult, was placed in the community. Five children went directly into adoptive homes. Six returned to the orphanage briefly and then were placed in adoptive homes.

All of these 13 children were reexamined approximately two and a half years after the experimental period closed for them. The interim experience consisted of life in an adoptive home for 11 of the children and continued residential care for two of them.

The follow-up examination showed that on the average the intervention group continued to gain. At an average age of nearly six years, the mean IQ was 96, or a total gain of 31 points from the first examination. Individual gains between pre- and post-placement test ranged from 2 to 61 points (with losses, however, occurring in the two children who remained in institutions and in one child placed in a distinctly below average adoptive home).

After a lapse of twenty to twenty-five years, these children— now adults in their 30's—were again visited. In spite of many moves, and changes of names through marriage, it was possible to locate every member of this intervention group. Either the parents or the child, usually both, were interviewed. Intelligence tests were not given to the "children" (now adults) but tests were administered to *their* children.

All of the 13 members of the experimental group, including the two who had spent a number of years in institutions, are self-supporting and independent. The three men include one in educational administration, one who is a sales manager of a moderately large organization, and one noncommissioned career military service man. Eight of the ten women are married. They include an elementary school teacher, a registered nurse, a beauty operator, a dining room hostess, a nurse aid, and two with no work history except homemaking. Of the two who are unmarried, one is a licensed practical nurse and the other is in domestic service. This latter is one of the two who was in institutional care until adulthood.

The educational record of the 13 is consistent with their present occupations. The two who had been in the institution had completed sixth grade. Three of the adopted had ended school in the tenth or eleventh grade. Eight graduated from high school. Of these, four had education beyond high school, some as much as three years of college, and one had a master's degree—that is, six years beyond high school.

The spouses of all are of educational and vocational status comparable to their partners. The institutional resident who was placed in adulthood as a nurse aid is married to a laborer. The teacher is married to a mechanic, the noncommissioned officer to a lab technician, the nurse to a real estate salesman, the beauty operator to a semi-skilled mechanic, the education professional to an advertising writer, and the clerical worker to a printer.

Nine of the experimental group had a total of 28 children. The IQ's of these children ranged from 86 to 125, with a mean of 104. Those who were in school were doing well and all are described as attractive, normal children.

Of this group, who began life with a major developmental delay but who experienced a highly stimulating, planned adult-child relationship for some period of their lives, none are retarded or dependent. None have experienced discernible mental health problems and none have had social or emotional problems beyond those encountered in everyday living.

Of the 13 mothers of these individuals, two were described as "psychotic with mental retardation." IQ's of five of the mothers ranged from 55 to 106, with 66 as median. Education ranged from second to eleventh grade, with a median of eighth. Paternity was unestablished in 7 of the 13, and the remaining included printer, salesman, and farm laborer. Even from this meager evidence, the group would be regarded as at high risk for below-average development.

In contrast, the adoptive parents had median educations of twelfth grade or better and were at the farm owner, insurance adjuster, independent trucker level or better. They met the usual criteria for the selection of adoptive homes.

Comparisons of outcome leave little doubt that the children, now adults, more nearly resemble the adoptive families in education, occupation, and life competence than they do their natural families.

The Fourth Group

The final group consists of 12 children who had been normal as infants, but who for one reason or another were not placed for adoption. Most commonly the delay was the product of legal problems associated with commitment, and later exposure to infectious illnesses which interfered with placement. By the time these problems were solved, as much as two to four years had passed and it was found that the child was no longer normal in mental development.

These 12 children remained in the orphanage and in the course of time entered the kindergarten and first grade. Tests given at a mean age of 7 years resulted in a mean IQ of 66, with average gains of 6 points since the next preceding test, a finding consistent with other studies which show a gain in IQ at beginning of school. Comparison between the 7-year test results and the initial scores, however, showed that losses were still the rule, with one child losing 64 points. This child at age 14 months had been described as a normal infant with IQ of 99. By three and a half years of age he had an IQ of 54, and by five years, 35.

These 12 once normal children showed increasing inability to cope with school or cottage demands, and by the age of eight years, 9 of the 12 had been transferred to an institution for the mentally retarded as residents, not with therapeutic intent. One was paroled to his grandparents, but at eight years of age was still in first grade and was recommended for institutional placement by the school psychologist. Three children continued in the orphanage. One completed kindergarten at six years of age, and one had a delayed school entrance and was nine years old in the second grade.

In contrast to the difficulties in locating the intervention group as adults because of their mobility, it was possible to locate all of the 12 contrast group members through institution records. It was found that 10 of the 12 had spent all, or nearly all, of their lives in institutional care in the twenty-year interval.

One had died in an institution for the retarded at adolescence of complications following surgery for a liver disorder. Four of the surviving 11 (36 percent) have remained institutional residents, unable to adjust in the community at any level. Four others have been "rehabilitated" at considerable expense and over a long period of time, from a life in the institution into jobs as dishwashers or part-time cafeteria helpers in the community. One more is unable to adjust in the community but is employed as assistant gardener in the institution where he lived for many years. None of these are married. One who remained in the orphanage until late adolescence now lives as a floater, working here and there as a handyman or porter. He was married briefly, but deserted his wife and mentally retarded child.

All of these, or 10 of the surviving 11, fit the classical stereotype of the mentally retarded, minimally skilled, unemployed or unemployable individual. They had a singularly barren, affectionless, detached childhood and as adults they are dependent and socially ineffective.

The one remaining contrast group member is consistently the exception. He is the only one who is employed, and employed in a highly skilled and well paying technical specialty. He is the only one with a sound marriage, a home of his own, and four attractive children with IQ's of 103 to 119. He not only graduated from high school, but had some college and trade training, and in every respect is a substantial, well-adjusted citizen and a contributing member of society.

A review of his experiences as compared with the others in the contrast group shows that up to the age of six he, too, had the same barren institutional existence. As a preschooler he had an IQ of 87; by six, his IQ was 67. Then, by chance selection, he was included in an intensive stimulation program as part of a doctoral research that emphasized language training and cognitive development. When he entered the regular school he was found to have a sensory defect. This was no major handicap in everyday life, but it qualified him for admission to a special boarding school. While there, he received personal attention from the dormitory supervisor and became an informal member of her family. In effect (though at a much later age), he experienced the intellectual stimulation and received the emotional acceptance which had been the therapeutic formula for the group previously discussed.

Assessment of family backgrounds suggests that compared with adoptees in general, the members of this group were somewhat more disadvantaged. Maternal IQ's, available for 8 of the 13 cases, ranged from 36 to 85, with a median of 65. Education ranged from less than fifth grade to twelfth, with a median of eighth. Maternal occupations, except for one clerical worker, were either nonexistent or in housework. Natural father occupations, known for 11 of the 13, were all in unskilled labor except for one carpenter.

There were of course no adoptive families to give stimulation, affection, or support.

The orphanage in which these children lived was, at that time, seriously overcrowded and understaffed. There was neither time nor inclination to give affection or attention to individual children. Toys were few and quickly broken. Language development was seriously retarded at all age levels for all children in the orphanage. There was little or no personal contact between children and adults. A more barren or unstimulating existence would be difficult to describe.

If one were to compare only the initial description of the family background and the current adult status of these individuals, it would be easy to claim excellent prediction from the parental data: a high risk family and the expected outcome. Evidence from other studies suggests that children from similar subaverage backgrounds are substantially below the general average in intelligence, school achievement, and vocational success, though not usually to the degree of deficit shown by the 10 individuals. This study goes beyond that and demonstrates that when the environment is singularly restricting, emotionally barren, and the opposite of challenging and supportive, the individual's response adequacy can be so curtailed and become so rigid that he cannot function as a normal adult. Whether mentally retarded or intellectually paralyzed becomes of little significance. He is dependent on society for care.

SUMMARY AND CONCLUSIONS

On the basis of family data—parental education, occupation, social history—all four of these groups of children would be identified as at high risk for retardation and/or maladjustment if they remained in the original parental environment.

All of them experienced a marked change in life setting. For two groups, early placement in adoptive homes moved them into situations offering a great deal of affection, general economic security, and intellectual and cultural opportunities which were above average for the community and in the opposite direction from the offerings of the natural family. The third group, even more at risk in view of initial delays in development, experienced specific programs which effected marked changes in the developmental course and made adoptive placement possible. The fourth group, in addition to adverse family background, had life experiences which accentuated the chances for retardation and adjustment difficulties.

The favorable results of adoption for children from initially disadvantaged family backgrounds when they are placed in homes of average or better opportunities are evident. It suggests the general principle that the home in which the adoptee is placed, the experiences he undergoes, and the reciprocal and ever-changing relationship between the adoptee and the significant persons in his life may be more important than information about his natural family and their socioeconomic status.

The evidence from these four groups speaks for itself. Children in families in which low intelligence, poor school achievement, and social and economic inadequacy are prevalent have repeatedly been shown to follow the same familial pattern. When drastic changes in life circumstances occur early in the formative period, there are marked changes in the subsequent intelligence, educational, vocational, and social achievements of the child, with prevention of inadequacies predictable from the original family history. The responsiveness of the human organism to both facilitative and repressive influences was further underscored in the tragic histories of children once assessed as normal, whose early promise was obliterated by circumstances. The significance of primary prevention needs no further emphasis.

In looking back on these particular adoption follow-up studies, the wisdom of hindsight suggests many things that might have been improved in the interests of scientific purity. Yet, burdened with the constraints of laboratory type research, the studies might never have been made at all. The periodic intrusions into the lives of the children and the adopting parents were friendly, turned out often to be supportive and helpful, and resulted in evidence that has helped influence public policy. Thus it has had a bearing on the lives of others. These studies, it is hoped, will encourage investigators to explore real-life situations and thus augment our knowledge of the modifiability and the responsiveness of the human organism in the direction of happier, more effective, and healthier lives—the true aim of preventive efforts.

Interpersonal Problem Solving Thinking and Adjustment in the Mother-Child Dyad

**Myrna B. Shure and
George Spivack**

One way parents can affect the behavior of their children is to tell them what to do, then give praise when they comply and use discipline when they do not. Another way is to help them think about how their actions affect others, and then guide them toward deciding for themselves what to do and what not to do. The first way focuses directly on behavior itself; the second, on the process of the child's thinking. When the child experiences problems involving other people, it can make a difference which approach the parent takes. Based on the position that children's ability to solve typical interpersonal problems can affect the quality of their social adjustment, the intervention we have developed has been designed for mothers to help their children learn to think; it focuses specifically on the problem solving approach to child-rearing.

A training program for mothers has evolved as a logical step from a series of research studies and demonstration projects which have examined ways in which specific interpersonal cognitive problem solving (ICPS) skills relate to overt criterion measures of human adjustment. People over a broad age range, from diverse socioeconomic groups, of both sexes, and across a broad span of adjustment levels, who exhibit healthy, adaptive behaviors have consistently demonstrated markedly superior ICPS ability compared to those who manifest some degree of behavioral maladjustment (Spivack and Shure, 1974; Spivack, Platt, and Shure, 1976).

Within groups of normal children, Shure, Newman, and Silver (1973) and Shure, Spivack, and Jaeger (1971) have differentiated youngsters efficient and deficient in ICPS skills as early as age four. Regardless of IQ (PPVT, Slosson, Stanford-Binet), youngsters who display varying degrees of behavioral difficulties—particularly those characteristic of impulsivity or inhibition—are consistently more deficient than their better adjusted classmates in two thinking skills: (1) alternative solution thinking (ability to generate different ways of solving an interpersonal problem) and (2) consequential thinking (ability to foresee what might happen next if a solution is carried out).

The importance of such thinking became increasingly evident when it was shown that within a wide IQ range (70 to 120+) teachers could improve both impulsive and inhibited behaviors in four-year-olds (Shure and Spivack, 1973) and in five-year-olds (Shure and Spivack, 1975 [c]) by enhancing ICPS skills through specifically designed three-month intervention programs (see Shure and Spivack, 1974 [a]; Shure, Spivack and Gordon, 1972; Spivack and Shure, 1974). Relative to controls, improvement of ICPS-trained youngsters lasted at least one year and, for many, two years beyond termination of training. Most important, in both age groups, trained youngsters who improved most in the trained ICPS skills also improved most in social behavior. This linkage supports the theoretical position which underlies the intervention—that *specific ICPS skills function as significant mediators of healthy social adjustment.*

Given that teachers could affect classroom behaviors of young children vis-à-vis ICPS training, the next step was to learn whether mothers, assumed to be in a unique position to affect such skills, could also become successful ICPS-change agents. In one study, Shure and Spivack (1975 [b]) found that by applying an adapted version of the teacher program script, twenty inner-city mothers could transmit ICPS skills to their four-year-olds. Significant behavioral improvement occurred. Nothing, however, was known about whether interpersonal thinking skills could be abetted in these mothers, or whether any change would affect the thinking and behavior of their children.

THE PRESENT STUDY

The present study investigated a new group of mothers, who in addition to administering ICPS-games and dialogues to their children, were given ICPS training of their own. Questions asked were: (1) could training increase mothers' ICPS skills? (2) could mothers' ability to guide their children in solving real problems (child-rearing style) be enhanced? and (3) how might change in mothers' problem-solving thinking and child-rearing style affect their childrens' ICPS ability and/or school behavioral adjustment?

❖   The Methods and Results sections of this paper have been omitted. The complete version of this paper can be found in *Social Competence in Children,* eds. Martha Whalen Kent and Jon E. Rolf, Hanover, N.H.: University Press of New England, 1979.

DISCUSSION AND CONCLUSIONS

ICPS training clearly improved impulsive and inhibited behaviors of inner-city four-year-olds. The strongest direct ICPS-mediator of these behaviors studied to date is children's ability to think of alternative solutions to interpersonal problems, and secondarily, their ability to foresee possible effects of their own actions on others (consequences). ICPS and behavorial changes in children trained by their mothers were remarkably similar to those in youngsters trained by their teachers, despite the larger research sample in the latter groups.

One important result is that children exposed to ICPS training in one environment (the home) improved in their behavior as observed in a different one (the school). The finding is particularly important because the behaviors were judged by teachers unaware of the training procedures and goals. It seems reasonable to assume that, because children learned how to think and were not taught specific solutions to specific problems, they were able to apply their own thinking skills to new problems when they arose, wherever that happened to be. With problem solving thinking ability giving children skills which would create a greater likelihood of success in solving a problem, as well as increased ability to cope with frustration, impulsive children had less need to show anger or impatience, and inhibited children less need to retreat from confrontation with others.

It is particularly encouraging that inner-city mothers, many of whom displayed deficient ICPS skills at the start, could success-fully improve their own skills as well as those of their children in a period of only three months. Also, typical pretraining child-rearing interviews which reflected a "telling-the-child-what-to-do" style of interaction changed to a style reflecting significantly more guidance in helping their children think through and solve their own prob-lems. While this latter skill did have some direct impact on the child's behavior, mothers' ICPS skills and child-rearing style also had direct impact on the child's thinking skills—skills which in turn played a significant role in the child's ultimate behavioral adjustment.

Given that the child's solution thinking is most related to behavior before training, most changed by training, and most directly related to mothers' ICPS ability and style of direct com-munication with the child, the stated sequence of events is logical and consistent. This consistency suggests that improvements were not due to mere "attention," where changes and relationships in all trained skills between mothers and their children would probably have been random. Also, both mothers and children improved most in those skills emphasized in training. The fact that mothers showed little or no improvement in their ability to solve adult-relevant problems, and that their children did not improve in cognitive sensitivity to interpersonal problems (skills not emphasized in training), suggests that mere attention alone could not have been a major factor in the results. When a placebo-attention group was studied (Shure, Spivack and Gordon, 1972), it was evident that such groups did not change ICPS skills or behavior in the same manner as those exposed to specific ICPS training.

Intervention incorporating interpersonal problem solving think-ing skills has been found adaptable for older children as well. To date it has been applied by teachers in hyperaggressive seven-year-olds (Camp and Bash, 1975), in normal five- to-eight-year-olds (Kirschenbaum, et al.), in normal third-graders (Gesten et al., chapter 11 below; Larcen, in Allen et al., 1976), in normal fourth-graders (McClure, 1975), and in retarded-educable youngsters six to twelve years of age (Healey, 1977). Elardo and Caldwell (in preparation) have identified specific classroom behaviors which most improve in normal fourth- and fifth-graders when trained in a program combining social role-taking and alternative solution thinking skills (Elardo and Cooper, in press). These behaviors are respect and concern for others, ability to function without teacher guidance, involvement in and tendency to initiate classroom discussions, and general attentiveness or decrease in tendency to lose attention or appear oblivious.

Evidence to date suggests that obstreperous or impulsive behaviors similar to those measured in younger children are slower to change, suggesting perhaps the need for extending the period of training for latency-aged youngsters, particularly the retarded-educable ones. That youngsters in various age groups can respond to problem solving training suggests the potential application of ICPS programming for the entire family.

Implications for the prevention of social incompetence

Previous research has provided another insight into the value of ICPS training. Not only does the problem-solving approach help youngsters already experiencing varying degrees of behavioral difficulties: it has a preventive effect as well. Teacher-trained four-year-olds showing no noticeable behavioral problems during the nursery year were significantly less likely than controls to begin showing varying degrees of behavioral difficulties a year later in kindergarten (Shure and Spivack, 1975 [c]). Trained youngsters whose impulsive or inhibited behaviors decreased were likely to have maintained adjusted behavior for at least two years without further training. There is no reason to believe the same would not occur for youngsters trained by their mothers. However long the impact of teacher training lasts without later reinforcement, the ultimate impact for a mother-trained child would probably have maximum potential if the mother continued to problem solve with her child at home.

One question unanswered by the present research is the effect a problem-solving trained child can have on his mother. Mothers of teacher-trained youngsters interviewed informally (see Spivack and Shure, 1974) indicate that a good problem solver can affect the way a mother handles problems that come up (see also Shure and Spivack, in press). While a cyclical effect must be present when a mother is also trained, it would be of interest to systematically measure changes in mothers unaware of the training procedures and goals as the child learns these skills in school. Nevertheless, the present group of mother-trained youngsters did increase their solution skills significantly more than the previous group of twenty children trained by mothers not receiving ICPS training of their own. While both mother-trained groups of youngsters improved more than untrained controls, these findings suggest that greater impact on children occurs when mothers as well as children are taught how to think. The mediating effects of children's ICPS skills on their behavior have clear implications for a new approach toward optimal mental health programming for mothers and their young children.

REFERENCES

Allen, G., Chinsky, J., Larcen, S., Lochman, J., and Selinger, H. *Community psychology and the schools: A behaviorally oriented multilevel preventive approach.* Hillsdale, N.J.: Earlbaum, 1976.

Camp, B. N., and Bash, M. A. *Think Aloud Program Group Manual.* Boulder: University of Colorado Medical Center, 1975. (Available from the authors at 4200 E. 9th Avenue, Denver, Colorado, 80220)

Elardo, P. T., and Caldwell, B. M. The effects of an experimental social development program on children in the middle childhood period. Manuscript in preparation. (Available from the authors at Center for Early Development and Education, University of Little Rock, Little Rock, Arkansas, 72204)

Elardo, P. T., and Cooper, M. *Project AWARE: A handbook for teachers.* Reading, Mass: Addison-Wesley, in press.

Gesten, E., De Apodaca, R. F., Weissberg, R., Raines, M., and Cowen, E. (Chapter 11 of this volume, below.)

Healey, K. An investigation of the relationship between certain social cognitive abilities and social behavior, and the efficacy of training in social cognitive skills for elementary retarded-educable children. Unpublished doctoral dissertation, Bryn Mawr College, 1977.

Kirschenbaum, D., Bane, S., Fowler, R., Klei, R., Kuykendal, K., Marsh, M., Pedro, J., and Reed, Y. *Social Skills Development Programs: Handbook for Helping.* Cincinnati: Department of Health Professional Services Division, (Available from Author Kirschenbaum at 411 Oak Street, Suite 204, Cincinnati, Ohio, 45219)

McClure, L. F. Social problem solving training and assessment: An experimental intervention in an elementary school setting. Unpublished doctoral dissertation, University of Connecticut, Storrs, 1975.

Platt, J. J., and Spivack, G. *Manual for the Means-Ends-Problem-Solving*

Procedure. Philadelphia: Department of Mental Health Sciences, Hahnemann Community Mental Health/Mental Retardation Center, 1975. (Available from the authors at 314 N. Broad Street, Philadelphia, PA, 19102)

Shure, M. B., Newman, S., and Silver, S. Problem solving thinking among adjusted, impulsive, and inhibited Head Start children. Paper presented at the meeting of the Eastern Psychological Association, Washington, D.C., May 1973.

Shure, M. B., Spivack, G., and Jaeger, M. A. Problem-solving thinking and adjustment among disadvantaged preschool children. *Child Development*, 1971, *42*, 1791–1803.

Shure, M. B., Spivack, G., and Jaeger, M. A. Problem solving thinking and tive mental health program for preschool children. *Reading World*, 1972, *11*, 259–273.

Shure, M. B., and Spivack, G. A preventive mental health program for four-year-old Head Start children. Paper presented at the meeting of the Society for Research in Child Development, Philadelphia, March 1973.

Shure, M. B., and Spivack, G. *A Mental Health Program for Kindergarten Children: Training Script.* Philadelphia: Department of Mental Health Sciences, Hahnemann Community Mental Health/Mental Retardation Center, 1974. (a) (Available from the authors at 314 N. Broad Street, Philadelphia, PA, 19102)

Shure, M. B., and Spivack, G. *Preschool Interpersonal Problem-Solving (PIPS) Test: Manual.* Philadelphia: Department of Mental Health Sciences, Hahnemann Community Mental Health/Mental Retardation Center, 1974. (b) (Available from the authors)

Shure, M. B., and Spivack, G. *A Mental Health Program for Preschool and Kindergarten Children, and A Mental Health Program for Mothers of Young Children: An Interpersonal Problem-Solving Approach Toward Social Adjustment.* A Comprehensive Report of Research and Training. No. MH-20372. Washington, D.C.: National Institute of Mental Health, 1975. (a) (Available from the authors)

Shure, M. B., and Spivack, G. Training mothers to help their children solve real-life problems. Paper presented at the meeting of the Society for Research in Child Development, Denver, March 1975. (b)

Shure, M. B., and Spivack, G. Interpersonal cognitive problem solving intervention: The second (kindergarten) year. Paper presented at the meeting of the American Psychological Association, Chicago, August 1975. (c)

Shure, M. B., and Spivack, G. *Problem solving techniques in childrearing.* San Francisco: Jossey-Bass, in press.

Spivack, G., Platt, J. J., and Shure, M. B. *The problem solving approach to adjustment.* San Francisco: Jossey-Bass, 1976.

Spivack, G., and Shure, M. B. *Social adjustment of young children.* San Francisco: Jossey-Bass, 1974.

Peer Relations and the Growth of Social Competence

Willard W. Hartup

Social scientists have long stressed the importance of parent-child relations in human development. The capacity to create sustained and mutually regulated relations with others, achievement of effective modes of emotional expression, and accurate social/cognitive reality-testing have been believed generally to be legacies of family interaction. But extensions and elaborations of the competencies that emerge from parent-child interaction also emanate from peer relations. Experiences with other children contribute, too, to one's capacity for relating to others, to the effectiveness of emotional regulation, and to the cognitive styles that constrain the child's adaptation to the environment.

These secondary competencies are no less essential to child development than the competencies emerging from adult-child relations, even though this fact is seldom acknowledged in the psychiatric and pediatric literature. Usually, the child's relations with other children (i.e. siblings and peers) are assumed to represent complex extensions of initial accommodations to adults and to be similar to them in essential ways. Whether the theoretical formulation rests on notions of libidinal vicissitude (Freud, 1963) or notions like stimulus generalization (Gewirtz, 1961), peer relations have seemed mostly to constitute secondary elaborations of social adaptations worked out within the family.

Empirical research, however, does not strongly support the hypothesis that social competencies emerge through such an elaborative process. In fact, the contemporary evidence suggests that peer relations contribute unique variance to individual differences

Preparation of this manuscript was assisted by funds from Grant No. 5-P01-05027, National Institute of Child Health and Human Development.

in children's social and intellectual competencies. Although peer-based contributions to the child's socialization may be synergistic with those deriving from contacts with the adult culture, such contributions cannot be regarded as simple extentions of adult-child relations.

❖

PEER RELATIONS: THEIR SIGNIFICANCE IN CHILD DEVELOPMENT

Having established that adult-child relations and peer relations are neither wholly independent nor wholly interdependent, it remains to be argued that peer relations contribute essentially to social competence. No one doubts that peer interactions are common events in childhood. An occasional reader may recall a childhood in which other children occupied only a minor role but, most likely, no reader will recall a childhood that involved no contact with other children. And yet, social scientists have not given much thought to the functions of peer relations in child development. They have described the various forms that such interaction takes, but what are the consequences of sociability with other children? What attitudes and orientations typify the child who is not involved in social activities with peers, as contrasted with the child who occupies a central niche in the social world? Is the isolate at severe risk for psychopathology? Is the risk more serious in certain behavior domains than others?

The following is a letter from an Indiana farmer that summarizes, idiographically, the current evidence dealing with the significance of peer relations in child development.

Dear Dr. [   ]:

I read the report in the Oct. 30 issue of [   ] about your study of only children. I am an only child, now 57 years old and I want to tell you some things about my life. Not only was I an only child but I grew up in the country where there were no nearby children to play with. My mother did not want children around. She used to say "I don't want my kid to bother anybody and I don't want nobody's kids bothering me."

. . . From the first year of school I was teased and made fun of. For example, in about third or fourth grade I dreaded to get on the school bus to go to school because the other children on the

bus called me "Mommy's baby." In about the second grade I heard the boys use a vulgar word. I asked what it meant and they made fun of me. So I learned a lesson—don't ask questions. This can lead to a lot of confusion to hear talk one doesn't understand and not be able to learn what it means. . . .

I never went out with a girl while I was in school—in fact I hardly talked to them. In our school the boys and girls did not play together. Boys were sent to one part of the playground and girls to another. So, I didn't learn anything about girls. When we got into high school and the boys and girls started dating I could only listen to their stories about their experiences.

I could tell you a lot more but the important thing is I have never married or had any children. I have not been very successful in an occupation or vocation. I believe my troubles are not all due to being an only child . . . but I do believe you are right in recommending playmates for preschool children and I will add playmates for the school agers and not have them strictly supervised by adults. I believe I confirm the experiments with monkeys in being overly timid sometimes and overly aggressive sometimes. Parents of only children should make special efforts to provide playmates for [their children].

Sincerely yours,
[signed]

Most of the research evidence that supports this letter derives from correlational studies. While causal direction may not be inferred from such data, the linkages they reveal are convincing. First, lack of sociability in both boys and girls is associated with discomfort, anxiety, and a general unwillingness to engage the environment. Bronson (1966) found that young children who were rated as "reserved-somber-shy" were inward-looking, highly anxious, and low in social activity. In later childhood, the correlates of reservedness included vulnerability, lack of dominance, nonadventuresomeness, and instability. The socially rejected child is very much like the socially inactive child: he is neither outgoing nor friendly; he is either very high or very low in self-esteem; he is particularly dependent on adults for emotional support; he is anxious and inappropriately aggressive (Hartup, 1970).

Second, scattered evidence suggests that children master their aggressive impulses within the context of peer relations. This evidence derives from studies of both children and nonhuman primates and need not be summarized here (cf. Hartup, 1976). It is doubtful, however, that mastery of the complex emotions and behaviors related to aggression could be achieved in the absence of early opportunity to interact with others whose developmental status is similar to one's own.

Third, sexual socialization probably cannot take place in the absence of peer interaction. Other children are implicated in the complex processes known as gender typing (Kobasigawa, 1968) and the contributions of the peer culture also extend to the socialization of sexual behavior.

> *Children are the most frequent agents for the transmission of the sexual mores. Adults serve in that capacity only to a smaller extent. This will not surprise sociologists and anthropologists, for they are aware of the great amount of imitative adult activity which enters into the play of children the world around. In this activity, play though it may be, children are severe, highly critical, and vindictive in their punishment of a child who does not do it "this way" or "that way." Even before there has been any attempt at overt sex play, the child may have acquired a considerable schooling on matters of sex. Much of this comes so early that the adult has no memory of where his attitudes were acquired. (Kinsey, Pomeroy, and Martin, 1948)*

Blinded by the belief that the peer culture is an unreliable context for socialization, many adults have felt that it would be better if more sexual information were given to the child by parents and/or teachers than by other children. In spite of their best efforts, though, sex educators cannot provide the child with the trial and error, the modeling, and the vast store of information needed for ultimate determination of the individual's sexual life style. Given the taboos that have evolved to prevent sexual activity between adults and children, it is only through interaction with agemates that these opportunities can be found.

Fourth, while peer relations do not make a direct contribution to measured intelligence or to school achievement (Hartup, 1976), such experiences are related to the ability to "put oneself in someone else's shoes." Children who are better role-takers are more sociable and more competent in their social interactions than children who are less capable role-takers (Gottman, Gonso, and Rasmussen, 1975). Furthermore, children who are leaders exhibit advanced levels of social responsibility (Gold, 1962) and relatively high levels of moral reasoning (Keasey, 1971). It may be true that intelligence, narrowly defined, is not affected greatly by opportunities to interact with other children, but the effectant use of intellectual abilities is.

Finally, children who are rejected by their peers have higher delinquency rates as adolescents (Roff, 1961), are more likely to drop out of school (Roff, Sells, and Golden, 1972), and are at risk for emotional difficulties, including serious forms of mental illness (Rolf, 1972; Cowen et al., 1973).

This evidence cannot be interpreted easily. Are children made vulnerable to stress by poor peer experiences, or, alternatively, do behaviors associated with vulnerability to mental illness "turn off" other children and produce poor peer relations? Does social withdrawal incite social rejection, or does a history of failure in peer relations lead to shyness, low social activity, and inability to handle aggressive feelings? Definite answers to these questions elude us. The evidence overwhelmingly suggests, however, that success in peer relations is embedded centrally in the socialization of the the child and is not a peripheral feature of social development.

❖

In summary, peer interaction is central in childhood socialization, contributing to the acquisition of social and communicative competencies in a manner that is unlike the contributions made by interaction with adults. The literature shows that it is unwise to regard child-child relations as a realm of experience secondary to the main course of socialization. Indeed, it is difficult to imagine effective social adaptations developing in children who lack peer interaction. Peer relations are necessities rather than luxuries in child development (Roff, Sells, and Golden, 1972).

WHY ARE PEER RELATIONS UNIQUE?

Why should child-child relations contribute so uniquely to normal development? The answer is, at once, both simple and complex. Human beings live in multiple social environments involving individuals of a wide range of ages, roles, and statuses. For this reason, the cognitive schemas undergirding effectant social behavior must be heterogeneous. Imagine how the social world would be perceived by an individual who became adapted to an environment that was populated only by adults! The research literature does not furnish us with information about singleton children reared in isolation, for example 200 miles northeast of Eagle, Alaska. Nevertheless, were such children to be found and suddenly moved to Minnesota School District 623 (Roseville), we can predict that they would be as socially vulnerable as the peer-isolated monkeys in the Madison, Wisconsin, experiments. This is not to say that such children would exemplify psychopathology in any classical sense. It is only to assert that adaptations acquired solely within the context of adult-child relations are unlikely to work in environments that include children as well as adults. And such rearing environments are unlikely to fit the individual, in the long term, for the wide variety of social relations that must be managed once adulthood has been reached.

Current research suggests that *egalitarianism* is the quality in peer relations responsible for their unique contributions to social development. Peer relations *are* egalitarian, in spite of the fact that every children's group is hierarchized and that at least one grain of truth resides in the *Lord of the Flies*. Peer relations contain large residuals of reciprocity (give-and-take). Children contribute to their own socialization through the provision of role relations that cannot ordinarily be provided by adults. What chance exists, for example, between a seven-year old boy and his father for effective aggressive socialization—for either the trial-and-error necessary to the acquisition of effective motor behaviors or the internalization of controls over aggressive affect? How can a morality of reciprocity (Piaget, 1932) emerge from authoritarian social contexts like families? How can sexual behavior be learned in an environment constrained by authoritarianism? How can one learn to care for the younger generation through interaction with adults? Imitation may be a powerful force in human socialization, but it cannot substitute for direct experience.

We argue, then, that adult-child relations are not always the best adapted context for social development. Whenever give-and-take (reciprocity) is an essential element in social adaptation, peer relations have a special value. How long can the mature adult maintain a child-like posture in rough-and-tumble games and still maintain the cognitive and affective equilibrium that make him an adult? How can the family attachments that enhance the child's survival be maintained during unrestrained aggression? No, parents cannot function as parents and, at the same time, create the give-and-take necessary to foster social competence. The value of peer interaction, then, derives from two sources: (a) the egalitarian features existing in the interaction between individuals whose behavioral adaptations exemplify equivalent complexity; and (b) the lack of constraints, imposed by both attachemnts and hierarchization that mark the child's relations with adults.

PROMOTING COMPETENCE THROUGH PEER INTERACTION

Behavior modification

Social reinforcement techniques. Considerable success has been achieved in modifying early peer interaction by means of social reinforcement. The earliest studies date from the 1930's and include the prototypic investigations by Jack (1934) and Page (1936). Increased ascendance in peer relations was sought through adult-child interaction rather than directly through experience with peers. First, ascendance was assessed by means of situational tests. Experimental groups were stratified according to these scores and next supplied with "confidence training" in the use of various play materials. The training consisted of graduated success experiences in telling stories, making flowers, and constructing wooden toys. Training effects were consistently found for nonassertive children (as compared to nontrained children) although less consistently obtained for children whose baseline scores indicated initially high levels of assertiveness.

These studies were extended, 30 years later, in a series of well-known investigations designed to increase the rate of social activity in socially withdrawn children and/or to modify the child's social repertoire. Allen, Hart, Buell, Harris, and Wolf (1964) worked with a four-year-old girl whose baseline scores showed interaction with peers only 10 percent of the time but interaction with teachers approximately 40 percent of the time. During a series of experimental sessions, teacher attention was withdrawn when the child made social overtures to adults and delivered contingently only when social overtures were made to peers. Interaction with children then increased to nearly 60 percent while interaction with adults declined to less than 20 percent. A reversal period re-established the baseline levels of social behavior toward adults and and peers, but reinstituting the experimental sessions increased peer interaction once again. Parallel studies, with similar results, were conducted with other isolate or passive nursery school children (Harris, Wolf, and Baer, 1967). Follow-up studies of the children in such experiments indicate the results to be relatively unstable (e.g. O'Connor, 1972). Apparently the reinforcement intrinsic in peer interaction does not "fade in" when short-term modifications of adult attention cease abruptly. Very gradual fading out of the adult attention, though, produces longer-lasting effects (see Baer and Wolf, 1970).

Scott, Burton, and Yarrow (1967) used similar techniques to reduce the aggressiveness of a preschool boy. Ground rules established for this experiment necessitated incomplete withdrawal of adult attention on occasions when other children were in danger. The strategy was successful, nevertheless, in decreasing the subject's aggressive outbursts. The behavior modification actually promoted social competence more broadly; ordinary reversal of the contingencies of adult attention failed to reinstitute high levels of aggression because peer attention, in the meantime, had established constructive social behaviors that were incompatible with the aggression.

Peer reinforcement may be used directly to promote social competence. Wahler (1967) determined baseline rates for speech, cooperation, isolate behavior, and dramatic play among five preschool children, identifying response classes associated with high rates of peer reinforcement for three of them and response classes linked to low reinforcement rates for two. The experimenter next recruited a small group of each child's peers as confederates, inducing them to ignore the high-rate subjects when the targeted behavior occurred while, at the same time, maintaining social interaction when other classes of behavior were exhibited. Low-rate subjects were treated similarly. Concordant results were obtained for all subjects. First, the instructions worked: selective attention could be utilized by the young children's playmates. Second, increases (or decreases) were observed in the selected response classes during the experimental period. Third, reversal resulted in rapid changes toward the baseline rates. Later, Solomon and Wahler (1973) demonstrated that selective use of peer rewards could be induced in sixth-graders to reduce disruptive activity in school classrooms. While virtually nothing is known about the generalization of these peer-induced effects—either across situations or across time—peer reinforcement is well established as an efficacious tool for promoting social competence.

Modeling. A vast literature documents the many ways that modeling affects children's social activity. Whether models are TV characters, live adults, or live children, imitative influences extend from the affective domain to cognitive abilities, and have direct effects on children's social relations (cf. Bandura, 1969). The literature on peer modeling is relatively small, but it suggests that systematic exposure to other children as models would add appreciably to our armamentarium for promoting social competence. Neither teachers nor therapists currently use modeling to the extent warranted by the evidence.

Peer modeling, like contingency management, has been used to modify both general sociability and the nature of the child's social repertoire. In O'Connor's (1969) work, isolate nursery school children were exposed to movies showing effective peer interaction. The movies began with relatively low levels of interaction (e.g. sharing toys) and increased over time in both tempo and number of children involved. Control children saw a film about dolphins. Classroom observations subsequently showed increases in the sociability of the children who had viewed the peer interaction but no increases among the children who had watched the dolphins.

Specific behavior systems shown to be sensitive to peer modeling range from altruism to cognitive styles. Exposure to films of fear-resistant children reduces animal phobias in young children (Bandura, Grusec, and Menlove, 1967); altruistic peer models promote increased sharing (Hartup and Coates, 1967); "reflective" peer models increase the latency of problem-solving among "impulsive" problem-solvers (Debus, 1970); disinhibition of inappropriate sex-typed behaviors is increased following exposure to models who display such disinhibition (Kobasigawa, 1968); and inhibiting models promote resistance to deviation (Grosser, Polansky, and Lippitt, 1951). Long-term consequences of peer modeling have not been studied extensively, but explicit use of modeling procedures seems to enhance generalization of the effects (Asher, Gottman, and Oden, 1976).

Conglomerate interventions

Coaching. A conglomerate intervention known as "coaching" has received considerable attention as a method for promoting competence in social relations. It involves demonstration (modeling), rational methods (discussion), and shaping—thereby combining elements shown elsewhere in the literature to be effective in behavior modification. So-called assertiveness training is another example of this type of intervention.

Chittenden's (1942) study was a pace-setter in this area. Baselines for dominance behaviors were established by observing the children who served as subjects both within a nursery school and in a laboratory session with another child. The intervention was a mixed procedure involving direct tuition and symbolic modeling based on story materials that were graduated in complexity. The leading characters (dolls) in the stories were portrayed as (a) instigated to assertiveness, (b) debating the merits of more constructive behavior, and (c) deciding to behave constructively. The experimenter conducted discussions with the child in addition to serving as the dramatist. Subsequent observations, in both the laboratory and the nursery school, showed diminution of assertive behavior in the experimental subjects, as contrasted with no-treatment controls. The nursery school effects were visible two months after the intervention was terminated.

❖

Peer Tutoring. Peer tutoring has a long history in educational practice (Allen, 1976) but it has gained new popularity during recent years. The new enthusiasm derives from two sources: (a) tutoring utilizes the potential existing in peer interaction for constructive educational ends and augments the efforts of certified teachers; (b) the tutoring situation is thought to enhance the social competencies of both tutor (the teacher) and tutee (the child being taught).

Ample evidence shows that children can teach things to other children in more or less formal situations (Allen, 1976). Tutoring relations are complicated, however, and few across-the-board statements can be made about them. Relatively common results include the following. (a) Children prefer to teach children younger than themselves but to be taught by children who are older. (b) Children prefer same-sex situations to opposite-sex situations. (c) Tutors do not like to participate in the evaluation of their tutees, especially if it will determine something that really matters to the tutee. Children's attitudes about tutoring and its effectiveness are also related to the competencies of both tutor and tutee; consequences are different when programs involve learners who are failures and learners who are not (Allen and Feldman, 1976).

The benefits to the tutor in this type of peer interaction are numerous. The teacher role carries with it status, attention from adults, and deference from other children. Such experiences can enhance self-esteem and change attitudes toward authority figures, the school, and society. Tutoring also provides role-taking opportunities, assists in the acquisition of helping behaviors, and effects a general attitude change concerning nurturance and sympathetic behavior.

The tutee's benefits are usually conceptualized in terms of cognitive learning—increases in reading skills, mathematical competencies, or whichever abilities the tutoring is centered upon. The effectiveness of such tutoring derives from several factors, most saliently the individual instruction. Peer tutoring, however, involves reciprocity in role relations not found in other teaching/learning situations, and herein must lie some of its unique potential for the tutee. All in all, this recent work shows that conglomerate interventions in peer interaction are reasonable alternatives to "pure" techniques for promoting social competence.

Non-programmed interventions

In 1935, Helen L. Koch gave a paper at the annual meeting of the American Psychological Association (Koch, 1935) evaluating an attempt to improve experimentally the attitudes and practices of "distinctly unsocial children." Seven unsocial children were selected for treatment, along with seven others who were studied as matched controls. For 30 minutes every day for 20 days, each "experimental" child was removed from the nursery along with one sociable child and surrounded by play materials thought to stimulate cooperative play. The members of the pairs were thrown together as much as possible. Observations were conducted when the children had been returned to the nursery school to establish the time spent in cooperative play, the frequency of conflict, and amount of conversation. The published report is sketchy, but "changes in the direction of increased sociability were cumulative throughout the investigation" (as reported by Page, 1936).

In 1972, Harlow and his colleague Suomi published a protocol for reducing the effects of social isolation in young rhesus monkeys (Suomi and Harlow, 1972). Over the years, Harlow and his colleagues tried many different methods for rehabilitating these socially withdrawn animals but with little success; interaction with neither adult animals nor agemates would restore social competence in the isolates. But, using four experimental animals that had spent their first six months in isolation, the investigators tried a new intervention: successive exposure to normal infant monkeys who were only three months old (three months younger than the subject). The results were astounding. Self-stimulation, huddling, and other isolate behaviors declined; locomotion and exploration increased; social contacts and social play emerged. Replication work (Novak and Harlow, 1975) involving animals whose isolation extended over 12 months also showed that social competencies could be established by means of cross-age techniques. The model invented by Koch (1935) thus is an effective primate model generally, but with one exception: the most productive interaction for the social isolate may involve not agemates but younger individuals.

Mixed-age social interaction differs qualitatively and quantitatively from same-age interaction (cf. Lougee, Grueneich, and Hartup, in press) and much of children's socialization occurs in mixed-age rather than same-age situations (cf. Konner, 1975). Does play with younger children have the same kind of therapeutic potential for a socially isolated human child that it has for the socially debilitated rhesus monkey? Can a protocol be devised that demonstrates the efficacy of this intervention strategy in human development? Using double-blind procedures and an appropriate control group, we have studied the effectiveness of the Wisconsin intervention with 24 socially withdrawn children (Furman, Rahe, and Hartup, in preparation). The children were located in five day-care centers and were identified on the basis of observations conducted over two weeks. Our subjects may be described as noninteractive and resemble, in some respects, children to whom labels like socially withdrawn, socially isolated, or nonsociable are attached. They may not be described as autistic or disturbed. In fact, we doubt that they constitute any kind of diagnostic group, although no information on home backgrounds or life histories is available to verify this. In all cases, they were observed to engage in social interaction in less than one-third of the observation periods conducted on each of them.

The intervention for eight children consisted of participation in 15 daily play sessions with another child who was 18 months younger than the subject. For another eight children, the intervention involved playing with another child who was within four months of the subject's own age. The remaining eight children received no treatment. The center personnel did not know which children were selected for the research or their experimental assignment, nor did the members of the research staff who conducted the post-session observations. Preliminary analyses show significant improvement in sociability by the children in both experimental groups, but greater improvement among those with younger "therapists" than among those with same-age "therapists." No change occurred among the children in the control condition. Longer-term follow-ups of these children have been conducted, but results are not available. Even now, however, our results indicate that nonprogrammed interaction with younger children promotes social competence in ways that do not duplicate the effects of experiences with agemates.

CONCLUSION

Social competencies derive from the child's interactions with other children as well as from family interaction. Good adjustment to the peer culture is facilitated by good family adjustment, but the contributions to socialization made through peer interaction are unique. Aggressive socialization, sex-role learning, affective adaptation, and moral development would be incomplete in the absence of experience with other children.

Both programmed and nonprogrammed strategies are available for the promotion of social competence. Intervention must begin during early childhood and entails complex processes, accompanied by many evaluative and management decisions. But the literature provides good guidelines for utilizing children as both formal and informal agents in their own socialization. No program in the primary prevention of psychopathology is complete without close evaluation of peer interaction in relation to the individual child and without sensitive planning based on these evaluations.

REFERENCES

Allen, K. E., Hart, B. M., Buell, J. S., Harris, F. R., and Wolf, M. M. Effects of social reinforcement on isolate behavior of a nursery school child. *Child Development*, 1964, *35*, 511–518.

Allen, V. L. (Ed.). *Children as teachers*. New York: Academic Press, 1976.

Allen, V. L., and Feldman, R. S. Studies on the role of tutor. In V. L. Allen (Ed.), *Children as teachers*. New York: Academic Press, 1976.

Baer, D. M., and Wolf, M. M. Recent examples of behavior modification in preschool settings. In C. Neuringer and J. L. Michael (Eds.), *Behavior modification in clinical psychology*. New York: Appleton-Century-Crofts, 1970.

Bandura, A. Social-learning theory of identificatory processes. In D. A. Goslin (Ed.), *Handbook of Socialization Theory and Research*. Chicago: Rand McNally, 1969.

Bandura, A., Grusec, J. E., and Menlove, F. L. Vicarious extinction of avoidance behavior. *Journal of Personality and Social Psychology*, 1967, *5*, 16–23.

Baumrind, D. Child care practices anteceding three patterns of preschool behavior. *Genetic Psychology Monographs*, 1967, *75*, 43–88.

Bronson, W. C. Central orientations: A study of behavior organization from childhood to adolescence. *Child Development*, 1966, *37*, 125–155.

Chittenden, G. E. An experimental study of measuring and modifying assertive behavior in young children. *Monographs of the Society for Research in Child Development*, 1942, *7*, (1).

Cowen, E. L., Pederson, A., Babijian, H., Izzo, L. D., and Trost, M. A. Long-term follow-up of early detected vulnerable children. *Journal of Consulting and Clinical Psychology*, 1973, *41*, 438–446.

Debus, R. L. Effects of brief observation of model behavior on conceptual tempo of impulsive children. *Developmental Psychology*, 1970, *2*, 22–32.

Dolhinow, P. J., and Bishop, N. The development of motor skills and social relationships among primates through play. In J. P. Hill (Ed.), *Minnesota Symposia on Child Psychology*. Vol. 4. Minneapolis: University of Minnesota Press, 1970.

Eckerman, C. O. The human infant in social interaction. In R. B. Cairns (Ed.). Social interaction: methods, analysis, and illustrations. *Monographs of the Society for Research in Child Development*, in press.

Eckerman, C. O., Whatley, J. L., and Kutz, S. L. The growth of social play with peers during the second year of life. *Developmental Psychology*, 1975, *11*, 42–49.

Freud, A., and Dann, S. An experiment in group upbringing. In R. Eisler et al. (Eds.), *The psychoanalytic study of the child*. Vol. 6. New York: International Universities Press, 1951.

Freud, S. *Introductory lectures on psychoanalysis. The standard edition of the complete psychological works of Sigmund Freud*. Vol. XVI. London: Hogarth Press, 1963.

Furman, W., Rahe, D., and Hartup, W. W. Social rehabilitation of low-interactive preschool children by peer intervention. Minneapolis: University of Minnesota, in preparation.

Gewirtz, J. L. A learning analysis of the effects of normal stimulation, privation and deprivation on the acquisition of social motivation and attachment. In B. M. Foss (Ed.), *Determinants of infant behaviour*. Vol 1. London: Methuen, 1961.

Gold, H. A. The importance of ideology in sociometric evaluation of leadership. *Group Psychotherapy*, 1962, *15*, 224–230.

Gottman, J., Gonso, J., and Rasmussen, B. Social interaction, social competence, and friendship in children. *Child Development*, 1975, *45*, 709–718.

Gottman, J., Gonso, J., and Schuler, P. Teaching social skills to isolated children. *Journal of Abnormal Child Psychology*, 1976, *4*, 179–197.

Grosser, D., Polansky, N., and Lippitt, R. A. A laboratory study of behavioral contagion. *Human Relations*, 1951, *4*, 115–142.

Harlow, H. F. Age-mate or peer affectional system. In D. S. Lehrman, R. A. Hinde, and E. Shaw (Eds.), *Advances in the study of behavior*. Vol. 2. New York: Academic Press, 1969.

Harris, F. R., Wolf, M. M., and Baer, D. M. Effects of adult social reinforcement on child behavior. In W. W. Hartup and N. L. Smothergill (Eds.), *The young child: Reviews of research*. Washington: National Association for the Education of Young Children, 1967.

Hartup, W. W. Peer interaction and social organization. In P. H. Mussen (Ed.), *Carmichael's manual of child psychology*. Vol. 2, New York: John Wiley, 1970.

Hartup, W. W. Peer interaction and the behavioral development of the individual child. In E. Schopler and R. J. Reichler (Eds.), *Psychopathology and child development*. New York: Plenum, 1976.

Hartup, W. W., and Coates, B. Imitation of peers as a function of reinforcement from the peer group and rewardingness of the model. *Child Development*, 1967, *38*, 1003–1016.

Heathers, G. Emotional dependence and independence in nursery school play. *Journal of Genetic Psychology*, 1955, *87*, 37–57.

Jack, L. M. An experimental study of ascendant behavior in preschool children. *University of Iowa Studies in Child Welfare*, 1934, *9*, No. 3.

Keasey, C. B. Social participation as a factor in the moral development of preadolescents. *Developmental Psychology*, 1971, *5*, 216–220.

Kinsey, A. C., Pomeroy, W. B., and Martin, C. E. *Sexual behavior in the human male.* Philadelphia: W. B. Saunders, 1948.

Kobasigawa, A. Inhibitory and disinhibitory effects of models on sex-inappropriate behavior in children. *Psychologia*, 1968, *11*, 86–96.

Koch, H. L. The modification of unsocialness in preschool children. *Psychological Bulletin*, 1935, *32*, 700–701.

Konner, M. Relations among infants and juveniles in comparative perspective. In M. Lewis and L. A. Rosenblum (Eds.), *Friendship and peer relations.* New York: Wiley and Sons, 1975.

Lieberman, A. F. The social competence of preschool children: Its relation to quality of attachment and to amount of exposure to peers in different preschool settings. Unpublished doctoral dissertation, The Johns Hopkins University, 1976.

Lougee, M. D., Grueneich, R., and Hartup, W. W. Social interaction in same- and mixed-age dyads of preschool children. *Child Development*, in press.

Novak, M. A., and Harlow, H. F. Social recovery of monkeys isolated for the first year of life. 1. Rehabilitation and therapy. *Developmental Psychology*, 1975, *11*, 453–465.

O'Connor, R. D. Modification of social withdrawal through symbolic modeling. *Journal of Applied Behavior Analysis*, 1969, *2*, 15–22.

O'Connor, R. D. Relative efficacy of modeling, shaping, and the combined procedures for modification of social withdrawal. *Journal of Abnormal Psychology*, 1972, *79*, 327–334.

Oden, S. L., and Asher, S. R. Coaching children in social skills for friendship making. *Child Development*, 1977, *48*, 495–506.

Page, M. L. The modification of ascendant behavior in preschool children. *University of Iowa Studies in Child Welfare*, 1936, *12*, No. 3.

Piaget, J. *The moral judgment of the child.* Glencoe, Ill.: The Free Press, 1932.

Piaget, J. *Play, dreams, and imitation in childhood.* New York: W. W. Norton, 1951.

Roff, M. Childhood social interactions and young adult bad conduct. *Journal of Abnormal and Social Psychology*, 1961, *63*, 333–337.

Roff, M., Sells, S. B., and Golden, M. M. *Social adjustment and personality development in children.* Minneapolis: University of Minnesota Press, 1972.

Rolf, J. E. The social and academic competence of children vulnerable to schizophrenia and other behavior pathologies. *Journal of Abnormal Psychology*, 1972, *80*, 225–243.

Rosenthal, M. K. The effect of a novel situation and of anxiety on two groups of dependency behaviors. *British Journal of Psychology*, 1967, *8*, 357–364.

Scott, P. M., Burton, R. V., and Yarrow, M. R. Social reinforcement under natural conditions. *Child Development*, 1967, *28*, 53–63.

Solomon, R. W., and Wahler, R. G. Peer reinforcement control of classroom problem behavior. *Journal of Applied Behavior Analysis*, 1973, *6*, 49–56.

Suomi, S. J., and Harlow, H. F. Social rehabilitation of isolate-reared monkeys. *Developmental Psychology*, 1972, *6*, 487–496.

Wahler, R. G. Child-child interactions in five field settings: Some experimental analyses. *Journal of Experimental Child Psychology*, 1967, *5*, 278–293.

Winder, C. L., and Rau, L. Parental attitudes associated with social deviance in preadolescent boys. *Journal of Abnormal and Social Psychology*, 1962, *64*, 418–424.

Whiting, B. B., and Whiting, J. W. M. *Children of six cultures: A psychocultural analysis.* Cambridge: Harvard University Press, 1975.

Zahavi, S. Aggression control. Unpublished master's thesis, University of Illinois, 1973.

The Empty Nest: Beginning or Ending?

Lillian B. Rubin

For many years, we have been hearing of the *empty-nest syndrome*—a package of depressive pathology that supposedly afflicts middle-aged women when their children leave the family fold (Bart, 1968, 1970, 1971; Curlee, 1969; Deykin, Jacobson, Klerman, and Solomon, 1966; Harkins and House, 1975; Jacobson and Klerman, 1966; Powell, 1977; Spence and Lonner, 1971; Weissman, Pincus, Radding, Lawrence, and Siegel, 1973; Weissman and Paykel, 1974). Until quite recently, this stage of women's lives was the province of clinicians. If a woman became depressed after her children left home, the relationship was assumed to be one of cause and effect. Children's leave-taking, they said, causes depression, a particular kind of depression that even warranted its own name. The empty-nest syndrome, they called it. Nothing to worry about, they assured us. It is a loss like any other. And as with any loss, the normal processes of grief and mourning would produce their healing effect. Sometimes the healing did not come. Instead the women were characterized as neurotic—pathological in their inability to separate from their children, in their incapacity to manage internal conflict without breakdown. Even then few questioned the theory.

There are some notable exceptions in the work of Deutscher (1969) and Neugarten (1968a, 1968b, 1974), Neugarten, Wood, Kraines, and Loomis (1968), and Neugarten and Datan (1974). Over a decade ago they showed that most women accept the departure of their children with equanimity, if not relief. But

The material presented here is taken from the author's book, *Women of a Certain Age: The Midlife Search for Self* (New York: Harper and Row, 1979). It is based on research supported by the Behavioral Sciences Research Division, National Institute of Mental Health, Grant No. MH 28167.

these findings were paid scant attention, probably because they flew in the face of established stereotypes and preconceptions. As recently as 1974 Neugarten noted that regardless of what the stereotype indicates, in reality we do not hear women mourning the loss of their role as mother, or their reproductive capacity. Yet, so pervasive are notions about the empty-nest depression that researchers continue to express doubt about their own findings when their data contradict the preconception. Thus Glenn (1975) found that women in the postparental stage reported greater marital happiness than those who were in the parental stage, but tempered his conclusion with the caution that "the empty-nest syndrome may still be prevalent enough to warrent concern." And Lowenthal, Thurnher, and Chiriboga (1975) heard the women they interviewed say they were looking forward to the children's departure, and concluded that their anxiety and despair about the empty-nest was too deep to be tapped by their interviews.

As consciousness heightened about the nature of the life problems that women face, as more women moved into the social sciences, where such theories are born, the empty nest depression underwent a reinterpretation. Now the pathology was located not in the woman, but in the system of social roles and arrangements that makes it always difficult, sometimes impossible, for a mother to develop an identity that rests on alternative roles.

An important shift in understanding this, but not yet enough, for these new formulations still rest on the same unspoken assumptions as the old ones—assumptions that depression in mid-life women is linked to the departure of their children, that it is the loss of the mothering role that *produces* the sadness and despair. Like the old ideas, these new ones too often take as given the belief that a woman is little more than the builder of the nest and the nurturer of the young, that her reason for being is in that nesting and nurturing function.

Bart (1968, 1969, 1970, 1971) is an important exception to these comments. Her pioneering work offers a complex and subtle analysis of social role which few of those who followed her have matched.

Think about the language we unquestioningly use to characterize this period of life: *the empty nest*. Not the *awakening*, not the *emergence*, not words that might suggest that inside that house all those years there lived someone besides a mother. No, we say the *empty nest*. And think, too, about the associations of those words. When we hear the phrase *empty nest*, we do not think of a father, because the "nest" is so intimately associated with mother that it is difficult to separate the two. Indeed, the very words "empty nest" conjure up a vision of a lonely, depressed woman clinging pathetically and inappropriately to a lost past—a woman who has lived for and through her children, a woman incapable of either conceiving or desiring a "room of her own."

That is the stereotype that permeates the culture, dominates our image of women at midlife. It is so consonant with our view of Woman-as-Mother—a view so widely shared and, until recently, so unconsciously held—that the phrase *empty-nest syndrome* has slipped into the language as if it speaks to an enternal and unvarying truth. What we have failed to notice, however, is that most of the ideas we have about depression in midlife women come from research done on hospitalized patients (Bart, 1968; Deykin, Jacobson, Klerman, and Solomon, 1966; Jacobson and Klerman, 1966; Weissman and Paykel, 1974).

Over the last few years other investigators have begun to suggest that in fact the departure of the children brings both an increase in marital satisfaction for women and an increased sense of well-being (Fuchs, 1977; Glenn, 1975; Lowenthal, Thurnher, and Chiriboga, 1975; Lowenthal and Weiss, 1976; Maas and Kuypers, 1975; Sales, 1977). These new research findings have received relatively little attention compared to the old ones, which are closer to the myth and stereotype about the nature of woman and the naturalness of motherhood.

Does this sad creature of the stereotype exist in the larger world where women live their lives and dream their dreams? This was one of the questions I brought to my study of midlife women. I wanted to know how women handle the midlife transition—how they respond to the end of their active mothering years, whether this life stage catches them unaware, as so much writing suggests, or whether, in fact, the process of living, growing, changing itself provides some preparation even if not consciously planned.

To this end I conducted intensive, in-depth, focused interviews with 160 women whose average age was 46.5 years—women who were or had been married, had borne and raised children, and (except for ten) had none under thirteen years old left in the home. They were and are women whose class backgrounds range from working class to professional upper-middle class. But they share in common the fact that they all gave up whatever jobs or careers they may have had in their youth to devote themselves to full-time mothering and housewifery for at least ten years after the first child was born.

Currently, almost half work in paid jobs outside their homes. Most are secretaries, clerks, receptionists; a few are factory workers, a few professionals. Of the rest, about a quarter are heavily committed volunteers, fewer than 15 percent have returned to school to prepare for a career, and most—well over half—call themselves "homemakers."

All have children in varying stages of leaving the nest. For some, the children have all been gone for a few years, and for others, only several months. A few still have one or more children living at home, but most can anticipate their departure within the next year or two.

It is true that some are sad, some lonely, some even depressed. It is true also that some are hesitant, some are unconfident, and most are frightened as they face an uncertain future. But except for one, none suffers the classical symptoms of the empty-nest syndrome (Bart, 1968, 1970, 1971; Deykin et al., 1966; Jacobson and Klerman, 1966). Those symptoms are a profound clinical depression, usually characterized by several serious psychiatric symptoms, such as deep sadness and despair; sleeplessness; loss of appetite; loss of sexual desire; retardation of initiative, thinking, and motor abilities; severely low self-esteem and self-confidence; little or no interest in daily life and ordinary affairs; an incapacity to experience pleasure or joy; and an inability to engage in anything that requires sustained effort or attention.

Certainly, there are differences among them—differences related to how long the children have been gone or whether they are yet gone (Harkins and House, 1975), differences related to how successfully a woman feels she handled the tasks of mothering, how she feels about her adult children (Spence and Lonner, 1971); differences related to how a woman has lived her life until this period, how she has prepared for the transition, how she feels about her marriage—or her divorce—as the case may be (Powell, 1977). Important differences, these, which merit attention and

392   LILLIAN B. RUBIN

examination. But underlying all those differences is a more important similarity. *Almost all the women I spoke with respond to the departure of their children—whether actual or impending—with a decided sense of relief.*

Among those whose children are already gone, almost every one is unequivocal in those feelings:

> I can't tell you what a relief it was to find myself with an empty nest. Oh sure, when the last child went away to school, for the first day or so there was a kind of a throb, but believe me, it was only a day or two.

Even those most committed to the traditional homemaker role—women who have never worked outside the home in the past and do not intend to in the future—speak in the same vein:

> When the youngest one was ready to move out of the house, I was right there helping him pack. We love having the children live in the area, and we love seeing them and the grandchildren, but I don't need for any of them to live in this house ever again. *I've had as much as I ever need or want of being tied down with children.*

A few—generally those who are a little closer to the time of the transition—are more ambivalent:

> It's complicated; it doesn't just feel one way or the other. I guess it's rather a bittersweet thing. It's not that it's either good or bad, it's just that it's an era that's coming to an end and, in many ways, it was a nice era. So there's some sadness in it, and I guess I feel a little lost sometimes. But it's no big thing; it comes and goes.

Even women who have not yet watched a child leave home speak with hunger of their readiness to turn their attention to their own lives:

> From the day the kids are born, if it's not one thing, it's another. After all these years of being responsible for them, you finally get to the point where you want to scream, "Fall out of the nest already, you guys, will you? It's time." It's as if I want to take myself back after all these years—to give me back to me, if you know what I mean. Of course, that's providing there's any "me" left.

But what about women who are divorced? Although just over 20 percent of the women in this study are divorced, see Rubin (1979) for more detailed discussion of divorced women at this stage of the life cycle. Would not women who have no husbands around to claim their attention—perhaps no prospect of marriage in sight—find the departure of the children more troubling? Surprisingly, the answer is *no*. For whatever the problems divorced women suffer, the departure of the children is not high among them. Like their married sisters, they are relieved to be freed of the responsibilities of mothering, glad to be able to call their lives their own:

> I thought it would be hard when they left, but it's not. I was talking to a friend about it just yesterday, and she said, "Why should it make a difference if the kids are home or not? They don't warm up the bed."

Are there no women, then, who experience feelings of loss at their children's departure, none who feels the grief and sadness that inevitably accompanies such loss? Of course there are. Most women do. But there is wide variation in the duration of those feelings—some speaking of days, or weeks, much more seldom of months. And whatever the intensity of the feelings, they rarely devastate women, rarely leave them depressed and barely functional.

Sometimes the leave-taking is more problematic for working-class than for middle-class mothers (Bart, 1968, 1971; Weissman and Paykel, 1974; Weissman, Pincus, Radding, Lawrence, and Siegel, 1973). But notice first the word "sometimes." And notice also that this says nothing about depression. In fact, in those instances where such problems exist for working-class women, they are almost always short-term and of limited intensity. Still, there *is* a difference—a difference related to the *process* by which the children of each class generally leave home.

Almost from birth, most middle-class parents know when the big break from the family will come—at eighteen, when the child leaves for college. There is plenty of warning, plenty of time to get ready. But in working-class families, college attendance is not taken for granted—often these days it is not even desired (Rubin, 1972)—and children are expected to live at home until they marry. Indeed, even among those working-class girls and boys who are

394   LILLIAN B. RUBIN

college bound, most know they will live at home during those years—both because it is part of the family expectations, and because generally they cannot afford to do otherwise (Rubin, 1976). Because the age of marriage is not clearly fixed, the time of departure is also indefinite, for both parents and children—somewhat like living with an indeterminate prison sentence rather than a firm release date that has been agreed upon and understood by all. That difference alone, the unpredictability of the departure date, makes preparation for separation more difficult in working-class families. Indeed, often middle-class mothers speak of the child's senior year in high school as the year in which much of the separation work was done—what sociologists call "anticipatory socialization."

> By the time my daughter left for college, I had already dealt with the issues. From time to time in her senior year in high school, I'd get a pang thinking about what was coming. I must admit, though, that by the time it actually happened, even I was surprised at how easy it was. I guess I had just grown accustomed to the idea by then.

But for the working-class woman there is no such clear marker, no date known years in advance when she can expect a child's departure. For her, therefore, preparation is different, separation perhaps more difficult for some brief period of time. Almost always the difficulty *is* brief, however, and it surely does not approach anything that could rightfully be called a depression.

In fact, regardless of class, those who suffer most are women who are disappointed in their children, whose relationships with them are unsatisfactory, whose disapproval of their life style makes the relationship difficult and tenuous, at least for the moment. Those are the most difficult times for a mother—the times when she looks inside herself and thinks, "It didn't work out the way I planned." Partly, that is because it is almost impossible for a mother to experience that disappointment in her children without blaming herself. After all, if her main task in life is to raise the children and it does not come out right according to her standards, whom else can she blame? Indeed, who else will be blamed? (Abramowitz, 1977; Bernard, 1975; Rich, 1976). On the other hand, Bart (1967, 1971) suggests that whether mothers have satisfactory or unsatisfactory relationships with their children makes little difference in their adjustment and suffering at the time of the children's departure. The difference between us may be due to the fact that the women she studied were hospitalized patients suffering a severe clinical depression, while the women I talked to were coping well and functioning normally. In a recent telephone conversation with Bart, she suggested that the changed cultural context—that is, the difference between the experience of being a midlife woman in the 1960's and the 1970's, after the changes wrought by the women's movement—could also be a factor in accounting for the differences in our findings about the prevalence of the empty-nest depression. Although this is reasonable speculation, it is not convincing, since it does not take into account that even in the 1960's research findings challenged the belief in the empty-nest syndrome.

I lie awake many a night wondering what I did wrong that my daughter lives the way she does—the dope and the living together, and all that kind of thing. I don't know; I couldn't stop her. God knows, I tried. I try to tell myself it's a different world and it's not my fault. But it's hard to believe that. It just feels like I failed at my job.

It may not be reasonable that women shoulder that burden. There are, after all, fathers who, by their absence if not by their presence, must take some responsibility for how their children grow and develop, for what kinds of adults they become. And there is a society outside the family with which children interact from very early childhood—schools, classmates, peer groups, each with a culture that helps to shape and mold its members. Yet from all sides the finger of blame is pointed at mothers—blame that, until now, they have accepted and internalized unquestioningly.

But there is more than pressure from external sources, there is more involved than blame and its companion, guilt. When most midlife women became mothers, they aborted their own hopes and dreams and invested them in their children—an investment whose costs lie heavily on both mothers and children, since it asks nothing less than that the child validate the mother's life.

My only career has been my children. If I can't find success in raising them, then what? Where am I going to look for any sense of pride or fulfillment? There's nothing else I've done that I can judge myself by. My husband has his career, and he finds success and fulfillment in that. He's proven himself someplace, so he doesn't feel the disappointment the way I do. For me, it's the only thing I tried to do, and I failed. You know, when you look at your children and see that they're not going to be what you dreamed, when those fantasies and illusions go out the window, it's hell.

"My only career has been my children"—words that suggest that if a woman has another "career," she can more easily tolerate the disappointement of her dreams for her children, that it will not be such "hell." And if it is possible to measure hell, that is probably true. Women who have work from which they get substantial independent gratification *can* more easily avoid the pain by burying themselves in this work. They have other things to think about, other ways of relating to the world and to themselves. They have at least the beginning of another identity, an emerging sense of their own separateness. That developing identity may not yet stand firmly, but its existence alone is enough to make a difference. It is demonstrable proof that a self lives apart from the children, clear evidence that a future exists.

Important though it may be, however, who suffers more from such disappointments and who less is not the central issue here. The question is: How do women handle the departure of their children under these circumstances? The answer: With pain, but also with relief:

It hurts that he's gone because things are terrible between us now, and he doesn't come around much any more. But, I don't know, I think it's better since he's gone. It's a relief, you know, not to have to see him every day. Oh, I don't know. What can I say? It hurts not to see him, but it hurts more to see him and be reminded.

She is relieved that he has gone—glad not to be burdened by his presence, not to be reminded daily of her pain. But it hurts, too—hurts because even though he is not there, she cannot help remembering, cannot help believing she failed, cannot help reflecting on the past with regret, cannot help wondering how it could have been otherwise.

There is something else. Those memories, those questions, mean also that the separation from the child is more difficult than usual, because she is stuck with feelings of incompletion— with the sense that one of life's tasks is not finished, yet is now outside her control. It is akin to dealing with the death of a parent with whom conflicts remain unresolved. Even though the departing child is not dead, the psychological experience of the loss can be the same; the last chance to heal the divisions, the last chance to make peace. The departure of a child with whom there is conflict means that the loss is experienced even more keenly, and the grief is more difficult to manage and work through.

With all this—whatever the disappointments, the sense of failure, the loss, whatever the time span of the suffering or the intensity of the pain—one thing is certain: The women I met are not debilitated by it. Indeed, they cope quite well with what- ever feelings of failure, disappointment, and loss they may suffer, for alongside them, there exists another, at least equally powerful set of feelings which helps to neutralize the pain. Alongside them there is the longing for freedom, the wish to find and claim a well defined and differentiated self, and the belief that finally this may be possible. These are the feelings which dominate the transition period and beyond, a struggle that engages women perhaps for the rest of their lives. "If it's hard now, it's because I don't know what I'll be doing, not because the children are gone. Their going is a blessing; it's time. But I'm scared."

How then can we account for the persistence of the myth that inside the empty nest lives a shattered and depressed shell of a woman—a woman in constant pain because her children have left her roof? Is it possible that a notion so pervasive is, in fact, just a myth? No simple questions, these; and no easy answers, for they touch the deepest layers of social structure and person- ality, and the interconnections between the two.

To start, let us grant that, as with all stereotypes, there is a kernel of truth in this one. The midlife transition is, in fact, difficult for most women—a time often filled with turmoil and self-doubt, a time when old roles are being shed and the shape of new ones are not yet apparent; a time of reordering long-held priorities, of restructuring daily life. From that small truth, however, has grown a fabrication based on the one-sided and distorted view of women and womanhood; a view that insists that womanhood and motherhood are synonymous, that motherhood is a woman's ineluctable destiny, her sacred calling, her singular area of fulfillment. Until recently (Bernard, 1975; Easton, 1976; Lazarre, 1976; McBride, 1973; Rich, 1976; Wortis, 1974), this view has remained largely unchallenged—one of the accepted verities on which our social and economic system is built. Man worked outside the home, woman inside. Her biological destiny was to nurture, his to provide the safety within which she could do it.

Never mind that it did not really work that way, that the ideology and the structure of the economy are at odds. Never mind that most men in this society cannot provide that safety, not because they do not want to or are lacking in skills, but because there are not enough jobs. Never mind that even where jobs exist, most do not pay enough to ensure much safety for the family. Never mind that poor women have always had to work, or that among married women with children under six years old, well over one third now work outside the home— most of them because of economic necessity. Never mind that this represents a threefold increase over the last two and a half decades, and continues to rise as inflation pushes the cost of living even higher. The myth lives—a kind of cultural conspiracy that blinds us all to such realities.

That myth—the image of the madonna-mother—has prevented us from knowing that just as men are more than fathers, women are more than mothers. It has kept us from hearing their voices when they try to tell us of other aspirations, other needs; kept us from believing that they share with men the desire for achievement, mastery, competence—the desire to do something for *themselves* (Baruch, 1976; Laws, 1976). It has aided and abetted the distortion of feminine consciousness—a distortion that makes it difficult, indeed, for women to accept and acknowledge their inner experience, whether in relation to their own aspirations or to their feelings about the end of their active mothering years. "I felt terrible when I didn't feel bad enough when the last of my children left. I'd walk around wondering 'What kind of mother are you?' "

But even when a woman can say clearly that she is glad it is over, rarely can she let the statement stand without qualification or equivocation. Instead, she covers it at once with some "evidence" that she really is a good and loving mother: "I mean, I really love them. You know, I gave them my life for all those years. And I miss them, too; I really do."

Why the hasty retreat? Partly, it is because she is concerned about the impact of her words on her listener. More importantly, it is because the acknowledgment of those sentiments—the act of speaking them aloud—activates her own guilt and discomfort, violates her own expectations about how a good mother should feel. Still, the relief is so powerfully felt that she cannot help adding with a self-conscious smile and a self-deprecating air— a manner suggesting that *these* words about to be spoken are not to be taken too seriously: "It's just that it's nice to have the house to ourselves."

By such comments we can come to understand a woman's yearning to comprehend the totality of the experience of motherhood and the profound ways in which it colors daily life. By such comments we come to know something of the things she holds dear. Yet because they are so incongruent with the set of expectations we bring to the situation, these are the very words we too often fail to hear; these are the words whose real meaning eludes us.

Often enough, as well, we are not told. It is difficult to speak of such feelings in the face of the myth. Often they are repressed and denied long before they ever surface into consciousness. When that does not work, the guilt that attends them can be excruciating, and the fear of being found deficient—"unnatural"—is felt keenly enough to still the tongue. A 51-year-old mother whose last child had left home a year before speaks compellingly about just those fears:

I sometimes worried that I was unnatural, so I didn't really like to talk about it. You know, when you hear all around you that women are pining for their children, you feel as if there's something wrong with you—that you're not a natural mother—if you don't.

What do women mean by "natural mother"? Why is it that about one fourth of the women I met admitted guiltily, almost fearfully, that they do not consider themselves "natural mothers," do not feel that they were "made for motherhood"?

Perhaps because the ideal we all hold is anything but "natural." In our minds lives the madonna-image—the all-embracing, all-giving tranquil mother of a Raphael painting—one child at her breast, another at her feet; a woman fulfilled, one who asks nothing more than to nurture and nourish. This creature of fantasy is the model—the unattainable ideal against which women measure not only their performance but their feelings about being mothers. Who, under those circumstances, is "made for mother-hood"? And who, under those circumstances, can acknowledge—let alone speak easily—of her real feelings?

Everyone knows there is more talk now about such issues, more public discussion, more critical examination of long-cher-ished ways of thinking about women and femininity. If the new feminist movement has done nothing else, it has raised these issues and forced us into a national dialogue about them. And, indeed, often enough women now say that they know others who feel relief at the departure of the children. But whether speaking of self or friends, rarely is it said without some sign of distress. Always there is the sense that perhaps it is true that other women share these feelings, but no one can be quite certain that it is right. Thus, when discussing the subject, women often look about uncertainly, lower their voices, and generally give signals of discomfort—as if they fear being overheard. Typical is a forty-five year-old who leaned forward in her chair as if to bestow an important confidence, dropped her voice to just above a whisper, and said:

> To tell you the truth, most of the time it's a big relief to be free of them, finally. I suppose that's awful to say. But you know what, most of the women I know feel the same way. It's just that they're uncomfortable saying it because there's all this talk about how sad mothers are supposed to be when the kids leave home.

"Most of the women I know feel the same way." How is it, then, that this woman, like so many others, does not really know what she knows? Why the discomfort with her own feelings? Why the guilt? Some women respond to those questions by denying the reality of what they hear: "Well, people say that now because, you know, women aren't supposed to be such gung-ho mothers any more. We're supposed to be liberated and all that stuff." Others simply label themselves and their friends as deviant or aberrant, assuming that the rest of the world is different:

> I don't think my friends are typical or representative, or anything like that. I think most women still are in very traditional places, and most women really do miss their children terribly when they go. It's as if their lives just end. I'm different, and so are my friends. That's because I picked them, I suppose.

All this suggests the enormous complexity of interaction between cultural expectations, their internalization, and personal experience. For what I have been saying is that, at one level, it is no big news to women who live it that the empty-nest syndrome does not exist for most of them. At another level, however, they are so mystified by the ideology of motherhood that they deny their own inner experience as well as the evidence their eyes and ears bring to them from the outer world.

It should come as no surprise to anyone that the end of the active mothering function is greeted with relief. Only someone who has never been a mother would fail to understand how awesome are the demands of motherhood as they are currently defined in our culture—demands and obligations that, for most women, are rooted deeply enough to color not only their living in peace but their prospects for dying in peace:

> Maybe you'll think I'm crazy, but when they were younger, I used to worry about what would happen if I died. Don't misunderstand me, I'm not ready to die. But if I have to die now, at least I can go knowing my kids could tolerate it, and that they don't really need me any more. *What a relief to know that!* It would be a tragedy, wouldn't it, to be a mother and die before you thought your kids were ready?

A tragedy? Perhaps. But at least equally tragic is the burden she carries. One might ask: What is so special about *her* burden? Do fathers not also feel keenly their parental responsibilities? We all know men, after all, who are encumbered with the need to plan for death as well as for life—men who struggle not only to make a living today, but to provide for tomorrow as well. Insurance companies grow rich as they offer to protect against just those fears—fears that are the price men pay for their unquestioning acceptance of the present division of labor in the family. With a wife and children wholly, or even largely, dependent upon him, a man works all his life partly, at least, to ensure their support when he dies. And that, of course, is the crucial difference. A mother fears leaving her children before they are emotionally ready, a father before they are financially ready.

This is not to suggest that mothers feel more deeply about their children than fathers, nor that the differences in their responses—the nature of their concerns—belong to natural differences between women and men. There is nothing natural about mothers being caregivers and fathers being money-givers. Rather, these are social arrangements—both women and men responding to long-established, socially defined roles and functions within the family. As a consequence of this family structure, however, a father can feel he has fulfilled his responsibility if he leaves enough dollars behind him. But what replaces a mother? What can she plan to leave behind to help her children until they become emotionally independent adults?

They carry with them heavy costs, these social arrangements—burdening both women and men in painful, if different ways. Mothers suffer when they bear the burdens of child-rearing alone, it is true. But the reward is an intimate connection with their children. And fathers? Contrary to all we hear about women and their empty-nest problems, it may be fathers more often than mothers who are pained by the children's imminent or actual departure—fathers who want to keep the children in the home for just a little longer:

For me, it's enough! They've been here long enough—maybe too long. It's a funny thing, though. All these years, Fred was too busy to have much time for the kids, and now he's the one who's depressed because they're leaving. He's really having trouble letting go. He wants to gather them around and keep them right here in this house.

Another, 48 years old, whose first child was married a year before we met, says:

My son's marriage was very hard on my husband—very hard on him. He was terribly upset. I was so shocked, I could hardly believe it. She's a beautiful girl and we both love her, so it wasn't that. I couldn't figure it out for a long time, but after a couple of months, we finally talked it out. It turned out he was suffering because he felt like it was the end of our little family. He felt terrible because it would never be the same again. He doesn't say much about it any more, but I can just tell it's still hard for him. My daughter is going with a very nice young man now, and it's quite possible that they'll get married. But Alex ignores it; I mean, it's like he pretends it isn't happening; you know, like if he doesn't look, it'll go away.

Interesting observations, these. And surprising—until I stopped to reflect on the different experiences men and women have in the family in general and in parenting in particular. Then it seemed reasonable that fathers would suffer the loss of children, sometimes even more than mothers. Foremost among those differences, perhaps, is the fact that for mothers the departure of their children comes as the culmination of a developmental sequence, the result of a natural process in which they have participated, rather than a sudden break—a fact that empty-nest theorists generally ignore: "Mother nature had it all figured out. By the time they're ready to go, you're ready to see them go." Indeed, she figured it out well from first separation to last. By the time the ninth month of pregnancy arrives, a woman does not object to birthing the child. She does not suffer from an empty womb, she rejoices in a full crib. This is not to deny the existence of postpartum depression in some women. It simply asserts that no matter how much a woman may enjoy and appreciate the experience of pregnancy, no matter what feelings the separation of the birth may eventually evoke, by the time she has carried a child to term, she is ready to give it up. So it is through all the stages of a child's development. Each stage brings with it some loss, some sadness. Each brings also some joy, some pride, some sense of accomplishment—another step taken, another phase negotiated successfully. And in each there is preparation for the next—an ending, but also a beginning—not alone for the child, but for the mother as well. Children crawl before they walk, walk before they run—each generally a precondition for the other. And with each step they take toward more independence, more mastery of the environment, their mothers take a step away—each a small separation, a small distancing. The child moves from its mother's arms, to the floor, to its own two feet—for mother and child a shared miracle which is, also, a shared separation. By the time a mother sends a little one off to school for the first time, she is ready—a readiness born of the experience of hundreds of such small separations, of her intense involvement in each stage of the child's growth which already foretells the next. For her, then, the preparation for the child's eventual departure is continuous, even if not always experienced consciously, its inevitability long ago etched in her psyche.

I've been thinking a lot about how I'll feel when they go because it seems as if it won't be hard for me. I've been wondering about that, and thinking about whether I'm just kidding myself. But you know, you grow toward it all the time you're raising your children. Where I wasn't ready to lose them a few years ago, I've grown now to where I look forward to it.

It is this developmental process that too often is missed by those who write and speak of the pain of the empty-nest stage— this process which makes it possible for a mother to speak of relief while acknowledging the sadness; this process which suggests that there are no shocks, no surprises, no sudden jolts. Certainly, there are moments of heightened realization, when the knowledge of change in the family is hammered home—a child goes to camp for the first time, an older one to college, another marries. But even these moments of high drama take place in the context of a long and subtle process that usually happens outside the immediate awareness of the people who live it, one they may understand only in retrospect.

Compare this with father's experience in the family. While mother has been feeding, tending, nurturing, teaching, watching, and sharing inside the home, father has been working outside. Sometimes he spends most of this time at work because work is the major emotional commitment in his life, sometimes simply because it is his job to ensure the family's economic stability. More often, it is probably some mix of the two.

But whatever his feelings about his work, he generally spends most of his life at it—most of his emotional and physical energy is spent in the pursuit of economic security for the family. Consequently, he is not there when his children take that first step, or when they come home from school on that first day. He is not there to watch their development, to share their triumphs and pains. Then, one day, it is too late: they are gone—before he had a chance really to know them. For him, indeed, it must seem sudden. For him there is nothing natural about the process because he has not watched it, has not shared in it. One can almost see him passing his hand over his eyes wearily, wondering, "How did it all happen so fast?"

Long ago he had a dim sense of being cheated, a wish to relate more and differently to his children. Long ago he promised himself he would—some day, when he was not so busy, not so tired. But there was never the time or the energy, and he never quite knew how to relate to them, what to say; how to play with them when they were little, how to talk with them as they grew.

Over and over, women—paradoxically, even those married to child psychiatrists and psychologists—tell of being the interpreter between father and children, the buffer, the mediator, the one whose task is to explain each to the other.

I always felt as if I had a foot in two different worlds, as if I was the one who walked across that no-man's land that always seemed to exist between them. Oh, it was better at some times than others; I mean, they were able to talk to each other some of the time. But even at its best, I was always there as mediator and explainer, the one who knew what the other wanted and tried to explain it.

True, women complain a good deal about this: "I *hated* always to have to explain the kids to him. They're his kids too. Why couldn't he take the trouble to get to know them?" And it is true also that, with all their complaints, it is a role they often hold onto because it gives them a sense of power, of mastery in a world where, in fact, they have little:

Was it only that you resented being in that position, or were there elements of it that you also liked?

Well, when I could make it work, I have to admit it could be very satisfying. It's like in a job you set out to do—when it works, it's just fine. You feel challenged and useful and important, as if there's at least one thing you can do that nobody else can. I guess in order to give up that role, you have to know there's something else waiting for you; I mean, you have to know there's something you can do as well.

On the surface it looks like a functional division of labor—both parents get what they want or need at the moment. She gets to feel important; he gets left alone to do his work. But the cost, especially for the father, is high. Just when he has more time, just when the children are old enough to be talked to like real people, just when he is beginning to notice what he has missed—they are gone.

Since mothers usually do not miss any part of the process, the end of active mothering does not come with any sudden wrench. Indeed, for women who can look at their children and think, "There a job well done," the sense of accomplishment transcends any feelings of loss; the relief is unequivocal. For those who suffer disappointment, the relief is mixed with painful feelings of failure. Yet not one of those women yearned for another chance. For good or ill, they were glad the job was done, ready to move on to the next stage of life.

That does not mean there are no problems with this life transition; it means only that the problems are in contemplation of and confrontation with the next stage of life, only that the problems have to do with anxieties about the future, not nostalgia for the past.

Some women talk of fears for the marriage. It has been so long since there were just the two of them, will they know how to relate to each other without the children mediating?

I'm fond of saying, "You start with the husband. Then, the kids are around for a few years. Then, you pick up with the husband again." So intellectually, I feel my first role should be as wife, but when you think of how much time being a mother takes, I know it hasn't been that way. Now, when the last of my kids go, I'm going to have to learn to be a wife again—just a wife. I don't know how graceful I'll be at it; I'm not very practiced.

Will they be able to talk? "It isn't that I want to hold the children here, it's just that I worry about what our life will be like. I don't know what we'll talk about, just the two of us, after all these years."

Alongside those fears there is excitement—each vying with the other as women contemplate an unknown future. For many families, especially those in the working class, there is some financial freedom for the first time in their years together— sometimes for the first time in their life together. That means there are possibilities for adventure, freedom, travel—possibilities that until now existed only in fantasy. And there is more. The departure of the children also means the possibility for the flowering of the marriage relationship in new, even undreamed-of ways, and for the development of a self only hinted at until now. Recall the woman who said: "I want to take myself back after all these years—to give me back to me." And recall, also, her fearful caveat, that inner voice warning her against expecting too much: "That's providing there's any 'me' left."

All these possibilities are exciting, yet frightening. How will it be? What kind of changes will it require, in him, in her, in their marriage? For her, the greatest unknown—and the central problem of her life right now—is what the next thirty or forty years will look like. What will be their shape and texture? What will be their daily flavor? Frightening questions, exciting possibilities.

The children's leaving hasn't been traumatic at all. What has been and still is traumatic is trying to find the thing I want to do, and being able to pursue it to a successful conclusion. I'm an artist—a good one, I think. But it's hard to make the kind of commitment that real success requires. I'm afraid of what it'll do to my marriage, and also to the rest of my life. And I suppose I'm afraid to really try and fail. But that's the stuff that's so hard and painful right now; it's not knowing what I'll be doing, or even what I *can* do. And from forty-five to seventy-five is a lot of years if I don't have something useful to do.

The ending, then, is difficult, not because the children are gone, but because it brings with it a beginning with the potential for adventure and excitement, but at the same time the possibility of failure. Some will negotiate it successfully, some will not. Sometimes the failure will be theirs; more often it will lie in the social constraints by which women's lives have been and continue to be hemmed in. But for all women whose central life task has been bearing and raising children, one question is heard like an urgent demand: "What am I going to do with the next thirty years of my life?" It is not an empty nest that plagues them, but the problems that stem from one that has been full too long.

REFERENCES

Abramowitz, C. F. Blaming the mother: An experimental investigation of sex-role bias in countertransference. *Psychology of Women Quarterly*, 1977, *2*, 23–34.

Bart, P. B. Depression in middle-aged women: Some sociocultural factors. (Doctoral dissertation, University of California at Los Angeles, 1967). *Dissertation Abstracts International*, 1968, *28*, 4752-B (University Microfilms No. 68–7452).

Bart, P. B. Why women's status changes in middle age. *Sociological Symposium*, 1969, *3*, 1–18.

Bart, P. B. Portnoy's mother's complaint. *Trans-action*, 1970, *8*, 69–74.

Bart, P. B. Depression in middle-aged women. In V. Gornick and B. K. Moran (Eds.), *Women in sexist society*. New York: Basic Books, 1971.

Baruch, G. K. Girls who perceive themselves as competent: Some antecedents and correlates. *Psychology of Women Quarterly*, 1976, *1*, 38–49.

Bernard, J. *The future of motherhood*. Baltimore: Penguin Books, 1975.

Curlee, J. Alcoholism and the empty nest. *Bulletin of the Menninger Clinic*, 1969, *33*, 165–171.

Deutscher, I. Socialization for postparental life. In R. S. Cavan (Ed.), *Marriage and family in the modern world*. New York: Thomas Y. Crowell, 1969.

Deykin, E. Y., Jacobson, S., Klerman, G. L., and Solomon, M. The empty nest: Psychosocial aspects of conflict between depressed women and their grown children. *American Journal of Psychiatry*, 1966, *122*, 1422–1426.

Easton, B. L. Industrialization and femininity: A case study of nineteenth century New England. *Social Problems*, 1976, *23*, 389–401.

Fuchs, E. *The second season: Life, love and sex—women in the middle years*. Garden City, N. Y.: Anchor Books, Doubleday, 1977.

Glenn, N. D. Psychological well-being in the postparental stage: Some evidence from national surveys. *Journal of Marriage and the Family*, 1975, *37*, 105–110.

Hammer, S. *Daughters and mothers: Mothers and daughters*. New York: Signet Books, 1975.

Harkins, E. B., and House, J. S. Effects of empty-nest transition on self-report of psychological and physical well-being. *Gerontologist*, 1975, *15*, 43.

Jacobson, S., and Klerman, G. L. Interpersonal dynamics of hospitalized depressed patients' home visits. *Journal of Marriage and the Family*, 1966, *28*, 94–102.

Laws, J. L. Work aspirations of women: False leads and new starts. *Signs*, 1976, *1*, 33–49.

Lazarre, J. *The mother knot*. New York: Dell Publishing, 1976.

Lowenthal, M. F., Thurnher, M., and Chiriboga, D. *Four stages of life*. San Francisco: Jossey Bass, 1975.

Lowenthal, M. F., and Weiss, L. Intimacy and crises in adulthood. *The Counseling Psychologist*, 1976, *6*, 10–15.

Maas, H. S., and Kuypers, J. A. *From thirty to seventy—a forty-year longitudinal study of adult styles and personality*. San Francisco: Jossey Bass, 1975.

McBride, A. B. *The growth and development of mothers*. New York: Harper and Row, 1973.

Neugarten, B. L. The awareness of middle age. In B. L. Neugarten (Ed.), *Middle age and aging*. Chicago: University of Chicago Press, 1968a.

Neugarten, B. L. Adult personality: Toward a psychology of the life cycle. In B. L. Neugarten (Ed.), *Middle age and aging*. Chicago: University of Chicago Press, 1968b.

Neugarten, B. L. The roles we play. In American Medical Association (Eds.), *The quality of life: The middle years*. Acton, Mass: Publishing Sciences Group, 1974.

Neugarten, B. L., Wood, V., Kraines, R. J., and Loomis, B. Women's attitudes toward the menopause. In B. L. Neugarten (Ed.), *Middle age and aging*. Chicago: University of Chicago Press, 1968.

Neugarten, B. L., and Datan, N. The middle years. In S. Arieti (Ed.), *American handbook of psychiatry* (2nd ed., Vol. 1). New York: Basic Books, 1974.

Powell, B. The empty nest, employment and psychiatric symptoms in college-educated women. *Psychology of Women Quarterly*, 1977, *2*, 35–43.

Rich, A. *Of woman born: Motherhood as experience and institution*. New York: W. W. Norton, 1976.

Rubin, L. B. *Busing and backlash: White against white in an urban school district*. Berkeley: University of California Press, 1972.

Rubin, L. B. *Worlds of pain: Life in the working-class family*. New York: Basic Books, 1976.

Rubin, L. B. *Women of a certain age*. New York: Harper and Row, 1979.

Sales, E., with the assistance of R. B. Katz. In I. Frieze, J. Parsons, P. Johnson, D. Ruble, and G. Zellman (Eds.), *Women's adult development*. New York: W. W. Norton, 1977.

Spence, D., and Lonner, T. The empty nest: A transition within motherhood. *The Family Coordinator*, 1971, *20*, 369–375.

Weissman, M. M., and Paykel, E. S. *The depressed woman: A study of social relationships*. Chicago: University of Chicago Press, 1974.

Weissman, M. M., Pincus, C., Radding, N., Lawrence, R., and Siegel, R. The educated housewife: Mild depression and the search for work. *American Journal of Orthopsychiatry*, 1973, *43*, 565–573.

Wortis, R. P. The acceptance of the concept of the maternal role by behavioral scientists: Its effects on women. In A. Skolnick and J. H. Skolnick (Eds.), *Intimacy, family and society*. Boston: Little, Brown, 1974.

Promoting Competence and Coping through Retirement Planning

Ruth Glick

❖

    For most people retirement is a major economic, social, and psychological event. This is true whether it is welcomed or dreaded; whether it is, as officially defined, departure from the labor force or a silent and unconscious shifting down as in the case of a wife who has never worked outside the home but now enters with her retired husband into the new status.

    There is no longer an institutional role to carry out. Income is reduced by a half to two thirds. Day to day routines are dramatically altered. The old center of life is gone, and another must be carved out if days are not to be shapeless. Finally in our culture retirement formally ushers in the period of life called old age, and the knowledge of death lurking must somehow be worked through.

    It seems logical to prepare for so new and different a status; to seek and process needed information; discuss it with others; understand ramification, risks, and realities; consider the options; weigh the trade-offs; and create bridges for a successful transition. It appeals to our common sense that this should be done. (I once had a professor who used to snarl: "Don't bring common sense into my class. I want evidence.")

    Is retirement planning a means of promoting competence and coping in later life? To reply at all, it is necessary to cast the issue somewhat differently, because the crucial question is not what effect will this program or that legislation or such-and-such a policy have on older people, but rather how should old people live?

    I am indebted to Harry Moody (1976) for giving us a way of looking at the matter which takes it out of the everyday realm of social planning or intervention models or increased services to older people. It is Professor Moody's thesis that the kind of social policy which a society adopts for its old is a function of the importance it gives to the very existence of old people, its view of human life as a whole, the significance it assigns the experience of aging. For Moody, public policy on old age in any society is rooted in basic attitudes toward old age, in certain assumptions about old people, and in systems of belief about human potential and human values.

Moody has set forth four patterns or stages or ways in which old people are perceived, and has tied these to corresponding characteristics of policy, treatment, and consequence. His Stage I is called *Rejection*. Here the old are seen as a drag and a drain, a parasitical body that consumes rather than produces and is useless in a technological society. Stage I stops just short of the ice floe. Its axiom, if it had one, would be: "No deposit, no return." The old are like the empty bottles thrown into the trash heap or tossed out of moving cars into the gutter.

Stage II is *Social Services*. It developed in reaction to the devastation wrought by Stage I. Remedial measures born of the liberal ethic and social conscience produced relief in the form of social security, welfare, food stamps, nursing-home care, senior centers, day care, nutrition programs, subsidized housing, and so on. Under this ethos the elderly become a special constituency with their own bureaucracy, their own lobbyists and professional service providers. The style of Stage II is prescriptive, its message simple—stay busy, there are 1001 things to do. These are called leisure time activities.

Stage III is *Participation*. It rejects the interest group liberalism of Stage II and its domination by middleman policies and programs, feeding the horses to feed the chickens. It rejects the passivity engendered by social services and advocates wide-randing changes within the society which have brought the old to their present pass. It demands, for instance, that the goals set forth in the Older Americans Act be carried out forthwith. It asks for an end to poverty, a comprehensive national health care program, the abolition of mandatory retirement, the opportunity for new careers, and the right of older persons to participate as they wish and can in the mainstream of the culture. Stage III is sometimes radical, always activist. *Priorities and Options* is its axiom. It says that if you need 1001 things to do, it is because you cannot find a few that have meaning. Following Simone de Beauvoir (1972), Stage III states that "There is only one solution if old age is not to be an absurd parody of our former life, and that is to go on pursuing ends that give our existence a meaning—devotion to individuals, to groups and to causes—social, political, intellectual and creative work" (p. 540).

Stage IV is called *Self-Actualization*. Moody wonders how this can be described in a society such as ours which has no image of life at full length, no role unique to the old, no philosophy of old age, as in ancient India, for example, where the old retreated in the final stage of life into the forest for contemplation and meditation in quest of spiritual deliverance—moksha. He reminds us of the patriarch, the guru, the archetype of the wise old man in many traditional societies. In these the old person symbolizes the completeness of the life cycle, the spiritual goal of existence, something more than a middle-aged person who has had a long, long, life—however productive. Only Stage IV acknowledges old age on its own terms.

Looking back over these stages, I suggest that in view of the greater visibility of the aged in recent years, and massive government expenditure, it may seem that Stage I is gone, and only tiny pockets of extreme deprivation and neglect have survived. But this is not the case. Fifteen percent of the aged still live in devastating poverty (Brotman, 1978). Most of these elderly poor are women who have worked all of their lives in low-paying jobs or as housewives. Some of these old women, especially the black isolates of the inner city—the poorest of the poor—live in danger of victimization and violence by hoodlums and junkies. A more recently revealed atrocity against the frail elderly is physical abuse by their own adult offspring. The calamitous conditions of nursing homes and the misuse of commitment procedures are documented. Despite staggering amounts of money spent, Stage I has not been obliterated.

It is true, however, that a wide variety of Stage II benefits have been made available to older people. Many, not old and needy, have benefited—the pharmaceutical companies, the medical profession, nursing home operators, politicians, the aging bureaucracy, researchers in the field of gerontology, and those who provide the social services of Stage II. The beneficiaries of this charitableness of a benevolent government and a rich society are everywhere.

The Stage II ethos fosters segregation, caretaking, and dependency, and weakens the natural support systems—family, church and synagogue, neighbors, friends, community. Much Stage II programming for the elderly, however well meant, also deals them out of the game, limits their freedom, limits their autonomy, limits their dignity. And some policies, although alleged to be in the best interests of the elderly, are not well meant. In the years preceding the fight against the 1978 amendment for the Antidiscrimination in Employment Act, which raised the age of retirement to 70 and abolished it altogether for federal employees, the powerful lobbies for industry and business and the labor unions which fought the new legislation argued that mandatory retirement is in reality an act of kindness, because it protects all workers from the shock of sudden retirement; if the workers know what to expect they can plan ahead with certainty, and the unfit and incompetent are protected from the humiliation of being weeded out because all men and women are treated equally.

Most retirement planning is a Stage II operation. One form of the art consists mainly of a series of pamphlets to be read and digested. The purpose is to give information—in some cases, it seems, all the information the individual is going to need in the next twenty years. This material, which is sold to industry and mailed at regular intervals to the worker's home, also sells a postretirement gift program to which many companies subscribe for their already retired employees.

In some large and prestigious organizations, everyone due to retire within the next year or two is herded into an auditorium. There, over a period of one, two, or three days, a panel of "resource people" has assembled to funnel into the pre-retirees' heads information about financial matters, health, Social Security, Medicare, physical fitness, consumer fraud, housing, peace of mind, wills. They talk about budgeting and about recreation and about volunteerism, and they tell them and tell them and tell them.

In a great many companies, maybe in the majority, preretirement counseling is one to one. Typically in the individual approach, a month or two before the big event, the prospective retiree is called in and informed about company benefits—pension, and insurance etc.—Social Security, Medicare, and whatever general information the teller happens to have. I met a union fellow at a retirement conference who told me he "counsels" 2500 prospective retirees a year, a half-hour at a time. I asked: "What do you tell them?" He said: "I tell 'em everything."

The economist Malcolm Morrison (1976) has shown that employees are seriously handicapped with respect to planning ahead for income adequacy, the number one problem in retirement. They lack the necessary information as well as the necessary skills to interpret and make use of the information. A recent study of trends in planning early retirement (Barfield and Morgan, 1978) reports that the number of respondents professing ignorance about the amount of retirement pension they could expect was so great that the investigators could not use the amount in the analysis. Many people still believe that pension, Social Security, and savings will yield enough for comfortable living to the end of their days. But only about 20 percent of retirees even receive a pension today (Morrison, 1978). Furthermore, early retirement means about a 20 percent permanent reduction in Social Security benefits. And then there is inflation. Morrison's blue collar workers are not the only ones who do not know that a $600 pension at age 62 in 1978 will be worth $306 at age 72 and $155 at age 82, given an expected continuing 7 percent rate of inflation. Many people say that they expect to earn money after retirement, as though the labor market is all that accessible to aging workers. Furthermore, the projected replacement earnings are as unrealistic as the projected accumulated savings. Listen, my friends, it may be that in old age money is one's best friend.

We are in Stage II on the growing edge of Stage III. Stage III concepts grow out of respect for the capacity of older people to take responsibility for themselves. The new legislation raising the age of retirement to 70, or abolishing it altogether, is a Stage III concept. The last of the legalized discriminations is on its last legs. Workers will be employed as long as they can do a job. The waste of healthy vigorous people will stop. Talent and experience will be valued. Competent workers will be able to decide for themselves whether, when, and how they will leave the labor force, rather than having to make the best of someone else's decision.

Stage III advocates treatment of older workers which is equitable with other workers; training and retraining; job redesign; and job development. It advocates alternatives to retirement which permit greater flexibility and increased opportunities for choice between leisure and work. Stage III options include retiring, taking early retirement, continuing to work full time, phasing out gradually from work, job shifting as people's ages and capacities changes, increasing the availability of part-time work, and providing the opportunity for a person to take time off for a while and then return to work (Morrison, 1978).

The new law finds many workers not prepared to make the most of the freedom to choose between options. This should have been built in over the years. Many workers are not prepared for flexible work schedules. In a study of the Steel Workers Union's extended vacation plan for older workers with seniority (Parker, 1971), it was found that most of the workers did not know what to do with their bonus time. They used it as regular vacation time and many admitted to boredom and were glad to get back to the job. George Steiner says we have not begun to understand the vacuum that is going to come on society given the glut of leisure it does not know how to use (Hall, 1973).

Stage II's conception of leisure is a mishmash of taking it easy while keeping busy. A little this, a little that. Busy. Busy. The more activities, the richer the life. Maggie Kuhn says that we are the only society that sends its babies to school and its old people out to play. What is interesting about these "leisure" activities is that they are usually the same pursuits that were carried on during the work life in a relatively small amount of free time. Why they should still be called leisure-time activities in the retirement years is a mystery, since in one sense it's all leisure. A vacuous design for living is conveyed in the popular retirement rhetoric: Golden Days, Harvest Years, the Next Promotion, Retire to Life, Retire to Action, The Best Is Yet to Be. Reading, you think you will drown in a sea of golden age garbage. Life itself is ultimately a leisure-time activity.

Pre-retirees also need substantive information about aging to which retirement is ineluctably linked, and here again they receive little help. Growing old. People are not sufficiently awed by how tough it is until they come to it themselves. Several months ago I was asked to speak at a conference, the title of which was "The Bright, Bright Future of Aging." I asked the 33-year-old program chairman who had invited me if he did not think one "Bright" would do it. He did not. I tried again: "E. M. Forster wrote a book called *Two Cheers for Democracy*. If he could knock out a "Cheer," can't you knock out a "Bright?" But he would not yield, so I had then to set to the task of ferreting out the possible sources of these brightnesses. I had to think long and hard on it, seek out the evidence, weigh it, and keep an open mind. Because I am not by nature cheerful and optimistic, I had to guard against a bias.

What can we say about old age in America today? What is the condition of the old among us? Are they the victims of neglect, resentment, and discrimination? Is the distance between the generations growing? That Americans hate old age is clear enough. Do they also hate old people? Is the society agist through and through?

Or as some believe, is there gradually evolving a more just system in which most older people are receiving a fair share? Does the fact that the young old (55–75) and an increasing minority of the old old (75 plus) are stronger, healthier, better educated, more vigorous, and more independent than their parents and grandparents ever dreamed of—does this mean that older people in the richest society in the world are better off than ever before?

One eminent student of aging, Leonard Hayflick, says to be old in America is unpleasant; to be old and poor, a tragedy (Hayflick, 1977, p. 9). Another gerontologist, perhaps even more eminent, Bernice Neugarten, says the old are in good shape today and getting better (Neugarten, 1974, p. 198). It is the worst of times. It is the best of times.

An unemployed school teacher applied for a position in a small midwestern city. A member of the school board interviewing him asked: "Do you believe that the world is round or that the world is flat?" The school teacher answered: "I can teach it both ways."

Old age is hard—and the people cope. Even when the last decades are not a catastrophe, even may be good, for the majority the rewards dwindle, social isolation increases in the wake of retirement, the loss of friends, the fading of emotional support, as children live their lives and grandchildren move away. Health, vigor, and perceptual acuity decline in varying degrees. Loss, loss. Worst of all is the threat of diminished intellectual competency, the specter of dependence, the possibility that one may not make it to death's door in control of one's own body and one's own mind.

What can talkative retirement planning accomplish in view of this? It can do some things. It can inform, it can advise, it can teach. How it informs and what it advises, what information it gives is, as I have tried to suggest, more than a matter of teaching styles.

Who will teach? I am surprised at how little even educated people know at this late date about aging. Full professors, including psychologists, still ask questions revealing that they do not know the difference between gerontology and geriatrics. The people in industry who are designated to conduct the retirement planning programs are ignorant as owls about the subject. You can imagine. Typically the job is passed to some young person from Pensions and Benefits or maybe to a superfluous person in the late fifties whom the company is trying to dump. As in medicine and psychology, anything to do with aging is low status. These trainers are not exceptional in their ignorance. I give a true-false questionnaire to university students of all ages, to young and old service providers to the elderly, to decision-makers in the aging bureaucracy, to individuals training to be retirement planners, and to planners who have been in the business for years, and I find the picture of older Americans drawn by them not too different from that revealed by the now famous Harris Poll Survey (National Council on Aging, 1975), an utterly false portrait of old people rotting away in poor health without proper medical care or enough money to live on: 30 percent are incarcerated in institutions, senility is a common condition, old people think a lot about death, we lose 100,000 brain cells a day. All false but frequently marked true. One item is detected as false every time— "Old people have little or no interest in sex." An odd picture this, of a population of demented, poverty-stricken, sick, old people, obsessed by death and apt to end up as vegetables in a nursing home, but jumping into bed to make love despite all the adversity. It is not really hard to understand. The sexual act is life itself. We should not be surprised that people in the last years of life cherish it as much for its symbolic as for its more obvious values. Schopenhauer (1928) said that the sexual impulse in itself is the expression of the will to live.

Retirement planning could debunk a lot of this stereotypy and misconception. There is no way to talk meaningfully about retirement without discussing aging. People need to know what is error and what is reality and what is as yet unknown. We are battling centuries of antipathy. Research into aging by the social historians and other humanists tells us that what is felt and said today about old age is no different than what has come down through the ages. There is no pattern, no progression whether we look at children's literature or history or philosophy from Plato to Sartre. There never was a Golden Age.

Against ignorance, fear, and anxiety, however, the sober realistic initiating of the planning process with accurate information can be corrective. Stage III programs can heighten the awareness of their situation and encourage older people to take action.

One example of the difference between a Stage II and a Stage III approach to a single problem illustrates this well. Older people often need drugs and medication, the cost of which is beyond their means. A Stage II solution is the enlistment by politicians of pharmacists who will give discounts to the elderly. Scrounging for discounts from all merchants and purveyors is Stage II's idea of a social invention. Stage III, also recognizing that older people need drugs and medication the cost of which is beyond their means, advocates political action. In Cleveland a group of mostly older people calling themselves "Active Clevelanders Together" banded together and, armed with irrefutable evidence that generic drugs could safely replace name-brand drugs, pushed through the legislation making it legal for every pharmacist in Ohio to dispense the generic drug at a fraction of the cost unless the physician has handwritten instructions disallowing it. And this is for people of all ages, not only for the elderly.

Can retirement planning programs help older people to cope more effectively with the problems of retirement? Well yes, but that is because they are already coping. That is how they come to be in the program.

Research (Kasschau, 1974) tells us that those who fare best in retirement are those who are favorably disposed toward it, and those are precisely the ones who tend to prepare ahead. The participants in the programs are all volunteers. Individuals with negative attitudes are unlikely to attend. A commonly reported problem by the researchers is that satisfaction or adjustment levels were initially so high on pre-program tests that there was nowhere to go on the post tests.

There is no scholarly body of research on retirement planning. The subject is not listed in the index of the *Handbook of Aging and the Social Sciences* (1976), nor is it mentioned in the chapter on work and retirement by Harold Sheppard in that volume.

A few studies have attempted to measure changes in attitude or behavior. Kasschau (1974, p. 47), summing them up, said, "The hit or miss character of the evaluation research seems intimately tied to the hit or miss fashion in which these programs are administered." Elsewhere she writes (p. 46): "Even the best company programs involve only one and one half to two hours weekly group sessions for five to twelve weeks. How can individual attitudes toward life, work, and retirement change from such brief impersonal encounters?" In the same article she reviews the retirement adjustment literature, most if not all of which reveals a high degree of satisfaction with retirement. A warning from Carl Eisdorfer (1977) about the discrepancy between self-estimates of health and objective criteria may be relevant here. Despite moderate to severe chronic illness as measured by objective criteria, a great majority of old people in the studies he reviewed did not identify themselves as significantly impaired but rather saw their symptoms as the limitations of normal old age. So it is with self-estimates of adjustment or life satisfaction. What does it mean if a 65-year-old person checks good or very good or excellent on a scale when asked how he finds life in retirement? The old joke serves us well—compared to what? To Joe who has terminal cancer? To Alice who has been dead a year?

The Moody model does not quite work. Stage III presents a conceptual problem. Participation seems to be a substage of a larger, more generic progressive principle. It is only one option, one avenue in the direction of self-actualization. Moody himself admits that Stage III denies the aging process with its insistence on continued activity in later life.

There is a general tendency today to decry solitude as unhealthy and looking inward, and disengaging as morbid. But a good measure of solitude is necessary for reflection. Introspection is a requisite of psychological growth, and the constructive use of experience depends first of all on one's awareness of that experience in some focused, holistic way. Stage III points to Arthur Rubinstein and Miz Lillian as examples of the ideal. Indeed, many gerontologists believe that the ideal old age is an extension, a stretching out of a good middle age. But Moody suggests that there is something *uniquely possible* in old age that is possible only at this point in the life cycle.

Self-actualization reaches its fullest explication in the thinking of the psychologist Abraham Maslow (1954). Maslow early in his career thought that self-actualization was the ultimate development of one's capacities and abilities. He thought it was the goal to be sought. In his maturity he said he realized that self-actualization could not be sought, but that like happiness it would elude us if we made its search the objective of our lives. Self-actualization comes as a by-product of something else that we do or that we are.

Maslow early in his career thought that self-actualization could occur in young people. In his maturity he wrote that this could not happen. Why? I give you his answer (1970, Preface, xx):

> Because in our culture at least, youngsters have not yet achieved identity or autonomy, nor have they had time enough to exper- ience an enduring, loyal, post-romantic love relationship, nor have they generally found their calling, the altar upon which to offer themselves, nor have they worked out their own system of values; nor have they had experience enough (responsibility for others, tragedy, failure, achievement, success) to shed perfectionist illusions and become realistic; nor have they generally made their peace with death; nor have they learned how to be patient; nor have they learned enough about evil in themselves and others to be compassionate; nor have they had time to become postambivalent about parents and elders, power and authority; nor have they generally become wise; nor have they generally acquired enough courage to be un- popular; to be unashamed about being openly virtuous . . .

In the final analysis the best thing about old age is experience. It is incontrovertibly the one thing old people have more of than young people. You do not live two thirds of a century for nothing. You learn how to cope.

Ethel Shanas (1975) says that when one interviews the old old, the very old in their 80's and 90's, a common statement is: "I never expected to live so long." These old pioneers reached extreme old age unexpectedly, you might say, and so had to invent coping mechanisms and behaviors and styles.

Do not reckon without the host The old person is not at this party as a pauper, but as a survivor. "Sobre viviente" the Spaniard says. He has continued to live in spite of, and after.

Could better, earlier, longer, more rational planning promote coping and competence in older adults? Again, yes. One thinks of long-term financial planning, health education, education about life span development, and the constructive uses of time. But if one thinks about the creative uses of experience, of self-knowledge, changing human relationships, life tasks, and values and meaning, then we are not talking about retirement planning.

Da capo. How do we view life as a whole? What significance do we assign the experience of aging? How should old people live?

REFERENCES

Atchley, R. C. *Social forces in later life: An introduction to social gerontology*. Belmont, Cal.: Wadsworth, 1972.

Barfield, R. E., and Morgan, J. N. Trends in planned early retirement. *The Gerontologist*, 1978, *18*, 13–18.

Beauvoir, S. de. *The coming of age*. (P. O'Brian, trans.). New York: Putnam, 1972.

Binstock, R., and Shanas, E. (Eds.). *Handbook of the aging and the social sciences*. New York: Van Nostrand Reinhold, 1976.

Brotman, H. *Money income and poverty status of family and persons in the United States: 1977*. Current population reports, consumer income series (P-60, No. 116), advance report. U. S. Dept. of Commerce, Bureau of the Census, July 1978.

Eisdorfer, C. The meaning of retirement. In R. A. Kalish (Ed.), *The later years*. Belmont, Cal.: Wadsworth, 1977.

Frost, R. Provide, Provide. In E. C. Lathem (Ed.), *The poetry of Robert Frost*. New York: Holt, Rinehart and Winston, 1969.

Hall, E. The freakish passion: A conversation with George Steiner. *Psychology Today*, February 1973, pp. 56–58, 60, 62, 64, 66–69.

Hayflick, L. Perspectives on human longevity. In Committee on Human Development, *Extending the human life span: Social policy and social ethics*. Chicago: University of Chicago Press, 1977.

Kasschau, P. L. Reevaluating the need for retirement planning programs. *Industrial Gerontology*, 1974, *1* (1), 42–59.

Maslow, A. H. *Motivation and personality*. New York: Harper and Brothers, 1954.

Maslow, A. H. *Motivation and personality* (2nd ed.). New York: Harper and Row, 1970.

Moody, H. R. Philosophical presuppositions of education for old age. *Educational Gerontology: An International Quarterly*, 1976, *1*, 1-16.

Morrison, M. H. Planning for income adequacy in retirement. *The Gerontologist*, 1976, *16*, 538-543.

Morrison, M. H. *The retirement revolution*. Unpublished manuscript, 1978.

National Council on Aging. *The myth and reality of aging in America*. Washington, D. C. 1975.

Neugarten, B. Age groups in American society and the rise of the young-old. *Annals of the American Academy of Political and Social Sciences*, 1974, *415*, 198.

Parker, S. *The future of work and leisure*. London: MacGibbon and Kee, 1971.

Prentis, R. S. *National survey of Fortune's "500" pre-retirement plans and policies*. Ann Arbor and Detroit, Mich.: University of Michigan and Wayne State University Institute of Labor and Industrial Relations, July, 1975.

Sandburg, C. 107, *The people, yes*. New York: Harcourt Brace, 1936.

Schopenhauer, A. [The metaphysics of the love of the sexes.] In W. Durant (Ed., R. B. Haldane and J. Kemp, trans.), *The world as will and idea* (Vol. 3). New York: Simon and Schuster, 1928.

Shanas, E. Aging in the year 2000; A look at the future. *The Gerontologist*, 1975, *15* (1), 38.

United States Civil Service Commission. *Retirement planning: A growing employee relations service*. Washington, D. C.: U. S. Government Printing Office, 1961.

VI. Improving Self-Esteem and Fostering Support Systems and Networks

The final section of readings is concerned with self-esteem and support networks in relation to primary prevention. The authors in this section address social and political realities that affect self-esteem. Strategies for improving self-esteem and fostering social support networks are discussed. All the interventions described in this section involve adult populations, but the concepts, approaches, and applications can be generalized to populations of children as well.

In the first paper in this section, Klaus K. Minde and his colleagues describe their research program for parents of low birth weight infants. The program incorporates features of both support groups and educational approaches to effectively improve self-esteem and sense of autonomy among mothers.

Grace K. Baruch and Rosalind C. Barnett examine the potential role of work in enhancing the psychological well-being of adult women. By considering self-esteem and role-pattern satisfaction of working and nonworking mothers, they succeed in shattering assumptions that female involvement in multiple roles primarily serves to produce conflict and distress.

The next paper is also concerned with women's issues. Betty Friedan considers the effects of women's roles and the process of liberation on self-esteem. She discusses the complexities of women's new roles and concludes that coping with new patterns has been liberating and has improved mental health.

The next two papers provide a consideration of how human sexuality is related to self-esteem and how social and religious repression of sexuality interferes with human fulfillment. Brian R. McNaught describes the psychological costs of being gay in our society. Like Friedan, he sees liberation as a positive process. Education and social support are discussed as crucial steps in the liberation process that promotes personal growth and improves self-esteem.

James B. Nelson examines sexuality as it relates to religion. He concentrates on the Judeo-Christian tradition, exposing its part in such "sins" as sexism, homophobia, and genitalization of sex. He develops the scholarly argument that while these sins have their heritage in the Judeo-Christian

426

tradition, the tradition also contains positive resources for sexual health which, for the most part, have been overlooked in the past.

In the final paper, Douglas W. Bray and Ann Howard examine the findings of their longitudinal study of the lives and careers of white male managers in the Bell system. They discuss the characteristics that appear to be related to managerial success. Their study provides insights into the relationships between life satisfaction and career success and the determinants of adjustment and happiness during adulthood.

The Effects of Self-Help Groups in a Premature Nursery on Maternal Autonomy and Caretaking Style 1 Year Later

Klaus K. Minde, Nancy E. Shosenberg, and Peter L. Marton

The recent literature suggests that parents of premature infants find it more difficult to look after their infants than do parents whose children were born following a normal gestation (Brown and Bakeman, 1980; Goldberg, 1978; Klaus and Kennell, 1976; Minde, 1980). The question of why this is so has been of interest to a number of investigators. Some have reported these infants' apparent lack of responsiveness to be a source of distress and consequent maladaptation for their parents. (Als and Brazelton, 1980; Field, 1979). Others have pointed out that difficulties in the mothers' past life or a lack of early intimate contact between mothers and their infants influence later maternal caretaking abilities (Hunter, Kilstrom, Kraybill and Loda, 1978; Minde, Marton, Manning, and Hines, 1980a). In addition, a number of authors have emphasized that many mothers of premature infants perceive themselves as having failed in their biological role to bear a "complete" infant (Kaplan and Mason, 1960; Seashore, Leifer, Barnett, and Leiderman, 1973). Consequently they feel inadequate and depressed and often see themselves as personally responsible for the early birth of their infant (Shosenberg, 1980). It appears that, although there is presently no clear agreement about the relative contribution of any of the above-mentioned factors for later parenting disorders, all authors who have written about this area agree that the birth of such a small infant is an extremely stressful event for any parent.

The assistance given to the families of these babies by physicians or other health care professionals has often been determined by whichever deficit an author assumed to be operative. For example, investigators who have stressed the inadequate postnatal environment of these infants have typically provided extra stimulation to them (Masi, 1979). Others who felt that the premature birth had prevented the parents of such infants from forming a stable bond gave mothers an opportunity to have ready access to their infants after birth (Klaus and Kennell, 1976; Leiderman and Seashore, 1975).

Although both types of intervention have been shown to benefit these infants initially, any long-term effects on both the infants and the parent–child relationship have been found to be associated with a continuing active involvement of the mother in the treatment process. For example, the best results of infant stimulation programs have been obtained when mothers were taught, and then themselves carried out, the suggested stimulation programs both in the hospital and later at home (Chapman, 1979; Rice, 1977; Scarr-Salapatek and Williams, 1973). It is possible and likely that the execution of these stimulation programs, in addition to benefiting the infant, also gave these mothers the feeling of competence; that is, that they were needed, important, and did a good job.

Similarly, early maternal visiting may have affected later caretaking behavior not primarily because of the establishment of a stronger early mother–infant bond but because these initial visits allowed mothers to handle their infants more and consequently increased their feelings of competence (Seashore et al., 1973). It is of interest to note that the above-mentioned studies either did not provide any long-term follow-up or the initial differences in the mothers' behaviors toward their premature infants disappeared after 1 month at home.

Although the above interventions were compatible with the notion that the maternal caretaking changes were caused primarily by inadvertently improving the self-esteem or the feeling of autonomy of the mothers of these very small infants, at least initially, the authors of these studies never mention this possibility. In addition, both types of program seem to have one other potential shortcoming. They only provide parents with *either* short-term specific emotional support (Klaus and Kennell, 1976; Leiderman and Seashore, 1975) *or* practical suggestions in regard to their infant's special needs (Field, 1979; Rice, 1977; Scarr-Salapatek and Williams, 1973). In contrast our own clinical experience had suggested to us that families of such high-risk infants were in need of both emotional and practical support for the task of parenting such small infants.

In an attempt to see the effect of such comprehensive care, we evaluated an intervention program in which peer-oriented, self-help groups served to assist the parents of premature infants. We chose this approach because of the following:

●our wish to avoid labeling parents as patients

●our clinical impression, supported by the work of Dumont (1974), Caplan (1974), and Powell (1975), that parents would be more accepting of supportive teaching from peers than from health professionals

•the evidence reported by Bronfenbrenner (1975) that the most successful long-term enhancement of the reciprocal mother–infant interaction is brought about by regular contact of mothers with specially trained peers during the first 3 years.

Subjects

Our study sample consisted of 57 very low birthweight infants and their mothers, assigned to experimental (N=28) and control groups (N=29) on the basis of their time of admission to the hospital. A more detailed discussion of our methodology can be found in previous publications (Minde, Shosenberg, Marton, Thompson, Ripley, and Burns, 1980b). In short, the selection criteria were as follows: for infants, birthweight less than 1,501 grams; singleton birth; weight appropriate for gestational age; absence of physical malformation and of serious medical complications, such as respiratory distress requiring ventilatory assistance or convulsions, at 72 hours of age; and for parents, their intent to keep the infant; ability to speak English; and domicile within 15 miles of The Hospital for Sick Children. The sample thus constituted a group of very small premature infants who had a relatively good medical prognosis and were unlikely to have suffered gross cerebral damage.

Setting

The study was conducted in the Neonatal Intensive Care Unit of The Hospital for Sick Children in Toronto, Canada. This unit has an annual admission of about 1,300 infants, about 350 of which weigh less than 1,500 grams and 110 less than 1,000 grams at birth. It has a nursing staff of approximately 150, placing it among the largest neonatal units in North America. Parental visiting and stimulation of the infants by parents are actively encouraged by all staff.

Method

All parents assigned to the experimental group were met by the group coordinator (N.S.) at the time of their first visit to the hospital and informed about the availability of the group. Each group consisted of 4 to 5 families who met once weekly for 90 to 120 minutes for 7 to 12 weeks following the birth of their infant, together with the group coordinator who was an experienced neonatal nurse and with a "veteran mother". The veteran mother had similarly had a small baby in the nursery during the previous 9 to 12 months and was known for her general sensitivity and integrity. She was seen as the official animator of each group.

The initial objective of the groups was to provide the parents with a forum within which they could talk about their intense feelings of fear, guilt, and depression about having given birth to such a small baby.

Once they had shared these feelings with each other and, as a consequence, begun to trust each other, the parents were exposed, with the help of specific resource personnel, to more didactic materials. These included films and slide presentations highlighting the developmental and medical needs of premature infants. Assistance was also provided for such concrete tasks as getting babysitters, finding better accommodations, or applying for unemployment benefits. Finally, the families were made familiar with local community resources for family support, and much time was spent on discussing issues such as working mothers, the role of the father in infant care, and the way parents can become emotionally available to their infants. In addition, the group coordinator was also available to the parents between group meetings to answer questions about specific medical problems of their infant and to provide individual support. About 60 percent of the parents made use of this opportunity at one time or another.

Parents in the group received only the routine ward care.

Summary of Previously Reported Results

In a previous publication (Minde et al., 1980b) we reported some findings suggesting that the 28 families who participated in these groups visited their infants significantly more in hospital than did the 29 control parents. They also touched, talked to, and looked at their infants in the en face position more during their visits and on a rating scale rated themselves as more confident in taking care of their infants at the time of discharge. Three months after discharge of the infants, group mothers continued to show more involvement with their babies during feedings and were more concerned about their general development.

In a follow-up study 1 year later, which included all but 2 of the original sample of 57 families, we again found significant differences between the mothers who had participated in the group meetings and their controls (Minde, Shosenberg, and Thompson, in press). For example, a statistically significant 69 percent of the mothers in the experimental group perceived the development of their infants at an age corrected for their gestation and adjusted their expectations accordingly. Only 37 percent of the control mothers did so. The experimental mothers at 1 year also gave their infants significantly more floor space to play, disciplined them less, and in general were more free in expressing concerns they had about them. When observed during a routine feed, the experimental mothers were also found to spend less time feeding their children, instead allowing them to feed themselves more. During a play session these mothers also vocalized and played more with their infants. We interpreted these findings to mean that the experimental mothers gave their infants more general freedom and stimulation and judged their competence more appropriately to their biological abilities.

During these same observations the infants of the experimental families in turn spent significantly more time sharing food with their mothers during their meals and during the play sessions played more and touched their mothers more frequently. When the infants were reunited with their mothers after a 5-minute separation, the experimental mothers hugged and kissed their infants significantly more. In contrast the control mothers showed their joy at reunion by doing many instrumental tasks with their babies, such as changing their diapers or combing their hair.

These results suggested to us that the experimental mothers were more socially stimulating with their infants and shared their feelings with them more easily. Their children reciprocated by showing more social and independent behaviors such as general playing, food sharing, and self-feeding.

We next considered the possibility that the experimental mothers had experienced a significant improvement in their interpersonal relationships as this in turn could have generalized to the care they provided their infants. When we enquired about any changes the mothers had felt in their relationships with members of their own family or with the husband or the father of the premature infant, we found that the experimental mothers indeed reported significantly more often that they had experienced a positive change in their relationship with one or more significant persons in their life.

The individual clinical summaries of those mothers who had reported an improvement in their relationships with others important to them also showed that five experimental mothers versus none in the control group had left their husbands or companions during the past year. Although such a separation is usually seen as a sign of deteriorating mental health, it seemed that in all these cases the woman had deserted a man who had been physically abusive to her or who had a history of severe alcoholism or who had a criminal record. This suggested to us that some of our mothers had become more self-sufficient and more autonomous in their actions in that they insisted on safeguarding their needs and those of their infants with fewer compromises. In order to verify this clinical impression we devised a global 5-point rating for autonomy. The descriptions of each point of this rating were derived from the work of Lozoff (1973), Anderson (1973), and Baker-Miller (1976) and private discussions between Minde and 20 women actively engaged in contemporary women's issues.

The following descriptions for a rating of 1, 3, and 5 on the global autonomy score were finally agreed upon, with a rating of 2 and 4 falling in between.

•1 = A woman who has been chronically abused either in her working or in her personal relationships since her childhood. She does not report awareness of any alternatives to this type of life, or she thinks that they do not apply to her.

•3 = A woman who has established herself in some area of her life, such as a job or volunteer activity, but who uses the potential advantages this gives her primarily either to maintain a basically dependent status quo or to identify with and hence adopt the traditional model of male independence.

•5 = A woman who has established herself in some area of her life and has acknowledged or overcome the guilt induced by this step. Nevertheless she is aware of her femaleness and in that sense has demonstrated an authenticity which in turn has allowed her to avoid copying the traditional male model of independence. Furthermore, she can give up outward signs of independence such as a job for some time to look after an infant or other significant person in her life or is able to tolerate the attachment of her child to surrogate caretakers.

Taking these criteria, the two senior authors independently rated all mothers on the clinical transcripts of the initial and 1 year follow-up psychiatric interviews.

Table 7 shows the results of these ratings and indicates that a significantly higher number of group mothers were seen to have achieved a positive change in their autonomy during the first year of their infants' life.

This differential change was not related to any initial differences in the degree of autonomy between the groups since both groups initially had very similar autonomy scores with group mothers scoring a mean of 2.4 (S D 0.83) and control mothers 2.5 (S D 0.86). Furthermore, the control mothers showed no change in their mean score after 1 year (mean: 2.5, S D 0.82) while the experimental mothers increased their mean autonomy score to 3.0 (S D 0.92). The changes in the autonomy scores of the experimental mothers can therefore not be seen as a result of regression toward the mean. In fact, some further data appear to validate this concept of autonomy, especially since they were arrived at independently of the global autonomy score. Table 8 shows that more group than control mothers had not returned to work at the 1 year interview (7 group and 5 control mothers had never worked and were therefore excluded from the analysis). Since all but two group mothers who returned to work did so after their infant was 7 months old and the return to work in neither group was associated with socioeconomic class, number of children at home, and the high, medium, or low activity status of the mother, these figures may well indicate yet again, that the group mothers in this study had become more autonomous and consequently more free to choose their own lifestyle.

Table 7 Changes in Maternal Autonomy at One Year

	No change or decrease	Increase
Group	16	12
Control	25	4

$X^2 = 5.95$ $df = 1$ $p < .02$

Table 8 Mothers Return to Work within One Year

	Yes	No
Group	12	9
Control	8	16

$X^2 = 2.75$ $df = 1$ $p < .1$

Discussion

The present study indicates that women who 1 year earlier took part in a peer self-help group following their premature infants' birth differ from a control group on a number of behaviors. In particular they show a higher degree of personal autonomy, a particular attitude towards their work, and positive changes in their relationships with other people. Although these findings are obviously not based on hard data, especially since our definition of autonomy may not be shared by others, we can speculate that this sense of maternal autonomy may also have been responsible for some of the changes we found in the behavior of these same mothers with their infants in our previous reports on the results of this self-help group experience. The increased social behavior of both mothers and infants during the observations at 1 year, as well as the increased ability of our group mothers to demonstrate their affection and concern for their infants which was seen during the early home visits and at 1 year, can be interpreted as a direct result of this changed self-concept of these women. This would also confirm some of the recent writings of Baker-Miller (1976) who states that autonomy and personal authenticity do not automatically imply lessening in activities traditionally associated with maternal caretaking behavior. In fact, the gain in autonomy, according to this writer, may allow a woman to utilize her interpersonal abilities and sensitivities with more ease and less conflict and in this sense make her into a more caring mother.

The question arises why this type of self-help experience should have had such a global impact upon these mothers. Even though a clear answer to this question is obviously not yet possible, we hypothesize that this group contact allowed us to take care of these families in a way that went beyond the "biomedical" model of traditional medicine. This traditional model, which applies the classical Western scientific "factor analytic" approach to medicine, basically assumed the "science" alone will finally deal with all the problems of both the body and the mind. In contrast, Engel (1977, 1980) in some important recent papers has presented an alternative model of medical care and called it the biopsychosocial model. This model sees "illness" and "distress" as disturbances in a complex integrated system. A particular illness is then seen at the same time as a component of a higher disturbance or a system, in the same way that a person is a component of his or her family or of society at large, as well as of lower systems such as the organs of a person which are made of cells. Engel states that the system-oriented clinicians will be aware that their primary task is the identification and characterization of the constituent components of the system they have to deal with. They will then intervene at the system(s) level most appropriate for the disorder at hand but will always remain conscious of changes within other systems which may affect the future process of the disorder.

It is clear that an awareness and understanding of these systems is especially important in medical conditions that affect the whole ecology of a person. For example, any type of chronic illness or physical handicap would have important repercussions on the total life of an individual and consequently he or she would be affected by the reactions of those sharing his/her life. Similarly, prematurity is a condition affecting far more than the biology of the infant (Als and Brazelton, 1980; Field, 1977; Frodi, Lamb, Leavitt, Donovan, Neff, and Sherry, 1978; Klaus and Kennell, 1976; Shosenberg, 1980). For example, some mothers may have precipitated their premature labour by not availing themselves of proper prenatal care for other than medical reasons. Others may find themselves depressed and anxious following the birth of such an infant, which compromises their ability to look after such a baby. In addition, there is good evidence that the future biological, social, and psychological functioning of these infants to a large extent depends on systems other than those associated with the specific biological impairment of the infant. In fact, the biological impairment that can be measured at birth is a very poor predictor of the future general functioning of these infants, while the attitudes in child-care practices of their primary caretakers are significantly correlated with later functioning in these areas (Cohen and Beckwith, 1979; Fitzhardinge, 1976; Littman, 1979; Sigman and Parmelee, 1980).

In summary, we feel that the self-help groups constituted one practical application of Engel's biopsychosocial model. The infants were given exemplary traditional medical care during their hospitalization, although at the same time their parents were allowed initially to mourn the loss of their hoped for full-term infants and to deal with other areas of this emotional crisis. In addition, they could all share concerns about both medical care and feelings with each other, such as their difficulties in providing their infants with breast milk and in getting clarified potentially confusing information from staff, to mention just two commonly encountered issues. Hence the groups allowed care to go on at various systems levels and converted a potentially very disorganizing and disintegrating experience into one which taught these parents competence and self-reliance.

In keeping with this model we argue that parents were able and willing to learn through videotapes, slides, and lectures about the common characteristics and problems of their infants only after their initial emotional crisis had been dealt with through group discussions and private meetings with the group coordinator. This approach, in our estimation, gave them a sense of mastery, especially since their interest and concerns were appreciated and reinforced by the professional staff and, later on, by their infants. The veteran parents (in five groups both the father and the mother acted as veterans) were crucial agents in this process as they could bridge the gap between the "professional" and the "patient" and communicate our concern and interest in the various systems implicated in this life crisis and also model a sense of potential mastery for the new parents. Since some sort of awareness in the various ecological systems influencing human behavior and development is an important aspect of any positive interpersonal relationship, we hypothesize that the increase in the group mothers' autonomy may be a direct result of our systems-oriented treatment program, although a replication of our study in another setting is clearly warranted.

An indication of this program's potentially long-term impact on the autonomy of these women has been the recent formation of the Toronto Perinatal Association. This organization of parents who initially benefited from these group meetings continues to make self-help groups available for families with premature infants in our hospital and has also become increasingly involved in the shaping of future perinatal service in Ontario.

References

Als, H., and Brazelton, T. B. A new model of assessing behavioral organization in preterm and full term infants. *Journal of the American Academy of Child Psychiatry*, 1980, 20, 239–263.

Anderson, J.V. Psychological determinants. *Annals of New York Academy of Sciences*, 1973, *208*, 185–193.

Baker-Miller, J. *Toward a new psychology of women*. Boston: Beacon Press, 1976.

Bronfenbrenner, U. Is early intervention effective? In B. Z. Friedlander, G. M. Sterritt, and G. E. Kirk (Eds.), *Exceptional infant assessment and intervention*. New York: Brunner/Mazel, 1975.

Brown, J., and Bakeman, R. Relationships of human mothers with their infants during the first year of life: Effects of prematurity. In R. Bell and W. Smotherman (Eds.), *Maternal influences and early behavior*. New York: Spectrum, 1980.

Caplan, G. *Support systems and community mental health*. New York: Behavioral Publications, 1974.

Chapman, J.S. Influence of varied stimulation development of motor patterns in the premature infant. In *Newborn Behavioral Organization: Nursing Research and Implications*. The National Foundation March of Dimes Birth Defects: Original Article Series, Vol. 15, Alan R. Liss Inc. 1979.

Cohen, S.E., and Beckwith, L. Preterm infant interaction with the caregiver in the first year of life and competence at age two. *Child Development*, 1979, *50*, 767–776.

Dumont, M. Self-help treatment programs. *American Journal of Psychiatry*, 1974, *131*, 631–635.

Engel, G.L. The need for a new medical model: A challenge for biomedicine. *Science*, 1977, *129*, 129–136.

Engel, G.L. The clinical application of the biopsychosocial model. *American Journal of Psychiatry*, 1980, *137*, 535–544.

Field, T.M. Effects of early separation, interactive deficits, and experimental manipulations on infant–mother face-to-face interaction. *Child Development*, 1977, *48*, 763–771.

Field, T.M. Interaction patterns of preterm and term infants. In T. M. Field, A. M. Sostek, S. Goldberg, and H. H. Shuman (Eds.), *Infants born at risk*. New York: Spectrum, 1979.

Fitzhardinge, P. Follow-up studies on the low birth weight infant. *Clinics in Perinatology*, 1976, *3*, 503–516.

Frodi, A., Lamb, M., Leavitt, L., Donovan, W., Neff, C., and Sherry, D. Fathers' and mothers' responses to the faces and cries of normal and premature infants. *Developmental Psychology*, 1978, *14*, 490–498.

Goldberg, S. Prematurity: Effects on parent–infant interaction. *Journal of Pediatric Psychology*, 1978, *3*, 137–144.

Hunter, R.S., Kilstrom, N., Kraybill, E.N., and Loda, F. Antecedents of child abuse and neglect in premature infants: A prospective study in a newborn intensive care unit. *Pediatrics*, 1978, *61*, 629–635.

Kaplan, D.M., and Mason, E.A. Maternal reaction to premature birth viewed as an acute emotional disorder. *American Journal of Orthopsychiatry*, 1960, *30*, 539–547.

Klaus, M.H., and Kennell, J.H. *Maternal–Infant bonding*. Saint Louis: C. V. Mosby, 1976.

Leiderman, P.H., and Seashore, M.J. Mother–infant neonatal separation: Some delayed consequences. In Ciba Foundation Symposium No 33. *Parent Infant Interaction*. New York: Elsevier, 1975.

Littman, B. The relationship of medical events to infant development. In T. M. Field, A. M. Sostek, S. Goldberg, and H. H. Shuman (Eds.), *Infants born at risk*. New York: Spectrum, 1979.

Lozoff, M.M. Fathers and autonomy in women. *Annals of New York Academy of Sciences*, 1973, *208*, 91–97.

Masi, W. Supplement stimulation of the premature infant. In T. M. Field, A. M. Sostek, S. Goldberg, and H. H. Shuman (Eds.), *Infants born at risk*. New York: Spectrum, 1979.

Minde, K. Bonding of parents to premature infants: Theory and practice. In P. Taylor (Ed.), *Monographs in Neonatology Series*. New York: Grune and Stratton, 1980.

Minde, K., Marton, P., Manning, D., and Hines, B. Some determinants of mother–infant interaction in the premature nursery. *Journal of the American Academy of Child Psychiatry*, 1980, *19*, 1–21. (a)

Minde, K., Shosenberg, N., Marton, P., Thompson, J., Ripley, J., and Burns, S. Self-help groups in a premature nursery—a controlled evaluation. *Journal of Pediatrics*, 1980, *96*, 933–940. (b)

Minde, K., Shosenberg, N., and Thompson, P. Self-help groups in a premature nursery—infant behavior and parental competence 1 year later. In E. Galenson and J. Call (Eds.), *Frontiers of infant psychiatry*. New York: Basic Books, in press.

Powell, L.F. The use of self-help groups as supportive reference communities. *American Journal of Orthopsychiatry*, 1975, *45*, 756–762.

Rice, R. Neurophysiological development in premature infants following stimulation. *Developmental Psychology*, 1977, *13*, 69–76.

Rutter, M. Invulnerability or why some children are not damaged by stress. In S. J. Shamsie (Ed.), *New directions in children's mental health*. New York: S.P. Medical and Scientific Books, 1979.

Scarr-Salapatek, S., and Williams, M.L. The effects of early stimulation on low birthweight infants. *Child Development*, 1973, *44*, 94–101.

Seashore, M.J., Leifer, A.D., Barnett, C.R., and Leiderman, P.H. The effects of denial of early mother–infant interaction on maternal self-confidence. *Journal of Personal and Social Psychology*, 1973, *36*, 369–378.

Shosenberg, N. Self-help groups for parents of premature infants. *Canadian Nurse*, 1980, July–August, 30–33.

Sigman, M., and Parmelee, A.H. Longitudinal evaluation of the preterm infants. In T. M. Field, A. M. Sostek, S. Goldberg, and H. H. Shuman (Eds.), *Infants born at risk*. New York: Spectrum, 1979.

On the Well-Being of Adult Women

**Grace K. Baruch and
Rosalind C. Barnett**

The major theme of this paper is that in our society the psychological well-being of women is facilitated: (a) by the development of occupational competence and of the capacity for economic independence; and (b) by involvement in a variety of roles. With respect to the first point, we shall argue that neither psychological well-being nor full social competence in adulthood is compatible with occupational incompetence and economic dependence. Unfortunately, women still fail to grasp this social reality and thus do not prepare for it. Many women, therefore, find themselves unable to cope successfully with the circumstances in which they find themselves. They are at high risk for psychiatric symptomatology, poverty, and diminished well-being, especially as they grow older. As for the second point, we shall argue that when one considers the whole life span, the gratifications provided by multiple role involvement usually outweigh any conflict and stress such involvement may entail.

We begin by discussing the social changes that have made occupational competence and economic independence critical for women's successful adaptation. We then review evidence about the effects of multiple role involvement on psychological well-being in a group of married women with young children who differ in employment status. Women who occupy the traditional pattern of wife and mother are compared with those who combine these roles with that of paid worker, a pattern shared by increasing numbers of women.

The issues to be discussed must be viewed in the context of at least two sets of social changes. The first set includes the ability to control fertility, the problems of overpopulation, and the lengthening life span. An increasing proportion of women need no longer face frequent or unpredictable childbearing (Hoffman, 1977), and the social value of children has decreased. Furthermore, female life expectancy now exceeds 75 years, of which perhaps 10, or no more than about 1/7 of a lifetime, may be spent in intensive child-rearing, and that not for all women. A view of women that focuses on the wife and mother role and socializes girls mainly for such a role reflects serious lags in our perceptions, beliefs, and, perhaps most important, our emotions.

The second set of social changes revolves around what is really not a change at all, but a return to the way things have usually been in human history. We refer to the increasing participation of women, including mothers of young children, in the paid labor force. What is old about this is the restoring to women of their historic role as economic providers. In hunter-gatherer and agricultural societies, which together have constituted the human life style for over 90 percent of our history, women have always provided a substantial proportion of the economic basis for survival and for support of their families through food-gathering, farming, and other economically productive activities.

The East African women studied by the anthropologist Beatrice Whiting (1977), for example, grow crops on small plots, earn cash, and provide food and clothing required by their children. Doing their work in the company of other adults, they spend four or five hours a day away from their children, yet their lives provide what Whiting sees as the critical components of human well-being: a sense of competence—that is, having a valued impact on one's environment; sufficient variation in stimulation; and the assurance of support and comfort. But as their husbands move into stable paid employment in urban settings, the women follow, leaving their family farms. Landless and jobless, they become economically dependent for the first time and must take sole, full-time responsibility for the care of their children in isolated homes. Boredom and irritability increase; self-esteem decreases; well-being suffers. But to take on eight hours a day of poorly paid work in the labor force is not an answer to their demoralization. Such work creates overwhelming difficulties with child care, fatigue, and other problems so familiar to many women in our society. What should strike us is that these new social changes in Kenya that trouble Beatrice Whiting so much are frighteningly similar to our norm, indeed our social ideal, for the American family: the man as sole economic provider, the woman, jobless and in sole charge of children, economically dependent and isolated in her own home.

But for women not to be involved in economically productive work is in fact a new-fangled pattern in human society. With a cross-cultural perspective, we can see that our pattern, which otherwise might appear to reflect some kind of natural law about the division of labor between men and women, may actually be very unstable as well as painful and dysfunctional.

Of course, which patterns are adaptive and which are not depends obviously upon the social context, but given the context we have described, we believe that all adults must be able to function as economic providers. This simple idea is a cliché if one is thinking about men, but it remains controversial when applied to women. When men cannot support themselves or their families, we read about it in the newspapers. And as such cases multiply, they command the attention of social workers and economists, psychiatrists and senators. When a woman is unable to provide for herself and any dependents, that is as expected, unless and until she enters particular social categories of persons who threaten to impinge upon public monies: separated mothers, pregnant teenagers, elderly widows. Like magic, her economic dependence suddenly becomes all too visible and regrettable, attaining the status of a social problem, a label that is a passport to social concern. But this concern should have been present in the minds of parents and educators, mental health workers and public officials from her cradle days on. Yet the situations of the divorced mother, the unmarried pregnant teenager, the poor elderly widow, the battered wife unable to leave home—all are simply visible crises that punctuate the course of an otherwise undetected disease. The twin components of this disease are occupational incompetence and economic dependence; among the various milder manifestations are low self-esteem and depression.

Much current literature on mental health and well-being documents these and other negative impacts of what we might call our recent "traditional" patterns, and conversely, the positive consequences of "nontraditional" lifestyles. For example, when the famous group of gifted children first studied by Terman was followed up recently—they are now in their 60's—the women in the group were asked to describe their life pattern and their satisfaction with it (Sears and Barbee, 1977). The women who reported the highest level of satisfaction were income-producers, that is, they were working for pay, and were heads of households, that is, not currently married. These findings were contrary to expectations, perhaps because our psychological theories (and national mythologies) say that marriage and children are the route to a sense of well-being. These women, of course, were very able and in many cases were relatively successful occupationally. But in a study of working-class women all of whom were married and had children, Myra Ferree (1976) found that despite the routine nature of their jobs, those who worked felt happier and had higher self-esteem than did the unemployed housewives.

A second illustration is the work of George Brown and his colleagues (Brown, Bhrolchain, and Harris, 1975). Their study of the development of psychiatric symptomatology in women living in London showed that among women most at risk—that is, those with small children, who did not have a confidante—employment was a powerful antidote to stress; psychiatric symptoms developed in 79 percent of those women who were not employed, compared with only 14 percent of those employed.

Finally, in a large-scale study of households in the Chicago area, Frederic Ilfeld (1977) found that women have higher rates of symptomatology than do men. However, the only group of women with symptomatology rates as low as those of men were those who worked in high-prestige occupations. The mental health implication, Ilfeld concluded, is to get more women into high-status jobs.

Intellectual well-being, we believe, is also a component of mental health. Consider a very disturbing longitudinal study of children given IQ tests in the 1930's (Kangas and Bradway, 1972). Results of a follow-up when the subjects were in their middle years showed that the brighter a man was as a youngster (in terms of IQ scores), the more he had gained in IQ with age; the brighter a woman, the less she had gained. Since the patterns of "average" women resembled those of men, biological differences are an unlikely explanation for the results found for the bright women. Therefore it may be that their lives had not provided the elements necessary for cognitive growth. On this point, Melvin Kohn and his associates (Kohn and Schooler, 1977) have recently demonstrated that the structure of work affects aspects of personality previously thought to be relatively stable and fixed early in life. The cognitive complexity of the work their subjects did was found to be related both to their intellectual flexibility and to their self-esteem. For those engaged in repetitive work, as are some housewives, the implications for well-being are ominous.

Furthermore, while the family is often viewed as a valuable refuge from the occupational world, we often forget that the workplace can be a valuable refuge from family life, from strong emotions, conflicting demands, petty annoyances. Work can provide variety, challenge, clear-cut responsibilities, even respectful underlings. Certainly if unemployment can contribute to mental illness, employment, for women as well as men, can contribute to mental health. Yet we rarely conceptualize unemployment as a social problem for women. Their unemployment is often hidden; analyses of the National Longitudinal Survey data (Blau, 1978) suggest that the effect of recessions, at least among white women, is to discourage them from entering the labor force. Furthermore, among black women, those who want to work form a larger group than those who actually hold jobs (Sullivan, 1977). When employed women lose their jobs, moreover, the social supports available are minimal (Warren, 1975) compared to those available to men.

It is almost a cliché now for people who work long hours at demanding jobs, aware of what they are missing in terms of time with family, long talks with friends, concerts, all kinds of opportunities for leisure, to express the sentiment that "there is more to life than work." The problem is that life *without* productive work is terrible. We assume this for men in thinking about their unemployment and their retirement, but we do not think about the situation of women in this way. We want to stress here that as Linda Fidell (1978) has shown, for some women the activities associated with child-care and home-making are truly productive and satisfying in terms of engaging their interests and talents, at least for part of their lives, as are volunteer activities. However, for others, the lack of economically productive work is associated with the absence of one or more of the previously mentioned requirements postulated by Beatrice Whiting (1977): a sense of competence; support and comfort; and variations in stimulation.

Many women settle for support and comfort at the expense of their other needs.

Unfortunately, our norm of married women economically dependent upon their husbands is not viable in many circumstances. Husbands lose their jobs or die without leaving an adequate estate; inflation makes two incomes increasingly necessary; and perhaps most important, marriages dissolve. It is projected that 40 percent of current marriages will end in divorce. Divorce too often brings poverty to many middle-class women who thought it could never happen to them. About half of the women now on welfare are separated or divorced, and the situation of divorced and separated women *not* on welfare is precarious. Dorothy Burlage (1978) in a new study of such women asks the question, How do these women manage to avoid welfare? The answer is, barely and painfully, and by being breadwinners. Their major source of support is their own earnings, not alimony or child support. Their economic situation after divorce is much worse than before, and considering income in relation to need, is much worse than that of their ex-husbands. Because of the limitations of their training and experience and the absence of social supports, many are living out Beatrice Whiting's nightmare alternative for mothers: eight hours of paid drudgery. The low pay of women's occupations, the need to work full time to receive not only income but desperately needed health benefits, and barriers to further education constrain both their current and future income. In their book *Time of Transition*, Heather Ross and Isabel Sawhill (1975) report finding that of separated women who are on welfare, only about one quarter could earn even $1000 more a year than welfare provides.

So we return to the question of occupational competence, and to its roots in socialization, because in mentioning such phenomena as divorce and widowhood, one is reciting the list of disasters that young girls are warned may force them to work. Thus they are encouraged to prepare themselves for some sort of fall-back occupation. In this way economic independence is associated not with pride and pleasure but with misfortune, stigma, and failure. For girls to develop maximum occupational competence has been a goal neither for them nor for their parents. The images of girls as future wives and mothers and boys as

economic providers are powerful influences on the values, attitudes, practices, and feelings of parents, who have been very
concerned not to jeopardize the wife-and-mother part of a girl's
future role. We are only now beginning to think about what may
jeopardize optimal development of a girl's occupational life.
The problem may be seen in a study by Barnett (1975), who
found that when one ranks occupations in terms of how prestigious they are, the more prestige an occupation has, the more
boys, but not girls, desired to enter it. For girls the more prestigious an occupation, the more they expressed an aversion to
entering it. Traditional parental values and attitudes can therefore be hazardous for daughters' future occupational options.
Having a challenging and satisfying occupation can be a central
source of self-esteem, identity, and satisfaction and it is increasingly important that women derive these from sources beyond
the roles of wife and mother.

Theoretical and empirical literature relevant to these topics
is unfortunately inadequate. Depending upon whose book one
is reading, one is told that marriage and children are a health
hazard for women, that career-oriented women are unhappy,
neurotic, conflicted about femininity, and so forth. Available
data are limited in various ways, but at least researchers are
asking important questions, such as whether marrying and having children are necessary for well-being.

On the question of marriage, studies of depression indicate
that among married people, women are more depressed than
men; among the unmarried, men are more depressed than women.
In reviewing these data, Lenore Radloff (1975) concluded that
marriage is a mental health advantage to men, but not to women.
However, a large-scale survey by Angus Campbell and his associates (1976) found no evidence that women were less satisfied
than men, and married women were more satisfied and happier
than unmarried women. So far, then, the data on marriage are
mixed.

Data on the relationship between rearing children and well-
being are somewhat clearer. Depression and a lower sense of
well-being are associated with caring for young children; indeed,
women in the so-called empty nest years are in fact lower in risk
for depression and higher in sense of well-being (Radloff, 1975).

Thus intensive involvement in child care is no sure route to happiness for women.

Work, in contrast, has until recently been seen as peripheral to women's well-being. Moreover, even studies that do focus on women's employment status tend to ignore variations among employed women which are due to differences in occupational status and in commitment to work (Campbell, Converse, and Rodgers, 1976; Kanter, 1977). Similarly, Linda Fidell (1978) has recently pointed out that women at home are not all alike; some are committed to the role of housewife, some want to work, and these variations affect well-being.

INVOLVEMENT IN MULTIPLE ROLES

It has been assumed that involvement in multiple roles, a phenomenon particularly relevant to women, is primarily a source of conflict and distress; multiple role involvement is rarely examined as potentially enhancing one's life and one's well-being. Yet in 1973 Gove and Tudor attributed the superiority of men's mental health to their involvement in the arenas of both work and family. The previously mentioned study by Brown et al. (1975) also indicates the benefits of multiple roles, since for married women with children, work was found to mitigate the consequences of stressful life events. And in her study of able women in midlife, Birnbaum (1975) found that compared with educated married women who had not worked since the birth of their first child, married professionals were higher in self-esteem and satisfaction.

In our own research we were able to examine the relationship of multiple role involvement to psychological well-being, indexed by self-esteem and role-pattern satisfaction, in a group of mothers who differed in employment status. Data were collected from women and their husbands, who were parents of preschool girls and boys, all of whom participated in a larger study of family and school influences on the competence-related behavior of preschool girls. Our sample included 142 white, married, middle-class women who had at least one child enrolled in a preschool in the Greater Boston area. All the women were in first marriages, and they were relatively well educated; 62 percent had at least a bachelor's degree. The homogeneity of the sample, while limiting generalizability, allowed us to see important differences that would otherwise be obscured.

Our focus was on comparing employed and unemployed mothers, both to determine any differences in the level of their role-pattern satisfaction and self-esteem and to investigate the differences between the groups with respect to the correlates of each of these outcome variables. The employed women met the criteria of working at least ten hours a week in paid employment for at least the year prior to the data collection. About 35 percent of the mothers in the sample, or 50 women, were classified as employed, and about 60 percent (n = 86) were classified as "at home." The remainder were students and were omitted from this study. The two subgroups of women did not differ with respect to age, education, or number of children. The women at home were occupying the pattern that has traditionally been commended to women, particularly if they have young children, while the group who were employed represented a nontraditional but increasingly popular pattern: that of working at least part time while caring for young children. If involvement in multiple roles is primarily a source of conflict and stress, without compensatory gratification, mothers who work should be lower in psychological well-being than those at home who are not confronted with potential role conflict and who are living out the socially prescribed life style.

[A thorough discussion of the method used to measure variables and the relationships between them has been omitted.]

Perhaps the most important finding of this study concerns the sources of self-esteem and satisfaction available to married women with young children. The well-being of nonemployed women is highly dependent upon their husbands' approval of their pattern, or, more accurately, on their (the wives') perceptions of his approval. Employed women are also sensitive to their husbands' attitudes, although considerably less so. But, in addition, their own commitment to work and their satisfaction with their current job contribute heavily to both indices of well-being. These work-related variables are clearly more under the women's own control, more independent of others, and thus may be more stable bases for well-being. Heavy reliance on external sources, on sources out of one's control, for one's self-esteem is highly problematic, especially in light of the high rate of marital dissolution.

A second important implication of our findings is that even while women are intensely concerned with the demands of young children, involvement in multiple roles need not result in debilitating conflict, strain, and dissatisfaction. At later stages of the life cycle, involvement in multiple roles may even protect against such stress as that associated with the empty nest and aging (Bart, 1972).

Our work supports, at least indirectly, the value of preparing girls from childhood on to develop and exercise occupational competence. In fact, in individual interviews many of the unemployed mothers who had daughters expressed similar sentiments. When asked how they would like their preschool daughter's life to be similar to theirs and how they would like it to be different, they stressed the importance of evaluating life choices before making commitments:

I hope she decides to get into some career *before* marriage, or at least before she has children—it would just make things a lot easier on all concerned.

I would like her to find a satisfying career which she can combine with being married and having a family, if she chooses to have one. I feel it is extremely important for her to have a fulfilling career for her to establish a real sense of worth as an adult woman. I do not feel I am as career-oriented and ambitious as I would like to be. I would like Debbie to be more so.

REFERENCES

Bailyn, L. Personal communication, 1978.

Barnett, R. C. Sex differences and age trends in occupational preference and occupational prestige. *Journal of Counseling Psychology*, 1975, *22*, 35–38.

Bart, P. Depression in middle-aged women. In J. M. Bardwick (Ed.), *Readings on the psychology of women*. New York: Harper and Row, 1972.

Baruch, G. K. Feminine self-esteem, self-ratings of competence, and maternal career-commitment. *Journal of Counseling Psychology*, 1973, *20*, 487–488.

Baruch, G. K. Girls who perceive themselves as competent: Some antecedents and correlates. *Psychology of Women Quarterly*, 1976, *1*, 38–49.

Birnbaum, J. A. Live patterns and self-esteem in gifted family-oriented and career-committed women. In M. Mednick, S. Tangri, and L. W. Hoffman (Eds.), *Women and achievement: Social and motivational analysis*. New York: Hemisphere-Halstead, 1975.

Blau, F. D. *The impact of the unemployment rate on labor force entries and exits*. Paper presented to Secretary of Labor's Invitational Conference on the National Longitudinal Surveys of Mature Women, Washington, D.C., 1978.

Brown, G. W., Bhrolchain, M. N., and Harris, T. Social class and psychiatric disturbance among women in an urban population. *Sociology*, 1975, *9*, 225–254.

Burlage, D. *Divorced and separated mothers: Combining the responsibilities of breadwinning and childrearing*. Unpublished doctoral dissertation, Harvard University, 1978.

Campbell, A., Converse, P. E., and Rodgers, W. L. *The quality of American life*. New York: Russell Sage, 1976.

Coopersmith, S. *The antecedents of self-esteem*. San Francisco: Freeman, 1968.

Ferree, M. M. The confused American housewife. *Psychology Today*, 1976, *10*, 76–80.

Fidell, L. *Employment status, role dissatisfaction and the housewife syndrome*. Unpublished manuscript, California State University, 1978.

Gove, W. R., and Tudor, J. F. Adult sex roles and mental illness. *American Journal of Sociology*, 1973, *78*, 812–835.

Hoffman, L. W. Changes in family roles, socialization, and sex differences. *American Psychologist*, 1977, *32*, 644–657.

Ilfeld, F., Jr. *Sex differences in psychiatric symptomatology*. Paper presented at American Psychological Association meeting, San Francisco, 1977.

Kangas, J., and Bradway, K. Intelligence at middle age: A thirty-eight-year-follow-up. *Developmental Psychology*, 1972, *5*, 333–337.

Kanter, R. M. *Work and family in the United States: A critical review and agenda for research and policy*. New York: Russell Sage Foundation, 1977.

Kohn, M. L., and Schooler, C. *The complexity of work and intellectual functioning*. Paper presented to American Sociological Association meeting, Chicago, 1977.

Lipman-Blumen, J. *The vicarious achievement ethic and non-traditional roles for women*. Paper presented to Eastern Sociological Association, New York, 1973.

Macke, A. S., and Hudis, P. M. *Sex-role attitudes and employment among women: A dynamic model of change and continuity*. Paper presented to Secretary of Labor's invitational conference on the National Longitudinal Surveys of Mature Women, Washington, D.C., 1978.

Radloff, L. Sex differences in depression: The effects of occupation and marital status. *Sex Roles*, 1975, *1*, 249–265.

Rosenkrantz, P., Vogel, S., Bee, H., Broverman, I., and Broverman, D. Sex-role stereotypes and self-concepts in college students. *Journal of Consulting Psychology*, 1968, *32*, 287–295.

Ross, H. L., and Sawhill, I. V. *Time of transition: The growth of families headed by women*. Washington: The Urban Institute, 1975.

Sears, P. S., and Barbee, A. H. Career and life satisfaction among Terman's gifted women. In J. Stanley, W. George, and C. Solano (Eds.), *The gifted and the creative: Fifty year perspective*. Balitmore: Johns Hopkins University Press, 1977.

Spence, J., and Helmreich, R. The attitudes towards women scale: An objective instrument to measure attitudes towards the rights and roles of women in contemporary society. JSAS *Catalog of Selected Documents in Psychology*, 1972, *2*, 66.

Sullivan, T. A., *Black female breadwinners: Some intersections of dual market and secondary worker theory*. Paper presented to American Sociological Association, Chicago, 1977.

Treiman, D. J. Problems of concept and measurement in the comparative study of occupational mobility. *Social Science Research*, 1975, *4*, 183–230.

Warren, R. B. *The work role and problem coping: Sex differentials in the use of helping systems in urban communities*. Paper presented at meeting of American Sociological Association, San Francisco, 1975.

Whiting, B. B. Changing life styles in Kenya. *Daedalus*, 1977, *106*, 211–225.

Women—New Patterns, Problems, Possibilities

Betty Friedan

Ultimately I am going to hint at new patterns and problems and pleasures and possibilities in the relations of women and men, but having as-
siduously tried to do some research on your own experience of these
phenomena during the five days of this conference, I have decided that
we are not there yet. And that I had better spend most of the time giving
you concrete proof of primary prevention of psychopathology through
social change and political action as it really happened this last twenty
years in this country through the Women's Movement. I can bear witness
from my original training as a psychologist and from my nearly twenty
years as a social change agent, founding and leading that movement to
the complex interrelationship between psychology, social change, and
pathology that we mutually confront, dealing with the concrete human
being in the process of making and surviving the change, and evolving
strategies for the next stage of human liberation.

First I want to remind you, because a lot of you here are too young to
remember and others would just as soon forget, where we were twenty
years ago, when I, as a young housewife-mother guiltily hiding my free-
lance writing from my suburban neighbors like secret drinking, was
starting *The Feminine Mystique*. I want to remind you where we were vis-
à-vis psychology, psychopathology, and women. There was, if you will
remember, at that time, a single image of woman—the happy housewife-mother—who was always 25 with three children under six, who
was fulfilled as a wife and a mother solely through those emotions having to do with her sexuality, her husband, her children, her home: her
peak experience, her orgasm, was throwing the powder in the dish-
washer. The fact that so many women were already working outside of
the home did not affect that image. And it was, above all, in its per-
niciousness, a psychological image. Remember *Modern Woman, The Lost
Sex* (Farnham and Lundberg, 1947)? A whole slew of books had come
out using or twisting Freudian psychology to say that the previous cen-
tury-long battle for women's rights—the vote, careers, higher education—had made modern women terribly neurotic, maladjusted in their

proper role as women, which was to live passively, vicariously through men and children, through feminine fulfillment as a life-long housewife-mother. Heeding that message, younger women, 20 years ago, were happily marrying and being told to marry at 17, 18, 19, giving up their own education to put their husbands through, and making a career of three, four, five children—the new happy, happy housewives.   '

The fact that overwhelming fortunes were being made selling tranquilizer pills mainly to women; the fact that women made up the great majority of the patients in every doctor's office; and, of course, the clients of the burgeoning psychological industry was not supposed to belie that happiness. Further, if you read the magazines, if you listened carefully to the messages in the mass media, no matter how happy, happy, happy she was supposed to be, the woman was also suffused with life-long guilt because she was the culprit of every psychological case history. Something wrong with the children—what was wrong with the mother? Can this marriage be saved—adjust, the wife, adjust! The neurotic, frustrated American "mom" had been discovered as the massive cause of GI malfunction in World War II. But in this new image of woman, she was *fulfilled* as a housewife, totally fulfilled as a wife and mother.

Twenty years ago when I started interviewing suburban housewives, this image, which I called the "feminine mystique," was so pervasive in the mass media, in conventional sophisticated psychological and sociological thought, that there simply was no name for the malaise so many women suffered that did *not* have to do with children or husband. I called it "the problem that has no name," but every woman knew what I was talking about. Anything that had to do with the self of women was more repressed 20 years ago than sexuality had been repressed in the Victorian era.

The modern women's movement, as the history books say, began as a change of consciousness with my book, *The Feminine Mystique.* It made conscious the urgent need of women to break through that obsolete image that had confined their energies and kept them from facing their real problems and possibilities and opportunities in this changing world. You will remember or you will have heard from others, the relief it was to realize that you were not alone, that what you suffered was not necessarily your own personal sin or guilt to be confessed in the confessional, or on the couch, but a general social and political, economic and psychological condition that you shared with other women and that could be changed—that urgently had to be changed.

The modern women's movement had to happen when it did basically because of the evolution of human life. It was not an accident that when I began the change in consciousness I was in my mid-30s with my youngest child off to school . . . and over half of my life left ahead of me.

With a life expectancy now of 81 years, there was no way that women could any longer define themselves as life-long mothers. They had to grow beyond the age-old practice of defining women through their child-bearing function. They had to move to a definition of themselves as persons. The post–World War II feminine mystique, misusing Freudian psychology and all the rest, was a last gasp of reaction that temporarily seduced women to evade the risks of personhood. The women's movement was a necessity in evolutionary terms, which I and others put into words. To remind you what happened, once we declared that women are people—no more, no less—then it was simply our American and human birthright—equality of opportunity, freedom, independence, our own voice in society. At first we followed the model of the Black movement, and made some mistakes by assuming too literal an analogy with it and with the labor movement. The modern women's movement began, above all, as an American movement. Its ideology was simply that of American democracy, the respect for the individual, human dignity, human freedom, equal opportunity, the right to fulfill your potential, the right to have a voice in your destiny. They said it was a movement without an ideology, but then I think they mistook what the ideology was.

The real ideology of the women's movement was simply the values of democracy applied to women, not a 10 percent minority, but a 52 percent majority. But when have the values of this, or any revolution been applied in the unique way that came from women's experience, not as an abstract doctrine, but concretely, to the dailiness of human life as it is lived in the home, in the bedroom, in the kitchen, in the office, hospital, classroom, and, therefore, immediately affecting everyone, changing everybody's life. It spread faster than could be believed, faster than any organization could contain. There was never any money. It was a miracle, and perhaps a paradigm of a new kind of human politics. All right. From 1966 to the present, a dozen years or so, there has been this movement, which used laws, which used the methods of the Civil Rights movement and then invented methods of its own, raising the consciousness of women, confronting the barriers of society. We got the laws and imperfectly got them enforced—against sex discrimination in education, employment, and credit. And enormous changes began to happen.

You are witness to these changes. The massive increase in the number of women who for economic reasons have to work outside the home now have a new sense of possibilities. In law schools and medical schools, women are no longer one, two, three percent of the class, but 30 percent and more. Every profession is now open to women. Sports are no longer just for boys, from the Little League up to national basketball. The breakthroughs against sex discrimination in employment are real breakthroughs, not just tokenism. But for many women now going to work as mothers after years at home, the only jobs they can get are low-paying sales or clerical jobs, which are paid less because they have been held primarily by women. So in average wages, it looks like women are getting paid *less* in comparison with men than before. That obscures the movement of younger women to equal opportunity, and the whole new consciousness of sex discrimination, sexism, in every profession. And the new expectation of equality in marriage and the family.

The psychological effects of all of this may be quite different, in reality, from the doom and gloom predictions of reactionary social biologists or the simplistic preconceptions of radical feminists. Those who proclaim the natural inevitability of patriarchy are sure that equal opportunity for women will destroy culture itself. Certain sociologists say that the family is a disappearing species because of these selfish women that want to do other things with their lives than stay home all the time with their children. Certain psychologists proclaim widespread male impotence because of the new aggressiveness of women. The rising divorce rate and every other psychologically bad thing that is happening to people today is blamed on the women's movement. But the women who have moved know in their hearts, know in their guts, the rightness, the urgency, the life-opening exhilaration of their own moving.

As I go around this country, lecturing, every year more women of all ages come up and say, "It changed my life, it changed my whole life." (That's the title of my second book; *It Changed My Life: Writings on the Women's Movement.*) When I ask one of these women "What are you doing now?" she starts telling me the new problems: juggling work, her job, and the housework, the children, putting it all together with Band-Aids. New problems of divorce or husbands being threatened, economic problems, time problems; cheerfully, cheerfully, she tells me about all these new problems. "Sometimes it seems like the problems increase geometrically." But I never hear recriminations, regrets. I ask, "Would you go back where it was simpler, more secure?" And she says, "Are you kidding?" No woman would go back, despite the many new problems that women have today. It is better to be a woman today. You feel better being a woman today. You might have *more problems* being a woman today, but you are more alive. And the new problems are much more interesting than the old problems.

I could be accused of being prejudiced, self-serving in this proclamation so, therefore, I want to give you some new national statistics gathered by psychologists that confirm my personal experience and observations. Before I wrote *The Feminine Mystique,* I was in my late 30s and I felt old. I felt like it was all going to be downhill. When I look back, I felt older at 38 than I felt at 48 and a lot older than I feel now at 58. I noticed something interesting when I began looking for women that were moving beyond the feminine mystique. In the mid-60s, right after my book came out, I went around the country, much as I went around this conference, looking for new patterns. It was before we even had a women's movement, and of course, I did not find any new patterns. It was too soon. I did find some individual women who were putting their lives together in new ways, and they had a lot of problems because there were no social patterns, not in this country yet. One thing I did notice about those women—they looked vital, they looked alive. They tended to be a little older than the suburban housewives I had interviewed for *The Feminine Mystique* because this was a time when women in their 20s, in their 30s, were all home with kids. (Only the exceptional one was out there, then, and she might not even have kids.) The few women that had been combining marriage and motherhood and profession were in their menopausal years. But they looked and sounded more vibrant, vital, than the younger trapped housewives I had been interviewing who had all these vague syndromes and symptoms. They might not even wear as much make-up but their skin looked younger!

I started asking them about the menopause and they'd say, "Oh, I don't remember." or "I haven't had it." And I'd say, "What do you mean, you haven't had it?" I would figure out the woman was 50 or whatever. She did not remember when she stopped menstruation because she actually had not experienced the symptoms, traumas, and depression that were supposed to characterize menopause. In other words, menopause was a syndrome that did not exist for such women. What they experienced was a vitality, as if they were growing again.

Then, the women's movement really took off, and women in great numbers began to go back to school, go to work. And even if they continued to write "housewife" on the census blank, they began to feel differently about themselves. It was like a phenomenon you do not even notice because it is so large—that women after 40, after women's life was supposed to be over and downhill, were growing and moving with incredible zest and vitality. Recently, the various fashion magazines showed women now in their 40s and 50s against pictures of themselves in their 30s, and commented that the women really did look younger now. And it was not just a question of the styles that used to make women try to look younger. This was something different.

I began to ask a lot of questions about this "x" that was making some women experience menopause differently, women growing instead of deteriorating with age. I did not know how pervasive it was. Coincidentally, just in time for this conference, some figures were released that are really mind boggling. A repeat was done of the classic midtown Manhattan study (Srole, 1975), which in 1954 showed mental health impairment increasing with successive age groups, and women much worse off than men. In this and another comparable study by the National Center for Health Statistics, women were so much worse off than men for every possible index that could be associated with mental health, from insomnia and fainting to inertia, depression, and feeling about to have a nervous breakdown, that Jessie Bernard wrote a book dooming the future of marriage because she concluded that while marriage seemed to be okay for a man, it was driving women crazy.

The men and women originally studied were aged 20 to 59. At each 10-year interval their rate of impairment had increased: mental health deteriorated with age, and more acutely for women. They repeated the Midtown study in 1975, 20 years later. Instead of finding the expected increase in impairment, to their utter amazement, it looked as if mental health had stopped getting worse with age. After 20 years of wear and tear of living, the deterioration of mental health that had been expected had not taken place. They could not believe it. Then they began to analyze the statistics more carefully to see what had happened. The impression that mental health no longer deteriorated with age had come completely from *a massive improvement in the last 20 years in the mental health of women over 40* (Srole, 1975).

Whereas in 1954, 21 percent of women 40–49 had shown what they called impairment of mental health, compared with 9 percent of men, by 1974 the women who had been 20–29 or 39 in the first study, showed no worse mental health, or slightly better, at 40–49. Furthermore, the women now 40–49 showed enormous improvement in mental health compared with the women 20 years ago aged 40–49. Only 8 percent of women were now impaired compared with the 21 percent in 1954. In other words, the women had caught up to the men. They showed, in fact, less impairment of mental health with age than the men. The psychologists who analyzed these statistics concluded that something really massive must have been happening to women in the last 20 years that was not happening to men.

All right. What does all this mean? Now I am drawing on my participant-observer knowledge, and from my own interviews of women over the years. It has been good for women to have more self-respect and independence as people, more freedom and options to move on their own in society. It has been good for women to get out the aggression that they used to turn against themselves in self-hate and self-denigration, in masochism, the impotent rage they used to vent on their own minds and bodies. It has been good for women, psychologically, economically—and economics is the bottom line in this. I cannot possibly stress too much the importance of having some independence and ability to support themselves. It has been good for women to come out of those tight, confining masks and be who they really are, to let it all hang out. It has been good for women to be part of a movement, to feel that they are supported by a great movement of other women, even to be able to share feelings without necessarily paying $50 to $100 an hour to do so. It has been good for women not only to be able to assert the self but to be a part, as many have been in one way or another, of a movement beyond the self. It has been good for women, finding the power to change their own lives and recognizing their power to change society.

It is already visibly good for women to have new options, but we are only beginning to know something about the potentials of human growth in females, about the healthy, active, fully grown personhood of women. At this time, certain transitional phenomena can obscure some of this. For instance, you have to be careful to distinguish in your own clinical work, or sociological or psychological analysis, phenomena of reaction, of defensive reaction, and understand that these may be temporary way stations to the real human autonomy and self-definition that women are seeking. Some of the extreme hostility against men that gave a bad image to "women's lib," which is a term I myself do not use, is not liberation, though the rage may be a real and even necessary stage in liberation. Some of that hostility and its acting out or the rhetoric that expresses it came from an ideological mistake, reducing the relationship of woman and man with its complex biological, psychological, social, and sexual dynamic by too literal an analogy to the relationship of worker and boss, or black and white. The separatism that resulted is not synonymous with liberation. To deny the psychological and biological and human interconnectedness of woman and man, to deny all the feelings that women have had about men, love, children, and home is to deny a part of woman's own nature.

It was reaction; women had to get their anger out; better than taking it out on the self. But an excess of that reaction is very similar to machismo. It hides enormous insecurity. Woman's worst problem today is the lack of confidence in herself. Having seen, maybe in your mother or your sister, that powerlessness, that trapped-housewife desperation, being afraid, still, that you might be pinched back into it, being unsure, still of your own ability to move in this complex society, in panicky defense you want to throw out all of the things that characterized woman in the past. Women are afraid of the softness; to hide their own inadmissible need for dependence, now they have to be more independent than any man. Be tough! Tough! Or we risk losing this hard-won autonomy.

But the more the woman moves, the more sure she is of her ability, the more she can afford to also admit her vulnerabilities and her weaknesses. And the more real she becomes. So you must not confuse the reaction, which is another kind of mask, with her real self that is not yet fully liberated. You must look for female machismo, as well as male machismo, and for what is hidden behind that facade.

In the discussions at the conference, I was a little disturbed (as I see that others of my generation are) by the seemingly utter preoccupation with the self, the selfishness, of some of the young women. They are choosing not to have children. They are only concerned with their careers, or they are only concerned with themselves. Now, a certain amount of selfishness is healthy for women. As one of the first woman theologians said, the sin of woman has been selflessness, too much selflessness, evasion of the risks of self by living through others. That can be a sin, you know. In my own origins there is a wonderful saying, "If I am not for myself, who will be for me? But if I am only for myself, what am I?" Woman has to be for herself, or she cannot really be for anyone else. You know from the psychopathology that you used to deal with, and may still be dealing with, what happens to the children when the woman has to use them for her own self-aggrandizement or to fulfill her own needs. She had to be for herself to really be there for her children.

❖   Some of you have worried that this negotiating of contracts about who is going to do the housework is taking all the spontaneity out of love and marriage. I will tell you something about this. When you do not negotiate, when the woman is the resentful martyr and feels like a service station as the women that I interviewed 20 years ago used to put it . . . that is really bad for the spontaneity of love and marriage. Why in those years did so many books become best sellers that sold "88 New Ways to Make the Act of Love More Endurable"? Why did the vibrator seem for a while to be more titillating for some women than the human penis? It was not good for love, marriage, spontaneity of sex for women to feel like a service station. The negotiation is an improvement.

I discovered some interesting things in my new interviewing of young women in Vermont and elsewhere. They had been through these knock-down-drag-out fights every time the garbage had to be taken out or dinner cooked: Why should I do it. . . . You've got to do it equally. He won't do his share. Or he wouldn't do it right, and so on and so forth. Until, she tells me, "I suddenly realized that I still was the one really running the house. Maybe I didn't want to give up that power. But in order to do my other work, I simply couldn't be the one that was responsible for it any longer. I couldn't be the only one that everyone would look to. I really had to give up that power. And once I gave it up, then we were able to negotiate." She goes on: "Negotiate, we don't even negotiate any more. It flows. Whoever is able to do it at that time does it, and half the time we don't even bother to negotiate."

In other words, the psychology of power. In recompense for the lack of power in society, women had to have this absolute domination in the home. And that was the American "mom," and you are still dealing with the effects of that in psychopathology. In the last decade, research began to show that when women worked from choice and not from absolute, dire desertion of the husband or whatever, their husbands had more decision-making power in their own homes, compared with the husbands of full-time housewives. In the new families that may evolve as women begin to move to a more equal role in society, carrying a greater share of the economic burden, the power of the woman in the home will be less destructive. As many young men are now finding, sharing the intimate, active life and nurturing of the home and children has its own power and rewards. There may be a virtual disappearance of certain kinds of psychopathology that resulted from the powerlessness (power lust) of women and the absent, passive father. (Incidentally, *Time* magazine a few months ago ran a cover story called the depression of psychiatry. The psychiatry business is evidently down. Most of the patients used to be women. In addition to inflation, the gurus, and disillusionment with the psychological panaceas, have you ever thought that the women's movement itself is helping to put psychiatry out of business?)

I will tell you a new problem I worry about: the conscious or not conscious conflict or choice not to have children at all that may be one cause of the stress for the younger women. "Up Against the Clock," a new study that has come out of the University of California at Santa Cruz (Fabe and Winkler, 1979), shows women, in agonizing conflict over the choice as they approach 35 whether to have a baby or not. I do not want to go back to a mystique, and I do not think that a human being has instincts the same way that animals do, but I do not want to see women choosing not to have children for the wrong reasons. I want them to have the choice. I do not want them to have to have children to justify their existence. But I think there is a powerful generative need or impulse, in women and in men, that is not lightly denied.

I am not even talking now about reproducing the human race or deploring a situation in which the best or the brightest are not having children. I am talking about the woman herself and the woman's total personhood, which surely includes that powerful generativeness. I do not like the discussions in some of the feminist psychotherapy in which the self is defined apart from love, from nurturing, as if the self for woman were only the career, or only the work. As if the self were not also defined in the nurturing of the children, the intimate relationship with the man, whoever. Because if it was denying a part of the personhood of woman when she had to deny those human assertive needs to grow and act and have a voice and use the abilities that she shared with men, it is also perhaps denying a part of the personhood of woman if she denies the powerful needs and abilities and fulfillment of mothering. Motherhood is more than a mystique. But I am not blaming the victim here.

❖   I am leery of the *mea culpa* kind of men's liberation. I do not think that men are going to do an awful lot to change, just to please the women. They will do some things to please the women. They will have to. But that is patronizing in a way. Let the men change because they need to change, to live their own lives well. Again going back to biological statistics, it is not good that men are dying 10 years younger than women of their age group, that the age discrepancy of men and women at death is widening, that men did not show that great improvement in mental health in this 20-year period. Men have got to make a breakthrough comparable to women's. It is not the same one, it will not have the same confrontational aspects. Men have got to break through the machismo, the competitiveness, the denial of their own real feelings and fears, and they are beginning to do it.

I think you may get shorter and more flexible working hours and less slavery to the corporation—not necessarily because of women moving into corporations, because a lot of women think they have to do it better than the man at this point. But because men, liberated from the whole earning burden and expected to share the parenting, are beginning to say their own "no" to living a whole life just for the corporation. Men's mid-life crisis—there is fire underneath all that smoke. There is a value change taking place among men. The next step of human liberation will be made by men.

Finally, I want to say just one word about feminist psychotherapy. I am a feminist. I was originally trained as a psychologist. I think that any good psychotherapist today must in a certain sense be a feminist, but what that means is simply this: that we listen very, very carefully and sensitively to the woman where she is now. To the woman, herself, whether or not she fits Freudian or feminist book definitions, with respect for her own authenticity or integrity. Taking her seriously, her totality as a person, a woman, and realizing that we do not know all the answers yet, that she is still *evolving*, that we have not even seen yet the limits of women's possibility, but we must respect the reality of her life, here and now.

And if you are a good feminist psychotherapist, you also have to look and listen with the same sensitivity to men, to men where they are now. Realizing that men also have been oppressed, truncated, by sex roles and obsolete definitions of masculinity, that men have all kinds of human potential, similar to women, that they have not been allowed to express or experience. And if you are also committed to the family, as the ground soil, the nutrient for mental health, then you have to realize that your commitment is to the evolving family. That there is no way to go back to the mom-the-housewife, dad-the-breadwinner, Junior-and-Janie-for-ever-children, Good-Housekeeping-seal-of-approval family that only 7 percent of Americans now live in. That we have to look with respect and sensitivity at all the ways that people are moving to live together, to meet their needs for intimacy and mutual support, in all the stages and the new length and complexity of the life span. There are old value judgments having to do with marriage, with divorce, with all sorts of things that were good and that were bad, which we have to hold in abeyance in order to understand where women, men, and the family really are, here and now, and where they are moving. It is going to require every bit of our ability, everything that has been learned in all times to really understand this fast-evolving reality—the changing woman, the changing man, the changing family.

I welcome this community of psychotherapists that were part of the problem 20 years ago, that helped perpetrate the mystique that kept women down. I welcome your embrace of the great human movement of social change, of the women's movement as a primary prevention of psychopathology.

References

Bernard, J. The future of marriage. New York: World Publishers, 1972.

Bird, C. The best years of a woman's life. Psychology Today, 1979, 13, 20–26.

Fabe, M., and Winkler, N. Up against the clock. New York: Random House, 1979.

Friedan, B. The feminine mystique. New York: W. W. Norton & Co., 1963.

Friedan, B. It changed my life: Writings on the women's movement. New York: Random House, 1976.

Lundberg, F. G., and Farnham, M. F. Modern woman: The lost sex. Philadelphia, Penn.: Richard West, 1947.

Singer, E., Garfinkel, R., Cohen, S. M., and Srole, L. Mortality and mental health: Evidence from the Midtown Manhattan restudy. Social Sciences and Medicine, 1977, 10, 517–525.

Srole, L. Measurement and classification in socio-psychiatric epidemiology: Midtown Manhattan study (1954) and Midtown Manhattan restudy (1974). Journal of Health and Social Behavior, 1975, 16, 347–364.

Overcoming Self-Hate through Education: Achieving Self-Love among Gay People

Brian R. McNaught

When the American Psychiatric Association's board of directors voted unanimously in December 1973 to remove homosexuality from its *Diagnostic and Statistical Manual of Psychiatric Disorders*, it did not "cure" the nation's 22 million gay men and women overnight.

When Ford and Beach demonstrated in 1951 that homosexual behavior is evidenced in every species of mammal, gay people did not suddenly think of their sexual activity as "natural."

When the Catholic Theological Society of America's Committee on Sexuality insisted (Kosnick, Carroll, Cunningham, Modras, and Schulte, 1971) that scriptural passages traditionally used to condemn homosexuality had been taken out of context and misinterpreted, gay men and women did not suddenly feel loved and accepted by God.

Despite all of the advances in the last 60 years in our understanding of human sexual response; despite the studies and subsequent statements by social scientists which underscore the appropriateness of homosexual behavior for some persons; despite evidence of an increased tolerance of gay people in many segments of society, including some quarters of the Catholic Church, I believe self-hate continues to be the biggest hurdle for many gay people. Ignorance, I believe, is the creator of this hurdle and therefore the enemy of gay men and women and of all those persons who are dedicated to serving the needs of gay people, such as counselors, clergy, therapists, educators, and social workers.

Despite all the public emphasis on civil rights, I suggest that the greatest goal of gay men and women today is to love and to be loved maturely. In conquering self-hate through education, the gay person begins the important process of growth toward love of self and of others, and learns to overcome the obstacles which currently discourage meaningful relationships.

These conclusions are drawn from the observations of personal experi-

462 BRIAN R. MCNAUGHT

ences and through written and verbal communication with a large cross-section of gay men and women throughout the United States and Canada. The communication with the gay people resulted from articles I have written, speeches I have given, or media interviews with me on the subject of homosexuality, conducted since 1974.

Seven years ago, on a nondescript Saturday morning, I grabbed a bottle of paint thinner and drank it. At the time, I seemingly had everything for which to live. I was 26 years old, attractive and intelligent. I was an award-winning columnist on the staff of a Catholic newspaper, a frequent host of a church-sponsored television talk show, and a popular speaker at parish functions. My family celebrated my presence, even when I was accompanied by my handsome and articulate lover, a minister.

My goal in life was to be God's best friend, or a "saint" as we would say in the Catholic Church. I desperately wanted to be loved and associated love with approval. The approval of others, I reasoned, was the only sign we had that it was appropriate to like yourself. In my attempt to experience self-love, I eagerly sought the approval of everyone I encountered, from aunts and uncles to grocery store clerks. If I could make them smile, I must be a person worthy of love, I insisted. I was good at getting smiles, but they were never enough. People who find their worth in the approval of others, I learned, have an insatiable appetite.

Of particular concern to me was the approval of my church, the institution around which nearly all our family social life revolved; the institution which had educated me for 16 years and nurtured in me the idea I was special. Considered a "prince of a boy" by the nuns in grade school, the brothers in high school, the Catholic readers of my weekly column, I was polite, creative, sensitive, and likeable. Nevertheless, I lacked an important sense of self-worth.

I am convinced that my lack of self-esteem resulted from my lifelong awareness of homosexual feelings. To be sexual at all in an Irish Catholic environment in the 1950s was discouraged. Sex was an inappropriate topic for discussion. Because no one ever spoke of homosexuality (boys loving boys and girls loving girls) except in the crudest jokes, I kept my feelings a secret from the time I developed my first crush on a male lifeguard at age 9 and dreamed at night about sleeping with Tarzan.

Like every gay person with whom I have talked, I did not think of myself as a "queer" when I was a youngster; at least I would not accept the term as an accurate description of my feelings. Queers were "sissies" and I was no sissy; I excelled in a variety of sports. Queer boys were supposed to hate girls and at the same time want to be a girl. I liked being a boy and had lots of girl friends. "But if I'm not a queer, what am I?" I wondered.

The myths surrounding homosexuality were presented as truths when I was in grade school and, in many places in this country, they continue to be. Children with a homosexual orientation grow up thinking there is something "queer" about their feelings; something sick and immoral; something which when revealed will eliminate the love and respect of their parents, siblings, and friends.

By the time I entered high school, I figured out that my feelings for other men—my attraction to the male aura—made me a homosexual. Still, I did not see the contradiction between liking the bodies of other boys and eventually getting married. Like millions of other gay people throughout history, I reasoned that I must be the exception.

I do not remember reading anything in popular literature about homosexuality. There was no available book or copy of the *Saturday Evening Post* to which I could turn. Outside the office of the guidance counselor there was a rack of pamphlets on a variety of subjects like drinking, dating, and drugs but nothing on homosexuality; nothing that could answer my questions.

"If you come into my office and tell me that you've screwed a chick, I'll talk to you," declared the guidance counselor in a talk to my all-male senior class, "But if you tell me you're queer, I'll kick you out of the office." Until he made that announcement, I had seriously considered telling the counselor my long-held secret. He frightened me into maintaining silence, which I was as good at as I was in securing his approval of me in other areas. When I graduated, the guidance counselor was one of the faculty members who voted unanimously to honor me with the Christian Leadership Award.

The process of learning to hate myself was well underway. I knew, for instance, that I would never win the high school award if I revealed my sexual feelings. Even though I felt I was a good person, insofar as I kept the Ten Commandments, discouraged "impure thoughts," and enthusiastically performed various "acts of charity," I began to believe that homosexuals, as a group, were bad people and that I shared somehow in that sin.

I lived two lives—a public one which drew positive attention and a private one which was tormented with fear and anxiety. When I drank the paint thinner, I did so to escape the contradiction between my public and private self. I feared losing the affirmation of others and at the same time could no longer bear lying about my sexual orientation. As far as I was concerned, I was going home to God to whom I would explain myself and from whom I would seek an answer to my pain. How could a father who loved his child allow him or her to be a homosexual?

As I had my stomach pumped, I decided that my secret was literally killing me and that if I cared to live, I had to learn to be myself, accept myself, and love myself regardless of the consequences. It was while sitting on the table in the emergency room of the Catholic hospital that I decided never again to live my life based on other people's expectations. Shortly thereafter, I broke up my relationship because it was beyond repair; I started reading about homosexuality and I joined an organization of gay Catholics called Dignity. After attending a conference on Christian ministry to the homosexual, I wrote a column for the Catholic newspaper on the beauty of gay love. I formed a chapter of Dignity in the city and told the editor and each of the staff people about my homosexuality.

Within a month of opening my new inner-city apartment as a center for gay people, I agreed to be interviewed in a daily newspaper. The next working day, my column was dropped from the Catholic newspaper. In the following weeks, I began legal proceedings against the Church, organized pickets of the newspaper, and began speaking publicly about homosexuality. Three weeks after my column was dropped, I undertook a hunger strike in protest of the sins of the Church against gay people. The fast ended after 24 days when the bishops of Detroit wrote me a letter in which they pledged to work to educate the clergy about homosexuality. The following day I was fired from the remainder of my responsibilities at the newspaper.

In the process of this public ordeal, I alienated my family, most of my readers, and my television viewers. All of the signs of my sainthood, my acceptance, were stripped away. I lost my job, my friendships with many gay and nongay people, the approval of my Church, and my high school Christian Leadership Award (for a period of time). Yet, for the first time in 26 years, I felt authentic, adult, and worthy of admiration and love.

Today, I am in a relationship with another man which is honest, open, sensitive, and supportive. I have many friends who love and support me as a whole person. While I may lack many of life's traditional signs of success, like write-ups in the alumni newsletter and a healthy salary for my work, I have never contemplated suicide again, and I feel fully alive.

My understanding of my homosexuality today is that it is a natural variation; that the genital expression of same-sex feelings ought to be responsible; that gay people are beloved children of God and, like heterosexuals, are called to reach our full potential. My position on the Catholic Church's official teaching is that they are in error when they suggest homosexuality is an "abomination," and that they will one day change their stand.

For me, the process of emerging from an image to a reality, from a secret to a song, from self-hate to self-love is ongoing. Frequently there are temptations to be inauthentic, to return to the closet, or to an image for the sake of approval. The tools I use to continue that growth process remain the same. The most important step I took was educating myself to the truths about homosexuality, truths which tore down the myths of the past and helped me rebuild a positive self-image.

The negative self-image frequently manifests itself in alcohol and drug abuse, irresponsible contact with sexual partners by individuals who know they have a venereal disease and, certainly the most tragic, the physical abuse of one homosexual by another. Humphreys and Miller (1980) found evidence to suggest that homosexual victims of violent crimes are most often those most fearful of being identified as gay. For this reason, gay men and women who seek my help receive homework reading assignments. There are a variety of worthwhile books on the market which I can enthusiastically recommend.

Young people who are confused by their sexual feelings are encouraged to read *A Way of Love, A Way of Life* by Frances Hanckel and John Cunningham (1979). I also encourage teachers of high school and college students to show the filmstrip *The Hidden Minority: Homosexuality in Our Society* (Guidance Associates, 1979).

As general resource books I suggest Tripp's (1975) *The Homosexual Matrix; Society and the Healthy Homosexual* by George Weinberg (1972); *Loving Someone Gay* and *Living Gay* by Don Clark (1977, 1979); and *Positively Gay*, edited by Robert Leighton and Betty Berzon (1979).

Women who are interested in reading more about the lesbian experience are encouraged to read *Our Right to Love: A Lesbian Resource Guide*, edited by Ginny Vida (1978); *The Joy of Lesbian Sex* by Emily Sisley and Bertha Harris (1977); and Rita Mae Brown's (1973) *Rubyfruit Jungle*.

Materials recommended for men include *The Joy of Gay Sex* by Charles Silverstein and Edmund White (1977); *Men Loving Men* by Mitch Walker (1977); *The Best Little Boy in the World* by John Reid (1976); and *The Front Runner* by Patricia Nell Warren (1974).

Religion, I have found, is a critical area for many gay people. Too many educators and therapists who are not interested in religion overlook the tremendous influence a religious background can have upon an individual's sense of self-worth. Today, especially, with the so-called Moral Majority and other reactionary groups using the Bible as a weapon in their war against gay civil rights, it is important that gay people and their families have accurate information about the Scriptures and their approach to homosexuality.

Most of the books I recommend are by Catholics but, because of their treatment of both the Old and New Testament, I feel they are helpful to persons of both Christian and Jewish backgrounds. By far, the most important book on the subject is *Christianity, Social Tolerance and Homosexuality* by John Boswell (1980). Also quite helpful are *The Church and the Homosexual* by John McNeill, S.J. (1976); *Embodiment* by James Nelson (1978); and *Human Sexuality: New Directions in American Catholic Thought*, a study commissioned by the Catholic Theological Society of America (Kosnick et al., 1977).

Another critical area of concern for gay people which often influences their ability to love themselves is the response of their families to homosexuality. My parents had many questions, which I attempted to answer, but they seemed to be especially helped by reading books by "impartial" observers whom they could trust. Of particular help at the time was Laura Hobson's (1976) book, *Consenting Adult*. Since then, Betty Fairchild and Nancy Hayward (1979) have written *Now That You Know: What Every Parent Should Know about Homosexuality*, a book which has been successful in moving many parents from a position of fear to one of understanding.

It is not uncommon to hear skepticism from a gay person who has read his or her first book on homosexuality. The opinions of one author who affirms homosexuality are welcomed but distrusted by readers who have spent 18, 30, or 50 years learning to approach their sexuality negatively. However, learning positive new things about one's sexual orientation is not unlike eating peanuts: it is not easy to stop. The people with whom I have worked generally ask for a more extensive book list, with fiction, poetry, history, and biographies included.

A second step which I took and which I recommend to people seeking to build positive self-images is associating with other gay people. I met my minister lover in a bar to which I vowed I would never return once I had "roped" him into a relationship. I viewed the people in the bar as the pathetic "queers" who had been described to me throughout my life and with whom I could not relate. Had I attempted to talk with them, I would have made new friends and therefore probably would not have felt so trapped in my relationship. However, I saw my lover as "not like those others," and I did my best to keep us both away from their influence.

When I broke up my relationship, I soon began meeting a variety of gay people. Some of them I liked very much and some of them I did not, but I came to a growing awareness that "gay" is an adjective and not a noun; that I was a gay man who was part of a community. I met other gay Catholics and gay atheists. I talked with gay Republicans, Democrats, and also gay anarchists. I listened to people defend monogamy and defend open relationships. In this process I felt liberated to choose my own path, to say "I am doing this because it is 'Brian's way' and not because it is the 'gay way.'"

The knowledge which I accumulated by reading enabled me to feel more secure when I encountered other gay people and nongay people. It enabled me to begin taking *responsibility* for my life, to see the need to *care* for my uniqueness, and to *respect* myself. The gay men and women I encourage to join local gay organizations, attend religious services for gay people, and participate in gay social functions return with similar stories. Some people begin dressing in clothing they prefer as opposed to the clothing they wore because they thought it was "gay." Those who find the gay bars to be compromising situations or places in which they are prone to drink too much begin to avoid them and feel better about themselves for doing so. Other people report that while they used to use terms like "queen," "faggot," "fruit," and "fairy" to describe themselves and their friends, they no longer see these terms as humorous or appropriate.

In order to find the gay organizations, the gay religious services, or the social functions sponsored by the community, I suggest that people purchase a copy of the *Gayellow Pages*. This national directory lists all the organizations, publications, and services for gay people in each city in the United States and Canada. It is an invaluable resource for gay men and women and for professionals seeking to meet their needs.

Although I would avoid at all costs "pushing" someone out of the closet, I do believe that "coming out" is an important part of the self-affirmation process. Individuals who are constantly forced to lie to parents, peers, and fellow workers about their social life are denying the joy and beauty of their same-sex feelings and undermining the positive attitudes they might have developed through private reading. While some persons find leading a double life a small price to pay for a successful career or similar goal, most persons with whom I have talked seem unwilling to play the games. Those persons who have "come out of the closet"—who have affirmed their sexual orientation to themselves and to significant others—frequently pay an initial price of rejection by some people, but at the same time they report a unique sense of self-determination, worth, and honesty.

In addition to coming out, I believe participating in your own liberation is important to the notion of care, respect, and responsibility. For many years, I had worked with other disadvantaged minorities in their struggles for civil rights. I did so as a white, presumed-to-be-heterosexual male. As such, my privileged status was maintained, and I was limited in my ability to feel the sense of growth experienced by those more intimately involved. When I lost my column, and then my job, however, I had to begin fighting for my own rights and, in so doing, experienced the same pride which I had seen in the faces of the black people, the Hispanics, and the women with whom I had marched.

There are two national gay organizations which I encourage gay people and their supporters to join. The first is the Gay Rights National Lobby (GRNL), located at 930 F Street, N.W., Washington, D.C., 20004. GRNL is the organization which lobbies Congress to pass legislation favorable to the civil rights of gay people. The National Gay Task Force (NGTF), located at 80 Fifth Ave., New York, N.Y., 10011, is the organization which monitors the media's presentation of homosexuality, works to educate the general public, solicits nondiscrimination clauses from major corporations, and acts as a liaison with the White House and others on issues of concern to the gay community. Persons interested in working for changes in their respective churches are also encouraged to join the gay caucuses which exist in nearly every denomination. Their names and addresses are available in *Gayellow Pages*.

From my discussions with various gay men and women, I suggest that the primary concern today for gay people is being enabled to love and be loved maturely. I have read that one-third of the population (gay and straight) wants a long-lasting relationship with another person, one-third says they want one but are unable to maintain a committed relationship, and one-third has no interest in being involved with the expectations and demands of a one-on-one marriage.

Perhaps because of my reputation as a gay man who supports relationships, the majority of the people with whom I have talked want to be in a committed relationship and dream of it lasting the rest of their lives. Although the men tend to be more flexible than the women on the subject of genital exclusivity, members of both genders talk enthusiastically about having one special person whom they would love and by whom they would be loved. The two questions most frequently asked are: "How do I meet a potential mate?" and "How do I maintain the relationship when there are no role models and no support systems?"

Professionals who would like to assist gay people in this process need to remember that most gay people have been denied the important period of dating and have missed the many lessons such a period teaches. Because most gay people were confused and closeted in high school and college, they generally faked the dating ritual and frequently selected a safe companion for the sake of appearances. When an individual comes out at age 21, he or she has probably never had the experience of kissing, holding the hand of, or even dancing with a person of his or her choosing. The male or female walking into their first gay bar has never had the intimate opportunity to learn that the most sexually attractive person does not necessarily possess the best personality, that race, religion, sense of humor, intelligence, and economic background frequently influence whether or not one person will be compatible with another. Furthermore, many gay people do not have a sexual experience with another homosexual until they have come out of the closet. When they do finally emerge into a gay social scene, they frequently conduct themselves like children in a candy shop, or, as I did, rush into a relationship merely for the sake of affirmation and security. Both the gay person and the professional should be aware that individuals who have only recently come out of the closet will need a period of time for social and sexual adjustment; to expect otherwise is to invite disappointment and more negative self-images.

Because of social attitudes toward homosexuals, the number of healthy social settings available to gay people are limited, though they have increased tremendously since 1969, the birth year of the modern Gay Pride Movement. Gay bars continue to be the most popular meeting places but are not always conducive atmospheres for getting to know another person. In fact, some gay people complain they have never had an intelligent conversation in a gay bar, due in no small part to the loud music, dim lighting, and sexually tense aura of most gay bars.

Gay newspapers (also listed in *Gayellow Pages*) generally record weekly or monthly social activities, such as picnics, sporting events, parties, and so forth, which are designed to meet the needs of the community. They also list organizations such as the gay mountain climbing group, the lesbian mothers' group, and the gay college athletes' association. These different organizations enable gay people to come into contact with people of similar interests. Each year, new social and professional groups are formed, offering that many more opportunities for gay people to find someone with whom they might establish a relationship.

Maintaining a relationship in a society which discourages permanence is difficult enough for heterosexuals, but for gay people who generally receive no support for their efforts from family, employers, the church, or the state, the task can seem impossible. They are forced to make choices. With whom should they spend the holiday—unsuspecting parents or a lover? With whom do they attend office social functions—lover or friend? How do they make sacred their commitment, when their church discourages their union? How do they share a home when some communities will not sell to two unrelated persons of the same gender and many apartment owners prohibit rentals to the same? Is it any wonder that many gay people find it difficult to maintain a committed relationship?

On the other hand, because there are no preconceived notions or role models for gay relationships, they are free to grow into their own unique shapes. Gay couples most successful at maintaining a committed relationship discourage roles and insist on open, honest communication. With increasing frequency, gay couples and liberated heterosexual couples are seeing that their relationships are virtually the same. They share the same goals, many of the same problems and frustrations, and the same joys.

Successful gay relationships are those in which the individuals are sensitive to each other's needs, share tasks equally, leave space for growth, and encourage each other's creativity. If sexual activity is to be engaged in outside of the relationship, it is done with mutual consent.

In this paper I have concerned myself mainly with encouraging gay people to love themselves by eliminating negative self-images through education. My approach has been to destroy the myths of the past through the reading of current literature and contact with other gay people and to encourage in the gay person respect, care, and responsibility. A person who has learned to love himself or herself is able to love another person maturely.

But what about our efforts in behalf of those boys and girls who are aware of homosexual feelings but have not yet had those feelings polluted by ever present myths? While it is important that we meet the needs of yesterday's and today's victims of hatred, fear, and ignorance, it is essential that we not merely try to repair their wounds, but also get about the business of primary prevention.

Young people need to learn at an early age that it is OK to be different from the majority; they need to know that there is no such thing as an unnatural thought. From their school texts, the attitudes of their teachers, sex education courses, television programs, magazine and newspaper articles, popular songs and church sermons, youngsters need to learn that it is all right to be homosexual. Although some parents seem concerned that presenting homosexuality in a positive light will encourage their children to become homosexual, no study supports such fears. On the contrary, healthy, broad-based sex education tends to create healthy, confident people, regardless of their sexual inclinations. Sexually mature people are not intimidated by the sexuality of others.

Educators and others with access to the public need to include "gay people" in sentences where appropriate, have books and other resources available for interested persons, and discourage the telling of antigay jokes. Persons interested in helping homosexual men and women develop positive attitudes toward sexuality and self should diligently watchdog the media, praising the networks and commercial sponsors when the gay subject matter is handled well and criticizing them when it is not, or when there is no attention given to gay people. Letters to the editor in local and national publications which comment on a gay news event or feature are another means of raising public consciousness, eliminating ignorance, and guaranteeing that more people will grow up with a healthy attitude toward themselves and others.

Finally, I applaud the courage of heterosexual men and women who publicly support the healthiness of homosexuality and who champion gay civil rights at the risk of being identified and scourged as homosexual. Although whites can march with blacks, and men can march with women without losing their "privileged status," nothing separates the heterosexual from the homosexual in the front page photo of a gay pride march.

In the same breath, I suggest that professionals, such as my high school guidance counselor, who ought to be comfortable with gay men and women but are not, should examine other career options.

References

Boswell, J. *Christianity, social tolerance and homosexuality*. Chicago: University of Chicago Press, 1980.

Brown, R. M. *Rubyfruit jungle*. New York: Daughters, 1973.

Clark, D. *Loving someone gay*. New York: Signet, 1977.

Clark, D. *Living gay*. Millbrae, Calif.: Celestial Arts, 1979.

Fairchild, B., and Hayward, N. *Now that you know: What every parent should know about homosexuality*. New York: Harcourt Brace Jovanovich, 1979.

Ford, C. S., and Beach, S. A. *Patterns of sexual behavior*. New York: Harper and Bros., 1951.

Fromm, E. *The art of loving*. New York: Bantam Books, 1967.

Gayellow Pages. (Obtainable from Renaissance House, Box 292, Village Station, New York, N.Y. 10014. Published annually.)

Guidance Associates. *The hidden minority: Homosexuality in our society*. White Plains, N.Y.: Guidance Associates, 1979.

472   BRIAN R. MCNAUGHT

Gutiérrez, G. In Sr. C. Inda and J. Eagleson (Eds. and trans.), *A theology of liberation*. Mary Knoll, N.Y.: Orbis, 1973.

Hanckel, F., and Cunningham, J. *A way of love, a way of life*. New York: Lothrop, 1979.

Hobson, L. *Consenting adult*. New York: Warner Books, 1976.

Humphreys, L., and Miller, B. Lifestyles and violence: Homosexual victims of assault and murder. *Qualitative Sociology*, 1980, *3*, 169-185.

Kosnick, A., Carroll, W., Cunningham, A., Modras, R., and Schulte, J. *Human sexuality: New directions in American Catholic thought*. New York: Paulist Press, 1971.

Leighton, R., and Berzon, B. (Eds.). *Positively gay*. Millbrae, Calif.: Celestial Arts, 1979.

McNeill, J., S.J. *The church and the homosexual*. Mission, Kans.: Sheed, Andrews and McMeel, 1976.

Nelson, J. *Embodiment*. Minneapolis: Augsburg, 1978.

Reid, J. *The best little boy in the world*. New York: Ballantine, 1976.

Silverstein, C., and White, E. *The joy of gay sex*. New York: Crown, 1977.

Sisley, E., and Harris, B. *The joy of lesbian sex*. New York: Crown, 1977.

Tripp, C. A. *The homosexual matrix*. New York: McGraw-Hill, 1975.

Vida, G. (Ed.). *Our right to love: A lesbian resource guide*. Englewood Cliffs, N.J.: Prentice-Hall, 1978.

Walker, M. *Men loving men*. San Francisco: Gay Sunshine Press, 1977.

Warren, P. N. *The front runner*. New York: William Morrow, 1974.

Weinberg, G. *Society and the healthy homosexual*. New York: St. Martin's Press, 1972.

Religious Dimensions of Sexual Health

James B. Nelson

Religion is a terribly ambiguous human enterprise, and it ought never to be confused with God. Religion is the patterning of human responses to what is *perceived* to be the divine, responses that take shape in doctrine, moral instruction, patterns of worship, styles of piety or spirituality, and religious institutional life. The power of religion for good is that the divine life does indeed break through these human forms in ways that fulfill persons, create life-giving human relationships, and transform social structures. But the power of religion for evil is just as great. The religious enterprise, that most dangerous of human enterprises, is always tempted to claim ultimate authority and sanction for its humanly constructed doctrines and precepts. Nowhere is all of this ambiguity more apparent than in sexual matters.

While I write here as a Christian, I believe that these observations will have considerable applicability to Judaism as well. Somewhere in the first few centuries of the Christian church, the patristic era, there arose two lists: the seven deadly sins and the seven virtues. As I attempted to formulate my observations about the religious dimensions of sexual health, two things occurred. First, I could not talk about the positive elements without talking about the ways in which Western religion has contributed mightily to sexual disease. Second, I discovered that my points fell, quite miraculously, into two groups of seven. Although these make no attempt to reflect the early Christian lists, I submit seven deadly sins which Western religion has contributed to sexual disease, countered by seven virtues (or positive resources) which the Judeo-Christian tradition offers to sexual health.

All of this is predicated upon certain assumptions about sexual health. The definition offered by the World Health Organization (WHO) (1975) is useful: "Sexual health is the integration of the somatic, emotional, intellectual, and social aspects of sexual being, in ways that are positively enriching and that enhance personality, communication and love" (p. 6).

That is a remarkable definition, not only because it affirms the multi-dimensional and relational aspects of sexual health, but also because it is (to the best of my knowledge) the first time any major health organization has used the concept of love in a health policy statement. Not incidentally, the WHO definition reflects the best in the Judeo-Christian tradition concerning sexuality and leaves out the worst! Now to the sins and virtues.

The first two deadly sins—spiritualistic dualism and sexist dualism—are the most basic, fundamental sins, and they are counterparts of each other (Ruether, 1975). Yet, for the moment they can be viewed separately. Any dualism is the radical breaking apart of two elements which belong together; it is seeing the two dimensions of life coexisting in uneasy truce or open conflict.

Spiritualistic dualism, the first deadly sin, was quite foreign to the Jewish Old Testament heritage. However, through the impact of the Greco-Roman culture and its Hellenist philosophy, it found its way into early Christian life and thought. The spirit was viewed as eternal and pure, while the physical body was seen as temporal, material, corruptible, and corrupting. Whatever salvation meant, it somehow involved escape from the distractions and temptations of bodily life into the realm of the spirit. Although, as we shall see in a moment, this spiritualistic dualism ran counter to the most basic insights of both Jewish and Christian traditions, it had an enormous impact, particularly upon Christian life, which is still with us.

Such dualism has multiple results. The body is viewed with suspicion, and its sexual feelings must be denied in favor of the higher life. A ladderlike image of true spirituality emerges, with celibacy reserved for the higher rungs. The alienated body produces a mind detached from the depth of feelings. Dichotomized thinking emerges from the mind-body dissociation; we become resistant to ambiguity, seeking simple and single reasons for understanding things. Both the body and its sexuality are depersonalized; the body is seen as a physical object to be possessed, controlled, and used by the self. Such are the wages of this deadly sin, spiritualistic dualism.

But what of the positive resources? Israel of the Old Testament knew nothing of this body-spirit split. It regarded the person as all of one piece. With a strong doctrine of the goodness of all of creation, Israel could not denigrate the body and its pleasures. They were gifts of God.

And what of Christianity? In spite of the fact that Hellenistic dualism made dramatic inroads, Christianity nevertheless remains a religion of incarnation. In its central affirmation, Christianity claims that the most decisive experience of God comes to us not principally in doctrine, not in philosophic abstraction, not in mystical otherworldly experiences, but *in flesh*. Even if ancient heresies (Gnostic and Docetic) still cast suspicion upon the goodness of material, bodily life and still question the full humanity of Jesus of Nazareth, the mainstream of Christianity has attempted to say that the most decisive, memorable, revelatory meeting place of God with humankind is in the meeting of flesh with flesh. And that has something to do with our sexuality.

So, the good news, the virtue (as opposed to this first sin) is this: the fully physical, sweating, lubricating, ejaculating, urinating, defecating bodies that we are are the vehicles of the divine experience. God continues to be most decisively experienced in the fleshly, embodied touching of human lives. The Word still becomes flesh and dwells among us, full of grace and truth.

Word becoming flesh: this is the mystery of communication and communion. The secret of our sexuality is our need to reach out to embrace others physically, emotionally, spiritually. The good news of a Jewish creation-affirming faith and a Christian incarnationalist faith is that our body-selves with all of their rich sexuality are God's way of inviting us into authentic humanness, through our need to reach out and embrace. Our sexuality is the divine plot to tease us into becoming "body-words of love." Our sexuality is both the physiological and the psychological grounding of our capacity to love. It is that basic. We who take these core religious affirmations seriously are bidden to celebrate the body as a means of grace. That is good news from religion for sexual health.

The second deadly sin is sexist or patriarchal dualism. It is the twin of spiritualistic dualism in some basic ways. For centuries men have assigned to themselves the primary characteristics of spirit and mind, and have labeled women as body and emotion, hence inferior and needing to be subdued by the higher powers.

If spiritualistic dualism was foreign to the Hebraic Old Testament culture, sexist or patriarchal dualism was not. Women were second-class citizens in the community of faith and much of the time looked upon as male property. The patriarchal culture continued its influence into the Christian era and is still pervasive. The essence of sexist dualism is the systematic and systemic subordination of women by men in institutional life and in interpersonal relations.

That this is a deadly sin in regard to the health of women hardly needs elaboration. That it is a deadly sin for males, also, is true. Unquestionably, women have borne the brunt of the manifold forms of injustice. For both women and men, the sexist estrangement takes its toll in patterns of dominance and submission. Women compete with women for male acceptance, which they have been taught is essential for their self-worth. Men find emotional intimacy and tenderness with other men to be threatening to the masculine, heterosexual image. Spouses find it difficult to speak honestly with each other about their sexual needs and anxieties, and performance fears invade their sexual love making.

What is the good news, the virtue that Western religion might contribute here? The Apostle Paul expresses it: "There is neither Jew nor Greek, there is neither slave nor free, there is neither male nor female, for you are all one" (Galatians 3:28).

The internalization of this reality makes possible the growth of our androgyny. (I realize that "androgyny" is an ambiguous term, inasmuch as it trades upon the very sexual stereotypes which it attempts to overcome. Nevertheless, it is a useful interim word, reminding us that societal sterotypes do not define our authentic being.) None of us is intended to be either rational or emotional, either assertive or receptive, either cognitive or intuitive, either strong or vulnerable, either initiating or responding, but all of these. A core religious affirmation is the *oneness* of human being and human becoming. Actually, we do not have to become androgynous, for each of us essentially is. We only need to be allowed to be actually what we are essentially, and the religious affirmation is important here (Singer, 1976, p. 333).

Moreover, the Judeo-Christian understandings of God are crucial to our own self-understandings. Stereotypically, masculine language and images have shaped that perception: God is "He" and "Him." Masculine titles have predominated: God is King, Lord, Master, Father. But, one of the best kept secrets in the Bible (particularly the Old Testament) is the abundance of feminine images for God. God is there likened to a woman in childbirth, bringing forth new creation; God is there as a nursing mother drawing humanity to her full breasts; God is there as a seamstress clothing her children with garments in the wilderness (Russell, 1973, pp. 97ff).

If this kind of religious imagery is internalized and experienced, it can lead to a more androgynous experience of the self. It might lead, also, to a more androgynous spirituality. A masculinized imagery and spirituality has emphasized God as structure, judgment, law, order, intellect, and logic. A feminist imagery would lead to the experience of God as nature more than society, as mystical oneness more than cognitive analysis, as flow and change more than structure, as immanence more than transcendence. Both dimensions are needed for sexual health, for each of us is created with androgynous capacities destined to be realized in unique ways.

The third sin is homophobia. The word was coined a few years ago to denote an irrational fear of homosexuality (Weinburg, 1973, Chap. 1). It has been, tragically enough, part of the Judeo-Christian legacy. Nevertheless, the antihomosexual bias simply cannot be justified by careful biblical interpretation (Boswell, 1980, Chap. 4; Nelson, 1978, Chap. 8). The Bible does not actually deal with homosexuality as such. This understanding of a psychosexual orientation toward those of one's own sex is distinctly modern. Furthermore, when the Bible deals with homosexual acts (as distinguished from orientation), it deals with them in the context of lust, idolatry, rape, and with the notion of leaving, giving up, or turning away from one's natural orientation. Thus, heterosexual orientation is presupposed. There is no biblical guidance on the matter of same-sex expression for those so oriented, within a context of mutual respect and love.

If the biblical legacy does not explain our persistent homophobia, misogyny (male distrust, fear—even hatred—of women) does. Patriarchal control idealizes a disembodied, detached rationality and enforces compulsory heterosexuality for both men and women. The only respectable alternative to heterosexuality is either celibacy or asexuality. Harrison (1981) writes:

> More than anything else we now need a clearer historical appreciation for the ways in which this long-standing and deeply rooted antipathy toward women in the Western Christian tradition interfaced and interacted with anti-body and anti-sensual attitudes. The fact is that the stigma of homosexuality in this society incorporates and encompasses all of the power dynamics of misogyny. Until we recognize this fact, we will not even begin to grasp why homophobia is such an intense and 'nutty' madness among us. (p. 8)

The antihomosexual attitudes of the dominantly Christian West thus cannot be explained simply by historical influences. As Boswell's (1980) careful study has pointed out, misogyny is a more consistent trend in Christian history than is homophobia. The connection, however, is quite clear. In male homosexual activity there is the stigma that some men must be passive, act like females, that is, like "failed males."

If both Jewish and Christian cultures have been dominantly homophobic, there are, nevertheless, positive resources for sexual health within these traditions. First, there is biblical affirmation of same-sex loving relationships. This material is usually overlooked by the antihomosexual proof texters, but it is there. For example, the close emotional bonding of David and Jonathan, of Ruth and Naomi, of Jesus and the beloved disciple are celebrated by the biblical writers. These are not, I assume, accounts of genital expression, but that is not the point. The point is that careful biblical scholarship simply cannot sustain the sweeping condemnation of all deep same-sex feeling which often has been asserted in the name of the Bible.

Another religious resource follows upon the recognition that the Bible does not deal with the issue of same-sex genital expression in the context of mutual respect and love. That resource is the affirmation that the morality of homosexual genital acts must be judged by the same fundamental criterion as the morality of heterosexual genital acts. To this theme I will return later.

In terms of the psychodynamics of homophobia, there is a more basic religious resource still. It is the message of God's radical affirmation of each and every person. In both Old and New Testaments this is called grace. It is the spontaneous, unmerited acceptance of the self by God. Here is the foundation for a sense of personal security in the self.

One of the strong dynamics of homophobia seems to be insecurity about one's own sexual identity and, hence, the tendency to condemn in another what is feared in the self. For the one, however, who has discovered a basic sense of inner worth through the divine acceptance, there is less need for fear. As a male I need not fear "the woman" within. As one predominantly heterosexual, I need not fear the homosexual feelings within. Nor need I be envious of the apparently greater sexuality of gays and lesbians (for our stereotypes constantly draw our attention to what they do in bed).

A common dynamic of what the religious tradition calls "sin" is thus false security. It is a false security rooted in an inner insecurity which then attempts to punish those who seem to threaten the self. That the security-creating divine acceptance, grace, can undercut this destructive dynamic is good news, indeed.

The fourth deadly sin which contributes to sexual disease is guilt over self-love. Christian theology has not had a good record in dealing positively with self-love. The dominant interpretation has seen self-love equivalent to self-centeredness, hence incompatible with the religious life. Self-love has been interpreted as acquisitive, individualistic, concerned with the self's private satisfactions, and prone to use others as tools for one's own desires. Thus, a sharp disjunction has been drawn between *agape* (selfless, self-giving love perceived in God and held normative for the faithful) and *eros* (human desire for fulfillment). Although, to be sure, a more positive appreciation of self-love has been present in certain elements of the tradition, the negative evaluation has been dominant.

When a suspicion about self-love combines with a suspicion of the body and of sexual feelings, there is a sure formula for sexual disease. The self-hate which emerges is usually of an indirect sort, but it *is* a rejection of one's actual self. Alongside this is often an idealized image of the self, but, since this is unattainable, hurt pride and self-hate emerge together.

In sexual expression, such self-rejection (or rejection of self-love) finds guilt in spontaneous sexual pleasure. Masturbation is an obvious arena of guilt, simply because giving oneself sexual pleasure is understood as sheer self-centeredness. But there is also a "works-righteousness" syndrome which becomes performance anxiety in sexual relations with the partner. In performing I always split myself into two people—one doing the performing, the other watching both the performance and the audience response. Such self-conscious splitting, watching, and judging further nurture my anxiety and undermine my capacity to commune with the other.

If guilt over self-love is a deadly sin, the good news from the religious heritage is that love is indivisible and nonquantifiable. Jesus said, "Love your neighbor *as* yourself," not "instead of yourself." It is not true that the more love we save for ourselves the less we have for others. Authentic self-love is not narcissism nor is it a grasping selfishness. Rather, it is that self-acceptance which comes through the affirmation of one's own graciously given worth and (in spite of all our distortions and flaws) our creaturely fineness.

Self-love is not only basic to personal fulfillment, but also to the capacity for authentic sexual intimacy with the partner. If I cannot say yes to myself, I cannot offer myself fully to another. I can surrender to the other, but I will have lost the gift I was asked to bring. True sexual intimacy depends upon a solid sense of identity in each of the partners. The entanglements in which identity is confused and diminished become symbiotic relationships in which one person becomes an extension of the other.

Sexual intimacy is love's communion, not unification. Sexual intimacy, then, rests in some large measure upon each partner's sense of personal worth. Without this we easily elevate the other into the center of our lives, hoping that the other's affirmation of us will assure us of our own reality. But this is too large a burden for the partner, for then the beloved has become idolatrized and confused with the divine.

Genuine self-love, furthermore, personalizes the body. When we can love ourselves as body-selves, we are aware of bodily tensions and their causes. There is more spontaneity of the body-self, for when we find the security not to demean ourselves we need not deaden any aspects of ourselves or dissipate our energies in useless rituals. Self-acceptance brings with it the profound sense that I am the body which I live, the sense that I have a real self with which to relate to others. I do not desire to absorb or be absorbed by another. I am a unique self interested in communication and communion, not in conquest and dependency. And that points to sexual health.

The fifth deadly sin is a legalistic sexual ethics. Legalism is the attempt to apply precise rules or laws to actions regardless of the unique features of the context. Legalism is the assumption that an objective standard can be applied in the same way to whole classes of actions without regard to the meanings those actions have to persons.

Many adherents of both Jewish and Christian faiths in our society have fallen into more legalism about sexual morality than virtually any other arena of human behavior. If one looks at such issues as masturbation, homosexual expression, and, in fact, virtually any form of genital expression outside heterosexual marriage, it is easy to find the legalistic posture in Orthodox and Conservative Judaism, in the official natural law stance of Roman Catholicism, and in a variety of conservative Protestant groups.

Adding to the confusion of this ethical scene is that some of the stringent sex rules of traditional orthodox religion have been based, at least in some significant measure, upon erroneous biological assumptions. Jews and early Christians alike made the biologically inaccurate and patriarchal assumption that the male semen was the carrier of life, the woman furnishing only the ground into which the seed was planted. Furthermore, it was frequently assumed that in any one male the total amount of semen was limited. Add to these assumptions the quite understandable concern of these early religious peoples for reproduction and the survival of the tribe in a threatening environment, and it is not difficult to understand why any deliberately nonprocreative male sex act was anathema.

The virtue which speaks to this deadly sin of legalism is love. Our sexuality is intended to be a language of love. Our sexuality is God's way of calling us into communion with others through our need to reach out, to touch, and to embrace—emotionally, intellectually, physically. It is God's beckoning us into the communion of love.

Since we have been created with the will to communion, the positive moral claim upon us is to become what we essentially are: lovers—in the richest, most inclusive sense of that word. The negative side of this, sin, is not basically a matter of breaking moral codes or disobeying laws (though it may involve that). More fundamentally, it is the failure to become what we are. It is the alienation which inhibits fulfillment and communion. It is the failure of love.

The values which emerge from love are several, and they become those criteria by which specific sexual acts might be measured in a nonlegalistic manner (Kosnick, Carroll, Cunningham, Modras, and Schulte, 1977, pp.

92-95). These values apply equally, I believe, to both heterosexual and homosexual expression. First, love is self-liberating. In a sexual act it expresses one's own authentic selfhood and yearns for further growth. Moreover, such love is other enriching; it has a genuine concern for the well-being and growth of the partner. Also, sexual love is honest; it expresses as candidly and truthfully as possible the meaning of the relationship which actually exists between the partners. Further, it is faithful; love expresses the uniqueness of the relationship, yet without crippling possessiveness. In addition, sexual love is socially responsible, aware of, and concerned for the larger community to which the lovers belong. It is life serving; the power of renewed life is shared by the partners. Finally, true sexual love is joyous, exuberant in its appreciation of love's mystery and life's gift.

An ethics centered in this kind of love will not guarantee freedom from mistakes in the sexual life, but it will serve the sexual health of persons crippled by legalism. It will serve their human becoming and their maturation as lovers after the image of the Cosmic Lover by whom they were created.

The sixth deadly sin of which our religious traditions are often guilty is a sexless image of spirituality. This has been more a bane of Christianity than of Judaism, for the church far more than the synagogue has been influenced by the Hellenistic, Neoplatonic split between spirit and body. Consequently, in the early Christian era a ladder image of spirituality emerged. True virtue was associated with movement upward, away from the earth. Bodily mortification and celibacy were elevated as particularly honorable. Even among married Christians, those who abstained completely from sex were deemed more virtuous than those who had intercourse with the intent to procreate. And those who made love in order to express affection and because they enjoyed it were least meritorious of all.

The good news, however, is that a sensuous, body-embracing, sexual spirituality is more authentic to both Jewish and Christian heritages. A clue is found in an Old Testament book, the Song of Songs. Here is a biblical love poem celebrating the joys of erotic love between a woman and a man. Although much of Christian interpretation over the centuries allegorized this poem into a symbol of "the purely spiritual" relation of the soul and God, devoid of any carnal reality, it is, in fact, a sexual story. The setting is an erotic garden. The lovers delight not only in each other's embodiedness, but also in the sensuous delights surrounding them: flowers, fruits, trees, fountains. Here there is no body-spirit split. Here there is no sexist dualism, no hint of patriarchy, no dominance or submission. The

482   JAMES B. NELSON

woman is fully the equal of the man. She works, takes initiatives in their meetings, and has an identity of her own apart from her lover (Nelson, 1981, pp. 90-91).

It is true, there is another garden story in our religious heritages, the Garden of Eden. Here the sexual dualisms have become apparent. There is shame in nakedness. Childbirth and daily work alike are cursed by pain, and the woman is derivative from the man. While the erotic garden of the Song of Songs represents a creation-centered spirituality, the Garden of Eden in Genesis represents a sin-and-redemption-centered spirituality. While the latter type has clearly dominated the notions of Western Christian spirituality, it is not the only (or perhaps even the most authentic) type.

We are beginning to realize that repressed sexuality "keeps the gods at bay" and that repressed human development does not bode well for the human-divine relationship. We are beginning to see that the bodily dimensions of feeling and emotion, longing and desire, are not foreign to but rather essential to a healthy spirituality. Such a spirituality will help men and women "discover that their flesh and its desires are not inherently evil, but are sharings in the passionate longings of God...to relate to creation, sharings in God's own lust for life. Spirituality must show forth that God who is shamelessly, even scandalously, in love with earth" (Deschene, 1981, p. 33).

The seventh deadly sin of our religious traditions has been the privatization of sexuality. Here, my pun is intended. Sexuality has been located essentially in "the privates," and hence our understandings of its dynamics have been restricted to the domain of private, interpersonal morality. But such a genitalization of sexuality in itself is a mark of sexual sin and alienation. For our sexuality is far more than genitals; it is our way of being in the world as female or male persons, our capacity for sensuousness, our self-understanding as body-selves, that deep inner drive toward communication and communion with the earthiness of earth and earth's Creator-Spirit. As such, our sexuality pervades the whole of life, including all of our social and institutional relationships.

To the extent that we can transcend a narrowed privatization in our understanding of sexuality, we can also comprehend the fact that an enormous range of social justice issues are at stake. Some are more obvious than others: justice for women, gays, and lesbians; commercialized sex; sexual abuse of women and minors; abortion; population control; the sexual rights of the aged, the handicapped, and the institutionalized. Moreover, a wholistic view of sexuality can help us all see more clearly and respond more effectively to those sexual dimensions present in social issues which appear to have little to do with our subject.

White racism in American society is one such issue. Historically, the schizophrenic attitudes of white males toward women ("there are two kinds—the good ones and the bad ones") were organized along racial lines. The white woman was elevated as the symbol of purity, and the black woman ("the other kind") was used for economic and sexual purposes. Then white male guilt was projected onto black males, who were fantasized as dark sexual beasts never to be trusted around white women. Further, the insecurity of many white people with their own flesh (for the respectable notion of religious virtue does not seem to accommodate many body feelings) frequently led to a "dirty body" image of those whose skin is so obviously different. These sexual dynamics, unfortunately, are still virulently alive in white racism.

Social violence is another issue with important sexual dimensions. The fact that violent crime in this society is overwhelmingly a male phenomenon is no accident. Nor is it an accident that men are directors of an insane global arms race ("my rocket is bigger than your rocket"). The machismo cult of competitiveness, toughness, superiority, potency, and homophobia is terrifyingly present. We are also beginning to learn about the interconnection between the deprivation of body pleasure and tendencies toward physical violence.

The list could be extended. The links between a Western white culture's inability to live in ecological harmony with the earth and our proneness toward self-body dissociation may be significant. The connections between a pervasive consumer mentality and our sexual alienation might also need more understanding.

Religion, then, is an ambiguous human enterprise. There are at least seven deadly sins, and perhaps even more, which certain elements in the Judeo-Christian heritage have contributed to our sexual disease. But speaking from faith's perspective, I am even more convinced of the positive resources of this religious tradition for sexual health. For, God the Cosmic Lover has a passionate love for this earthy creation and has made our sexuality a fundamental dimension of our own passion for wholeness, health, and love. This God somehow keeps breaking into our ambiguous religious ways with fresh resources for our healing.

References

Boswell, J. *Christianity, social tolerance, and homosexuality.* Chicago: University of Chicago Press, 1980.

Deschene, J. M. Sexuality: Festival of the spirit. *Studies in Formative Spirituality,* 1981, *2* , 25-38.

Harrison, B. W. Misogyny and homophobia: The unexplored connections. *Integrity Forum,* 1981, *7,* 7-13.

Kosnick, A., Carroll, W., Cunningham, A., Modras, R., and Schulte, J. *Human sexuality: New directions in American Catholic thought.* New York: Paulist Press, 1977.

Nelson, J. B. *Embodiment: An approach to sexuality and Christian theology.* Minneapolis: Augsburg, 1978.

Nelson, J. B. Between two gardens: Reflections on spirituality and sexuality. *Studies in Formative Spirituality,* 1981, *2,* 87-97.

Ruether, R. R. *New woman, new earth.* New York: Seabury Press, 1975.

Russell, L. *Human liberation in a feminist perspective.* Philadelphia: Westminster Press, 1973.

Singer, J. *Androgyny: Toward a new theory of sexuality.* Garden City, N.Y.: Anchor Books, Doubleday, 1976.

Weinberg, G. *Society and the healthy homosexual.* Garden City, N.Y.: Anchor Books, Doubleday, 1973.

World Health Organization. *Education and treatment in human sexuality: The training of health professionals.* Geneva: World Health Organization, 1975.

Career Success and Life Satisfactions of Middle-Aged Managers

**Douglas W. Bray and
Ann Howard**

Some 22 years ago, the Bell System began a long-term study of the lives and careers of managers called The Management Progress Study. The participating managers, originally 422 young white males from six telephone companies, are now middle-aged and in mid-career, and a new phase of research is in progress to determine what this stage of life means to them. The preliminary data from this midlife research allows the exploration of the relationship between career success and life satisfactions reported here.

The Management Progress Study (MPS) participants have undergone a rigorous schedule over the years. Their introduction to the study brought them in groups of twelve to a three-day management assessment center between 1956 and 1960. At the assessment center, the first of its kind in industry, the participants underwent a series of individual and group exercises. These included simulations (an In-Basket exercise, a short business game, and a leaderless group discussion), interviews, aptitude tests, attitude and personality questionnaires, and projective techniques (the Thematic Apperception Test and sentence completion blanks). Behavior in the exercises was observed by a trained staff of psychologists and reported in an "integration" session, where each participant was evaluated individually. The assessors pooled their judgments and rated the assessees on a number of dimensions like leadership skills, planning and organizing ability, and primacy

The authors thank Louise DuBois for her conscientious research assistance in the analyses of these data.

of work. Finally, overall predictions were made about each participant's future as a Bell System manager.

The data from the original assessments were securely filed away and individual results kept confidential from both management and the participants themselves. Annually, for the next seven years, each participant was interviewed by a psychologist while a representative of the company was interviewed about him independently. Eight years after the start of the study, the participants were reassessed in a center similar to the one they had gone through initially. Following this, the interviewing program became triannual with the participants and with their bosses, and was expanded to include telephone interviews with participants who had terminated their employment with the Bell System.

Twenty years after the first assessment another close look at the participants was in order. The original plans had called for another management assessment center to evaluate changes in their management skills over the twenty-year span. But as the time drew near, it appeared that a great opportunity would be missed by merely continuing the study in the same direction. For this was the mid-1970's, when midlife and its crises were consuming the attention of writers and theoreticians, and the middle-aged male was threatening to replace the white rat and the college sophomore as the dominant research subject in psychology. The Management Progress Study was redirected toward studying its participants as middle-aged people and not just managers.

❖

THE SUCCESSFUL MANAGER

Because the original assessments in the Management Progress Study were conducted over a five-year period, the twentieth-year reassessments will span the years 1976 to 1980. At the time of this writing, MPS:20 assessments have been completed for the 1956 and 1957 samples, a total of 80 college graduates. These men had varying degrees of success in advancing from the first level of telephone company management to a possible maximum of seventh level, which is the President. Of the 80, 22 had been promoted to the fourth and fifth levels and can be counted as definitely successful. Another 39 participants had made the third level, which is the entry into middle management, and might be called moderately successful. The less successful were still at the first and second levels of management; there were 19 of these men. A comparison of results for these three groups of managers permitted an investigation of factors associated with managerial success.

A cross-sectional sample of successful managers was also obtained for corroborating data. This consisted of 35 participants in the Bell Advanced Management Program (BAMP). This group of high potential fourth and fifth level managers (all but two were white males) had been selected to participate in a one-month advanced training program at the University of Illinois in 1978. Although time constraints did not permit a full assessment of these managers, some of the same paper-and-pencil exercises used in the Management Progress Study were administered. This second sample permitted identification of any results in the Management Progress Study which seemed to be atypical; it turned out that this was seldom the case. Thus data were available for two groups of managers identified as "successful": 22 from the Management Progress Study and 35 from the BAMP program.

The typical successful manager at MPS:20 was, by virtue of sample selection, a white male college graduate with 20 years in the Bell System. He was married, had three children, and was 44 years of age. In contrast, the BAMP managers were slightly younger, with an average age between 39 and 40. Average tenure for the BAMP managers was 16 years.

Management Progress Study results have previously identified high levels of managerial abilities and motivations that characterize successful managers (Bray, Campbell, and Grant, 1974). Factor analyses of ratings of the dimensions in the managerial assessment centers showed seven major categories of success-related characteristics. Compared to less successful managers, successful men have greater administrative skills, stronger interpersonal skills as shown in face-to-face leadership, and greater intellectual ability. Their performance is more stable in that they are less likely to suffer performance decrements due to stress and uncertainty. Their work motivation is high, meaning that they get a lot of satisfaction from the work area compared to other areas of life, and they have their own high work standards. Their career orientation is toward advancement in management, and they are relatively independent of others.

Analyses of scores from individual exercises provide more specific data about the characteristics of successful managers. The Edwards Personal Preference Schedule showed similar personality/motivational structures for the fourth and fifth level MPS:20 men and the BAMP managers. Their average scores on six scales were notably different from the Bell System norms of 585 college recruits surveyed in 1958. The successful managers were particularly high on needs for achievement (accomplishing difficult tasks), dominance (the need to lead and direct others), aggression (the tendency to express hostility), and autonomy (the need to be independent of others). Both groups scored rather low on need for deference (desire to please others) and affiliation (need for friendships).

It is not really surprising to find that successful managers describe themselves as independent men who do not want to be controlled by the organization or bosses. Moreover, they respond to the challenge of doing a difficult job well and seem to enjoy taking leadership roles. Their tendency not to need or value friendships was less obvious, however. Although the men often appeared quite sociable in casual encounters, deep and meaningful friendships do not seem to be one of their major sources of life satisfaction.

Another unanticipated finding was the high average score on need for aggression. This is not just an assertiveness scale, but implies being rather nasty, hostile, and willing to tell people off. The notion that middle-aged people or managers who have achieved success then relax and nurture their subordinates as they move into a fatherly or mentor-like role is certainly not supported by these data, at least not for men in their forties.

Another strong characteristic of the successful manager is that his job involvement is quite high. When sequences of interviews with the MPS men were rated by a clinical psychologist on "life themes" (Rychlak and Bray, 1967), the successful managers were found to be highly involved on the occupational life theme. In other words, their interviews revealed that they were highly concerned with and talked a lot about their jobs, their bosses, salary, promotions, the company, and other work-related events. On a questionnaire administered with their 19th-year interview, these men rated career as one of the most important things in their lives, and they indicated that they work more hours at home than do less successful managers. The BAMP managers responded similarly to the same questionnaire items.

Successful managers are not just involved with the company, however, but are apt to expand their lives more than do other managers. As reported earlier (Bray et al., 1974), the type of man known as the "enlarger" seems to extend himself toward achieving in many areas of life, and this was more characteristic of the successful men. In contrast, the less successful were more likely to be "enfolders," those who stabilize and build on existing life structures.

As evidence of the successful men's enlarging tendencies, ratings of the MPS:20 dimensions showed them to have a broader range of interests. They were also rated higher on involvement in affairs of the world and the community. Analysis of the sequences of interviews found that the successful men rated higher on what was called the ego functional life theme—that is, they were more concerned with improving their intellectual abilities and emotional and physical health. Finally, on the 19th-year questionnaire the successful men reported a greater interest in current events, a finding replicated with the BAMP managers.

    [A section discussing the determinants of current characteristics of successful managers has been omitted.]

RECAPITULATION

What then do we conclude of career success and life satisfactions among middle-aged managers? The major tie, and apparently the only tie, between them is career satisfaction. As shown in Figure 6, career satisfaction acts as a bridge between career success and life satisfactions. Although career satisfaction relates significantly to both career success (measured by management level achieved) and life satisfactions (measured by ratings on happiness), the two primary concepts are not significantly related to each other. The more successful are more apt to be satisfied with their careers and the happier people are more likely to be satisfied with their careers as an important aspect of life, but this link is not strong enough to establish a significant relationship between advancement and general life happiness. Other considerations intervene.

Various assessment dimensions and test scores that form the substance of the ratings on career satisfaction help show the composition of the small area of overlap in the three circles diagrammed in Figure 6. Both the highly successful and the highly satisfied with life show increasingly positive attitudes toward work and the company as a place to work, as evidenced by ratings on primacy of work, scores on the need for achievement scale of the Edwards test, ratings on Bell System Value Orientation, and scores on the General Management Attitude scale. Both derive pleasure from leading others: the most successful were initially higher on the dominance scale of the Edwards and became increasingly so; the happiest and best adjusted were not initially higher but became so over time. Both the successful and the happy tended to have fewer financial worries also; the successful presumably because they have more income, the happy because they have fewer worries in general.

❖ Related positively to career success but not adjustment and happiness were cognitive abilities and administrative skills—intellectual ability, planning and organizing ability, and creativity in the solution of business problems. The more successful tended to enlarge their lives by their interest in a variety of fields of activity and were concerned with expanding their skills, knowledge, or personality. They tended to function independently of others, as shown by lower ratings on need for superior and peer approval by the assessment staffs and by low scores on the need for deference scale of the Edwards Personal Preference Schedule. The most successful managers were "organization men" only in the sense of dedication to work and organizational identification; they did not kowtow to authority but remained their own men.

❖ One interpretation of this constellation of scores is that the best adjusted and happiest individuals are not particularly evaluative or critical about life. Their outlook is positive, whether directed toward themselves, their careers, others, or life in general. Although they obviously must attend to problems in order

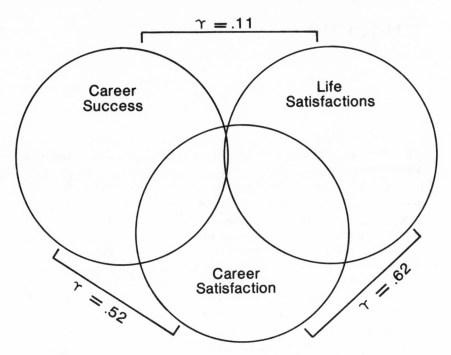

Figure 6. Career Satisfaction as a Bridge Between Career Success and Life Satisfactions

to resolve them, they do not ruminate about what life is all about but accept it as it is.

❖   The implication of these results with middle-aged managers is that career success does not necessarily lead to happiness. Contrary to those who find all good things in the same baskets (cf. Vaillant, 1977), these results indicate that career success relates to satisfactions only in the career area of life. Since work is increasingly being found a highly critical area of life, this relationship is not to be discounted. These data show, however, that the most successful at work are no more likely to be the most successful in marriage and family life or in recreational pursuits. Nor are they more likely to feel more positive about life and the nature of man or be able to avoid the feelings of crisis that sometimes accompany middle age.

Epilogue

The foregoing papers should leave most readers with few doubts that research demonstrates that the prevention of psychopathology is possible. Enough evidence has been reported in our series of volumes on this topic to convince all but the most intransigent holdouts that sufficient knowledge is available to achieve a reduction in the incidence of several categories of mental disorder and emotional disturbance.

The present volume has reviewed some of the basic concepts, theories, and approaches to the prevention of organic factors that contribute to disturbance, to the role of stress and efforts at reducing avoidable stress, and to strengthening the host through the fostering of coping skills, self-esteem, and support networks. It is clear that the technology for primary prevention exists and that successful applications of this technology are being made in a variety of areas.

There is a major aspect of primary prevention that we have largely left out of the present volume. The missing topic is a consideration of the importance of social change and political action in achieving successful efforts at prevention. Because primary prevention efforts are proactive and require approaches to relatively large groups, many prevention efforts involve more or less controversial attempts at changing environmental stresses, life-styles, and even at achieving a redistribution of power. There is a strong tendency in our society to try to separate and isolate various social problems and stresses. We identify a social problem labeled violence against children in the family, and another social problem labeled spouse abuse, and we describe others that we call sexism, racism, abuse of elderly persons, family disruption, poverty, unemployment, the incarceration and decarceration of persons labeled mentally ill, the neglect of the mentally retarded and the isolation of the physically handicapped. This by no means exhausts the list of groups with social problems that often involve increased levels of psychopathology.

What do all of these problems, involving all these different groups, have in common? We suggest, for your consideration, the best answer we can come up with. It is *powerlessness*. People without power are commonly exploited by powerful economic groups who explain the psychopathology that results by pointing to some defect in the victims. The rest of us do not rush to the defense of the victims because we are caught up in the ideology that puts "justice" in the hands of those with power. We tend to join those groups that "blame the victim."

If the foregoing analysis is accurate, it makes little sense to develop separate programs directed at the prevention of child abuse, spouse abuse, elder abuse, the exploitation of women, of minority groups, of migrant farm workers, of the physically handicapped, the mentally ill, and the mentally retarded. If we view all of these groups as more or less powerless because of socioeconomic conditions, then a logical approach is to determine whether there might be some way to achieve an equitable redistribution of power. The slogan of the 1960s was "Power to the People!" Another piece of conventional wisdom holds that "Money is power." Without meaning to be simplistic, we would like to suggest that we might well examine the arguments for a redistribution of power through a redistribution of wealth in our society.

When confronted with the issue of powerlessness, many psychologists have tended to approach it as a question of individual aberration or misperception of reality. The optimism of such a view is commendable, but the resulting attempt to alter people's perceptions of their ability to affect their own lives is often not only misguided but counterproductive and ultimately damaging. Several of the authors in this volume document the fact that many people in our society, in a great many situations, are powerless. If such people believe that they cannot do much to affect their life circumstances, to alleviate their misery, or to build a better world for their children, it is not because they perceive contingencies incorrectly, but because their perceptions are in fact accurate. They see themselves as powerless because they have no power. Without question this perception itself further exacerbates their feelings of hopelessness and further reduces the likelihood of their being able to make the necessary effort on those few occasions in their lives when they might be able to act effectively. If so, something might be said in favor of "therapy" to make them feel less powerless. But therapists are in short supply and rarely available to those who concern us—and anyway, they read a different agenda.

After considering this issue, we decided that a second volume of readings was needed and so we have developed a companion volume to the present one. The other volume is entitled *Readings in Primary Prevention: Social Change and Political Action,* also available from the University Press of New England. It provides the broader context in which to view and evaluate the approaches, concepts, and programs described herein.